AN APPROACH
TO THE ASIAN DRAMA

Methodological and Theoretical

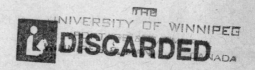

PRINCIPAL ASSISTANTS

William J. Barber, Professor of Economics,
Wesleyan University, Middletown, Connecticut, U.S.A.

Altti Majava, Demographer, National Planning Office,
Helsinki, Finland

Alva Myrdal, Cabinet Member, Minister for
Disarmament, Stockholm, Sweden

Paul P. Streeten, Professor of Economics,
University of Sussex, Brighton, England

David Wightman, Reader in International Economic History,
University of Birmingham, England

George W. Wilson, Chairman, Department of Economics and Division of
Economic Research, Indiana University, Bloomington, Indiana, U.S.A.

AN APPROACH TO THE ASIAN DRAMA

Methodological and Theoretical

Selections from *Asian Drama: An Inquiry Into the Poverty of Nations* A Twentieth Century Fund Study

by **GUNNAR MYRDAL**

 **VINTAGE BOOKS**
A Division of Random House
New York

PREFACE TO THE VINTAGE EDITION

As I explain below in my preface to the complete work, the length of it is abominable. The publication in one volume of only those parts, which are of a more methodological and theoretical character, has been urged upon me by colleagues who wanted to use my book in their classes without having their students buy and carry the awkward three-volume edition.

When sending out this volume I want to make a few reservations. As I explain in several connections, the bigger book, in spite of its length, consists of broad generalizations only, and they make up a "theory" in my conception of this term: a logically correlated system of questions to the empirical material. The question of what to take out for the present book has therefore not escaped arbitrariness.

More particularly, I should mention that in many chapters of a more factual character, not included in the present volume, I have discussed, usually in the beginning of a chapter, concepts used and statistics available. The two topics are closely related, as part of the deficiencies of the statistics is due to their collection and analysis under concepts that are not adequate to reality. Examples are to be found in Chapter 11 on National Output and Structure of Economy, Chapter 12 on Levels of Living and Inequity, Chapter 13 on Foreign Trade and Capital Flows, Chapter 17 on Concepts and Practices of Socialism, Chapter 18 on Concepts and Practices of Democratic Planning, Chapter 24 on The Industrialization Issue, Chapter 25 on The Case for Crafts and "Small-Scale Industry," Chapter 27 on Population Prospects, and Chapter 30 on Health.

Cross references, even to parts of the complete work that are not included in the present volume, are reproduced in their original form. In an appendix the analytical content of the complete work is reproduced. For author index and subject index I refer to the complete work.

The selections used in this volume are based solely on the three volumes of *Asian Drama*. Since its publication I have written another work, *The Challenge of World Poverty: A World Anti-Poverty Program in Outline*. (Pantheon, New York, 1969) which summarizes the findings of *Asian Drama* and goes on to propose specific policies which I think ought to be followed. I am not incorporating any material from this later work in the pages which follow.

GUNNAR MYRDAL

The Stockholm University Institute for
International Economic Studies
March 1, 1969

PREFACE

Habent sua fata libelli — books have their own destiny, even while they are being written and before they are published. Often, the simplest way of explaining what a book is about and what it aims to achieve is to tell why and how it came to be written.

After the Second World War I became increasingly interested in the economic problems of the underdeveloped countries. This was not in any way an extraordinary and original bent of mind; it followed closely the general reorientation of the social sciences in the post-war period on which I comment in Section 2 of the Prologue to this book. The same inclination manifested itself in the secretariat of the Economic Commission for Europe, which came into being in the spring of 1947 with myself at the head. Its work was to a considerable extent oriented toward the study of the development problems of the underdeveloped countries in Southern and Eastern Europe; it also investigated similar problems outside Europe in cooperation with the secretariats of the Economic Commissions for Asia and the Far East and for Latin America.

In connection with the E.C.E.'s particularly close cooperation with ECAFE and at the instigation of P. S. Lokanathan, who was then Executive Secretary of ECAFE, I made a six-weeks' tour of South Asia in the autumn of 1953, visiting Pakistan, India, Burma, Thailand, and Indonesia. I had consultations with my colleagues on the ECAFE staff in Bangkok, with government officials, and with other indigenous and foreign experts at the universities and in the field; as is my custom, I also visited industries and villages. In short, in the limited time available I tried in every way to familiarize myself with the economic, social, and political problems of the countries in the region. Since that visit I have never been free of an intense awareness of the momentous human drama of the desperate strivings for national consolidation and economic development in the South Asian countries. I decided then that as soon as I could free myself with good conscience from my duties with the E.C.E., I would return for a couple of years to these countries and devote myself to studying their problems of economic underdevelopment, development, and planning for development.

My own readings and writings during the next few years were almost exclusively directed toward preparing myself for this task,[1] and I made

[1] See, in particular, *An International Economy*, Harper, New York, 1956, and *Economic Theory and Under-developed Regions*, G. Duckworth & Co. Ltd., London, 1957 (published in the United States under the title *Rich Lands and Poor*, Harper, New York, 1957).

two more visits to the region. I also had the opportunity to make a similar tour of seven weeks in the adjacent region, which I then called the Near and Middle East but which I have now grown accustomed to calling by the more appropriate name of West Asia. There I met the same basic problems as in South Asia, though in a somewhat different political, social, and economic setting. In the spring of 1957, before I left the position I held with the E.C.E., my horizons were further enlarged by an exploratory visit of several weeks to the Soviet Central Asian Republics.[1] An eight-weeks' visit to Australia as Dayson Lecturer in the early autumn of 1957 gave me some idea of how Asian problems appear in the perspective of a continent that is geographically almost a part of Southeast Asia yet is very different and distant. From my earlier life and work I was, of course, intensely aware of the West European and East European perspective and the American as well. And so I felt, when in the late autumn of 1957 I became free to take up full-time work on the study that has resulted in the present book, that I had for a long time been circling around the task and was at least somewhat versed in the world setting of South Asia's economic problems. The next step was to tackle these problems directly, and to this end I spent the larger part of the next three academic years living and working in the region.

My intention was to write a general book focussed on actual conditions in South Asia, the prospects for development there, and the main policy alternatives facing the national governments. The attempt to do this, I felt, should not be deemed pretentious. Books and articles are continually being produced which are even more general in scope, as they concern the economic problems faced by all the underdeveloped countries in the world; indeed, I had myself been guilty of occasional contributions to this literature. The defense of these even more general studies has been — and I believe it is a fully valid one — that they provide a broad conspectus of what we know about these countries and their problems. That conspectus is needed for the guidance of practical policy in underdeveloped and developed countries; policy formation cannot wait until relatively complete information is available, but must be based on a provisional assessment of everything that is known in a general way. From a scientific point of view, a more essential function of studies following a generalizing approach is to provide a logically correlated system of questions to be answered by further detailed research, a "theory" in other words. In a sense, this study was designed to occupy a middle ground, slightly nearer the concrete facts than the most general literature on the development problems of underdeveloped countries. It was thought that by concentrating on the underde-

[1] The results of this visit, which I made in company with three members of the E.C.E.'s research staff, were published in the November, 1957, issue of the *Economic Bulletin for Europe*, Vol. 9, No. 3, under the title "Regional Economic Policy in the Soviet Union: The Case of Central Asia."

veloped countries in one region — which, though heterogeneous, are more similar than underdeveloped countries in widely separated parts of the world — one might hope to reach a somewhat deeper understanding of the common problems.

The foregoing paragraphs are an attempt to state and explain how the idea for the study took shape in the mind of the author. Meanwhile the Twentieth Century Fund, which had concentrated its work during the prewar years on major problems in the United States, had undertaken a few studies of other countries, and was beginning to enter into broad regional studies. As the plans of the Fund's Trustees for a study of South Asia agreed with my own ideas, the Fund undertook the study in its own program, as is its regular practice when supporting scholarly work, and appointed me director of the project. This relationship with the Fund continued after my return to Stockholm at the beginning of 1961, when the work remaining to be done on the study became a major part of the research program of the newly created Stockholm University Institute for International Economic Studies, of which I became the director. The Trustees and staff of the Fund have been extremely helpful in all respects, and were understanding when it turned out that the work on the book would take much longer than originally planned. In accordance with its rules and general practice, the Fund has not interfered with either the approach chosen or the conclusions reached and the manner of expressing them; responsibility for these matters was left entirely to me.

One preconception of mine deserves mention, as it determined my approach to the task. My personal journey through life and work, from early youth when my research interests were focussed on economic theory in a very narrow sense, had instilled in me an increasingly firm conviction that economic problems cannot be studied in isolation but only in their demographic, social, and political setting. Like all others who keep alive their interest in contemporary world history, I felt that crucially important things were happening in the region of South Asia. As I had been molded by my particular research experiences, I felt at the outset of the study that only by means of a broad institutional approach could I understand and explain the economic underdevelopment in the region, as well as what there is of economic development and planning for development. As my work proceeded and I saw how significant are levels and modes of living and attitudes and institutions in relation to underdevelopment and development in South Asia, I became even more convinced that such an approach was necessary to give realism and relevance to research. In general terms, the reasons for this orientation of my work — and my objections to the usual "modern approach" that is embodied in the structure of the plans and in the scientific and popular discussion of the economic problems of these countries — are spelled out in the Prologue; in specific terms they are developed in all of the chapters and in the methodological Appendices 1 to 8.

It is not altogether a pretentious metaphor when I describe my endeavor to apply an institutional approach in this study as an attempt to analyze the development problems of South Asia in the manner that Adam Smith studied England's development problems two hundred years ago. Smith, of course, never dealt with economic problems as purely "economic," and the same can be said in general of the whole classical school, including toward the end Karl Marx. John Kenneth Galbraith has stressed this aspect of the classicists' approach:

The principles of good government, the inducements to individual performance, the role of popular enlightenment, the foundations of thrift, the effect of competition and of monopoly, the relation between social classes, the reasons why some people, notably the English, worked hard and others, notably the Irish, were idle, were all grist for their highly diversified mill. Anything that was deemed to have a bearing on economic advance came into the discussion. The only test was broad relevance to the questions: What made for economic progress? Or, on the other hand, what led to stagnation — to the much discussed stationary state?[1]

The classicists had "concerned themselves with the aggregate requirement of progress." From this vantage point, Galbraith sees "some serious shortcomings in the modern discussion" of the underdeveloped countries, and states: "We have given too little attention to inquiring whether [the things that contribute to economic development] are being employed in a context that is favorable to development."

But Adam Smith's England contained only about 7 million people, while the present study concerns a fourth of mankind; and the fact that there is a vast amount of literature relating to various aspects of the South Asian situation proved to be a mixed blessing. I frankly confess that I found my task much more difficult than I had expected. Although I have not spared myself, but have worked harder than ever before in my life, this book, with all its shortcomings, has taken me four times as long to produce as I thought it would.

The length is abominable. The question can, indeed, be raised why I did not break it up into five or six books on separate topics. But the central idea in the institutional approach is that history and politics, theories and ideologies, economic structures and levels, social stratification, agriculture and industry, population developments, health and education, and so on, must be studied not in isolation but in their mutual relationships. Incidentally, one consequence of this approach was that I found myself constantly laboring to adjust all of the several chapters; none was considered complete until the entire manuscript reached the final stage. As I realize that the interests of many readers will tend to be restricted to particular parts

[1] *Economic Development,* Harvard University Press, Cambridge, 1964, pp. 38–40.

of the study — the chapters on health and education, perhaps, or the methodological discussions in the Prologue, some of the appendices, and portions of certain chapters — I am happy to report that consideration is being given to making some of the more specialized material available in separate volumes, where references to other parts of the study will underline my basic conception that all problems in these countries are closely interrelated.

I met some difficulties besides those I inflicted upon myself by choosing to deal with a whole region and electing to view the economic problems in their total demographic, social, ideological, and political setting. One was the extremely frail basis for factual knowledge about the South Asian region, of which I was not fully aware when I began the study. Wherever I turned, I found that any statistics available had to be scrutinized most severely before being used; at best they were highly uncertain and not as specific as the analyst would desire. Most of the general figures so confidently quoted in the literature, such as those pertaining to trends in income, population, literacy, and school enrollment, proved to be no more than extremely crude guesses, often palpably wrong. To establish this was itself a time-consuming process. When, instead, I made my own more specific estimates on the basis of meager statistics — as, for instance, in regard to schooling — they were of necessity extremely tentative, often having as their main purpose to indicate more clearly the sort of data that should be produced by further research.

Worse still, as I worked on I became increasingly aware that many of the concepts and theories commonly used in analyzing the problems of the underdeveloped countries in South Asia broke down when criticized from the point of view of their logical consistency and their realism, that is, their adequacy to reality. To work my way through what I gradually came to view as severely biased preconceptions — many of which I had shared with most of my fellow economists — was again a slow and painful process. This analytical deficiency has had a crucial effect on the character of the study. It is not unrelated to the statistical deficiency, as the weakness of much of the data stems from the fact that inadequate concepts and theories provided the framework of categories used in their collection and analysis.

So the work went on far beyond any deadlines the Twentieth Century Fund and I had set for the study, which in my work life was a unique experience. And instead of producing the facile but, as I had hoped, still respectable book on the main development problems of South Asia I had set out to write, I found myself engaged in a study where the main concern was methodological — how to cleanse concepts and discard theories and then state problems in a logical and realistic way — and where the results were very often merely a demonstration of our ignorance and a clearer statement of what we do not know. It is in this way that the work on the study became to me personally a destiny, the course of which I had not foreseen or planned from the beginning. I sincerely believe that at the present stage an important contribution to the advance of knowledge about these countries is the negative act of destroying constructs that we have rapidly put together and exposing to criticism masses of more or less worthless statistics collected within the framework of these constructs, which we are using all too confidently. I believe this because these constructs and statistics now stand in the way of scientific progress.

The chapters in Part Two on the political problems and several chapters or sections in later parts, particularly, may seem to belong to the type of book I originally intended to write — and may to an extent serve the purpose of such a book — as they consist of generalizations about conditions in the several countries of the region which I believe are broadly valid. But, as I explain in Section 7 of the Prologue and Section 2 of Chapter 1, from a methodological point of view my main purpose in stating these generalizations, especially in fields outside the main focus of the study, is to set down logically and explicitly the ideas that have determined my approach to the more intensive study of some particular problems. In a sense, what I have reached for in this book, beyond mere criticism, is a tentative "theory," one that coordinates in a systematic manner a general conception of what is happening in the region of South Asia. I tried to make this theory realistic; more specifically, I tailored it to fit the facts, so far as I knew them.

"Theory" in this context means nothing more than a logically correlated system of questions addressed to the material. It is in the nature of this conception of theory — which will be further developed in the Prologue — that the author of a theory should not fear, but expect as a perfectly normal consequence of fresh research, that further insights into various components of the complex of social interrelationships about which he has tried to inform himself will invalidate his theory, perhaps in fundamental respects.

I would like to emphasize that I am deeply conscious of the fact that I have myself shared many of the ways of thought that I criticize in this book. This has, I hope, saved me from falling into a polemical mood. Also, it has made it subjectively easier to simplify the text. Thus I have not, except on a few occasions, found it necessary to quote extensively from the literature in order to exemplify the views I am criticizing. I have been more concerned with a main line of thought than with the variations on the theme by individual authors. In this connection I should stress that I am well aware that most of the elements of which my own approach is composed have found expression in the observations, qualifications, or reservations of other writers. If the book has any degree of originality, it is as a total composition and in the insistence upon following the basic institutional approach through to its consequences.

New primary research was never contemplated and could not have been carried out without a much bigger research apparatus than I had available; it could not in any case have been more than extremely spotty. As I was determined to achieve realism, i.e., adequacy to the facts, as well as logical consistency, I have naturally tried to delve as deeply into the many diversified and involved conditions in the several countries as time and ability permitted. But the scope of the study was so wide that the results have had to be presented on a rather abstract level and the treatment has had to be selective. Many very important problems — including, I realize, many that have been given primacy in the economic literature — could only be hinted at and their place in the system abstractly demarcated, as for instance those of taxation (Appendix 8, Section 8). Thus this book is not in any sense a survey.

The "theory" I have tried to formulate relates to the South Asian region, which is the only one I have kept under close observation. I have not in general felt it within my province to inquire in this study whether the theory, or any part of it, is valid for other underdeveloped regions in the world. To stress this limitation is felt to be the more imperative as I come to the conclusion that a major vehicle for introducing serious biases into research on South Asian problems has been the uncritical application of concepts and theories that have been developed in, and have validity for, another region or group of countries, viz. the rich Western or Communist countries.

Theory is always tentative and provisional. No publication is ever the final one (though reviewers occasionally say as much about a particular book), and undoubtedly there are differences in regard to how much is left open for further research. In this particular case I want to confess that never have I felt so far from being able to present something resembling the final truth about a matter. It is my conviction that in twenty or even ten years' time we shall have different approaches and use quite different concepts and theories from those we have been accustomed to using. This book aspires to do little more than speed up the reorientation of economic and social research on South Asia. In this situation my findings can only be suggestive and tentative, and I expect that they will soon be lost like the memory of a variation of a melody in a mighty fugue of thinking and research which will proceed and never reach a finale.

In working on this book I have been reminded of a friend of mine who long ago wrote a doctoral thesis on the fiscal problem as one of the collective satisfaction of individual needs, and in the preface told a story from the Icelandic Aesir sagas. Thor, the god of war and manly prowess of the pagan Scandinavians, paid a visit to the Giants in Utgård. While they were eating and drinking, the Giants teased Thor about his physical prowess and challenged him to lift a cat that lay purring in a corner of the hall of feasting. Irritated, Thor rose to toss the cat out of the window, but however much he exerted himself, he could only get the cat to stand on its legs. Finally, by using all his strength he succeeded in lifting it so that one of its feet was for a moment a hairsbreadth off the floor. When the exhausted Thor returned to the table, he found, however, the Giants upset and showing signs of fear. The saga explains that the Giants had distorted Thor's vision. What he had been challenged to lift was not any normal animal but the mythical Great World Serpent swaddling the earth seven times, its tail firmly gripped in its jaws. If in the beginning of this study I was naive like Thor, at the end I am humble. I shall be satisfied if I have succeeded in indicating the nature of the problems of underdevelopment, development, and planning for development in South Asia, stating more systematically the immense scope of our ignorance, and hinting at the most profitable areas for further research.

A detailed account of the contributions of my assistants is given in the complete work on pp. xiv–xviii.

Contents

AN APPROACH
TO THE ASIAN DRAMA
Methodological and Theoretical

Prologue

THE BEAM IN OUR EYES

1   *A Plea for a Sociology of Knowledge*

Through the pursuit of social study, human beings and their interrelations in society, like other natural phenomena, are increasingly brought under scientific observation and analysis. What is scientific about this scrutiny and can justify its being called "social science" is its underlying assumption that the way an individual in a society feels, thinks, and acts is not a singular and haphazard phenomenon but one with definite causes and effects. Contained in this assumption is the idea that if we had complete knowledge, every state or change of mind and body could be fully explained and related to every other phenomenon in the world. We would know not only *how* people feel, think, and behave, but *why* they feel, think, and behave as they do, and *with what consequences* for themselves and for others. Without ever approaching such total knowledge, we attack our problems on that assumption and organize our findings accordingly, in terms of observed regularity and causal necessity.

Proceeding along these lines, the social sciences are now penetrating every corner of society and every phase of human life. Taboos are gradually being broken down. Their destruction in order to rationalize common sense has become a major aim of Western social science. We realize that all problems of living are complex; they cannot be fitted into the pigeonholes of our inherited academic disciplines, to be dealt with as economic, psychological, social, or political problems. Sometimes — for teaching purposes and for greater efficiency in research, through specialization — the old disciplines have been retained and even separated into sub-disciplines; however, we do not attach the same significance to these divisions as in earlier times. Today, for instance, no one would draw inferences about social reality from the concepts of economics alone, although this was done frequently two generations ago. To avoid a superficial and one-sided approach, the specialized social science disciplines cooperate in research. In addition, one discipline, sociology, focusses on the totality of social relations and takes special responsibility for those fields of social reality that are less closely scrutinized by the other disciplines. This development has been prominent in America for some time.

Thus we economists and other social scientists are now studying intensively how people behave, and how they are motivated and then conditioned both by their inherited constitution and by their environment. We are interested in the selective processes operating on the young as they find their way in life and are guided into different occupations. We are examining the formation of opinions and attitudes, especially decision-making by public administrators, business managers, employers and employees in the labor market, and political leaders and their followers. We are observing how people spend their leisure time, how they marry and pursue family life, how some become criminals, vagabonds, or prostitutes. In short, we are concerning ourselves with human behavior and motivations, in whatever profession, social class, or geographical location.

Only about the peculiar behavior of our own profession do we choose to remain naive. How we as scientists operate in seeking to establish knowledge is largely shielded from the searchlight of social study. But, surely, though we are seeking truth, we are not less conditioned by our mental make-up and the society in which we live and work than are other men. Social scientists are human; some, as we know well, are "all too human"; and they are part of a social system and a culture. Our research interests, the particular approach we choose, the course we follow in drawing inferences and organizing our findings, are not determined by facts and logic alone. We are not automatons like the electronic machines we increasingly use to master large masses of data. And yet, although literature and art have long been considered in relation to the psychology and the environment of their creators, our writings have not been.

Our lack of curiosity about our own peculiar behavior as researchers should be surprising. As a group we are certainly as interesting and important to the dynamics of the social system as are maladjusted girls, new immigrants, and other special groups in society that we are studying more and more intensively; we perhaps even rank with business managers, professional politicians, or creative artists. Our behavior can be easily ascertained from our writings. A deeper study would, of course, entail investigation of our personal history and our present inclinations as these are influenced by our relation to the class structure and our cultural and social milieu.

The desire to make money is naturally a strong determinant of the behavior of men in business and of all of us when we are acting in the "economic" sphere; so the desire to find truth affects the behavior of scientists and, indeed, of all men when they try to form a correct view of reality. As scientists we are not blind to the fact that in the economic sphere there are also other motives. No longer do we assume that in their economic pursuits people have the singlemindedness of the "economic man" of classical economic theory. Recognizing that even in their economic choices people are conditioned by their total mental make-up and, in particular, by the community in which they live, that they are motivated in a variety of ways as are all human beings in all their behavior, we are directing our attention more and more to the interplay of all these forces. But the "scientific man," thought to be conditioned by nothing except his desire to discover the true nature of things, is still commonly taken much for granted. No great effort is made to spell out that abstraction itself, and thereby give it a precise meaning, as the classical economists tried to do for the "economic man." The concept of the "scientific man" exists simply as an observed taboo.

It is clear, of course, that with few exceptions, we want to make scientific study as "pure" as possible, in the sense that it should render as accurate a picture of reality, when looked at from a particular viewpoint, as is attainable. Other influences, external to this objective, acting on our minds during scientific inquiry are irrational: they cause us to take a view that is biased in some direction. There are devices of logic by which we can attempt to purge our research of biases. But as part of the naiveté we retain about our own behavior in social study, those problems of the philosophy of knowledge, of the logic of social study, are usually kept in the shadow. We shall return to them in Sections 7 and 9.

Our main interest in this Prologue is in the sociology of knowledge, which is concerned with causation. The point is that we could better avoid biases, and could therefore expect more rapid progress in the social sciences, if we were a little less naive about ourselves and our motivations. A minimal desideratum is that we be always aware of the problem and attain some degree of sophistication about the operation of the personal and social conditioning of our research activity.[1] From this should rationally follow systematic inquiry into this important part of social reality. That would

[1] The American novelist, Richard Wright, who in his book *White Man Listen!* tried to deal with a problem in general terms, was conscious of the need to watch the way he was conditioned in his views: "I state that emotion here precedes the idea, that attitudes select the kind of ideas in question. . . . We are human; we are the slaves of our assumptions, of time and circumstances, we are the victims of our passions and illusions, and . . . our critics can ask of us . . : Have you taken your passions, your illusions, your time, and your circumstances into account? This is what I am attempting to do." (Richard Wright, *White Man Listen!*, Doubleday and Company, New York, 1957, p. 64.)

A social scientist should not be less humble and assume that he is purely "factual and objective." He cannot, in any case, escape valuations, as he needs explicit, or implicit, value premises even to ascertain the facts; see below in Section 9.

require the firmer establishment of a hitherto much neglected discipline: the sociology of knowledge.

These forces working on our minds, which cause irrationality if not recognized and controlled, are exceptionally strong and insidious in our approach to the problems of underdevelopment, development, and planning for development in the underdeveloped countries of South Asia. On this fact rests the defense for beginning our book with the general observations just made.

2 The Spurt of Interest in the Problems of Underdeveloped Countries

There was little scientific interest in the underdeveloped countries of South Asia, or elsewhere, almost until the Second World War. Since then a swelling flood of research has been devoted to their problems. Many of our resources in the social sciences are now employed in the study of underdeveloped countries. The tide is still rising, and we economists are riding the crest of the wave. Before the war the most intensive work in the underdeveloped world was done by the cultural anthropologists, sent out from centers of learning in the rich Western countries. They described for us, usually in static terms, the structure of institutions and attitudes by which people in those countries live, work, and survive. Now the lead is taken by economists, studying the dynamic problems of underdevelopment, development, and planning for development.

This tremendous re-direction of our work has not been an autonomous and spontaneous development of social science, but a result of vast political changes. Three changes, closely interrelated, stand out sharply: first, the rapid liquidation of the colonial power structure; second, the emergence of a craving for development in the underdeveloped countries themselves, or rather among those who think, speak, and act on their behalf; and, third, the international tensions, culminating in the cold war, that have made the fate of the underdeveloped countries a matter of foreign policy concern in the developed countries. So far as Western countries, scholars, and scholarly institutions are concerned, it is clear that the third cause has been foremost in arousing interest in the problems of the underdeveloped countries. In the underdeveloped countries themselves it is fairly well understood by their intellectuals — and has occasionally given rise to slightly cynical comments — that the readiness to give aid and, more fundamentally, the interest of both the West and the Soviet Union in their conditions and problems were largely due to the world tensions that give significance to their internal affairs abroad.

It should be remembered that the economic and social conditions of the

South Asian countries today are not very different from those existing before the disintegration of the colonial power system. The only major change has been the recent rapid acceleration in the rate of population increase. But the outburst of scientific interest in their economic problems preceded this acceleration, and, even more, our full awareness of it. On the whole, the masses in South Asia in pre-war times were as poor and their lives as miserable as they are now. Their poverty and misery did not, however, induce economists to take any great interest in their situation, let alone concentrate attention on the practical problems of how to engender development through economic planning and coordinated large-scale state intervention. Practical action along such lines was then not within the realm of political feasibility. Still less was there a feeling of urgency about such action.

The lack of interest among social scientists, particularly economists, in the extreme poverty and economic stagnation in the underdeveloped countries and in their problems of economic development was clearly a reflection of the existing world political situation. More specifically, this lack of interest reflected the character of the colonial regimes and their effect on us as well as on the subject peoples: these regimes were not such as to call forth large-scale research on economic underdevelopment by giving political importance to these problems.

What has happened in this field of study is, of course, a glaring indication of a much more general relationship. For social scientists it is a sobering and useful exercise in self-understanding to attempt to see clearly how the direction of our scientific exertions, particularly in economics, is conditioned by the society in which we live, and most directly by the political climate (which, in turn, is related to all other changes in society). Rarely, if ever, has the development of economics by its own force blazed the way to new perspectives. The cue to the continual reorientation of our work has normally come from the sphere of politics; responding to that cue, students turn to research on issues that have attained political importance. Theories are launched, data collected, and the literature on the "new" problems expands. By its cumulative results, this research activity, which mirrors the political strivings of the time, may eventually contribute to a rationalization of these strivings and even give them a different turn.

So it has always been. The major recastings of economic thought that we connect with the names of Adam Smith, Malthus, Ricardo, List, Marx, John Stuart Mill, Jevons and Walras, Wicksell and Keynes were all responses to changing political conditions and opportunities. Of these great scholars not only List and Marx but also Smith and Keynes, even, to an extent, John Stuart Mill, were aware of the political background of their contributions. The expanding volume of literature on development problems represents a more profound re-direction of economic science, indeed of all social science. A collective effort involving many workers, it cannot be ascribed to any one man or group of men. We are almost all participants in this revolutionary reorientation of research interests.

3 Sources of Bias: The World Conflict

To obtain a more sophisticated picture of research in the social sciences, we must first acknowledge that the changed world political situation is responsible for our shift of emphasis to the problems of the underdeveloped countries. Once we admit the importance of this influence, we must ask whether it does not affect the manner in which research is conducted as well as the field of research chosen. Although this shift of *field* represents a rational adjustment of our work to the needs of our society, we must suspect that the effect on the *approach* used in our research efforts may be to introduce irrational biases. The epistemological implications of the latter type of influence are quite different from those of the former. The merely selective — negative or positive — conditioning of the choice of research problems does not, in itself, invalidate the research that is done; the fact of such conditioning, however, should make us wary of less tangible influences on the content of our research.

One source of bias is the involvement of our society in the political changes referred to and the tensions they generate, along with our personal involvement. As mentioned above, the world political situation since the Second World War has been characterized by the almost complete liquidation of the colonial power system. The colonies have been replaced by independent nation-states in which influential groups are pressing, with varying success, for state planning to bring about economic development that would lift their countries out of stagnation and poverty. Concomitant with these two major changes has been another set of changes: the rise to power of the Soviet Union; the staggering gain in the size of territories and populations under Communist governments, especially the emergence of Communist China; and the ensuing cold war. To both sides in the world conflict the political allegiance — or at least the neutrality — of the underdeveloped countries has become a stake in the struggle for security and power. Concern is not restricted to the foreign policy of the underdeveloped countries. Their attempts at national consolidation and economic development have also become aspects of the cold war in the sense that the effectiveness, the speed, and, even more, the direction of their reforms have become politically important to the contending power blocs.

The current international political situation bristles with tensions and emotions of the most violent kind. Governments and nations feel their vital interests to be involved. And quite apart from any formal or informal pressures from the authorities or from public opinion, the individual scientist is himself usually deeply engaged in these momentous events. As an American, a European, or a national of one of the underdeveloped countries, he is bound to be anything but indifferent to the theoretical and practical findings of his research. This must have an influence on his inclinations in research and on how he presents his results to the public — unless he exercises the utmost care to avoid a biased view.

In the Communist countries, bias is massively and systematically incorporated in the approach to all social, economic, and political problems and has been hardened into a stale dogma. In these countries, scientific as well as literary writings are programmatically expected to contribute to the fight for Communism.[1] This limitation has virtually eliminated social science as we know it. It has stifled even that sophistication with which laymen approach social problems and which in democratic countries is continually fed by, and in turn stimulates, social research. Another sobering thought for social scientists is that there can be rapid economic development and flourishing progress in the natural sciences and in technology while the social sciences are represented by little more than a crude, teleological doctrine plus a highly developed economic technocracy.

The cramped situation of the social sciences in the Communist countries is explained, of course, by the absence of democracy. In order to exist and function, the social sciences more than other sciences require the freedom of thought and expression that we associate with democracy. At the same time, they themselves fulfill an essential function in a democracy and, on a level of highly trained rationality, they actually represent the democratic way of thinking and living. It is no accident that we may search in vain for important and original contributions by social scientists in the Communist countries to the scientific discussion of development problems in the poor countries.

Gradually, as the degree of personal security and independence is heightened, such contributions may and probably will be forthcoming. The trend toward greater freedom of expression seems sure to continue, as it is spurred by the rapid rise of educational levels in these countries, which is the real force behind de-Stalinization in its broad sense. There have been signs both in the Soviet Union and in some of the East European countries, though not as yet in poverty-stricken China, of greater willingness to allow objective research in the social sciences. Until now, however, the signifi-

---

[1] In Khrushchev's words: "The impact of the social sciences will increase steadily in the study of mankind's historical path to Communism . . . in moulding the materialist world outlook in people, in the education of the man of Communist society and in the struggle against bourgeois ideology. . . . Literature and art will play a big part in moulding the new man. By asserting Communist ideas and genuine humanism, literature and art instil in Soviet man the qualities of builders of the new world . . ." (Nikita S. Khrushchev, "Report on the Programme of the Communist Party of the Soviet Union," as delivered to the Twenty-second Congress of the C.P.S.U., *Soviet Weekly*, Supplement, October 18, 1961, p. 15.)

cant modern contribution to the scientific discussion of underdevelopment and development has come from students in the Western democracies and in the underdeveloped countries themselves, a very large part of it from the United States. It is in relation to these research efforts in the non-Communist world that the problem of biases is raised here.

This is not to say that bias arises in the perception of national interest only when it is raised to the pitch of cold war. It stems also from internal interests and pressures exerted by the dominant social strata. In retrospect we can see that even economic studies conducted during the long and care-free era of nineteenth-century liberalism were not free from biases.[1] The present world tension must be expected to be a powerful additional source of bias, particularly in the study of the underdeveloped countries.

4 Political Strategy and Diplomacy in Research

Impelled by the immense interests at stake, it is natural that the national authorities, the institutions sponsoring and financing research, and, indeed, public opinion in the West all press for studies of the problems of the underdeveloped countries. This clamor for research is entirely justified, as these problems are of increasing political importance to the Western countries themselves. But the studies are also expected to reach opportune conclusions and to appear in a form that is regarded as advantageous, or at least not disadvantageous, to national interests as these are officially and popularly understood. Such community pressure for opportunistic research operates in all Western countries, especially in the larger ones actively involved in the cold war. It operates also, though occasionally in a different direction, in the underdeveloped countries themselves. Their institutions and authorities and their educated class — whose views are commonly referred to as "public" opinion — are becoming more and more touchy about most questions dealt with in social study.

The most perceptible political influence on the research approach in Western countries to the problems of South Asian countries is the predominant role given to considerations of national power and international power relations. In a world full of perils to national security and survival, this tendency is understandable; it is often asserted to be a more realistic direction of social research. The implication is, however, that studies of the problems of underdeveloped countries are now undertaken, not with a

---

[1] Gunnar Myrdal, *The Political Element in the Development of Economic Theory*, Routledge and Kegan Paul, London, 1953; cf. two other works by the same author: *Economic Theory and Under-developed Regions*, Duckworth, London, 1957, Part II (in America: *Rich Lands and Poor*, Harper, New York, 1957); and *Value in Social Theory, A Selection of Essays on Methodology*, Paul Streeten, ed., Routledge and Kegan Paul, London, 1958.

view to the universal and timeless values that are our legacy from the Enlightenment, but with a view to the fortuitous and narrow political or, narrower still, military-strategic interests of one state or bloc of states. All sorts of studies are now justified by, or focussed on, their contribution to the "security" of Western countries. This officious accommodation by the scholarly profession to a new political "realism" in research often borders on the ridiculous. Even a respectable biologist's compilation of available research on the influence of climatic factors on organisms in the tropics may be introduced by and interspersed with glib and, understandably, inexpert reflections concerning the political effect on the "free world" of economic development there.

Often this is no more than a confession of faith by a troubled soul. At other times it may be intended to provide a mantle of respectability in an emotional environment dominated by non-professionals. Most of the time it turns out that the political or even the military-strategic interests of one's own country are taken to consist in the preservation of very general values. The "best interests of the United States," for instance, dictate the establishment and growth in the underdeveloped countries of what many people there themselves strive for: a stable and, where possible, democratic regime in a consolidated nation capable of economic development. This would be an interesting and, we believe, a broadly valid formulation of how American democracy evaluates the underdeveloped countries in the long run. Applied, as it frequently is, to a contemporary short-term perspective on American foreign policy at a time of fluid conflicts and tactical alliances, the proposition is less evidently valid in the policies pursued and is often clearly belied by them. In any case, it is difficult to see the relevance of this assumption about American society, or American interests, to the scientific study of an underdeveloped country's own experiences and problems. If, nevertheless, it *is* given relevance, the door is opened to all sorts of extraneous influences on research approaches, in other words, to biases.

A major source of bias in much economic research on poor countries is thus the endeavor to treat their internal problems from the point of view of the Western political and military interest in saving them from Communism. Sometimes this intention is stated, though not in the form of a reasoned presentation of specific value premises logically related to the definition of the concepts used.[1] More often it remains implicit in the approach, though the study is interspersed with suggestive formulations. This type of reasoning must often make the public and scholars in the underdeveloped countries suspicious and irritated, as they naturally want their problems analyzed from the point of view of their own interests and valuations. The taking of an outside view does not in itself constitute a fault in

[1] Chapter 2, Section 1.

the methodology of scientists, whose criterion of validity cannot be the acceptability of approaches and conclusions to the people concerned. What is important is that the practice usually goes hand in hand with a retreat from scientific standards, which permits the entrance of uncontrolled biases — and this, of course, gives substance to the suspicion and irritation in underdeveloped countries.

Consideration of Western political and military interests in saving the underdeveloped countries from Communism invites inhibitions, for instance, about observing and analyzing the shortcomings of political regimes in those countries — provided, let it be noted, that they are not friendly with the enemy in the cold war. An indication of such tortuous reasoning, which lends itself to opportunistic arrangement of the facts, is the use even in scholarly writings of labels like "the free world" or "the free Asian countries" to denote, not that people are free in the ordinary sense of the word, but the purely negative fact that a country's foreign policy is not aligned to that of the Communist bloc or blocs. This is not an innocent terminological matter; such practice hides shifts in the meaning of concepts. And, as the literature abundantly proves, this kind of reasoning tends to give strength by association to an assortment of loosely argued and inexplicitly stated value preferences even in matters of internal policy — economic policy in regard to foreign trade and exchange, public versus private enterprise, and so on.

This opportunistic approach to a research task is not necessarily, or even ordinarily, egoistic and hard-hearted in its conclusions. A study may have as its purpose to discover better based and politically appealing reasons for giving more generous aid to the underdeveloped countries. The political influences on Western social research do not usually encourage unkind treatment of underdeveloped countries — as long as they are not hopelessly lost to the enemy bloc. On the contrary, what national communities more or less overtly demand from their social scientists are essays in practical diplomacy pleading certain directions of external and internal policy and giving a more solid and scholarly foundation to such pleas. When, as often happens, social scientists resist having their work turned into diplomacy, the pressures on them may nevertheless force them to engage in research on particularly innocuous problems in an underdeveloped country that have less immediate connection with political issues. They become accustomed to bypass facts that raise awkward problems, to conceal them in technical terminology, or to treat them in an "understanding" and forgiving manner. These are also biases in research. Conditioning that results in omissions rather than commissions nonetheless erodes the basis for objective research. The scholar should not be made to speak with tongue in cheek.

These remarks are not intended to isolate the economic problems of underdeveloped countries from the ideological and power constellations of world politics. The cold war has, of course, considerable bearing on events in the underdeveloped countries of South Asia; and their political allegiance to a power bloc, or their neutrality, is worth studying. Most certainly, the drift of its economy and the social and economic policies it pursues can affect such a country's alignment in the cold war, though this problem is often oversimplified. An underdeveloped country that, for whatever reason, comes under Communist rule will apply Soviet methods of planning for economic development, and this will bring about a major change in the situation under study. In the same way a country's dependence on credits and gifts from the Western bloc may influence its internal policies and thereby affect the social reality we are studying. But to recognize these causal relations is not to say that the Western interest in winning the underdeveloped countries as allies or at least keeping them neutral is an appropriate value premise for the study of their development problems. If it *is* chosen as a value premise, it should be chosen openly and operate in a logical way that does not detract from scientific objectivity.[1] Diplomacy is essential to national policy, but it is disastrous when it dominates the work of social scientists.

The tendency to think and act in a diplomatic manner when dealing with the problems of the underdeveloped countries of South Asia has, in the new era of independence, become a counterpart to the "white man's burden" in colonial times. No one with any critical sense can be unaware of this trend. I can myself testify that British and American and other Western scholars confess and defend as a principle — when speaking "among ourselves," that is, among us who are from the rich and progressive countries — the necessity to "bend over backwards." Not only politicians but also scholars, in public appearances, will apologize for making even slightly derogatory remarks and suggest that as foreigners they should not venture to express a view on the matter. In the literature such discretion leads to the avoidance of certain problems and the deliberate understatement of negative findings. I have often heard writers explain that they did this in order not to hurt feelings. A Russian scholar addressing a South Asian audience is equally tactful now that the policy of the Soviet Union has become friendly to the "bourgeois-nationalist" regimes in the region.

I am here not arguing against diplomacy, except in scientific research. A scholar should work and express himself identically at home and in a foreign country. As a scientist he should, of course, have no loyalty other than that to the truth as he perceives it. When speaking in a wealthy, powerful country like the United States this is easy, as I know from experience. The situation is apparently felt to be different in the underdeveloped countries. But it should be understood that diplomacy of this kind is tantamount to condescension, while to speak frankly is to treat the nationals of these

[1] Chapter 2, Section 1.

countries as equals. If South Asians realized this, they should be offended by such diplomacy.

An example of how our thinking has become biased in this direction is the escape into terminology that is thought to be more diplomatic than the ordinary usage, as when one or another euphemism is preferred to "underdeveloped countries." For a discussion of the logical embarrassment into which such attempts lead, see Appendix 1, "Diplomacy by Terminology."

5 Another Source of Bias: Transference of Western Concepts and Theories

Another primary source of bias of special importance to the study of the underdeveloped countries of South Asia may appear to be more mechanical, a function merely of the rapidity with which we have undertaken massive research in a previously almost uncultivated field. As research must of necessity start from a theory, a set of analytical preconceptions,[1] it was tempting to use the tools that were forged in the West and that, in the main, served a useful purpose there,[2] without careful consideration of their suitability for South Asia. Thus a Western approach became incorporated into the mainstream of the discussion of development problems in South Asia, both within the region and outside it. Indeed, Western theoretical approaches have assumed the role of master models. For reasons we shall go into at considerable length in the body of the book, a Western approach must be regarded as a biased approach. Let us attempt to understand how this transfer came to pass.

Economic theorists, more than other social scientists, have long been disposed to arrive at general propositions and then postulate them as valid for every time, place, and culture. There is a tendency in contemporary economic theory to follow this path to the extreme. For such confidence in the constructs of economic reasoning, there is no empirical justification. But even apart from this recent tendency, we have inherited from classical economics a treasury of theories that are regularly posited with more general claims than they warrant. The very concepts used in their construction aspire to a universal applicability that they do not in fact possess. As long as their use is restricted to our part of the world this pretense of generality may do little harm. But when theories and concepts designed to fit the special conditions of the Western world — and thus containing the implicit

[1] Section 7 below.

[2] Throughout this book I am making the generous assumption that the Western approach is fairly adequate to Western conditions. This might be an overstatement. In any case, this is a book on South Asia, and I have not felt it to be my task to go into a critical analysis of the use of Western concepts and theories outside the region I am studying.

assumptions about social reality by which this fitting was accomplished — are used in the study of underdeveloped countries in South Asia, where they do *not* fit, the consequences are serious.

There is a conservatism of methodology in the social sciences, especially in economics, that undoubtedly has contributed to the adherence to familiar Western theories in the intensive study of underdeveloped countries. Economists operate to a great extent within a framework that developed early in close relationship with the Western philosophies of natural law and utilitarianism and the rationalistic psychology of hedonism. Only with time has this tradition been adapted to changing conditions, and then without much feeling of need for radical modifications. That economists work within a methodologically conservative tradition is usually not so apparent to the economists themselves, especially as the tradition affords them opportunity to display acumen and learning and, within limits, to be inventive, original, and controversial. Even the heretics remain bound by traditional thought in formulating their heresies.[1] As circumstances, particularly political ones, changed, there was room for a shifting of emphasis and approach. When theoretical innovations lagged far behind events, such adjustments sometimes took on the appearance of definite breaks, as in the so-called Keynesian "revolution." The new thoughts were soon integrated into the traditional mold, slightly modified to better suit the environment, the changes in which were themselves largely responsible for inspiring fresh thinking.

Occasionally a breakthrough established new lines of thought that contrasted more sharply with tradition. The most important challenge came, of course, from Marx and his followers. But Marx, at the base of his constructs, retained much of classical economic theory. And gradually economists remaining within the fold incorporated large parts of what was or seemed novel in Marx's approach, not least in regard to the problems of development, as we shall see. For both these reasons we should not be surprised to find that the biases operating on Western economists often tend to converge with those conditioning economists in the Communist countries. These assertions will be exemplified in various contexts in this book.

When we economists, working within this tenacious but variegated and flexible tradition of preconceptions that admittedly are not too badly fitted to our own conditions, suddenly turn our attention to countries with radically different conditions, the risk of fundamental error is exceedingly great.[2] This risk is heightened by the dearth of empirical data on social

---

[1] See Myrdal, *Economic Theory and Under-developed Regions*, pp. 129 ff.

[2] "One ever-present problem is the possibility that a conceptual scheme will imprison the observer, allowing him to see only what the scheme directs him to see and ruling out other interpretations of data. It is readily admitted that this danger is implicit in all a priori thinking." (Richard C. Snyder and Glenn D. Paige, "The United States Decision to Resist Aggression in Korea: The Application of an Analytic Scheme," in *Administrative Science Quarterly*, Vol. 3, No. 3, December, 1958, p. 358.)

realities in the underdeveloped countries of South Asia, which enables many biases to be perpetuated that might be questioned and corrected if concepts and theories could be exposed to the challenge of concrete facts. The problem is compounded by another consequence of the Western-biased approach. When new data are assembled, the conceptual categories used are inappropriate to the conditions existing: as, for example, when the underutilization of the labor force in the South Asian countries is analyzed according to Western concepts of unemployment, disguised unemployment, and underemployment. The resulting mountains of figures have either no meaning or a meaning other than that imputed to them. Empirical research then becomes faulty and shallow, and, more important in the present context, less valuable for testing the premises latent in the Western concepts that have guided the production of new statistics. The very fact that the researcher gets figures to play with tends to confirm his original, biased approach. Although it is the confrontation with the facts that ultimately will rectify our conceptual apparatus, initially the paucity and flimsiness of data in underdeveloped countries leave ample opportunity for biases, and the continuing collection of data under biased notions only postpones the day when reality can effectively challenge inherited preconceptions.

The danger of bias does not necessarily arise from the fact that students from the rich countries in the West inevitably face the problems of underdeveloped countries in South Asia as strangers. If anything, the outsider's view has advantages in social research. There are two ways of knowing a toothache: as a patient or as a dentist, and the latter is usually not the less objective. The white Southerner's conviction that he, and he alone, "knows" the American Negroes because of his close association with them has been proved erroneous. The stranger's view may be superficial, it is true, but superficiality is not the monopoly of strangers; it is a matter of the intensity and effectiveness of research. There is thus no necessary connection between superficiality and the extent of bias. Indeed, biases in research have no relation to superficiality *per se*. They emanate from the influences exerted by society, from our personal involvement in what we are studying, and from our tendency to apply approaches with which we are familiar to environments that are radically different. Biases can be present or absent as much when we are strangers to the country we are studying as when we are its nationals and as much when the research undertaken stretches over long periods and is conducted with a huge apparatus as when it is simply a journalist's attempt to put his impressions and reflections in order.

Nor are Western economists uniquely subject to the specific biases emanating from our methodological conservatism. Our confreres in the South Asian countries are afflicted as much, if not more, with them. Many have been trained at Western centers of learning or by teachers who acquired their training in the West. All have been thoroughly exposed to the great economic literature in the Western tradition. Familiarity with, and ability to work in accordance with, that tradition is apt to give them status at home. Their motivations for sharing in this bias are fairly independent of their political attitudes. Part of the explanation, as will be shown in the next section, is that application of the Western approach serves both conservative and radical needs for rationalization in the South Asian countries.

That the use of Western theories, models, and concepts in the study of economic problems in the South Asian countries is a cause of bias seriously distorting that study will be a main theme of this book. For the moment a few *obiter dicta* must suffice to outline this general criticism.

The concepts and the theory of unemployment and underemployment rest on assumptions about attitudes and institutions that, though fairly realistic in the developed countries, are unrealistic in the underdeveloped countries.

The neat division of income into two parts, consumption and saving, is realistic in Western societies where the general levels of income and a stratified system of income redistribution by social security policies and other means have largely abrogated any influence of consumption on productivity. This is not the case in the underdeveloped countries.

Marx's assumption, so widely adopted by Western economists, that the effects of industrialization and, indeed, of investment generally — in the final instance Marx's changes in the "modes of production" — spread quickly to other sectors of the economy and to institutions and attitudes, may be fairly realistic for Western countries, both now and when they started their rapid economic development. But as these "spread effects" are a function of the level of living and of the general culture, the assumption is not valid for most underdeveloped countries, particularly when the sectors of change are small in comparison with the total community. This should be obvious after many decades of colonial history during which the modern enterprises remained enclaves in a largely stagnating economy, but it is seldom given the recognition it deserves, either in economic analysis or in planning for development.

The lack of mobility and the imperfection of markets in underdeveloped countries rob the analytical method of aggregation of magnitudes — employment, savings, investment, and output — of much of its meaning. This conceptual difficulty is in addition to the statistical one already pointed out: that the data aggregated are frail and imperfect, partly because their categories are unrealistic.

The list could be made much longer, as will be seen in this book. Our main point is that while in the Western world an analysis in "economic" terms — markets and prices, employment and unemployment, consumption and savings, investment and output — that abstracts from modes and levels of living and from attitudes, institutions, and culture may make sense and lead to valid inferences, an analogous procedure plainly does not in underdeveloped countries. There one cannot make such abstractions; a realistic analysis must deal with the problems in terms that are attitudinal and institutional and take into account the very low levels of living and culture. The newest attempts to analyze education (and health) in terms of "investment in man" do not even state the problem in a rational way. The "non-economic" facts do not adjust smoothly to economic changes, but set up inhibitions and obstacles to them, so that often the "economic" terms cannot even be given a clear meaning. A practical corollary is the much greater need for coordination of planning in the "economic" and the "non-economic" fields.[1] Acknowledgment of this important difference is frequently made by way of qualifications and reservations. But the basic approach, not least in regard to the problems of economic planning, has remained a rather simple application of Western concepts and theories.

6   The Western Approach Serves Deeper Inclinations to Bias

The temptation to apply the Western approach was said above to be almost mechanical, a function of the speed with which research was begun in a nearly untouched field and our natural inclination to utilize research methods with which we were familiar. The urge to do so was the more impelling as no other kit of tools was available for bringing a semblance of order into the analysis of the complex conditions in South Asian countries. But the matter is not so uncomplicated. The appeal of the Western conceptual approach draws further strength from the fact that it is well fitted to the rationalization of opportunistic interests both in the developed Western countries and among the influential intellectual elite in the underdeveloped countries themselves.

Generally speaking, the Western approach abstracts from most of the conditions that are peculiar to the South Asian countries and are responsible for their underdevelopment and for the special difficulties they meet in developing. These conditions and difficulties are all of a type that South Asians and their foreign well-wishers must desire to forget. They were the features of the social structure that were prominent in the thoughts of the European colonial masters, both in their stereotypes and in their more sophisticated reasonings. Exaggerated emphasis on these impediments to development served their need for rationalization. It explained away their

---

[1] See Appendix 2, Section 19.

"For all practical purposes growth and development in the less developed parts of the world seem to depend rather upon the speed and efficiency with which given attitudes and institutions can be and actually are modified and changed. Viewed in its truly dynamic dimension the process of economic growth and development is and always has been a problem of political and socio-cultural change." (K. William Kapp, *Hindu Culture, Economic Development and Economic Planning in India,* Asia Publishing House, Bombay, 1963, p. 69.)

responsibility for the backwardness of colonial peoples and their failure to try to improve matters. Both the post-colonial ideologies and the ideologies of the liberation movements were deeply stamped by protest against that thinking.[1] And so the pendulum of biases swung from one extreme to the other. The intellectuals in these countries want to rationalize in the contrary sense, and it serves their needs to make the abstractions implied by Western economists. Genuine sympathy, in addition to reasons of diplomacy, brought Western economists under the same spell of opportunism. The fact that what they were applying was established theory, which had been successfully used in the Western countries, made the entrance of this systematic bias the easier.

It was an approach that appealed to both radicals and conservatives in South Asia. The radicals, partly under the impact of Marx's thinking, were prone to exaggerate the rapidity of adjustment of the entire social system to changes in the "economic" sphere; conservatives, averse to direct policy intervention in modes and levels of living, attitudes, and institutions, welcomed an approach that placed these matters in the shadow. Concerning the radicals, we must also remind ourselves of the similarities, particularly in basic concepts, between Marx's and Western economic theorizing. These have already been referred to and are illustrated in many contexts in the ensuing chapters.

There are also differences in approach, however, and it should be clear that certain elements of Marx's economic speculation often seem to fit situations in South Asia much more closely than those in the rich modern welfare states of the West: for instance, the apparent existence of a "reserve army" of idle, or largely idle, workers; the existence and the increase of a dispossessed proletariat; the often frank exploitation of workers by employers; and the big and widening gap between a few rich individuals or families and the masses of very poor people. It is remarkable that very little fresh analysis of the problems of the region in Marx's terms is forthcoming, while essays in the Western pattern are abundant. We thus often find at the universities in South Asia economists who are strongly anti-Western in their sympathies and politically far to the left, even avowed Communists or fellow-travellers, but who are yet eager and proud to place the emphasis of their teaching on the latest abstract and formal growth models developed at Cambridge or Yale, and whose ambition is to write articles resembling those in the Western journals and, hopefully, to publish them there.

In attempting to understand this bent of mind of the radicals we must take into account the virtual bombardment of massive Western research on the underdeveloped countries in recent times, while the literary output on their problems in Communist countries has been small, polite, but un-

[1] Chapter 21, Section 7 *et passim*.

inspiring. An additional factor is, however, that pursuit of Marx's particular approach referred to above would inevitably have led to a consideration of "non-economic" factors. The competitive strength of the Western approach is, at bottom, that its abstractions give an optimistic slant to the thinking about the development problems in the underdeveloped countries of the region.

Optimism, and therefore approaches that make optimism seem more realistic, is itself a natural urge for intellectuals in South Asia. That all planning in the region tends to err on the side of optimism is rather palpably clear.[1] The leaning toward diplomatic forbearance in the Western countries fits equally well with biases toward unwarranted optimism among their economists. In Western countries, especially America, optimism is even prized, as a foundation for enterprise and courage; it is almost part of the inherited cultural pattern — what George F. Kennan once called "the great American capacity for enthusiasm and self-hypnosis."[2] In the contest for souls, it is felt to be to the interest of the West that the underdeveloped countries outside the Communist sphere have development and be made to believe in it. In the West there is also a natural wish, and so a temptation to believe, that the underdeveloped countries in South Asia will come to follow policy lines similar to those of the Western countries, and that they will develop into national communities that are politically, socially, and economically like our own. For this reason, too, there is a normal tendency to use a Western approach in studying these countries, as to do so is to play down the initial differences and make such development appear more feasible.

The two main sources of bias in the Western countries thus strengthen each other in that their influences tend to converge. As we saw, the international power conflict and the tensions and emotions associated with it have influenced the study of the problems of the underdeveloped countries in South Asia in the general direction of diplomatic kindness and tolerance — again, provided that these countries are not on the wrong side in that conflict. Many of the conditions peculiar to these countries are highly undesirable; indeed, this is what is meant by their being underdeveloped.[3] Therefore, the other source of bias with which we dealt in the last section — the tendency to use the familiar theories and concepts that have been used successfully in the analysis of Western countries — exerts influences

[1] India's First Five Year Plan would seem to be an exception, as it underestimated the growth of output. But the surpassing of estimates was largely due to unexpectedly favorable monsoons and other accidents. The targets in regard to the policy measures actually making up the plan, and in particular the investments, were not met.

[2] In the Soviet Union uncritical optimism is programmatic, and realism, when it does not lead to optimistic conclusions, is considered a "bourgeois" deviation; this constitutes one of the many similarities in cultural situation between the United States and the Soviet Union.

[3] Appendix 2, Section 5.

in the same direction. For when using the Western approach one can more easily soften the bite of these peculiar and undesirable conditions.

We have wanted to stress the political urges behind these tendencies that affect research on underdeveloped countries in the region. But these tendencies have at their core a compassion that makes them almost irresistible. Quite aside from the cold war and the opportunistic tendencies to bias emerging from it, we of the West are by tradition disposed to be friendly to peoples in distress, once we begin to take an interest in their condition. And it is our earnest hope, apart from all selfish interests, that they will succeed in their development efforts. That we wish them to develop into national communities as similar to our own as possible is a natural ethnocentric impulse that would make itself felt in the calmest world situation. Perhaps it should be stressed again that the concern of the West about the possibility of Communist expansion in underdeveloped countries is also understandable, and from the viewpoint of our own interests valid. And these interests justify using our influence to stop it. Still less can one criticize the human sympathy that characterizes the Western attitude toward these countries.

Nevertheless, we must not let these understandable and genuine feelings influence our perception of the facts. It is the ethos of scientific inquiry that truth and blunt truth-speaking are wholesome and that illusions, including those inspired by charity and good will, are always damaging. Illusions handicap the pursuit of knowledge and they must obstruct efforts to make planning for development fully effective and successful. For this reason, the present book is intended to be undiplomatic. In our study we want to step outside the drama while we are working. We recognize no legitimate demand on the student to spare anybody's feelings. Facts should be stated coldly: understatements, as well as overstatements, represent biases.[1]

[1] In regard to issues that have been felt to be awkward and threatening — for instance, the Negro problem in America — biases toward forbearance and optimism have been quite general in the social sciences. A "balanced view" on such issues tends to be a view that soft-pedals difficulties and causes for worry. Understatements, though in principle just as damaging to the establishment of truth as overstatements, are considered more "objective" and certainly give more respectability. When working without explicit value premises, "the optimistic bias becomes strengthened, paradoxically enough, by the scientist's own critical sense and his demand for foolproof evidence. The burden of proof is upon those who assert that things are bad in our society; it is not the other way around. Unfortunate facts are usually more difficult to observe and ascertain, as so many of the persons in control have strong interests in hiding them. The scientist in his struggle to detect truth will be on his guard against making statements which are unwarranted. His very urge to objectivity will thus induce him to picture reality as more pleasant than it is." (Gunnar Myrdal, *An American Dilemma, The Negro Problem and Modern Democracy,* Harper, New York, 1944, p. 1039.)

"I have often observed that social scientists who are responsible for the publication of other authors' works or who utilize them in their own writings, when they apprehend biases, believe that these can be 'edited away,' by modifying certain expressions used or cutting out or revising certain practical conclusions drawn. Similarly, a general tendency toward understatement is observable in most social science literature. When

One more point should be mentioned before we leave this attempt to characterize briefly the forces tending to create biases in research on development problems in South Asia. As these biases engender an over-optimistic view of development prospects, they sometimes provide encouragement; but mainly they are apt to create undue complacency. In any case, a more realistic view makes it clear that *development requires increased efforts: speedier and more effective reforms in South Asia and greater concern in the West.*

7   A Note on the Unavoidable A Priori

Our criticism of the tendency to take the Western approach in studying the conditions and problems of the underdeveloped countries in South Asia should not be understood as a denial of the right to start out with a theoretical preconception about how things are or, indeed, of the necessity of doing so. Questions are necessarily prior to answers, and no answers are conceivable that are not answers to questions. A "purely factual" study — observation of a segment of social reality with no preconceptions — is not possible; it could only lead to a chaotic accumulation of meaningless impressions. Even the savage has his selective preconceptions by which he can organize, interpret, and give meaning to his experiences. On a fundamental level modern social science is no different from the magical thinking of primitive man. Scientific data — facts established by observation and classification — have no existence outside the framework of preconceptions. Generalizations about reality, and their organization within an abstract framework of presumed interrelations, precede specification and verification. They constitute "theory" in research.

In strict logic a non-theoretical approach in scientific work is thus impossible; and every theory contains the seed of an *a priori* thought. When this theory is stated explicitly, we can scrutinize its inner consistency. This immanent criticism does not take us beyond the sphere of abstract logical relationships; it conveys nothing about empirical reality. But it is also a first principle of science that facts are sovereign. Theory, therefore, must not only be subjected to immanent criticism for logical consistency but must constantly be measured against reality and adjusted accordingly.

The two processes go together. As we increase the volume of observa-

an author has set down something which he feels to be unfavorable about a social class or a region, he looks for something favorable to say in order to 'balance the picture.' A 'balanced view,' a colorless drawing, is considered to be more 'scientific.' Particularly in governmental investigations great care is usually taken to spare the readers. The deliberate attempt that is made in such reports not to offend anyone will often make them difficult to use for scientific purposes. This tendency is, of course, not only ineffective in mitigating biases, but, even worse, it is itself one of the main types of bias in research." (*Ibid.*, p. 1043.)

Concerning the general problem of bias, see the same work, pp. 1035–1045.

tional data to which we are led by our analytical preconceptions, our original theories are refitted in order to make sense of the data and explain them. This is the crux of all science: It always begins *a priori* but must constantly strive to find an empirical basis for knowledge and thus to become more adequate to the reality under study. This is also the reason why we can never achieve perfection — merely an approximate fitting of theory to facts. But there are differences in how close we can come to the facts. In the underdeveloped countries of South Asia, most of the crucial data are deficient in scope and reliability. Moreover, such data as exist are heavily prejudiced by inadequate preconceptions, and we must always be on guard against biases arising from this source.

Theory is thus no more than a correlated set of questions to the social reality under study. Theory always has its essential function in relation to research still to be carried out. As greater realism is approached, theory becomes better equipped to fulfill this function. "Pure" and unrestricted model-building *pro exercitio* may have its aesthetic or pedagogical value, but it is a diversion from serious research.

What must be emphasized is that *all knowledge, and all ignorance, tends to be opportunistic*,[1] and becomes the more so the less it is checked and reconditioned by solid research directed to the empirical facts. Through wide and arduous travelling, which seldom means taking the shortest route, students undoubtedly will be forced gradually to correct their preconceptions, however deeply rooted in opportunism these may be. Until the approach is better tailored to reality, the data fail to fall into place, the facts rebel, and the logic is strained. In the longer time perspective I see no reason for pessimism about the study of the underdeveloped countries in South Asia. Inherent in all honest research is a self-correcting, purifying force that in the end will affirm itself.

An interesting parallel comes to mind — namely, the history of research on inherited group differentials in aptitudes, especially intelligence. This to me has always stood as one of the great monuments to the ethos of truth-seeking and its intrinsic quality of leading, in the end, to truer knowledge. The psychologists who more than half a century ago set out to measure innate differences in intelligence between whites and Negroes, men and women, rich and poor, had no doubt that such differences existed and that they were pronounced. There is truth in the biblical saying that "he that seeketh, findeth"; but if a scientist seeks what isn't there he will find it only as long as empirical data are scanty and the logic is allowed to be forced. As the researchers amassed their observations and as they refined their tools for observation and analysis, they found what they had *not* been seeking and what, indeed, was contrary to their preconceptions: the differences disappeared, or at least could not be scientifically established.

We shall in time come to see a similar change in the approach to the

[1] Myrdal, *An American Dilemma*, pp. 40–42 *et passim*.

study of the underdeveloped countries in South Asia. The more we labor with these problems, the more evident will become the necessity to modify the analytical preconceptions that are now dominant. But this process of improvement can be speeded up if we help by scrutinizing our approaches for irrational influences that are working on our minds. This is why I have asked for greater interest in the sociology of knowledge. Such an inward turn of research interests would pay large dividends in more rapid scientific progress.

8   A Plea for an Institutional Emphasis

As we are far from satisfied with the conventional approach to the development problems in South Asia, it is incumbent upon us to sketch an alternative theory that can serve as an analytical framework for the conduct of this study.

We shall use as a starting point the incontrovertible fact that the basic social and economic structure of the countries of South Asia is radically different from that existing in advanced Western countries. Conditions in the rich Western countries today are such that, broadly speaking, the social matrix is permissive of economic development or, when not, becomes readily readjusted so as not to place much in the way of obstacles in its path. This is why an analysis in "economic" terms, abstracting from that social matrix, can produce valid and useful results. But that judgment cannot be accurately applied to South Asian conditions. Not only is the social and institutional structure different from the one that has evolved in Western countries, but, more important, the problem of development in South Asia is one calling for induced changes in that social and institutional structure, as it hinders economic development and as it does not change spontaneously, or, to any very large extent, in response to policies restricted to the "economic" sphere.

This view, of course, has been implicit in our criticism of the adequacy of Western conceptual approaches and it forms the essential preconception running through the body of this study. We do not preclude the possibility that, at a future date, the institutional structure of the South Asian countries may be such that some of the Western tools of analysis, at present woefully inadequate, will come into their own. Neither this possibility nor a defense sometimes offered for the current use of Western concepts — their potentiality for defining the targets these countries are seeking to hit — justifies the use of modern Western preconceptions now. The essential first step toward an understanding of the problems of the South Asian countries is to try to discover how they actually function and what mechanisms regulate their performance. Failure to root analysis firmly in these realities invites both distortions in research and faults in planning.

So our approach is broadly "institutional," and we plead for greatly intensified research efforts along these lines. We should remember that to be really fruitful this new approach cannot be restricted to the insertion of qualifications and reservations meant to take into account the things left out by conventional economic analysis along Western lines. As the very theories and concepts utilized in that analysis guide it away from those "non-economic" factors, what is needed is a different framework of theories and concepts that is more realistic for those societies.[1]

Building such a framework, however, is a very large order; it is understandable why it has not been met and why, perhaps, its demands will not be satisfied until much more solidly based empirical work has been done. In this situation even the negative accomplishment of demonstrating the inadequacy of our inherited economic theories and concepts, and thereby discovering that we know much less than we pretend to know, is worthwhile. But, of course, our goal is also the more ambitious one of replacing conventional theories and concepts by other, new ones better fitted to the reality of these countries. And we need not only to establish the mechanisms that can explain the unique properties of these economies but also to build an analytical structure fitted to the dynamic problems of development and planning for development.

In the latter respect the Western economic approach has an alluring appearance of superiority, as it provides a simple system permitting generalizations and, more particularly, one that can fit the needs of dynamic analysis in terms of planning for development. In addition to the influences of theoretical conservatism and of opportunistic interests of various types, as analyzed in Sections 4–6 above, these properties seem to provide more objective reasons for adhering to the Western approach and accounting for its lack of realism by means merely of qualifications and reservations. One might have expected the behavioral disciplines, particularly social anthropology and sociology, to provide the more broadly based system of theories and concepts needed for the scientific study of the problem of development. Unfortunately, they have not done so. The tradition of social anthropology has been to work in static terms, attempting to explain the structure and internal relations of societies in what we now call a state of stagnation or

---

[1] "We all agree that the basic requirement of any model is that it should be capable of explaining the characteristic features of the economic process as we find them in reality. It is no good starting off a model with the kind of abstraction which initially excludes the influence of forces which are mainly responsible for the behavior of the economic variables under investigation; and upon finding that the theory leads to results contrary to what we observe in reality, attributing this contrary movement to the compensating (or more than compensating) influence of residual factors that have been assumed away in the model. . . . Any theory must necessarily be based on abstractions; but the type of abstraction chosen cannot be decided in a vacuum: it must be appropriate to the characteristic features of the economic process as recorded by experience." (Nicholas Kaldor, "Capital Accumulation and Economic Growth," in *The Theory of Capital,* Macmillan & Co. Ltd., London, 1961, pp. 177–178.)

"low-level equilibrium." Much sociological research has remained within this tradition. It is, for instance, surprising how little attention has been devoted in village surveys to the effects of population increase on social stratification. And when studies in these disciplines are focussed on change, as they increasingly are, the emphasis is not often placed on development, much less on framing a more comprehensive system of theories and concepts suited to the needs of the planner.

For this there may seem to be an obvious explanation, that the factors abstracted from in the economic analysis — attitudes, institutions, modes and levels of living, and, broadly, culture — are so much more difficult to grasp in systematic analysis than are the so-called economic factors. They undoubtedly are. But if the view propounded in this book is correct, it simply follows that the problems of underdevelopment, development, and planning for development in South Asia are themselves exceedingly difficult and that they have yet to be mastered. An artificial restriction of "reality" to that which is seemingly easier to grasp misses the central point. For in the South Asian countries the "economic" facts cannot be studied in isolation from other social facts.

To the economists belongs the credit for spearheading the attack on the dynamic problems of underdevelopment, development, and planning for development. Economists have always been the cavalry of the social scientists and have enjoyed the status corresponding to this role. It is to us the politicians turn for advice; it is to us they listen. The doctrine of the preponderance of economic factors has been blamed on Marx. However, it was devised before his time and, as is obvious from national and international political debate, it is adhered to with few reservations by politicians in all countries. Economists dominate fact gathering and planning in every country, and when an international organization is set up, everyone agrees that it must have an economic research unit. For more than two hundred years economists have advised both those in power and those in opposition; some of us have been members of parliaments and governments. By comparison, the other social sciences have been "poor relations."

Our strength in all generations has been our singular sensitivity to the political needs of the time and our courage in offering theories that, though sufficiently complicated to flex our intellectual muscles and to impress the multitude, have been communicable in essence to the public and capable of suggesting solutions to practical, political problems. We have been a fighting church with a message, albeit one with much disputing among sects. When we turned decisively to the dynamic problems of underdeveloped economies after the Second World War, problems that were at the same time of great political significance, this was in keeping with our traditions. Our confreres in the other social sciences noted, as they often have, our impetuous sweep and occasionally warned us that we ought to consider certain matters excluded from our framework of analysis. Administrators and other men of practical affairs also went outside our framework when dealing with such issues as community uplift, educational advance, or land reform. But seldom, and never effectively, did either of those two groups, both of which were in closer touch with reality, formulate their skepticism as a challenge to our fundamental approach. And they had, in any case, no other system of theories and concepts to offer for tackling a problem as political and dynamic as that of development.

In this book we argue that there is a need not merely for qualifications and reservations, but for a fundamental change in approach. If we are correct, there is room for more interdisciplinary research, and we should welcome efforts by sociologists and others to improve our system of theories and concepts. The fact is, however, that a political and dynamic point of view is embedded in the tradition of economics, and less so in the other social sciences. As it is we economists who have inherited that viewpoint, the main hope must be that the economics profession will gradually turn to remodelling our framework of theories and concepts in the direction characterized above as institutional. Just as general philosophy failed to provide economics with a ready-made methodology, with the consequence that economists were left very much on their own to cleanse the metaphysical conception of value (a task they have far from accomplished), so the responsibility for working out a more realistic approach to the problems of underdevelopment, development, and planning for development must rest with economists. Despite the strivings for "cross fertilization" and interdisciplinary research, the barriers hampering transmission of ideas among our disciplines remain considerable. And the new approach must concentrate on the dynamic problem of development, an emphasis that does not come naturally to those brought up outside the tradition of economics.

Certainly we hope to gain support from the practitioners of behavioral research. With strong ideological influences and vested interests working to retain the Western approach of economic analysis, as shown in the foregoing sections, attempts to change it will meet resistance from a majority of both the producers and the consumers of economic research in South Asia, as well as in the West. If the present study, by placing the economic problems in their wider setting, can stimulate researchers in other disciplines to focus their work more directly on issues relevant to economic research, planning, and development, it will have made a contribution.

In the body of this book, we attempt to plot the course in which we believe further research efforts can most profitably be steered. The difficulties in formulating a satisfactory alternative theory of the processes of underdevelopment and development are immense. We are seriously handicapped by the dearth of relevant empirical data; many important matters that we would like to qualify have not yet been measured. The general pattern of preconceptions underlying our approach — namely, that the institutional environment of South Asian countries is radically different from the one familiar in the West and that "economic" facts cannot be dealt with in isolation — is, however, firmly grounded in observation of life in the region. In attempting to fill out an alternative theoretical scheme, one aim is naturally to develop a broad set of generalizations about conditions in the region and about the mechanism of causal relations between them. Ideally, we should like to support each of these generalizations with a solid body of empirical data. Unfortunately, given the present state of knowledge, this is rarely possible.

For this reason, many of the specific generalizations advanced stem from what Marshall once described as "staple general reasonings." While we are confident that this approach leads us closer to the essential realities of economic processes in South Asia than does one inspired by current analytical preconceptions in the West, we make no claim to infallibility in the substantive content of our generalizations. At this stage, the fundamental merit claimed for an alternative approach is not that it yields answers to the urgent development problems of South Asian countries, but that it raises the right questions.

We regard the generalizations making up our "theory" as highly tentative and often conjectural. Many will challenge them; it is healthy that they should. For an essential ingredient to progress toward an understanding of the complexities of the development process is the dialogue in which generalizations are advanced, challenged, and then modified and corrected. In this fashion, the sources of differing interpretations and conclusions can be isolated and inspected. This function of generalizations should be borne in mind by readers of this book. That the text is not splashed with question marks but, for convenience, is largely written in declarative form should not obscure the role and function of the generalizations contained in it.

A few remarks on what an institutional approach is *not* have their place at the end of this section. It is not an indulgence in "loose thinking," as some of the conventional economists would be apt to think; on the contrary, it imposes the demand that theories and concepts be logically consistent as well as adequate to reality. Anyone who reads this book, especially the methodological appendices, will find that considerable effort is devoted to clarifying the concepts used. Indeed, a major general criticism launched against the conventional approach of economists is that they have generally been very careless in their reasoning. Paradoxically enough, loose thinking is most often found when they have pretended to be strict and rigorous in their reasoning, but have not scrutinized it as they should by submitting it to transcendental and immanent criticism.

Neither can an institutional approach be characterized as reasoning in "qualitative" terms. If anything, his approach induces the institutional economist to press harder for research that can give quantitative precision to his theories and bring them to the empirical test. In our view, the idea that there is a sphere where "qualitative" reasoning can substitute for thinking in quantitative terms is mistaken. The goal must always be to quantify facts and the relationships between facts, and until we can measure them our knowledge has not proceeded far from the initial *a priori*. Moreover, the institutionalist, since he is basically more critical than the conventional economist, regularly finds the latter's claims to quantitative precision unwarranted, often on logical grounds.

Finally, the conventional economist, whose models we shall frequently have to criticize for loose thinking and unwarranted precision, should not conclude that the institutionalist is "adverse to models." Model-building is a universal method of scientific research, in the same way that quantifying knowledge is a necessary aim of research. As research proceeds, models can be made ever more useful tools in our work. Even if as yet we are in most respects far from the stage where algebraic master models for the whole economy, or large sections of it, have meaning, there are many specific relationships where, to the great advantage of further intensified empirical research, an algebraic statement of the problem can be useful. But to construct such models in the air, out of uncritically conceived concepts that are inadequate to reality and usually not logically consistent, and so pretend to knowledge when none has been established, does not represent scientific progress; it comes near to being an intellectual fraud.

9 *Valuations and Their Inevitability in Scientific Study*

This is the point when at last we have to raise the question of objectivity in research as a problem of logic.

In principle, it would seem easy to lay down the rules for objective research on the South Asian countries. The student should have no ulterior motives. He should confine himself to the search for truth and be as free as possible from both the pressures of tradition and of society around him and his own desires. More particularly, he should in his research have no intention of influencing the political attitudes of his readers, either inside or outside the countries whose conditions he is studying. His task is to provide factual information that will help them all reach greater rationality in following out their own interests and ideals, whatever those are. In his scientific work he should have no loyalties to any particular country or group of countries or any particular political ideology, whatever his own preferences. Indeed, he should have no loyalties at all except to the professional standards of truth-seeking.

These are laudable principles well worth expressing. But they do not solve the methodological problem of how to avoid biases. The problem of objectivity in research cannot be solved simply by attempting to eradicate valuations. Just as the fault with our general views is not that they are general but that often they are logically untenable and not adequate to reality, the fact that valuations are implied cannot be condemned as unscientific. On the contrary, every study of a social problem, however limited in scope, is and must be determined by valuations.[1] A "disinterested" social science has never existed and never will exist. For logical reasons, it is impossible. A view presupposes a viewpoint. Research, like every other rationally pursued activity, must have a direction. The viewpoint and the direction are determined by our interest in a matter. Valuations enter into the choice of approach, the selection of problems, the definition of concepts, and the gathering of data, and are by no means confined to the practical or political inferences drawn from theoretical findings.[2]

The value premises that actually and of necessity determine approaches in the social sciences can be hidden. The student himself may be unaware of them. In fact, most writings, particularly in economics, remain in large part simply ideological. Some two centuries ago, the modern social sciences branched off from the metaphysical philosophies of natural law and utilitarianism. As our heritage from these philosophies, we continue to attempt to "objectify" and "neutralize" the valuation viewpoints and the value-loaded concepts used in scientific analysis. Such attempts are, for instance, plainly visible in the so-called welfare economics, which has lately had a new efflorescence, but they are a much more general phenomenon. Throughout the history of social studies, the hiding of valuations has served to conceal the inquirer's wish to avoid facing real issues. As, for logical reasons, no one can approach a social problem and analyze it without valuations, the result of remaining unaware of these valuations by leaving them implicitly assumed is a concealed *non sequitur*, and thus a space for uncontrolled influences from the valuation sphere. I have seen few efforts in recent years by economists to reform themselves on this

[1] For substantiation of the views expressed in this section, see Myrdal, *Value in Social Theory, Essays on Methodology*, and earlier works cited therein. See also Myrdal, " 'Value-loaded' Concepts," in Hugo Hegeland, ed., *Money, Growth, and Methodology and Other Essays in Honor of Johan Akerman*, Glerup, Lund, 1961, pp. 282 ff.

[2] The terms "theoretical" and "practical" (or "political") are used in this book as they are in the discipline of philosophy. The former word refers to thinking in terms of causes and effects, the latter words to thinking in terms of ends and means.

To stress the subjectivity of the valuation process we deliberately use the word "valuations" rather than "values" — except in the combination "value premises," where certain valuations have been defined and made explicit for use in research. The common use of the term "values" invites confusion between valuations in the subjective sense, the object of these valuations, and indeed the whole social setting of valuations. The use of the term "values" also usually contains a hidden value premise, that a "value" *eo ipso* is valuable in some objective sense; this implies a bias of the *"laissez-faire"* variety. See Myrdal, *An American Dilemma*, p. 1031.

Concerning the relations assumed between valuations and beliefs, see *ibid.*, Appendix 1.

score, least of all among those devoting themselves to abstract economic theory.[1]

Efforts to run away from the valuations are misdirected and foredoomed to be fruitless and damaging. The valuations are with us, even when they are driven underground, and they guide our work. When kept implicit and unconscious, they allow biases to enter. The only way in which we can strive for objectivity in theoretical analysis is to lift up the valuations into the full light, make them conscious and explicit, and permit them to determine the viewpoints, the approaches, and the concepts used. In the practical phases of a study the stated value premises should then, together with the data — established by theoretical analysis with the utilization of those same value premises — form the premises for all policy conclusions.

We have argued here for making the value premises explicit that research may be objective. But we also need to specify them for a broader purpose: clarity and conclusiveness in scientific reasoning. Here we touch on the main problem of the philosophy of knowledge. There is this relation between that problem and the problem of the sociology of knowledge, which has been the focus of interest in this Prologue: that the elucidation of our general views and the definition of our specific value premises are more obviously imperative, and at the same time are made easier, once we realize that we must not naively expect our ideas, even in scientific re-

---

[1] The situation is aptly described by Paul Halmos, who rightly stated that "all social science is 'action research' no matter how etherealized." See "Social Science and Social Change," *Ethics*, January, 1959, p. 108.

He continues a few pages later (p. 117): "One may expect that the efforts of social scientists aimed at 'immunising' their communication from injunctive-normative tendencies will continue. The esoteric, highly speculative and often incomprehensible conceptual systems, the frantic search for specially coined terms free from associated 'value-dross,' the tendency towards explicit neutralism and relativism and the pretence that scientific honesty and loyalty do not belong to a wider context of values — all these and some other aspirations will not stop the positive social sciences from their fact-moulding and object-altering function, a function which the non-social sciences do not possess. There is no way of escaping from the issue of moral responsibility in social science communication, and there is no way of lowering an 'iron curtain' between social science and moral philosophy."

And he quotes David Riesman: "Some social scientists have sought escape from terms which common usage has loaded with values, escape into manufactured symbolism so lacking in overtones as to avoid connotations of praise or blame. In the spirit of certain schools of logical positivism, they want to make only 'meaningful' statements and only purely denotative ones. But, in my opinion, the relation of social science to its subjects, who are also its audience, forbids any such easy undialectical answer to the problem of the researcher's ethical judgments. Terminological opacity will itself be taken as a judgment upon the world, perhaps a manipulative, frightened or unsympathetic one. . . . Literate peoples are going to read what is said about them, no matter how many verbal formulae are set up as barriers, and what they cannot understand they may aggressively misunderstand. Communication involves 'noise,' redundancy — and overtones." (David Riesman, *Individualism Reconsidered*, Free Press, Glencoe, Illinois, 1954, pp. 12–13.)

search, to be unconditioned by anything other than our urge to find the truth.

In Chapter 2 we shall follow up this train of thought by attempting to define the value premises applied in the present study.

10 *The Conception of Drama*

The title of the book, *Asian Drama*, was chosen in order to express the conception of events in South Asia held by the author at the beginning of his work and fortified in the course of study. Behind all the complexities and dissimilarities we sense a rather clear-cut set of conflicts and a common theme as in a drama. The action in this drama is speeding toward a climax. Tension is mounting: economically, socially, and politically.

To some degree all of us are participants in this drama. It is as if the stage, set for South Asia, were enlarged and drew onto itself the entire world, so that no one could be merely a spectator. The growing Western literature on the problems of the underdeveloped countries in South Asia since the Second World War, to which this book is another contribution, is due to a heightened awareness of our stake in the dramatic happenings in these countries. As was pointed out in Section 2 the spurt of interest of the social sciences in their problems is not a spontaneous widening and deepening of research, but is politically determined. Despite the increased interest in South Asian problems in other parts of the world, the leading figures in this drama are the people of South Asia themselves, above all their educated class. The participation of outsiders through research, provision of financial aid, and other means is a sideshow of rather small importance to the final outcome.

This drama has its unity in a set of inner conflicts operating on people's minds: between their high-pitched aspirations and the bitter experience of a harsh reality; between the desire for change and improvement and mental reservations and inhibitions about accepting the consequences and paying the price. Such conflicts are a part of human life in all times and places; but in the countries under study, they have an exceptional, mounting intensity and assume a unique form.

Urged on by aspirations but curbed by material conditions and their own inhibitions, articulate individuals and groups in all these countries continually take decisions with the objective of resolving or accommodating the conflicts. The drama gains its fast pace from the terrific strength of the forces creating the conflicts. The lofty aspirations of the leading actors are separated by a wide gap from the abysmal reality — including the unreadiness of leaders, followers, and the more inert masses to accept the consequences of attempting to attain these aspirations. And that gap is widening. The movement of the drama is intensified as, through time, aspirations are inflated further by almost everything that is printed and preached and demonstrated, be it planned or not, while positive achievements lag. Meanwhile populations are increasing at an ever faster pace, making the realization of aspirations still more difficult.

This conception of the problems in South Asia is not a mere artifice but an image that comes naturally to an observer of the present life of these nations. No one who listens to the public proclamations, reads the papers, talks to people in various walks of life, watches the moves and countermoves in private and public affairs, compares pretensions with reality and declared aspirations with achievements, appraises the efforts and the fulfillments, contemplates the extraordinary disparities, discrepancies, and outright contradictions woven into that half-intentional or unintentional confusion present in almost everything that meets the eye, can fail to sense a fateful constellation of explosive potentialities for extremely rapid change and stubbornly formidable external difficulties and internal obstacles and inhibitions to change. One cannot escape feeling that what one is observing is precisely the unfolding of a drama in the classic sense. It is exceptionally intense, as well as immense in its involvement of hundreds of millions of people, but through its complexities and dissimilarities, as through a classical drama, runs an essentially simple theme.

Indeed, the whole public discussion, whenever it transcends the particulars, runs in terms of a momentous drama. Even debates on particular issues are readily cast in terms of a country's destiny. Wrapped up in the dramatic conception of the life of these nations is also the recognition, shared at bottom even by those who assert the opposite, that the outcome is anything but certain. The student knows, of course, that at some future date a backward glance will be taken, and today's choices will then seem necessary under the circumstances. For this is the way history is explained; everything that happened had its causes and exerted further effects in unending sequence.

In the classic conception of drama — as in the theoretical phase of a scientific study — the will of the actors was confined in the shackles of determinism. The outcome at the final curtain was predetermined by the opening up of the drama in the first act, accounting for all the conditions and causes of later developments. The protagonist carried his ultimate fate in his soul, while he was groping for his destiny. In life, while the drama is still unfolding — as in the practical phase of a study, when policy inferences are drawn from value premises as well as from premises based on empirical evidence — the will is instead assumed to be free, within limits, to choose between alternative courses of action. History, then, is not taken to be predetermined, but within the power of man to shape. And the drama thus conceived is not necessarily tragedy.

DIPLOMACY BY TERMINOLOGY

The Prologue of this book is devoted to an analysis of the influences toward bias that work on our minds when we appraise the economic problems of South Asia. It may serve the useful purpose of illustrating the general character of those irrational influences to dwell briefly on the term "underdeveloped countries," which we use in the present study, and its many synonyms.

This term, of fairly recent origin, has had an interesting history. Its appearance in popular and political as well as in scientific writings is a direct result of the vast political changes referred to in Section 2 of the Prologue. Most of the very poor countries now called "underdeveloped" were until recently not countries at all, but colonial dependencies under various appellations. In the literature before the Second World War, they were usually referred to as "regions"; rather than being called "underdeveloped," they were termed "backward."

Both the static concept "backward regions" and the dynamic one "underdeveloped countries" express the poverty of the people. But "underdeveloped countries" also implies that the areas concerned are now, and want to remain, independent political units and are anxious to rise out of their poverty. Indigenous intellectuals now conceive of their homelands dynamically as "underdeveloped countries" (or "nations"), with these political connotations. Before the Second World War such views were not commonly held, either in the areas themselves or in the West. (The development plans worked out in India by the Indian National Congress and others in anticipation of independent nationhood are exceptions that, by being exceptions, prove the general rule. And even they do not date far back.) When we in the rich Western countries accept the designation "underdeveloped countries," we also accept — at least in a general and noncommittal way — the implied valuation that these countries are, and should remain, independent and should develop: this valuation is what gives the term its meaning.

It should not in the least disturb our scientific conscience when a principal concept has political implications and is, in fact, defined in terms of a value premise. That a concept is "value-loaded" does not signify a lack of logical stringency, or a cause of bias; on the contrary, as discussed in Section 9 of the Prologue, biases creep into research when we attempt to avoid or conceal the valuations that are inherent in both theoretical and practical research. The trouble taken in much of the literature to give underdeveloped countries an "objective" definition, though misdirected, can do little harm, for, at least on the general plane of discussion, the implied valuation is clear-cut and fairly homogeneous.[1]

"Development"—means the process of moving away from "underdevelopment," of rising out of poverty; it is sought and perhaps actually attained by means of "planning for development." There is in the definition of "underdevelopment" and "development" considerable indeterminacy as to the relative weights to be given to different elements of unsatisfied desires that we conflate in the concept "poverty" and that motivate the craving for development out of poverty. Since poverty is deep and extensive in the countries we have in mind, this indeterminacy does not, as pointed out above, have great import for the definition of the concept "underdeveloped countries," when it is used only as a general characterization. But the concept "development," particularly when we attempt to assess a "rate of development," clearly suffers from indeterminacy. That problem is discussed in Appendix 2 (Section 7). As we there show, this indeterminacy is not so great as to render the concept "development" meaningless and thus useless for scientific analysis, but it is sufficient to make it vague. The vagueness has a factual basis in the relative lack of homogeneity in the valuations. To awaken our consciousness of that vagueness by determining its basis and its limits is then logical clarification. On the other hand, to define the concept "development" more precisely than is justified by the facts of relevant valuations is logically faulty.

What is actually meant in characterizing a country as "underdeveloped" is that there is in that country a constellation of numerous undesirable conditions for work and life: outputs, incomes, and levels of living are low; many modes of production, attitudes, and behavioral patterns are disadvantageous; and there are unfavorable institutions, ranging from those at the state level to those governing social and economic relations in the family and the neighborhood. They are evaluated as undesirable — or low or disadvantageous or unfavorable — from the standpoint of the desirability of "development" — a characterization afflicted with vagueness but definite enough to permit its use. There is a general causal relationship among all these conditions, so that they form a social system. It is the task of the study of underdevelopment and development to determine this relationship within that social system. This problem and ways to measure, or indicate, the level of underdevelopment and the rate of development will be discussed further in Part II of Appendix 2.

Meanwhile, diplomacy has entered the arena. In the rich countries, "underdeveloped" has been felt not to be a sufficiently tactful description of the position of the very poor countries. Increasingly, also, some of the nationals of the latter countries have felt inclined to substitute euphemisms, or at least to follow the Western lead, when discussing their countries' problems. This has been particularly true of those who are personally well off and versed in many phases of Western culture that are associated with the notion of a highly "developed"

[1] See also Gunnar Myrdal, " 'Value-loaded' Concepts," in Hugo Hegeland, ed., *Money, Growth, and Methodology and Other Essays in Honor of Johan Akerman,* Glerup, Lund, 1961, pp. 282 ff.

country. And so we find in the literature a florilegium of euphemisms,[1] intended to convey the same value-loaded idea though without stressing the initial status of underdevelopment. As the fact that the poor countries are underdeveloped is the fact the phrase-makers really want to put across, this diplomacy in handling the concept leads to logical embarrassment.

The now widely used term "developing countries" is one of these diplomatic euphemisms. As with few exceptions the countries in question are not developing very fast — if at all — while most of the rich Western countries are continuously developing at a comparatively rapid rate, the term does not serve to distinguish the very poor countries on whose behalf the demand for development is raised. Moreover, the really important aspect of their situation and the meaning that seeks expression is not that they are developing, but that they are underdeveloped, that they need to develop, and that they ought to develop, and in some cases are planning to develop.

Also, by using a term that presupposes that these very poor countries are now developing, and implies that they will continue to develop, an important question is begged. To ascertain whether development is under way, and to throw light on whether a country has real possibilities for further development, and on how this can be brought about, must be among the purposes of study. Definite answers to these questions should not, to say the least, be assumed *a priori* by means of a loaded definition of a country's present situation. The illogicality of the term is disclosed by the fact that it is utilized to cover all underdeveloped countries, and not restricted to those countries that *are* now developing and in the future *can* and *will* develop further.[2]

The term "newly developing countries" is, for the same reason, a logical misnomer. Terms such as "new countries," "emergent countries," "newly emerging countries," or — a label also occasionally tried out — "new democracies" do not always truly represent the situation. In a context where the focus is on the constitutional status of colonies that have won their independence recently, the grouped terms are, and the last term may be, correct. But in relation to the de-

---

[1] In popular vocabulary, though hardly to the same extent in scientific parlance, a parallel tendency to take refuge in ever less blunt euphemisms is noticeable in all matters that are felt to be awkward in polite society: ethnic origin and interracial relations, sex organs and sexual relations, the release of urine and excrements and the facilities provided for it, and so on. In Victorian and post-Victorian England, food, the intake of food, and the organs performing that function were not topics for conversation, at least not at meals. In Sweden, as an advanced welfare state, recent decades have seen the use of increasingly evasive terms for the dwindling group of persons employed as personal and household servants. The common tendency to vagueness, in the direction of understatement, with reference to a woman's age is the same type of verbal diplomacy. A closer parallel to the terminological trend referred to in the text is the promotion of the depressed areas in Britain since the thirties to "development areas."

[2] A generally false rationalization is, for instance, the following assertion: "The term 'developing countries' is used because most of them are already in the process of economic development . . ." (United Nations, ECAFE, *Economic Survey of Asia and the Far East, 1962*, Bangkok, 1963, p. 5.)

Besides containing a misstatement of the facts, it is illogical, for if that is the reason the term is chosen, it should not then be used so as to include those underdeveloped countries that have not yet started to develop.

velopment problem, these terms are irrelevant. "Lesser developed countries" and similar expressions are more accurate. But they are used in connection with a tendency to de-emphasize the actual differences between the rich and the poor countries, and they thus become misleading. All these terms express an escapist attitude. As things are, such an attitude is quite understandable, but it introduces a temptation to deviate from clear thinking, which must be bluntly honest and face the real issues.

The term "underindustrialized countries" does not have that fault, but it is too narrow to express the meaning really intended. Economic development is much more than industrialization. Indeed, the extent to which investments in industry give rise to "spread effects" as opposed to "backwash effects" is an important problem for study in evaluating the relation of industrialization to a country's economic development.[1] This study should not be prejudiced by the choice of terminology. As we demonstrate in the body of the book, there is a tendency in discussing and planning development to expect industrialization to improve drastically the general economic situation in South Asia. In consequence, too little emphasis is placed on agriculture, on raising levels of education and health, on increasing the volume of labor input, and on improving labor efficiency in the economy as a whole. Such a tendency toward irrational beliefs — apart from valuations that may be diverse — should not be fortified by using the term "industrialization" to mean "economic development."

This note on semantics throws light on the nature of the two closely related problems of the sociology and the philosophy of knowledge, touched on in the Prologue: the problem of understanding the forces tending to cause bias that work on our minds when we study the underdeveloped countries in South Asia, which certainly do not stop at the terminological level; and the problem of counteracting these forces by adhering to strict logic if we are to attain objective knowledge.

[1] Chapter 24, Sections 5–9.

Chapter 1

SCOPE AND DIRECTION

OF THE STUDY

---

1 The Regional Approach

The regional approach has no intrinsic justification. There are no mystical qualities in geographical proximity that make neighboring nations a "unit" in any real sense, culturally, politically, or economically. In the specific case of the South Asian countries many circumstances have combined to make their present-day mutual relations feeble. Economic planning and, indeed, all economic policies in the countries under investigation have a rather narrow nationalist horizon, and in recent years the trend has been toward a reduction in the scale of their economic inter-relationships.[1]

With the important exception of the studies carried out by the Economic Commission for Asia and the Far East, most economic research on South Asian problems has been "national" rather than "regional" in extent. For practical reasons, much of the voluminous literature on the plans and on evaluations of plan fulfillment has been confined to the problems of individual countries. Moreover, most research projects initiated abroad have been adjusted to this pattern in order to ensure maximum cooperation by national governments and research organizations and to enhance the immediate practical value of the research results. These reasons are admittedly valid. But the preoccupation of research with single countries has

[1] Chapter 13, Sections 4 and 6.

left a wide gap in the analysis of the more general problems that confront all South Asian countries. This study, embracing the whole region in its frame of reference, is thus partly justified by its attempt to draw analytical comparisons among the countries of South Asia. These countries display enough similarities in basic conditions to make comparisons relevant, and enough differences to make comparisons rewarding for an analysis of the main causal relations.

The regional approach was originally chosen for another reason as well: It was thought that regional cooperation might come to play a larger role in the struggle of these countries for economic development. This possibility was duly emphasized in the background work on their trade and exchange relations and in the analysis of their general problems of economic planning. However, the results indicate that, realistically, the scope for regional cooperation may be very narrow even in the future.[1]

In reporting our findings, we have attempted to follow the general practice of presenting the main facts for all the countries of the region, as defined below, in connection with each of the problems taken up for discussion. Paucity of reliable materials has, however, severely restricted our ability to make comprehensive comparisons in most cases. Thus discussion must often center on one or a few countries, or even districts of a country, that display features of particular interest or where the available material is more satisfactory. As our main concern is analytical rather than merely descriptive, we have not felt obligated to produce exhaustive factual details or to spread the discussion uniformly among the several countries of South Asia.

India, because of its huge population and its political importance in both South Asia and the world, looms much larger in the study than do the other countries. In addition, statistical and other materials are far more abundant and better organized there. India, furthermore, has the most advanced political and administrative machinery in South Asia, and most of the problems dealt with in this book have been discussed there much longer and at a higher level of sophistication than elsewhere. India's three Five Year Plans represent the most serious attempt at economic planning in South Asia, or in any underdeveloped country outside the Soviet orbit. To say that this book is mainly about India with numerous and systematic attempts at comparisons with other countries in South Asia would not be far from the mark.

India's neighbors, Pakistan, Ceylon, and to some extent Burma, have also been given rather close attention. Because of a dearth of material, Afghanistan and Nepal — and Sikkim and Bhutan — have not been considered. In Southeast Asia, Indonesia is a big country of great importance, and we have tried to keep its problems within the focus of our study, though we

[1] Chapter 13, Section 15.

have been unable to treat them as thoroughly as we would have wished. For Thailand, the Federation of Malaya,[1] and the Philippines, available material, at least in certain respects, has been richer. The problems of Singapore are so unusual that it has mostly been left outside the main focus. We reluctantly abandoned the original intention of encompassing the countries that emerged after the collapse of the French Indo-Chinese colonial empire — North and South Vietnam, Laos, and Cambodia — as some of them are primitive and all are in flux. Occasionally we have touched on the last three of these when information of interest was available.

All of West Asia and Iran have been excluded from the region studied, as have Japan, Formosa, the two Koreas, China, Hong Kong, the Soviet Union's North Asian republics, the Portuguese territories, the three British dependencies, and West Irian.

Thus in this study "South Asia," or "the region," takes in Pakistan, India, Ceylon, Burma, Malaya, Thailand, Indonesia, and the Philippines, and sometimes South Vietnam, Cambodia, and Laos as well. The subregion "Southeast Asia" excludes India, Pakistan, and Ceylon. The expressions "the Western countries" or "the Western world" refer in this study to the highly developed countries in Northwestern and West Central Europe (but not Eastern and Southern Europe), to the United States, and to those British Dominions populated by people of European stock, that is, Canada, Australia, and New Zealand; the latter are sometimes referred to as "the white dominions." South Africa is an anomaly and is not included in the classification.

Comparisons with the outside world have generally been restricted to Western Europe. This procedure is to an extent rational because most of South Asia until recently was dominated politically by countries in Western Europe and that domination had profound commercial, social, and cultural influences. In fact, the countries of South Asia have long felt the impact of that political relationship and its influences in all other spheres of life, and they continue to do so in large measure. Comparisons with the Communist world, especially the Soviet Union and China, and with Japan, would admittedly be relevant to a discussion of South Asian development and planning for development. When the writer has not pursued this line, his honest excuse is that while he knows the Western countries reasonably well, his knowledge of these other parts of the world is scanty.

In correcting the proofs of the book an attempt was made to carry the narrative to the beginning of 1966; no events later than that are taken into account, though sometimes more recent literature is discussed.

---

[1] The main work on this book was carried out before the formation of the Malaysian Federation. As we have not studied conditions in North Borneo and Sarawak — the two territories that, initially together with Singapore, were added to the Federation of Malaya — we shall in general refer to the latter political entity.

2   The Broader Setting

The central concern of this study is with the problems of economic underdevelopment, development, and planning for development. But it is
false to imagine that economic analysis unaided can probe exhaustively
into these matters. In reality, as we have taken pains to point out in the
Prologue, there are no exclusively "economic" problems; there are simply
problems, so that distinctions between "economic" and "non-economic"
factors are, at best, artificial. The very act of clarifying what we should
mean by "economic" problems or "economic" factors implies an analysis
that includes all the "non-economic" determinants. The only worthwhile
demarcation — and the only one that is fully tenable logically — is between
relevant and less relevant factors, and the line of demarcation will vary
with the characteristics of the environment under study.

Abstraction from part of the complexity of the real world does, of
course, have its uses in scientific analysis. But the scope for useful abstraction is far narrower under South Asian conditions than in the economic
and social environment of the West. Especially when problems are viewed
from a dynamic and policy perspective, a host of factors conventionally
excluded from contemporary economic analysis in Western countries have
a powerful influence in a South Asian environment — which means that attempts to isolate purely economic factors there are much more dangerous
for the validity and relevance of the analysis.[1] All the consequences the
writer draws from this methodological position may not now be universally
accepted. But as a general proposition, the need to account for more than
"economic" factors when studying the processes of economic underdevelopment, development, and planning for development is a commonplace in
the literature on these problems. An attempt to view those economic processes systematically in their broader setting should thus not be a radical
methodological innovation.

It is also worth noting that attempts in the region to formulate plans for
economic development often include programs for policy action extending over the entire field of social relations. These encompass not only programs for investment in physical facilities and for mobilizing resources
through savings, taxation, and foreign loans and grants, but also policies
directed toward population control, health, education, vocational and professional training, general civic culture, improvement in administration
and self-government, intensification of voluntary cooperation in various
fields, higher levels of social security and social conditions generally, protection and uplift of depressed classes, and so on. This inclusiveness in the
general layout of planning stands in rather sharp contrast to the tendency
to end up by laying the main stress in both research and planning on the

[1] Prologue, Sections 5, 6, 8; Appendix 2, Sections 19, 20.

"economic" factors, conceived in terms of the Western concepts of markets and prices, employment, savings, investment, and output.[1]

In the practical field, the inclusiveness, in principle, of planning in the region is a recognition of general interdependence among the factors involved in a process of social change. To engender and accelerate development, induced changes in *all* social conditions and relations must be assumed to be instrumental or even to play a strategic role in the cumulative causation of a development process. In Appendix 2 an attempt is made to elucidate the nature of those wider relationships within the whole social fabric of an underdeveloped country and thus give a tentative foundation to a general social theory of economic underdevelopment, development, and planning for development in the region.

While these convictions have determined the approach to the problems dealt with in this study, we cannot pretend to have come far toward formulating a completely general framework of analysis. In attempting to view the "economic" facts in their relation to all other social facts, we have been brought into contact with a wide range of problems and with a rapidly swelling literature. Despite its volume, much of this literature leaves us in great uncertainty, partly because we cannot master it, partly because its coverage is so spotty, and partly because the questions posed are often not directly relevant to the central concern of our study. *Essentially this remains a study of major economic problems in South Asia, though one that maintains a constant awareness of the broader setting of these issues.* Although we have been obliged to work under severe practical limitations, we have attempted to point out clearly and systematically the position within the broader set of social relations of the economic problems analyzed.

In its more intensive discussions the study is directed to the dynamics of the forces presently at play, chiefly their significance for the future. Wherever feasible — for instance, in Chapter 27 where we deal with population developments — we try to project trends. Alternative policies are also considered — as in the concluding sections of Chapter 26 on agricultural policies in regard to land ownership and tenancy. We are thus not primarily interested in the history behind the current situation and trends, though we must often make historical generalizations and include selected material of a historical kind in order to explain present conditions. We realize that the lack of historical depth in our approach restricts our understanding of the social reality we are investigating. This again is due solely to the practical limitations of time, research facilities, and technical competence.

Having stated these qualifications, we must add that the economic situations and trends in the several countries in the region are so immensely variegated and complex, and the data so weak, that a study of the magnitude

---

[1] Concerning these general points, see the Prologue, Section 5; Appendix 2, Sections 19–21; and Appendix 4. See also Chapter 15, Section 1.

of the present one cannot aspire to a high degree of intensity, much less to encyclopedic comprehensiveness, even in the economic field. We have consciously directed our inquiry toward analysis, toward the clarification of problems. The difficulties inherent in such an approach are, however, staggering. Even a map encompassing a huge territory should be correct. We have tried to steep ourselves in the empirical details thoroughly enough to prevent our going astray when seeking answers to relevant questions about broad interrelationships and trends. But many of the essential facts are elusive and unrecorded, and on many points the empirical evidence is contradictory.

The scope and focus of our study have prevented our undertaking new primary research. We have, of course, tried to avail ourselves of the findings of earlier detailed studies in the many fields included in our wide terms of reference. For our purposes, however, much of this material is deficient. Therefore we have often drawn inferences that are only indicative or suggestive and that, at times, have been based on our own impressions from looking at things and talking to people. The conclusions reached and the supportive reasoning are thus highly conjectural, as we shall often have occasion to remind the reader. It remains a worthwhile scientific task to state clearly what is not known but *should* be known in order to understand what is happening. Indeed, one of the main purposes of this book is to indicate gaps in knowledge and to spell out at some length a system of rational hypotheses for further research; and this can be done only by conjectural reasoning.

We are thus caught in a dilemma. We are seeking knowledge; this search must involve details that are not observed in a comprehensive way. Concurrently, because we insist on the general interdependence of all social factors, the scope of what should be studied is enlarged. The inevitable result is that considerable space in this book is allotted to such generalizing judgments, which are presented without the support of conclusive evidence.

3 *Dissimilarities in a Framework of Broad Similarities*

The countries with which we are concerned have proximity in space. All are located within the tropical, or subtropical, zone, though there are significant differences in climate among and even within the countries.

In each, the populations are "colored" or, as this expression has gone out of fashion in South Asia, "non-white." Although this fact is now usually played down, both in these countries and abroad, it gives an important undertone to most of their thinking about themselves and about their relations with the rest of the world. It is notable that their protests against colonialism regularly include the word "racialism."

But perhaps the strongest thread that binds these countries is the historical experience they have shared and its subsequent effects on their view of political problems and processes. All save one are ex-colonies. The periods of colonial rule, though of varying length, were of such duration and intensity as to leave a definite imprint on almost every aspect of their existence. Thailand, the sole exception, lived in the shadow of colonialism and its destiny too was molded by colonial intervention.

The recent liberation of these countries has been of tremendous importance to their entire national life. The process by which national independence was achieved differed radically from country to country, with major and probably lasting consequences for both their internal conditions and their relations with the outside world.

All these countries and nations owe their geographical definition and, indeed, their understanding of their own nationhood to the colonial era. Thus far only the partition of imperial India calls for qualification of this generalization. When now, as politically independent entities, they struggle for national consolidation within their boundaries, the relative strength of centripetal and centrifugal forces varies considerably from country to country.

Liberation came as a result of a world development in which these peoples played a secondary role. But in all these countries it is true that independence was in the end brought about by members of the small, articulate elite groups within the educated class — "educated" in the special sense the term has in South Asia, comprising only a small percentage of the total population. These elite groups now have the responsibility of consolidating the new nation-states. Among them, however, there were and are differing degrees of cohesion and internal unity behind the drive for consolidation.

Generally speaking, politics in its broadest sense — including all strivings for power and for changing or preserving economic, social, and cultural relations — increasingly absorbed the interest of the educated elite in all these countries as the hour of independence approached, and it has continued to do so. This interest has been diffused to at least some layers of society below the educated class, though to a varying degree in the different countries.

The fight for independence gave importance to politics and a high status to politicians. Their subsequent ascendancy to power and the exploitative use they have often made of it — or are suspected of having made of it — have tended to deflate this status and make it appear shoddy. But few people, even below the "elite" class, lack views on how things should and, particularly, should not be — even when they are frustrated, confused, apathetic, or cynical about their prospects for influencing conditions. Especially in the big urban agglomerations, people can readily be aroused to participate in public demonstrations that are something more than anarchic mob riots.

The idea of a self-regulating and self-reforming community is spreading, though it is not always or even ordinarily envisaged as a national community. For many generations history has evolved at a slow pace in these countries and in many ways it continues to evolve slowly even now. Of course, conditions were also far from static in colonial times; but with political control in the hands of foreign and, on the whole, authoritarian regimes, many social and economic relations became frozen. With the termination of colonial rule the realization that people can shape their own destiny, and have the responsibility to do so, has brought all relationships within society into challenge.

This fluid state has often been characterized as a "revolution of rising expectations." That the change in attitude has thus far mainly affected the educated class and scarcely touched the lower strata does not make it less important in countries where that class is dominant. These aspirations are bound to rise over time, and to spread to an ever larger part of the population. In a political sense, the aspirations now paramount have been formulated in terms of the modern democratic welfare state of the rich Western countries. In fact, they have their roots in the era of the Enlightenment that inspired the American and French revolutions. One of the ironies of history is that these ideas and ideals were brought to the countries of South Asia mainly by colonialism, which thereby unwillingly, and unwittingly, destroyed its own foundation.

Initially all these countries attempted to build their constitutional and civic structure on the lines of parliamentary democracy, based on free elections and adult suffrage for men and women, and on an extensive list of civil liberties. This was another influence from the peculiar but very real contact through colonialism with the newly democratic Western nations. In none of the South Asian countries has the experiment with ultra-modern political democracy been anything like a complete success; many of them have come under authoritarian rule of one shade or another, and this movement may still be in the ascendancy.

The ideals in regard to social and economic relations within these countries, adopted from the ultra-modern welfare state, had developed gradually in the rich, progressive nations of the Western world and began to be realized only during the past generation. Therefore it is natural that, particularly in this respect, a wide gap exists between aspirations and accomplishments.

There is a similarity in the basic economic conditions of the South Asian countries. All are very poor and, in general, the largest are the poorest. Social and economic inequalities are extreme, and are usually most pronounced in the poorest countries. All have endured a long period of stagnation in regard to the larger part of their economies, and in most of South Asia levels of living of the masses are either lower or not substantially higher today than they were before the Second World War. There are considerable differences among the individual countries, but the phenomena of poverty and inequality are universal.

All the new nations in South Asia are now pledged to the promotion of economic development through the planned and coordinated efforts of governments. Only a few, however, have come far in this direction. Even India has been unable to register a rate of progress comparable to that in the Western countries, either now or in earlier stages of their economic development.

The obstacles to rapid economic expansion are formidable and their significance must not be minimized. In the main they are rooted in the inefficiency, rigidity, and inequality of the established institutions and attitudes, and in the economic and social power relations embodied in this framework of institutions and attitudes. Again there are differences in degree among the several countries, but the point is that there is a fundamental difference in kind that distinguishes the economic environment of South Asia from that familiar in advanced Western economies.

These are sweeping generalizations, and this book will be concerned with expanding and documenting them and analyzing their implications. They are set out here in skeletal form because of their importance in determining the approach to the problem of underdevelopment and planning for development selected for this study.

Chapter 2

THE VALUE PREMISES

CHOSEN

In Section 9 of the Prologue we discussed the need to make explicit the value premises applied in a social study, for both logical clarity of the conceptual apparatus utilized in research and the avoidance of hidden valuations that lead to biases — that is, for the sake of relevance, effectiveness, and objectivity of research. All social study, even on the theoretical level where facts and causal relations are ascertained, is policy-directed, in the sense that it assumes a particular direction of social change to be desirable.

Ideally, sets of alternative value premises should be used; however, this usually presents a complication too great to contend with. It is true that by stating one set of value premises we not only inform the reader of the valuations implicit in a study but also make it easier for him to substitute another set. But the value premises used in the study do not lose their strategic advantage; it was that set that steered the interests and determined the approaches, the statement of problems, and the definition of concepts.

This is one reason why the student should feel bound not to select his value premises arbitrarily. They should be chosen because they are both *relevant*, in that they reflect actual valuations held by people who are concerned with the problems being studied, and *significant*, in that these people are influential in molding public policy.[1]

[1] For a fuller presentation and justification of these views on the methodological value problem see the writer's *Value in Social Theory* (American ed.), Harper &

1 The Logical Feasibility of External Value Premises

It would be perfectly feasible to carry out a quite objective scientific study of the problems of underdevelopment, development, and planning for development in the countries of South Asia from the point of view of Western or American political and military interests in the region, or from the viewpoint of those same interests on the part of the Communist countries, or some of them. Such an approach, however, should spell out these interests, clarifying their role as value premises in determining the direction of study. With the cards thus placed on the table, such a study could not be censured on methodological grounds.

From it could be also inferred the practical steps that should be taken by the outside country or countries concerned, in their own interest. Of course, the choice of steps is considerably narrowed by the political independence of the countries of South Asia; their policies cannot simply be bent at will, even though they are economically so very dependent on the policies of the developed countries. The choice is further narrowed if we exclude outright compulsion or threat of compulsion, fraud, corruption of individuals and groups, and other practices condemned by the ethos of Western civilization. Yet, barring such irregular practices, the policies of outside states can alter the conditions under which the South Asian countries exist and form their national policies, and can thus be influential, for instance, in keeping certain groups in power; they can even change the valuations held by these and other groups.

In the final instance, external policies must be shown to coincide, after the induced conditioning, with the valuations that actually are, or rather have been made to become, relevant and significant in the countries of South Asia. These other valuations thus become important for the rational consideration of the outside policy measures to be recommended as practical conclusions from a study undertaken from the valuational angle of the foreign country or bloc of countries. Such a coincidence cannot be casually assumed. It must be demonstrated by scientific analysis of the valuations and power relations, and their dynamics, that in such a study are conceived of as objects of foreign policy conditioning. Such an analysis has to be carried out, not from the viewpoint of the set of valuations, of ideals and interests, of the foreign observer, but from the viewpoint of those valuations that have relevance and significance in the countries of South Asia. In this specific sense the valuational angle of the South Asian countries themselves is more basic, even in a study pursued primarily from the valuational angle of the interests of a foreign country or bloc of countries.

Brothers, New York, 1959, particularly pp. 157 ff. These pages are reproduced from Appendix 2, "Facts and Valuations," in *An American Dilemma, The Negro Problem and Modern Democracy*, Harper, New York, 1944, pp. 1035 ff.

In the present study we have attempted to look at problems in the countries of South Asia as they appear from the point of view of the interests and ideals, norms and goals that are relevant and significant in these countries themselves. The interests of foreign countries are left out of consideration entirely, so far as the value premises are concerned.

2 *The Difficulties in, and Necessity of, Identifying Valuations in South Asia*

The task of specifying the relevant and significant value premises anchored on the valuations actually held by the peoples in the several countries of the region is an immensely difficult and challenging one — far more so than are similar exercises in Western countries. The three main reasons for this will here be stated in summary form; they will be elaborated in later chapters, especially in Part Four where we study ideologies thoroughly.

One reason is ignorance of how people in different occupations, social and economic strata, and locations really feel, the intensity and tenacity of their feelings, and the extent to which they can be influenced by policy measures aimed, directly or indirectly, at changing them. There are great lacunae in our knowledge of such matters in Western countries; what is ascertained about the public's valuations is often only vague and uncertain. But the difference between what we know about these valuations in a Western country and in any one of the countries of South Asia is, of course, very considerable. Research into public opinion has gone much deeper in the Western countries.[1] The use of such research methods for this purpose in South Asia is hampered at the start by our ignorance of how to classify people there, the actual size of the various groups we want to define, and, indeed, of the elementary facts of population size, age distribution, and vocational distribution.[2]

Moreover, in the Western countries a wealth of knowledge can be ac-

---

[1] A main criticism of opinion research is the common failure to distinguish between beliefs and valuations and between "personal" and "political" opinions. On this problem see *An American Dilemma*, Appendix 10, Sections 2 and 3; cf. also the Introduction and Appendix 1. Opinion research has not changed in these respects as much as one could have hoped since that work was written.

[2] "Another difficulty is the infrequency or absence of any of the more formal methods of assessing public opinion and relating it to social and political structure which are becoming more common and useful in the West. Progress toward careful assessment of Eastern public opinion is hampered by the simple absence of census data and other sociological information necessary to describe a population accurately enough to permit respectable sampling or reliable interpretation of the results of observation." (Charles A. H. Thomson, "Western Influence and Asian Opinion," in *Nationalism and Progress in Free Asia*, Philip W. Thayer, ed., The Johns Hopkins Press, Baltimore, 1956, p. 335.)

quired indirectly. With the far greater mass participation in public life in
a Western country — through elections to representative assemblies at
various levels, through organizations for the promotion of common interests and ideals, and through reflections of the public mind in the press —
the valuations of people in all stations of life are constantly manifested in
a manner amenable to study. There is also a large literature on the social
and emotional history of various movements and of changes in people's
attitudes induced by political and other means, counterparts of which are
almost entirely lacking in the countries of South Asia.

A second cause of difficulty is the fluid, uncertain, and, from an egalitarian point of view, biased character of the processes by which public
policies are decided in South Asia. Apart from the educated class, "citizen"
participation is low throughout the region, though not uniformly so in the
various countries. The rigid and inegalitarian social stratification and, in
particular, the social monopolies of property and education result in inequalities in power, whatever the constitutions prescribe. Real influence is
therefore more narrowly held than in Western countries.

By itself, this might seem to simplify the problem of discovering the relevant and significant valuations in the South Asian countries, as we could
focus our study on the small groups that hold most of the power. To some
extent such a focus is undoubtedly possible and important; but the precise
facts of this restriction of participation in power are difficult to assess. It
is also uncertain how much and how rapidly the spread of elementary education and other impulses from within these countries and from the outside
world will change the situation. Moreover, every government in the region,
whatever its actual degree of "democracy," has to consider the desires of
the broad masses of people and what they will tolerate. This is true even
where power is in the hands of the military. The masses may be "passive"
in regard to the collective processes of policy formation, but their passivity
includes more or less resistance to the effectuation of policies. And every
regime must reckon with the possibility that those inert masses will be
roused to activity. Non-participation thus constitutes a vast problem containing much uncertainty and much that is not known.

But there is a third severe obstacle to laying bare the actual valuations
of peoples in these countries and the selection of those valuations that are
relevant and significant: their immense heterogeneity. In the course of the
Great Awakening, aspirations, interests, and ideals have been exploding
in discrete sections of societies that are culturally and economically ill-
prepared to assimilate them systematically. One effect of the inverted and
telescoped historical sequence of social and economic development in
the countries of the region is that people in the various layers of society
live very different kinds of lives and consequently have very different outlooks toward their world. Indeed, most individuals, apart from those en-

tirely isolated by backwardness and stagnation, harbor within themselves sharply conflicting valuations.

In Western countries such differences also exist, but through a long process of national consolidation, or of what in India is called "emotional integration," these differences have tended to diminish. The modern democratic welfare states developed in the West during the past half century have a high degree of "created harmony" of interests and ideals.[1] It has thus become possible to study problems in the Western countries on the basis of a fairly explicit national creed that determines people's long-range strivings, if not always their daily conduct of life. This is true even when the problem concerns such departures from the creed as discrimination in America against Negroes and, particularly in earlier times, against Jews and immigrant groups. In the most advanced nations of Northwest Europe, the national ethos is seldom so explicitly formulated, mainly because it enjoys an even less questioned allegiance on the part of almost all citizens. The situation in the South Asian countries is, of course, utterly dissimilar. In none of them is the degree of national consolidation and "emotional integration" comparable to that in the Western countries, either now or when they were on the eve of their industrial revolutions.

The fundamental difficulties in identifying relevant and significant value premises do not relieve the student of the methodological necessity of attempting to discover them. On the contrary, the heterogeneity of actual valuations in South Asian countries and the magnitude of our ignorance about them and about the actual power relations make it the more essential to insist on clearly stated value premises. In Western countries, with their greater national consolidation and "emotional integration," it would be more reasonable to expect that the value premises used in a study, even if left implicit, would be likely to correspond broadly to commonly shared valuations. This is not a valid defense for leaving valuations hidden in implicit assumptions in studies referring only to Western countries.[2] But the core of "knowns" is sufficiently solid that less stringent methodological procedures are apt to have less disastrous effects on the clarity, effectiveness, and objectivity of research than in studies of South Asia.[3]

Most important is that those value premises that have actually determined the approach in a study be made explicit and permitted to fulfill their function. Whatever these value premises are, and however they were reached, this is what methodological clarity demands in the first place. It

[1] Gunnar Myrdal, *Beyond the Welfare State*, Yale University Press, New Haven, 1960, pp. 72–77 *et passim.*

[2] This is the argument in the writer's contributions referred to in footnote 1, p. 32.

[3] Gunnar Myrdal, "'Value-loaded' Concepts" in Hugo Hegeland, ed., *Money, Growth, and Methodology and Other Essays in Honor of Johan Åkerman*, Glerup, Lund, 1961, pp. 275–276.

should be clear from the foregoing that considerable doubt remains whether the value premises chosen *are* relevant and significant. Of this doubt the reader as well as the author should remain conscious.

3 *The Set of Value Premises Selected for This Study: The Modernization Ideals*

Among all the heterogeneous and conflicting valuations that exist in the countries of the region, we have deliberately selected the new ones directed toward "modernization"; they are specified in the next section. These valuations, which for brevity we label "the modernization ideals," were impressed on the nations of South Asia in the Great Awakening following independence, though people there had been gradually conditioned to them by influences from the Western world during colonial times, and more recently by influences from the Soviet Union. They have become the "official creed," almost a national religion, and are one of the powerful strands of the "new nationalism."[1]

Even before independence, the modernization ideals were prominent in the programs of the liberation movements. Later they were often inscribed in the new constitutions. They now appear as the declared main goals in the development plans with which all the countries of the region are equipped and in the introductions to reports by public commissions and committees considering questions of major reform. The programs and general pronouncements of the various political parties regularly adhere to them, or at least avoid contradicting them. They are reiterated in speeches, in leading articles in the press, and in the textbooks for schools and universities. They have, indeed, infiltrated the vocabulary of public discussion. In choosing these ideals as the value premises for our study we are, in a sense, taking these nations, or rather those who speak for them, at their word.

Although the relative homogeneity of this system of valuations is evident, there are differences among the countries in the region and among groups in a single country. The modernization ideals are expressed more clearly and are less confused with other valuations of the traditional type in India, Pakistan, Ceylon, and the Philippines than in Indonesia and Burma. In particular, emphasis on the several elements of the creed varies. In terms of the conventional Western axis of conservatism-radicalism, Pakistan, the Federation of Malaya, Thailand, and the Philippines give a more conservative slant to the modernization ideals, while the official creed of India, Ceylon, Burma, and Indonesia tends to be more radical. There are also movements in time along this axis. At least until recently, Ceylon and,

---

[1] See in Part Four, and see Appendix 9.

perhaps, Indonesia have moved toward the left, as has Burma, which for a time had tended toward the right. On the whole, India is still moving toward the left in public declarations, though hardly in practical politics.

Viewed in the light of prevailing conditions, however, the creed is radical throughout the South Asian countries, for even modest realization of the ideals would drastically change their economic, social, and political conditions. In fact, when abstractly presented — and very general pronouncements are much more common in South Asia than in the West — the modernization ideals are there ordinarily stated with a more radical flair. On this point there is an interesting parallel with the era of Enlightenment in the Western countries, when radical ideals — notably, but not exclusively, concerning equality — were commonly expressed more uncompromisingly in the literature than at present, although their society was much further from the realization of these ideals than is ours.[1]

As a matter of fact, it turns out that this official creed of the South Asian countries is composed mainly of the ideals long cherished in the Western world as the heritage of the Enlightenment and more recently realized to a large extent in the "created harmony" of the welfare state. These valuations have a long-standing association with thinking in the social sciences, particularly economics, though always with serious opportune compromises and even deviations, and without the methodological clarity of being stated as value premises.[2]

We have noted the relative heterogeneity of the official creed among countries and among groups of intellectuals within the countries. On the general level of valuations, where this creed exists, the ideals are also somewhat vague and indeterminate; at times, moreover, they are internally inconsistent. These logical deficiencies are part of the reality that must be faced; they cannot be disposed of by conceptual tricks that tidy the argument.[3] They indicate that the valuation viewpoint is not really a point but rather a limited space within which the key concepts are often blurred at the edges.

The modernization ideals are mainly the ideology of the politically alert, articulate, and active part of the population — particularly the intellectual elite. The judgments that follow refer to the opinions of these groups. Though their members are trying to spread their ideology to the whole educated class and to the masses of the population, their success in accom-

---

[1] Gunnar Myrdal, *Economic Theory and Under-developed Regions*, Duckworth, London, 1957, p. 112 *et passim*.

[2] See the works quoted in footnote 1, p. 12, particularly Myrdal, *Economic Theory and Under-developed Regions*, Part II, "Economic Inequalities, the Public Conscience and Economic Theory."

[3] "These conflicts cannot be concealed by such blanket terms as 'maximum welfare.' The main aims of economic policy have to be listed, their compatibility investigated, and where incompatibility remains, preferences have to be stated." (Paul Streeten, *Economic Integration, Aspects and Problems*, Sythoff, Leyden, 1961, p. 17.)

plishing this should not be exaggerated. The inclinations of the broader strata of the population, as yet only partially touched by the Great Awakening, greatly influence the prospects for initiating and implementing policies that conform to the modernization ideals. At least the masses can resist and create obstacles.

And we should also be aware that the modernization ideals have to compete with conflicting valuations. Even politically alert and active members of the educated class are often of two minds and engage in awkward and frustrating mental compromises. Although such conflicts are characteristic of ideologies of this nature,[1] in South Asia they are magnified by the vast distance between ideals and reality.

It should be stressed that endowing the modernization ideals with the technical function of serving as value premises for our study does not, in itself, say more about actual valuations and power relations in the countries under study than that these ideals are relevant because they are present among these actual valuations and that they have that significance of being held, or at least expressed, by social strata which exert most of the political power. Still less does this choice imply any *a priori* assumption that events must go in the direction of the realization of those ideals.[2] It means simply that we are looking at conditions and events from the point of view of the stated value premises, and that we are defining our concepts in terms of that viewpoint.

Naturally, the choice of this set of value premises would be more fully justified if our study were to indicate that their realization represented the trend of the future. This finding did not emerge. But one of the convictions we hold as a result of our investigation is that, particularly in view of the accelerating population increase, rapid strides toward the realization of the modernization ideals must be made in order to avoid increasing misery and social upheaval. They all have a rationale, as we shall point out in Part Four. This is what gives our set of value premises, or rather a study of the countries in the region undertaken from that angle, practical importance.[3] We should also bear in mind that, in one sense, they have all passed

---

[1] This is a main viewpoint in the writer's *An American Dilemma*, stated in the first section of the Introduction, p. lxix.

[2] The contrast to the writer's study of the Negro problem in America comes readily to mind. Not only were the set of value premises in that study, the "American Creed," much more firmly rooted in actually existing and powerful valuations in the whole population, but those valuations were so strong that — after study — they also stood out as determining the trend in the past and for the future. See *ibid.*, p. 23 *et passim*.

[3] The writer must in honesty add that the distinct aura of Enlightenment surrounding the modernization ideals in South Asia is congenial to him and to his collaborators, who are conservative in their moral allegiances and are personally deeply attached to those inherited radical ideals. Undoubtedly, this attitude made it easier to work with, and stick to, this set of value premises. As instrumental in this study they were not, however, selected on that personal ground, but rather for their relevance and significance in South Asia. The sympathy of the writer and his collaborators for those ideals may have been psychologically favorable to the conduct of the study but has in principle to be considered as accidental and logically irrelevant.

the point of no return. The modernization ideals are in effect in South Asia, at least to the extent of preventing these countries from reverting to their traditional undisturbed status. "Countries may never succeed in becoming modern, but they can never return to a traditional society or polity. A state which, however minimally, advances toward modernity . . . has irreversibly turned its back on the traditional oligarchic alternative."[1]

4 Summary Specification of the Modernization Ideals

In abstract form the modernization ideals making up the official creed in these countries have been given expression to an extraordinary degree. In various contexts, but mainly in Part Four, we shall examine the details of these ideals, their relation to other valuations held within the region, how they have come to play their role in the region, and what their effects are and can be expected to be in the future. We shall there stress that the role they now play in South Asian countries represents a significant difference in "initial conditions" as compared with the Western countries in their early stages of development. At this point in the argument, a condensed statement of the modernization ideals must suffice. It should be noted that many of these ideals overlap and, indeed, that they are regularly interdependent and mutually reinforcing, though occasionally conflicting.

a. *Rationality.* It is regularly assumed in public debate that policies should be founded on rational considerations. It is also taken for granted and often stressed that such a course represents a break with tradition. Superstitious beliefs and illogical reasoning should be eradicated.[2] This valuation is occasionally expressed explicitly, as in the statement that the nation is now entering the "scientific era."

An important element in this valuation is the need to apply modern technology in order to increase productivity, but it has been given a much broader interpretation embracing all economic and social relations.[3] His-

---

[1] Edward Shils, "The Military in the Political Development of the New States," in *The Role of the Military in Underdeveloped Countries,* John J. Johnson, ed., Princeton University Press, Princeton, N. J., 1962, pp. 60–61. See Postscript, Section 2.

[2] The following is a typical statement: "The new way of life is only possible through a deliberate cultivation of the scientific attitude that removes the deadwood of superstition, kills the fanaticism of the mind and kindles a new spirit of inquiry, analysis and objectivity. A mental revolution is necessary." (L. S. Chandrakaut, "Problems of Technological Change," *Yojana,* October 1, 1961, p. 73.)

[3] "But we have to deal with age-old practices, ways of thought, ways of action. We have got to get out of many of these traditional ways of thinking, traditional ways of acting, traditional ways of production, traditional ways of distribution and traditional ways of consumption. We have got to get out of all that into what might be called more modern ways of doing so. What is society in the so-called advanced countries like today? It is a scientific and technological society. It employs new techniques, whether it is in the farm or in the factory or in transport. The test of a country's advance is how far it is utilizing modern techniques. Modern technique is not a matter of just getting a tool and using it. Modern technique follows modern thinking. You can't get hold of a

tory, tradition, and indigenous attitudes and institutions are taken into account, in principle, only on the rational grounds that it is practical for the attainment of specific objectives to do so. No one publicly defends views while acknowledging them to be irrational.[1]

In the first instance, the quest for rationality implies that opinions about policies should be logically valid inferences rooted as deeply as possible in knowledge of the relevant facts. A corollary to this is that opinions, though founded on valuations of both goals and means, should form a logically coherent system. Another corollary is that, though logically the value premises are a volitional and *a priori* element in scientific study, the quest for rationality means that they nevertheless become dependent, to an extent, on the outcome of that study.

b. *Development and Planning for Development.* The desire for development and planning for development flows directly from the quest for rationality and represents in the economic and social field the all-embracing and comprehensive expression of the modernization ideals. Development means improvement of the host of undesirable conditions in the social system that have perpetuated a state of underdevelopment. Planning is the search for a rationally coordinated system of policy measures that can bring about development.[2]

c. *Rise of Productivity.* Higher output per head of the population or of the labor force is a commonly shared goal of development planning. It is generally assumed to be achieved primarily by improved techniques and increased capital intensity in all branches of production and by an improvement in what we shall call the modes of production.[3] These are in turn dependent on raised levels of living, improved attitudes and institutions, national consolidation, and, in fact, on the realization of all the other value premises listed below.

Output per head of the population or of the labor force can, with certain reservations, be taken as an indication of the level of underdevelopment, and the rate of upward change of that output as an indication of development.[4] But it can never serve as a satisfactory definition of these

---

modern tool and have an ancient mind. It won't work. We have 400 million people in India, very fine people, very capable people, very intelligent people, but people who have functioned for ages past in certain ruts of thought and action. Take our peasant; it is a matter of amazement and shame to me that any peasant should go about today with a plough which was used in Vedic times. There has been no change since then. It should have been a museum piece; yet the fact is, it is there. It astonishes me." (Jawaharlal Nehru, "Strategy of the Third Plan," in *Problems in the Third Plan: A Critical Miscellany,* Ministry of Information and Broadcasting, Government of India, 1961, p. 46.)

[1] Chapter 3, Section 2.
[2] Chapter 15, Section 1; and Appendix 2.
[3] Appendix 2, Part II.
[4] Appendix 2, Section 7.

concepts. As we proceed with our list of the modernization ideals, we shall note that changes in other conditions are important, not simply as instrumental in raising productivity but as goals in themselves,[1] and that the goals may sometimes conflict.

d. *Rise of Levels of Living.* That this valuation is commonly accepted is not surprising in view of the extremely low levels of living of the masses in South Asia, especially in the bigger and poorer countries.[2] Indeed, a main reason for desiring a rise in output per head is that it could raise levels of living.

It is commonly believed, however, that substantial improvements in levels of living must be postponed for some time to come in order to permit capital accumulation and even higher productivity and levels of living in the future. This need would assume a partial conflict, at least in the short run, between higher consumption and higher production. But there is also a positive relationship between these conditions to which we shall often call attention — that improved levels of living are a pre-condition for higher labor input and efficiency and, generally, for changes in abilities and attitudes that are favorable to rising productivity. This interdependence between productivity and levels of living is much stronger in the countries of South Asia than in Western countries, though the relationship is mostly obscured by application of the Western approach in the economic analysis of South Asian development problems.[3]

e. *Social and Economic Equalization.* In all the countries of South Asia the ideal that social and economic stratification should be changed in order to promote equality in status, opportunities, wealth, incomes, and levels of living is commonly accepted in public discussion of the goals for planning and for policies generally. In India, Ceylon, Burma, and Indonesia, this ideal has, on the general level of valuations, been carried to the point of a widespread acceptance of such radical policy formulas as "a socialistic pattern of society" and the "classless society." In the other countries — Pakistan, Thailand, the Federation of Malaya, and the Philippines — such extreme formulations of the egalitarian ideal are seldom granted the official imprint, though greater equality is given an important place in all statements of policy goals. Indeed, development is usually interpreted as creating the conditions for raising levels of income and living for the masses.[4]

Social and economic conditions are generally, though in varying degree, far from the realization of this ideal.[5] Recent changes have in fact probably tended to increase inequality, particularly in economic levels. Moreover,

[1] Appendix 2, Section 7 *et passim.*
[2] Chapter 12, Sections 2–6.
[3] Appendix 2, Section 21; and Chapter 21.
[4] Chapter 15, Section 1; and Chapter 16.
[5] Chapter 12, Sections 7 and 8.

specific policies, motivated by the equalization ideal, have often not been carried out, or else have benefitted people other than those at the bottom of the social and economic hierarchy.[1] Occasionally, non-realization of the equalization ideal has been excused, in a vague way, by references to the priority of raising output;[2] this explanation would imply a conflict between the ideals under *c* and *e*. But the opposite can be and sometimes is argued: in the conditions prevailing in South Asia, greater equality is a pre-condition for speeding up production and development.[3]

f. *Improved Institutions and Attitudes.* In general, it is held that social and economic institutions and attitudes should be changed, in order to: increase labor efficiency and diligence, effective competition, mobility, and enterprise; permit greater equality of opportunities; make possible higher productivity and well-being; and generally promote development. It is even quite common in all the countries of the region to discuss these desired changes as a social, as well as an economic, "revolution" and to proclaim that such a revolution is necessary for development.

In regard to institutions, perhaps the easiest way to illustrate the prevalent valuations contained in the modernization ideals is to picture the kind of national community implied in reasonings about the need for a social revolution and in the motivation for specific reform proposals. What is envisaged is a united and integrated national community within which there is solidarity and "free competition" in a much wider sense than the term implies in economic analysis. In such a national community the barriers of caste, color, religion, ethnic origin, culture, language, and provincial loyalties would be broken down, and property and education would not be so unequally distributed as to represent social monopolies. A nation with marked social and economic equality, high social as well as spatial mobility, and firm allegiance of the whole population to the national community is visualized. The desire for such a "modernization" of institutions is most clearly expressed in India,[4] where the barriers to free competition in this wider sense are strongest and most pervasive. The ideal is shared,

---

[1] Chapter 16, Sections 6–8, *et passim* throughout the book.

[2] Chapter 16, Section 3.

[3] Chapter 16, Section 3.

[4] "Let us be clear about our national objective. We aim at a strong, free and democratic India where every citizen has an equal place and full opportunity of growth and service, where present-day inequalities in wealth and status have ceased to be, where our vital impulses are directed to creative and co-operative endeavour. In such an India communalism, separatism, isolation, untouchability, bigotry, and exploitation of man by man have no place, and while religion is free, it is not allowed to interfere with the political and economic aspects of a nation's life." (Nehru's Convocation Address, Allahabad 'Varsity, December 13, 1947.)

In his *The Discovery of India* (4th ed., Meridian Books Ltd., London, 1956, p. 534), Nehru had already pleaded for a "functional organization of society" where "merit is the only criterion and opportunity is thrown open to everybody."

however, in the whole region, though in Ceylon and Southeast Asia with considerable reservation in regard to foreign ethnic groups.

The modern welfare state in the rich Western countries is, of course, much closer to the realization of this ideal, as are, at lower but rising levels of living, the Communist countries. From the valuation perspective of national consolidation, South Asian countries are all much more amorphous and splintered. The ideal system is viewed as a unified and integrated nation-state, branching out into smaller communities bound together by loyalties to the nation-state. In reality, however, the social and political framework is traversed by lines of interests and allegiances to other types of communities that do not fit into the ideal order but are inimical to it. Although these narrower communities for the most part have no formal existence in a constitutional legal sense, they greatly influence how people feel and think and what they are prepared to do or not do. Many of the proposed and partially enacted reforms of the institutional system — land reforms, tenancy legislation, attempts in India to break up the caste divisions, etc. — should be viewed in this broader perspective, as attempts to eradicate social monopolies and barriers against free competition in the pursuit of happiness, considered inimical to national consolidation, to equalization, and to advances in productivity and levels of living.

Attitudes, in turn, are understood to be supported by and at the same time to uphold established institutions. In regard to attitudes, the general ideal of a social revolution is commonly referred to as the creation of the "new man" or the "modern man," the "citizen of the new state," the "man in the era of science," the "industrial man," and so on. What is implied is illustrated below, though the list should not be regarded as complete, nor should the individual items be viewed as independent of one another:

(1) efficiency;

(2) diligence;

(3) orderliness;

(4) punctuality;

(5) frugality;

(6) scrupulous honesty (which pays in the long run and is a condition for raising efficiency in all social and economic relations);

(7) rationality in decisions on action (liberation from reliance on static customs, from group allegiances and favoritism, from superstitious beliefs and prejudices, approaching the rationally calculating "economic man" of Western liberal ideology);

(8) preparedness for change (for experimentation along new lines, and for moving around spatially, economically, socially);

(9) alertness to opportunities as they arise in a changing world;

(10) energetic enterprise;

(11) integrity and self-reliance;

(12) cooperativeness (not limiting but redirecting egoistic striving in a socially beneficial channel; acceptance of responsibility for the welfare of the community and the nation);

(13) willingness to take the long view (and to forego short-term profiteering; subordination of speculation to investment and of commerce and finance to production, etc.).

The desirability of changing attitudes, though accepted at a very general level, is usually played down in public debate.[1] Least of all does discussion take the form of demands for specific policy measures aimed directly at changing attitudes. Attitudinal changes are glossed over even in the formulation of educational policies.[2]

There are several explanations why a frontal attack on attitudes is avoided. First, it would wound national pride. The educated themselves, including the intellectual elite, are aware of the failure to live up to ideals in this respect. Even more important is the separation of this group from the masses. Conscious of the wide gap between their modes and levels of living, culture, and all circumstances of their life and work and those of the villagers and urban slum dwellers, the intellectual elite compensate for their alienation by romanticizing the plight of the masses. The demand for more efficient labor performance and greater enterprise is often countered by protests that the peasants are rational, intelligent, hard-working, and zealous.[3]

Another important determinant of such thinking is that it developed during the fight for liberation as a protest against colonial theories and stereotypes.[4] Europeans in colonial times typically described the "natives" of these countries as superstitious, lazy, careless, unenterprising, and merely survival-minded. These derogatory views were part of the rationalization of the prerogatives they took to themselves and were able to retain as a super-caste.

---

[1] Gandhi upbraided his people for wrong attitudes toward life and work much more frankly than have his followers. Occasionally, however, an Indian intellectual does not mince the subject but speaks out: "The young Indian must come round to a rational and objective view of material advancement. He must be able and willing to tear himself away from his family ties; flout customs and traditions; put economic welfare before cow worship; think in terms of farm and factory output rather than in terms of gold and silver ornaments; spend on tools and training rather than on temples and ceremonials; work with the low caste rather than starve with the high caste; think of the future rather than of the past; concentrate on material gains rather than dwell on *Kismet* (destiny). These are extremely difficult changes to envisage in the Hindu social structure and ideas. But they seem unavoidable." (D. K. Rangnekar, *Poverty and Capital Development in India,* Oxford University Press, London, 1958, p. 81.)

[2] Chapters 32–33.

[3] This tendency toward romantic pastoralism when viewing subordinate social strata is familiar from European history. It was particularly prominent in the eighteenth century, when the social system in Europe was somewhat closer to a surviving feudal order while the intellectuals were becoming radical in their philosophy.

[4] Chapter 21, Section 7.

It is obvious, moreover, that the attitudes that are thought to need changing are a function of the low levels of living and culture, and that these levels can only slowly be elevated. These attitudes are also fortified by the institutions in which they are molded and which they help to preserve. Together, the modes and levels of living, the attitudes, and the institutions form a complex social system that is difficult to change, particularly as all these countries are reluctant to apply compulsion.[1] In curious juxtaposition to this awareness of the complexity of the problem is the over-optimism, nurtured by Marx's thinking but largely taken over by Western economists — mostly only as an implicit assumption, revealed by immanent criticism — that economic development and, in particular, industrialization will automatically change both institutions and attitudes.[2] The escape from thinking or doing much about institutions and attitudes is made easier by the application in economic analysis and planning of the Western approach, which ordinarily takes into account solely the "economic" factors. Because it serves vested interests in the *status quo,* this approach appeals to the conservatives at the same time that it permits the radicals to be optimistic.[3]

To sum up: among the articulate groups there is unanimous support, on a very general plane, for changing institutions and attitudes, but there is also much escapism, particularly in regard to specific issues.

g. *National Consolidation.* Ideally, national consolidation means a national system of government, courts, and administration that is effective, cohesive, and internally united in purpose and action, with unchallenged authority over all regions and groups within the boundaries of the state. Consolidation is thus a pre-condition both for the preservation of the state as a going concern and for its efficient functioning as a matrix for the effective formation and execution of national policies, that is, for planning. National consolidation in this sense does not necessarily imply a highly centralized government.[4]

India comes closest to the goal of national consolidation in a restricted sense. Although its population is fragmented into particularist groups, the country as a whole has been relatively free of open rebellions. It is obvious that a still higher degree of national consolidation is needed, and, to support it, more "emotional integration" — which is to say changed attitudes among the people and, to make that possible, reform of the whole institu-

---

[1] Chapter 18, Sections 13 and 14; see below under *k*.

[2] See Prologue, Section 5; Appendix 2, Section 20.

[3] Prologue, Section 6.

[4] India, Pakistan, the Federation of Malaya, and Burma have federal systems of government, though much power is concentrated at the center. All the countries in South Asia are with varying success trying to build up more local self-government (see below under *j*). A federal system and, more generally, a certain independence of political units below the national level can be justified as being practical for good and effective government, even if it is often utilized for separatist aims.

tional system.[1] In its wider sense, national consolidation as an ideal thus coincides with the ideal of changed attitudes and institutions.

Throughout South Asia the idea of national consolidation, even in a narrow sense, is still being contested. In every country there are groups of people who want to dissociate themselves from the existing national entity; they demand autonomy or at least more independence than is compatible with a reasonable degree of national consolidation. Aside from such movements there are divisions of culture, religion, caste, and economic interests that work against national consolidation. In Ceylon and Southeast Asia, these divisions follow the lines of visible and recognized differences in ethnic origin. However, the ideal of national consolidation enjoys common allegiance among the intellectual elite, apart from those involved in separatist movements.

h. *National Independence.* This ideal is firmly adhered to and, of all the ideals, is given the most explicit expression. National independence, like a reasonable degree of national consolidation, holds a key position among the modernization ideals. Together the two are pre-conditions for planning, that is, the effective formation and execution of national policies aimed at realizing development and all that development includes.

In one sense, even the rebellions constitute no exception to the general urge for national independence. South Asian rebel groups are not shifting their allegiance to a foreign country, but are fighting for an autonomous existence. The ideal of independent nationhood — though not always associated with the boundaries demarcated on the attainment of independence — has been disseminated more successfully throughout the lower strata than has any other modernization ideal. The "new nationalism" is commented on further in Appendix 9.

i. *Political Democracy, in a Narrow Sense.* All the countries of South Asia began their independent existence by declaring their ambition to become democratic nation-states; they gave themselves constitutions, or began to work on constitutions, patterned on those recently evolved in Western countries, with representative assemblies founded on free elections and universal suffrage. They also attempted to establish legal guarantees for civil liberties and to give these a very inclusive interpretation. As these ambitions were thwarted in some countries in the region and their full realization curtailed or endangered in all of them, certain alternative ideals such as "guided democracy," conceived to be more compatible with the "genius" of the country, were substituted for the original Western ideals.

---

[1] "In India, the first essential is the maintenance of the unity of country, not merely a political unity but a unity of mind and heart, which discards the narrow urges which separate and disunite, and which breaks down the barriers which are raised in the name of religion or between State and State or in any other form." (Nehru's broadcast speech, December 31, 1952, "The Future Beckons to Us.")

Enough has been retained of the ideals of democracy and civil liberties, however, to support a common assumption that the national regime should not only be in accord with the interests of the people, as understood by those in power, but should be willingly accepted by the great majority, and that it should permit general freedom of thought and action, even if it engages in some suppression of public opposition.[1]

Yet it may be doubted whether this ideal of political democracy — with political power based on free elections and with freedom of assembly, press, and other civil liberties — should be given weight in formulating the modernization ideals. This is not because the ideal is at present not very fully met, and may not be met in the future: value premises represent merely an angle from which actual conditions are viewed and need not be "realistic" in that sense; many of those stated above are not. But experience has shown that, unlike the other value premises, this ideal is not essential to a system comprising all the other modernization ideals. National independence, national consolidation, changes in institutions and attitudes, equalization, rise of productivity, rise and redirection of consumption, and, more generally, planning for development can be attained by an authoritarian regime bent on their realization. On the other hand, the substitution of an authoritarian regime for a more democratic one gives no assurance that policies will be directed toward the realization of those ideals, or that, if so directed, they will be more effective.[2]

Granted that political democracy is not essential to a coherent system of value premises corresponding to the modernization ideals, it should be noted that as an abstract ideal it is sincerely adhered to by many, perhaps most, of the intellectual elite in those countries of the region where even the outer forms of democracy and full civil liberties have been sacrificed.

j. *Democracy at the Grass Roots.* Somewhat independent of the political forms and the power basis of a national government is the degree to which it is desired that responsibility for their own affairs be delegated to local and sectional communities and accepted by the people in those smaller communities. This ideal of local and sectional self-government and cooperation has much in common with the ideal of changed institutions and attitudes.

Under the actual circumstances in South Asia today, an oriental despotism of the type that existed in most parts of the region in pre-colonial

---

[1] Chapter 16, Part II.

This is also a common assumption in the Communist countries—many of which, incidentally, have equipped themselves with constitutions largely molded after the modern Western pattern, however un-Western the practices of the regime.

[2] The writer may be permitted the observation that few things in the outcome of this study have been more disturbing to him, in view of his own personal valuations, than the conclusion that political democracy is not a necessary element in the modernization ideals.

times, and to some extent in a few of the princely states during the colonial
era, is clearly no longer possible.[1] It could only be sustained when population growth was still effectively curbed by the intermittent appearance of
Malthusian checks — famines, epidemics, and wars — and when the masses
of people were cut off from the larger society, especially from the rest of
the world. The old-fashioned despotism was able to confine itself to preserving and protecting its power, to sanctioning a measure of internal
peace, and to extorting tribute for the expenses of a court and an aristoc-
racy, for wars, and for limited public works. South Asian governments
nowadays must strive for economic development, and successful development presupposes a rather high degree of popular acceptance of the development goals. All effective governments, whether democratically based or
authoritarian, must enforce some measure of social discipline through compulsion; but even an authoritarian regime cannot record major achievements unless it can somehow mobilize acceptance, participation, and cooperation among the people. Even the poorest and least articulate layers of
society have considerable potential for resisting and obstructing measures
intended to coerce them. As Nehru observed: "Nobody, not even the greatest autocrat or tyrant, can force vast numbers of people to do this or that."[2]

Thus it should not be surprising that this ideal, referred to in South Asia
as "decentralization" or "democratic planning," which is directed toward
the creation of conditions for popular cooperation and joint responsibility
in local and sectional communities within the nation, is — on the general
level — a more widely accepted valuation than any of the modernization
ideals other than the quest for independence. But, as we shall find in Chapter 18, no country in the region has progressed very far toward its realization. A number of serious and closely related obstacles stand in the way:
deficiencies in government and administration; social and economic inequalities; and, in general, vested interests in the *status quo,* and the traditions of a stagnant society.

k. *Social Discipline versus "Democratic Planning."* These countries are
all "soft states,"[3] both in that policies decided on are often not enforced, if
they are enacted at all, and in that the authorities, even when framing policies, are reluctant to place obligations on people. This reluctance, which
derives from the economic, social, and political structure of the South
Asian countries as they have emerged under the impact of colonialism and
the fight for independence, is then excused and, indeed, idealized. By
"democratic planning" is meant not only, and not even primarily, that poli-

---

[1] This has repeatedly been pointed out, particularly by K. M. Panikkar: ". . . it is
fairly certain that even if democratic institutions in Asia . . . get metamorphosed into
something quite different from their original shape and focus, or do not develop in the
spirit of genuine vigour, the principles of 'Oriental despotism' will not come back." (K.
M. Panikkar, *Asia and Western Dominance,* Allen and Unwin Ltd., London, 1953, p.
499.)

[2] Nehru, "Strategy of the Third Plan," *Problems in the Third Plan,* p. 43.

[3] Chapter 18, Sections 13 and 14.

cies should be decided on by democratic political procedures (under *i* above) and that they should, as far as possible, be implemented with the cooperation and shared responsibility of local and sectional communities (under *j* above). More specifically, it is implied that policies should not require compulsion, and this is often held to be a fundamental difference from the practice in Communist countries. The abstention from compulsion has thus been permitted to masquerade as part of the modernization ideals.

This problem will confront us often in the chapters that follow. For the present let it be said that this particular interpretation of the ideal of democratic planning is not among the value premises of this study. On the contrary, our investigation has convinced us that the success of planning for development requires a readiness to place obligations on people in *all* social strata to a much greater extent than is now done in any of the South Asian countries. It requires, in addition, rigorous enforcement of obligations, in which compulsion plays a strategic role. This value premise runs parallel to, and is partly identical with, the quest for national consolidation (under *g* above) and, in particular, effective government. It would not in principle conflict with the ideal of political democracy, which only concerns the manner in which policies are decided upon.

We cannot claim that this ideal of a more disciplined nation is shared by a large number of people, even among the intellectual elite in South Asia. It is another example of how our study has forced us to choose a value premise that is not widely accepted, in order that the system of value premises may be coherent and in accord with the primary quests for rationality and planning for development.

If this value premise does not conflict in principle with the ideal of democracy, it often does so in practice. Conflict arises when the modernization ideals do not have — and, with the means available in a democratic setting, cannot be made to have — enough force to induce people, including the intellectual elite, to voluntarily undertake diligent efforts toward their realization and to cast aside conflicting valuations.[1] This very serious problem should not be concealed. Under present South Asian conditions development cannot be achieved without much more social discipline than the prevailing interpretation of democracy in the region permits. An authoritarian regime may be better equipped to enforce social discipline, though its existence is no guarantee of this accomplishment.

1. *Derived Value Premises.* We have noted that the modernization

---

[1] Western aid is commonly argued in terms of making such efforts possible. For example: "Most underdeveloped countries today are determined to achieve higher standards of living and the events of the last twenty years have injected into their bodies politic the dynamics of economic and social change. Our task is to help these countries to attain their economic goals within a political and social framework that remains democratic." (Benjamin Higgins, *Economic Development*, W. W. Norton Co., New York, 1959, p. 438.) The point is that with or without foreign aid — the importance of which should not be overrated — the task may be impossible to effectuate.

ideals cannot be entirely independent and *a priori;* they are partly dependent on the outcome of the study for which they serve as value premises.
This is a corollary to the general quest for rationality and planning (under
a and *b* above). In one sense all of the modernization ideals are contained
in, and derived from, the ideal of rationality and planning — though usually
not entirely, as they mostly have an independent and not only an instrumental importance. It follows that as we take up concrete problems many
value premises that are more specific will come into discussion.

We may illustrate by referring to the ideal of spreading birth control
among the masses. Only a few South Asian governments — primarily India
but later also Pakistan and, more tentatively, Ceylon — openly supported
the spread of birth control among the masses until recently, and no government was willing, or able, to apply policy measures so effectively as to have
any great influence on population prospects.[1] Behind this fact is much
diversity and uncertainty about the valuations surrounding the population
issue, even among the intellectual elite, in all the countries of the region.
Yet population increase severely hampers the rise of output per head and
development in general.[2] As the rate of population increase in South Asia
is very high and rising rapidly, and as this rapid population increase is not
likely to be abated spontaneously,[3] the logic of the situation forcefully
demands the choice of this value premise. This conclusion is now becoming
accepted in all the countries of the South Asian region.

Redirection of consumption in order to raise productivity must also be a
value premise. While, as already stated, changes in levels of living (under
d above) have little importance for productivity in the Western countries
within practical limits, the opposite is true in the countries of South Asia,
particularly in the poorest of them. There are, however, differences in the
effects on productivity of a rise in levels of living according to the economic
strata and the particular item of consumption in which the rise occurs.
Generally speaking, the productivity effects of a rise in consumption
should be greatest in the lowest economic strata and in the items of food
intake, health care, and education. As productivity is very low everywhere,
with depressing effects on the levels of living of the masses, these differentials in the productivity effects of changes in consumption should be observed and policy measures directed in favor of those strata and those
items where a rise in consumption has the greatest productivity effects.
Such a redirection of consumption would be in the interest of the general
well-being and culture. In large part, though not entirely, this ideal runs
parallel to the equalization ideal (under *e*) or is, rather, an expression of
it; it gains support from the productivity ideal (under *c*). Although those

[1] Chapter 28, Sections 8 and 14.
[2] Chapter 28, Part I.
[3] Chapter 27.

differentials have not been in the focus of public awareness, it seems likely that, on an abstract and general level at least, this value premise would find wide acceptance among the intellectual elite. Its greater practical realization in specific policy fields would, however, encounter vested interests and other inhibitions and obstacles.

The presence of these hindrances does not fully explain why the reallocation of the nation's consumption has been given so little consideration in planning. Another part of the explanation is the application of the Western approach to planning. The whole conceptual apparatus, of income, consumption, savings, and investment, assumes the absence of productivity effects of consumption.[1] That this approach in turn serves to accommodate opportunistic interests was pointed out in the Prologue, Section 6.

With the same type of motivation, we have been brought to adopt a number of other derived value premises — for instance, that non-discriminatory controls are preferable to discriminatory ones,[2] and that popular education and the spread of literacy should have a leading role in education and reform.[3] We have also accepted the value premise that everything within practical limits should be done to improve health conditions and prevent premature death, independent of the consequences for fertility and mortality. This latter value premise is not derived; it stands as a moral imperative.[4]

[1] Appendix 2, Section 21 *et passim.*
[2] Chapter 19, Section 1.
[3] Chapter 32, Section 3.
[4] Chapter 28, Section 9; Chapter 29, Section 2.

2 *In Anticipation of a Possible Methodological Controversy*

In this study I have analyzed conditions and events in South Asia from the viewpoint of certain value premises for which I have accounted in Chapter 2 (Section 4). I have used these value premises not only when drawing practical, that is, political, conclusions, but even when attempting to ascertain facts and factual relationships. In the Prologue (Section 9), I argued the necessity of stating value premises explicitly in order to give objectivity to research and avoid biases. It is a truism that "Things look differently, depending upon where you stand." Since a view without a viewpoint is not feasible, a study devoid of valuations is inconceivable. Valuations always determine what the analyst is looking for and sees. If he ignores this fact he loses control of the value judgments that have actually been directing his work, and becomes defenseless against biases.

Even if this point is conceded, it is possible to doubt whether the modernization ideals that have been used as value premises in the present study are appropriate to the purpose. In particular, it can be argued that these ideals, which gradually developed in Europe, matured to a high degree of explicitness in the era of Enlightenment, and thereafter determined the main ideological structures of the developed Western and Communist countries, are foreign to South Asia. Admittedly, the choice of value premises is, to an extent, a volitional decision, and the criteria of relevance and significance allow for arbitrariness, particularly when one is studying countries where popular valuations are as diverse and as difficult to ascertain as in the South Asian countries.[1]

There were two main reasons for choosing the value premises applied in the present study. First, the modernization ideals are those actually proclaimed by the political and intellectual leaders in the region; they are implicit not only in the plans but also in the policy discussions in all of the South Asian countries. As was pointed out in Chapter 3 (Section 1), the traditional valuations cannot be used as a basis for comprehensive policy planning, and this gives the modernization ideals a strategic position. The second, and even more compelling, argument for choosing these value premises was that the South Asian countries, and particularly the bigger and poorer among them, have passed the point of no return. Given the present and foreseeable rate of population growth, the choice of remaining traditional societies is no longer open. Only by a fairly vigorous application of the modernization ideals — the internal coherence of which I have demonstrated in several contexts — can they hope to avoid not only stagnation, which might be bearable, but actual impoverishment with increasing misery for the masses (Chapter 2, Section 3).

I can foresee that some of my colleagues, even while admitting this, may see a contradiction between my use of the modernization ideals as value premises and my constant criticism of the "modern approach," which is the name I have given to the application of Western and Communist concepts, theories, and models to South Asian conditions. Value premises determine the point of view from which reality is studied; they do not determine how facts and factual relationships are to be ascertained. Thus, even though the analyst has decided upon certain value premises, he remains free to conduct his research in the manner he deems most appropriate. It is my firm conviction that social study must be comprehensive enough to be adequate to reality, and that this reality is very different in South Asia from what it is in the West. Therefore I have rejected the "modern approach," which abstracts from modes and levels of living and attitudes and institutions, and have adopted instead an institutional approach. This decision is in no wise inconsistent with the value premises I chose. The terminological similarity might seem to imply a logical connection between the modernization ideals and the "modern approach" but, in fact, none exists.

[1] Chapter 2, Section 2.

Chapter 3

THE WIDER FIELD

OF VALUATIONS

---

1 Relation of the Modernization Ideals to Other Existing Valuations

In the preceding chapter we endeavored to make explicit the set of value premises used in this study. We categorized them as the modernization ideals. They overlap in part and are generally interrelated, for two reasons: first, all conditions in a social system are causally interrelated[1] and, second, since all the more specific value premises should satisfy the first premise of rationality, they have to form a logically coherent system. As they all have an independent value and not only an instrumental one, the modernization ideals, though usually mutually supporting, occasionally conflict with each other. The system can be worked out, verified, and specified by analysis; but, except for the primary quest for rationality, these ideals are all somewhat indeterminate and vague. This fact should not be concealed by any conceptual tricks. It does not, however, seriously decrease their usefulness as value premises for scientific study of the problems. Generally speaking, their fuller realization is remote. In using the modernization ideals as value premises in our study we are simply assuming the desirability of bringing society closer to these ideals and the undesirability of a lapse backward.

[1] Appendix 2, Section 5 *et passim*.

The indeterminate and vague nature of the system of modernization ideals on the general level, which we have chosen for the technical purpose of stating the value premises for the present study, allows for differing views even in a discussion carried on within the framework of those ideals. Opinions differ, for example, as to the causal relationship between a rise in production and equalization and the relative importance of these two goals, and about the state's role in industrial production and the policy measures that should be applied. So long as the rationality ideal is accepted by the participants, this discussion turns very largely on what the facts are; but there are also various shades of valuations concerning both means and ends in planning for development. Communism, "the socialist pattern of society," "free enterprise," etc., are loose expressions for positions taken in this discussion, all with their own connotations of valuations. In the present study this discussion as well as actual policy trends will be treated in their common setting of the more general modernization ideals.

Outside the sphere of the modernization ideals are all the other relevant and significant valuations that should be accounted for in order to put our chosen value premises into perspective.[1] We shall try to consider other valuations in this chapter; the difficulties in doing so have been discussed in Chapter 2, Section 2. We shall find that not all of these other valuations conflict with the modernization ideals: some actually give support to them; some are neutral; and some are ambivalent and can be used both for and against attempts to realize these ideals.

Insofar as these other valuations clash with the modernization ideals, from the point of view of their effect on planning for development they act as *inhibitions* when held by members of government and by those who participate in shaping and carrying out government policies. They account for the hesitancy and the half-heartedness in making and executing plans. When present only among the majority of the people who are not active participants in policy formation and execution, these conflicting valuations act as *obstacles*. As such, they occupy in principle the same position in the analysis as do other obstacles — for example, climatic difficulties or a downturn in the demand for a country's export commodities. They must either be overcome by policy measures that constitute a rational plan or be circumvented, if planning as an expression of the modernization ideals is to forge ahead. The conflicting valuations can, of course, be both inhibitions and obstacles simultaneously, and they very often are. Planning and plan implementation are themselves instruments to break down inhibitions and obstacles.[2]

The dividing line between an active in-group and a passive out-group in regard to the formation and execution of policies — and thus the distinc-

---

[1] They have importance for planning; see Appendix 2, Section 13.
[2] See Appendix 2, Section 17.

tion between valuations as inhibitions or obstacles when they are not both — is vague throughout South Asia. In every country, to some extent, the government is dependent on acceptance of its policies by the people. This is true not only in countries like India or Ceylon where the government seeks its power basis in general elections but also in more authoritarian countries like Burma or Pakistan. On the other hand, in every country that has reached some degree of national consolidation, there is a government and an administration, and generally these depend more heavily on certain groups than on all other people. In the existing circumstances, as we said in Chapter 2 (Section 2), political power is much more concentrated in South Asia than in Western countries; it is held by a small, politically active and articulate group, most of whom belong to the educated class. The distinction in this study between "inhibitions" and "obstacles" is a somewhat simplifying, abstract model though we believe it represents a realistic approach.[1] It envisages a government and its entourage as the active subject in planning, and the rest of the people as the relatively passive objects of the policies emerging from planning. That the model does not encompass the complex reality in its entirety should be borne in mind.

The modernization ideals are all, in a sense, alien to the region, since they stem from foreign influences.[2] But they have come to be indigenous in the sense that they have been adopted and shaped by the intellectual elite, who, in turn, have endeavored to diffuse them throughout the population. The other valuations, held by the mass of people and in large part also by the intellectual elite, are mainly "traditional": they are part of an inherited culture long identified with a stagnating society. Related to this is another distinction. While the modernization ideals, both individually and as a system of valuations, are dynamic and interventionist, requiring changes through public policy,[3] all the traditional valuations, including those on the most intellectualized level, are static. Even when they are of such a nature as to lend support to the modernization ideals, they themselves are not the driving force. The static character of the traditional valuations is obvious when they appear as inhibitions and obstacles.

In all the South Asian countries the modernization ideals are so firmly fixed among the articulate elite that rationality and planning for development are the recognized precepts for policy-making, however unsuccessful the planning efforts are in practice. Even those traditionalists who oppose these ideals have not managed to produce a reactionary "plan" of their own; for this would necessitate organizing their valuations on the

[1] Appendix 2, Sections 12–13; Appendix 3, Section 8.
[2] See in Part Four.
[3] Chapter 15, Section 1.

principles of rationality.[1] Put another way, the impact of the modernization ideals has already placed the traditional valuations under the serious "inhibition" of being difficult to express in policy terms.[2]

As traditional valuations, unlike the modernization ideals, are ordinarily not subordinated to the rationality ideal — except on that "higher" level where they do not conflict with the modernization ideals — they cannot be synoptically classified. Many of them lead a shadow life, which is real although obscured from the analytical observer thinking in terms of a logical system. Frequently, they are not verbalized at all, let alone comprehensively articulated in public debate. It would thus serve little purpose to attempt an inventory of all the relevant and significant traditional valuations. Some of them, to be sure, find expression in the statements and writings of the articulate and literate, but the evidence afforded by these sources is, at best, only partial.

2 Traditional Attitudes on the "Higher" Level

At one level — that of the intellectual elite — some traditional valuations are articulated and thus available for inspection even if not for systemization. Although a few intellectuals are, or feel that they are, completely Westernized and secularized, most observe the prescribed rites of their inherited religion and are cognizant of the broad lines of its theology. They have a knowledge of their country's history, its architectural treasures, its literature and philosophy, music, drama, and dance, and its fine crafts, all of which have positive connotations and add to the richness of life. Their attachment to their nation's history, religion, and culture provides more than mere pleasure; it is a psychological necessity, the more so because of the long subjugation of these peoples and the shocked awareness of eco-

[1] "What weakens the Hindu parties in their political efforts is their failure to have a clear-cut political program for returning to the old order; theirs is to a large extent a kind of rear-guard action, aiming to prevent the passage of government legislation affecting the Hindu social structure, to minimize the use of English in the educational system, and more positively, to fight for the passage of legislation banning cow slaughter. (Support for such legislation has increasingly become a symbol of one's identification with the Hindu faith.)" (Myron Weiner, "Some Hypotheses on the Politics of Modernization in India," in *Leadership and Political Institutions in India*, Richard L. Park and Irene Tinker, eds., Princeton University Press, Princeton, New Jersey, 1959, p. 21.)

[2] Only in India have the traditional valuations emerged as a body of doctrine that posits a set of alternative guidelines to the direction of social change: Gandhi's political philosophy. But Gandhi's philosophy was dynamic and demanded radical change. At bottom he accepted most of the modernization ideals, though he succeeded in associating them emotionally with traditional views. This explains why many of his followers found it easy to become apostles of modernization and development, a role made easier by the many ambiguities in his policy prescriptions. The various aspects of Gandhi's political philosophy will be discussed in Part Four and in most chapters of this study.

nomic and social backwardness following upon acceptance of the modernization ideals. Just as an individual, during a crisis that demands a reappraisal of his way of life, needs to establish himself as a continuous personality, with a past and a defined relationship to his social and cultural environment, so the most enlightened intellectuals in these countries feel compelled to identify themselves with their nation.

Nehru described this involvement:

Yet the past is ever with us and all that we are and that we have comes from the past. We are its products and we live immersed in it. Not to understand it and feel it as something living within us is not to understand the present. To combine it with the present and extend it to the future, to break from it where it cannot be so united, to make all this the pulsating and vibrating material for thought and action — that is life.[1]

And again,

The rising middle classes . . . wanted some cultural roots to cling on to, something that gave them assurance of their own worth, something that would reduce the sense of frustration and humiliation that foreign conquest and rule had produced . . . The past of India, with all its cultural variety and greatness, was a common heritage of all the Indian people, Hindu, Moslem, Christian, and others, and their ancestors had helped to build it.[2]

[1] Jawaharlal Nehru, *The Discovery of India*, 4th ed., Meridian Books Ltd., London, 1956, pp. 6–7.

[2] *Ibid.,* p. 343.

The very title of Nehru's book, *The Discovery of India*, testifies to this search for identification. Nehru tells (p. 36) how this discovery "produced a sensation of pride in me as well as that of shame, for I was ashamed of much that I saw around me, of superstitious practices, of outworn ideas, and, above all, our subject and poverty-stricken state. As I grew up and became engaged in activities which . . . promised to lead to India's freedom, I became obsessed with the thought of India. What was this India that possessed me and beckoned to me continually, urging me to action so that we might realize some vague but deeply-felt desire of our hearts? The initial urge came to me, I suppose, through pride, both individual and national, and the desire, common to all men, to resist another's domination and have freedom to live the life of our choice."

And farther on (p. 522): "India must break with much of her past and not allow it to dominate the present. Our lives are encumbered with the dead wood of this past; all that is dead and has served its purpose has to go. But that does not mean a break with, or a forgetting of, the vital and life-giving in that past. We can never forget the ideals that have moved our race, the dreams of the Indian people through the ages, the wisdom of the ancients, the buoyant energy and love of life and nature of our forefathers, their spirit of curiosity and mental adventure, the daring of their thought, their splendid achievements in literature, art and culture, their love of truth and beauty and freedom, the basic values that they set up, their understanding of life's mysterious ways, their toleration of ways other than theirs, their capacity to absorb other peoples and their cultural accomplishments, to synthesize them and develop a varied and mixed culture; nor can we forget the myriad experiences which have built up our ancient race and lie embedded in our subconscious minds. We will never forget them or cease to take pride in that noble heritage of ours. If India forgets them she will no longer remain India and much that has made her our joy and pride will cease to be."

Or, in his address to the United States Congress, October 13, 1949, after pointing out

In South Asia, it is commonly assumed that a nation must identify itself with the past even while breaking away in new directions. As the then Vice President, later President of India, Professor Radhakrishnan, put it, in speaking to a meeting of state governors: "To survive, we need a revolution in our thoughts and outlook. From the altar of the past we should take the living fire and not the dead ashes. Let us remember the past, be alive to the present, and create the future with courage in our hearts and faith in ourselves."[1] Implied in this search for historical moorings and identification with inherited culture is a sense of national pride in them: "It is essential to awaken a sense of pride in our past and re-inforce the faith of the people in what India achieved in the past and what, by dint of intelligent effort, they could achieve in the future."[2]

Awareness of *history* and search for national identity do not in themselves endanger or even compromise allegiance to the modernization ideals, especially on a high intellectual plane. The fact that India and many other South Asian countries had advanced cultures at a time when the now rich and powerful Western countries were uninhabited, or were inhabited by barbarians who left no monuments or records, can be used to build up national pride. It also has an ornamental and ceremonial value that can be appropriated by the new governments.

Memories of the more recent colonial regimes and the process of gaining independence are, naturally, an important element in the consciousness of the politically alert. Insofar as the colonial period appears dark in retrospect, planning and development stand out as means for summoning energies and realizing hitherto unused opportunities. The colonial period is thus ordinarily viewed as a long stretch of time during which people were denied the chance to develop to the full extent of their capacities. The favorable aspects of the colonial system can be looked on as a foreshadowing of the urge for development along national and independent lines.

---

that the drafters of the Indian constitution had been greatly influenced by the American constitution: "Yet it is true that India's voice is somewhat different; it is the voice of the old world of Asia. It is the voice of an ancient civilization, distinctive, vital, which at the same time has renewed itself and learnt much from [America] and the other countries of the West. It is, therefore, both old and new. It has its roots deep in the past, but it also has the dynamic urges of today."

We quote Nehru rather extensively on this point, as we shall on others, for the reason that as an intellectual leader he imbibed the Western ideals very deeply, while as an active politician he was constantly occupied in trying to fit them into a national setting. Thus, and by his honesty and exquisite intelligence, he is an ideal type in Max Weber's meaning, setting forth in high relief what other intellectual leaders and most of the intellectual elite in the region feel and think with less lucidity and insight.

[1] Quoted in Romesh Tapar, "Wiffle Woffle in High Places," *The Economic Weekly,* November 4, 1961, p. 1683.

[2] Congress Planning Sub-Committee, *Report of the Ooty Seminar,* May 30–June 5, 1959, All India Congress Committee, New Delhi, 1959, p. 44.

Knowledge of pre-colonial history is usually so shaky that it lends itself even better to a rationalization of the modernization ideals. Idealization of past periods makes the modernization ideals appear both more urgent and more homespun.[1] In India, for example, there is a rich mythology about the ancient village as a perfect democracy with a rational cooperative organization of production and community life, where caste observance was less rigid and degrading and women enjoyed a higher status.[2] Virtually any cause can find sanction in "history," and the Indian mythology has its counterparts in other South Asian countries, especially Burma and Indonesia. Whether the "golden age myth" is founded on historical fact or is merely an imaginative interpretation is not of immediate consequence; as long as it renders a picture in accord with the modernization ideals, it can be used in their support. Of course, the opposing valuations can be supported by a different interpretation of the facts (or assumptions) about the glory and superiority of the past. Awareness of the past can provide a mantle for a reformer and planner like Nehru, but it can also be exploited by those who wish to clip his wings.[3]

[1] On this point Nehru quotes Aurobindo Ghose: "If an ancient Indian of the time of the Upanishad, of the Buddha, or the later classical age were to be set down in modern India . . . he would see his race clinging to forms and shells and rags of the past and missing nine-tenths of its nobler meaning . . . he would be amazed by the extent of the mental poverty, the immobility, the static repetition, the cessation of science, the long sterility of art, the comparative feebleness of the creative intuition." (Nehru, *Discovery of India*, p. 85.)

[2] About the secure position of women in ancient India, see S. N. Vyas, "Position of Women in Ancient India," *Social Welfare*, 3 (9), December, 1956, Delhi, pp. 36–37. See also Rattan Lal Khanna, *Panchayat Raj in India*, English Book Shop, Chandigarh, 1956.

"Incessantly, Indian women pointed out that their enslavement did not exist in the Vedic time of early Indian history, before the advent of the Christian Era. Indian historical evidence shows that there were many learned women and capable women rulers of this early period. It seems likely that child marriage was not practised at that time, and that widow-marriage was allowed.

"Marriage for girls was not compulsory during the Vedic period. Some women used to remain unmarried throughout their lives, in order to carry on their spiritual work. This tradition continued later on in Buddhist periods. Famous were the Buddhist welfare nuns, who lived in the convents." (Hurustiati Subdranio, "The Changing Social Position of Women in the East," *Eastern and Western World*, W. van Hoeve Ltd., The Hague, Bandung, 1953, p. 116.)

"Many Indians still refer to the old Vedic laws, in order to improve the conditions of women and other subjugated groups. They point out that the recently drafted Hindu Code Bill contains the essence of these ancient laws; only they should be interpreted apart from customs and usage, which came into existence at a later date. Women of the peasant and working classes have always enjoyed a greater freedom than high-ranking sisters, for whom 'purdah' and the veil have been regarded as the insignia of respectability." (*Ibid.*, p. 117.)

[3] Whether the intellectuals in South Asia have a special interest in ancient history, and what role a consciousness of this history plays in their attitudes toward current problems, is a moot point, worthy of empirical study. The illiterate masses are apparently static and backward-looking, but that they look so far into the past is questionable. One wonders what they feel and think about the monuments they often have in

The same can be said of *religion* in its more lofty meaning.[1] The basic doctrines of the old religions in the region — Hinduism, Islam, and Buddhism — are not necessarily inimical to modernization. For example, Islamic and, less explicitly, Buddhist doctrines are advanced to support reforms along the lines of the modernization ideals.[2] The modern constitution worked out for Pakistan prior to the 1958 military putsch was given a generally Islamic façade, as was the First Plan, though the rules laid down in the constitution and the policies prescribed in the plan were hardly influenced by it.[3] Much of the detailed work on the First and Second Plans was directed by American experts, who evidently had no difficulty in adjusting to the Moslem façade. That the Islamic character of the Pakistan republic was, especially in the beginning, played down by the military regime reflected the more secular views of those taking power, and their greater independence of the mullahs.[4] The slight reversion to stress on religion that later took place did not by itself necessitate any change in the regime's position on the modernization ideals.

---

the fields. The educated elite are in large measure engaged in accommodating to a contemporary situation in flux, and their interest in ancient history is perhaps slight. But there are always some who have an interest in history and cultivate it. They are furnishing the material needed for the alternative purposes referred to in the text. In comparing African intellectuals with those from South Asia, particularly those from India, one sometimes gets the impression that the former, because they do not carry the same pretensions of ancient history, religion, and philosophy, more easily accept the experimental and practical approach to life, and that they resemble ordinary farmers' boys who have made good in America or Sweden.

Memories of the recent colonial regimes and the process of gaining independence are, of course, more commonly present in the minds of the intellectuals. The question is how they are molded to suit present interests. Again there is need for empirical research to establish the facts. The outsider's impression is that while specific events in the recent past are rapidly receding from interest, a gradual stereotyping has taken place. In all probability these stereotyped beliefs and valuations will be vastly more significant in forming people's outlooks than is pre-colonial history, because the former ruling nations are still important partners in the outside relations of the South Asian countries.

[1] As Nehru pointed out: "Science today challenges the old concept of religion. But if religion deals not with dogmas and ceremonials, but rather with the higher things of life, there would be no conflict with science or *inter se* between religions." (Jawaharlal Nehru, *India Today and Tomorrow,* Azad Memorial Lectures, Indian Council for Cultural Relations, New Delhi, 1959, p. 32.)

[2] Attention is focussed mainly on the egalitarian ideals, but Islam, in particular, is used to support other modernization ideals as well. In Indonesia the first Sarakit Islam Congress in 1916 strongly criticized the improvidence and negligence of the Indonesians. "At the second Congress in 1917 it was stated that religion commands people to exert themselves in approved professions, such as agriculture, handicrafts, trade, etc., and strictly forbids laziness, idleness, resignation to poverty, and living off the charity of others. 'Religion prescribes all the people to acquire knowledge and to practise the sciences.'" (W. F. Wertheim, *Indonesian Society in Transition,* W. van Hoeve Ltd., The Hague, Bandung, 1956, p. 212 *et passim.*)

[3] See Chapter 8, Section 1.

[4] Chapter 8, Section 8.

In Burma, likewise, these ideals have been explained as an outgrowth of the teachings of Buddha. In fact, even more specialized views — on free enterprise or socialism, "Marxism" or "non-Marxism," and so on — have been held to be in conformity with Buddhism.[1] The greater syncretism and confusion in most Burmese pronouncements should not be attributed to Buddhism, but to other causes — the personality of U Nu, which is so different from that of the Indian and Pakistani leaders; the delayed development of higher education in Burma and the low standards of its university; the small number of Burmese trained for, and accepted in, higher positions in the British civil service; the upheavals and ideological adjustments due to the Japanese occupation; and the burdens placed on the intellectual leaders by the insurrections.

Much the same is true in the other South Asian countries. W. F. Wertheim makes this point about Indonesia: "As the claim for land distribution, springing from a desire to own a piece of ground of one's own, is quite reconcilable with Islamic teachings, it may well be, that the struggle between Left and Right in Indonesia will begin with a fight between Islam and . . . Islam!"[2]

Since independence and the death of Gandhi, less stress has been laid on the religious foundation of policies in India. But whenever references to religion are made on the abstract level, those who defend the moderniza-

---

[1] Particularly in the earlier years of Burma's independence, "Marxism" was rather commonly explained to be in full conformity with Buddhism. "Marxist theory is not antagonistic to Buddhist philosophy. The two are, frankly speaking, not merely similar: in fact they are the same in concept." (U Ba Swe, *The Burmese Revolution,* Union of Burma, Information Dept., Rangoon, 1952, p. 7.)

Later it became the fashion to stress that "democratic socialism" followed Buddhist lines. Meanwhile the Communists are careful not to attack religion. Frank Trager gives an amusing example of this:

"However much Marxism in the West was atheistic and anticlerical, and however personally secular the Marxists may have been, in Southeast Asia they carefully, except during the 'third period,' concealed or otherwise tempered classic doctrine on this point. The views put forth by Asian Communist leaders, such as Tan Malaka, at the Fourth Comintern Congress generally governed Communist tactics in Southeast Asia. More than most, Tan Malaka was keenly aware of the role of religion in a traditional society. Accordingly, Communist propaganda was designed to take into account this element. Schrieke quotes one of the propaganda leaflets used in Sumatra. By any standard an extremely skillful job, the leaflet attempted to show that 'religion, *adat* and prosperity' were one with Communism, and quoted directly from the Koran. The government and the capitalists were dubbed *Kafir,* or unbelievers. The word 'capitalist' was translated into the local language as equivalent to the money-grubbing unbeliever, *Kapisetali,* 'the skinflint *par excellence,* the tax-demanding government.'

"When, much later, anticlericalism crept into the writing of one leading Burmese Communist, a storm broke loose and he had to be publicly disciplined. Though some Burmese leaders attempted to reconcile 'Marxist theory and Buddhist Philosophy,' more recently U Nu, in distinguishing Socialism from 'Marxism' and in equating the latter with Communism, indicated that to identify Marxism with Buddhism was 'ill-considered and unfounded.'" (Frank N. Trager, ed., *Marxism in Southeast Asia,* Stanford University Press, Stanford, 1960, p. 260.)

[2] *Indonesian Society in Transition,* p. 227.

tion ideals can usually manage to quote the scriptures in support of them.[1]
Islam and Buddhism can provide support for one of the modernization
ideals in particular: egalitarian reforms. Hinduism is unique among the
great religions in having no central core of egalitarian doctrine that asserts
the fundamental equality of all human beings. This aspect of Hinduism is
generally played down in India, though Hindu scriptures are sometimes
strained to support even this modernization ideal.[2] Hinduism can also become identified with rationalism and social reform,[3] as can purified Buddhism.[4] On the other hand, religion, like history, can be used by the opponents of all or some of the modernization ideals for their own purposes;
as is said in the West, "the devil can cite scripture."

In South Asia the ancient *philosophies* and their more modern versions
are regularly of the *Welt-und-Lebensanschauungen* variety and are closely
related or identical to the religious doctrines on the "higher" level. They
are almost systematically inconsistent in the definition of concepts and,
like the religious doctrines, are held together by means other than simple
logic. In regard to the issues raised by the modernization ideals they share
the flexibility and ambivalence of the religious doctrines.

The higher forms of *esthetic expression*, such as sagas and poetry,
drama, music, dance, and the finer crafts, represent, of course, national
assets, and their preservation, promotion, and dissemination to broader
strata of the population are natural goals for rational planning. In South
Asia, as in the rest of the world, these efforts often require public support.
To the extent that such goals are incorporated in planned policies,[5] and

---

[1] In Section 7 below, we shall return to this subject and to the conflict between the
"pure" doctrines extracted from the ancient scriptures and the popular version of
Hinduism today.

[2] "Work without aiming at personal profit and with an eye only to the welfare of the
community is the way of life taught in the Bhagavad-Gita. It lays emphasis on the
equal dignity and sacredness of all labour that falls to one's lot, and on honest effort
with detachment and without agitation over results. Indeed, the Gita lays down in a
unique manner the socialist doctrine in terms of religion." (C. Rajagopalachari,
Vedanta the Basic Culture of India, Hindustan Times, New Delhi, 1946, p. 5.)

[3] "In India there is a religious philosophy as old as civilisation itself which, strange
as the claim may seem to outsiders, is remarkably consistent with science. Out of that
religious philosophy has been evolved a code of ethics which can be a firm spiritual
basis for a juster social and economic organisation. It is remarkable that the evolu-
tionary hypotheses and the rule of law as men of science know it were anticipated in
Hinduism." (*Ibid.,* pp. 3f.)

[4] "Buddha had the courage to attack popular religions, superstition, ceremonial, and
priestcraft, and all the vested interests that clung to them. He condemned also the
metaphysical and theological outlook, miracles, revelations, and dealings with the
supernatural. His appeal was to logic, reason, and experience; his emphasis was on
ethics, and his method was one of psychological analysis, a psychology without a soul.
His whole approach comes like the breath of the fresh wind from the mountain after
the stale air of metaphysical speculation." (Nehru, *Discovery of India,* p. 109.)

[5] In Communist countries artistic strivings are usually strongly supported. As these
pursuits require social investments or socially organized activity, and are often thwarted
by the competitive demands of a free-enterprise economy, Communist countries are
as a rule more successful in developing "national culture."

are, or become, cherished, they enhance the appeal of the modernization ideals. In no way are they intrinsically hostile to these ideals.

It should be noted that in the neutral, or rather ambivalent, value attached to history, religion, and other elements of the inherited national culture, South Asian societies are no different from those anywhere else. As we know, in all Western countries this type of association has been used both for and against the ideals we have selected as our value premises. From history are adduced arguments for radical change as well as for conservatism. Support from religious doctrines has been sought by those fighting for egalitarian reforms as well as by those who admonish the poor to be contented. If in the advanced welfare state the reform arguments have gradually become more prominent, this is a reflection of the general trend of opinions, and of social and political change. The elements of inherited folk culture, and of upper-class and even court culture, have inspired both education methods and industrial design and progressive forces generally; occasionally, however, they have been used to support resistance to industrialization and the spread of machines. The South Asian situation is much the same in principle.

3   *Valuations in Regard to the Indigenous Languages*

Rich in metaphors relating to ancient times and suited to the recounting of sagas and myths, the indigenous languages are understandably cherished, particularly after the long period of political domination by foreigners, who seldom were interested in their preservation and enrichment.[1] Thus, in principle, the value attached to them is no different from that attached to other elements in the inherited culture. However, there are some special complications in connection with the use of indigenous languages, and the problem is of considerable practical importance.

It should first be noted that furtherance of the modernization ideals requires the extended use of the indigenous languages. No real "emotional integration" of the new nations and therefore no secure national consolidation[2] is possible as long as the members of the tiny upper class in charge of administration, law enforcement, and modernized business and industry communicate in a European language and the masses speak only their native tongue. An elected assembly must be narrowly selective on a class basis rather than truly representative as long as law or custom decrees that the language of debate be foreign. The people cannot be brought to accept responsibility for their own local and provincial affairs and community cooperation — the "democratic planning"[3] so essential for develop-

---

[1] See, however, Chapter 31, p. 1638, footnote 1, on the active interest of European scholars in the history of the old cultures and in their languages.

[2] See under *g*, Chapter 2, Section 4.

[3] See under *j*, Chapter 2, Section 4; and see Chapter 18.

ment — unless they can deal with an administration that does its speaking
and planning in their language. The alternative would be virtual extinction of the indigenous language and wholesale adoption of a European
tongue, ordinarily English. Not only would such a policy be resisted on
national and cultural grounds; it would be a practical impossibility, even
in the Philippines where the literacy rate is high and English is taught
from the primary grades to the university level, and certainly in the other
countries of the region.[1]

On rational grounds, therefore, increased use of the indigenous language
must be part of the planning in all South Asian countries, both in the conduct of ordinary affairs and in businesses, governmental bodies, and, of
course, schools and universities. The language will have to be developed
to serve these purposes, and dialects will have to be standardized. In this
process problems will arise. Some rationalist language reformers will concentrate on making the language as easy and as serviceable as possible, by
sticking to common usage and by borrowing freely from other languages,
beginning with that of the former metropolitan country. Others will attempt to "purify" the language — in India and Pakistan by "Sanskritizing"
or "Persianizing" it — and will sometimes produce an artificial idiom hardly
more intelligible to common people than the foreign tongue. Rationalism,
of course, dictates the former course. Purification is a costly process, especially for the peoples of South Asia who already have to contend with
poverty and the many other obstacles to their rapid development. In deciding to give a wider and eventually an exclusive place to the indigenous
language the South Asian countries are following in the steps of many European countries — all of them, in fact, if we take into account their break-
away, after the Middle Ages, from the dominance of Latin in the church,
the law courts, diplomacy, and the universities. The European countries
also experienced difficulties and controversies in developing and stand-
ardizing a national language. The only difference is that the South Asian
countries cannot afford a process that takes centuries; they need much
quicker results.[2]

If we leave the thorny question of script for later consideration, the main
problem is that of accelerating the use of the indigenous language. In some
South Asian countries the broad issue is rather uncomplicated and the
process is well under way. Burma and Thailand are perfecting their na-

[1] Chapter 32, Section 4; Chapter 33, Sections 3, 4, 6.

[2] The closest parallel is, perhaps, Finland. When, after being split off from the wider
Swedish community, it began a hundred years ago to develop a national Finnish
language out of a number of local dialects with little written literature, the country
comprised only 1.7 million people. Finland has succeeded in that effort, though the
material and cultural costs were considerable. In retrospect there was clearly no other
way to achieve national consolidation, as about five-sixths of the people did not speak
Swedish, the language of the commercial and administrative upper class at that time,
or Russian, the other official language of the Grand Duchy of Finland before Finnish
gained that status, under an 1863 law, in 1883.

tional languages and getting them accepted and used in the representative assemblies, courts, administration, schools, and universities; although part of the trouble the Burmese government has had in enforcing its authority and gaining the loyalty of the people in outer regions stems from the language issue. In Indonesia there are many local languages and dialects, but Bahasa Indonesia (developed from Coastal Malay with a liberal admixture of Sanskrit, Arabic, Dutch, and English words) should in time prevail as the national language, provided Indonesia can master other disruptive political forces. In the Philippines, Tagalog is becoming more generally understood and may become the national language, though there is still resistance to it in regions where other dialects are spoken.

In Ceylon, however, the difference in language aggravates the struggle between the Singhalese majority and the Tamils. In Pakistan, Urdu was designated as the national language after partition; it was spoken mainly in West Pakistan but was nevertheless foreign to most of the inhabitants of that zone. In East Pakistan, Bengali is the common idiom and the language difference became a serious element in East Pakistani grievances against dominance and exploitation by the other half of the country.[1] The East Pakistanis were not satisfied even when the constitution finally adopted both Bengali and Urdu as national languages; English is the official language.

In Malaya, the almost equal division of the population between Malays, on one hand, and Chinese and Indians on the other, did not prevent the establishment of Malay as the national language. Possibly the Chinese and the Indians will in time be forced to acquire a working knowledge of Malay, but this will not keep them from communicating among themselves in their own language. As the Chinese dominate Malayan business and have a large majority in nearby Singapore, a very important part of the country's economic life will continue to be carried on outside the national language.

The language situation in India is especially complicated and hazardous for national consolidation and development. The Indian National Congress began even under British rule to divide the country into linguistic units; this was, indeed, necessary in order to get the fullest possible backing in the fight against the British. By repeated decisions it was also prescribed in the Congress program that independent India should be divided into states demarcated on language lines.[2] The Indian constitution designated fourteen official languages for administrative and educational purposes, including Sanskrit but not English. Among these languages Hindi in Devanagri script was to become the official Union language in 1965. Until then, and while knowledge of Hindi was spreading, both Hindi and English were to have official sanction as Union languages.

---

[1] Chapter 8, Section 3.

[2] The necessity for reorganizing the British provinces on the basis of language was in principle often recognized by the British from the beginning of the century.

Through a chain of decisions, marked by much strife and some bloodshed, a structure of linguistic states has come into existence, and the process may not yet be at an end. On the whole, this reorganization is a drastic simplification and rationalization achieved by suppression of the princely states and many of the arbitrary provincial boundaries of British times.[1] Many of these states have a population the size of the larger European countries.

The constitutional prescription that Hindi should become the Union language within fifteen years after independence has met, however, with greater difficulties in execution. For one thing, Hindi is admittedly less highly developed than, for instance, Bengali, Tamil, or Marathi. Furthermore, the split of the syncretized Hindustani into Hindi, Urdu, and Punjabi has produced a much smaller language in terms of popular usage. The Indian philologists who have devoted their efforts to improving Hindi have usually been purists, eager to cleanse it of foreign words, and to enrich it by adding words from Sanskrit. As a result Hindi has tended to become an increasingly strange language even to the people who live in the area that is officially supposed to be Hindi-speaking.[2] Even more important, however, is the resistance in the southern states where the official languages are Dravidian. Understandably people in these states feel that the efforts to make Hindi the all-Indian language provide an undue advantage to the northerners. This cannot be cancelled by the pious advice offered by Nehru and other appeasers: that the northerners should learn a southern language in exchange. The advice is seldom followed; nor would it effect a substantial change as, in any case, no southern language is privileged to be the Union language. These feelings of resentment, shared by people in West Bengal, present a serious barrier to the spread of Hindi since education is a prerogative of the states.

[1] Chapter 7, Section 2.

[2] All this was contrary to Gandhi's intentions. He wanted, instead, to unify and standardize Hindustani to include Urdu, Punjabi, and, if possible, other minor languages; he favored the study of additional Indian languages in order to strengthen the unity of the country. Nehru's ideas were along the same lines, and he particularly opposed the purist tendencies in the development of Hindi: ". . . an effort must be made to discourage the extreme tendencies and develop a middle literary language, on the lines of the spoken language in common use. With mass education this will inevitably take place. At present the small middle-class groups, that are supposed to be the arbiters of literary taste and style, are terribly narrow-minded and conservative, each in its own way. They cling to antique forms that have no life in them and have few contacts with their own masses or with world literature. . . . I would personally like to encourage Hindustani to adapt and assimilate many words from English and other foreign languages. This is necessary, as we lack modern terms, and it is better to have well-known words rather than to evolve new and difficult words from the Sanskrit or Persian or Arabic. Purists object to the use of foreign words, but I think they make a great mistake, for the way to enrich our language is to make it flexible and capable of assimilating words and ideas from other languages." (Jawaharlal Nehru, *An Autobiography*, The Bodley Head, London, 1953 ed., pp. 454–456.)

As a result of all this, the time is still far distant when India will have a Union language in effective use. In practice, English is the language of the higher courts, the Union administration, to a large extent that of the state administrations, and that of the Indian Parliament. It is also used by educated people generally when they gather together, particularly when they are from different parts of India.[1] English is still, in a sense, the cementing force in this huge country, as it is in Pakistan. Many of the intellectual elite, and not only those in the southern and western states outside the Hindustan tradition, conclude that English should be preserved indefinitely as the *de facto* national language. Meanwhile the state languages are developing rapidly, and their use in the press, state assemblies, administration, and universities is gradually expanding. Many more youths are now learning English, but only as a second or third language, and standards are continually sinking. One writer has observed that "As a result, all ten languages [i.e., excluding Sanskrit and Urdu, Punjabi and Kashmiri], not Hindi alone, are emerging as alternatives to English."[2]

Looked at from the point of view of the modernization ideals, which are the value premises of this study, the improvement and effective utilization of the state languages is not only desirable but necessary. The isolation of a small intellectual elite — defined and held together by mastery of a foreign language that can never become the popular idiom in any part of India — must be broken, and the masses brought into active participation. But there can be no real national consolidation and responsible participa-

[1] In the autumn of 1961 an all-India National Integration Conference was called together. "It was a large gathering of distinguished persons from different walks of life, political, social, economic and educational." (*Yojana*, October 15, 1961, p. 2.) The conference language was generally English — even in the discussion about whether and when and how to implement the constitutional prescription that Hindi should become the national language. The official organ of the Planning Commission, quoted above, commented as follows: "Fourteen years after Independence it looks as though the change-over is to be a prolonged and painful one, for even the first steps do not seem to have been taken. . . . It is obvious that in some subtle ways English and English ways of thought and feeling overpower us in our national affairs of the greatest importance. We persist in clinging to them almost unconsciously; such is their enchantment." (*Ibid.*, pp. 15–29.)

"The irony of the situation is that nothing more happened beyond this professed adoption of Hindi as our National Language. The Congress leaders went on making their publications in English, pouring forth their orations in English, drafting their resolutions in English, carrying on their debates in English and even conducting their informal *tête à têtes* in English. The espousal of Hindi by the Congress at this stage strikes one as a conjugal alliance without its consummation!

"And this state of affairs, it appears, would have carried on indefinitely. The Congress had its hands full with the struggle for Independence. And it was fantastic, anyway, to think of the Congress leaders, most of them the product of English universities, [willing] to give up the foreign language and switch over to Hindi. Therefore, it appeared that the newly-born babe of Hindi had been given an unobtrusive burial at its very birth." (T. S. Bawa, *Nehru's India*, Freeland Publication Private Ltd., New Delhi, 1956, pp. 160–161.)

[2] Selig S. Harrison, "The Challenge to Indian Nationalism," *Foreign Affairs*, Vol. 34, No. 4, July, 1956, p. 623.

tion in local and sectional self-government and in cooperatives if administration, representative assemblies, law courts, and schools continue to employ a language the masses do not understand. Gandhi fully recognized this crucial need; his promotion of the idea of a federal system and demarcation of states along linguistic lines was more than just a tactic to join all forces in the fight against the British.[1]

However, the development of the state languages implies a threat to the Union. Without an all-Indian language, understood by everyone, or at least by all who are taught in schools, it is difficult to see how the Union can be kept together. Present trends would seem to imply a gradual break-up of the relative unity and mobility of personnel in administration, courts, universities, and the professions.[2] The prospect of counteracting these trends by general and prompt acceptance of Hindi as a second language seems slight. Neither is continued reliance on English as a unifying upper-class language a permanent solution, since it is socially restrictive and does not meet the need for national consolidation and popular participation. As long as the debates in the Union Parliament, for instance, are conducted in English, national politics must remain a class monopoly estranged from the people. In the absence of an all-Indian language it would, indeed, be more appropriate to let everyone speak his own language and to have simultaneous translation, as in international organizations. As it is, all planning and policy-making under the Union government in New Delhi, as well as negotiations with state governments, are carried on in a language unknown to most of the people whose interest and cooperation are sought. Aside from the class problem — which is so important for national consolidation and popular participation — it would be strange if popular feelings in a newly liberated country were to permit the continuation of this system over the long run.

In the absence of a generally accepted all-Indian language as a unifying

[1] "It is evident that unless we advance this cause, we shall not be able to remove the growing intellectual and cultural gulf between our men and women and between the classes and the masses. It is also equally certain that the vernacular medium alone can stimulate originality in thought in the largest number of persons." (*Young India*, April 21, 1920.)

"Our love of the English language in preference to our own mother tongue has caused a deep chasm between the educated and the politically-minded classes and the masses. The languages of India have suffered impoverishment. We flounder when we make the vain attempt to express abstruse thought in the mother tongue. There are no equivalents for scientific terms. The result has been disastrous. The masses remain cut off from the modern mind. We are too near our own times correctly to measure the disservice caused to India by this neglect of its great languages. It is easy enough to understand that, unless we undo the mischief, the mass mind must remain imprisoned." (*Constructive Programme*, Navajivan Press, Ahmedabad, 1944, p. 16.)

[2] "It is . . . necessary to emphasise that the growth of these languages led to an integration of linguist nationalities in India, to the emphasis on the fissiparous tendencies of particularism, so that, moved by their pride in their language, the Gujeratis, the Marathas and the Kanarese, for example, began to feel different from each other in a way they had never done before." (K. M. Panikkar, *A Survey of Indian History*, Asia Publishing House, Bombay, 1954, p. 222.)

force, the Union's division into states along linguistic lines invites and strengthens the tendencies toward narrow sectionalism, inimical to national consolidation.[1] These centrifugal tendencies are magnified in India by their correlation with caste. It is not only that the caste structure is broadly regional and encompassed within the language boundaries; the existence and functioning of linguistically defined states adds opportunities for, and intensifies, conflicts between castes.[2] The constant appeals by national leaders rightly condemn "casteism, provincialism, and linguism." It is through these that attachment to one's own language, which is natural and could be consistent with the realization of the modernization ideals, comes into severe conflict with those ideals.

The language problem is complicated by differences in scripts. Such differences are less frequent, of course, in those countries that have or are on the way to having only one national language. Indonesia and the Philippines have simplified matters by adopting the Roman script for their national language, thereby enabling students to have English as a second language without learning a new script. In India not only are there a large number of indigenous languages, but most of them have their own scripts and a high cultural value is commonly attached not only to the languages but also to the traditional ways of writing them. In many parts of the country the public schools have to require the children to learn three languages; this places a heavy burden on the curriculum; but, under the circumstance explained above, can be justified on rational grounds. The burden is increased when children must be taught three scripts — the script of the state language, that of Hindi, which is supposed to become the national language, and the Roman script for English.[3] Teaching of other subjects has to be curtailed.[4] Another cost of this policy is the necessity for

[1] The Linguistic Provinces Commission, appointed by India's Constituent Assembly in 1948, warned that its inquiry "has in some ways been an eye-opener for us. The work of 60 years of the Indian National Congress was standing before us, face to face with centuries-old India of narrow loyalties, petty jealousies and ignorant prejudices engaged in a mortal conflict, and we were simply horrified to see how thin was the ice upon which we were skating. Some of the ablest men in the country came before us and confidently and emphatically stated that language in this country stood for and represented culture, race, history, individuality, and finally a sub-nation." (Harrison, "The Challenge to Indian Nationalism," *Foreign Affairs*, p. 621.)

[2] Chapter 7, Section 5.

[3] Not to mention a fourth language, another state language, as proposed by Gandhi, Nehru, and others. The situation is similar in Pakistan, where both Urdu and Bengali are now national languages. The *Overseas Hindustan Times*, of New Delhi, carried the following notice (on December 7, 1961): "Mr. Zabir Hussain, Pakistan's Minister for Home Affairs, said last week that the Government had asked experts to examine the possibility of evolving a common script of various Pakistani languages, especially Urdu and Bengali. He told newsmen at Larkana that a common script would foster greater unity among the people. He also made a plea for a simplification of the language, used by the Radio and the Press."

[4] Chapter 33, Sections 3, 4, and 6.

specially constructed typewriters, and many Indian scripts are not easily adjusted to typewriting. Moreover, the use of different scripts makes it all the harder for people who have learned only one or two languages to learn a second or a third.

Many national leaders in India, beginning with Gandhi and including the former and the present Presidents, have proposed the use of a single script for all the Indian languages, but this proposal has not met acceptance. It would certainly decrease the costs just described, but would not eliminate them. For knowledge of English is commonly agreed to be necessary for all students above the elementary level, and English cannot very well be written in any of the Indian scripts. Students must learn the Roman script in order to read the foreign literature; at the advanced level the literature in the Indian languages is meager and difficult to keep up to date. From the viewpoint of our value premises, the ideal solution would be to accept the Roman script for all languages, as has been done in Indonesia and the Philippines. Some intellectuals in India stress that this is an obviously needed modernization;[1] they would place scripts, if not languages, among things not deserving of emotional attachment. Thus Humayan Kabir, cabinet minister recently in charge of the Ministry of Scientific Research and Cultural Affairs in India, has argued that script "has no relation whatever to any language or to any alphabet . . . Any alphabet can be written in any script, provided the alphabet has the symbols for the necessary sounds. If it has not, such sounds may be added and visual symbols invented or adopted to represent them. The only basis on which to prefer a script should therefore be clarity, legibility and capacity for easy manual and mechanical manipulation."[2] He prefaced this declaration by pointing out that the languages of India have been written in different scripts throughout history.

But such arguments do not have much influence on those who are attached to a particular script. There is, of course, no difficulty in integrating a cultural preference of this kind in otherwise rational reasoning and in planning. However, the costs in terms of lost opportunities of an educational policy requiring different scripts for different languages must then

---

[1] It is often pointed out "that the single script for India is absolutely necessary and that the South will accept none other than the Roman or Indo-Roman." (Nomesk Thapa, "Sins and Sinners," *The Economic Weekly*, October 7, 1961, p. 1553.)

This is also the position of many intellectuals in West Bengal. It is open to doubt, however, whether even in these non-Hindi parts of India, this solution would be accepted, if the proposal were put to a decision. That it would meet fierce resistance in the Hindi parts of India is certain: so long as the constitution prescribes that the national language is Hindi in Devanagri script, they are *beati possidentes*.

"National integration does demand a certain degree of conformity in the interest of functional efficiency. Here the emphasis is not on meaningless 'codes' and 'pledges' but on matters such as a common script which is as important as a common currency or common weights and measures." (*Ibid.*)

[2] Humayan Kabir, "Language, Alphabet and Script," *Studies in Education and Culture,* pp. 208–209.

be accounted for. A similar calculation could be made for the costs of having to learn the several languages in the first place. But the national cost of the language issue in India is very different and much larger than the opportunity costs of having to learn more languages and scripts. It adds its load of irrationality and emotion to all other divisive forces in the new nation.

When on January 26, 1965, in accordance with the constitution and the Official Languages Act of 1963, Hindi was declared the official language of India, serious riots broke out in Madras and spread to other non-Hindi-speaking states. After long and acrimonious negotiations, the government was pressed to accept an amendment to the act, giving the force of law to Nehru's promise that English would continue to be an associate language as long as the non-Hindi-speaking people wanted it. At the same time the decision to have a tri-lingual basis for education – implying that Hindi states should teach a southern language in exchange for the teaching of Hindi in non-Hindi-speaking states – was confirmed, though without much hope that it would be carried into practice more effectively than before. The language issue has, in short, been left where it was, except that even more bad feeling has been generated. As one Indian weekly commented on the outburst of rioting early in 1965: "The painful logic of the language issue is such that the fanatics are easily able to force those who normally think and act rationally to yield to local and necessarily narrow sentiment."[1]

4 *The Hindu Taboo on Cow Slaughter and Similar* *Valuations of a Specific Type*

There are other specific traditional valuations that are widely held and articulated systematically enough to be easily observable. Sometimes they are given the force of constitutional prescript or law. Since they are specific they cannot remain flexible, indifferent, or ambivalent as can the "higher" valuations dealt with in Section 2. They must often conflict with the modernization ideals, and thus represent inhibitions and obstacles to planning for development.

From a practical point of view the most important of these valuations is the Hindu taboo on killing animals, epitomized in the ban on cow slaughter. India is estimated to have more than half as many cattle as human beings and, in fact, one-fourth of all the cattle in the world. Many of them are useless, or destructive since even wandering and half-starved animals eat something; almost all have a very low productivity. The cattle stock has recently been increasing; and there is a real danger that the number of unserviceable and unproductive cattle will increase even faster with control

[1] *Link*, February 21, 1965, p. 1.

of local famines and improved treatment of cattle diseases, particularly if the taboo should be strengthened by new and better enforced laws. This problem of cattle increase offers a somber parallel to the population explosion, which we shall discuss in Chapter 27. The religious taboo that places the life of cattle on a par with that of human beings finds expression in legislation throughout the country. In Chapter 26 (Section 7) we shall consider how this taboo affects productivity in agriculture; here we are interested in its valuative aspect.

The British, believing in non-interference in social and religious matters, had followed a *laissez-faire* policy, though they defended Moslem practices and, toward the end of the colonial era, even tried out, with the support of Indian representative assemblies, cautious legislation against the taboo on cow slaughter. Independence and the upsurge of Hindu nationalism gave the ardent supporters of traditional valuations an opportunity to strengthen the hold of this taboo. They succeeded in inscribing in the Indian constitution a Directive Principle (Article 48) instructing the states, as responsible for agricultural policy, both to endeavor to organize agriculture and animal husbandry on scientific lines and to prohibit the slaughter of milk and draft cattle. With the general backing of this Directive Principle, laws against slaughter of cattle have been enacted in a number of states and there is constant propaganda for such legislation in other states. The Indian Planning Commission commented dryly on the situation created by this Directive Principle and the ideological and emotional force behind it:

Famines and epidemics having been largely brought under control, there is a tendency for the number of surplus cattle to increase even in the ordinary course and this trend will become more marked owing to action taken in recent years to place a total ban on slaughter of cattle. Proposals for bans on the slaughter of cattle derive from a widely prevalent sentiment which has found expression in the Constitution and must inevitably also enter into national planning. . . . But in giving effect to this Directive Principle care has to be taken to see that conditions are not created which may defeat the very objective which the Constitution seeks to achieve.[1]

For the time being it seems impossible to effect a fundamental change in Indian legislation, or to test the strength of the taboo among ordinary people by offering economic incentives, through taxation and/or subsidies, for the slaughter of useless cattle. The only recourse is to circumvent the taboo. One proposal in the First Five Year Plan was to set aside special areas (Gosadans) where cattle could be left to die — possibly, cynics said, with some assistance from the tigers. But this scheme, continued in the Third Plan, is costly and has made little progress.[2] Another proposal has

---

[1] India, Government of, Planning Commission, *Second Five Year Plan*, New Delhi, 1956, p. 282.

[2] Chapter 26, Section 7.

been "birth control" through castration of bullocks. But that runs into the difficulty of lack of enough people qualified to perform castrations, and is limited also by a widespread popular taboo against their performance.[1] Since a cow must drop a calf each year if she is to produce milk steadily, it also would mean that still fewer cows would be in milk.[2]

In the circumstances, it is understandable that the designers of the Second Plan concluded on what sounds like a note of despair. "States should take a realistic view of the fodder resources available and the extent to which they can get the cooperation of voluntary organisations to bear the main responsibility for maintaining unserviceable and unproductive cattle with a measure of assistance from the Government and general support from the people."[3] The Third Plan abstained from any general judgment on the problem of cattle numbers apart from emphasizing its "seriousness"; it proposed an increase in the number of Gosadans and a large-scale program of castration of scrub bullocks.[4] The simple fact is, of course, that it is impossible to plan a rational policy for husbandry in India, if cattle cannot be selectively killed to the extent and at the age that is most advantageous economically. In asking for both rational husbandry and a ban on cow slaughter the Directive Principle is self-contradictory.

For India, with its large and growing number of cattle, many of which are surplus, and with so many other adverse conditions that keep the rural masses in poverty and backwardness, the ban on cow slaughter represents a very serious complex of inhibitions and obstacles to planning. Nehru, always adhering strictly to rationality, bluntly came out against this religious taboo on several occasions;[5] however, he did not find it feasible to make a major issue of it and demand a revocation of the ban on cow slaughter in the Directive Principles. It is known that he frequently fought for his view in the cabinet and with members of the state governments.

[1] The Third Draft Plan seemed to place its main hope in birth control, though it noted some difficulties: "The most effective way of checking the further multiplication of useless and inefficient cattle is . . . the castration of scrub and uncertified bulls commonly used in the villages. An all India scheme of Mass Castration for the sterilisation of undesirable males has been incorporated in the Third Five Year Plan. Its success will, however, depend on the active participation of the public and the availability of the requisite number of Burdisso castrators." (India, Government of, Planning Commission, *Third Five Year Plan, Draft Report,* New Delhi, May, 1961, pp. XX–7.)

[2] One writer estimates that at present only one-third of the adult cows are in milk, and that if birth control were adopted, "not even one-tenth of the cows could be kept in milk and it would be impossible economically to maintain such a herd of cows." (V. M. Dandekar, "Problem of Numbers in Cattle Development," *The Economic Weekly,* Annual Number, February, 1964, pp. 351–352.)

[3] India, Government of, *Second Five Year Plan,* p. 283.

[4] India, Government of, Planning Commission, *Third Five Year Plan,* New Delhi, 1961, pp. 348–349. See Chapter 26, Section 7.

[5] In a speech in his own constituency during the next-to-last election campaign, he dared to say that he saw no difference between a cow and a horse, and added that in India the cow is maltreated while kept holy. Louis Fischer reported:

"He has, for example, defeated a bill introduced in Parliament by Hindu extremists which would have banned the killing of any cow. Arguing against the measure, Mr.

Many intellectuals express views similar to Nehru's in private conversation but avoid taking a public stand, either because they do not dare or because they consider the situation hopeless.[1] Many more, and not only those who abhor cow slaughter, make valiant attempts to justify the taboo as economically advantageous, or at least compatible with rational husbandry. Numerous articles and books have been written in support of this opportune rationalization. Like other elements of irrationality in reasoning, it is damaging to logical thinking in general. It should also be noted that in India the taboo is often used to back up nationalist aggressions against the Moslem minority, which does not share in it. Not a few of the riots and fights between Hindus and Moslems have been touched off by incidents arising from their contrary views on cow slaughter.

In Ceylon and the other Buddhist countries there are like sentiments against slaughtering cattle, or killing any animal — broader sentiments that are also present in India. In regard to cattle, however, the taboo is not as damaging as in India, because the surplus cattle population is not as great. The numbers are kept down in part because the people in these countries, unlike the Indians, are averse to breeding animals in captivity, but principally because almost all Buddhists eat meat. The taboo mainly results in a kind of division of labor, with the actual killing left to foreigners — in Southeast Asia often to Indians — and to low-caste groups. There is, consequently, no general tendency to legislate a ban on cow slaughter.

The Moslems in Pakistan, Indonesia, Malaya, and elsewhere consider pigs unclean and have a strong aversion to eating pork.[2] This certainly in-

---

Nehru, according to an Associated Press report from New Delhi dated April 2, 1955, called the idea 'most silly. We are totally opposed to it,' he exclaimed. 'We stand or fall by it.'

" 'Shame, shame,' cried the obscurantist Hindus.

" 'I don't get excited over any animal,' the Prime Minister retorted, 'not even the cow.'

"It takes courage to make such a statement in India, and it is political dynamite. Hindu sentiment and religion are deeply opposed to ending a cow's life, even if its existence robs young cows of necessary pasture and fodder." (Louis Fischer, *This Is Our World*, Jonathan Cape Ltd., London, 1956, p. 470.)

Gandhi's support of the ban on cow slaughter is one of the few points where he deviated from the modernization ideals.

[1] The writer has seldom seen such a large exhibition of portraits of Gandhi as when he visited the Indian Veterinary Institute. It seems that veterinarians, because they are suspected of unconventional views on cow slaughter, are in particular need of a protective front.

[2] In the Soviet republic of Uzbekistan the farmers are almost all Uzbeks, who are Moslems; a large number of non-Moslem Russians work in industry and administration and live in the cities. The Uzbeks, as Moslems, don't eat pork, but since the Russians do, pig breeding is a profitable occupation. When visiting Uzbekistan the writer found that the collective farms had usually solved the problem in the following way: In a distant corner of the farms, far away from the houses where the farmers lived and worked, there were establishments for breeding pigs, the pork being sold in the cities. The breeding, feeding, and slaughtering of the pigs and the transporting of the meat were done by hired Russian workers, under the supervision of an Uzbek, who kept at a safe distance from the pigs.

terferes with the efficiency of peasant farming as the breeding of pigs is often an ideal supplement to raising crops; it also seems to improve health conditions since pigs are scavengers. But again this taboo is not as serious a deviation from rational planning as is the Indian taboo against cow slaughter. As it is the breeding and eating of pigs and not the killing of them that is disliked, and as this aversion rests on a doctrine that pigs are unclean and not that they are sacred, this taboo does not demand a legislative ban; its non-observance by people of other creeds is not felt to be a crime.

The conflict between articulated specific traditional valuations and the modernization ideals can be expressed in terms of the costs to the latter through lost opportunities. In the case of the ban on cow slaughter in India, these costs are very high, though never calculated. Other specific traditional valuations that are articulated appear to be fairly inconsequential for the modernization ideals. Some may be entirely in accord with planning. For example, the Directive Principle in the Indian constitution that the states should prohibit the manufacture and sale of alcoholic beverages may be rational, if the prohibition could be enforced and did not merely encourage disobedience of law and corruption of administrators. The remarkable thing about most traditional valuations of the specific type, however, is the infrequency with which they have been articulated in public discussion. Still less frequently have they been given sanction by constitutions and laws or have they overtly motivated public policies. With some few exceptions, of which the Indian ban on cow slaughter and the positions on the language question are the most important practically, the modernization ideals have reigned supreme in public discussion and overt public policy-making.

An example of formal repudiation of a traditional valuation is that of caste and caste observance in India. Although caste permeates Indian life, and although in private conversation many intellectuals are prepared to defend it as a useful institution, it is condemned in the constitution and by virtually everyone who speaks publicly or writes on the issue. Idealization of the caste system as it is supposed to have operated in the mythological past has its obvious emotional background in a different, and more "realistic," attitude toward it on the part of many of the intellectual elite, who come mainly from the higher and privileged castes.

5 The "Asian Values"

So far, we have dealt with verbalized valuations, made explicit by the small intellectual elite. They may be supported by similar feelings in the inarticulate broader strata, but about this we do not know much. That the two specific valuations dealt with in Sections 3 and 4 — in regard to indigenous languages and cow slaughter — have at least some popular backing is apparent. The valuations on the "higher" level, discussed in Section 2, seem to be restricted to the educated class, yet they are certainly not unimportant, as this class holds such a disproportionate share of the political power in South Asia. But an examination that confines itself to what is verbalized and explicit can convey only an inkling of the social significance of traditional attitudes and beliefs, some of which are very important inhibitions and obstacles to development. What is needed is intensive empirical investigation of these attitudes and beliefs in different strata of the population and their influence on behavior. At present, solid knowledge about this highly relevant matter is scanty. Our discussion must therefore be largely restricted to the statement of open problems and the formulation of reasonable hypotheses for further research.

Before taking up that discussion, in the next section, we need to dispose of a presumed short cut by way of generalizations about "Asian values," or the "values" of one or another of the religions or nationalities of the region. There is a large literature expounding this general theme, and many more works refer to these values in explanation of behavior. According to this view, people of one religion, one country, or of the entire region — meaning, usually, all Asia — have the same fundamental cultural and personality traits and world outlook: they share certain basic modes of thinking, feeling, and acting. These traits are supposed to emanate from their history and religion[1] — an explanation that recalls the attitudes discussed in Section 2.

Insofar as there are considerable and systematic differences in conditions among the several South Asian countries, there is undoubtedly something to the concept of a "national character." The same may be said of religions. And as the differences in conditions are much more pronounced between these countries as a whole and the Western world, there is room also for the concept of the "Asian" — or "South Asian" — mind. But these terms are not suitable for scientific use. They have been contaminated by being made to serve — in South Asia as in the Western world — specula-

---

[1] "Vedanta is the tap-root of Indian culture in the past as well as now. Whatever courage, heroism, self-sacrifice or greatness was shown by men and women in India, was all derived from Vedanta, the philosophy of the Vedas. Even now Vedanta is the living spirit and genius of the people of India. However much foreign civilisation or new aspirations may affect us, the main source has not decayed. The lives of the rich and the poor, of the leisured classes and the peasants and labourers, of Indus, Mussalmans and Christians, of the illiterate and the learned, of the honest and the dishonest, are sweetened alike by the pervasive fragrance of Indian philosophy. Vedanta is the basic culture of India." (C. Rajagopalachari, *Vedanta the Basic Culture of India*, pp. 7-8.)

Similar statements about the unity of culture among South Asians, directly related to history, religion, and ancient philosophy, abound. A Western scholar with a similar message is F. S. C. Northrop. See his *The Taming of the Nations*, Macmillan, New York, 1952.

tive, nationalist, aggressive, or apologetic ideologies. For convenience we shall refer to these values as "Asian values"; in criticizing them we have in mind South Asian, or more specifically Indian, conditions. These alleged cultural and personality traits all turn out to claim a special wisdom and, particularly, a superior moral status. In any case, they are flattering to the collective ego and, at the very least, excuse the shortcomings that exist in material conditions. This is the element of valuation in the belief in common traits. The "genius" of a country or of Asia — an expression with wide currency in the region — is understood to embrace all these characteristics.

For our purpose a summary of some of the most common attributions will suffice. No distinctions among the several countries in the region are acknowledged, since much the same traits are alleged to characterize them all. A central claim is that people in Asia are more spiritual and less materialistic than Westerners. They are other-worldly, selfless, and disposed to disregard wealth and material comfort. They sustain poverty with equanimity and even see positive virtues in it. They have a special respect for learning and a capacity for contemplation and meditation. Their intellectual strength lies in intuition more than in reason and hard calculation. In current affairs their main criterion is the moral worth of a person or a policy, and they are apt to censure expediency and opportunism in politics. With spiritual concerns and personal salvation paramount, the external world takes on an illusory and transient aspect. The attitude toward the environment tends to be timeless, formless, and therefore carefree and even fatalistic. The ideal is alleged to be detachment, withdrawal, if not renunciation and asceticism. This bent of mind, it is said, gives Asians serenity and the capacity to endure extreme physical suffering. They are pictured as tolerant, non-aggressive, and non-militant in their social relations and their international politics. They are said to dislike definitive legal principles and to prefer to settle conflicts by mutual agreement rather than by formal procedures; to regard status as more important than contracts; to desire peace with their neighbors and the world, and peace in their souls.

Stereotypes like these abound in the literature, and allegations of common traits are injected into almost all public pronouncements about Asian countries and their problems and policies. On a par with the modernization ideals they have, in fact, infiltrated the vocabulary of public discussion. Even those intellectual leaders who have questioned their accuracy in general or specific terms (see below) often refer to these "Asian values" in addressing their countrymen, as do visiting statesmen and scholars from the West.

An important field of study would be to cull from the literature and the public debate such statements about Asian cultural and personality traits, analyze them critically, in historical perspective and in their present political, social, and economic setting, and check by opinion surveys and other means the extent to which they coincide with the actual attitudes and behavior of people in different countries and different social and economic strata. As to the realism of the stereotypes, we shall offer here only a few broad observations.

The most cursory examination reveals that the alleged cultural and personality traits bear little resemblance to reality — as little as their counterparts in the Western world (see below). For instance, the charity and tolerance often attributed to the Indians is in direct contradiction to the extreme intolerance bred by rigid social stratification[1] and the callousness toward those in a lower social stratum[2] that is found among the most cultivated Indians and soon adopted by Westerners who live in India for any length of time.[3] That India's foreign relations have sometimes seemed to reflect tolerance is explained by national interests and the accident of Nehru's leadership.[4] In dealing with particular issues, especially with neighboring countries, Indians are generally felt to be haughty and intolerant; this is the consensus in South Asia and often also in the Western countries.

Non-violence, under Gandhi's intelligent leadership, was a broadly successful political tactic of the Indian liberation movement, as it has been for many other groups opposing organized social power, including workers in Western countries in the early stages of trade unionism when their struggle for collective bargaining rights was suppressed by the police and the military. To Gandhi personally, and to many of his followers, the principle of non-violence was undoubtedly a strong moral imperative, related to his philosophy of life and his religion. But non-violence is certainly not a national trait in India, as demonstrated by the Hindu-Moslem strife at

[1] Chapter 16, Sections 6–9.

[2] Arthur Koestler observes this, though, following convention, he promptly takes it as another, but different, expression of the Asian values; the Oriental attitude to the sick and the poor is notoriously indifferent, because caste, rank, wealth, and health are preordained by the laws of Karma. "Welfare work in the slums and care of the poor in general was, and still is, a monopoly of the Christian missions in Asia. Gandhi's crusade for the Untouchables and Vinoba's crusade for the landless are modern developments under Western influence — Gandhi himself acknowledged that he was inspired by Christianity, Tolstoy, Ruskin and Thoreau." (Arthur Koestler, *The Lotus and the Robot*, Macmillan, New York, 1961, p. 280.)

The explanation may sooner be found in the social relations that develop in a very poor country. See below and in Chapter 16.

[3] "This [individual-to-individual] callousness is . . . so strong in the country that it is the greatest danger for a foreigner living in India, for it is a frighteningly easy thing to find it creeping into one's own soul." (A. M. Rosenthal, "The Future in Retrospect, Mother India Thirty Years After," *Foreign Affairs*, Vol. 35, No. 4, July 1957, p. 623.)

This contaminating pattern of being crude and exploitative, while feeling guiltless, is one that all thoughtful Westerners become aware of and often touch on in conversation. Chapter 16, Section 6.

[4] Chapter 7, Section 2.

the time of partition and the conflicts of various types in India today.[1]
Buddhism, in particular, is supposed to cultivate non-violent attitudes.
But the incidence of recorded crimes of violence in the Buddhist countries
of South Asia is among the world's highest, and in Burma the rebellions
since independence fail to testify to a particularly tolerant and non-violent
national character. Former premier U Nu often referred to "the evil tradition of wresting power by force" in Burma: "Burmese history is full of
instances where a king is overthrown by a contender by force and who in
turn is similarly ousted by a still more forceful rival. Except for the glori-
ous periods of Anawrata, Bayinnaung and Alaungpaya, Burma has been
a battlefield for warring states, each cutting one another's throat."[2]

Similar conclusions can be drawn about all the other stereotyped pretensions to a national or regional personality. The widely accepted idea
that Asians are bent on settling disputes peacefully and by mutual agreement, without resort to legal procedures, is refuted by the popularity of
litigation in all South Asian countries once there is access to the courts.[3]
And the idea that, in the conduct of political life, they are preoccupied
with moral issues to the exclusion of expediency and personal advantage
is, of course, repudiated by the facts, as will be discussed in Chapters 16
and 20. That status means more than contract is generally true, but this
is not uniquely Asian; it is characteristic of all societies that have long
stagnated at low levels, especially when the social stratification is rigid
and inegalitarian.

Against the claim that people in Asia are peculiarly spiritual and non-
materialistic must be placed the common observation of a propensity for

[1] As one of India's foremost journalists has pointed out: "In the ten years of independence there have been more police firings on workers, students and other demon-
strators, admittedly obstreperous, than there were in the ten comparatively quiescent
years between 1932 and 1942 when the British *raj* held sway. . . . Of non-violence . . .
there is therefore little evidence inside India — which is not to say that a state of turmoil persists (it does not) but that authority as represented by those in charge of law
and order is more trigger-happy in independent than it was in British-ruled India."
(Frank Moraes, "Gandhi Ten Years After," *Foreign Affairs,* Vol. 36, No. 2, January,
1958, pp. 257–258.)

[2] Hugh Tinker, *The Union of Burma,* Oxford University Press, London, 1959, p. 384,
quoting U Nu, *Towards Peace and Democracy.*

[3] About Ceylon it is reported: "The inordinate desire of the Sinhalese for litigation
is pursued with undying zeal throughout life and cases where men have ruined themselves on account of this vicious habit are legion. Win or lose the result is inevitable.
It entails ruin from which one seldom escapes when one has commenced. Every little
misunderstanding has to be settled in the Courts. The frivolity can hardly be imagined.
Murders have been committed over an olive and whole fortunes have been lost in
litigating over a tiny bit of land. Unfortunately, the prevailing legal system provides
ample scope and no little facility for going to Courts. The peasant enjoys the novelty
of it. He is boastful of his association with reputed lawyers in town. He gets a lot of
fun by his visit to town. All the while he himself pays prohibitive sums to be humiliated
in Courts and inconvenienced in public." (N. D. Wijesekera, *The People of Ceylon,*
M. D. Gunasena & Co. Ltd., Colombo, 1949, p. 179.)

narrow materialism in all social strata — which is not surprising considering the general poverty and the strains of caste and social inequality. The great respect for learning in India, regularly referred to even by Nehru, tallies poorly with the low social and economic status accorded the village teacher and, increasingly, the college professor. Asceticism and the renunciation of material pleasures, often idealized as the "simple peasant life," is a typical example of making virtue out of necessity in very poor countries. Outward austerity, even on the part of those who could afford luxury, was propagated and observed by Gandhi, and was certainly in agreement with his personal ideals. Clearly, however, the continued observance of simple, folksy dress, for instance, which has become almost a uniform for popular leaders, is more a symbolic rite and a political device than a sign of a basic attitude.[1]

If these remarks — based on personal observation and on comments of journalists and others who do not pretend to write as professional social scientists — seem deprecating and unfriendly, that impression is unwarranted. They seem so only in juxtaposition to the completely unrealistic views commonly expounded as a defensive cover. When, later, we turn to the causes of these stereotyped views about cultural and personality traits of the people of Asia, their opportunism should be noted. An hypothesis for further research should be that their appearance and spread in the South Asian countries is ideological and acquires its driving force from the complex emotions we call nationalism. To indulge in this type of wishful thinking offers a particular temptation for the intellectuals in these countries, which were so long under Western political dominance and are now trying against heavy odds to rise out of their underdeveloped status by applying ideals and ideas largely borrowed from the Western world.

The fact that during colonial times the Europeans in South Asia generally ascribed to themselves traits superior to those of the natives partly accounts for the strength and tenacity of the myth of the "Asian values" during the fight for independence and since. The acceptance of these values is very much in the nature of a protest against the colonizers' opinions of the natives — and against the views Westerners are still suspected of harboring.[2] To acquiesce in the ideology of the Asian values is, of

[1] Frank Moraes, in the previously quoted article, says: "In the Mahatma's immediate entourage which adopted this repressive habit of life, these complexes and contradictions were abundantly manifest. They were by no means confined to an inner circle, for on the outer fringes there also popped up a series of minor Mahatmas who sought to mold themselves in their Master's image. Flaunting their outward austerity as a sign of inward grace, not a few of these individuals came to regard themselves as representing the authentic voice of the Mahatma. More than anything else this trend has been responsible for the slightly shop-soiled hypocrisy which characterizes some Congress circles, and detracts from the intrinsic virtue of much of what the Mahatma taught." ("Gandhi Ten Years After," *Foreign Affairs*, pp. 258–259.)

[2] However, this protest is often expressed — and often simultaneously — by the contrary ideology, that conditions and attitudes in South Asia are identical to those in the West. Chapter 21, Section 7.

course, easy for Westerners, who are in a position of strength and have, moreover, in the difficult period since the Second World War, felt a need for diplomacy.[1] This tendency may be observed in the conduct by UNESCO of world-wide conferences on how to reconcile the Asian values with those of the West.

In keeping with the psychology of biased ideologies, most Western writers, like their confreres in South Asia, do not consciously present false views to credulous readers, but, in perfectly good faith, deceive themselves. At the very least, they avoid questioning the reality of the "Asian values"; for this reason we have been unable to cite any work on that subject. The absence of critical study of their realism is rather surprising in view of the importance of these values in the literature and in public debate. Another opportune interest in the Western countries served by the "Asian values" is the belief that they provide immunity against Communism.[2] This view is never closely reasoned; it would be extremely shaky even if the "Asian values" should correspond to reality.

A nationalist ideology that ascribes wisdom, higher morality, and other flattering or apologetic traits to one's own people has, as we well know, its counterparts in the West. However, except in Germany under the Nazi regime, the myth of national superiority, or of the superiority of the West or of Christian civilization, was never allowed to reign unchallenged. It is perhaps even more remarkable that in the South Asian countries, where conditions so forcefully invite a compensating and protest ideology, so many intellectuals, particularly in India, have seen through this type of wishful thinking and have sharply criticized the attempts to present their own peoples as better than others. Nehru early took the lead:

---

[1] See the Prologue, Sections 4 and 6.

[2] An example of this unwarranted generalization, based on the Indian variant of the "Asian values," is the following passage:

"In India, Hinduism is still a tremendously strong tradition; if Indian society is reformed of its archaic excesses, Hinduism itself — or its basic concepts — may be strengthened because they will be less assailable. From the earliest days of Indian history Hindus have been concerned about the state of the individual human soul and have been hungry for individual salvation. In the course of centuries they have constructed sweeping metaphysical doctrines, some of which had as their base the belief that the world was in a sense illusory and that salvation was to be found by withdrawal, others the idea that salvation was to be found by action in the world. But whichever doctrine was accepted the emphasis was on personal salvation; each man had to live his own life and determine his fate by his own decisions; the drama of the individual human soul was, morally and metaphysically, of infinitely more importance than the vicissitudes of empires and the fate of mankind in the mass; these were but the setting, tremendously spectacular though they might be, for the personal drama. The great images of traditional Hindu thought — the images of the sadhu meditating on the mountain-side, of the Brahmin living in the world but without attachment to the world, of the warrior who fights because it is the predestined duty of his life, and all these and other castes by their different means striving to find salvation and peace — still live powerfully in the Hindu mind. While they do so it will be difficult to enclose India within a Communist straitjacket." (Guy Wint, *Spotlight on Asia*, Penguin Books, Middlesex, U. K., 1955, p. 213.)

A country under foreign domination seeks escape from the present in dreams of a vanished age, and finds consolation in visions of past greatness. That is a foolish and dangerous pastime in which many of us indulge. An equally questionable practice for us in India is to imagine that we are still spiritually great though we have come down in the world in other respects. Spiritual or any other greatness cannot be founded on lack of freedom and opportunity, or on starvation and misery. Many western writers have encouraged the notion that Indians are other-wordly. I suppose the poor and unfortunate in every country become to some extent other-wordly, unless they become revolutionaries, for this world is evidently not meant for them. So also subject peoples.[1]

Repeatedly he comes back to this theme: "I won't put it that way, that Indians are 'more spiritual.' I would say that a static society talks more about so-called spirituality."[2]

To Nehru, many of the alleged virtues attached to the ideology of the Asian values were, in fact, not virtues at all. Thus he occasionally spoke out against the idealization of poverty in terms of asceticism, differing with Gandhi on this point:

Nor do I appreciate in the least the idealisation of the 'simple peasant life.' I have almost a horror of it, and instead of submitting to it myself I want to drag out even the peasantry from it, not to urbanisation, but to the spread of urban cultural facilities to rural areas. Far from this life giving me true happiness, it would be almost as bad as imprisonment for me. . . . What is there in the 'Man with the Hoe' to idealise over? Crushed and exploited for innumerable generations he is only little removed from the animals who keep him company.[3]

Personally I dislike the praise of poverty and suffering. I do not think they are at all desirable, and they ought to be abolished. Nor do I appreciate the ascetic life as a social ideal, though it may suit individuals. I understand and appreciate simplicity, equality, self-control, but not the mortification of the flesh.[4]

Nehru was particularly outspoken in his criticism of the mythology of the Asian or Indian values, but several other Indian intellectual leaders have endorsed similar views and continue to express the same criticism.[5]

---

[1] *The Discovery of India*, p. 69.

[2] Tibor Mende, *Conversations with Mr. Nehru,* Secker & Warburg Ltd., London, 1956, p. 118.

[3] Nehru, *An Autobiography*, p. 511.

[4] *Ibid.*, p. 510.

[5] An Indian author, examining the impact of foreign study on Indian students, observes: "The contention of the superior spirituality of India has, of course, for a long time been the stock in trade of Indian critics of the West and its impact on India and the argument has been shared by Western critics of the West and admirers of India. The fact was that most of the Indian students [abroad] admitted that they wanted a foreign degree for quite secular reasons. For some, no doubt, their spirituality was an intellectual conviction, but for many it was merely an unthoughtout cliché. To some extent, it is a result of the feeling of national inferiority, a defence mechanism, against

In other South Asian countries there is seldom the same clarity of thought and speech. And so strong is the force of this nationalist ideology that even those who criticize it in general – including Nehru himself – cannot avoid, when facing a local audience, a tone of reverence toward one or another of the "Asian values" – the tradition of tolerance and non-violence, the inherited respect for learning, the spiritualism. In consequence, these myths are given some reinforcement, even by those who would like to dispel them.

A problem about which we know very little is whether and to what extent this ideology, which typically is a creation of the intellectual elite, has penetrated to the masses, and what changes it has undergone in the process. For the intellectuals it undoubtedly represents an attempt to identify with the masses, but there is no assurance of their response. A second problem, and the most important one in the present context, is whether and to what extent this ideology supports or conflicts with the modernization ideals chosen as the value premises for this study. The very fact that it is so often acclaimed by those who stand for the modernization ideals and is utilized for their propagation would indicate that this ideology has a high degree of flexibility, just as do the references on the "higher" level to history, religion, and inherited culture.[1] It undoubtedly is very flexible. But as it is irrational – in that it contains a false conception of reality – it must make for less rational study of goals and means of planning for development, and may even be presented in opposition to the modernization ideals. We find, for instance, that the alleged Asian (or Indian, etc.) acceptance of poverty, and interest in spiritual rather than material matters, is occasionally invoked as an argument against planning for development, the implication being that planning is an outflow of Western materialism. More often, this ideology is used to support a go-slow attitude toward planning or, what amounts to much the same thing, irrational compromises in framing public policies. The weaknesses of the "soft state" – the reluctance or inability to put people under obligations, to enforce obligations, or to apply effective measures against corruption, and so on – can be explained away or defended as expressions of Asian (or Indian, etc.) tolerance.

In the absence of empirical studies, we have very little organized information about these relationships.

---

the superiority of the West in earthly things and a sort of apology for Indian poverty. Professor Shils, I think, is right to suggest that the 'sense of national inferiority underlies the clichés in praise of India, which Indian intellectuals often put forward in public and which seldom find expression in private conversations – which are much more observable in Indian intellectuals abroad than in Indian intellectuals in India.' " (Amar Kumar Singh, "The Impact of Foreign Study: The Indian Experience," *Minerva*, Vol. I, No. 1, London, 1962, p. 47.)

[1] Section 2.

6 *Valuations on the Deeper, Everyday Level: The Problem*

If we are to do more than scratch the surface, we need to examine all the mental inclinations that determine the behavior of the peoples in South Asia. For that wider category we shall use the commonly accepted term "attitudes," meaning the totality of the beliefs and valuations[1] that cause behavior to be what it is. These are the attitudes behind all inarticulateness and all protective and rationalizing precautions, attitudes that have been molded by a long spiritual and material history and that are causally related to levels and modes of living and working and to the entire framework of institutions. As indicated in the preceding section, they are not meaningfully and accurately depicted by myths of the "Asian values" type, but this is not to imply that people's attitudes do not differ systematically, or that the differences do not influence their readiness to accept, and to permit the realization of, the modernization ideals. Attitudes such as these necessarily vary with geographical area and with the social and economic strata in each region and, indeed, in each village.[2]

To ascertain by scientific inquiry these attitudes on the deeper level of actual living patterns and determine their relations to the modernization ideals is, of course, particularly difficult in countries where the masses are illiterate, live within narrow confines, and have little conception of the state that is the matrix for the national policies of which they are the object. The effective attitudes among the intellectual elite or the whole of the educated class certainly cannot be considered representative, especially in South Asia with its sharp social and cultural divisions. Moreover, in these articulate strata, too, many attitudes are shielded from outside observation and often from full subjective awareness. One function of the generalizing rationalizations of the "Asian values" type is to conceal the true nature of people's attitudes from others and from themselves.

The need for scientific inquiry into actual and effective attitudes comes to the foreground in any realistic study of the problems of underdevelop-

[1] On the relation between beliefs and valuations, see Myrdal, *An American Dilemma*, Harper, New York, 1944, Appendix 1.

[2] "It is clear . . . that there is no uniformity yet in the prevailing value systems which determine not only a community's pattern of production and consumption, of farm management, marketing and even housing, but also its primary attitudes and wants. These vary greatly from one community to the next, within groups in the same region and even locality otherwise enjoying in all respects equal resources and opportunities.

"In the absence of common valuations, a uniform response to common incentives and stimuli cannot be expected. On the other hand, variations in the value system can make all the difference to the extent of success or failure of a development scheme independently of the material and natural resources. They can also defeat the central purpose of many of the reforms, policies and programmes — such as, for instance, the land reforms — which are centrally framed for universal and uniform application to all rural communities throughout the country." (Kusum Nair, *Blossoms in the Dust*, Duckworth & Co. Ltd., London, 1961, p. 191. See also the many examples given in her book.)

ment, development, and planning for development in the South Asian countries. We shall in this book be deeply involved in such an inquiry, as, for instance, in our study of labor utilization in Part Five. In the almost complete absence of intensive empirical inquiries aimed at revealing these attitudes, knowledge is scanty and uncertain; we cannot go much beyond formulating reasonable hypotheses for further research. Such research has to be specialized in particular sectors and strata of the national communities and particular types of behavior. But there is also room for a more general approach to these problems.

In both respects, some leads for research can be given. To begin with, research should be factual. It should not start out with the stereotypes illustrated in the preceding section. Neither are the traditional valuations or the "higher" level dealt with in Section 2 of much aid. History certainly becomes important, not as a source of generalizing rationalizations, but rather as the long sequence of ramifying causation that has culminated in present conditions. Myths and sagas are known and recited even among the illiterate villagers, and a common treasure of folklore does help bind together those who share in them; otherwise, their influence on attitudes toward the political, social, and economic issues posed by the modernization ideals should not be exaggerated.

Religion is, of course, crucial, but not the interpretation of old scriptures and the lofty philosophies and theologies developed over centuries of speculation. It is, indeed, amazing how much Western, as well as South Asian, writers think they are saying about the peoples in the region when they refer loosely to the impact of Hinduism, Buddhism, or Islam, which they think of as general concepts and often as intellectualized and abstruse. Religion should be studied for what it really is: a ritualized and stratified complex of highly emotional beliefs and valuations that give the sanction of sacredness, taboo, and immutability to inherited institutional arrangements, modes of living, and attitudes.

7   The Role of Religion

Understood in this realistic and comprehensive sense, religion usually acts as a tremendous force for social inertia. The writer knows of no instance in present-day South Asia where religion has induced social change. Least of all does it foster realization of the modernization ideals — though, of course, appeals to religious principles on the "higher" level can be used for, as well as against, those ideals, while cruder religious conceptions can be exploited to incite people to resistance or to demonstrations, riots, and lynchings. From a planning point of view, this inertia related to religion, like other obstacles, must be overcome by policies for inducing changes, formulated in a plan for development. But the religiously sanctioned beliefs and valuations not only act as obstacles among the people to getting the plan accepted and effectuated but also as inhibitions in the planners themselves insofar as they share them, or are afraid to counteract them.

Among the masses, these traditional beliefs that with their related valuations have religious sanction are normally irrational, for they are superstitious and imply a mystical rather than a logical way of thinking. Religious conceptions to that degree irrational have not commonly been held in the West for centuries. To a considerably lesser extent, irrational beliefs sanctioned by religion are also present among the educated class, including its intellectual élite. Even Islam and Buddhism, which at the rarefied "higher" level are so rational and free from iconism and magic, have, in the forms in which they actually influence life and social relations, become demonological and permeated by taboos, magic, and mysticism. In particular, social and economic stratification is accorded the sanction of religion. The attitudes, institutions, and modes of living and working that make up and are reflected in this stratification do constitute very real inhibitions and obstacles to planning and the execution of plans. Considerable differences exist among the countries of the region, but in general the inherited stratification implies low social and spatial mobility, little free competition in its wider sense, and great inequalities. This system of social relations is the product of history and is strongly supported by custom in traditional society; religious beliefs and valuations furnish the emotional support. It is evidence of the stability and strength of this social and economic stratification that it is not commonly challenged by the underprivileged and exploited lower strata but is generally considered by them to be natural and right — a fate ordained by the gods and the whole paraphernalia of supernatural forces. It is this feeling, for instance, that restrains the untouchables in India from pressing into the temples and using the wells of the higher castes.

In India, K. M. Panikkar was one of many enlightened Hindus who have tried to strip institutions such as caste and the subordinate status of women of their religious protection by stressing that Hinduism, as expressed by the scriptures since ancient times, does not sanction them; he concluded that "every kind of custom however poisonous, came to be tolerated and received sanction under the cover of [Hindu] religion."[1] Primary among the modernization ideals is the quest for rationality; hence efforts to realize these ideals conflict with religion, not necessarily or even ordinarily on the "higher" level, but religion as it exists among the people. Even aside from the factor of inertia, implying that the social and economic *status quo* has religious sanction, the permeation of religion, as it is commonly experienced, by irrational views and illogical thinking is inimical to the spread of

[1] K. M. Panikkar, *Hindu Society at Cross Roads*, Asia Publishing House, Bombay, 1955, p. 40.

the modernization ideals and to their realization by planning for development and the effectuating of plans.

An important problem for research is whether, to what extent, and how fast, secularization is diminishing the force of this source of social inertia and irrationality, as a result of the spread of the modernization ideals and of planning and other social and economic changes.[1] Probably, secularization varies in amount and speed both for different social groups and for the several countries in South Asia.[2] It should be noted that from the point of view of the modernization ideals what is needed is merely the eradication of the ballast of irrational beliefs and related valuations. As pointed out in Section 2, no religion on the "higher" level need be in conflict with the modernization ideals. But as religion is part and parcel of the whole complex of people's beliefs and valuations, their modes of living and work-

[1] See below in the next section.

[2] W. Norman Brown asserts that secularization all over the Indian peninsula had proceeded fast even in British times and that "With both Hindus and Muslims religion and magic are contracting into narrower and more sharply defined boundaries . . . Within the cities Brahmans are called upon less frequently for prayers and ceremonies in times of illness and misfortune. Brahmans add that in the cities witchcraft has come to hold fewer terrors for the populace, magicians are less patronized, and their own antidotes are less in demand. Muslims say that charm workers have fewer customers . . . urban temples and shrines seemed less frequented than in 1922 or 1928 or 1935." The observations he records are, however, qualified by the statement that they all refer to cities and towns: "There is no reason to think that any great change has taken place in the villages." (*The United States and India and Pakistan*, Oxford University Press, Oxford, 1955, pp. 50–51.)

An eminent Indian sociologist, M. N. Srinivas, states in the same vein: "Indians are still, by and large, a religious people, but large areas of life are becoming secularised." Contrary to Brown, he holds, however, that "pilgrimages have become more popular than ever before," and that the "demand for the services of the Brahmin priest is increasing among castes which hitherto did not resort to him." (M. N. Srinivas, "Changing Attitudes in India Today," *Yojana*, October 1, 1961, pp. 27–28.) As he attributes the former change to the development of communications and the latter to the "Sanskritization," meaning the imitating in lower castes of the rituals, customs, and way of life of the Brahmans, there need not be a contradiction implied.

The general question whether, how fast, and with what differences for the several countries and social and economic strata a secularization is taking place in South Asia, has not been made an object of scientific research. An example of the type of generalizing judgment that needs to be tested by empirical research, and that in this case relates broadly to "ancient civilizations," is an article by A. Vanistendael, "Thinking about Asia," in *World Justice*, Vol. I (1959–1960), No. 1, September, 1959, p. 73: "There are the ancient rites and old customs, to be sure, but these are mere gestures and customs. The political leaders and the intellectuals no longer believe in the absolute secret value of these rites and traditions. Do the young ones still believe in them with all the strength which is necessary for a favorable evolution? Again, I very much doubt it. The intellectuals whom I met are certainly very much permeated with Western ideas. Do they still consider themselves as Orientals differing from us in other ways over and above the opposition existing between them and us as whites, as Europeans, as Americans? Have they not become a rather sceptical group, a group of agnostics, who are forced to follow the current of customs and traditions, of social pressures the importance whereof is very rapidly increasing?"

ing, and their institutions, it needs to be reformed in order to break down inhibitions and obstacles to development.[1]

In India, from the beginning of the nineteenth century a series of religious reformers tried to modernize Hinduism.[2] They were under obvious Western influence and can indeed be regarded as harbingers of the spread of the modernization ideals. Their immediate appeal was to the intellectual elite; their message did not directly reach the masses. And, like other reformers in the same line, they evoked reaction. Gandhi himself was in this great line of religious reformers. By being sympathetic to a purified version of the old beliefs and, in particular, by identifying his message with Indian nationalism in the struggle for independence and coordinating these beliefs with his policy lines in this struggle, he appealed also to strata other than the intellectual elite.

Although recognizing that their basic approach was determined by Western influences, these reformers were able to find support for their ideals in the Hindu scripture from the ancient time of the Vedas; this, indeed, became their chief message.[3] They could also point to an ancient

[1] "The fight against such customs leads directly to the reform of religion. It is significant that every movement for religious reform in free society has been against traditionalism. The breakdown of religious *tabus*, priestly influence and of social practices having a religious sanction has been the noticeable characteristic of the establishment of liberal political institutions on a traditional society. Even in Islamic societies, there has been a notable trend against such institutions as polygamy, seclusion of women and similar customs. The purifying of religion and the revival of the great religions of the East have gone side by side with the development of liberal ideas in society." (K. M. Panikkar, *Afro-Asian States and Their Problems*, Allen & Unwin Ltd., London, 1959, pp. 94–95.)

[2] K. M. Panikkar, *Asia and Western Dominance*, Allen & Unwin Ltd., London, 1955, pp. 321ff. *et passim*.

[3] "As a religion Brahmo Samaj was based firmly on the Vedanta of genuine Hindu tradition, but its outlook on life was neither Christian nor Hindu, but European, and derived its inspiration from the intellectual movements of the eighteenth century.

"Thus it may be said that as early as 1820 India had come into the direct current of European thought and had begun to participate in the ideal. Its social message was Westernization, to purge Hinduism of the customs and superstitions with which it was overlaid, to raise the status of women, to bridge the yawning gulf between popular and higher Hinduism, to fight relentlessly against caste, social taboo, polygamy and other well entrenched abuses. To the educated Hindu, who felt unsettled in mind by the attack of the missionaries, the Brahmo Samaj provided the way out." (K. M. Panikkar, *Asia and Western Dominance*, p. 321.)

"This seemed all the more the right path since the Vedas gave no authority to the usages and superstitions that had come to be accepted by the masses as Hinduism. There was no sanction in the Vedas for caste, for the prohibition of the marriage of widows, for untouchability, for the taboo on food and the other characteristics of popular Hinduism which had been seized upon by the missionaries in their campaign and were being widely rejected by Hindu intellegentsia." (*Ibid.*, p. 323.)

"Ram Mohan Roy and his followers, petitioning for the abolition of *Suttee*, for education in English, for greater freedom for women, though they quote from Hindu scriptures in justification of their reforms, are really thinking in terms of Rousseau, watered down to meet Indian conditions. European inspiration of the Asian reform movements of the first half of the nineteenth century cannot be denied." (*Ibid.*, p. 484).

ideological lineage of reformers including Buddha. The present-day social reformers in India who, like Panikkar, attach interest to religion, follow this method of attempting to show that pure Hinduism in its original form did not sanction the popular prejudices and social arrangements they now want to change. Occasionally they express themselves as if the Hindu religion had no connection with attitudes, customs, and institutions, and maintain that they are out to reform not religion but society;[1] this may be good tactics, but it is bad sociology. Religion as a social fact cannot be identified with, and has, indeed, very little relation to, the religion on the "higher" level that they want to preserve.

A remarkable situation has gradually come about in South Asia. First, practically no one is attacking religion.[2] Even the Communists do not take

[1] This was Gandhi's position. "Caste has nothing to do with religion," he said. "It is harmful both to spiritual and national growth." Later Panikkar made himself the principal protagonist for this view:

"The major difficulty of Hinduism which had made it a wild jungle growth of widely varying customs, usages and superstitions was lack of a machinery of reform and unification. The institutions of Hinduism, which in a large measure got identified with the religion itself, were the results of certain historical factors. They were upheld by law and not by religion. Vivekananda put the point well when he wrote: 'Beginning from Buddha down to Ram Mohan Roy, everyone made the mistake of holding caste to be a religious institution . . . But in spite of all the ravings of the priests, caste is simply a crystallized social institution, which after doing its service is now filling the atmosphere of India with stench.'" (*Ibid.,* p. 327.)

"Among the more enlightened Hindus themselves, at one time this view gained wide acceptance. Most of the reform movements of the last century were, it would be remembered, directed against orthodox Hinduism. They proceeded on the assumption that what was necessary was a purification of the Hindu Religion. The Brahmo Samaj, the Arya Samaj and other similar movements, which were started with the laudable object of reforming Hindu society confused the main issue and organised themselves on the basis of a reform of religion. This basic misconception had two very significant results. It aroused the dormant powers of the Hindu religion which called forth from its ancient armoury all its weapons to defend its institutions, right or wrong. Practices which had authority neither in religion nor in tradition, came to be regarded as fundamental. Even the self-immolation of widows, which was never widely prevalent and which certainly had no sanction in religion found its defenders at one time. Secondly, it made even the internal reorganisation of Hindu society difficult as reformers came to be identified with the thought and practice of other religions." (Panikkar, *Hindu Society at Cross Roads,* p. 1.)

"It is a religion giving sustenance to every aspect of human life, and the modification of laws or the abolition of customs will no more adversely affect the religion of Hinduism than the discarding of old and dirty clothes and wearing of clean and new ones affect a man." (*Ibid.,* p. 88.)

"The attack on religion has definitely failed now. Even the most ardent workers in the mission field do not have any longer the hope of converting India to Christianity. Equally decisive has been the failure of movements from inside which aimed at a large-scale reform of religious ideas. Hindu religion has emerged triumphant from the struggle and today does not feel her supremacy challenged from any. side. But the problem of the Hindu social organisation has remained materially unchanged except that it has now come to be recognised that its solution does not lie through the machinery of religion. It is the Hindu society that has to be basically reorganised and not the Hindu religion." (*Ibid.,* p. 2.)

[2] Nehru was almost alone in publicly admitting agnosticism, though he did not make an issue of it. He had stated in his autobiography, however: "The spectacle of what is called religion, or at any rate organized religion, in India and elsewhere, has filled me

a stand against religion in any of the South Asian countries.[1] In spite of
its obvious relevance for all those who want to modernize South Asian
society, Marx's declaration that religion is the opium of the people is never
quoted. What is insisted on in India and constantly preached by those intellectual leaders who support the modernization ideals is that religion
should be relegated to private life; it should not influence those in public
life. While occasionally a bow is made to religion in the abstract as a force
for creating good citizens — which from their point of view must be contrary to truth, if popular religion is meant — the secular character of the
state, public institutions, education, politics, and business is constantly
stressed. Any division of people according to religious creed is branded as
"communalism" and put on a par with "casteism, provincialism, and linguism" as a danger to national consolidation. This position cannot be shared,
of course, by the leaders of the communal political parties; yet even they
mostly play down the religious issue publicly and use it in an almost
underhanded way. The official views, which are a legacy of the liberation
movement, do not prevent all political parties, including the Communist
Party, from exploiting religious communalism for their own purposes in
elections, despite public condemnation of such maneuvers.

The situation is, of course, different in Pakistan, because it was created
as an independent state for the Moslems; its Islamic character at first was,
however, played down by the military regime that took power in autumn
1958. In Ceylon, the dominant Singhalese group identifies itself openly
with Buddhism, while the Tamil minority stresses its Hinduism. In Indonesia, one of the five guiding principles is "belief in God," which to the
Moslem majority implies that Indonesia is basically an Islamic country,
though this is not much stressed. In Burma, Buddhism was by gradual
steps made the state religion; nevertheless, as in all the other countries,
religious freedom is an accepted principle. In both Indonesia and Burma
there has been what may be called a religious revival. In Indonesia, though
not in Burma, this is a reversal of earlier tendencies toward religious skepticism among the intellectuals.

Secondly, there are now very few organized attempts at religious reformation in any South Asian country. In India, there is a definite retreat
from the nineteenth century movements to purify Hinduism; a hands-off
attitude is observed by the intellectual elite, who do not even carry forward Gandhi's criticism of the filth in the temples and of all the supersti-

---

with horror." (*An Autobiography*, p. 374.) In his last will and testament he wrote:
"I wish to declare with all earnestness that I do not want any religious ceremonies performed for me after my death. I do not believe in any such ceremonies and to submit
to them, even as a matter of form, would be hypocrisy and an attempt to delude ourselves and others." (*Indian and Foreign Review*, June 15, 1964, p. 4.) On this point
his will was not respected.

[1] Section 2.

tions connected with popular religion.[1] To the progressive rationalists among the intellectual elite in India who are working for modernization, avoidance of any interference with religion, even in its most irrational manifestations, and the relegation of it to private life is the way to achieve progress: let sleeping dogs lie.

These tactics undoubtedly have some pragmatic basis. Important legislative reforms — for instance in regard to family legislation — are being carried out, and support for them is found in the "higher" forms of religion now prevalent among the intellectual elite, while silence is preserved about the fact that popular religion is different. The hope is that through these and other reforms, and through education, religious reformation will take place without a frontal attack. In fact, this ideological and political process started under British rule.[2] There are, however, the urgent problems of whether "communalism" can be eradicated; whether the reform legislation will be observed in practice; whether, more generally, people will change in the way development requires; and whether all these changes will happen rapidly enough, without a deliberate reformation of popular religion that would drive out superstitious beliefs and elevate in their place the cherished rites, philosophical thoughts, and general moral precepts accepted by most of the intellectuals. But there may well be no basis for a reformation of religion, in which case a choice of this alternative to the present tactical policy of the intellectual elite in India could bring about a violent reaction that would spell disaster for all the efforts toward modernization and development.

By characterizing popular religion as a force of inertia and irrationality that sanctifies the whole system of life and work, attitudes and institutions, we are, in fact, stressing an important aspect of underdevelopment,[3]

---

[1] Gandhi was in many ways more courageous than later popular leaders; he also upbraided the people for disorderliness and laziness.

[2] "The unifying doctrine was the Vedanta, but the abstract conceptions of this philosophical approach could only appeal to the elite. Popular Hinduism continued in the old way, sectarian, devotional and based on daily rituals. But it also underwent extraordinary changes. The gnarled branches of this ancient tree either fell away by themselves or were chopped off by legislative action promoted by the reformers. Child marriage, which many Hindu communities considered as an essential part of their religion, was abolished by law through the insistence of popular agitation. The remarriage of widows was permitted. Social disabilities based on caste vanished by themselves, and the occupational basis of caste-communities was weakened. Temples were thrown open to the untouchables, and in the most orthodox province of Madras, Hindu religious endowments were placed under the control of public bodies. The movement for the regeneration of the depressed classes assumed a national character, and their participation in social and political life became a major factor in the last days of British rule. Popular Hinduism had a more vigorous life than it ever had in the immediately preceding times, but it had in the course of a hundred years changed its character and temper, though it had kept much of its form." (Panikkar, *Asia and Western Dominance*, p. 326.) This account may have an element of truth, though it displays exaggerated optimism on every single point.

[3] Appendix 2, Section 5.

namely, the resistance of that system to planned, induced changes along the lines of the modernization ideals. This wider definition of popular religion by the social scientist is defensible on the ground that any narrower definition is arbitrary and does violence to reality.

It should be noted, however, that not all elements of that system are necessarily irrational from the point of view of the modernization ideals. Some beliefs and practices undoubtedly represent a pragmatic accommodation to actual conditions and are in accord with rational considerations in planning. For example, the ritual washing of the body observed by some castes in India and by groups in other South Asian countries can certainly be a health-protecting custom. It can also be a basis for attempting to educate people to more hygienic habits. Likewise, the vegetarian diet, observed by many in the higher and middle castes in India, particularly in the South, and increasingly by some lower castes, has a justification in terms of planning in a country as poor as India where climate makes the preservation of animal food so difficult and where vegetable crops can be grown that are high in protein and vitamins and cheaper than animal food. Often the positive valuations attached to various elements of the inherited culture in the broad sense of the word are irrelevant from the point of view of the modernization ideals.[1] This is true of dress, for instance. An old custom is often based on utilitarian considerations that justify it from a modernization point of view. We now realize that this is true of many of the inherited customs in the construction of buildings.

Other traditional attitudes related to religious beliefs and valuations are not inimical to rational planning in the present stage of development in South Asian countries. Thus, as long as there is so great a scarcity of trained doctors and nurses prepared to serve in the villages, the popular emotional attachment to indigenous systems of medicine is harmless, or even advantageous, especially if public policy is directed to improving the

---

[1] This is, essentially, what Kingsley Davis means in the following passage:

"First, from any standpoint as fundamental as that which we are pursuing, much of so-called cultural change is irrelevant, because it has little to do with the kinds of national requirements just described. Important social changes may occur while countless cultural elements remain stable. For instance, neither the Russian language nor the Russian tea-drinking habit changes much despite the whole Communist revolution in Russia. Conversely, cultural changes may occur with no significant national or social consequences. Whether women wear skirts or pants, whether they believe in one god or three, smoke pipes or cigarettes, or prefer cubistic to representational art, it is hardly of significance to a nation. Only when such cultural traits take on some kind of national significance may their change become relevant. Then they are important for what they mean not in economic or technological context, but in a ritual or emotional context in which case it is the national or international context that makes them important, not the traits themselves. For this reason, when we approach the subject of change from the standpoint of a systematic discipline — political science, sociology, or economics — we are not faced with the encyclopedic task of talking about the endless variety of 'cultural change.' Our interest lies specifically in *social* change, and with criteria of relevance plainly in view." (Kingsley Davis, *Identification of Fundamental Social Changes which Condition Inter-Nation Relations*, 1958, roneod.)

training of the practitioners of these ancient arts of medicine. Furthermore, it has been found that the use of modern medicines and, in particular, inoculation, does not arouse much resistance, for the masses rapidly incorporate the new medications into their old magical way of thinking about illnesses and their cure.

Relatively innocuous too is the belief in astrology and horoscopes, often entertained even by intellectuals. In all South Asian countries one meets politicians, businessmen, doctors, engineers, and experts of every kind who are rational and effective in their particular vocation but hold such beliefs and conduct their private affairs accordingly. And it is never made a public issue. Even when politicians are occasionally moved to arrange public events in accordance with the advice of astrologers, this usually does not greatly upset rational planning. Among the lower strata these beliefs are cruder and probably more important in their life and work, though not too consequential. Nevertheless, a considerable increase in general well-being, productivity, and savings would result if people in all strata spent less money on weddings, funerals, and other social events, to which custom and tradition, usually with some religious sanction, commit them.[1] Unnecessary family expenditure for social — or, rather, status — purposes is paralleled by extravagance in official functions in all South Asian countries.

As a whole, however, this combination of attitudes, institutions, and customary modes of living and working, sanctioned by popular religion, creates a tremendous weight of social and political inertia, which planning for development must try to lift. And the irrational elements in people's thinking about themselves and society erect a wall of confusion that makes the very idea of planning difficult to disseminate rapidly and effectively. After all the diligent efforts to popularize the Indian development plans, one wonders how much has taken hold in the minds of villagers and slum dwellers, and how this thinking in terms of planning, if transmitted, has been molded by the transference. Among the educated and the intellectuals the irrationality inherent in traditional thinking undoubtedly con-

---

[1] "Still greater effort is involved when a change in what may be called social mores is required. An instance is the reduction of expenditure on social events or religious ceremonies. If this were achieved on a large scale, a substantial contribution to capital formation might be made in many rural areas. It is obvious that such an advance depends entirely on educative effort in the widest sense of the term. There have been isolated cases of success in this type of effort in India. For example, among one large semi-aboriginal tribe the alcohol-drink habit was almost eradicated in one area through the efforts of an indigenous social and religious leader. For sustained progress over a wide area, however, the emergence of local leadership alone cannot be depended upon. Success can be achieved only by a national movement conducted on a moral or spiritual plane such as to attract and inspire local leadership everywhere. A beginning in many directions in this wider field can be made only by a wide national movement which may or may not be directly sponsored by the State. Obviously, political, social and religious leaders would all have to come together in such efforts." (D. R. Gadgil, *Economic Policy and Development,* A Collection of Writings, Gokhale Institute of Politics and Economics, Sangam Press Ltd., Poona, 1955, p. 148.)

tributes to the relative lack of interest in facts and straight reasoning from facts that has been commonly observed as a regional characteristic.

A most important general problem for investigation is whether whatever attitudes, institutions, and modes of living and working should prove to be peculiarly South Asian are primarily a function of South Asian poverty and low levels of living, including poor educational facilities. For instance, the survival-mindedness of the people, their unresponsiveness to opportunities for betterment, and their scorn of manual labor, especially work for an employer, may result, directly or indirectly, from long ages of hopeless poverty. The fact that they are not very different, at least in the type, from those that prevailed in pre-industrial Europe, and that were widely discussed in the Mercantilist literature, rather supports this view.[1] The inegalitarian social stratification, in particular, may partly be a result of stagnation in poverty. We shall comment on these behavioral peculiarities in other parts of the book. The intensity and stale forms they have acquired in South Asia may be due to the much lower economic levels that have long been the rule in most of the South Asian countries and to the absence until independence of a functioning and self-reforming national community.

In any case, it is completely contrary to scientific principles to follow the easy, speculative approach of explaining the peculiarities in attitudes, institutions, and modes of living and working by reference to broad concepts of Hinduism, Buddhism, or Islam, or to personality or cultural traits such as abstention, spiritualism, lack of materialism, and other allegedly "Asian values." And it is not accidental that these broad generalizations can so easily be shown to be unrealistic. It should rather be an hypothesis for further study that people in this region are not inherently different from people elsewhere, but that they live and have lived for a long time under conditions very different from those in the Western world, and that this has left its mark upon their bodies and minds.[2] Religion has, then, become the emotional container of this whole way of life and work and by its sanction has rendered it rigid and resistant to change.

8   The Dynamics of Social Change

This research on attitudes in their total social setting needs to be pursued within the framework of social change. Almost nothing is known

[1] Chapter 21, Section 3.

[2] "Europe and Asia are divided chiefly by time. Between them lie barriers still more effective than oceans — the Industrial Revolution, the growth of modern science, and the evolution of modern parliamentary government. The antithesis of East and West refers ultimately to the consciousness of different stages of political and economic development; it distinguishes a world which has already experienced those metamorphoses from a world which, for the most part, has yet to undergo them." (John M. Steadman, "The Myths of Asia," *The American Scholar*, Spring, 1961, p. 175.)

about how all that is continually happening in South Asia affects the attitudes of different groups and strata. Some happenings are in the stream of events that are not directed by the governments; some are planned as intentionally induced changes; ideally, planning should control all the changes taking place and direct them so that they are most favorable for development. These changes will be commented on in detail in the appropriate chapters. A condensed and therefore superficial enumeration of some of the most important categories of influences must suffice for the present.

The creation in colonial times of an educated class and an intellectual elite implied a gradual enlargement of a very tiny group of people who, through education and by their contacts, received ideological impulses from the Western world, and later also from the Soviet Union. Over the decades their minds reflected the major world events with a selection, relative emphasis, and interpretation that were molded by their special situation and differed in various strata and in the several countries. It was in this way that the modernization ideals spread and became integrated in the "new nationalism," which, however, also contained other ingredients. Newspapers made their appearance; they enjoyed, in spite of occasional attempts at suppression, a large degree of freedom, often more than they do today. The liberation movements, which were strong in India, Burma, and Indonesia but weak in Malaya and Ceylon, opened possibilities for spreading nationalism in some measure and in some form to the broader strata. Occupation of Southeast Asia by the Japanese in the Second World War stirred up conditions for almost all people in that area, as did their forced departure, and, in Indonesia, the warfare against the Dutch and finally the rebellions there and in Burma. The partition of British India into two countries was, of course, a traumatic experience for the population in the whole subcontinent, especially its northern parts.

In the economic and social field, the colonial governments had generally followed a *laissez-faire* policy, but the foreign business enterprises, the accomplishments in the field of expanding public activities, particularly in transport, and the pursuance of other policies implied changes of conditions, ordinarily in the direction of greater mobility and monetization of markets. Urbanization was proceeding. Legislation was used against some traditional abuses. Immigration of Indians and Chinese to Ceylon and the Southeast Asian countries was encouraged. Generally, with all its shortcomings, the colonial period provided these countries with more "development" than they had ever had, though not always in the direction that now seems desirable.

The winning of independence, the coming to power of independent national governments of new would-be nation-states, and the regular routines of political activities, including elections, implied in themselves big changes, which in some measure touched the broader strata of the populations. So did the spread of the ideals of planning, welfare, and democracy.

Many of the new governments instituted legislation aimed at greater equality or against the interests of the foreign groups in the population. Quite generally, moves were made to increase the health and educational facilities more rapidly. The spread of communications, particularly radio and film, was a common experience, as were improvements in transportation facilities: airplanes were flying in the sky. Urbanization was given a new spurt. New industries were promoted. In agriculture attempts were made, with varying success, to raise productivity through agricultural extension, community development and cooperation, and, more generally, to uplift the rural population.

To this should be added the effects of the new international relations that developed after independence at the peculiar juncture of world politics in the post-war era. To the intellectual elite, especially its higher strata, the new experience of sending and receiving diplomats and the policies pursued through these channels and in the international assemblies were of considerable importance. The large number of technical assistance experts sent by individual nations or through the international organizations and distributed throughout all the South Asian countries had their "demonstration effects" even outside each one's special mission.

The various impulses mentioned are not abating, but are bound to accelerate. What they signify is uncertain. The assertions frequently made in the literature about their effects on people's attitudes must for the time being remain unsubstantiated. These range from assertions that attitudes are in rapid flux to statements that these impulses are not of much import and that people remain fairly unchanged in their attitudes, particularly in the rural districts.

In our list of new impulses we did not mention the population explosion in recent years, which constitutes by far the most important social change in South Asia, overshadowing everything else that has happened. Contrary to most of the other changes, its general effect has been to delay economic and social advance for the masses of people and to solidify all institutions and attitudes.

A common assertion in much of the literature is one variant or another of the statement that what we are seeing is a "revolution of rising expectations." Even if for the time being this meant a widening gap between aspirations and realizations, it would not be a bad thing from the point of view of the modernization ideals, and is apparently not so considered by those in the intellectual elite who are pushing planning for development. They know that complacency among the masses is a main enemy of development, and that only by rousing the people from apathy to aspire after something better can they hope to overcome the strong forces of resistance. But they must also know that if actual trends do not somewhat keep pace, the results would then be increased strains on their political systems. The relative stability of a country's development process should thus be considered as consisting in a delicate blending of rising expectations sufficient to press and permit development with enough complacency to prevent political explosion.

The concept of "rising expectations" is, however, rather loose and borders on meaninglessness unless it is quantified. The prefixed substantive "revolution" suggests that the changes in attitudes are great and proceeding fast. In the present context only one preliminary remark need be added. Without doubt, the idea of the rising expectations as a revolutionary movement among the masses is in large part a false rationalization. It reflects the Western observer's and the indigenous intellectual's feeling of how he would react if he had to live in the dire poverty of the masses, and his bad conscience when confronted by this extreme inequality. Among other things, the radical tone of most South Asian political proclamations is difficult to understand unless it is assumed that in them speak the members of a privileged class, who wish to identify themselves with their nation and, despite the great social distance, are aware of the misery of the broader strata. It represents how they themselves would react if they had to live under similar circumstances.[1] The actual feelings of the masses must be ascertained, however, by studying the attitudes of these people with a minimum of sentimentality and preconceived ideas; this is not done to any large extent.[2] We need only note here that in none of the South Asian countries has a political regime been unseated by means of a popular revolt.[3]

When this problem of social change is, instead, viewed from the practical angle, the attitudes and institutions and the modes of living and working should be studied as the objects for intentional planning, that is, for rationally coordinated policy measures, inducing changes that go in the direction of development. One fundamental question then becomes whether it is more difficult to cause a big and rapid change in that direction than a small and gradual one. This is in another and more appropriate sense the problem of revolution versus evolution, posed as a policy choice.[4] Through our study we have grown more and more convinced of the realism of the hypothesis that *often it is not more difficult, but easier, to cause a big change rapidly than a small change gradually*. This problem is related to another one: what policy means are felt to be available for carrying out reforms. The bigger and more rapid change ordinarily must be attained by resolutely altering the institutions within which people live and work, instead of trying, by direct or indirect means, to induce changes in attitudes while leaving institutions to adjust themselves to the changed attitudes. But institutions can ordinarily be changed only by resort to what

[1] Chapter 16, Section 13.
[2] Kusum Nair, *Blossoms in the Dust*, Chapter XXIV *et passim*.
[3] Chapter 16, Section 12.
[4] Appendix 2, Sections 19–20.

in the region is called compulsion — putting obligations on people and supporting them by force.

On a general level, the public debate in the countries of South Asia is filled with pronouncements that a social and economic revolution is needed. A study of their actual conditions can hardly avoid strengthening this view. In particular, the recent and continuing very rapid rise in the rate of population increase must make radical changes seem necessary to avoid a much too slow advance or even a disastrous decrease in economic levels. But in practice the policies resorted to are piecemeal and gradualist, often to the extreme. All these countries remain "soft states" — as defined under *k* in Chapter 2, Section 4 — much more so, in fact, than the Western world, with its inherited legalism and recently won political democracy.[1] The results of their policies are also most often disappointing, as we shall find in the course of this study.

The adherence to the gradualist approach to this extent and in this manner in spite of the common recognition of the need for revolutionary change must, of course, be explained by the social situation in these countries, especially the innumerable inhibitions and obstacles that rational planning meets. There are always strong interests opposing changes, particularly of institutions, and particularly those institutions that relate to property and the stale and inegalitarian social stratification; these are traditional and so are protected by religious sanction. As we must constantly bear in mind, the intellectual elite who, on one hand, are the vehicles for the modernization ideals, on the other hand, largely belong and/or have numerous ties to the privileged groups that have vested interests in the institutional *status quo,* at least in the shorter view.

Many other things support the over-gradualist approach. The historical development in the Western countries was on the whole one of social evolution. With this fact the intellectuals in South Asia are familiar through their Westernized education and contacts. The fundamental differences in initial conditions[2] fade from their thoughts more easily by the common use of the Western approach in research and planning. Western students of South Asia are biased by their own background in favor of a gradualist approach. They as well as their South Asian confreres are also aware that the introduction of sudden changes has often caused disruption, demoralization, and rootlessness. The history of early English industrialization and its serious social effects was widely publicized by Marx and before him by contemporary English students of social conditions. The general thesis has been confirmed by anthropological and sociological studies of isolated and stagnant communities upon which modern Western culture has intruded. It is mostly forgotten, however, that these disrup-

[1] Chapter 18, Sections 13–14.
[2] Chapter 14.

tions are all examples of the effects of change under *laissez faire*, or at least in the absence of adequate planning to avoid them.

When faced with the realities of the "soft state," Western students are, moreover, apt to play down their observations for reasons of diplomacy. For economists, in particular, this tendency is abetted by their Western approach, which — except for some general qualifications and reservations injected in their analysis — implies an abstraction from those types of social facts that represent resistance to change: modes of living, attitudes, and institutions. The indigenous students are under strong Western influence in their thinking; moreover, on this particular point, their national pride encourages this approach. Insofar as the social realities are taken into account, they tend but to offer another reason for a very gradualist approach. The South Asian countries are regarded as unable to master, administratively and otherwise, a policy of more rapid induced change — except by relying on totalitarian and monolithic methods. "Democratic planning," with reliance on persuasion, is thus rationalized, to defend the avoidance of radical reforms through changing the institutions — to which mostly those with an interest in the *status quo* would, of course, not voluntarily agree, even after ever so much persuasion. Although the idea of "democratic planning" is stretched to exclude many social controls that have been resorted to freely and successfully in the Western democracies, it usually is sympathetically received in the Western world — by social scientists as well as others — because it is associated with resistance to Communism; this association tends to emasculate criticism.[1]

And so the South Asian planners remain in their paradoxical position: on a general and non-committal level they freely and almost passionately proclaim the need for radical social and economic change, whereas in planning their policies they tread most warily in order not to disrupt the traditional social order. And when they do legislate radical institutional reforms — for instance in taxation or in regard to property rights in the villages — they permit the laws to contain loopholes of all sorts and even let them remain unenforced. This contradiction is intellectualized in two opposing views, simultaneously held, on what planning for development really requires in the way of social change. On the one hand, it is propounded that social change must be radical and go very deep. On the other hand, it is stressed that it must proceed with the utmost caution, upsetting the inherited traditional social setting as little as possible.

This internal contradiction is usually bridged by an over-optimistic assumption about the magnitude and rapidity of the spread effects from

[1] Chapter 18, Section 13.

It is apparent, though, that even Western students of a conservative leaning, who cannot be suspected of any Communist sympathies, have begun to ask themselves whether a social revolution is not necessary in order to set the South Asian countries firmly on the road to progress. See below in Chapter 16, Section 18.

development spurts in industry — a confidence, as we point out elsewhere,[1] that is rooted in Marx's thinking but is widely shared by Western and South Asian economists and all other planners. The general assumption is slipped in without evidence that it is realistic; it is, in fact, most often left implicit. It does not agree well with South Asia's historical experience. And it is certainly not in accord with what little we know about attitudes, institutions, and levels and modes of living and working in the region.

9   The Role of the "New Nationalism"

As rationality is the first among the modernization ideals, they are all logically interrelated and can intellectually be contained within the ideal of planning for development. Thus, as soon as policies are discussed in terms of ends and means, the modernization ideals gain a strategic advantage over the traditional valuations, for these can be presented, not in the dynamic terms of planning, but only in the static terms of permitting or resisting change.[2]

Emotionally the traditional valuations are contained in religion, in the wider sense of people's actual experience of sanction given to existing modes of living and working, attitudes and institutions. This sanction — irrational or a-rational, that is, outside the sphere of rationality — is what gives the traditional valuations their strength to act often as inhibitions and obstacles to planning for development. The corresponding emotional container of the competing modernization ideals, or, as these ideals are dynamic, the vehicle for them, is nationalism. Some of the modernization ideals directly need nationalist emotions in order to be grasped. People must have a conception of the nation as a whole and attach positive valuations to this idea before they can feel that national independence and national consolidation[3] are goals worth striving for and that all the other modernization ideals can only be realized in the setting of an independent and consolidated nation-state. Part of their emotional appeal stems from the expectation that as these ideals begin to be realized the nation-state will become stronger, more united, and better consolidated. Nationalism, therefore, is commonly seen as a force for good by all those in the intellectual elite who are bent on planning policies aimed at development. To them, fostering nationalism will provide the means of breaking down inhibitions and obstacles.

Like the modernization ideals, nationalism in South Asia, in the main, has spread rather recently under influences from abroad, mainly from Europe. These influences were negative as well as positive. In South Asia,

---

[1] Prologue, Section 6; Appendix 2, Section 20; and Chapter 24, Section 7.
[2] See above in Section 1.
[3] See under *g* and *h* in Chapter 2, Section 4.

where the primary national goal had to be liberation from colonial bonds, nationalism was alloyed with resentment against the Western countries and the former metropolitan country in particular, though in this respect there is much ambivalence. As in Europe, nationalism began in the higher, though not usually in the highest, social strata, but sought identification with the common people, and it seems to be the one valuation in line with the modernization ideals that has with some success been disseminated in the broader strata, changing, it is true, in filtering downward.

In spite of its association with romanticism, nationalism in Europe tended to be secular and rational; it was often tinged with anti-clericalism. To serve in South Asia as the emotional vehicle for the spread of the modernization ideals, which are also imported from the Western world, it would need to have the same character, and it often does with a limited group of Westernized intellectuals. More generally, however, nationalism in South Asia became associated with religion. In the educated class where religion often has been purified and raised to what we have called the "higher" level, this does not substantially diminish the ability of the new nationalism to be the emotional carrier of the modernization ideals. But when the new nationalism spreads to broader strata, where religion is of the type described in Section 7 above, its chance of serving this purpose is seriously impaired, even in regard to its primary function of keeping the new nation-state united.

The essential dissimilarity is due to the historical fact that the development of nationalism, which in Europe spanned centuries and proceeded step by step, in South Asia is violently telescoped and then becomes confused and chaotic, as events and situations tumble over each other with no orderliness of historical precedence. In Europe the strong independent state with a fairly effective government and a common pattern of law enforcement and observance preceded nationalism, and both preceded democracy. The states in South Asia were created anew, partly as an effect of rising nationalism. And they were immediately given a ready-made democratic ideology, if not much democratic reality. The practical problems in South Asia are: how to consolidate and strengthen the newly created states brought into existence by the collapse of the colonial power system under the onslaught of nationalism; how, at the same time, to make governments in these new, not very advanced, states stable and effective; and how to do all this in the turmoil of nationalism with some degree of democracy from the beginning and attempts at what we have called democracy at the grass roots.[1]

It is, then, not only a telescoping in the sense that the changes are concentrated in a shorter time span, but there is also a break in the order in which the changes occur. What could in Europe unfold gradually and proceed as a grand symphony with one movement following the other in

[1] See under *j* in Chapter 2, Section 4.

thematic sequence[1] is by destiny syncopated in South Asia into almost a
cacophony. Little wonder that Western observers often confess confusion
about this new nationalism. And less wonder that South Asian writers,
who exaggerate at least as much the analogy that is evidenced by use of
the same term for the two phenomena and are under an inner compulsion
to seek and convey a meaning and a telos to the life of their nation, are
usually no more successful in analyzing it for us.[2]

There certainly is a melody of progressive and rational ideas in the new
nationalism in South Asia, soaring above the tumult of noises. And, as we
shall shortly discuss, almost everything there depends on whether this
melody will be able to ring out loudly enough to become the main theme.
This is the nationalism that appeals to unity and condemns all internal,
spatial, religious, and social particularisms. It stands for rationalism against
superstitious beliefs, and expresses the will to modernize society and to
achieve economic development. But this is not the sole component of
South Asian nationalism, and in many countries and at many junctures not
even the dominant one.

For it is also a brand of nationalism when the East Bengalis are agitated
by what they regard as the inferior status afforded their language and
their region in Pakistan; or when Dravidians in Madras demonstrate
against North India, against the higher status given the Hindi language
and the power and privileges of the Brahmans, and when occasionally they
go so far as to burn the flag and the constitution of the Indian Union; or
when Sikhs march in protest against the Gurdwara Act and in support of a
separate Sikh state in Punjab; or when loyalties of caste, religion, and language dominate elections in India; or when in Ceylon the Singhalese rise
and demand the only true citizenship of the island; or when the Tamils then
stand up against the Singhalese; or when the Karens or the Shans in Burma
fight against the national government; or when everywhere in Southeast
Asia protection for "nationals" against the "foreign group" is demanded;

---

[1] We are, of course, speaking relatively and abstracting from the wars and the frequent suppressions of national minority groups and also from reactionary throwbacks
as under Nazism in Germany.

[2] Nehru, with his usual intellectual honesty, explained his bewilderment in a speech
to a Scandinavian audience:

"Now it is in the minds of men, hundreds and millions in Asia, that changes have
taken place and are taking place. . . . It is difficult for you to understand. It is difficult
for me to understand, much more so to persons coming from afar, but the main point
is that something has happened, and it had to happen. You cannot keep a whole continent bottled up. The bottling up process is ended, and great forces have come out,
and they have to make changes. They are making changes. Changes are happening.
What direction those changes will take depends on so many factors, primarily of
course on those very people, those very countries. Secondarily, on what other countries do or do not do; also, of course, if there is peace or war in the world.

"So I want you to appreciate this. I myself am a seeker after this, and I try to
understand what is happening in my own country. I know something about my country, but I do not understand it even now fully, much less do I understand the other
countries of Asia." (Information Service of India, Stockholm, *Nehru in Scandinavia*,
1958, pp. 36–37.)

or when those groups then resist.[1] It is nationalism, though it distracts from and distorts the wider nationalism that is represented by what we called the melody of progress and rationalism.

It is, of course, totally unrealistic to study the new nationalism in South Asia except as a composite of a great variety of collectivist emotions that have emerged in the long historical process, some of which are not directed to unifying and strengthening the nation, defined as all the people who live within the state boundaries. Even those feelings that come closest to such an all-embracing nationalism often contain traces of separateness and exclusiveness directed at some group of people within their boundaries. But the most important thing is that so many of those feelings, and so many of the strongest ones, are not focussed on the new nation-state and its development, but conflict with that type of nationalism and consequently are inimical to national consolidation and to planning for development.

Realistic studies of attitudes in their over-all social setting must be focussed also on that aspect of social reality which is represented by this new nationalism in the South Asian countries. The remarks in this section and in Appendix 9 on the new nationalism in South Asia are made for the primary purpose of spelling out reasonable hypotheses for these studies. It is apparent that they should start out from a dynamic conception of a complex of diverse emotional pressures for change working in a framework of strong inhibitions and obstacles; these pressures will take different courses, depending on how they are channelled. South Asian nationalism harbors conflicts that must rage within the minds of the individuals themselves. Even though one of its sources has been precisely the influence of nationalism in Europe, this new nationalism in South Asia has a very different historical determination from that of the emerging nationalism in Europe long ago. Important problems are: how the stream of ideas from that source joined with the urges from traditional society, especially inherited religious and other attitudes of an anti-rational and separatist nature; how it was tainted by all sorts of aggressive impulses, some of them directed against the Western world and some against neighbor countries or groups within the particular country; how it then resulted in inner conflicts; how nationalism differs in different countries, different areas within a country, different ethnic groups, different social and economic strata, and different generations; how ideas are diffused from one group to another and how they tend to change in transference.

The main practical problem from the point of view of the modernization ideals that are the value premises of this study is whether and how

[1] ". . . the separate regional patriotisms within India represent just as authentic expressions of nationalist spirit as the broader pan-Indian ideal. Independence offered the opportunity for each region to assert its own interests in the name of the golden age that each can summon forth from the millennia of Indian history." (Harrison, "The Challenge to Indian Nationalism," *Foreign Affairs*, p. 622.)

this complex of emotions can be controlled in the interests of national consolidation, rationalism, planning and coordination of national policies for development. In these long-stagnant countries, the dynamic nationalism of various sorts represents a flood of intense emotions that, unlike the traditional valuations generally, are not necessarily indifferent to the modernization ideals or bent on preserving the *status quo.* If this flood could be harnessed to produce energy for reform, national planning for development and induced changes would be more feasible and more successful. From the point of view of the value premises selected for this study, this must be the new nationalism's functional role.

In all the South Asian countries there are leaders and groups in the intellectual elite who are aware of the need to harness the nationalist emotions in a productive system of channels, consolidating and strengthening the new nations, making possible more effective government, and rendering national policy more feasible and successful. The urge must be to counteract the feelings of exclusiveness, separateness, and particularism and convert them into allegiance to the entire entity of peoples living within the new state's boundary. Such a more inclusive nationalism then becomes a force for progress — not for reaction, as it now so often is in Western countries. It becomes a vehicle for rationalism and for the ideals of planning, equality, social welfare, and perhaps democracy. We know that a channelling and redirection of emotions often occurs without the causal mechanism of this psychological process being fully exposed. As a practical act this is being attempted on a large scale in South Asia, and Gandhi and Nehru were only the most outstanding of the leaders in these efforts. How far such efforts will be successful is uncertain, but they are an essential phase of the drama that is unfolding in these countries, and will determine its outcome.[1]

[1] This redirection and consolidation of the mixed complex of emotions in the new nationalism into a productive ideological channel is what Kingsley Davis has in mind in the following passage:

"Under these circumstances, how is a program of rapid industrialization to be accomplished? How are poor people to be induced to keep limiting their consumption when they see shiploads of goods coming into the country and bales of money coming from the government printing presses? How are they to be induced to give up their time-honored but inefficient customs, beliefs, and techniques? How are those who hold a high stake in the old order to be liquidated or compensated without interfering with the purpose for which they are being dispossessed? How are the popular demands for equality, democracy, social security, full employment to be contained? Presumably the only way is through the sway of a dominant but new and appropriate ideology, which displaces the concern with individual wants to some higher and more collective level. To assume that the motivation to achieve economic development is itself 'economic' is a contradiction in terms. The motivation must lie outside of and above the economic if industrial development in an agrarian country is actually to take place.

"At present there are two dominant motivational systems that seem to be capable of justifying the authority necessary to enforce the sacrifices. They are communism and nationalism. Both of course have implications for international relations, but . . . neither in itself can be described as 'economic' . . . Suffice it to say at this point that the requirement of cohesion within a nation is not some sort of idle abstraction dreamed

10 Asian Nationalism

Nationalism is fundamentally a feeling of solidarity with a group of people. As we have seen, this group can be, and in South Asia very often is, smaller than the entire population within a state's boundaries, but it can also transcend them. It is worth considering briefly how far the new nationalism in South Asia includes feelings of unity with other peoples in the region, or in all Asia, or poor peoples all over the world — who are also mostly colored and also have recently won independence or are in the course of winning it.

The early existence of such solidarity would seem natural, because of the resentment against the rich Western countries marking nationalism in South Asia.[1] Such a wider solidarity is often expounded by South Asian writers.[2] Western writers testify that they have observed signs of it.[3] The reality of that wider nationalism, encompassing Asia or the entire world of colored people who have been or still are under colonial rule, is indi-

---

up by the sociologist. It is an absolute essential of rapid industrialization in any contemporary underdeveloped agrarian country. The contrary point of view — which actually is the dominant though seldom articulated point of view — is a major cause of false predictions in international affairs." (Davis, *Identification of Fundamental Social Changes which Condition Inter-Nation Relations.*)

Of course, communism and nationalism are not mutually exclusive but may go together.

[1] "Pan-Asian sentiment has been the result of anti-European sentiment — not its cause." (Steadman, "The Myth of Asia," *The American Scholar*, p. 173.)

"If nationalism developed directly by resistance and indirectly by the recovery of historical sense and pride in cultural achievement as a result of Western contact, the sense of Asianism is exclusively the counterpart of the solidarity of European feeling. Before the end of the nineteenth century there was no such feeling as Asianism. But in the beginning of this century we find the great Japanese artist Okakura Kakuzo opening a book with the startling declaration 'Asia is one.' Undoubtedly there is much that is common in the tradition of non-Islamic Asia, in religious approach, social organization, art, and so on. . . .

"The idea that there is no common social or spiritual background for an attitude of Asianism to develop is . . . not wholly correct. In any case, if it did not exist, the common experience of a hundred years has created a political background. All the Asian countries have had to go through the same suffering, fight the same battles and meet the same enemy. The evolution towards political freedom has been, generally speaking, on parallel lines. The racial arrogance of the Europeans, their assumed attitude of intellectual and moral superiority, and even the religious propaganda to which all the Asians were subjected, gave rise to a common political outlook in the Asia of the twentieth century. Books like the *Futurism of Young Asia* by the Indian Socialist, Benoy Kumar Sarkar were indicative of this change of attitude." (Panikkar, *Asia and Western Dominance*, pp. 493, 494.)

[2] Sir John Kotelawala, *An Asian Prime Minister's Story*, G. G. Harrap & Co. Ltd., London, 1956, p. 172.

[3] Thus Louis Fischer says: "I was astounded when I first went to India in 1942, how often the Russo-Japanese War of 1904–5 came up in conversation. It was the first time a coloured people defeated a white country, and Indians said it had stimulated their nationalism. On subsequent study trips to the Orient I noted deliberate efforts to weld the consciousness of colour with the protest against poverty and the dislike of Western imperialism into an Asian mood, a sense of Asianhood. It is coupled with an

cated by the wide use of the terms "colonialism" and "racialism," usually together, and by a uniform stand taken in the United Nations and elsewhere on issues relating to the liberation of the last vestiges of colonial empire. Even those South Asian countries that have military alliances with the United States and the former colonial powers seldom deviate from this unity.

These attitudes, however, do not seem to penetrate much beyond the level of general principles and the position taken on the struggle of other peoples who are still under the colonial yoke. There can be a shared common resentment against the West without much positive solidarity among these nations themselves. It is notable that the Bandung Conference and other similar encounters have never managed to produce more than rather platitudinal and non-committal resolutions in regard to economic cooperation between the participant governments. The regional cooperation in the United Nations Economic Commission for Asia and the Far East has not really come to grips with concrete questions of cooperation,[1] and the fault was not only that of the non-Asian members. In none of the South Asian countries today is such cooperation a live political issue. From a practical standpoint Asian nationalism is hardly more than a phantom, and it is regularly catered to only by a select group in the intellectual elite.[2]

This is not difficult to understand. The colonial power system involved a peculiar organization of the dependent people's outward contacts. On the one hand, their relations with the metropolitan country were forcibly stimulated; on the other, their mutual relations were not developed, not even very much within individual empires. This was, to begin with, true of their commercial relations.[3] But it was equally true in regard to political, social, educational, and broadly cultural matters. When the South Asian countries now emerge as independent nation-states, they bear, as we shall find, deep imprints of the pattern of international relationships established

---

attempt to make Africa a sentimental peninsula of Asia. This Pan-Asia, if achieved on an emotional or political or any level, would by its very nature constitute a bloc of brown, black, and yellow races antagonistic to the white West. The prospect presents the world with a subtle problem transcending in importance most of the tasks that now occupy overburdened foreign offices and state departments.

" 'Asia is one by its culture and art,' said C. Rajagopalachari, then India's Minister of Education, at a conference on Asiatic Art and Culture in Calcutta, in January, 1947." (*This Is Our World*, p. 140.)

[1] David Wightman, *Toward Economic Cooperation in Asia, The United Nations Economic Commission for Asia and the Far East*, Yale University Press, New Haven and London, 1963. See Chapter 13, Section 15.

[2] As Louis Fischer aptly puts it, the unity of Asia "is a myth, and those who speak in its name are spinning fantasies. The desire to unify Asia politically is the pursuit of an abstraction." He adds that it is "a type of endeavor in which, alas, quite a few Indians gladly indulge." (*This Is Our World*, p. 145.)

[3] "By its very nature . . . western influence, which was largely confined to commercial exploitation by a number of rival interests, national or otherwise, continued with the passage of time to wrench even farther apart the disjointed and artificial units

in colonial times. Least of all, of course, were the colonial powers interested in promoting a consolidation of feelings of unity in the region. The
liberation movements, as they got under way, provided a reason not to
encourage such feelings. There was little contact among the liberation
movements in the several countries, even if the achievements of the Indian
National Congress — as of the Kuomintang revolution — were admired
widely in South Asia. After independence both the close relations with the
former metropolitan countries and the isolation from the neighboring
countries were preserved, and in some respects intensified. In commerce,
for example, dependence on Western countries has increased, while intra-
regional trade has decreased.[1] A factor contributing to the persistence of
the pattern is that planning in the several South Asian countries has been
narrowly nationalist and usually pursued even without much knowledge
of what was being done in the neighboring countries.

The heritage from the colonial era has resulted in situations and developments in individual countries that are bound to create animosity toward, and conflict with, other countries in the region. Leaving aside the
strained relations between India and Pakistan, the presence of Indians in
Burma and the departure of most of them during and after the Japanese
occupation did not contribute to warm feelings between India and Burma.
Generally speaking, the presence of large Indian and Chinese communities
in Ceylon and Southeast Asia has resulted in a narrow nationalist outlook
among the majority populations in these countries; their treatment has not
endeared these countries either to India or to China. After independence,
the Western countries' eagerness to involve as many countries as possible
in military alliances, while India, Ceylon, Burma, and Indonesia preserved
various and changing sorts of neutrality in the cold war, has further under-
mined what basis there was for regional solidarity. From the other side,
China has figured differently — and changeably — depending on many
factors: the position of a particular country in the cold war, whether or not
it has a large Chinese minority, and China's policy toward this minority
and in regard to boundary disputes.

---

which it had established for its own purposes." (W. Gordon East and O. H. K. Spate,
eds., *The Changing Map of Asia*, 2nd ed., Methuen & Co. Ltd., London, 1953, p. 223.)

"In the years prior to 1942 there had developed, apart from the limited measures
of co-operation inaugurated by the world economic crisis, only superficially important
links between the several territories. Economically, like the republics of South America,
they faced the world, turning their backs to one another; their indigenous subsistence
economies were self-contained, and in respect of commercial products the political
units were competitive rather than complementary. The simple radial or even more
skeletal rail networks, draining each country's wealth out through one or two large
ports and, excepting the link between Siam and Malaya (which in any case originated
in a German project designed to oust British influence from southern Siam), completely
unconnected with one another, epitomize this fragmentation." (*Ibid.*, p. 222.)

[1] Chapter 13, Sections 6 and 12.

See the complete work for Chapters 4-13.

A COMPARISON OF EUROPEAN AND

SOUTH ASIAN NATIONALISM

The new nationalism in South Asia is compared with European nationalism in Chapter 3, Section 9. The purpose of this appendix is to enlarge somewhat on that brief discussion.

Like the system of modernization ideals discussed in Chapter 2, nationalism in South Asia received most of its initial impetus from Europe.[1] To elucidate the similarities and the dissimilarities, a few basic facts about the emergence and growth of nationalism in Europe should be recalled.

In the Europe of the Middle Ages, nationalism, or even a conception of individual nationhood, scarcely existed. People's lives, thoughts, and feelings were overlaid by, and contained within, the hierarchical and richly diversified institutional patterns of the universal Church and the feudal power structures — in which we here include the islands of the free cities as well as the guilds and other occupational urban associations.

Nationalism in Europe came into being only after two great secular changes had occurred and their effects had had time to accrue. One change was the series of intellectual revolutions, the Renaissance, the Reformation, and the Enlightenment, that gradually broke the Church's domination and opened the way to rationalism. The other, more or less simultaneous with the liberation of minds from Church domination and related to it but also to the availability of new military techniques, was the creation of fairly stable states, capable of control-

---

[1] Not all resistance to the colonial conquerors was inspired by the West. Thus there were early rebellions against the Dutch in the Netherlands Indies that cannot be attributed to a spread of Western ideas. And the Vietnamese resisted the French colonialists from the beginning. As Brimmell points out, not only were the Vietnamese "profoundly conscious of having been conquered by an alien power"; they were "conscious of a marked degree of national unity too, being of one race, speaking one language, and possessing traditions of previous united struggles against foreign domination. There was, therefore, no question of the appearance of nationalism in Vietnam as a result of external stimulus; it was already in being." (J. H. Brimmell, *Communism in South East Asia*, Oxford University Press, London, 1959, p. 96.)

ling and gradually taking over even local government from its feudal organization. Nationalism as a movement could then start to bud. It began among the intellectuals, and only much later became a more popular movement. As somewhat broader layers of the population gradually came to identify themselves with the "nation" and, partly for this reason, gradually won participation in political power, the strong state took on a new meaning and import. Under the influence of Enlightenment, the stirrings of the French Revolution and of the Napoleonic Wars, nationalism finally reached fruition in the nineteenth century. Thus when we speak of European nationalism we use a term that has a rather clear meaning; it refers to a well-known political process whose historical background has been carefully studied and is understood.

In the recent developments in South Asia there are parallels to what once took place in Europe so striking as to make it natural that the stirrings and the movements there are also called nationalism. In Europe nationalistic ideas gained ground as the economic development toward industrialization gathered momentum. This development is historically associated with the emergence of a new social class — the "middle class" — and its elbowing for influence in society. In many European countries that class was more responsive than others to the nationalistic ideas. Only in the setting of a consolidated national state could this new class unfold its economic, cultural, and political ambitions. In South Asia demands for industrialization, modernization, and economic development — though different in form from those several generations earlier in Europe — became, together with the craving for independence, important features of the nationalist strivings. The educated class and, within it, the intellectual elite became the prime vehicle for articulating these strivings and pushing them forward. Like the "middle class" in Europe, the intellectuals in South Asia also needed a national stage for the realization of their ambitions. As their education was Western in character, they imbibed all the ideological traditions of the earlier European growth of nationalism. In line with this analogy to the history of Europe, this elite group, along with the whole educated class, referred to itself, and does so today, as the "middle class," despite the inappropriateness of the label in view of the group's very small relative size and the extreme poverty of the common people in the region.[1] In the conditions existing in South Asia the intellectuals and the educated are all members of what we should more correctly call the upper class.

In South Asia, however, the commercial and industrial base was much smaller, and is smaller even today, than it was in Europe at the inception of nationalism. There did emerge a few indigenous businessmen in the modern sense, who backed the nationalist movement — unlike the feudal landlords and the businessmen in the ethnic minority groups, who commonly stayed away from it and relied on the foreign masters for their protection. But the larger number in the new "middle class" that formed the backbone of the nationalist movement were of a different variety. They were, first, people in the professions and, secondly, those in the administration who were not held back

[1] This term has even won adoption in the scientific literature. It is equated with the present middle class in Western Europe and is itself an indication of the misleading strong Western impact on thinking in the region.

by loyalty to the foreign governments they were serving or by fear of losing status and other advantages. Only after independence were the latter released from inhibitions in that regard. The number of indigenous professionals and civil servants had been increasing much more rapidly than at a comparable stage in Europe. Since independence the growth of this group has been still more rapid. A leading social class of this composition is bound to be oriented ideologically toward reliance on the state, on planning, and state interference. That orientation differs from the European situation.[1]

In Europe nationalism was among the forces that brought wars to the continent. It sometimes became allied to, or was utilized in the service of, reactionary causes, for instance the suppression of minorities and the spread of anti-Semitism and other anti-liberal ideas. The "new imperialism" in regard to the backward regions on other continents from the 1870's onward was, of course, also partly an offshoot of European nationalism. But more often, particularly in its earlier manifestations, it was a movement for liberalism and emancipation. Earlier, too, it became closely associated with attempts to win greater appreciation for the qualities and cultural traditions of the common people. In line with those strivings it was, at the same time, directed to tearing down social barriers that tended to split nations internally. At least this was one powerful branch of early nationalism. National languages and folklore were cultivated and romanticized. In its intent nationalism tended to be in that sense "popular." Politically this main branch of nationalism later became identified with the strivings that gradually led to the democratization of political power. Social reforms together with defense and aggrandizement of the state became nationalist targets in many European countries.

In South Asia, even before independence had been won, the nationalists had accepted the principle of full democracy, with universal suffrage for men and women, and the new states tried to give this ultra-modern principle practical reality. For the most part these ideals have yet to be put into practice, as have the radical social and economic reforms that were also demanded. On a deeper level the attempt of the intellectuals to arouse the masses, which assumes an attempt to identify with them, a trait so prominent in European nationalism, was equally characteristic of the nationalist movements in South Asia. However, until nations are far more consolidated and education is far more widespread, the basis for rational attitudes among the masses must remain extremely weak, and the social distance to those masses extremely wide. As a result, these attempts at identification with them cannot avoid creating inhibitions of various sorts and a split mind in the intellectual elite. While in all South Asian countries, and most obviously in India, there are exquisitely accomplished intellectuals who are rational in their thinking, the masses everywhere are steeped in ignorance and superstitions to a far worse degree than was true in Europe at that fairly late stage when democracy was being propagated. In Europe the ground for rationalism was soon prepared by compulsory universal education (England lagged in this respect compared with other West European countries) and, before that, by the secularization of society, a develop-

[1] Chapter 15, Sections 1 and 2.

ment not yet fully accomplished even among the intellectual elite in South Asian countries. In the relations of the tiny elite class to the masses there are easily detected elements of both attraction and repulsion that were largely absent in Europe.

In Europe, nationalism, despite its association with romanticism, remained secular and rational at its core. In South Asia the spread of the ideology of planning represents an injection of radical and ultra-rational attitudes in regard to society and its dynamics. For advance in this direction and toward economic progress, equality, social welfare, and democracy, and all the other national goals comprised in the modernization ideals, education of the people is relied on as it once was by the nationalist movements in Europe. The constitutions of the new states were all given a basically secular character, with little more than formal and ceremonial deviations in those countries where it was necessary to pacify religious groups. For a number of reasons, to which we refer in many contexts in this book, the rational aspect of South Asian nationalism has had to be curtailed very severely in practice, however.

Nationalism in South Asia began as a movement for independence from foreign domination. European nationalism's first imperative was also, of course, national independence and national consolidation and strength. And it was with the intellectual weapons forged in Europe, where liberalism had become the middle-class ideology, that the liberation movements rose in South Asia and fought their way to a vision, and later the realization, of full independence, implying the formation of would-be nation-states. Nevertheless, today it must mean a considerable difference in emphasis and flavor of the new nationalism in South Asia that until very recent years most of the countries there were colonies and had been under colonial rule for generations or centuries. In Europe boundaries had been altered from time to time as a result of wars, or obliterated to make national unity possible, as in Germany and Italy. But, on the whole, the peoples had been politically independent to begin with, even if disunited. If they were subdued by a foreign power, it was not a power that made them feel a different and inferior race, and the subjugation never endured for long. What subjugation meant in South Asia is suggested by the words of a sensitive foreigner: "We have never been called 'natives'; no people from the other end of Asia came to put signs at the entrance of our parks that 'dogs and Europeans are not admitted'; no foreign race ever stepped over our starved bodies to reach its gay night-clubs; we have never been forced to live for centuries with the humiliating knowledge that our colour or birthplace condemned us to be second-class citizens."[1]

This difference in historical experience is of importance for the strength and

---

[1] Tibor Mende, *South-East Asia between Two Worlds*, Turnstile Press, London, 1955, p. 292.

Foreign rule of the colonial type was perhaps experienced to a degree by some of the peoples of Southeastern Europe that were under the Turks; even now they do not belong to the Western world as we define it in this study. A more striking exception, though one of short duration, was the treatment of the Germans by the Western occupying powers after the Second World War. The memory of this is now repressed by most Germans and by their new allies.

character and, especially, the direction of the resentment that is an ingredient of nationalism in the South Asian countries. Resentment was almost regularly an ingredient of European nationalism as well; it was seldom a simple, positive patriotism. But in Europe the resentment was directed against one or several neighboring countries, or against a majority or minority group, in opposition to which the nationalist feelings were organized. There is plenty of that type of resentment in South Asia too — Asian or South Asian solidarity is largely a myth.[1] But in addition there is resentment toward some far-off country that until recently ruled the territory and whence, usually, it imported the modernization ideals and the nationalist ideology itself. Particularly as the colonial governments and all the people from the metropolitan country had extended to other Europeans entrance to their own social and economic privileges in a colony, and as all Western countries from a South Asian view must seem basically similar in their conditions and their outlook on the world and on life, this resentment is naturally directed toward all the rich Western countries.

The intensity of resentment toward the Western world in South Asia — usually rationalized as opposition to "colonialism" and "racialism" — varies considerably among countries, depending on their experience under colonial rule and on the circumstances under which they won their independence. While in South Asia it has not generally reached the pitch of the xenophobia one often meets in West Asia, it is nevertheless strong in Indonesia, and also in Burma. In India, Pakistan, Ceylon, Malaya, and, especially, the Philippines it is less strong and more often ambivalent.[2] This resentment is most prevalent among the intellectuals; they were the ones who directly experienced discrimination and who have been thinking about what colonialism implied to the subdued peoples.[3] It is quite possible that in many parts of South Asia the masses

[1] Chapter 3, Section 10.

[2] Richard Wright, who had some personal experience in his homeland to build on, explains in *White Man, Listen:* "A certain degree of hate combined with love (ambivalence) is always involved in this looking from below upward and the object against which the subject is measuring himself undergoes constant change. He loves the object because he would like to resemble it; he hates the object because his chances of resembling it are remote, slight." (Richard Wright, *White Man, Listen*, Doubleday, New York, 1957, p. 28.)

[3] Tibor Mende, in discussing the conditioning role that resentment plays in Asian nationalism, writes: "*We* think of the generous institutions which helped colonial societies; *they* remember roadside incidents which humiliated and infuriated individuals. We could hardly be expected to appreciate the part played by anti-colonial passions." (*South-East Asia between Two Worlds*, p. 292.)

Writers in the region usually look at this resentment from a positive angle, stressing how it can be used as an emotional basis for national consolidation and development.

"The Ceylonese also began to dream of a future, enjoyment of freedom and revival of national consciousness. They realised that as a subject race it was not worth living because of the ignominious treatment meted out to them at home and elsewhere. They also felt a pride in their culture, history and race as the others did. Such thoughts were confirmed during periods of sojourn in foreign lands. On return home the position is realised in its true perspective. The injustice of the whole thing begins to react and leads to a mental conflict and a physical contempt for the European and his culture. The spirit of nationalism is engendered and develops.

"The bitter memories of the past suffering generate sufficient courageous energy

rather appreciated the white colonizers as just and benevolent and, in particular, as prepared to defend them against arbitrary and oppressive actions on the part of their indigenous masters. About this we know little in the absence of intensive research. However, the general impression gathered when surveying what has been happening in South Asia is that resentful nationalism is an attitude more easily spread to the lower strata than a simple, positive patriotism.

It is an inescapable fact that the modernization ideals, almost without exception, lack national tradition in societies that have long been stagnating, economically, socially, and culturally, and also that their acceptance must regularly imply a violent break with national tradition; at the same time, they so apparently originated abroad, in the very power that colonized the country. Valiant attempts are made to rationalize history in terms of the golden age myth and to reinterpret ancient scriptures so as to reveal a divination of and insight into modern science and society, as we illustrate in Chapter 3 (Section 2) and in many other contexts in this study. It is all a pathetic attempt to escape the truth of Harrison's dictum that "Southeast Asia's revolt against Western rule was not the only, or even the most important, symptom of revolution; at least equally significant was the revolt of Southeast Asia against its own past."[1] To an extent this was so in Europe too in every single country; Esaias Tegnér, a great Swedish poet of the early nineteenth century who was definitely in the nationalist tradition, wrote that only barbarism was once national. But the reforms needed in Europe, and pushed by the nationalists, could be less radical and abrupt. They could be allowed to grow and, in growing, to create a new national tradi-

---

which if wisely directed must lead to a national regeneration. Various critical stages of the long struggle have been passed. The Ceylonese have witnessed their subjection by military conquest and assimilation of an alien culture. They are now witnessing their own reaction and conflict. The psychological forces behind such a movement are tremendous and ere long will be translated into a physical conflict unless the alien and the national find an honourable basis of agreement for a satisfactory solution. Nationalism must bring about freedom or chaos. Our position cannot be more aptly described than by a modern folk song which says: 'All our virtuous customs have been cast aside. All that was good has been spoilt by Westerners. All that is bad in us and in the foreigner has been accepted as good by us. We have become a laughing stock to the world around us.' " (N. D. Wijesekera, *The People of Ceylon*, M. D. Gunasena & Co. Ltd., Colombo, 1949, pp. 219–220.)

"Also the French, anxious to maintain their prestige on which, as they learnt from their British friends, depended the authority of the European in the East, developed an attitude of racial superiority. This attitude is well described in a pamphlet of Phan Tsu Trinh. After noting the contempt for the Indo-Chinese, which the Frenchman in the Colony did not consider even necessary to conceal, the writer says: 'In your eyes we are savages, dumb brutes incapable of distinguishing between good and evil. You not only refuse to treat us as equals, but even fear to approach us as if we were filthy creatures. . . . There is a sadness of feeling and shame which fills our hearts during the evening's contemplation when we review all the humiliations endured during the day. Caught in a machine which saps our energy, we are reduced to impotency. This explains why beggars only dare show themselves in the offices of the French.' " (K. M. Panikkar, *Asia and Western Dominance*, Allen & Unwin Ltd., London, 1955, p. 217.)

[1] Brian Harrison, *South-East Asia — A Short History*, Macmillan & Co. Ltd., London, 1957, p. 236.

tion. And they emanated from a cultural and intellectual interplay within a Western civilization in which every European nation felt a part-ownership, as did also the European settlements in the New World.

This cannot be so in South Asia, though the cultural distance from the Western world is much greater in Burma and Indonesia than, for instance, in the Philippines. In India, the intellectual elite feels strongly that it has inherited an old, distinct culture that is not generally rational in the Western sense, even if on the "higher" level it can be presented as rational, or at least innocuous, from the viewpoint of the modernization ideals (Chapter 3, Section 2). It is also true that the necessary compromises are not always very difficult. Moreover, as we point out in Chapter 3 (Section 7), many elements of the traditional culture, such as dress and food habits, are not in conflict with the modernization ideals, or can with slight adjustment be made to fit them.[1] It is on the deeper level of modes of living, institutions, and attitudes, all sanctioned by popular religion, that the conflicts cannot be resolved and that they result in what we call obstacles and inhibitions to planning and policies.

The importance of this national rootlessness of the rationalist ideals becomes clearer as one probes more deeply into the new nationalism in South Asia. At this stage we shall only observe that when adoption of the imported modernization ideals turns out to be less prompt than expected, as has regularly been the case, there is a strong temptation to conceal the failures by turning away from Western rationalism and seeking guidance in what in the region is commonly referred to as the "genius" of one's own country or of Asia. As, however,

---

[1] Frank Trager succinctly describes the types of compromises or rationalizations that are worked out:

"The varieties of Burmese national dress for both males and females are vigorously maintained and encouraged, though elsewhere in Southeast Asia this cultural phenomenon is more frequently left to females. The traditional arts and crafts are being revived where necessary and nurtured where they continue to exist, but adaptations of non-indigenous art and literary forms are also approved. Praise of customary law may be heard, but little effort is being made to use it in place of concepts of law derived from the Western colonial experience. Education is not being returned to the monastery school or to the Islamic academy, though these institutions continue their educational functions. The precolonial lunar calendar, which still conditions the life of the people, will not be substituted for the Western import. Folk medicine, which remained the practice in colonial societies having a ratio of one trained physician for from fifteen to twenty thousand people, may be 'investigated scientifically,' but otherwise Western medical science is being extended as fast as circumstances permit. When Indonesia adopted as its national motto 'Bhinneka Tunggal Ika' (There Is Unity in Diversity), it was careful to point out that the phrase came from a Madjapahit poet, Empu Tantualar. But this phrase is also a variation of *E Pluribus Unum*.

"In brief, the attempt to be rid of alien domination in the political, economic, racial and cultural aspects of life is giving rise to some as yet incomplete synthesis between indigenous traditions and external influences." (*Marxism in Southeast Asia*, Stanford University Press, Stanford, 1960, p. 257.)

As Trager is fully aware, there are deeper conflicts that cannot so easily be resolved. One example is the Indian position on cow slaughter; see Chapter 3, Section 4, and Chapter 26, Section 7. Still more important examples of indigenous traditions that must be transformed in order to make development possible are the caste system and the economic power system generally, particularly in regard to land ownership and tenancy, and the attitudes toward manual work.

modernization is necessary for progress, and as in any case the intellectuals are deeply Westernized, this does not solve their practical problems. As one of the most sincere thinkers of India, Professor D. R. Gadgil, explains:

The nationalist movement, especially in those under-developed countries which have older traditions, must willy-nilly make a new synthesis. The real problem of these societies is that of finding the terms on which they can coexist honourably with the technology and civilisation of the West. There is no question of rejecting the latter; at the same time, however, it is not possible for these societies to accept the West completely — to forget their own past.[1]

Nationalism in Europe was from the beginning focussed on a conception of the nation-state. This focus became stronger as nationalism grew and as the ideal of national self-determination received ever wider support. But, as we know, the Poles were for long periods denied a state of their own and were divided up between the neighboring states. The German people were united in a state only for a short period between Bismarck and Hitler; even then this did not include the German-speaking Austrians. The old Austro-Hungarian empire, as long as it lasted, was a conglomeration of different peoples, so that nationalism there consisted mainly of a number of movements directed against the existing state. The Belgian state, when newly created in the 1830's, had its boundaries dictated by geographical, strategic, and political interests of foreign countries rather than by national, religious, or linguistic ones, and even today there is probably more Walloon and Flemish than Belgian nationalism in Belgium.

Yet, taking all this into account, it must be recognized that minority problems in the South Asian countries, particularly in Ceylon and Southeast Asia, are more grave, as the minorities there represent ethnic groups of very much greater economic, social, cultural, and religious differences. In Malaya the almost equal balancing of people of Malay and of Chinese and Indian origin prevented, to a much greater extent than in Belgium, the growth of a nationalism that took the new state as the focus of loyalty.

Again, in most of the European nationalist movements, in spite of the historical relation to anti-clerical rationalism, religion continuously played its role, even if a comparatively minor one. This became most evident when a nation-state was fairly homogeneous in religious adherence so that one religion could be, in law or in fact, the state religion (Lutheranism in Scandinavia, for example) and when that religion was not tied to a supra-state church. Less often, religion was among the ties that held a majority or minority group together. In South Asia the general pattern was not different, except that the religious component of nationalism was usually much stronger. This is not difficult to understand, as the religions there were almost always different from the religion of the colonial power against which nationalism was a protest movement. If nationalism generally was, and is, weaker in the Philippines than elsewhere in the region, this was undoubtedly in part because the great majority of the population there had become Christians long ago, as were their American over-

[1] D. R. Gadgil, *Economic Policy and Development* (*A Collection of Writings*), Sangam Press Ltd., Poona, 1955, p. 150. Cf. Chapter 3, Sections 1 and 2.

lords, though a more important influence was the understanding and sympathy that the Americans, as anti-colonials, showed from the beginning to nationalism in their own colony.

But in Indonesia and among the Malays in Malaya the Moslem creed became an important ingredient in the growing nationalism, as did the Buddhist creed in Burma, Thailand, and Vietnam. In Indonesia, Islam served as a unifying force and a refuge, and its spread — from the arrival of the Portuguese until late in the nineteenth century — was partly a reaction against the foreign colonizers.[1] In Burma, more particularly, nationalism can even be said to have had its beginning as a religious movement, and the Buddhist establishment there consequently has a place in the public mind similar to that enjoyed by the Orthodox Church in Bulgaria because of its leadership in the struggle for freedom from Turkish rule. It fitted well the fact that Burmese nationalism from the beginning was anti-Indian as well as anti-British. In Ceylon Singhalese nationalism, which is a comparatively late development, is identified with Buddhism, as Hinduism is with the resistance movement of the Tamils. The Pakistan state came into being in order to provide a national home for the Moslems.

In India itself the early rise of aggressive nationalism in the last decades of the nineteenth and the first of the present century was dominated by orthodox Hinduism.[2] Gandhi, as the recognized leader of the nationalist movement from the twenties, was much more modern; in regard to social stratification and economic inequality, he was almost revolutionary. He stressed religion as the basis for political thought and action, but embraced in it all creeds. It is true that there remained a Hindu flavor in the nationalist movement he led, and this was probably not without responsibility for the failure of the Congress Party in the end to prevent the Moslems from breaking off, thus necessitating partition.[3]

Unlike the purified doctrines on the "higher" level, popular religion in South Asia is imbued with demonology and magic, vastly more than it ever was in Europe, at least since the early Middle Ages. This popular religion also gives sanction to a stale social and economic stratification and other non-rational elements in the national cultures. It follows that in South Asia inhibitions and obstacles to rational thinking[4] are much greater than they had been in Europe. This cannot be without influence on South Asian nationalism. Even during the Middle Ages, before nationalism was born, Europe was better off in this regard than South Asia is today. And in South Asia there is not, as there was then in

[1] "One can, indeed, sustain the paradox that the expansion of Islam in the Indonesian archipelago was due to the Westerners." (W. F. Wertheim, *Indonesian Society in Transition*, W. van Hoeve Ltd., The Hague, Bandung, 1956, p. 196.)

[2] Bal Gangadhar Tilak, nationalist leader of the time, was a commentator of the Gita, and though in several respects his interpretation of the teachings of that sacred book was in line with the needs to modernize Indian society, it must not be forgotten that he fought against the bill that sought to raise the age of consummation of marriage for girls to twelve years, and stood for religious idolatry and animal sacrifice, which nowadays are seldom if ever defended publicly by intellectuals. He was also strongly against cow slaughter. Gandhi later was, too; but otherwise, under all the cover of religious morality, Gandhi was fundamentally a post-Victorian liberal, as we have many occasions to point out in this book.

[3] Chapter 6, Section 2.

[4] Chapter 3, Sections 6 and 7.

Europe, only one universal church, whose wings had to be clipped as a pre-condition to a nationalism focussed on the nation-state. There are, instead, several different religions, whose adherents are entrenched in intolerance of each other. India and Pakistan are extreme examples, but Ceylon and the Southeast Asian countries are not far behind on account of the Indian and other minority groups that are both foreign and of a different religion.

Beyond the broad distinctions between groups of different faiths, religion gives sanction to important and multifarious divisions in the South Asian countries. In India and, to a lesser extent, in Pakistan, the caste system and all the other social and spatial barriers, and the differences in attitudes and modes of living and working that go with these institutions, create unbridgeable chasms and inequalities that split the new nations much worse than the feudal system ever did in medieval Europe. In Ceylon and the Southeast Asian countries there are similar barriers, notably the strained and stratified relations between the indigenous majority and groups of foreign origin. Moreover, in Europe, nationalism had not arrived even as an idea at that time; it did not become a force until feudalism and clericalism had been nearly liquidated. In those countries of South Asia where the liberation movement was strong and effectively directed with the purpose of keeping it unified, and particularly in India, the fight against the foreign colonial power, conceived of as a common foe, helped to keep the centrifugal forces under control and neutralized; in India, the breaking off of the Muslim League was the principal failure. Now that the foreign rulers have gone and no longer present a common target for aggression, these internally divisive forces have been much more freely released and must be fought directly by government policies.

National leaders, who support national consolidation, attempt to wage this fight. When religion weakens allegiance to the now independent would-be nation-state, they strike out against "communalism" as they do against the other particularist tendencies, founded on other non-rational divisions in traditional society — in India, "linguism," "casteism," and "provincialism." But the fact that they do have to keep up this fight proves that this new nationalism, which as earlier in Europe is essentially secular and rational, meets strong forces of resistance. In Brian Harrison's words: ". . . while the mechanism of the modern nation state is being more or less faithfully reproduced, complete with signs and symbols, the sense of nationality is only at an early stage of development. . . . It does not seem at all likely, in view of the conditions actually discernible today, that the pace of national integration in Southeast Asian countries can be very rapid."[1] The one thing we should not miss is that these frustrating and dividing forces in South Asia also commonly take the form of nationalism.[2]

Thus, in spite of all the parallels to European nationalism, the new nationalism in South Asia is something very different. It differs in many more respects and for more fundamental reasons than appears from the qualifications just listed.

[1] Brian Harrison, "Problems of Political Integration in Southeast Asia," in Philip W. Thayer, ed., *Nationalism and Progress in Free Asia*, Johns Hopkins Press, Baltimore, 1956, p. 143.

[2] Chapter 3, Section 9.

The fundamental reason is that an historical process that in Europe spanned centuries is telescoped within a few decades and that the order of the happenings is deranged.

There is no practical possibility in any of the South Asian countries of chaining the forces of nationalism and inaugurating a sequence of events like that in Europe where first the feudal order was overcome by the strong states and the Church gradually weakened. In these states nationalism could thereafter grow while the time ripened for political democracy founded on general literacy, and for egalitarian reforms.[1] Even if it were possible, which it is not, to stamp out nationalism, the events that unfolded in this sequence in Europe would not occur — in any case not so rapidly as South Asia requires because of the population explosion and for many other reasons.

Nationalism there is needed to provide the impulse for change — indeed, for all the necessary changes, and concurrently. The difficulties in this syncopation of policies, the historical necessity of which is seen by all the enlightened intellectual and political leaders in the region, are immense.

[1] Chapter 3, Section 9.

Chapter 14

DIFFERENCES IN

INITIAL CONDITIONS

In our analysis we often resort to comparisons, either explicit or implicit, between the underdeveloped South Asian countries and the highly developed Western countries. Such comparisons are valid and relevant inasmuch as the differences between the two groups of countries are, on the whole, much greater than the differences within the groups.

Two types of comparisons can be made, both of which are important: Present conditions in South Asia can be compared either with present conditions in the Western countries or with conditions in the Western countries on the eve of their rapid economic development, particularly their industrialization. In this concluding chapter of Part Three on economic realities in South Asia, we shall concentrate on the second type; that is to say, we shall attempt to spell out the main differences in "initial conditions" for economic development between the South Asian countries and the developed Western countries. This type of comparison has been considered relevant to the problem of formulating economic policy in South Asia. The countries of the region recognize that they are underdeveloped and should develop: their plans all are built on a desire for modernization, especially industrialization, and it is natural to believe that they could learn a great deal from the experience of the developed countries.

The general conclusion we shall reach is that the differences in initial conditions are extremely significant and that they regularly work to the disadvantage of the underdeveloped countries in South Asia. Furthermore, the differences are in many instances of such a nature as to prohibit a pattern of growth analogous to that experienced by the developed Western countries. It is important to take note of the newness of the development problems confronting the countries of South Asia today — and most other underdeveloped countries — because of the tendency to overlook their uniqueness that is inherent in the biases common in research and prevalent also in planning and, generally, in public discussion. These biases are discussed in the Prologue (Sections 3–6), and we shall come back to them often in later chapters.

1   *The Problem*

In the modern approach to the economic problems of the South Asian countries, the two types of comparisons are logically related to each other by the assumption, either stated or implied, that the present differences represent a time lag in development. This was not the assumption when, in pre-war and pre-independence times, "backward regions" was the term used to signify what are now referred to as "underdeveloped countries," or even as "developing countries."[1] The change in approach is related not only to the greater awareness of, and concern for, the economic problems of underdeveloped countries but also to the optimistic biases just referred to. The modern approach is widely rationalized in the theory of "stages of growth" with the implied assumption that there is a predetermined sequence of stages. Although by no means new, this theory was usually extended in earlier times only to the Western world and some countries on its fringe, and not to "backward" areas like South Asia — except by a few radical thinkers like Marx. We have noted throughout this study how often modern Western economists have taken over theories from Marx, usually without crediting him with them. Sometimes they are unaware of their intellectual debt, and sometimes they deny it exists and call themselves non-"Marxists."[2]

The concept of a time lag implies that in the history of the West there was a period — somewhat differently located on the time axis for the several countries — when conditions were essentially "comparable" to those that now exist in South Asia — again with individual variations among countries. The concept of a time lag also implies that it is possible to postulate a fairly uniform development for countries, which in turn implies that

---

[1] Appendix 1.

[2] "The country that is more developed industrially only shows, to the less developed, the image of its own future," wrote Marx in the Preface to *Das Kapital*. (Karl Marx, *Capital*, translated by Samuel Moore and Edward Aveling, edited by Frederick Engels, Allen & Unwin Ltd., Woking, 1957, p. xvii.)

the entire set of conditions relevant for development move together with a degree of internal harmony. Differences in development are believed to have a "dimensional," not a "qualitative," character. When applied to a single South Asian country or the region, the concept of a time lag implies, finally, that the present world environment, if not identical to what it was in the Western countries in the period of comparison, is at least not so much less favorable as to block or seriously hamper its development.

The logical weakness in this theory is at once apparent when we try to determine more precisely the appropriate period of comparison, that is, the period in history when the Western countries were underdeveloped in the same sense that the South Asian countries are underdeveloped today, and after which they, successively, began to develop. One thing is certain: at the beginning of what we recognize as the industrial revolution – or, more precisely, their industrial revolutions – the Western countries had behind them many years – in some cases centuries – of social, political, and also incipient economic development;[1] in a number of ways they were already much more favorably situated for further development than South Asia is today. In many respects, therefore, the period of comparison should be fixed centuries before the industrial revolutions in the West. In other respects conditions in South Asia are comparable to those in Western countries at any time in recent history. And in still some other respects conditions in the South Asian countries are more comparable to those existing now in the West, or at least at periods much later in the Western development process.[2] Efforts to define the time of "take-off" in the Western countries assume a basic similarity among them in initial conditions and in the process of development – an assumption that is open to question. Be that as it may, to use this Western concept of a "take-off" and

[1] The point is succinctly made by Simon Kuznets: "If the 'earlier situations' in the presently developed countries that could be viewed as examples of underdevelopment existed three centuries ago or possibly even earlier, it follows that these older units of the European community must have had a long period of development and rise before the coming of the economic and technological revolutions. It also follows that when the recent rapid pulse of economic growth began, the countries now in the forefront probably were also among the advanced units of that time." (Simon Kuznets, "Underdeveloped Countries and the Pre-Industrial Phase in the Advanced Countries: An Attempt at Comparison," U. N., *Proceedings of the World Population Conference*, 1954, Papers: Vol. V, Meeting 26, New York, 1955, pp. 952–954.)

[2] These modern characteristics have been pressing themselves upon the region. They reflect the impact of the whole modernization movement, on everything from ideologies and political institutions to industries. How disparate conditions are is suggested by Kuznets when he writes that birth rates in the underdeveloped countries, compared with Europe's in pre-industrial times, "may be said to reflect the lower economic level of many of the currently underdeveloped countries as over against that of older European units in their pre-industrial phase. On the other hand, their lower death rates may be said to reflect the more recent date for which we observe them in the underdeveloped countries of today – mortality thus mirroring the advantages of the technological advance made since the pre-industrial phase of the now developed countries." (Kuznets, "Underdeveloped Countries and the Pre-Industrial Phase," p. 965.)

attempt to locate on an assumed general development axis the "stage" at which any South Asia country now is, is to do violence to the facts.[1]

When in the ensuing discussion we leave the period of comparison in the history of the Western countries vague, we do so intentionally. Realism and logic preclude the determinateness aimed at in the theory of stages of growth. In some instances — as in regard to climate or population increase — this indeterminateness presents no problem, as the differences in conditions are very largely independent of time. In other cases we shall have to establish the period of comparison in a specific context. Particularly because of the change in world environment and the "qualitative" as well as "dimensional" character of the differences, we shall, however, be skeptical about our inferences. And we shall not put them in the quantitative form of a model, since to do so would give them what in this study we often refer to as unwarranted precision. One major set of differences between the South Asian countries today and the developed Western countries in the past will not be touched on in this chapter, except incidentally; namely, differences in policies and in the ideological outlook that influences policies. Part Four will be devoted to an intensive analysis of this important complex of problems. The present chapter will be restricted to those conditions that policy is designed to change or that it must at least take into consideration.[2] Since most of these "initial conditions" are examined in detail in earlier or later chapters, we shall aim here at a synoptic treatment. In a sense, then, this chapter is one presenting conclusions from our study, placed in the middle of the book instead of at the end and dealing with a set of conditions that excludes for the most part ideologies and policies.

2   Some Constants or Quasi-Constants: Natural
Resources and Climate

There are some differences between South Asia and the Western world that are constant or quasi-constant in time. To this group belongs, first of all, the natural resource endowment.

In Chapter 11 we pointed out that, so far as we now know, South Asia as a region is poorly endowed with resources. Only India is known to have both coal and iron ore in sufficient quantity to provide a basis for heavy

[1] It is a procedure associated with the common biases analyzed in the Prologue (Sections 3–6) and, in particular, with the tendency to analyze South Asian problems in Western terms and to underestimate differences; logically, it is based on metaphysical preconceptions of the teleological variety. On the theory of "stages" see Appendix 2, Section 3.

[2] Conditions under 1–5 in Appendix 2, Section 5.

industry. Scattered deposits of many metals and minerals have been found throughout the area but they do not seem to be large; thus far they have not been very intensively exploited. There does not seem to be much oil anywhere in the region except in Indonesia. Land resources, by and large, are poor, either because they were so to begin with or because they have been damaged by overcrowding and the climate (see below). Ceylon, however, possesses excellent though limited land for the cultivation of tea, cocoanuts, and rubber, and Malaya and Indonesia also have excellent land, less limited in extent, for the growing of rubber trees. Large forested areas, not yet fully utilized, remain in Malaya, Thailand, Burma, Ceylon, and the Philippines.[1]

The fact that some countries without abundant natural resources have succeeded in creating a flourishing industry, mainly by importing raw materials — notably Switzerland, Denmark, and Japan — does not necessarily mean that South Asia could readily do the same. The difficulties in relying on imported raw materials are greatest at the beginning of industrialization, and are probably more severe for late-comers. Once a country is further along in the development process, the costs of such imports can be borne more easily, for then capital investment and consequently relative capital cost, and particularly wage rates, have reached levels sufficiently high that raw material costs constitute a much smaller portion of total production costs.

Of course, large areas of South Asia have not been thoroughly surveyed. It is for this reason that we characterize the endowment of natural resources as a quasi-constant factor. Through systematic efforts, hidden resources may come to light, but it seems improbable that most of the countries will ever equal the average Western country in raw materials.

Climate, insofar as it affects the productiveness of resources, might be treated as an aspect of the natural resource endowment. But as it also affects the productivity of labor, it is more accurately treated as a separate set of conditions. Although we have little knowledge of its precise implications for development, climate constitutes another major difference between South Asia and the Western world that is a constant or quasi-constant in time. The South Asian countries are situated in the tropical or arid subtropical zones — as, indeed, are almost all the underdeveloped countries of the world. It is a fact that all successful industrialization in modern times, including that of Japan and the Soviet Union, has taken place in the temperate zones; in China, too, industrialization has been attempted mostly in the northern provinces. This cannot be entirely an accident of history but must have to do with some special handicaps, directly or indirectly

[1] Chapter 11, Section 7.

related to climate, faced by countries in the tropical and subtropical zones.[1] It should also be noted that almost all Western countries initiated economic development and industrialization from a base of self-sufficiency in food, and sometimes a surplus; generally speaking, an agricultural revolution preceded their industrial revolution. Although the agricultural sector in South Asian countries is very large in terms of the labor attached to it, yields are mostly so low that the region as a whole has become a deficit area in foodstuffs, and is in large part becoming more so. Again this contrast suggests the importance of climate to development, for extremes of temperature and rainfall have obvious effects on the productivity of both labor and land in agriculture.

It needs to be explained, therefore, why the climatic factor is almost entirely neglected in the literature on development problems in South Asia and in the underdeveloped countries generally,[2] why there is so little specialized research on the economic effects of climate and the possibilities for their amelioration, and why the development plans of these countries are almost entirely silent on this subject.

This present-day lack of interest in climatic conditions is in sharp contrast to the thinking about underdevelopment in pre-independence times. Among the stereotyped opinions then elaborated to explain the poverty of the underdeveloped countries — more specifically, the lack of drive, enterprise, and efficiency of their peoples — were theories that all this was attributable to the unbearable climate and its effects on soils, crops, animals, and people, and on the pattern of civilization in general. These popular theories were regularly reflected in the pre-war scientific literature and

---

[1] In refutation of the argument that climate is important in development it is often pointed out that great civilizations sprang up in tropical areas in ancient times and lasted for centuries. How this was possible and how it can be reconciled with the generalization in the text lies outside our analysis in this book, which is restricted to modern times. Probably, however, these ancient civilizations differed in fundamental ways from modern ones; also, they often grew up in smaller regions favored by exceptional climatic conditions; soil erosion and deforestation had not proceeded so far, and so on.

[2] Of the several general texts available, G. M. Meier and R. E. Baldwin, *Economic Development: Theory, History, Policy* (Wiley, New York, 1957) has no reference at all to climate, nor has W. W. Rostow, *The Stages of Economic Growth* (Cambridge University Press, London, 1960) or A. O. Hirschman, *The Strategy of Economic Development* (Yale University Press, New Haven, 1958). W. A. Lewis devotes about six pages at various places in *Theory of Economic Growth* (Allen and Unwin, London, 1955) to very general points about climate — in a book of 450 pages. Benjamin Higgins in *Economic Development* (Norton, New York, 1959), a work of over 770 pages, provides a very interesting condensed discussion of the climatic factor, but one entirely directed toward criticism of geographic determinism (pp. 265–274) and giving no attention to climate as a complex of conditions for production. W. E. Moore's *Industrialization and Labor* (Cornell University Press, Ithaca, 1951) provides a standard discussion of socio-economic problems of labor efficiency in "developing" countries but is totally without mention of climate. The best selections of readings — Amar Agarwala and Sampat Singh, eds., *Economics of Underdeveloped Areas* (Oxford University Press, London, Bombay, 1959) and L. W. Shannon, ed., *Underdeveloped Areas* (Harper, New York, 1957) — contain only the most perfunctory mention of climate.

were often supported by statistics.[1] There is a tendency in this pre-war literature, represented by Ellsworth Huntington's *Civilization and Climate,*[2] toward pessimistic geographical determinism. As popularized, it was a doctrine consonant with the vague beliefs in the racial inferiority of the colonial peoples.[3] In any case this pessimism supported the common view, badly needed as a rationalization of Western colonial policy, that little could be done to improve the productivity of the colonies and the life of the colonial peoples. That this interest in the climatic conditions, and especially the glib popular theories concerning their effects, served opportunistic ends should not, of course, be taken to mean that these conditions are unimportant or even that all the observations made in the pre-independence era were incorrect. Yet the reaction to this type of thinking has been so complete that, as we have pointed out, climate is no longer discussed as an important factor in economic development.[4]

We observed early in the book that the post-war approach to economic development problems in South Asia has been in the nature of a protest movement on the part of the intellectuals to which Westerners, both in public discussion and in scientific literature, have deferred for reasons of both sympathy and diplomacy.[5] The treatment of climatic conditions is typical of this new, opposite bias. Indeed, it is an extreme example of the effects of this all-pervasive bias. For, although research, planning, and public discussion that are based on Western concepts, theories, and models tend systematically to bypass the complications arising from attitudes, institutions, and modes and levels of living, the relevance of these to prob-

---

[1] Chapter 21, Sections 6 and 7.

[2] 3rd ed., Yale University Press, New Haven, 1924.

[3] This view is occasionally expressed even in works written after the Second World War.

"But there is something lacking, some mental or spiritual attribute which has in the past weakened in the races of India the powers of cohesion, of citizenship, of corporate resistance to outside influences. There is in the Urdu language a word 'ghabhrana,' which has no exact English equivalent, but which may be approximately translated as 'to fall into a state of mental confusion.' It is significant that the principal language of northern India should include this word. It is an indication that this state of mind is sufficiently common, this lack of mental stamina so universal a feature of everyday life as to require a special word to describe it.

"What then is the reason for this peculiar mentality? To anyone who has lived and worked for many years in India and with Indians, there is a very simple answer to this question, too simple perhaps to be wholly satisfying. It is the environment and particularly the climate in which the people of India live and have lived for countless generations." (Sir William Kerr Tytler, *Afghanistan, A Study of Political Developments in Central and Southern Asia,* 2nd ed., Oxford University Press, London, 1953, p. 289.)

[4] There are, however, signs of renewed interest on the part of geographers, at least, in problems of underdevelopment as related to environment, an interest that is free of any naive environmental determinism. See, for example, Norton Ginsburg, ed., *Essays on Geography and Economic Development,* Department of Geography, University of Chicago, Research Paper No. 62, Chicago, 1960.

[5] Prologue, Sections 4 and 6. For an elaboration of this point, see Chapter 21, Section 7.

lems of development is at least "accounted for" by interspersed reservations and qualifications and by the habitual admission that development is a "human" problem. Climatic conditions, on the other hand, are either ignored or casually dismissed as being of little or no importance.[1]

There can be only one scientific attitude: to shun easy and obviously incorrect generalizations about climatic conditions and their economic effects and to make these the subject of empirical study. Such research is especially important in view of the fact that climatic conditions are only quasi-constants. It is possible, in some small measure, to alter the climate; more important, the effects of climate on the productivity of land, capital, and labor can be changed in many ways, and both production and consumption can be better adapted to the climate. It is, indeed, altogether wasteful to attempt to plan economic development in the South Asian countries without taking climatic conditions into consideration. There is here a vast, unexplored field for economic and social engineering, requiring close cooperation between the natural and the social sciences. In Appendix 10 we have tried to outline its scope, without pretending to do more than scratch the surface. Almost any generalization about climatic conditions must for the time being be uncertain or merely suggestive. One difficulty should be emphasized: the effects of climate can rarely be isolated from the effects of other conditions. Some of these, like the levels of nutrition and health, and, to some degree, all other conditions as well, are causally related to climatic conditions. But, as we have said, all conditions tend to be causally interrelated.[2] The main reason for the difficulty in arriving at well-founded generalizations about the effects of climate is simply that little empirical research has been devoted to study in this field.

Nevertheless, it is possible to say that the extremes of heat and humidity in South Asia seem to contribute to deterioration of the soil and of many kinds of material goods; to be partly responsible for the low productivity of certain crops, forests, and animals; and not only to cause discomfort but also to impair health and efficiency. Almost all of these unfavorable effects can be in large part avoided or counteracted by planned policies. It is true, of course, that to overcome the difficulties — and occasionally turn them into advantages — would require expenditures, and sometimes very high expenditures, often of the investment type. And since capital and all other

---

[1] From the many examples available we need cite only two:

"Climate . . . is a convenient bogeyman to be blamed for psychological difficulties whose real origin is much more personal." (D. H. K. Lee, *Climate and Economic Development in the Tropics*, Harper, New York, 1957, p. 104.)

"Because economic growth is currently most rapid in the temperate zones, it is fashionable to assert that economic growth requires a temperate climate, but the association between growth and temperate climates is a very recent phenomenon in human history." . . . "The climate hypothesis also does not take us very far." (Lewis, *Theory of Economic Growth*, pp. 53, 416.)

[2] Appendix 2, Section 5.

real cost elements such as administration are scarce, climatic conditions impose serious obstacles to development and constitute an important difference in initial conditions between South Asia and the Western world.

3   *Population*

The basic facts in regard to population will be analyzed in detail in Part Six of this book; some of the pertinent historical data have been dealt with in Chapter 10 (Section 5). In the present discussion, which is simply intended to catalogue the main differences in initial conditions, only a few of the generalizations that are substantiated in these other chapters need be set forth.

In pre-industrial times the secular trend of population growth in Western Europe had been comparatively slow, though it rose somewhat as the industrialization phase was approached. By contrast, the population of all the South Asian countries has been increasing over a very long period, though not as rapidly as today. As a result, those of the South Asian countries that contain most of the region's population now start out with a considerably higher man/land ratio than did the European countries, at the same time that their supply of industrial natural resources, as we have noted, is inferior to Europe's. This disproportion of population and resources in itself puts South Asia at a considerable disadvantage in regard to development prospects. To this must be added the effects of the population explosion, which in recent years has raised the average rate of population increase in the region to well above 2 percent a year and in some of the countries to 3 percent or even higher. Moreover, the rate of population increase is still rising.

A spontaneous spread of birth control practices is not in prospect; indeed, in the Western countries it took place on a large scale only when they had reached a much higher level of development, characterized by higher living levels and more rational attitudes. And even in those South Asian countries where dissemination of birth control information among the masses is accepted government policy, the policy measures taken have nowhere had substantial effects. Because of the youthfulness of the South Asian populations, the inhibitions and obstacles encountered, and the administrative difficulties, a continued rapid, even a more rapid, increase in the population, and especially in the labor force, can be expected for a considerable time to come.

The present population density and the prospective population trend thus constitute a very important difference in initial situation. The South Asian countries, none of which has as yet experienced a rapid economic development and some of which are stagnating or retrogressing, have and will continue to have an annual rate of natural increase in population and in the labor force double, or more than double, that in the countries of Western Europe when they were already well on their way to rapid development.[1] Europe, moreover, had an escape hatch for its increasing population in emigration to the New World: Western Europe would now have almost 100 million more inhabitants if there had been no emigration and if other vital factors had remained the same. No such possibilities of escape exist for South Asia. Even such migrations within the region as could lead to a more favorable allocation of labor force to land and other resources are virtually excluded as between countries and are possible within countries only to a rather limited extent and usually at very high cost.[2]

By any criterion these population trends present a serious impediment to development prospects in South Asia[3] and constitute one of the principal differences in initial situation.

4   *International Trade and Capital Movements*

It is commonly recognized that expansion of export outlets played a crucial role in the early period of development in all the now highly developed Western countries. In Dennis Robertson's phrase, international trade was the "engine of growth."[4] As far back as 1890, Alfred Marshall had concluded that "the causes which determine the economic progress of nations belong to the study of international trade."[5]

Rising exports — and imports — characterized not only the early spurts of rapid development but its successful continuation in all the now developed Western countries. In the nineteenth century, as one country after another had its industrial revolution — which for those in the New World and some others included the production of primary products for the export market — international trade increased faster than the sum total of gross national products in the several countries. There was mutual stimulation in this process for which foreign trade was the main vehicle. "Growth through trade" aptly describes much of the economic progress of the nineteenth century.

[1] In the United States, the rate of natural population increase was much higher. Similarly the other "younger" developed economies of the New World — Canada, New Zealand, and Australia — had growth rates higher than those of Western Europe. However, the experiences of these countries, where population increased also through immigration from already developed countries, are for this and many other reasons hardly relevant to South Asia.

[2] Chapter 27, Section 16; Appendix 11; and Chapter 26, Section 6.

[3] Chapter 28, Part I.

[4] Dennis Robertson, "The Future of International Trade," *Essays in Monetary Theory,* King & Staples Ltd., London, 1940, p. 214.

[5] Alfred Marshall, *Principles of Economics,* 8th ed., Macmillan, London, 1920, p. 270.

South Asia was not unaffected by this movement. As we observed in Chapter 10, there was a period when all South Asian countries, in some degree, experienced a pattern of development that corresponded rather closely to the early development spurts in the West. The introduction of plantation agriculture, mining, and, in a few colonies, forestry, and the rise of commercial rice production in Burma and Thailand, could not have taken place without the opening up of export markets. The fact that at first this external demand stimulated the production and export of only a few products was not extraordinary at that period, nor would this alone have precluded a later, more balanced and diffused economic growth. But, for reasons mentioned in Section 8 of Chapter 10, this development was largely abortive in South Asia. The initial spurts in production for export did not trigger a cumulative process of development in other sectors. Even when, as in plantation agriculture and mining, the colonial enterprises were of an "industrial" kind and were complemented by the creation of ports, railroads, and financial and commercial institutions, they did not produce much in the way of spread effects but remained enclaves amid backwardness and stagnation. Enterprise and investment were merely bubbles on the surface; they filtered down hardly at all to stimulate indigenous entrepreneurial activity.

In any event, the epoch of rapidly growing export markets has ended — except perhaps for Malaya where rubber may still be subject to an increase in demand if it can compete with artificial rubber in the world market,[1] and possibly also Indonesia if internal order and efficient government could be achieved. Generally speaking, the South Asian countries have in recent decades seen the demand for their exports shrink relative to the development of world trade. Their terms of trade have not deteriorated sharply, but this is because the increase in their production of export products has been slow, and is thus not a source of much satisfaction. The outlook for their export earnings is not bright.

The forces responsible for the unfortunate trading position of the South Asian countries have been analyzed in Chapter 13; in the present chapter we have already touched on one of these forces. The accelerating rate of population increase, in conjunction with the slow rise of agricultural production, has decreased the ability of these countries to export foodstuffs, or increased their need to import them, with the result that the region as a whole is now a food deficit area. More important, however, have been the changes in the demand for their exports. Rapid and all-around technological development has decreased the demand for these in the Western countries by raising agricultural productivity at home, by providing industrial substitutes for some important imports, by permitting substantial cut-backs in the amount of raw materials used, and by inducing a

---

[1] This is a precarious assumption, as scientific and technological advances will almost certainly lower the costs of production of artificial rubber. See Chapter 13, Section 13.

switch in demand from goods requiring large amounts of imported raw materials to those whose raw material content constitutes a small part of their value. Furthermore, with the exception of rubber, most goods traditionally exported by South Asia have a low income elasticity of demand and almost none are products the demand for which is rapidly rising as a result of economic development in the developed countries; discriminatory tariffs — which rise in line with the stage of processing — hamper the development of export industries. The export of manufactured products from South Asia is not very significant and is concentrated on a few cheap, low-quality goods for which the world market is not expanding; many of these exports meet rising protective walls. The increase in the volume of international trade since the end of the Second World War has been mainly in other industrial products, and in trade between the developed countries. We have seen also that there are serious hindrances to efforts by the underdeveloped countries in South Asia to basically improve their export situation through diversification of their products and markets. Rigidity and lack of adaptability are two characteristics of economic underdevelopment. Above all, the possibility of building up a manufacturing industry that could successfully compete on the world market is severely limited by the markedly superior conditions under which the entrenched industries in the developed countries operate — the advanced skills and other external economies, the heavy investments in research, and the ever more rapidly accelerating technology.

The whole climate for development through trade has also changed fundamentally since the nineteenth century, which, seen in historical perspective, we now know to have been an era of unequalled freedom of international trade. The Western countries that led in the development process, all small in population, stood out like islands in an ocean of backward peoples. Having the field of international trade virtually to themselves, they could and did exploit the resources and peoples in the huge backward areas of the world and kept them politically and economically dependent. Now that these large areas are trying to emerge from political and economic dependency, they cannot simply repeat the development process of the developed countries. While being a late-comer in the nineteenth century was not a disadvantage but often quite the opposite, it is in the twentieth century a serious disadvantage. As the South Asian countries do not enjoy the stimulation from rising demand for their exports at a time when their import needs are increasing, they are forced to direct their development efforts toward something hitherto untried—import substitution. Protectionism played its role in many of the now developed Western countries, but all of them, unlike the South Asian countries today, had access to growing export markets. There is no historical example in the Western world of economic development based on a policy of self-sufficiency and import substitution.

The development of the Soviet Union since the end of the 1920's is somewhat similar to the South Asian situation, at least insofar as the Soviet
Union did not utilize international trade as the engine of growth. Had it
attempted to do so, it would probably have run into political and economic
difficulties, especially after the onset of the Great Depression in the Western countries. Instead, it instituted state control of all foreign economic relations and central planning of a much more exacting type than any South
Asian country has contemplated. Moreover, the Soviet Union started from
a higher level of industrial and pre-industrial development, was better endowed with natural resources, was initially a food surplus country, and
had not the climatic handicaps of the South Asian countries.

One dilemma inherent in the attempt to industrialize by means of import
substitution, to which the South Asian countries are forced, is that the
initiation of new industries requires large imports of capital goods, and
often continuing imports of spare parts, raw materials, and semi-manufactured goods; the building up of ancillary industries to make the countries independent of these other and continuing import needs will again
create a need to import capital goods. Even if the final result should be a
saving of foreign exchange, the initial effect is invariably to increase import needs, usually for a not inconsiderable period. This augments the
tendency toward a negative balance of payments already inherent in the
lagging export demands and the increased food needs consequent upon the
population explosion. This gap between import needs and export possibilities has been widening and is bound to widen further. While the
obvious remedy is capital inflow to cover the deficits and enable the South
Asian countries to import essentials for consumption and the capital goods
necessary in furthering import substitution, the deterioration in their
trading position is itself likely to decrease the availability of foreign capital.

Although it is true that Britain and Japan, for example, managed to develop with few or no capital imports, foreign capital played a major role
in the development of most other countries. The relationship to the trading
position was very close. The early spurt in exports and the outlook for rising exports created, at home and abroad, a confidence in future growth
that enabled these countries to borrow from abroad, often to the extent that
a major result of the initial increase in their exports was the possibility of a
still greater increase in their imports. Although the initial change was an
increase in exports, their balance of trade could then become negative. It
was through this mechanism, whereby the expansion of export outlets
made possible large-scale borrowing abroad, that the development spurts
could gather momentum and permit the increase in foreign trade to exceed
the growth in national product for a long time. The capital movements
flowed mainly between the Western countries—those that developed early
and the late-comers—but some also flowed to the underdeveloped South

Asian countries during that early period when their export production was rising rapidly. Ragnar Nurkse has commented on these capital movements and the change in recent times:

The 19th century pattern of development in outlying areas was geared to export markets for primary staples. This mechanism of growth transmission is now at a comparatively low gear. Nor is this all. Conditions in the trade field have some influence on international investment. The vigorous expansion of demand for primary commodities induced a massive flow of private capital to peripheral areas in the past. Conversely, the lag observed at the present time in the export trade of most of the less developed countries provides a simple explanation for the lack of incentive for private foreign investment.[1]

Even had the international capital market remained intact, the deterioration in their trading position and, in particular, the contraction in the demand for their export products would have made it almost impossible at the present time for the South Asian countries to rely on foreign capital in their development efforts. This situation therefore constitutes a difference in initial conditions to the great disadvantage of these countries.

In fact, however, the old competitive international private capital market, particularly for long-term capital at fixed interest rates, has almost disappeared. After a brief revival in the years following the First World War, the crisis in international payments, culminating in 1929, resulted in the almost total extinction of that market, which had earlier furnished developing countries with long-term credit at very low interest rates—sometimes less than half the rate of interest that the World Bank, working with guarantees from the governments of the rich countries, today charges for its loans (which in view of the need for guarantees cannot be considered loans on commercial terms). As long as the South Asian countries were colonies and their money and banking systems were integrated with those of the metropolitan countries, even they had benefitted from this easy access to cheap foreign capital. Behind the virtual collapse of the international private capital market lie many fundamental changes in international relations. It is certain that in the Western countries the tendencies toward autarkic policies have been much stronger in the financial than in the trade field. Through the exigencies of wars and business crises, states have become much less inhibited by the taboos of liberalism than before the First World War, and they are especially likely to interfere in foreign exchange and payments relations. The unstable international political situation has discouraged private loans to foreign countries. And the political and economic uncertainties in newly independent countries such as those of South Asia have weakened confidence that obligations to foreign capitalists will always be honored.

While long-term private lending to South Asian countries has almost disappeared, there is some direct investment in the region, but on a very small scale since opportunities for enclave enterprises in oil and other dynamic extractive industries are rather limited. In addition to the discouraging effects of bleak export prospects, foreign businessmen are wary of nationalization and other policies that could lower the profitability of investments.

A new element in the situation, however, has been the flow of capital in the form of grants and loans from foreign governments and intergovernmental agencies. Such aid has been virtually a necessity because of the deteriorating trading position, the widening gap between exports and imports, the demise of the international private capital market, and the actual or assumed uncongenial climate for direct investment in South Asia. While most of the Marshall Plan aid to Europe was given in the form of grants, the tendency at present is to favor loans. Insofar as payments of interest and amortization are expected, increasing burdens are placed on the payment balances of the South Asian countries in future years. Particularly in view of their unfavorable export prospects, the limits to what many of them can borrow in this way are being reached.

These problems are dealt with in detail in Chapter 13. Here we need only recognize that the closely interrelated developments in trade and in capital movements must be regarded as a difference in initial conditions that is very much to the disadvantage of the South Asian countries.

Approaching the subject imaginatively, and assuming the same type of human solidarity with respect to the underdeveloped countries in South Asia as has developed within the individual rich democratic welfare states of the West — as well as in the Communist countries — it is not difficult to frame policies that could counteract the disadvantageous commercial and financial conditions under which South Asia now labors. In the field of trade, the developed Western countries could not only initiate effective international action to stabilize their imports of primary products; they could give the South Asian countries preferential treatment in a number of ways. South Asian products, both primary and manufactured, could be granted freer entry to Western markets. The Western countries could take measures to reduce domestic production in fields where the South Asian countries have the best chance of becoming competitive; they could even subsidize imports from these countries. In the field of finance, they could make much more capital available to the South Asian countries as grants or loans with low or no interest rates and extended repayment provisions.

Substantial changes of this type in the trade and financial policies of the developed countries are not to be expected within the foreseeable future. But the *ability* to offset some of the most serious disadvantages of the South Asian countries in trade and in capital movements clearly exists. It can be done if the developed countries are willing to make the attempt against strong internal opposition.

5   *Economic Levels, Social Structure, and Attitudes*

Heroic efforts have been made to compare levels of income per head in South Asian countries today with those in the Western countries in pre-industrial times.[1] But comparison of these aggregates between different regions in different historical eras raises formidable problems. Quite apart from the difficulty of defining a time period in the Western countries appropriate for this type of comparison and the unsatisfactory primary data, it is difficult to see how any index could have much meaning. As, presumably, the differences between the two regions not only are large but point in different directions for different items of "income," and as the climatic, economic, social, and cultural settings are so dissimilar whatever period of comparison is chosen, it is more revealing to compare modes and levels of living and working in specific respects. Even such specific, and therefore more realistic, comparisons can yield only vague and tentative conclusions about the relative levels of welfare. Logically viewed, an overall index figure must be regarded as unwarranted precision.[2]

Our very broad impression, supported by the above-mentioned studies and by everything else we know, is that on the Indian subcontinent the masses live in worse poverty than did those in the Western European countries at any time during several centuries before the industrial revolution. In Malaya, on the other hand, the economic level even of the bulk of the population may be as high as and possibly higher than it was in Western European countries even in late pre-industrial times. The other South Asian countries would fall somewhere between these two extremes.

But what significance do income levels have for development prospects? When references are made in the literature to income differences in time and space, it is usually assumed that the level of income has a direct bearing on a country's ability to support the savings needed for those investments considered to be crucial for development. However, this savings-centered approach to the problem of economic development is highly questionable for several reasons, which we touch on in many contexts in this book. First, savings and investment do not play the exclusive role for development assumed in most economic writings on the problems of South Asia; this is one point where the approach is clearly influenced by modern, Western preconceptions. Attitudes and institutions are more important in the region — even, incidentally, in determining savings ratios — than are levels of income *per se*. Second, what is saved out of income,

---

[1] Phyllis Deane, "The Industrial Revolution and Economic Growth," *Economic Development and Cultural Change*, Vol. V, No. 2, January, 1957. Simon Kuznets has presented a series of essays entitled "Quantitative Aspects of the Economic Growth of Nations" in *ibid.*, Vols. V through XI. See also his "Essays in the Quantitative Study of Economic Growth" in Vol. IX, April, 1961.

[2] Chapter 11, Section 1.

whether it is high or low, depends very much on the direction and effectiveness of government policy. And finally, low income levels probably hamper development more by keeping down consumption than savings, because inferior living conditions, particularly poor nutrition, reduce labor input and efficiency.[1] Strangely, this point is overlooked in most comments concerning the effect of low income levels in South Asia.

The emphasis on the low levels of income of the South Asian masses, the strained comparison with Western levels of income at an earlier period, and the Western approach to income, savings, and investment in South Asia, all represent attempts to apply an over-simplified and narrow formula to what in reality is an intricate complex of social, economic, and even political conditions that impede development. But even if we reject the savings-centered approach, and remain skeptical of the inter-regional comparison involved, it is true that the great poverty in South Asia, particularly in those countries containing the bulk of its population, is itself a major barrier to development. Moreover, the present and foreseeable increase in population noted in Section 3 must there lead to a decline in the already low levels of living unless resolute development policies are pursued. This worsening trend implies a difference in initial conditions, detrimental to all the South Asian countries, that is fairly independent of the period in Western history chosen for comparison.

We have still less information that would enable us to judge whether economic inequality today is greater in South Asia than in the Western countries in pre-industrial times. It is probable, however, that on the Indian subcontinent social inequality is more pervasive and more detrimental to free competition, in the wider sense of the term, than anywhere in the Western world in recent centuries. As both economic and social inequality in our conception[2] hinders economic progress, this would put India and Pakistan, at least, at a disadvantage in initial conditions compared with Western Europe, again fairly independent of the comparison period. This judgment would be less true of the other South Asian countries.

We are thus led to the major question of whether in South Asia today the complex of political, social, and economic institutions and the attitudes underlying and deriving from these institutions represent greater inhibitions and obstacles to development than did those in the Western world in earlier times. In accordance with our approach to the development problem,[3] these conditions in South Asia enter into our discussion in almost every chapter. We have not, of course, been able to investigate the Western countries in the same way, least of all for periods preceding their industrialization. A more definitive study of the difference in initial conditions

[1] Appendix 2, Section 21.
[2] Chapter 16, Section 3.
[3] Prologue, Section 8.

in these respects would have to take account of many more things than can be suggested in the few cursory remarks to which we must here confine ourselves. On the whole, our research and observations incline us to the belief that attitudes and institutions in the South Asian countries are less favorable than were those in the now developed Western countries at the start of their industrial revolutions or in the centuries before. Like this statement, the illustrations below are in terms of the general pattern.

In regard to political institutions, one obvious difference is that the Western countries were independent and mostly had become consolidated nation-states, able to pursue national policies, well before their industrial revolutions. For centuries the feudal structure of society had been gradually breaking down, and even in medieval Europe, the free cities were strongholds of non-feudal attitudes and practices in industry and commerce. The Western countries formed a small world of similar culture within which people and ideas circulated rather freely. In this world, before the industrial revolution, rationalism was fostered and traditionalism weakened as the Renaissance, the Reformation, and the Enlightenment, successively, revolutionized concepts and valuations. Modern scientific thought developed in the Western countries, and modern technology was early introduced in their agriculture and industries. The great discoveries and the colonization of the non-European world had helped pave the way; they changed attitudes and institutions in the European countries more than in the territories colonized, except where the latter were sparsely populated, as in the New World.

By contrast, the South Asian countries have only recently become independent and have yet to become consolidated nation-states capable of pursuing national policies effectively. All of them have a Westernized educated class and an intellectual elite that understands and has assimilated the scientific spirit of the Western world. These educated Asians, however, are more a "part of the intellectual life of the cosmopolitan world than they are of their indigenous cultures."[1] They are the vehicle for impulses to change, but these impulses, since they are not indigenous as in the West but emanate from a totally different culture, encounter substantial resistance. Furthermore, change has to be rapid in South Asia instead of building up slowly as in the Western countries.[2] The necessity for speed is accentuated by the population explosion, which itself strengthens the resistance to change as, in a stagnant society, it tends to depress living levels and increase social and economic inequality. And so these new nations — as we shall illustrate when we get to Part Four on ideologies — are from the start attempting to apply, or pretending to apply, policies, and adopt institutions, that have been maturing gradually in the Western countries:

[1] H. L. Keenleyside, "Obstacles and Means in International Development," *International Development Review*, Vol. II, No. 1, 1960, p. 21.

[2] Section 9, the last section in this chapter, will enlarge on this point.

planning, political democracy, economic and social equality — in short, the whole apparatus of the modern democratic welfare state. Alien as they are to the attitudes and institutions pervading poor, traditionalist, and stagnant societies, these reforms often remain on paper, and inherited patterns of life and work persist.

Similarly with economic modernization. Only India and the Philippines have the nucleus of a national entrepreneurial class; Pakistan's smaller group of entrepreneurs consists mainly of refugee-immigrants from India. In all the other countries industry and business had been almost entirely in the hands of European, Chinese, and Indian minority groups. Efforts to encourage enterprise among the indigenous majority have been less successful in promoting development than discriminatory measures against foreign enterprises, stimulated by independence, have been in retarding it.

Obviously, South Asia is attempting to close a yawning gap in attitudes and institutions. In this as in other respects, those Western countries that, in their day, were also late-comers to industrialization were in a more advantageous position. First of all, they were not as late as South Asia. Secondly, the speed of change was not as great then as now. Finally, if among the Western countries technology had been advancing unevenly, attitudes and institutions had been advancing on a broad front; by the time the late-comers began to catch up industrially, their educational level, for example, was higher than England's had been at a similar level of economic development. The South Asian countries, however, have been losing ground for a long time. Everything they have to try to catch up with is moving ahead faster all the time. This fateful dilemma will be the subject of Section 9.

6 The Availability of Modern Technology

The differences in initial conditions accounted for so far all make the problem of economic development more difficult for the nations of South Asia than it once was for the now developed economies of the West. There is, however, one important difference that would seem, at least in part, to counterbalance these difficulties: technology has advanced far beyond its level in the nineteenth century or before. The South Asian countries need not go through a slow, painful process of experimentation; today, as Mason puts it, "a highly productive technology . . . is available for the borrowing." Mason notes that "if this technological heritage were not available, economic growth in the underdeveloped world would undoubtedly be even slower than . . . it promises to be."[1]

Of course, more than simple borrowing is involved. The technology has

[1] Edward S. Mason, *Economic Planning in Underdeveloped Areas: Government and Business,* Fordham University Press, New York, 1958, pp. 14, 47.

to be adapted to South Asian conditions. Moreover, the introduction of any new production process inevitably necessitates a period of learning, and a longer and more intense one if its users have not been instrumental in its creation. Despite these obvious caveats, the availability of a more efficient technology is clearly an advantage. Learning and modifying an existing technique must be less costly than developing a new one. As Mason points out: ". . . the underdeveloped countries . . . could hardly be at an absolute disadvantage, as compared with the initiators of industrial development, since they always have the alternative of devising techniques themselves, as their predecessors in development have done."[1]

The advantage of having an accumulation of technological knowledge to draw on was evident in the unprecedented rapidity of industrialization and general economic development in those Western countries that were latest to enter the development phase. South Asian planners are conscious of this fact of history and prone to see it wistfully as a sign of the future.[2] But it does not follow from past experience that the availability of a greater amount of technological knowledge necessarily works to the advantage of the late-comer nowadays. All writers on this subject — including Mason — set down a number of qualifications that tend to reduce this advantage. Unfortunately, in the absence of empirical studies of the relevant facts it is impossible to be more than tentative about the significance of such qualifications.

One main category concerns the nature of modern technology compared with that applied by the now developed countries in their early spurts of industrialization. For one thing, it is usually held that technological development has greatly increased the optimal size of plants or firms. With advanced techniques, the volume of output required to achieve minimum costs — or costs close to the minimum — will therefore often be in excess of what a limited domestic market can absorb. This creates a special hardship for those countries of South Asia — not always the smallest in population[3] — that have a particularly small aggregate monetized demand, actual and potential. The size of the domestic market is the more important because of the absence of regional cooperation and the generally unpromising outlook for manufactured exports: the South Asian countries are thereby forced to direct their industrialization efforts toward import substitution. It has been suggested that "the scope for developing new technological innovations, by modification and combination of various alterna-

[1] *Ibid.*, p. 85, f.n. 13.

[2] For example: "Countries which start later on their industrial career have some advantage in that they have, in the main, to take over and apply techniques that have been worked successfully in more advanced countries." (India, Government of, Planning Commission, *Second Five Year Plan*, New Delhi, 1956, p. 6.)

[3] This should be remembered when comparing countries like Malaya, Ceylon, and the Philippines with India or Pakistan.

tives, is considerably broader than was the case when the original technological changes were developed."[1] But such innovations require enterprise, fresh thinking, and a considerable effort of research, all of which are scarce in the underdeveloped countries (see below). Sometimes, on the other hand, the technique of the smaller optimal size — or the smaller size that is not very much more costly — may be simply a less modern one than is now used in the advanced countries under the pressure of labor scarcity. It has often been suggested, therefore, that the underdeveloped countries could with great advantage buy second-hand equipment; though obsolescent in the advanced countries, it would be more efficient than present techniques in the underdeveloped countries. The purchase of such equipment would not only reduce the initial investment but in many cases would also permit smaller plants.[2] However, acceptance of anything but the most up-to-date meets both with strong inhibitions and with other and more substantial difficulties in the underdeveloped countries.

In our opinion, the adverse economic impact of limited domestic markets tends to be overemphasized in the literature. At least, the impact is different in different industries, and is often greater in heavy than in light industry. But much more detailed research is needed before one can gauge the true significance of market size for the optimum size of plant or enterprise. Not enough relevant information is available to warrant the blanket assertions so many writers make, and sometimes embellish by mathematical models based on abstract assumptions not tested in regard to their relevance and realism.

Another aspect of modern technology usually thought to add to the difficulties of its adaptation in South Asia is its requirement of large initial investments. Since present-day technology is mainly a product of economies that have a scarcity of labor and a relative abundance of capital, it tends to be labor-saving and capital-intensive. Much of it may therefore be beyond the means of the very poor, capital-starved economies in the region. In any case, the necessity of large capital investments may severely limit the scope and rate of their industrialization. But the sweeping assumption often encountered, that modern technology has become more capital-intensive than in the earlier phases of Western industrialization, is another proposition that requires more specific evidence and is certainly not valid in every instance. Many branches of industry using modern technology are capital-saving in the important sense of consuming less capital per unit of output. Neither is it universally true that modern technology requires larger units of capital initially, especially in light industry. Again, as in the case of optimal size, intelligent adaptation to the different factor propor-

---

[1] C. Wolf and S. C. Sufrin, *Capital Formation and Foreign Investment in Underdeveloped Areas,* Syracuse University Press, Syracuse, 1955, p. 40.

[2] United Nations, *Report of Expert Group on Second-Hand Equipment for Developing Countries,* December 7–22, 1965, New York, 1966.

tions and other conditions in South Asia might enable modern technology to be utilized in such a way that less, rather than more, capital is required. The usual broad generalization seems, therefore, to be hazardous and somewhat misleading. Nevertheless, technology today may and probably does entail more investment in transport and power than in earlier periods. If so, and if these magnitudes are somehow allocated to new industries, then new production techniques can be said to require a heavier initial investment. Even this generalization must be tentative, however, for much of the early industrial development in England involved canal building, which at the time represented a substantial investment; and the countries of Western Europe and the New World that industrialized later had to invest in railways.

One can be more certain that there are tremendous external economies for an industrial enterprise growing up in an already developed industrial surrounding. Conversely, there is great difficulty in starting even one industry without the support of that surrounding. As Everett Hagen points out:

. . . every Western industry depends for its efficiency on other industries. It assumes the ready availability of materials, components, and tools. It depends also on auxiliary enterprises which can provide technical, financial, and managerial services on demand; on a complex network of communication and transportation facilities; and on an intricate system of business practices. A Western economy is a technical (and cultural) complex, not a set of isolated pieces of technology. In an underdeveloped society the auxiliary industries are missing and the framework of business practices is different. One piece cannot be detached from the complex and used efficiently elsewhere without skillful adaptation.[1]

This interconnection of the economic system makes the beginning stages of industrialization much more difficult today, particularly when shortages of capital, enterprise, and skills set narrow limits to the scope of the industrialization efforts.

The shortage of skills, indeed, represents a third main difficulty for the underdeveloped countries of South Asia in advancing to a higher technological level. The use of modern technology calls for a certain minimum supply of various skills that are generally lacking in the region. Not only is a somewhat more skilled labor force needed, but a greater number of technicians and managers as well. Achievement of the requisite skill levels of all kinds necessitates substantial efforts in education, using the word to include a widespread attack on illiteracy, academic study in science, and much for-the-job and on-the-job training. Managerial and engineering skills, in particular, can be perfected only after actual working experience.

[1] Everett E. Hagen, *On the Theory of Social Change, How Economic Growth Begins*, The Dorsey Press, Cambridge, 1962, p. 31.

Also, the possibility of adapting modern technology to the smaller plant size and lower capital intensity often appropriate in South Asia rests on the availability of engineers and managers in sufficient number to explore and experiment with modifications of all kinds. If imagination and enterprise are wanting, the South Asian countries may settle for adopting the techniques of the advanced countries without making adjustments to their conditions, and the difficulties already mentioned would then be more valid and relevant. Thus limitations of their domestic markets will pose a greater problem if managerial and engineering skills are scarce. Larger plants and firms may, indeed, provide a means of economizing these types of rare skills. For the same reason, these countries may be compelled to use more capital-intensive techniques than would *per se* be economic; in the same way lack of a skilled work force may induce more capital-intensive production techniques. Obviously, too, without trained managers, engineers, and workers it is impossible to strive for the optimal complex of industries and auxiliary enterprises. It can be said, therefore, that *the lack of skills is a fundamental hindrance to progress.*

There can be little doubt that the educational level of management, technical personnel, and workers now considered minimal for successful operation of a modern industrial establishment is substantially higher than it was in the early period of Western industrialization. Most of the technical innovations of the late eighteenth and nineteenth centuries were mechanical inventions whereas today and increasingly they grow out of discoveries concerning the structure of matter and energy, chemical processes, metallurgy, and so on. In the early phase of the industrial revolution it was the entrepreneurs themselves, in textiles and other industries, who had to make the machines needed for their factories. They were capable of doing this because the new machinery "involved no principles that an intelligent merchant could not grasp. Indeed, much of the mechanical invention of these years was simply the result of the harnessing of the traditional skills of clockmakers, millwrights, blacksmiths, and the like to the needs of the entrepreneur."[1] Or, in the words of Mason, "the early developments in industrial technology were undertaken not by men of science who discovered the practical application of general principles but by skilled artisans and thinkers working in the eighteenth-century equivalent of the twentieth-century garage."[2] Successful adoption and adaptation of present-day technology requires a much greater knowledge of general science. The connection between science and technology (to be discussed in Section 9) is probably closer now than ever before in history. An economy whose

[1] Charles Wilson, "Technology and Industrial Organization," in Charles Singer, E. J. Holmyard, A. R. Hall, and Trevor I. Williams, eds., *A History of Technology*, Vol. V. *The Late Nineteenth Century c1850 to c1900*, The Clarendon Press, Oxford, 1958, pp. 799–800.

[2] *Economic Planning in Underdeveloped Areas*, p. 32.

work force is largely unskilled and illiterate and whose managerial and engineering talent is in short supply is therefore severely handicapped.

7   In Regard to Agriculture

Industrialization is unquestionably of crucial importance for long-range development, but the more immediate problem in the South Asian countries is agriculture. It contains the vast majority of the labor force and must absorb most of the increase in the labor force for decades to come, even if industrialization should proceed at a faster rate than at present.[1] The problem of using modern technology in agriculture is altogether different from that of its utilization in industry. In industry, it is feasible and may be advantageous to set up a new plant basically along Western lines; in fact, industrialization implies that many such plants are established, selected, and coordinated so as to form a complex containing as many external economies as possible. Modern technology in Western agriculture, however, has been directed toward raising yields, while the labor force engaged has been rapidly and steadily declining. Technological development in this pattern simply does not fit South Asian conditions.

Apart from the institutional barriers that would stand in the way — much more so than in industry since the modern industrial sector is new — the application of this pattern on a large scale in South Asian agriculture would rob the labor force imprisoned there of its meager livelihood. Generally, most land is cultivated; if more can be cultivated this is costly and there is usually labor pressing to use it following more or less the old pattern of labor intensity. The proportions of land and labor are thus in the main given, and on the whole changing in a way to increase the need for a much bigger labor input per unit of cultivated area. The improvement of productivity in agriculture has to adjust to these existing and foreseeable factor proportions, as well as to the fixed institutional conditions that limit technical advance in various ways. In consequence, the larger part of modern agricultural technology is unadaptable to South Asian conditions, and a new technology has to be devised, as we explain in Chapter 26.

A second reason why adoption of modern agricultural technology from advanced countries is not very practical is that this technology is based on research directed, quite understandably, at a kind of agriculture that operates under climatic and soil conditions different from those in South Asia — except insofar as it relates to plantation culture, which has been of direct economic concern to investors in the Western countries. Some specific techniques, such as artificial insemination and new methods of preventing plant diseases, are applicable, but even these often have to be radically

[1] Chapter 24, Sections 5 and 6.

adjusted to local conditions. The institutions in the region that are working on basic or applied research in agriculture — or in forestry — are far too few and ineffective to have had any major impact. Moreover, like economic research, their work is too much under the spell of Western science and technology. Often their ambition is to produce results more in line with the Western tradition than with the needs of their own countries. In Section 8 we shall have something to say about the kind of research that is needed.

The improvement of agricultural productivity requires not only research but also vigorous public policies. It may be noted in passing that this is only one of many ways in which the effort to advance production techniques in the South Asian countries tends to induce the state to become much more involved in development than was true in the Western countries in their early phase of development. This problem will be discussed in the next chapter.

8   *Criticism of the Static Approach*

Despite the reservations we have noted as to the difficulties of adapting modern technology to South Asian conditions, the availability of this technology, and the scientific knowledge on which it is based, should constitute a net advantage in initial conditions. The qualifications mentioned above refer essentially to the differences between modern technology and the technology applied when the now developed countries were beginning to industrialize. They should not obliterate the fact — which in itself should constitute a difference in initial conditions favorable to the underdeveloped countries in South Asia — that individual entrepreneurs and states now have access to scientific and technological knowledge vastly superior to that accessible to the Western countries during their pre-industrial phase of development.

But this whole approach to the problem is, in a sense, static. The important thing is not that science and technology have achieved a much higher level, which South Asia can try to approach by adoption and adaptation, but that they are continually and rapidly moving toward ever higher levels. This dynamic quality of technological change may seem to be adequately acknowledged by occasional assertions that the problem "is not merely one of introducing some degree of improvement in techniques; it is a matter of raising the *rate* of technological progress."[1] It is frequently added that a high rate of technological progress in the South Asian countries will require far more advanced research facilities than were needed in the Western countries in the early phases of their industrialization; and

---

[1] Higgins, *Economic Development*, p. 185.

also higher levels of education generally and more rational and enterprising attitudes, particularly among administrators and business entrepreneurs. This thinking is then rationalized in demands for a more scientific outlook and the emergence of a "scientific man" or an "industrial man."

The trust in further scientific and technological progress has been the basis for the optimism implied in the planning ideology, which we shall scrutinize in the next chapter. This optimism regarding the role of science and technology in economic development in South Asia has often been given pathetic expression by intellectual and political leaders in the region, including Jawaharlal Nehru; and the hopes expressed have been endorsed unreservedly by Western statesmen. Nor have Western economists been eager to dampen such expectations, except occasionally by the type of qualifications we noted in Section 6 above. No one, surprisingly enough, has pointed out the importance of the world environment within which the advances in enterprise, the innovations, and research in the South Asian countries must take place. In the developed countries, with huge resources at their disposal, science and technology are now progressing at an ever faster pace. This activity is naturally directed toward the interests and industries of the developed countries themselves. Only to a very minor, almost infinitesimal, extent does it have bearing on problems of direct importance to South Asia.[1]

What is, almost inexplicably, concealed in economic writings is the obvious fact that *scientific and technological advance in the West has had, and is having, an impact on the South Asian countries that is very detrimental to their development prospects*: only in regard to specific problems is this negative impact registered and analyzed. The general point that technological development continually creates new or increased impediments to economic development in South Asia is regularly missed. This is another example of the working of the optimistic bias we noted in the Prologue (Sections 4–6), common to Western economists and their South Asian colleagues.[2]

The deterioration of the trading position of the South Asian countries since soon after the First World War, which we discussed in Section 4, is

[1] There are, of course, exceptions such as the growing concern for water scarcity that has led certain Western nations to invest heavily in research on desalination of sea water. If efficient means to use sea water were developed, the arid regions of, say, West Pakistan might be rendered productive.

[2] The truth is glimpsed more often by the philosopher-historian than by the economist. Thus Panikkar, referring to the negative impact of technology, writes: "Briefly it may be stated . . . that the world is on the doorstep of a great transformation which will make the gap between the scientifically advanced and the scientifically backward nations deeper and wider; making the latter more than ever dependent for all essential things on the more powerful nations." (K. M. Panikkar, *Afro-Asian States and Their Problems,* Allen & Unwin Ltd., London, 1959, p. 80.) The only fault with Panikkar's statement is that this impact is not new, but dates far back. Like the widening gap, the process has been going on for a century or more.

thus in large part due to scientific and technological advances in the developed countries, which have made possible the rapid rise in agricultural productivity there, substantial reductions in the use of raw materials imported from South Asia for industrial production, and the substitution of synthetic products for other imported raw materials. Similarly, the population explosion in South Asia has been due to advances in medical science and technology that have lowered mortality rates. Since the development of science and technology is rapidly proceeding, not abating, its detrimental impact on the economies of South Asia can be expected to continue. As by far the greater part of all research is carried on in the developed countries and is financed by their governments, their foundations, universities, and industries, it would be unreasonable not to expect the research efforts to be directed to their advantage. Moreover, it would be contrary to our belief in progress, the very spirit of our civilization, to argue that, as a protection to underdeveloped countries, these advances should be stopped or their results should not be used.[1] We will continue to raise agricultural productivity, make savings in the use of raw materials, and develop substitute products; we may, for instance, as the report of a committee of the U. S. Congress suggests, produce synthetically at some not too distant time not only coffee but also tea and cocoa. And to prevent and cure disease and prevent untimely deaths, and to do this ever more effectively in the underdeveloped countries as well, is an even more intrinsic part of the ethos of our civilization. These efforts will continue, though they accelerate the population increase in a region like South Asia and build up ever greater impediments to economic progress.

Although restriction of scientific and technological advance is out of the question, its unfortunate impact could be counteracted by deliberately increasing research activity and directing it toward problems the solution of which would be in the interest of the underdeveloped countries. This would imply aid of another type by the developed countries, and aid on a larger scale than anything previously done or now contemplated in the way of technical assistance. In agriculture there are vast needs for scientific and technological research. Studies are needed, for example, about the attributes of soils in various tropical areas and their reaction to diverse

[1] This was stressed in the Secretary General's report to the United Nations Conference on Trade and Development in 1964, though with a reservation: "In no circumstances could we seriously entertain the thought of restraining technological advances. That does not mean, however, that it is advisable to encourage types of research which should not, for the time being, enjoy any priority whatsoever, as, for instance, research into substitutes for coffee. Moreover, in some cases, the transition might be made easier for the producing countries if minimum proportions were established in the use of the natural product, just as minimums are fixed in some cases in the use of certain national primary products in relation to imported commodities." (*Proceedings of the United Nations Conference on Trade and Development*, Vol. II, New York, 1965, p. 25.)

patterns of rainfall; about drainage, irrigation, and fertilizers; about improved seeds and animal stocks, cropping patterns, the use of agricultural implements, the prevention of plant and animal diseases, the storage of perishable products. Localized and intensive study of such problems in the temperate zones has made possible dramatic increases in yields of land and animals with steadily decreasing inputs of labor. It is no exaggeration to say that the efforts to raise agricultural productivity in South Asia by extension services and other means have so far been based on very limited knowledge of the fundamental facts regarding the physical, social, and economic conditions peculiar to the region. Much more research should also go into planning irrigation schemes and the use of energy from wind and even the sun and tides. In industry there is the whole problem, referred to in Section 6, of adjusting plants, machines, tools, and materials to the climatic and other conditions in South Asia, including consideration of the relative proportions of labor of various kinds and other factors of production. In the population field the problem, of course, is primarily one of improving contraceptive techniques and extending the practice of birth control in order to bring births into some kind of balance with deaths.

In all these respects — except perhaps the last — very little has as yet been accomplished. What is needed is clearly much more research systematically directed toward solving the problems of the underdeveloped countries. Some of this research could be carried on in the underdeveloped countries themselves, but hardly on a scale that would even come close to balancing the detrimental effects of the scientific and technological development in the advanced countries without considerable outside assistance in the form of research personnel and funds. Unless the research effort is very large and in the right direction, *the dynamics of technological progress will work to the ever greater disadvantage of the underdeveloped countries, increasing their difficulties and decreasing their development potential.*

9   *The Acceleration of Technological Advance and the Quickening Pace of History*

The true significance of the foregoing observations can only be grasped when we realize that technological advance, now proceeding so rapidly in the developed countries, can be expected to proceed ever faster in the future. In a sense, the most fundamental difference in initial conditions between the South Asian countries today and the Western countries in any period of their pre-industrial phase is the difference in the pace of history. A telescoping of change has become the only alternative not only to continued stagnation but to regression. In the final analysis, this situation is a result of the high levels of economic development now achieved by the developed countries and the accelerating speed with which they continue to develop.

Change was not rapid in the beginning of Western development prior to industrialization. It is, indeed, difficult to overestimate the importance of gradualness in the early development of the Western countries where "economic development" originated. All the major "revolutions" of the West — religious, intellectual, geographic, and even political (the emergence of consolidated nation-states) — occurred long before the industrial revolution, and they proceeded slowly, thereby permitting a relatively smooth adaptation of all relationships in society. Thus Western Europe had several centuries in which to become accustomed to, and prepare for, change. It is as if the "coefficient of changeability,"[1] starting at a low point in the Middle Ages, rose and then continued to rise at an ever faster rate. And so the ideas of change, adaptability, and mobility were gradually accepted as a way of life, until Westerners became accustomed to the kind of "permanent industrial revolution" in which they live today.

It is generally recognized that progress in science and technology was a result of and, at the same time, a driving force in this gradual development. From the viewpoint of the economist and the economic historian, the improvement of the methods of production was of primary importance. The industrial revolution was understood to have required a number of "inventions" of new production methods — over and above the changes in social and economic conditions, among which were the advances in rationality and in scientific knowledge that made the inventions possible and, even more important, led to their application and widespread use. During the nineteenth century, when economics took shape as a science, and before the speed of technological change had become so pronounced, it was natural for economists to lean toward the view that the great and radical inventions had already been made and that only "improvements" remained to be added. This is the impression that comes to mind on looking backward and discovering how often a large number of improvements branched out from earlier innovations; with hindsight, these appear to be consequential, indeed radical, technological breakthroughs. Although nineteenth century economists produced very little explicit discussion of technological advance — less than their forerunners from Adam Smith's time — this was the usual implicit assumption. It was this way of looking at things that made it natural to assume that there would be no alteration "in the state of the arts." This assumption permeates classical and neo-classical economic analysis. We see it reflected today in the regular type of quasi-static analysis of the underdeveloped countries' problem of adopting the modern powerful technology of the advanced countries (Section 6). The assumption also fits the common bias of assigning to savings and investment the

---

[1] The term is Gerschenkron's. (A. Gerschenkron, *Economic Backwardness in Historical Perspective*, Harvard University Press, Cambridge, 1962, Chapter 3.)

crucial and almost exclusive role in economic development; it still dominates planning and most economic analysis of the development problem.

But this view of technological advance should now be excluded by our
experience of living in a society where technological advance is so very
rapid and is, in fact, constantly accelerating. More and more it becomes an
almost automatic process driving development forward. The reality of the
situation is blurred by saying that we are living through a new industrial
revolution. Whatever measure we apply, the Western world has had many
"industrial revolutions" since the first, each following more closely upon
the preceding one. Indeed, we have good reason to expect that the great
technological breakthroughs are yet to come. One element in this process,
pointed out in Section 6, is that scientific research is playing an ever larger
and more direct role in technological advance. This advance is increasingly
characterized by systematic and coordinated innovations, founded on
newly acquired scientific knowledge often of the basic type, while the role
of invention as such is decreasing. J. P. Corbett has described this transformation:

Of course, this new cooperation between theory and practice was, at first, extremely loose and unsystematic. The practical problems of navigation were indeed a powerful stimulus no less to astronomical enquiry than to the improvement of clocks. Even in the absence of such precise connexions, there was, no
doubt, throughout the early period, a constant vague pressure of science and production on each other. At the very least they can be said to have flourished in
the same climate of opinion. Yet such a crucial invention of the early industrial
revolution as the steam engine was developed very slowly by practical engineers,
on the basis of general mechanical knowledge, but without any rigorous scientific
analysis; and much the same appears to have been generally true of the other
inventions of that period. With the nineteenth century, however, the pace began
to change. The old and influential but still very loose connexion between science
and production began to be much more effective and direct. Over an ever widening field the achievements of research paved the way for production, and the
problems of production called successfully upon research. Thus electrical generators were in economic use within a few decades of the fundamental work of
Faraday which made them possible in theory. In our day, finally, this cooperation
between the producer and the theorist has reached a very high level of efficiency.[1]

This increasingly close relation between science and technology has certainly been a major cause of the acceleration of technological advance. It
also gives us reason to expect the curve to be of the exponential variety.
Without wanting to press the analogy too far — as we are not in a position
to define either knowledge or the increase of knowledge in terms permitting quantitative measurement — it is reasonable to assume that the growth
in scientific knowledge is proportional to the sum of knowledge previously

[1] J. P. Corbett, *Europe and the Social Order*, A. W. Sythoff, Leyden, 1959, p. 20.

acquired. Knowledge should thus grow at a compound rate of interest, and technology should advance along a parallel, or more steeply rising, line.[1]

Taking as given the civilization within which it takes place, the accelerating growth of scientific and technological knowledge becomes a force, speeding up and bending the course of history in a way that is largely outside our control. Even in the field of armaments and war preparations, where the mutual interests in control are immense, the difficulties of carrying it out in practice loom so large that few are optimistic. In other fields a slowing down of the practical application of science and technology in production and consumption is not even desired. It could not be, given the spirit of our civilization and the competitive co-existence of nations and political blocs under which we live. The effects on our societies of this force for change, however, are beyond our perception. Historians and philosophers themselves have generally shied away from attempting to analyze in more specific terms its implications for the sort of society we will be living in. However, the speeding up of history is clearly visible even if we do not perceive its direction.

Until now, the modern democratic welfare states of the West have been able to contain the dynamics of scientific and technological change without bursting. This is undoubtedly due to two facts: first, from the beginning that kind of change was indigenous to these countries; secondly, it had a slow beginning over many centuries, during which it only gradually gathered its present explosive momentum. Society has adjusted to it; at least it has succeeded in doing so up to now. As for Russia, it was part of Europe and always had scholars and technicians active in the development of science and technology. The Soviet state has directed its planning so that it has its full share in scientific and technological advance, and even leads the march in one field after another. It has the resources to do this, and by means of its political system can allocate them effectively for this purpose.

The underdeveloped countries cannot possibly realize their aspirations in the same way, except in very limited, indeed insignificant, fields. Modern science and technology is to them a force emanating almost entirely from outside. And these countries are not afforded the opportunity for gradualness in development that typified the now developed countries. Technological advance is experienced as a shock administered by external forces. Meanwhile scientific and technological advance in the developed world has had, and continues to have, the detrimental effects on their de-

---

[1] William Ogburn was probably the first social scientist to think systematically along this line. In support of his view he pointed to the fact that new knowledge tends to develop simultaneously through the work of many researchers in different places. See William F. Ogburn, *Social Change*, The Viking Press, New York, 1928.

velopment prospects that we pointed out in Section 8. The foreseeable acceleration of this advance makes it probable that these effects will be increasingly detrimental.

There is little the South Asian countries can themselves do to prevent this. And we have assumed that any restriction on these advances, in order to protect the underdeveloped countries, is excluded. The only possible "control" is a positive one, through massive research directed toward solving the problems of the South Asian countries. At present, making this possibility explicit — as its realization on such a scale is not in sight — is only to underline the additional difficulties that the increasingly rapid technological development in the developed countries is bound to create in South Asia.

Even apart from this consequence of the dynamism of technological advance, the adoption and adaptation of modern technology in South Asia is very difficult, as we pointed out in Section 6. In colonial times, attempts to do it mostly resulted only in the creation of enclaves that left the larger part of the economy stagnant. A danger facing the independent governments in South Asia today is that their development efforts will have a similar effect: small islands of more or less modernized industrial production may be created, while the larger part of the economy remains backward. We shall return to this problem in Chapter 24; the special difficulties facing a modernization policy in the large sector of agriculture will be studied in Chapter 26.

 The need is for telescoping changes, for having them take place faster than they ever did in the early development of the Western countries, faster even than they are now taking place in those countries. But the long stagnation in the underdeveloped countries has solidified institutions and attitudes, and hardened resistance to change in all strata of their population. The onslaught of modernization from outside, without the gradual transition experienced by the Western countries and in the presence of a population explosion, leads to a situation where elements of modernism are sprinkled through a society in which many conditions have remained almost the same for centuries. As Nehru said of India: "Our country at the present moment is a very mixed country. Almost every century is represented in India: from the stone age in which some tribals live, you may say, to the middle of the twentieth century. We have atomic energy and we use also cow dung."[1] To take the optimistic view that these spurts of modernism are "growing points" or provide a "base for further advance" is to assume a number of things: that the hampering effects of the population explosion at home and of the ever more rapid technological advance in the developed countries can be overcome, and that the spread effects within the South Asian countries themselves can be made to operate with much greater effectiveness than they have done up to now.

[1] R. K. Karanjia, *The Mind of Mr. Nehru,* Allen & Unwin Ltd., London, 1960, p. 38.

It is evident that these things will not come about by a process of "natural" evolution, and this constitutes the case for radical state policies. The aim of planning is to engender by state intervention development *in spite of* the greater difficulties we have noted throughout this chapter. What is attempted through planning is something entirely different from the mainly self-propelled economic development of the Western countries a hundred or two hundred years ago. Their development came about through a process of industrialization that was kept moving by the widely scattered activities of individual entrepreneurs bent on utilizing individual new techniques, as they became available, for their own profit. The emergence of the ideology of state planning for development thus itself constitutes a difference in initial conditions, to which we shall devote the next chapter.

Part Four

A THIRD WORLD

OF PLANNING

In the last chapter of Part Three we tried to account in an abstract and summary way for the main differences in initial conditions between the South Asian countries today and the Western countries at the time of their emergence from relative economic stagnation into the era of industrialization and rapid development. So far we have not considered policies.[1] The task in Part Four is to study this category of conditions for development. In this and the next four chapters we shall focus our attention on one of the determinants of policies, namely, ideologies.

An ideology can be studied from two different angles. One is its content of ideals and ideas. The ideology is then itself viewed as a "theory." It is tested in regard to its logical consistency, the adequacy to reality of its ideas about facts and about the causal relations between facts, and the significance and relevance of its ideals as value premises for practical conclusions and political action in the particular society. This approach is the traditional one for economists.[2] In studying an ideology as a theory,

[1] Chapter 14, Section 1; Appendix 2, Section 5.

[2] Except that the value premises have usually been "objectified" by means of a metaphysical construct; see Prologue, Section 9, and Appendix 2, Section 14 *et passim*.

an economist may dismiss it as untrue or irrelevant, or he may modify it and develop it into a more accomplished theory. This is what the whole post-war discussion of planning for development is about. In Appendix 2 (Parts III and IV) and in Appendices 3 and 4 we examine the ideology of planning as a theory. But an ideology should also be looked on as a fact — as an aspect of the social reality from which policies emerge that, in their turn, influence actual development. Like other social facts it has to be ascertained, and also to be explained in terms of its origins and its spread and influence, that is, in causal terms. It is a guiding principle of this book that in studying underdevelopment, development, and planning for development in South Asia, the ideologies must be counted among the social facts.

We shall find that in these countries, policies develop in the context of totally different ideologies from those in the Western countries in their early stages of development. In this introductory chapter we shall start our analysis by considering the general ideology of planning for development because it holds a central position among the modernization ideals.[1] In Chapters 16–19 we shall then study how other ideological elements, the ideas of equality, socialism, and democracy, have been integrated into the ideology of planning. In regard to all these ideological elements, we are interested in their conceptual content, in their rationale from the point of view of our main value premises — broadly, the modernization ideals — in the causes of their spread as a result both of domestic conditions and influences from abroad, and in the relationships between them, causally as well as "theoretically." We are interested also in how the ideals expressed in ideologies compare with actual conditions in the South Asian countries and, even more, with the development of those conditions; and in the role of ideologies in the determination of policies.

As the field of study so outlined is immense, our analysis will have to concern itself with only the essential and common features and will often be focussed mainly on India, where the ideological discussion is fuller and carried on in more explicit terms. Even there we shall be interested only in the main line of thinking and not take into account diversity of ideologies.

[1] Chapter 2, Section 4.

Chapter 15

SPREAD AND IMPACT
OF THE IDEOLOGY
OF PLANNING

1   *An Interventionist and Rationalist Approach*

The basic principle in the ideology of economic planning is that the state shall take an active, indeed the decisive, role in the economy: by its own acts of investment and enterprise, and by its various controls — inducements and restrictions — over the private sector, the state shall initiate, spur, and steer economic development. These public policy measures shall be rationally coordinated, and the coordination be made explicit in an over-all plan for a specified number of years ahead.

The whole complex ideology of planning, in all its manifestations, is thus essentially rationalist in approach and interventionist in conclusions. It is committed to the belief that development can be brought about or accelerated by government intervention. Economic conditions, in particular, need not remain as they are or evolve under the influence merely of "natural forces." Instead, it is felt that these conditions and their evolution should be under state control so that the economic system can be moved in a desired direction by means of intentionally planned and rationally coordinated state policies.[1] The strategy for these policies would emerge as a set of practical inferences from rational analysis of the facts in a country's situation and the positing of certain development goals.[2] All those in the South Asian region who urge state economic planning agree, in principle, that it should benefit the common people, concentrate on raising the levels of living of the poorest strata in the nation, and express the will of the nation as a whole. These and some other ingredients of the modern planning ideology as it is propounded in the region are separately considered in Chapters 16–19. In the present chapter, we shall be concerned with the more technical aspect of the planning ideology: its demand for coordination of policies by means of a plan.

This interventionist and rationalist idea of state economic planning represented the more of a break with the past as the South Asian countries — outside the foreign enclaves — were, and are, so largely stagnant, with most of their people traditional in outlook and inclined to accept things as they are. Its appearance in this Rip Van Winkle world, among people still drowsy with the slumber of centuries, makes the challenge of state economic planning all the more dramatic.

Once the possibility of change by means of rationally coordinated state actions is accepted, many, indeed most, social and political conditions in these countries begin to appear undesirable and in need of reform.[3] As the modernization ideology spreads, changes in almost every respect beyond the purely "economic" come to be regarded as themselves desirable goals for policy. It will seem necessary, for example, to improve levels of nutrition, housing, health, education, and general culture; to break up the rigidities of social stratification; to equalize opportunities and increase social mobility; to make local and sectional community organization more effective; to extend and intensify participation by the people in such communities as well as in the national community; and to base that participation on more rational considerations of their true interest. State policies that aim at improvements such as these in "non-economic" conditions have, in addition to their independent value, an instrumental value since the same conditions that are regarded as undesirable in themselves also act as obstacles and inhibitions to economic development; changes in them are therefore means for attaining economic development. Causa-

[1] "Planning consists of integrating and having an over-all view of the general conditions and then trying to progress all along the line, given certain priorities." (Jawaharlal Nehru in a speech before the Economic Planning Conference, New Delhi, 1950.)

[2] "But, there is no doubt that if economic and social problems are analysed objectively and assessed in terms of certain well-defined criteria, a course of action best calculated to produce the desired results could be mapped out. Society is no longer content passively to evolve; it wants to develop. Planning is thus purposive adaptation of resources to social ends." (India, Government of, Planning Commission, *The First Five Year Plan, A Draft Outline,* New Delhi, 1951, p. 8.)

[3] The points made in the remainder of this section are developed technically and in greater detail in Parts II and III of Appendix 2.

tion is circular: not only would improvement in these conditions make possible, or speed up, economic development, but the engendering of economic development would tend to improve these other, non-economic conditions.[1]

In this way *planning becomes the intellectual matrix of the entire modernization ideology.*[2] And the demand for national development comes to encompass all strivings for political, social, and economic reform. In the public discussion it is now taken for granted that many, or indeed all, of those undesirable conditions that together constitute underdevelopment do not exist independently of each other, but are interdependent.[3] Economic development is thus understood to be a "human" problem.[4] This is, of course, the view taken by social scientists whenever they leave narrow and technical economic questions and deal with planning as an integral whole. Development plans often explicitly define planning as a comprehensive attempt to reform all unsatisfactory conditions.[5] This view is reflected also in the broad goals and ambitions of most of the plans, which go beyond economic policies in the narrow meaning.[6]

Various kinds of biases get in the way of this broader vision. These biases are discussed in the Prologue and in Appendices 2, 3, and 4,

---

[1] A model of circular causation with cumulative effects, implied in this approach, is sketched in Part II of Appendix 2.

[2] Chapter 2, Section 4.

[3] "The inter-relationship between many aspects of the development of human resources can be readily demonstrated. When vast numbers of the population are undernourished, ill-clad, illiterate, sick, under-employed and poor, the energies of the people are necessarily at a low ebb. One deficiency leads to another in an endless cycle of contagion. Economic and human aspects of the Plan programmes are also interdependent. Productivity is affected by conditions of health, education, and welfare among the workers and their families. The success of health measures, in turn, is partly contingent upon improvements in housing and public sanitation and in levels of literacy and understanding among the people. . . . The emphasis on literacy, and the relative weighting of technical and cultural components at the various levels of education, must be related to the need for better productivity and incentives for higher living standards among various groups of the community." (Pakistan, Government of, Planning Commission, *Second Five Year Plan (1960–65)*, Karachi, June, 1960, pp. 329–30.)

[4] "Finally, national planning in India is based on a coordinated approach to economic and social problems. 'The problem is not merely one of developing resources in a narrow technical sense but of improving the quality of human life and of building up an institutional framework adequate to the wider ends in view. . . .'" (Baljit Singh, "Institutional Approach to Planning," in Baljit Singh, ed., *Frontiers of Social Science*, Macmillan, London, [no date], p. 369.)

[5] "Development . . . touches all aspects of community life and has to be viewed comprehensively. Economic planning thus extends itself into extra-economic spheres, educational, social and cultural." (India, Government of, Planning Commission, *Second Five-Year Plan*, New Delhi, 1956, p. 1.)

[6] "Any program of national economic development must cover the social and political spheres as well as the economic." (Philippines, Government of the, National Economic Council, *The Five-Year Economic and Social Development Program for FY 1957–1961*, Manila, January, 1957, mimeographed, p. 9.)

and we shall return to them later in many connections; their general effect is to turn interest away from levels of living, attitudes, and institutions. This particular line of criticism will not be pursued in the present chapter. We shall instead talk of "economic" development as if it embraced the whole purpose of planning.

2 Another Difference in Initial Situation

In South Asia as elsewhere, this interventionist and rationalist approach to economic development, which views it as a proper concern of the state and a matter for planning, originated within the small intellectual elite of the educated class. Through many mechanisms, and with transformations and dilutions, the view then spread horizontally among the educated class, and gradually something of it percolated down to broader strata. The liberation movements, the flush of elation at the time of winning independence, and thereafter the processes of politics and administration in the states and their subdivisions were vehicles of this sideways and downward transit. Superficially at least, the planning ideology now rules supreme in the South Asian countries. It provides the terms of reference of much of the public discussion of their social and economic issues — in the literature and press of these as of all other countries participating in that discussion, in the pronouncements of political and intellectual leaders, in the deliberations of political assemblies and other organized, official or non-official, gatherings, and in the propaganda of all, or nearly all, political parties. These nations, or those individuals in them who are at all articulate, are in various degrees becoming "plan-conscious," and this is commonly asserted to be a good thing — with qualifications that will be discussed later.

Leaving aside for the moment the question of shades and gradations, already the appearance in underdeveloped countries of the demand for economic development and still more the assumption that it is the concern of the state to engender development by means of planning is a new event in history, so far as the non-Communist world is concerned. Were there no other differences in initial conditions, this ideological commitment alone would make it inappropriate to assume that the countries in South Asia will follow a course of development similar to that of the Western world. The industrial revolution in the Western countries did not — and, more important when we discuss ideologies, was never thought to — come about as a result of state planning in the modern sense. More specifically, economic development was never given the same prominence as a principal goal for state policy. Insofar as economic development was conceived of explicitly as something that was happening or ought to happen, it was understood to be a process initiated and continually spurred on by the individual and dispersed activities of a large number of entrepreneurs, each seeking his own profit. New techniques were continually applied, as they came into existence through invention and improvement, as a consequence of competition among these entrepreneurs. When new techniques were imported from abroad, as happened often in the countries that started to industrialize later, this was also supposed to depend on the initiative of the entrepreneurs and to be done at their own responsibility and risk. And the imported techniques were usually not radically different from those they replaced. As an explanation of the industrial revolution in the West, this conception of the process of development is, of course, a vast simplification — an "ideal type" in Max Weber's terminology. But it has a core of truth relevant to our present comparison between the initial conditions in the South Asian countries today and the Western countries then. The ideological and political milieu of economic development in the latter was that of the liberal interlude between Mercantilism and the modern welfare state. It is true that there was a considerable amount of state intervention, particularly in those countries that arrived later at their industrial revolutions, that is, the countries in northwestern and central Europe and in the New World.[1] But for the most part, this intervention was limited to miscellaneous *ad hoc*, and even provisional, policy measures, and, in any case, was not programmatically encompassed in a comprehensive state plan for economic development in the modern sense. It was never given that form and motivation.[2]

The difference in initial conditions introduced by the political idea of state economic planning is, potentially at least, of considerable significance. It is, as already pointed out, a further addition to the catalogue of differences in material and other conditions for economic development, itemized in the previous chapter, between the underdeveloped countries

[1] Pre-industrial development in Europe occurred within a framework of close state regulation that occasionally deserves to be described as statism. Liberalism brought general freedom of enterprise, but regulations and restrictions on foreign trade and on the exportation of technological know-how and skills lingered on well into the industrial age. The direct contributions by the state were also considerable, however. Thus the German states organized and protected cartels, and, there as elsewhere, the building of railroads and public utilities was undertaken by public authorities. Even in the United States, where such investments were largely left in private hands, they could not have come about without extensive state intervention.

The liberal conception of economic growth has colored the writing of much economic history, and the inclination has often been to assume that all state intervention was misguided and retarding. In recent decades, however, there has been a general awakening to the crucial role that governments played in the process of industrialization.

[2] In Japan, state intervention played a larger role in the early phase of industrialization than in northwestern Europe or the New World. A large portion of capital formation and industrialization was directly undertaken by the state, which functioned in a highly centralized and authoritarian manner. But not even there was the transformation of the economy dressed in anything like the ideology of planning that prevails in South Asia at the present time.

in South Asia today and the Western countries when they entered upon a phase of rapid economic progress.

Only a few of the South Asian countries have made really serious attempts to bring their economic life under the discipline of economic planning; and even in these the scope and effectiveness of coordinated state controls is not great. But the idea of planning represents an attitude, rather commonly shared by both governments and their opposition, about how state policies ought to be viewed. Even when there is little actual planning, and still less implementation, the ideology of planning serves as a rationalization for interventionist practices. No government in South Asia operates under the ideological assumption that it should stay out of economic life, giving free play to the forces in the market, and that interference is *per se* regrettable. Rather, every government wants to be able to claim large-scale state intervention as an accomplishment of planning for economic development, even when the planning and coordination have been very deficient. Every advance in the economy is presented as a result of successful planning. At the same time, the planning ideology gives a rationale for austerity and makes it more possible for the government to explain why living conditions are not improving or are not improving more rapidly. The appeal for sacrifices can also be used to cover up development slower than that promised, almost regardless of whether this is due to adverse circumstances or deficiencies of planning. Such deficiencies will be pointed out in political discussion in terms of the need for more perfect planning. The planning ideology thus tends to provide the terms of reference in every controversy over public policy.

There is also a difference in the general international setting in which the governments of South Asia operate. For today no other governments, either in the Western or, of course, the Communist world, abstain, or even pretend that they mean to abstain, from intervention in economic life so as to engender and steer development. Leaving the Communist countries apart for the moment, the rich Western countries — which represent our main point of comparison in this as in the foregoing chapters — have all gone a long way indeed toward state planning, and in its course have equipped themselves with appropriate ideological tenets. But the impulses toward economic planning in the Western countries stem from their present life, not from an ideological tradition of policies that determined their early development. In state planning for economic development, the South Asian countries may not be so very different — at least in intent — from the Western countries today; but this similarity, so far as it exists, is precisely what represents a difference in initial conditions. And while some Western countries play down what economic planning they have, and try to convince themselves that theirs is a "free economy," the South Asian countries tend to play it up, and pretend that their planning amounts to much more than it does. They have accepted planning as an idea even before they are able to translate much planning into reality.[1]

3   The Reasons for Economic Planning

Since the idea of economic planning is essentially a rationalist idea, an attempt to spell out the general reasons for planning in the South Asian countries has its place at this stage of the argument. These reasons become causes for its spread, insofar as people are motivated rationally.

The need for economic development — though not necessarily for engendering it by means of state planning — is, in itself, a rational inference from the realization of the abject poverty in these countries. The further idea that large-scale state intervention, coordinated in a plan, is needed to bring about economic development follows as an inference from the realization that these countries have long remained in a state of relative stagnation, while the Western world has for many generations developed rapidly. A strong, induced impetus is needed to end that stagnation and bring about economic progress, which apparently is not coming spontaneously, or at least not rapidly enough.[2] This argument is strengthened by closer study of the actual conditions for development. In the last chapter we surveyed the differences in initial conditions between the South Asian countries today and the rich Western countries when they were in a more or less comparable situation of economic underdevelopment and, one after another, entered upon an era of rapid development. We found that these differences are fundamental and mostly of such a nature as to make development much more difficult for the countries in South Asia. Generally, they alone make it unlikely that these countries will develop in the Western pattern. Indeed, they make it unlikely that many of these countries will develop at all unless the new element, state planning, is vigorously applied.[3] Moreover, in the climate of independence,

---

[1] Sections 7 and 9.

[2] "For let us be clear on one point: if the pattern of individual preferences was such as to produce economic growth, we would have it now. The present situation in underdeveloped countries is the result of *somebody's* decisions. And no government can launch economic growth where it does not exist without 'interfering in the market' in a sense quite different from the intervention involved in the nostrums of welfare economics. We have seen that launching a take-off is not merely 'patching the market.' Even raising the ratio of effective savings and investment to national income to finance a 'minimum effort' involves an element of intervention; it would not occur through market forces alone." (Benjamin Higgins, *Economic Development*, W. W. Norton Co., New York, 1959, p. 435.)

[3] "One thing seemed clear. Without a system of comprehensive State planning these countries could not emerge out of their economic backwardness." (K. M. Panikkar,

the demand is not only for development but for rapid development. When Prime Minister Nehru opened the 1956 session of the Economic Commission for Asia and the Far East, he declared: "We are not going to spend the next hundred years in arriving gradually, step by step, at that stage of development which the developed countries have reached today. Our pace and tempo of progress has to be much faster."[1]

The population trends strongly increase the urgency of effective state planning to spur economic development. In Part I of Chapter 28, which is devoted to a study of the economic effects of these population trends, it will be seen that throughout the region the rapid and accelerating population growth tends to lower incomes per head, levels of living, labor input and efficiency, and productivity. It generally makes rapid economic development more difficult and thus less likely to occur spontaneously. If the rate of population growth were not so rapid and were not expected to rise steeply in the near future, there would be less need to feel hurried. Indeed, if an Asian country had a stationary population, the need for planning would be considerably less urgent, even in the poorest countries, India and Pakistan. The realization after the new censuses that population increase is rapidly accelerating and has already reached a very much higher rate than was foreseen only a few years ago, gives much more force to the rational reasons for comprehensive planning.

Several of the other differences in initial conditions discussed in Chapter 14 push the state toward taking more responsibility for economic development, and call for state intervention that should be rationally planned and coordinated. The radical difference in regard to international capital movements works in this direction. Even though most of the loans in colonial times went to governments or needed their guaranty, they came

<hr />

The Afro-Asian States and Their Problems, Allen & Unwin Ltd., London, 1959, p. 45.)

As we shall discuss below, the South Asian intellectuals find support for this conclusion both from the Soviet and the Western world.

"In the socialist countries and in the countries following a national revolutionary pattern we plan economic development, because economic development would not, under historic conditions existent, take place by itself automatically. Consequently it must be planned." (Oskar Lange, *Economic Development, Planning and International Cooperation,* Central Bank of Egypt, Cairo, 1961, p. 10.)

[1] Jawaharlal Nehru, Prime Minister of India, *Address* at opening of 1956 session of the Economic Commission for Asia and the Far East, Bangalore, February, 1956.

Around the same time the Indian Planning Commission held that "for India the next few years are the crucial years. India's social stability, its future as a democracy, its freedom as a nation depend upon the speed with which, in the next five and ten years, it pushes the pace of its social and economic growth." (India, Government of, Planning Commission, *The New India — Progress Through Democracy,* Macmillan, New York, 1958, p. 3.)

The then prime minister of Burma, U Nu, addressing a gathering of American businessmen, stated in the same spirit: " 'We have been in a hurry. . . . We have waited for a long time and we feel we must accomplish a great deal in a short time.' " (Quoted in Hugh Tinker, *The Union of Burma,* 2nd ed., Oxford University Press, London, 1959, p. 382, f.n. 2.)

from the private capital market. Now the larger part of the capital inflow that is needed for development has to be negotiated with other governments or with intergovernmental organizations. Capital grants, and even most of the loans, are not acquired on a strictly commercial basis. Different from the private investors of earlier times, the lenders now want to see large-scale "projects" that are part of a development plan. Even when the capital inflow finances private investment, indigenous or foreign, the government of the recipient country becomes deeply involved as the authority sponsoring a plan. As capital inflow from abroad can never be more than supplementary, there also remains the difficult problem of how to squeeze and twist consumption so as to provide for development. The recognition that this is necessary in order to speed development implies again a need for planned state intervention on a large scale.

In regard to foreign trade, the fact that the export outlook for most of these countries is bleak means that, instead of a rising demand for exports aiding the early stages of industrialization as in most Western countries, exports must be pushed by systematic government action. Whatever effect such a state-directed export drive may reasonably be expected to have, these countries will, in the main, have to create space for industrialization by keeping out, again through state intervention, imports for which production at home can substitute. The actual circumstances press them thus to frame their policies toward nationally planned economies with much more self-sufficiency and autarky.

It was also noted in the last chapter that in various ways modern technology shows an inherent tendency to draw the state into large investments and into economic enterprise. Thus once a government has decided on economic development, there appears a great need for overhead investments in transportation, power plants, and irrigation. They must be undertaken by the state because they are too big for private enterprise and would not be profitable except under conditions not usually acceptable to the governments. Various industrial undertakings can be expected to produce large external economies that do not add to the profits of the individual enterprises. Moreover, the need for research and for training of workers and specialists on all levels cannot be expected to be filled by industrial entrepreneurs. Even for a large private enterprise, it would imply bearing overhead costs not only for the enterprise itself but also for the economy as a whole. This widens the field where the state finds reason to become involved.

All these reasons for state intervention, and consequently for state planning, are present in any economy, but they are, of course, much more important in an underdeveloped country bent on rapid economic development. To the list must be added: the relative lack of entrepreneurial talent and training in the private sector; the disinclination of most of those who are wealthy to risk their funds in productive investment and their preference for speculation, quick profit, and conspicuous consumption and investment; and, finally, the tendency in underdeveloped countries for any large-scale enterprises to acquire an extraordinary degree of monopoly or oligopoly. For these reasons, which vary in strength among the several South Asian countries, the state will either find cause to make the industrial starts itself or else to regulate and control the entrepreneurial activities in order to obtain the most rapid development in the desired directions. This is what Edward S. Mason refers to when, in writing about planning in the region, he says that "government dominated almost by default."[1]

Attempts to realize in any substantial measure the ideals of social and economic equality and welfare, which are declared policy goals in all the South Asian countries, would also necessitate large-scale state intervention. In poor countries especially, such policies need to be integrated with all other measures in a general plan, both to be effective and to spur rather than endanger economic development. We shall come back to these problems in later chapters. Here it is sufficient to say that many of the inherited inequalities and rigidities are adverse to economic development and need to be mitigated by coordinated state policies if development is to be achieved. At every stage, planning can also be expected to have some educational effect. To prepare a plan, publish it widely, and have it discussed should force people to think rationally in terms of means and ends. All the leaders in South Asia know that development requires fundamental changes in people's attitudes toward life and work and that the grip of traditionalism must be broken.

The argument for state planning, which we have tried to spell out from the viewpoint of the conditions, the problems, and the interests of the people in South Asian countries themselves, is strongest for India and Pakistan, the poorest and most populous nations. Ceylon has a higher average income, but the population increase is so rapid and the spontaneous forces for industrialization — outside the plantations, where possibilities of expansion are limited — so weak, that even there the case for planning is very strong. Countries like the Federation of Malaya, the Philippines, and Thailand[2] perhaps have the potential for a more spontaneous development, somewhat similar to the historical Western type. But the rapid population increase can be expected to bring even these less poverty-stricken countries to the point at which large-scale planning becomes necessary. Particularly the Federation of Malaya would seem,

---

[1] Edward S. Mason, *Economic Planning in Underdeveloped Areas: Government and Business,* Fordham University Press, New York, 1958, p. 57.

[2] As a matter of fact, Thailand has had much state interference, though very little state planning, in consequence of its peculiar authoritarian structure and a general desire to hold down Chinese influence in the country; see Chapter 9, Section 13, and Chapter 17, Section 14.

however, to have relatively good prospects for development of the semi-spontaneous type: income levels are much higher; natural resources are still abundant in relation to the size of the population, though it is growing rapidly; export possibilities appear brighter; and the large Chinese population provides industrial enterprise to an extent that is exceptional in the region.[1] Provided Malaya could preserve a measure of internal unity and political stability, it might consequently have greater possibilities than other South Asian countries of continual economic development without a high degree of state planning, at least in the near future.

Successful economic planning, with all its implications of conditioning and directing economic life — and, indeed, the prior ability to reach operational agreements — requires a stable and effective, internally united government, conditions of law and order, social discipline, and, more generally, national consolidation. Even spontaneous, or nearly spontaneous, economic development, given the other necessary conditions, is hardly possible without a considerable measure of political stability. Economic planning needs even more. But, after some time, the rationale of economic planning also contains the idea that planning itself is a principal means of reaching a higher level of national consolidation: first, because it will create a new institutional structure to articulate government policies; secondly, because the result, when planning is successful, will be higher economic levels, greater opportunities for the people, and a symbol of national achievement. Also, when planning brings people from different social strata into the dynamic processes of social and economic advance, their sense of involvement and allegiance to the new nation-state should be strengthened.

The formulation of a national plan should, then, in itself, enhance the feeling of nationhood. On the other hand, a government without the cohesion and effectiveness to frame and carry out a policy for economic development will thereby tend to perpetuate, and perhaps increase, that lack of national consolidation which was, in the first place, the cause for its failure to plan. In this way planning comes to demarcate the difference between two kinds of cumulative processes: a virtuous and a vicious one. There is a threshold to pass and planning for development has to overcome and compensate for inertia and for forces working against it.[2] To

---

[1] The last factor is probably not the least important. Ceylon, which is similar in so many other respects, has not had, and has not now, the same amount of private enterprise on all levels as Malaya has, thanks to the many enterprising Chinese there. T. H. Silcock even makes the extravagant assertion that "Malaya suffers from an excess rather than a deficiency of enterprise." (T. H. Silcock, *The Commonwealth Economy in Southeast Asia*, Duke University Press, Durham, N.C., 1959, p. 128; compare his *The Economy of Malaya*, rev. ed., Donald Moore, Singapore, 1956, p. 44.) He has to be understood to mean that ideally the overflowing enterprise should be differently directed.

[2] Appendix 2, Sections 9–11 and 18.

start planning for economic development and to persevere in the effort
are recognized as important objectives in themselves, testifying to the
strength of government and also — in the normal case — actually strengthening the government. This political relation between planning and national consolidation is undoubtedly part of the planning rationale. And
the consequences of circular causation with cumulative effects, favoring
the more successful while frustrating the weaker and less fortunate, stand
out plainly in the differences in achieved development planning between
South Asian countries on different levels of national consolidation.

4 The Causes of the Spread of the Planning Ideology

This attempt to sketch in abstract terms the rationale of the strivings
for state planning of economic development in South Asia does not, of
course, explain the actual emergence and spread of this ideology. In
reality these nations, or their leaders, did not simply form a clear picture
of their situation and draw the logical conclusion that they needed state
planning to overcome their difficulties and develop as rapidly as possible.
The spread of the idea of planning for economic development has a much
more complicated causation.

To begin with, knowledge about the true conditions in these countries
is not only incomplete, even among their leaders, but also biased in an
optimistic direction. Most public officials have shielded themselves from
realistic awareness of the serious implications of the population trends.
Almost everywhere, there has been a consistent tendency even to minimize the rate of population growth, usually by a delay in taking notice
of newer estimates. In India, almost up to the publication of the preliminary results of the new (1961) census, it was still common to refer
to a yearly increase of population of four to five million, though the rate
of increase was about twice that amount.[1] Even now when the very rapid
population increase is accepted as an abstract fact, its serious implications
are seldom considered and all sorts of false ideas are entertained as protection against the truth.[2] A similar tendency to understate or to try to
evade can be observed in regard to most other adverse circumstances.

---

[1] The *Hindustan Times* of December 12, 1959 reported a speech of the Indian
President, at the opening of the World Agricultural Fair in New Delhi the preceding
day, in which he referred to "the rapidly expanding population" and said that "we
are adding to this population at the rate of something like 4 to 5 million every year."
  Similar rates were being cited by students of India: "India's population, which is
increasing at the rate of five million a year, constitutes an oppressively major problem." (Frank Moraes, *India Today*, Macmillan, N.Y., 1960, p. 184.) ". . . the population rises every year by over 4½ million." (D. K. Rangnekar, *Poverty and Capital
Development in India*, Oxford University Press, London, 1958, p. 4.)

[2] Chapter 28, Section 13 *et passim*.

This is so in India as elsewhere in South Asia even though information about social and economic conditions flows more freely there and the level of scientific analysis of social and economic problems is, generally, much higher. The inhibitions and obstacles to raising production posed by attitudes, institutions, and low living levels, particularly in regard to nutrition, health, and educational facilities, which should rationally motivate much more incisive remedial policies, are generally kept somewhat outside the main focus of the plans; and the application of Western models in terms of employment, savings, investment, and output is helpful for rationalizing this common bias.[1]

Furthermore, those who think, speak, and act for the new nations — politicians, planners, administrators, professionals, industrialists, and businessmen — are only a minute upper stratum in the total population. Forming a rather secluded circle and living fairly comfortably, they must be inclined to protect themselves by a system of illusions in whose preservation they have a vested interest. Some of them have been educated in the Western countries; even when not, their education has been under the strong influence of ideas and styles of thought uniquely relevant to conditions in the Western world. Consciously or unconsciously, they want to deal with their own countries' problems in terms as similar as possible to those of the countries by whose culture they are so deeply influenced. This is usually true also of those who are radical nationalists and take a less friendly attitude toward the West. Together, these tendencies often give a wistful note of make-believe to the public discussion of domestic problems and the whole intellectual debate.

But when all this is noted, the fact remains that the practical difficulties confronting the leaders of these nations are so different and in many ways so much greater than those the Western nations are or ever were faced with, that in the end they tend to come out with a different appreciation of their situation and with different conclusions in regard to policy. One such general conclusion, which embraces many others, tends to be the necessity of economic planning. In this way the logical reasons for state planning enumerated in the last section come to function as causes.

<hr/>

[1] Prologue, Section 6; Appendix 2, Sections 19–21; Appendix 4, Sections 1 and 2.

The errors in all estimates in the plans thus acquire a systematic optimistic bias. It is occasionally argued that, given South Asian conditions, greater optimism than the facts warrant is almost a precondition for working effectively and undespairingly. It also serves a political purpose — to get the governments committed to a bigger push.

A prominent Indian economist who supported the high targets of the Second Five Year Plan explained to the writer that he had been fully aware of its unrealistic assumptions in regard to the rate of population growth and many other things and had lent his support in order to push the government into difficulties that it could not overcome except by taking more vigorous action. In Chapter 27, Section 1, we report the confession by the chairman of the Pakistan Planning Board that when producing the First Five Year Plan he deliberately underestimated the population growth, because "Hope builds while knowledge destroys."

From its beginnings, the idea of state planning for economic development was an element of the "new nationalism."[1] This gave the idea of
planning an emotional momentum that it would never have obtained
merely as a rational conclusion from knowledge of the facts. In all these
countries, on the eve of emancipation from colonial domination the idea
of state planning tended to merge with the fight for independence, though
to a very different extent: much less, for instance, in Jinnah's Muslim
League than in Gandhi's and Nehru's National Congress.[2] In the nationalist setting, the ideology of planning expressed the protest against the particular brand of *"laissez faire"* that was natural to the colonial regimes.[3]
The idea of state planning for national development tended thus to become a symbol of how independence, once it was won, should be used
for the benefit of the nation. How the planning idea then became a main
bridge to join nationalism with social and democratic ideals will be discussed in the following chapters.

One particular nexus with nationalist ideologies should, perhaps, be
mentioned here. In the preceding section we stressed that, in most South
Asian countries — given their economic structure, especially their trading
position and the difficulties of increasing their exports substantially within
the foreseeable future — import substitution is almost the only way to
economic development and, in particular, to industrialization. Import
substitution is already a dominant consideration in the policies of India
and Pakistan and it will increasingly affect Ceylon and the other South
Asian countries, with the possible exception of Malaya. Since autarky
needs to be planned, the foreign trade outlook becomes one of the rational
reasons for planning, as we have said. In addition, we must now note
that on the psychological and ideological level, self-sufficiency tends to
have a much more positive value connotation in South Asia than in the
Western world. This is true particularly of India, but holds also, in varying
degree, for the other countries of the region. In South Asia, foreign trade
was almost entirely dominated by foreigners and was naturally associated
with colonialism. The importation of cheap manufactured goods was also
seen to be a main cause of the deterioration in indigenous crafts and thus
of impoverishment, especially in the rural areas. To develop animosity
to the use of imported goods and a preference for indigenous fabrics and,
occasionally, to organize a boycott against imports were prominent tactics
in India's fight for liberation under Gandhi's leadership.[4] The Western

[1] Chapter 3, Section 9, and Appendix 9.

[2] Chapter 6, Section 2, and Chapters 7 and 8 *passim*.

[3] Chapter 17, Section 1 *et passim*.

[4] Usually Gandhi's autarkic views are presented in relation to specific issues, but
sometimes he gives a general formulation: "Therefore, real planning consisted in the
best utilization of the whole man-power of India and the distribution of the raw
products of India in her numerous villages instead of sending them outside and re-
buying finished articles at fabulous prices." (*Harijan,* March 23, 1947, p. 79.)

countries as well always have had elements of a similar autarkic ideology, operating as motivations for protectionist policies in favor not only of agriculture but also of many industries. Mercantilist ideology still survives in the urge to keep down imports, as is symbolized by the characterization as "favorable" of a trading balance that gives a country an export surplus. But in modern times this preference for autarky on nationalist grounds has never been so strong in any of the Western countries, not even Germany and the United States during their industrial revolution. We are here discussing a relation on the psychological and ideological level, and thus not on the level of rational reasons but pertinent to the causes of the spread of the ideology of planning. How in the South Asian countries, in their special trading position, the traditionalist ideology of self-sufficiency, strengthened during the fight for liberation from colonialism, works to influence the modernization ideology and, in particular, planning in regard to industrialization will be explained in full in our more substantial discussion of problems of planning in the next part of the book.[1]

We should next observe that political independence forced the leaders of the liberated countries to frame, and begin to implement, policies to serve their national interests. No longer would a metropolitan power make decisions for them. Alternatives were thrown open. They could not escape from formulating national policy goals and explaining by what policy means they intended to reach them. They had to plan. The impact of this necessity was demonstrated by the fact that everything, including the broadest issues, was debated. The long introductions to many of the planning documents testify to this need of clarifying principles. While in the Western countries agreement on practical policy measures is often facilitated by keeping silent about the implicit general value premises, we find in all the South Asian countries an intense interest in arguing, and making explicit, fundamental goals for society. They want to link them with actual policies. Since those goals were high-pitched (as all general goals are apt to be when they are formulated), and conditions were clearly miserable by the standard of their own goals and in comparison with the rich countries that provided the norms for the participants in this grand debate, the practical conclusion that pressed for expression was the need for great changes. Such changes could not be expected to come about by the people's own initiative, and therefore had to be induced from above, by coordinated state policies. Independence offered new opportunities, and

---

[1] A more general point may be made in this connection. Gandhi's influence on Indian planning has been to make the planners more conscious of the need to encompass in planning much more than "economic" factors. He saw development as a process comprehending the entire social system, and in this respect, therefore, his influence has been toward what we called the element of rationalism in planning. As, however, he relied entirely on moral suasion and the voluntary undertaking of greater social responsibilities by individuals, modern planning in terms of state intervention represents a sharp deviation from Gandhi's teaching.

in the beginning the leaders generally underestimated the difficulties they would meet in implementing policies. But the need to discuss general issues and principles worked forcibly in favor of the spread of the planning ideology.

The fact that, as a legacy from colonial times, the South Asian countries, and particularly India, Pakistan, and Ceylon, were better endowed with competent administrators than with entrepreneurs was an additional cause — and partly a reason — why it was natural to rely more on state policies than on private initiative for attaining economic development. The disdain of the majority of the educated class for private businesses and business-men worked in the same direction. Large-scale private enterprise and capitalism were associated with colonial domination and imperialism. It is true that the administration also was a legacy from foreign rule, but it had been rapidly taken over, "nationalized" under the government, while private business for the larger part had not. In the Southeast Asian countries, most of the industry and trade that was not carried on by Europeans was in the hands of the Chinese or Indians, who also were the moneylenders.

Beyond doubt, the ideology of planning contained an element of resent-ment against private, especially foreign, business; this resentment was a force for its rapid spread, particularly among the intellectuals. For reasons we shall discuss later,[1] the purge of foreign or other private business did not go very far in most South Asian countries; but antagonism to it was an emotional attribute of the general planning ideology and remains so today, even when public declarations and policies seem friendly enough. This antagonism gives ground, for instance, to the suspicions, particularly in America, that India is "socialist" in more than verbal formulas and "anti-Western." And since the emotional charge is always present and may intensify, the suspicion might have a rational basis, however grossly inappropriate it is to present conditions and policies.

Even in this very condensed exposition of the factors causing the spread of the planning ideology, one must include the inclinations and patterns of paternalism and authoritarianism carried over from colonial and pre-colonial times. They helped to give the idea of state planning easy entrance and were conducive to its popular dissemination and acceptance. In a poor and backward country submissiveness to authority is often combined with sullen dissatisfaction, resistance, and general lack of discipline. This malaise was skillfully utilized in the fight for liberation, particularly under Gandhi in India. But these negative traits are only seemingly a contradic-tion to the basic trait of authoritarianism. For mixed with the suspicion and bickering, and, indeed, affording them their motivation, is an extraor-

[1] Chapter 17.

dinary optimism about what state functionaries can do, and a feeling that it is up to them to organize things for the people. The inherited dependence on authority, and the attitudes arising from it, are a tremendous impediment to local self-government and cooperation. But they are at the same time among the factors that made the lower layers of the population at least submissive to the planning ideology.

Corresponding to the submissiveness of the masses of people is the willingness to give direction and command among the upper echelons of administrators, political manipulators at various levels, and experts employed in preparing the plans. In South Asia, as everywhere in the world although more so, administrators — and, on the whole, politicians and experts — if they are at all awake to the need for changes, are naturally inclined to be "planners" of a sort in their own sphere of competence. This inclination was frustrated in colonial times by the prevalent *laissez faire* attitude of the foreign rule and its preoccupation with merely preserving law and order. Much of that "habit of negation," as an Indian scholar once described it, lingered on and still characterizes the national administrations to a considerable degree. But when after independence administrators began to think of national development, it seemed natural to conceive of a state that planned for development, and of themselves as the planners for the people. Undoubtedly the fact that so many of the educated class in South Asia belong to this group, or take their systems of valuations from it (plus the corresponding weakness of an entrepreneurial class), contributed to the easy rise of the planning ideology to its present dominance. The custom of management even came to condition the approach of industrialists and businessmen when they were brought into negotiations with politicians and the government authorities. In India, especially, the big entrepreneurs were early participants in planning.[1] The idea of planning thereby tended to become more of an operational principle than a deeply felt social and economic urge; but the facts of mass poverty and the blatant need for economic development continually work to preserve its emotional charge.

Once planning has become a going concern, this will in many ways tend to strengthen its hold in a country, as we shall note in Section 8. There will then be pride in having a plan and an urge to take it seriously. The Indians soon became aware that their plans were praised abroad — both in the West and in the Communist countries — and that the other countries in South Asia were less successful in planning than they.

[1] See Sections 7 and 8 below.
The Bombay Plan of 1944 was prepared by a group of industrialists and economists. It planned to double income per head in fifteen years and envisaged an increase of 130 percent in agriculture, 500 percent in industry, and 200 percent in services. (Cf. Nabagopol Das, *The Public Sector in India*, 2nd ed., Asia Publishing House, London, 1961, p. 5.)

5   Influences from Abroad

So far we have dealt with causal factors originating within these countries themselves. But from the beginning the ideological influences from abroad have, of course, been paramount. The rationalism that is inherent in the planning ideology and makes it, on the practical plane of state policies, the main container of the whole modernization ideology has been the cumulative result of generations of Western education and Western contacts, ordinarily channelled through the cultures of the metropolitan countries. In more specific terms, the ideology of state economic planning has then converged on the peoples in the region from all sides, first from the Communist countries and later from the West.

That the ideological influences from the Communist world have been strong is quite apparent. Very generally, but particularly in India, Burma, and Indonesia, the intellectual and political leaders had received strong impulses from the Russian revolution and from the writings of the Russian Communists and Western leftist socialists. This is true, incidentally, even of many leaders of the new, anti-socialist Swatantra Party in India, the first organized party to take a stand in principle against planning. Among the pioneers, the idea of state planning for economic development had definitely a radical — socialist, usually "Marxist"[1] — motivation. The five-year

---

[1] "Marxism" is a most confused concept and will not be used as a technical term in this book.

Marx was not a planner, and his ideology in its more undiluted forms was not a planning ideology. (See Gunnar Myrdal, *Beyond the Welfare State,* Yale University Press, New Haven, 1960, pp. 4ff. See also Appendix 2, Section 20.) As one of the great classics, Marx has probably had a greater influence on Western "bourgeois" economists than on their colleagues in the Communist countries, as the former are concerned with a society more like the one Marx was studying and do not propound comprehensive and central state planning.

For the planning ideology in South Asia as it actually developed, however, Marx's thoughtways had a sort of general importance, both because of their stress on the economic factors and their awareness of the social forces and the general interdependence in the entire social system, and also because of the emotional load. Lenin's theory of imperialism as a late phase of capitalism has had a greater and more specific influence on the doctrines implied in South Asian ideologies. (See below Chapter 17, Section 1 *et passim.*)

It is true, however, that Marx loosely assumed a new organization of society after the bourgeois state was liquidated, when there would be a rational order, developing naturally and democratically once exploitation of labor was ended. Engels was more explicit and even used the term "planning," but he remained still on a very abstract level: "Darwin did not know what a bitter satire he wrote on mankind, and especially on his countrymen, when he showed that free competition, the struggle for existence, which the economists celebrate as the highest historical achievement, is the normal state of the animal kingdom. Only conscious organisation of social production, in which production and distribution are carried on in a planned way, can lift mankind above the rest of the animal world as regards the social aspect, in the same way that production in general has done this for mankind in the specifically biological aspect. Historical evolution makes such an organisation daily more indispensable, but also with every day more possible. From it will date a new epoch in history, in which mankind itself, and with mankind all branches of its activity, and particularly natural

plans of the Soviet Union were recognized as the pioneering attempt of an underdeveloped country to engender economic development by state planning,[1] and have been a decisive influence, which has not spent its force. This influence is being reinforced by Communist planning elsewhere. China's emergence as an independent Communist country that has put its stake in comprehensive state planning has been a potent influence in the same direction, particularly in India and the other neutralist countries.[2] The notion, supported by the West, of a race between Communist planning and "democratic planning" could only strengthen the impact of the idea that planning is necessary. There is a lively realization that China is an Asian country, trying to master problems similar to those of South Asia.[3]

But planning has also gradually spread and manifested itself in the coordination of public policies in the Western countries, which have all become welfare states.[4] As scanned by the Asian intellectuals, who naturally sought all that might be relevant to the circumstances of their own countries, the Western progression toward planning and, even more, the discussion about coordination of public policies had influences not altogether different from those emanating from the Communist world, at least with respect to the general idea of the desirability and usefulness of state planning. The Asian intellectuals' close association with and dependence on the radicals in the metropolitan countries, who were usually ardent planners, have been pointed out in other chapters of this book.

These two streams of ideological impulses were represented in the intellectuals' application to their own development problems of policies

---

science, will experience an advance that will put everything preceding it in the deepest shade." (Friedrich Engels, *Dialectics of Nature*, Foreign Languages Publishing House, Moscow, 1954, p. 49.)

[1] "The Russian experiment in planning had shown the way, and one of the major influences in nationalist thinking in the period before the war in India was the achievement of the successive five year plans in the Soviet Union which had converted the semi-colonial economy of Czarist Russia into one of the leading industrial nations of the world." (Panikkar, *The Afro-Asian States and Their Problems*, p. 45.)

[2] "An added urgency was given to this problem by the revolutionary changes in China. Though China's own industrial planning came a few years later, the Communist Government in China forced the problem of economic betterment on the new nationalist States of Asia. It became clear that unless radical changes were brought about in the economic conditions prevailing in these States and the living standards of the masses were greatly improved it would be difficult to avoid the danger of the Communist ideas spreading among the people. Planned economic development became, therefore, not a distant ideal but an immediate necessity." (*Ibid.*, p. 46.) Cf. Rangnekar, *Poverty and Capital Development in India*, p. 258.

[3] China's more recent economic difficulties and the border conflict with India have hardly weakened the trust in planning as such, and certainly not in India; the border conflict was commonly cited as a reason for strengthening planning. If and when China again makes progress, it will not only be a force in support of planning in the region but will probably influence its direction and means as well.

[4] Myrdal, *Beyond the Welfare State*, Part I. See Section 9 below.

and theories from the Soviet Union and the West that were usually not concerned primarily with these problems. In the post-war period, Western authors, including an ever larger number of economists, turned their attention increasingly to the development problems of South Asia. In the present context, the important point about this growing literature on South Asia's problems is that, on the whole, it has strengthened the hold of the ideology of state planning in the countries of the region. In spite of the tendencies toward bias, to which we have referred,[1] few serious students have been able to escape the conclusion that very little takes care of itself in most of the countries in the region. The rationale of planning, as stated in Section 3, is strong. This conclusion is unavoidable because there is an obvious paucity of self-propelled initiatives and private enterprise, both in industry and agriculture; a weak entrepreneurial middle class of the kind that played such a prominent role in Western development; and many other social and economic conditions adverse to development. Although the full consequences are by no means always accepted when advice is given on particular issues, it has now, on a general level, become something of a *consensus sapientium* that the countries in the region — especially the poorest and most populous, in which prolonged social and economic stagnation has fortified the impediments to economic development — will have to rely on the state for initiative, investment, enterprise, direction, and over-all planning.[2]

Today the ideology of state planning is also supported by pressures from intergovernmental organizations, governments, and even private business abroad. That credits and technical assistance to build up new enterprise from the Soviet Union and other Communist countries have worked in that direction is not surprising, given the donors' ideological commitments and the institutional structure of their agencies for economic and financial international relations. But in the West as well private capital is no longer on tap, and the governments and intergovernmental organizations that now furnish the bulk of the credits and grants naturally deal with South Asian governments, who usually also negotiate whatever private direct investment there is. As already indicated, both private business and governments in the West, when dealing with the South Asian governments, are interested in the existence of an over-all plan into which the special projects are fitted and which can render it more likely that they will not fail. Quite apart from, and often contradicting, their ideological preferences at home, all Western governments as well as their business people are supporters of state planning in South Asia. Where planning has lagged, as in Ceylon, Burma, and Thailand, the International Bank has been prepared to send experts to help formulate a plan. Throughout the region, the intergovernmental organizations, governments, private foundations, and universities have supplied personnel for planning. As

[1] Prologue, Sections 3–6; Appendix 2 *passim*.

[2] For exceptions to this statement see Appendix 2, Section 19.

these countries become increasingly dependent on foreign grants, loans, and, to an extent, foreign enterprise, it is only to be expected that this pressure for state planning, exerted in strange unison from both the Communist and the Western spheres, will be strengthened.

6   Counterforces

There are, however, factors in the social and political situation of the South Asian countries that have been adverse to acceptance of the planning ideology. One would expect that a fundamental inhibition would stem from adherence to traditional valuations in a largely stagnant society. But among the educated class and, in particular, the intellectual elite, this inhibition seems to be of minor importance. Even a modicum of Westernization has apparently made people ready to accept, in principle, the rationalist and interventionist idea that development can and should be spurred and guided by policy measures. This ideology is flexible enough to permit, according to one's inclination, an anti-Western or an anti-Communist slant or a mixture of both, as we shall find in the following chapters when we discuss the politically more substantive elements of the planning ideology. Moreover, when ideas that are felt to belong to the inherited culture are intellectualized, they are easily adjusted to fit the modernization ideals.[1] On the ideological level there has, in fact, been astonishingly little articulate resistance to planning as such, though of course plenty against the particular policies in the plans and their implementation or lack of implementation.

It may, nevertheless, be the case that preoccupation with traditional ideals, particularly those of a religious and social character, somehow decreases the eagerness to induce change intentionally, which is the essence of the planning ideology. We know very little about this. We know still less about the spread of the planning ideology, and the basic recognition of the need for development, among the masses. In popular and scientific discussion, both in South Asia and in the Western countries — and, of course, in the Communist world — it is fairly common to speak and write as if these masses had suddenly woken from centuries of slumber and begun rationally to demand rapid development in order to improve their miserable lives.[2] The expression "the revolution of rising expecta-

---

[1] Chapter 3, Section 2.

[2] The following passage is an example chosen at random (italics have been added): "Planning for economic development goals has a strong hold on the imagination of *people* and government in India. The economic plans which were so highly publicized in the years just preceding Independence were expressive of rising *popular* expectations, of the revolution of demand for rapid economic development." (Merrill R. Goodall, "Organization of Administrative Leadership in the Five Year Plans," in Richard L. Park and Irene Tinker, eds., *Leadership and Political Institutions in India*, Princeton University Press, Princeton, N.J., 1959, p. 314.)

tions" is indicative of this apperception of social reality in South Asia. This view represents a rather complete misunderstanding of conditions in a stagnant society. Apparently it is seriously held by South Asia's political leaders, however. Political parties are eager to play up planning in the party programs before elections, even though, when it comes to the contest for votes, propaganda at the local level turns to quite different issues.

More generally, the inclination to preach planning and the entire gamut of modernization ideals to the masses is certainly in part motivated by a desire to educate them and to spur them to act in their own interest. It also represents, however, a rationalization by those who are much better off about how people living in utter poverty and deprivation should feel. The great social and psychological distance of the elite from the masses causes them to impute to the masses attitudes they themselves might have if they were forced to live under similar conditions. That Western observers of the South Asian scene do the same is very apparent. This detachment from reality is evident, for instance, in the initial high hopes attached, both in South Asia and in the West, to the effects of community development and other efforts to change rapidly and radically the villagers' whole outlook and their way of living and working. As experience shows, these expectations were exaggerated.

What we see in all the South Asian countries — though in different degrees and configurations — is a small intellectual elite that has imbibed planning ideology and modernization ideals and is trying to disseminate these concepts among the masses. To the extent that this effort is not entirely fruitless, an important question is what transformation the planning ideology undergoes in its spread. We have already noted that the inclinations and patterns of paternalism and authoritarianism carried over from pre-colonial and colonial times facilitate mass acceptance of the planning ideology. At the same time they must be assumed to influence its content. The masses are led to expect or demand that the government do more for them, without showing greater readiness to change their own ways. This does not help the cause of development, as planning in a stagnant and poor society aims at getting people to rationalize their attitudes and, in particular, to work harder and more purposively to improve their own lot. We shall say more about these problems in Chapter 18.

The spread of the planning ideology in the South Asian countries is, of course, also influenced by the extent to which that ideology actually is translated into policy. To these problems we now turn.

7 Economic Planning in Practice

As we would expect from the summary of the reasons for planning in Section 3, there is in fact a good correlation between the impact of the ideology of planning and a country's relative degree of poverty and lack of spontaneous development. In India, and subsequently in Pakistan, the very low income levels plus the weakness, in the large agricultural sector, of self-generating forces for development made the political leaders more conscious of the need for planning efforts. In the Federation of Malaya, the Philippines, and Thailand, on the other hand, the more favorable conditions mentioned in Section 3 made it natural for the political leaders to place greater trust in market forces. As for actual accomplishments in the field of planning, there is — as we should expect — an equally strong, or perhaps even stronger, correlation with the degree of national consolidation and unified, effective government. These determine both the amount of public interest that can be given to economic planning and the possibilities for effective action. A plan is essentially a political program that requires a sequence of clear-cut political decisions.[1]

These two correlations conflict to some extent, but not entirely. Despite its poverty, India has gone further toward consolidation and effective government than any other country in the region. In Pakistan, serious planning began with the ascendency of the military regime, which, at least for a time, imposed more direction and discipline on the country.[2] The fact that efforts to plan have been so unsuccessful in Burma and Indonesia is clearly related to the insurrections and the continuous struggle to maintain unity and effective government in these states. In Ceylon, the absence of much development outside the plantation sector and the growing population pressure — especially in the rice districts — make planning a pressing need in spite of the higher levels of income, but the debilities of the political process have so far been an obvious hindrance.

A third correlation is with the supply of expert personnel needed both for planning and execution, and with the relative prevalence of a rationalist milieu, created by Westernized intellectuals. In these respects as well, India is in the lead, although Ceylon, the Philippines, and the Federation of Malaya (particularly when taken together with Singapore) do not lag far behind. The lower level of public discussion of planning in Burma and Indonesia — so bound by traditional inhibitions, often clad in odd nationalist and religious slogans and generally more emotional — cannot be explained only in terms of political difficulties. More accurately, these difficulties have been much increased by the dearth of highly educated, rationalist individuals with long experience of participation in colonial government and administration or with professional competence, and by the excessive number of leaders with training chiefly as plotters, schemers, agitators, and fighters.

In fact, planning can be considered a going concern only in India and

[1] See Appendix 2, Section 15.
[2] Chapter 8, Section 7.

Pakistan at the present time. As an ideology, however, it everywhere has a hold over the articulate upper stratum, gives form and direction to public discussion, and has led to the establishment of governmental planning agencies. These agencies have all published plans that show a major effort to survey conditions and outline policies for development. The plans have been used as a guide and reference, and it may be that its inclusion in a plan contributes to the eventual realization of a given project. But outside of India and Pakistan — and the Philippines and Malaya, where planning is less far-reaching — there have been few commitments on the part of governments to carry out any plans, and these few have seldom been acted on. Sometimes the plans have been too fanciful; sometimes administrators, managers, experts, and skilled workers have not been available; sometimes exigencies such as a sudden deterioration in the terms of trade, or an internal rebellion, have halted action. Often, inaction can be laid to a combination of these causes. In their absence, or alongside them, responsibility for unfulfilled plans may lie with rivalries between parties or ministers.[1]

It is indicative of the foregoing that only in India and more recently in Pakistan have there been serious and regular attempts to check on plan fulfillment by evaluation reports.[2] Even in India, plan fulfillment has

[1] A plan that for these and other reasons remains a castle in the air may *for the same reasons* be quite beautiful from a formal point of view, while a plan that is really a government program and means something for the development of policy in a country may have less attraction to the plan and model addicts. Edward S. Mason notes about Pakistan's First Five Year Plan: "No leading political figure has espoused the cause of economic development in Pakistan, and no political party has made the promotion of development a central objective in its program. The importance of the political element in central economic planning is well illustrated by the difference in the character of the development programs in India and Pakistan." (Edward S. Mason, *Economic Planning in Underdeveloped Areas: Government and Business*, Fordham University Press, New York, 1958, p. 70.) Later (p. 78) he makes the reflection: "The lack of political support, already mentioned, for *any* development program in Pakistan allowed the technical personnel of the Planning Board a somewhat freer hand than their counterparts in the Indian Planning Commission appear to have had. Political intervention came later, in the implementation of the Plan."

The designers of Ceylon's Ten Year Plan enjoyed during the work an even greater disinterest on the part of the — shifting — governments of the time. This is not unrelated to the fact that from a formal point of view it is one of the most accomplished planning documents produced in the region. Cf. Appendix 2, Section 15.

[2] Mason, after a survey of the planning efforts in the region, concludes: "In a number of Asian countries . . . it is unnecessary to ask how good is the advice because there is little discernible relation between what is contained in the x year plan and what in fact gets done." (*Ibid.*, p. 61.)

The secretariat of the Economic Commission for Asia and the Far East observed: "In Indonesia, for example, because of the Government's preoccupation with the maintenance of political stability and security, the First Five-Year Plan was reduced to sheer administrative exercises. It would not be of much sense to compare the targets of a totally inoperative plan with what actually happened. Judging from the status of the plan, perhaps only China's mainland, India and Japan, and to some lesser extent, Burma and Pakistan, can serve as good causes for an appraisal of achievements."

(*Footnote continued on following page*)

regularly fallen short of the targets for public investments in basic facilities and in industry. As for the dispersed and less calculable public efforts in agriculture, rural uplift, and education, the distance between plans and accomplishments is even wider. The relevant chapters in the Indian plans often have an abstract and unrealistic tone of academic propaganda, as does the public discussion.[1] To an extent the failure of plan fulfillment is often hidden by discussion couched in terms of aggregate financial magnitudes like investment and the rise in national output, while of course planning concerns the coordination of policy measures and the proportions within the aggregates. It is not to be denied, however, that in India, as in no other country of the region save Pakistan in later years, planning has become an important part of the national political life. It is true, as one observer puts it, that "In India the Plan is the focus of public life, a tenet of national faith."[2]

This is in part due to India's relatively long familiarity with planning endeavors. Several plans were produced before independence, and the colonial government was for a short time, between 1944 and 1946, even induced to set up a Department of Planning and Development.[3] Since independence, three Five Year Plans have been worked out and put into effect and a fourth is in preparation. In each case, a strong effort has been made to involve the public in the preliminary discussions. And the plans have been taken seriously, even though the targets have often not been met. Ultimately, the greater acceptance of planning and its increased relevance to actual policies in India reflected India's possession of a larger and more accomplished group of intellectuals and the relatively firm, centralized leadership of the Indian National Congress and the Congress Party, particularly in the early days of independence. Beyond doubt the more intense identification with the planning ideology in India has been among the important causes of the advance of actual planning. But

---

(United Nations, ECAFE, *Economic Bulletin for Asia and the Far East,* XII, No. 3, December, 1961, p. 18.)

[1] One observer comments: "Talking with officials in the Ministry of Education we had the impression of enthusiasm, feverish activity, and farreaching plans. It seemed that all programs were being overhauled in order to bring them closer to life and reshape them in the spirit of Indian tradition. The new programs were designed to raise the children to a higher level of physical, intellectual, moral, and aesthetic development, to stimulate harmonious growth of all their abilities. These plans were as inspiring as the people who developed them, believed in them, and were eager to implement them. Yet there was something unreal about them. Talking with Indian educators and reading their pamphlets, reports, and memoranda, I could not help thinking of the rural schools which we had visited shortly before." (W. S. Woytinsky, *India: The Awakening Giant,* Harper & Bros., New York, 1957, p. 131.) See Chapter 33.

[2] *Ibid.,* p. 56.

[3] About the precursors in pre-independence times to the five-year plans in India, see A. H. Hanson, *The Process of Planning: A Study of India's Five-Year Plans 1950–1964,* Oxford University Press, London, 1966, pp. 27ff.

it is equally certain that this political development has strengthened the hold of the planning ideology. Planning became a going concern with a momentum of its own when, in India and, later, in Pakistan, the idea of planning became firmly established in economic and political life.

8   Planning as a Going Concern

When that happens, it implies a number of things. Planning has then created new institutions and, more important, has changed and molded the existing ones to serve its progress. An ever larger part of the articulate upper stratum of the nation has been acquiring vested interests in planning. With growing effectiveness the planning ideology sets the frame of reference in every controversy over public policy.

The effect of planning on the institutional structure, its tendency to create vested interests, and its influence on people's ways of thinking and acting impinge first on the officialdom around the government. Indeed, the entire government becomes involved and begins to operate as part of a huge planning machinery. Preparing, arguing, and implementing the plan become their main function, and increasingly all government policies are presented from the perspective of the plan. Official publicity organs begin to popularize the idea of planning as a general principle and, even more important, to present all the particular policy efforts of the government as an outgrowth of planning. Planning then involves a growing number of people — not only through the implementation of government policies and their public discussion and the elections, if they are held, of parliament and other representative bodies, but also through people's participation in institutions beneath the government level. Planning will itself be a force in building and strengthening that institutional infrastructure.

Planning must continually reconcile competing interests and determine precedence among them. This is, of course, true already for the variety of interests within the government itself, operating within and beneath every ministry and for the bigger arena where multiple interests are represented by the several ministries and by the state governments. Where planning is a going concern, these interests must be argued within the context of the national plan. But planning and the resolution of interest conflicts must extend beneath the level of government: geographically, to districts and localities, and sectionally, to different economic pursuits. The idea of planning implies that all economic and many other types of activity in a country should be coordinated; it is by this coordination that the plan is produced and put into effect.

The political and institutional structure in all countries of South Asia permits only a limited degree of coordination by means of central government command. That degree should be higher under an authoritarian regime, as in Pakistan, but in this particular respect the difference must not be exaggerated. So long as a measure of autonomy for states, provinces, and municipalities is preserved, and, more important still, so long as production and trade have not been collectivized and brought under direct control of the central government, the regular mode of operation in preparing a plan and implementing it becomes essentially that of negotiation with all sorts of collective organizations beneath the central government, implying consultation and persuasion, bargaining and cooperation. In these negotiations the government should have the upper hand and be able, to an extent, to induce these other collective organizations to fall in line with its purposes. It can exert authority — which means much in countries with a legacy of authoritarianism from pre-colonial and colonial times — by playing off interests against each other, and by arming itself with the statistics and the research that give force to the proposals. It has also at its disposal a number of levers of control — inducements as well as restrictions — which it can, when necessary, increase. How powerful the central government's upper hand is depends on its political stability and internal unity and the effectiveness of its administration, as well as on the personal factors of leadership and ability. But the central government can use its upper hand to the full only in negotiation.

Planning, when under South Asian conditions it becomes a going concern, consists largely of negotiations by the central government with governments of the constituent states and business interests. It must also try to reach down to the people in the districts and the villages. As planning becomes a going concern and focusses on inducing change throughout the national community, its implementation increases the need for collective institutions that can represent local and sectional interests at those levels. Yet, for various reasons, as we shall see in Chapter 18 where these problems are discussed in more specific terms, it is in the South Asian countries a most difficult task to make provincial and local self-government and cooperation effective. A vast and growing number of officials are needed to persuade people to adjust their life and work in accordance with the plan, and nevertheless the success is only very partial. The problems raised by these attempts at self-government and cooperation are usually discussed in terms of "decentralization" in India, while the authoritarian regime in Pakistan has invented the phrase "basic democracy." Under the conditions prevailing throughout South Asia, no clear distinction can be made between the efforts to induce cooperative organization in agriculture, small-scale industry, crafts, and trade and those to organize political units on the provincial and local levels.

In sum, two points must be stressed at this stage of the argument: when economic planning becomes a going concern it has to face the necessity of "democratic planning" through regional and functional organization; and old, revitalized and remolded, collective institutions as well as newly created ones become extensions of an institutional infrastructure, intended to become the instrument for people's participation in planning and, particularly, the implementation of planning. The huge army of officials employed to accomplish this, and all the non-officials who participate more or less actively in these institutions, have their perspective increasingly dominated by the planning ideology, and they acquire vested interests in its pursuit.

The organized groups in the higher strata of the nation, especially those representing commerce and industry, and individual big enterprises or business complexes, are much more easily involved as participants in economic planning, once it is on the way to becoming a going concern.[1] Their integration therefore is not stressed in the public discussion of "democratic planning." Indeed, these business groups have the strongest reasons to exert influence on policies and their implementation; lobbying for advantages at all stages of the planning process becomes one of the most important parts of the pursuit of business. In the course of India's first three five-year plans, organized participation by business has become ever more effective.

The mode of participation is negotiation — the only alternative to a wholesale nationalization of production and trade. But whereas, in its negotiations with the masses, the government's main interest is to urge their participation in implementing a predetermined plan (which in advance has taken into account not only the national interest but also the presumptive interests of the several groups to whom it is appealing), in dealing with business and, generally, people in the articulate strata, it meets potent negotiating partners. They can influence planning more directly than by simply remaining apathetic. They can, and regularly do, take initiatives, so that the negotiations turn into real bargaining. Given a measure of political unity and determination, the central authorities will retain the lead, for reasons already given. They can pit interests against each other and, through the various controls at their disposal, influence the conditions under which industries and business firms operate.

The end result is a compromise that gives consideration to the organized private business interests. But whatever the outcome, in the process of these consultations and bargainings these interest groups have become a part of the institutional system molded by planning as a going concern. By a continuous widening of the network of participation, the whole

---

[1] "An essential element in the Plan will, therefore, be the creation of suitable machinery for such consultation and collaboration. In the field of organised industry this presents little difficulty." (India, *First Five Year Plan, Draft,* p. 25.)

"The Plan has been formulated after detailed discussions with Central and State Governments and private industries." (*Ibid.,* p. 36.)

structure of political and economic institutions thus becomes involved in the planning process, and thereby strengthened. The multitude of persons involved in this extended planning activity acquire a stake — to earn an income, make a profit, exert influence, and gain prestige, or to widen the opportunity for realizing cherished ideals. This continual increase of persons and institutions with very real vested interests in planning, and the corollary increase in emphasis on planning in all public discussion, again tend to strengthen the hold of the planning ideology.

There always will be opposition to the actual policies pursued, and it will always be nurtured by interests who find themselves slighted in some respect. But more important here is whether the government meets only scattered opposition on specific issues or conflicts with well-consolidated interests, bent on inhibiting its planning activity and therefore deprecatory of the planning ideology itself. Systematic opposition might well be expected from the relatively wealthy groups. In the first place, it is on them that the effects of planning are most likely to impinge through a plethora of direct and discriminatory controls. Secondly, the planning ideology throughout South Asia is committed to the improvement of mass welfare. Greater economic and social equality, including downward levelling, and prevention of the concentration of power are proclaimed aims of public policy. In all the countries of the region the planning ideology has been slanted toward social and economic radicalism.[1] In India, Ceylon, Burma, and Indonesia, "socialism" has been accepted as the frame of the future society, and the relative scope of the public industrial sector is to be increased.[2] It is a fact, however, that almost nowhere has any of this radicalism met with much opposition on the ideological level.

Most of the benefits from these policies do not reach the poor, even if such is the proclaimed aim and motivation. As will be a main theme in the following chapters, the benefits accrue instead to the strata above them. More generally, the policies pursued have nowhere[3] led to greater economic equality and a lessening of concentration of economic power. This reflection of the actual power structure explains why the promise of greater equality need not elicit opposition to planning from the upper strata: what planning there has been in South Asia has generally been to their advantage. Neither has socialism and the planned enlargement of the public sector as yet gone against the interests of big business or any other group above the masses. There has been complaint about the infringements on the freedom of private entrepreneurs by all the controls that have accompanied planning. In Chapter 19 where we shall deal with this problem we shall find, however, that these controls mostly work in

[1] Chapter 16.

[2] Chapter 17.

[3] Except possibly in Ceylon; there, however, planning has never been important, at least until recently; cf. Chapter 9, Part I.

favor of established business, and particularly big business. Even the high
rates of taxation are not as burdensome as they look, because of many
loopholes in the taxation laws and the opportunities for tax evasion.

Against this background it becomes more understandable why businessmen and other inherently conservative strata do not offer more opposition
to equalization, socialism, and the plethora of direct and discriminatory
controls implied in the South Asian version of the planning ideology.
The fact is that these policies either are to their immediate benefit or disturb them little. What opposition there is serves chiefly to keep the government on the alert and warn it against more radical adventures.

9   A Third World of Planning

As has already been mentioned, in the Western countries today there
is a considerable amount of over-all economic planning, though there was
but little when they were in the early stages of development. A rapid
acceleration of the trend toward planning has come only in recent decades.

It has been impelled by major forces and changes that have interacted
and had complex, cumulative effects on state policies. Among these forces
and changes in the Western countries ultimately leading to planning on
a large scale were: the unending sequence of violent international crises
of the last half century, including the two world wars and the Great
Depression in between; the oligopolistic organization of all markets as a
result of both the appearance of large-scale enterprises and the development of associations for the purposes of cooperation, protection, and
collective bargaining among people otherwise competing on the supply
or demand side in the markets; the continued rationalization of people's
attitudes toward their participation in economic life and toward state
authority; and the democratization of the powers of the state. Ordinarily,
public, quasi-public, and private *interferences* with both the institutional
framework of the market and its operations *preceded planning* and, indeed, caused planning by necessitating coordination of these various
interferences to avoid economic disorganization. This statement about the
mechanism of the growth of economic planning in the West and some
further remarks in this section concerning the present character of Western planning will be left as *obiter dicta* in the present context, since the
social and economic analysis that could verify them would take us too far
afield.[1]

Economic planning in the Western countries was thus a *consequence*
of industrialization and the social and economic changes related to the

[1] For what is said in this section, see Myrdal, *Beyond the Welfare State*, Part I.

emergence of a more mature industrial society. In the underdeveloped
countries of South Asia planning is, instead, applied *before,* or at a very
early stage of, industrialization. Furthermore, in South Asia planning, in
principle and in approach, is thought to *precede* organized acts of control
and *interferences* with markets. Planning cannot be left to grow prag-
matically, as in the Western countries, by a "natural" process (however
different from the "natural" economic processes of the classical economists) through cumulative *ad hoc* adjustments caused by gradual compromises between the interest groups in the national community, and
driven forward by the necessity to reach some reasonable coordination
of all the existing private interferences and public policies. Planning in
South Asia is thus not the result of development, but is employed to foster
development. It is envisaged as a *pre-condition* — indeed, is motivated by
the assumption that spontaneous development cannot be expected. The
underdeveloped countries in the region are thus compelled to undertake
what in the light of Western history appears as a short-cut.

Moreover, in all the South Asian countries the *idea* of planning *precedes*
attempts at its *realization.* Planning does not, as in the Western countries,
force itself on a national community through a gradual process of all-
embracing social change, which finally results in a high level of planning
as a *fait accompli,* while the community often still remains largely unwilling to accept planning as an idea. In the West, planning is therefore
unprogrammatic and pragmatic. By the very logic of their situation,
planning in the countries in South Asia becomes *programmatic.* This all
follows as a consequence of the fact that planning is introduced at an
earlier stage of development, and that their conditions for development
demand planning. The logic of their situation also implies that this programmatic planning in principle should be *comprehensive* and *complete,*
not partial and piecemeal as in the Western countries — or rather as comprehensive and complete as their governments can succeed in making it.

In the Communist world, however, programmatic and comprehensive
planning has been used for the very purpose of engendering and directing
economic development from a state of underdevelopment that is sought
by the underdeveloped countries in South Asia.[1] It can be said with a
good deal of truth that what the underdeveloped countries in the region
are attempting, with greater or lesser success, is to use elements of the
Communist techniques for programmatic and comprehensive state planning to promote development, but to avoid some of the conditions under
which these techniques have been put into use in the Communist coun-

---

[1] "Both the socialist and the national revolutionary pattern have one feature in
common. Economic development is not spontaneous as in the classical capitalist pattern but is consciously achieved through planning." (Lange, *Economic Development,
Planning and International Cooperation,* p. 8.)

tries.[1] Thereby their attempts toward planning become different also from the Communist prototype. They are all intent on "democratic planning." Neither where political democracy has been faltering nor even in those countries that have come under a military dictatorship are the leaders prepared to enforce a totalitarian and monolithic regime. And even if they were so disposed, they are not constituted and equipped to impose the fanatical discipline of the Communist system. Aside from these fundamental political inhibitions, there is also a difference in their economic institutions. They have not, like the Communist countries, nationalized production and made state enterprise and collectivism the rule. Nor have they organized their foreign trade and exchange relations in a pattern of state monopoly.[2]

Their economic planning is thus of a third type, different from that of the Communist countries as well as that of the Western world.

[1] "It is a matter for serious consideration how far the techniques of mobilisation of resources utilised by centrally-planned economies can be grafted into schemes of planning in which the public, cooperative and the private sectors function side by side within the national plan. There would appear to be many steps which these countries could take to increase their resources without having to impose excessive strain on the people or to depart from freedom and democratic control." (Tarlok Singh, "Some Problems of Planning in India and South-East Asia," *Indian Year Book of International Affairs, 1957*, Madras, 1957, p. 5.)

[2] E. H. Carr shows that the Soviet Union was "forced" to apply its system of central planning (which was not contained in the doctrine inherited from Marx) because production and trade had been nationalized; see E. H. Carr, *A History of Soviet Russia*, Vol. 6, London, 1960.

See the complete work for Chapters 16-18.

THE MECHANISM OF

UNDERDEVELOPMENT AND

DEVELOPMENT AND A SKETCH OF AN

ELEMENTARY THEORY OF PLANNING

FOR DEVELOPMENT

I
Circular Causation

1 *Purpose and Scope*

This appendix will seek to formulate in simple terms the logic of underdevelopment, development, and planning for development. As in the rest of the book, we shall be concerned only with the region of South Asia. Although many of our arguments will apply also to other underdeveloped countries and regions, and occasionally even to all countries, whether developed or underdeveloped, and touch the foundations of economic analysis, we shall not pursue these wider implications but shall confine our analysis to concepts and causal relationships that could be used for the study of our particular region. Whether the empirical questions we shall raise, the logical criticism to which we shall subject prevalent approaches, and the alternative way of analyzing the problems we shall put forward — in short, whether our "theory"[1] applies to other parts of the world and other branches of economics is a question that lies beyond the scope of this book.

[1] See Preface and Prologue, Section 7.

Part I of this appendix deals with the basic notion of circular causation, which recurs, explicitly and implicitly, in much of the literature. Part II attempts to clarify the social processes of underdevelopment and development by examining certain categories of social conditions and their causal connections.[1] Parts III and IV deal with the theory of planning as an application of the preceding analysis to government action, that is, to conditions in which policies are adopted by public authorities with the specific intention of inducing change in the prevailing social conditions in order to engender and direct development.

A more technical treatment of economic models and their usefulness for planning in South Asia and, in particular, of the use of the concept "capital/ output ratio," elaborating on some ideas here discussed, has been relegated to a separate appendix, 3.

2 The Idea of a "Vicious Circle"

An idea fairly widespread in the recent literature on underdeveloped countries is that the social processes in such countries tend to be dominated by "vicious circles." Thus Ragnar Nurkse refers to the "vicious circle of poverty" and explains:

It [the concept] implies, of course, a circular constellation of forces tending to act and react upon one another in such a way as to keep a poor country in a state of poverty. Particular instances of such circular constellations are not difficult to imagine. For example, a poor man may be weak; being physically weak, his working capacity may be low which means that he is poor, which in turn means that he will not have enough to eat; and so on. A situation of this sort, relating to a country as a whole, can be summed up in the trite proposition: "a country is poor because it is poor."[2]

What Nurkse here describes is a *low-level equilibrium that perpetuates itself* and results in economic stagnation.[3] He assumes that his poor man produces

<hr>

[1] An early attempt to use in a more systematic fashion the idea of circular causation as the basis for a study of underdevelopment and development was made in the writer's *An American Dilemma, The Negro Problem and Modern Democracy,* Harper & Bros., New York, 1944, Chapter 3, Section 7, "The Theory of the Vicious Circle," pp. 75 ff., and Appendix 3, "A Methodological Note on the Principle of Cumulation," pp. 1065 ff., reproduced in *Value in Social Theory, A Selection of Essays on Methodology,* Paul Streeten, ed., Routledge and Kegan Paul, London, 1958. See also Gunnar Myrdal, *Economic Theory and Under-Developed Regions,* Duckworth & Co. Ltd., London, 1957. For a critical note to this earlier attempt by the writer, see below, Section 9, p. 1875, footnote 1.

[2] Ragnar Nurkse, *Problems of Capital Formation in Underdeveloped Countries,* Basil Blackwell, Oxford, 1953, p. 4. Cf. his book *Some Aspects of Capital Accumulation in Underdeveloped Countries,* Oxford University Press, Cairo, 1952.

[3] The idea of a vicious circle in this static sense of forces balancing each other so that the effect is stagnation, is now ubiquitous in the literature on underdeveloped countries. See H. W. Singer, "Economic Progress in Underdeveloped Countries," *Social Research,* Vol. 16, No. 1, March, 1949. The following are random examples:

"The term *vicious circle,* as it applies to the environment in underdeveloped countries, refers to an inextricable interrelationship of cause-and-effect that operates so as to imprison an economy in its own shortcomings. The notion is that a given effect, as evidenced by whatever it is that happens to exist, acts as the cause leading to a substantially similar effect. In essence, the status-quo tends to perpetuate itself — because

only enough food to keep himself in a state of health such as to maintain barely this level of production.

If, however, Nurkse had assumed that his man produced less than this critical amount of food, a *cumulative downward movement* would be established. It is this process that should properly be called a "vicious circle." Nurkse's poor man would become poorer because he is poor.[1]

---

of a process of circular causation." (Walter Krause, *Economic Development*, Wadsworth Publishing Company, San Francisco, 1961, p. 20.)

"The vicious circle operates on both the supply and the demand sides. First, low incomes lead to low levels of savings and investment. The low rate of investment in turn leads to the perpetuation of low incomes and the circle is completed. This is the vicious circle on the supply side. Second, the low rate of investment keeps productivity and incomes low. Therefore, the purchasing power of the people in real terms is low. This leads to a relatively low private marginal productivity of investment. Inducement to invest being low, low incomes are perpetuated. This is the vicious circle on the demand side." (Raja J. Chelliah, *Fiscal Policy in Underdeveloped Countries*, Allen & Unwin Ltd., London, 1960, p. 26.)

"Here, then, is one of the vicious circles so common in any analysis of underdevelopment: underdevelopment yields low agricultural productivity, yields malnutrition, yields low productivity, yields underdevelopment." (Benjamin Higgins, *Economic Development*, W. W. Norton Co., New York, 1959, p. 271.)

"If any attempt is made to lift any part of this mesh of interlocking vicious circles, there is usually such a pull downward that any sustained progress becomes almost impossible." (S. R. Sen, "The Strategy for Agricultural Development," Presidential Address to All India Agricultural Economic Conference, 1959, New Delhi, 1959, p. 3.)

"It is not easy to see how this shortage of entrepreneurs can be overcome. Education can do much, but the best school for businessmen is business itself. It is by operating in the business world that one gets knowledge and ideas about business. Here also we face the familiar vicious circle. No entrepreneurs, therefore no development. No development, therefore no entrepreneurs." (B. B. Das Gupta, "The Theory and Reality of Economic Development," in Philip W. Thayer, ed., *Nationalism and Progress in Free Asia*, Johns Hopkins Press, Baltimore, 1956, p. 172.)

"An underdeveloped area is like a circle compressed by a chain whose main links generally are poverty, overpopulation, ignorance and a static order evolved to fit the requirements of a non-industrialized subsistence culture. To break out of this rigid circle some link of that chain must be broken. Low food intake creates barely sufficient energy to sustain life. Unless a surplus is produced, there is no possibility to accumulate the savings necessary to create more efficient production which in turn would permit an accumulation of savings, neither is there enough to sustain the effort of breaking out of the rigid pattern of social behaviour which is created by, and sustains, the underdeveloped community." (Frank J. Moore, "Some Aspects of Industrialization and Cooperative Development in Underdeveloped Areas," *Indian Economic Review*, Vol. 1, No. 4, August, 1953, p. 1.)

"The utter inadequacy of the facilities [for education] that are being provided, in relation to the needs, is well known. The economic backwardness of the country is responsible, in part, for these deficiencies, but the low level of economic development is itself, in a measure, a result of insufficient and faulty education." (India, Government of, Planning Commission, *The First Five Year Plan — A Draft Outline*, New Delhi, 1951, p. 219.)

[1] This true vicious circle has been less frequently noted in the literature. Nathan Keyfitz gives an illustration of it:

". . . Java is overpopulated and poor; as its population grows further, there is pressure from squatters who need land desperately and who take over the forest reserves. The capacity of the soil to hold water is reduced and some of it is washed away, so the food available is further reduced and pressure to take over more forest increases.

"Other instances are not hard to imagine. Some corruption appears in a country; it

But the process can also be reversed and turned into a "virtuous circle." Nurkse's example would then read: if a poor man is given more to eat, his health improves; since he is physically stronger, his working capacity is greater, which in turn means that he gets more to eat; and so on. The system could, in other words, be thrown out of its low-level equilibrium of economic stagnation and induced to describe a *cumulative upward movement* by improving a worker's productivity. If he is a subsistence farmer, he could be provided with irrigation, fertilizers, better seed, and tools and could be taught improved agricultural techniques. He would produce more and have more to eat; his health would be better, his working capacity further increased, and so on. Soon he would be able to sell some of his increased produce and buy more in the market to improve his production and consumption. Nurkse's proposition would then read: a country is becoming richer because it is less poor and therefore becoming richer.[1]

Stagnation and the tremendous obstacles and inhibitions that thwart an underdeveloped country's attempts to emerge from stagnation and embark on economic development are such important parts of reality that low-level equilibrium is well worth studying. But Nurkse's metaphor explains very little — though it does bring out that there is generally a causal interdependence between the various factors in the social system even outside the so-called "economic factors," and that it is conceivable that the social and economic system remains in equilibrium. The problem is why in certain cases circular causation perpetuates stagnation, or permits only minor and temporary movements around a low-level equilibrium, but in others gives rise to a cumulative process downwards or upwards, that is, a true "vicious" or a "virtuous" spiral. Is the low-level equilibrium of stagnation "normal" in any particular sense? If so, why?

In every social system random changes are, of course, always occurring and we would expect their net effect to be the initiation of a cumulative process

---

gives people the thought that their government may not be stable and that ruin is ahead; this suggests to the individual the advisability of making something for himself while the opportunity lasts; the spread of corruption makes other individuals fear that the time of collapse is coming closer, and a vicious circle sets in which makes collapse inevitable unless some new force enters. Or in the matter of security of the currency: the word gets about that the currency is not safe; people start to buy goods, and prices begin to rise; there is fear of a further rise in prices, and further bidding for goods; the vicious circle of inflation and lack of confidence runs on." (Nathan Keyfitz, "The Interlocking of Social and Economic Factors in Asian Development," *Canadian Journal of Economics and Political Science*, XXV, No. 1, February, 1959, p. 39.)

[1] "Typical examples of such cumulative processes are the following: Capital supply: increased productivity: higher real income: higher capital supply, etc. Higher demand: higher incentive to invest: higher productivity: higher demand, etc. Improvements in the quality of the labour force (literacy, better knowledge, improved health, greater mobility): greater productivity of labour: more resources to improve education, health, mobility, etc.

"Reduced inequality: weakened revolutionary forces: stronger democracy: more concessions to equality, etc. Higher incomes: attraction of skilled men and capital: reduced costs of communal services: lower rates and taxes: higher incomes, etc." (Paul Streeten, *Economic Integration, Aspects and Problems*, 2nd ed., A. W. Sythoff, Leyden, 1961, p. 56.)

in the one direction or the other. If this does not happen, is it because of "thresholds" that prevent circular causation from initiating a cumulative process? If so, what constitutes a threshold? When and how does circular causation pass a threshold or thresholds and initiate cumulative change?

From the point of view of planning, the problem is how to break out of the equilibrium of stagnation and start a cumulative upward process. Nurkse was fully aware of this political and dynamic aspect of the problem of circular causation: "The circular constellation of the stationary system is real enough, but fortunately the circle is not unbreakable. And once it is broken at any point, the very fact that the relation is circular tends to make for cumulative advance. We should perhaps hesitate to call the circle vicious; it can become beneficent."[1]

3   *The Theories of "Stages of Growth"*

The idea of a "virtuous circle" has always been implied in the theories of "stages of growth" – though never systematically demonstrated. We are here concerned with two aspects of these theories: (1) the implied *theory* of circular causation with cumulative effects; (2) the implicit systematic *biases*. The biases operate through the *selection* of strategic *factors* on which interest is focussed and of *assumptions* about their role in historical processes. This selection of strategic factors and of assumptions about their role remains essentially *a priori*, however much illustrative material is amassed. It never is – and, in this teleological approach, it never can be – empirically verified or refuted. A fundamental preconception is, moreover, the *similarity of evolution* in different countries at different historical periods; this is why these theories can be, and are, used for prediction. But similarity depends on the level of abstraction and the choice of features compared. Such comparisons can be refuted only by demonstrating that other principles of selection and comparison are equally possible – and, of course, *ex post* that the predictions do not come true.

The theory that different countries at different times develop in a unidirectional process toward ever "higher" forms of production and society, so that their history and their destiny can be conceived in terms of identifiable "stages," goes back at least two centuries,[2] even if one does not count in the

---

[1] *Problems of Capital Formation in Underdeveloped Countries*, p. 11.

Or, as Harvey Leibenstein expressed it:

"If we continue to think in terms of vicious circles, and it is sometimes a convenient shorthand mode of thinking about the problem, at some point we have to explain how the vicious circle can be broken. It is here that the critical minimum effort idea appears. . . .

"From what has been said, it should be clear that the minimum effort idea is both consistent with the vicious circle notion and at the same time offers a way out. In other words, the only reason the vicious circles appear vicious is because it is so very difficult to find and marshal stimulants to development that are of sufficient magnitude." (*Economic Backwardness and Economic Growth*, John Wiley & Sons, New York, 1957, pp. 96, 98.) Cf. the writer's works cited in footnote 1, p. 1844.

[2] On the history of the doctrines of stages there is a large literature. For two more recent surveys see Edgar Salin, "Unterentwickelte Länder: Begriff und Wirklichkeit," *Kyklos*, Vol. XII, 1959, Fasc. 3, and Bert F. Hoselitz, "Theories of Stages of Economic Growth," in B. F. Hoselitz *et al.*, *Theories of Economic Growth*, Free Press of Glencoe, Ill., 1960, pp. 193–238.

speculations on the development from "the natural state" that were so prevalent in the writings throughout the Enlightenment era and were presented by Adam Smith in amplified form in his *The Wealth of Nations*. It represents a type of philosophizing or theorizing about history of which most historians are suspicious and critical: first, because in adjusting the facts to the theory it does violence to what they know actually happened; and, secondly, because it frequently serves transparent political aims. Historians do, of course, arrange their data by periods for purposes of description and presentation. The criterion of division is the occurrence of a major change in a sequence of events whose direction they are studying. But the demarcation is, in principle, assumed to be empirical; it does not stem from any consciously conceived "philosophy" or "theory" of history. Admittedly, some historians have strayed from this principle. Arnold Toynbee has done so on a monumental scale, and he has been severely censured by his professional colleagues for selecting his voluminous evidence to suit his "philosophical" or "theoretical" thesis. Ironically, the thesis he propounds is itself tautological, and hence neither provable nor refutable.

The grossly arbitrary selections of the "stage" builders convince the historians that their own empirical method is sound and that the "philosophical" or "theoretical" approach is unscientific.[1] So does the fact that the history of historiography demonstrates that, one after another, most of the "stage" theories, after a brief period of popular appeal and excitement, fall into oblivion, while the humbler and less dramatic efforts to establish "what actually happened" continue to increase our stock of historical knowledge. It is the journeyman

[1] This is the essence of Gerschenkron's criticism:

"The regularity [according to which all economies are supposed to pass through the same individual stages as they move along the road of economic progress] may have been frankly presented as an inescapable 'law' of economic development. Alternatively, the element of necessity may have been somewhat disguised by well-meant, even though fairly meaningless, remarks about the choices that were open to society. (See Rostow, *The Stages of Economic Growth*, pp. 118 f.) But all those schemes were dominated by the idea of uniformity. Thus, Rostow was at pains to assert that the process of industrialization repeated itself from country to country lumbering through his pentametric rhythm. Accordingly, Soviet Russia was like everybody else and rather confidently expected in the end to be propelled by the 'Buddenbrooks dynamics' into the fifth stage of 'high mass consumption.' Leaving erroneous literary allusions aside, there is, within a fairly wide margin, nothing wrong in principle with an approach which concentrates upon the interspatial similarities in industrial development. The existence of such similarities is very real. Their study yields attractive simplicities, but it does so at the price of dismissing some refractory facts which a historian will ignore at his own peril.

"There should be a fine on the use of words such as 'necessary' or 'necessity' in historical writings. As one takes a closer look at the concept of necessity as it is appended to prerequisites of industrial development, it becomes clear that, whenever the concept is not entirely destitute of meaning, it is likely to be purely definitional: industrialization is defined in terms of certain conditions which then, by an imperceptible shift of the writer's wrist, are metamorphosed into historical preconditions. (It is not surprising, therefore, to see Rostow at one point (p. 49) mix conditions and preconditions of industrial development very freely.)

"The recourse to tautologies and dexterous manipulations has been produced by, or at any rate served to disguise, very real empirical difficulties." (Alexander Gerschenkron, *Economic Backwardness in Historical Perspective*, Belknap Press of Harvard University Press, Cambridge, 1962, pp. 355, 357.)

craftsman, not the speculator, who to the ordinary historians represents the best tradition of historical research.[1]

Yet, for obvious reasons, the "philosophical" or "theoretical" approach to history appeals to social scientists trying to establish laws of change in society. The method of analysis by "stages" has tempted particularly those who have sought realistic explanations of economic and social processes by employing an institutional approach and drawing lessons from history. Among them have been some of the great geniuses of social and economic speculation like List and Marx, who were also accomplished craftsmen working on historical material. Within the framework of their arid theories of stages of development they have made important and lasting contributions in almost all fields of social and economic thought.[2] Indeed, as Knut Wicksell once pointed out, it is a hallmark

[1] As my colleague Professor Ernst Söderlund, himself an historian, pointed out when reading an early draft of this section, this is not to say that the ordinary "anti-philosophical" historian is free from preconceptions, even if he succeeds in hiding this fact from himself by being naive about the problem of value premises in social research. The view of history that is usually called the "empirical" but which he would prefer to call the "genetic" and that can be said to be the one adhered to by most ordinary historians is focussed on the facts and the inferred relationships between facts that have resulted in a situation, now or in the past. Since, however, the resulting situation is accepted as known and given, since the purpose of research is to demonstrate how it *must* have come about, and since the selection from a large number of equally possible sequences reflects a current interest, a normative element is concealed in the notion of inevitability. The (implicit) end is inherent in and predetermined by the "facts." A double bias pervades this approach, viz., the selection from facts and exclusion of hypothetical facts. Only *some of the facts* are selected to prove the non-purposive achievement of a purpose, and *hypothetical processes* of development, assuming different behavior by one or more actors in the historical drama, are ignored. When historians dismiss as "unhistorical" the question "what would have happened if . . . ?," which comes so naturally to the social scientists, the historical necessity implied in this dismissal is the "must" dictated by a purpose. All facts are contingent. Necessity and inevitability are characteristics of logical deduction, in this case from the "requirements" of the final situation. (Cf. Chapter 5, Sections 2 and 3.)

The anti-theoretical and anti-philosophical bias of many professional historians, especially in Britain, which leads them to suspect any attempt to move from the particular to the general, is thus at bottom a defense of their attempt to remain naive about that element of teleology that is the essence of the "genetic" approach, however empirical the presentation of what has happened. It is akin to a tendency in empirical economics, breaking through now and then, to claim that the researcher has been approaching the facts without any preconceived theory. (See Gunnar Myrdal, *Value in Social Theory*, pp. 232 ff. *et passim.*)

On the European continent and in America, the challenge of social science has more often forced historians to rise above details and reflect on the nature of historical explanation, the role of bias in historical research, and the selection of evidence in relation to interest and the questions asked. There can be no "purely objective" history in the sense of describing "what has actually happened." Ranke's *"wie es eigentlich gewesen"* calls for the impossible. All historical research, like other social research, must begin with questions guided by interest and must select, evaluate, and appraise. But to say that an object looks different from different angles is not the same as saying that the object can take on any shape. Full methodological clarity the historians will not achieve until they, too, recognize the necessity of working with explicit value premises and begin to clarify the role of these in objective research and the basis that should be found for them. See Prologue, Section 9.

[2] This is seldom fully recognized in modern writings, partly through ignorance, just as the origin of theorems is forgotten. But as always, ignorance is opportune (Pro-

of great scholars that, regardless of the approach and method they use —
sometimes despite them — they create new insights.

The multitudinous theories of development stages[1] share some general and
methodological traits worth noting. From an abundance of historical conditions
and events, the theories select and highlight *certain factors* thought to be
significant for development.[2] Secondly, they assume *certain relationships* between changes in those factors and between them and the entire social structure. From a logical point of view, the differences between their doctrines
appear as a consequence of differences in this *selection* of operational *factors*
and their *assumed* relationships. All exponents of this approach are, to some
degree, aware of its arbitrariness and try to protect themselves by numerous
reservations.[3] In fact, they often arrange their illustrations so as to show differences in the historical processes they analyze. But in spite of this insight, and
in clear contradiction to it, all of them are convinced that their analysis in terms
of stages is broadly true of what is empirically known.[4] They are even convinced that their analysis represents a valid *theory* of change in societies —
that is, of development.[5]

logue, Section 6; Chapter 21, Section 7), and this is particularly true in regard to the
non-recognition of the powerful impact of Marx on Western social science. Cf. Prologue, Section 6; and Section 20 below.

[1] The illustrations in footnotes to this and the following paragraphs are chosen from
a recent specimen of this doctrine of stages, W. W. Rostow's *The Stages of Economic
Growth, A Non-Communist Manifesto,* Cambridge University Press, London, 1960. As
we shall see, it reflects in its teleological aspirations what we have called "the modern
approach," to which critical references are made in several contexts in this book. In
particular, it reflects the systematic set of biases in the approach to the problems of
underdeveloped countries discussed in the Prologue. It has the virtue of illustrating
in a compressed and lucid form the methodological traits common to this approach
and brings out clearly the logical compromises and contradictions implicit in it.

[2] In Rostow's words: "We shall be concerned here, then, with certain 'particular
factors of reality' which appear to run through the story of the modern world since
about 1700." (*Ibid.,* p. 1.)

[3] Rostow's work contains the following: "I cannot emphasize too strongly at the outset, that the stages-of-growth are an arbitrary and limited way of looking at the sequence of modern history; and they are, in no absolute sense, a correct way." . . .
"Once again, history is full of variety: . . ." and: "The stages-of-growth analysis does
not pretend to explain all of history: there are factors at work, relating to the onset of
the great wars and power struggles of the twentieth century, which are quite independent of the analysis presented in this book." (*Ibid.,* pp. 1, 53, 118.)

[4] "This book presents an economic historian's way of generalizing the sweep of modern history." . . . "It is possible to identify all societies, in their economic dimensions,
as lying within one of five categories: the traditional society, the preconditions for
take-off, the take-off, the drive to maturity, and the age of high mass-consumption."
(*Ibid.,* pp. 1, 4.)

[5] "The exposition begins with an impressionistic definition of the five major stages-
of-growth and a brief statement of the dynamic *theory* of production which is their
bone-structure."

"These stages are not merely descriptive. They are not merely a way of generalizing
certain factual observations about the sequence of development of modern societies.
They have an inner logic and continuity. They have an analytical bone-structure,
rooted in a dynamic *theory* of production."

"They constitute, in the end, both a *theory* about economic growth and a more gen-

This presentation of the stages of development — from "lower" to "higher" — renders the whole approach teleological. By a teleological approach is meant one in which a purpose, which is not explicitly intended by anyone, is fulfilled while the process of fulfillment is presented as an inevitable sequence of events. Originally, the purpose was explicitly God's purpose unfolding itself in history. But with the growth of rationalism "nature" replaced God, and later such entities as "*Zeitgeist*," "history" itself, "progress," and more specific notions such as the "invisible hand," the "market," "the logic of events," appeared as secularized versions of Providence. Common to these various approaches are three features: *inevitability, unintended purposiveness,* and *implicit valuation* (though not necessarily that of the writer). The suggestion of *inevitability* gives the stream of historical forces a stickiness that reduces greatly the scope for maneuver, both in the past, ruling out hypothetical alternatives, and in the present, ruling out planning. The *unintended purposiveness* introduces terms like "natural progress" and "growth," in which *valuations* are disguised as descriptions, teleology as causality, and reason as nature.

As in Rostow's recent variation on this theme, so in those of List, Marx, and all the other great precursors, behind the reservations lies a doctrine of historical purpose inexorably unfolding itself. Each writer has a different destiny in view; each adjusts his theory and his selections of illustrative material to fit his preconceptions. Policies are allotted their role, positive and negative, together with other impulses and resistances to change. But in the teleological setting, policies are not presented as having been adopted by men and organizations that could have chosen differently. Instead, they are themselves part of "objective" processes that serve the unchosen purpose. Events, policies, and responses serving this purpose are presented as "functions" of certain situations, or as being "in the nature of things," or as "fulfilling certain requirements." What is "inevitable" is not merely what follows from certain causes but also what serves certain ends — though not willed by anyone — and the two are not clearly distinguished. It is as if we "explained" the fact that water is the only substance whose specific weight "must be" lighter when frozen than when liquid by the "fact" that otherwise we could not eat fish at Christmas.

The teleological approach leads to considerable logical confusion. On the one hand, it leads its exponents to regard policies as themselves caused by and emerging from development, or as mere elements in a historical process; on the other hand, the norms hidden in their teleological intentions often lead them to advocate certain policies as being "correct" from the standpoint of these implicit norms.[1] Because of its teleological framework and, more particularly, because of its basic assumption of similarity between development

---

eral, if still highly partial, *theory* about modern history as a whole." (*Ibid.*, pp. 3, 12, 1. Italics added.)

[1] This basic confusion is plainly visible in the works of List and Marx and, of course, Rostow. There are decisions, says Rostow, "that societies have made as the choices open to them have been altered by the unfolding process of economic growth; and these broad collective decisions, *determined* by many factors — deep in history, culture, and the active political process — outside the market-place, have interplayed with the dynamics of market demand, risk-taking, technology and entrepreneurship, to *determine* the specific content of the stages of growth for each society." (*Ibid.*, p. 15. Italics added.) Immediately after this statement, and apparently unaware that he is

processes in different countries[1] at different periods, the whole approach has an inherent tendency to play down the importance of policies,[2] or rather to organize them into the predetermined sequence of events. Even the "bad" policies — "bad" from the standpoint of the norms contained in the selected and assumed telos — are turned into servants of development.[3]

---

shifting his logical basis, Rostow raises a number of plainly normative questions in terms of "How . . . *should* the traditional society react to . . . ?" (Italics added.)

[1] In Rostow's variant also between the Soviet Union and the Western countries. "In its broad shape and timing, then, there is nothing about the Russian sequence of preconditions, take-off and drive to technological maturity that does not fall within the general pattern; although like all other national stories it has unique features, . . ." (*Ibid.*, p. 67; his Chapter 7. "Russian and American Growth," pp. 93 ff.)

[2] There is a *laissez-faire* element inherent in all teleological speculation, in the sense that the teleologician is confident that his scheme will be realized, and that interference with it is futile. According to the theories of stages, development is bound to take its course, predetermined by the teleological doctrine of the author. Marx, like the classical economists, was not a planner, although many popular and some learned writers assume that he was; see Gunnar Myrdal, *Beyond the Welfare State,* Yale University Press, New Haven, 1960, pp. 4 ff. ". . . the non-purposive achievement of a purpose through a natural development, moving towards an end which is inherent in, and predetermined by, the facts as they already exist, is the teleological conception underlying not only Marx's thinking but also the liberal economic doctrines in the classical . . . line. Indeed, Marx, and even more emphatically, Engels, condemned as 'unscientific' the free-wheeling schemes of economic planning embraced by earlier French and English socialists." (*Ibid.*, p. 7.)

Belief in inevitability or in a general pattern of events is incompatible with government planning toward freely chosen goals, yet it may inspire men to intense activity. Since the historical process acts *through* men, motives, organizations, and institutions, not apart from them, the belief in inevitability neither logically nor psychologically implies quietism. To be committed to the future, to speed up events, to acquire a vested interest in the inevitable, are natural reactions, as is shown by Islamic fatalist fanatics, Calvinists with their sense of predestination, and "Marxist" revolutionaries. The notion that the future is on their side gives them strength and courage to act and to force action through organizations, including the state. But, fundamentally, planning along the tracks of history can only speed up the historical process and planning against them is futile.

In the one view historical destiny shapes us, in the other we shape our destiny. In the teleological view, what will happen will happen; in the view of the planners what will happen is open and depends on what we choose to do.

[3] See also Hegel's antithesis, which turns the thesis into a "higher" synthesis, and his notion of the "cunning of reason" by which the worst misery serves the end of progress, the "rose of suffering."

In Rostow's formulation: "Although imperial powers pursued policies which did not always optimize the development of the preconditions for take-off, they *could not avoid* bringing about transformation in thought, knowledge, institutions and the supply of social overhead capital which moved the colonial society along the transitional path . . ." (*Stages of Economic Growth*, p. 27.) This statement is, of course, only a more diplomatic expression of Marx's harsher dictum: "England, it is true, in causing a social revolution in Hindustan, was actuated only by the vilest interests, and was stupid in her manner of enforcing them. But that is not the question. The question is, *can mankind fulfil its destiny* without a fundamental revolution in the social state of Asia? If not, whatever may have been the crimes of England she was the unconscious *tool of history* in bringing about that revolution." (Karl Marx, "The British Rule in India," written in London, June 10, 1853; published in the *New-York Daily Tribune*, No. 3804, June 25, 1853 — as quoted from K. Marx and F. Engels, *The*

The mainspring of Rostow's particular theory of the stages of development
— which has been quoted here because it is the last specimen of the genus
and because, despite the harsh criticism by historians, it has influenced many
politicians and economists and given them a new vocabulary for popular use —
is, of course, the rapid awakening in Western countries after the Second World
War of an intense interest in the development problems of the underdeveloped
countries, the political causes of which were suggested in the Prologue (Section
2). There we also sketched the nature of the specific biases that underlie what
we have called the "modern approach" and distort the views of students in both
Western and underdeveloped countries (Sections 3–6). This modern approach
tends to overlook or minimize the factors that make development so difficult in
the underdeveloped countries or, conversely, that should necessitate radical and
comprehensive policy measures. A teleological doctrine encompassing world history for the last two hundred and fifty years that, behind all its reservations,
assumes a fundamental similarity between different countries at different
periods and a uni-directional course of development toward ever higher stages
thus acts as a *deus ex machina.*

Interest has been primarily focussed on the stage that Rostow has ingeniously
called the "take-off," in analogy to the performance of an airplane that, after
accelerating on the runway, becomes airborne. Leaving aside the intricate
question of what precise meaning this concept can have,[1] a take-off into "self-
sustained" development is what the articulate elites of all underdeveloped countries want their own societies to achieve and what we all hope they will achieve
with the least possible sacrifice. The incorporation of this concept into a teleological doctrine of stages of development makes that prospect seem not only possible but probable, even inevitable. True, Rostow covers himself with the reservation that "it is still too soon to judge either the present Indian or Chinese
Communist take-off efforts successful."[2] But that is not the main drift of his argu-

---

First Indian War of Independence 1857–1859, Foreign Languages Publishing House,
Moscow, 1959. Italics added.) This is, of course, the "invisible hand" of Adam Smith
that, for instance, leads smugglers to perform a useful purpose in enlarging the market
and intensifying the international division of labor.

[1] See below, Section 18.

[2] *Stages of Economic Growth*, p. 38.

S. R. Sen points out: "Moreover, it is important to recognise that any 'take-off'
may not turn out to be a 'sustained take-off.' In fact, take-off may be of various types.
There may be an 'abortive take-off' reminiscent of Baudelaire's albatross. There may
be a 'hauled take-off' comparable to that of a glider which just helps to raise the
economy to a higher level but where further progress is limited. There is again the
'assisted take-off' as in the case of an aeroplane catapulted from an aircraft carrier
where the initial push is only a precursor of far reaching progress in future. Lastly,
there is the 'self-propelled take-off' of the space rocket which once it crosses the gravi-
tational pull will not come back to earth again. It is obvious that the strategy for agricultural development has to be so devised that the take-off is not of the first two types
and is at least of the third type, if not the fourth." ("The Strategy for Agricultural
Development," p. 6.)

"Some of the recent writings inebriated by growth models are too confident that
take-offs always result in soaring flights, forgetting that regions and economies can
'come a cropper.'" (Streeten, *Economic Integration, Aspects and Problems*, p. 60.)

Rostow can express his full agreement with such statements and he can point out
that he has made the same reservation himself.

ment. Thus a little further on in the text he speaks of "the *fact* that the whole southern half of the globe plus China is caught up actively in the stage of pre-conditions for take-off or in the take-off itself" and refers to "their [the under-developed countries'] foreseeable maturity."[1]

The observations made explain why the theory of underdevelopment and development as we conceive it (see Part II of this appendix) cannot employ the old framework of stages of growth. It must be purged of teleology and for-mulated in such a way that the valuations are brought out as explicit value premises.[2]

We must remember that the approach we have criticized contains the no-tion of circular causation, and this is the reason for the remarks above. More-over, insofar as its exponents have used illustrations from history or from con-temporary events, they have been concerned with the causal relationships between changes of conditions in the social system. Thus in the first stage, when society is stagnant, circular causation works to perpetuate the low-level equilibrium, as described in Section 2; this is what is usually, though wrongly, referred to as the "vicious circle." But when the social system starts moving

---

[1] Rostow, *Stages of Economic Growth*, p. 92. Italics added.

"For the central *fact* about the future of world power is the acceleration of the pre-conditions or the beginnings of take-off in the southern half of the world: South-East Asia, the Middle East, Africa, and Latin America. . . . Put more precisely, the take-offs of China and India *have begun*. Pakistan, Egypt, Iraq, Indonesia and other states are likely to be less than a decade behind — or at least not much more, given the acute pressures to modernize now operating on or within their societies." (*Ibid.*, p. 126. Ital-ics added.)

". . . it is *as sure as anything can be* that, barring a global catastrophe, the societies of the underdeveloped areas will move through the transitional processes and establish the preconditions for take-off into economic growth and modernization. And they *will* then continue the process of sustained growth and move on to maturity; that is, to the stage when their societies are so structured that they can bring to bear on their re-sources the full capabilities of modern technology." (Rostow, *The United States in the World Arena*, Harper & Bros., New York, 1960, p. 412. Italics added.) This is the language of the visionary teleologician as surely as was Marx's confident prediction of the proletariat in the industrialized countries "expropriating the expropriators."

Reflecting on the penultimate quotation, David Wightman, in a critical review of Rostow's book written from the historian's point of view, also raises the problem of the practical effects of the teleological doctrine: "To say, as Rostow does, that India is in the take-off stage may be very encouraging to those who are moved by magical phrases. But what if it proves to be wrong? What frustrations and disillusionments might follow? Rostow plays down the obstacles that might impede economic growth. The message derived from historical analysis appears to be that the trick is not too difficult, though it may appear so at the transition stage. This could be dangerous and misleading optimism. There is a tendency for underdeveloped countries to ac-cumulate technique and capital yet repudiate Western values, institutions and forms of government. These non-economic elements in growth are the most difficult to tackle. So they tend to be minimized by economic practitioners and theorists." (Da-vid Wightman, "The Stages of Economic Growth," *Il Politico*, Vol. XXVI, No. 1, Uni-versity of Pavia, 1961, p. 134.) I. M. D. Little makes a similar observation in "A Critical Examination of India's Third Five-Year Plan," *Oxford Economic Papers*, Vol. 14, No. 1, February, 1962.

[2] Prologue, Section 9.

upwards, circular causation engenders a cumulative process: the "virtuous circle." All the explanations of successive stages of development in these teleological speculations contain elements of analyses of just such a cumulative process.

On the one hand, the institutional and historical interests of these writers have tended to make the analysis of circular causation somewhat broader than traditional economic theory. This is one reason why the writings of some of them have had so substantial and healthy an impact on the development of social science. On the other hand, their arbitrary selection of significant factors and their assumptions about the interplay of these — a double bias that is neither made fully explicit nor always guided by their respective teleological intentions — have been detrimental to their research. In this respect, List and Marx delved deeper into the empirical material and tried harder to assimilate it and to clarify their concepts and terminology than did Rostow, whose approach is theoretically less rigorous, conceptually vaguer, and empirically more superficial.

We would emphasize, then, four features of the approach to development in terms of stages of growth:

(1) There is implied a political motivation, though it is concealed in the teleological reasoning of this approach suggesting inevitability, similarity, and powerful historical forces against which "non-historical" action is futile. (Rostow's subtitle, "A Non-Communist Manifesto," removes any lingering doubts on this score, so far as he is concerned.)

(2) This bias is in the direction of *laissez faire*, not in the ordinary sense of a do-nothing philosophy (List and Marx were certainly not adherents of *laissez faire* in this sense), but in the sense that it is considered futile and "unhistorical" for the state or any other group to intervene with the intention of promoting freely chosen objectives. If sufficiently compelling, the stages-of-growth prognosis may itself influence the programs and actions of people, parties, and governments and thereby alter the material analyzed in this prognosis. The logical role of policy remains ambiguous: it is both part of the process analyzed, in which the ends are implicit, and an advocated means to further these ends whenever they are made explicit.

(3) The doctrines cannot — and do not attempt to — "explain" events, least of all temporal or spatial differences in the character of development that do not fit their preconceived pattern.

(4) When challenged on this latter ground the doctrines tend to withdraw into qualifications and reservations that render them tautological and hence, though then foolproof against criticism, empty of empirical meaning.

It is, however, precisely this continual shift from a specious set of propositions to an empty tautology that may strengthen the survival value of this approach. The tautology lends it an air of scientific truth, the speciousness an impression of significance. Thus tautologies take such forms as the proposition that countries grow because they have propensities to grow, where the test of the presence of the propensity is actual growth;[1] or that civilizations flower be-

---

[1] "There are, then, two ways of distinguishing the propensities from the economic decisions to which they relate and of indicating the sense in which they may be regarded themselves as conceptually quantitative. . . . the propensities would define a

cause a suitable challenge meets with a proper response, where the test of the suitability of the challenge is the flowering of the civilization; or that it is the changing sequence of leading sectors that characterizes the stages of growth, where leading sectors are simply those that happen to be ahead of the others; or that industries are bound to grow at a decelerating rate beyond a certain stage, where the definition of industry abstracts from technical progress.[1] Clearly, all such propositions can be given empirical content. But insofar as the theories of the stages of growth contain empirical, and therefore refutable, propositions, they tend to select factors and to analyze their relationships in a manner that often neglects important differences in the experience of different countries at different periods.

It should not be concluded from what has been said that generalizing from empirical research or attempting to discover a common characteristic in the history and experience of different countries at different periods is either undesirable or impossible.[2] Scholars like Simon Kuznets have shown that such

---

relation between the level of real income and allocation of resources to fundamental science, applied science, and consumption. The propensity to apply potential innovations would show the quantitative relation between the level of income and the proportion of potential innovations accepted. With a given population, the propensity to have children would define the relation between changes in income and the number of births." (W. W. Rostow, *The Process of Economic Growth,* 2nd ed., Oxford University Press, London, 1960, p. 33.)

"By an alternative method, which is conceptually more precise but less susceptible of statistical investigation, one might regard the propensities as reflecting, for any short period of time, the response of a society to changes in the yields believed to be associated with the allocation of the resources in various directions. This approach involves certain difficulties." (*Ibid.,* p. 34.)

[1] E.g., Rostow, *Stages of Economic Growth,* p. 13, and *The Process of Economic Growth,* pp. 101 ff.

Whether, for example, the textile industry has followed a decelerating path depends on the definition used: if synthetic fibres are excluded, the proposition is true; if not, it is false. The more we disaggregate (e.g., specific processes of spinning or weaving wool or cotton), the greater becomes the number of decelerating growth paths in a growing economy if there is technical progress, and conversely. The succession: cotton, pig iron, steel, heavy engineering, shows deceleration in each sector, but if we chose clothing, transport, and all forms of engineering, it would not.

[2] ". . . there is, within a fairly wide margin, nothing wrong in principle with an approach which concentrates upon the interspatial similarities in industrial development. The existence of such similarities is very real. Their study yields attractive simplicities, but it does so at the price of dismissing some refractory facts which a historian will ignore at his own peril. Those who see the essence of industrialization in the establishment of a strong and independent manufacturing enterprise need only to look diagonally across the previous tabulation in order to find such an enterprise in existence everywhere — in advanced England as well as in lagging Germany or in very backward Russia. Seen *in latum et in longum* — which are the easy dimensions — Russia is like Germany and Germany is like England. But to say this is to debar oneself from looking into the *depth* of history, that is to say, from perceiving the industrialization in the making. What is the story of Central European industrializations without the role of the banks in the process? What is the Russian industrialization of the 1890s without the Ministry of Finance?

"The point, however, is not simply that these were important occurrences which

generalizations are both possible and valuable. Research into the changing importance of different sectors or the changing distribution of income by size, occupation, and region, or into sectoral savings, investment, capital/output ratios, population trends, urbanization, and so on, forms an essential part of any comparative analysis of development. But such comparisons, precisely because they try to take into account all relevant material, do not overlook differences in initial and subsequent situations or in their causes and effects. They yield no all-embracing explanations; only limited insights.

In Chapter 14 we discuss the differences in initial conditions as between the South Asian countries and the advanced Western countries when they were at a more or less "comparable" level of development. In doing so we make no use of the theory of stages of growth; in fact, the results of our analysis are not compatible with that theory.

4   The Malthusian Theory of Population and Other Models of Circular Causation

The notion of circular causation, discussed in Sections 2 and 3, covers instances in which a change in one condition causes changes in one or several other conditions *in the same direction* from the point of view of development. Thus in the second round the initial change is supported by consequential impulses, which in turn give rise to repercussions, magnifying the initial change. Circular causation thus starts a cumulative process in one direction or the other.

If, instead, an initial change in one condition gives rise to secondary changes going *in the opposite direction,* the cumulative process will be hampered or will even end in the restoration of equilibrium. The classical example of an economic model that postulates self-correcting movements within fairly narrow limits, so that equilibrium is restored, is Malthus' theory of population. Like the stage theorists, Malthus begins with a "propensity" and a "yield." The "propensity" is the "passion between the sexes," which he deems "in every age so nearly the same, that it may always be considered, in algebraic language, as a given quantity."[1] The "yield" is the limited "power of the earth to produce subsistence." It is, of course, well known that Malthus' predictions, which he derived from his model, were mistaken because his assumptions were both inadequate and faulty. In particular he ignored the growth of imports of cheap

---

have just claims on the historian's attention. What matters in the present connection is that observing the individual methods of financing industrial growth helps us to understand the crucial problem of prerequisites for industrial development." (Gerschenkron, *Economic Backwardness in Historical Perspective,* pp. 355–356.)

[1] In its simplest form, the theory assumes constant fertility rates and the tendency of food production to increase less rapidly than population. Anything that has the effect of raising real wages, whether redistribution from the rich to the poor, or a rise in labor productivity due to improved techniques or to an increase in cooperating factors, will tend to decrease mortality and speed up population growth. The resulting increase in the supply of labor will in time reverse the rise in wages and tend to lower them again to the level at which they are just sufficient to cover the cost of reproducing the labor force. Mortality would tend to rise to that rate at which equilibrium between the size of the labor force and the demand for labor is re-established.

food from abroad and underestimated the rapid rise of productivity in both agriculture and industry at home.

Leibenstein has recently formulated more rigorously the Malthusian model[1]
and other constructs. Some of his models are stable like Malthus', higher per
capita income leading to population growth through falling mortality, and
hence to a reduction in incomes. Others are stable within a range but unstable
outside it, because, for example, higher investment, induced by the rise in incomes, outpaces population growth.[2] Others again are unstable throughout.

Leibenstein's various models bring out the fact that the response to an initial impulse may either reinforce or counteract it. We can therefore construct
either Malthusian stable or fluctuating models or models of cumulative growth
or decline or, given certain thresholds, a combination of fluctuations and trends.
If one abstracts from all the other factors on which population growth depends,
everything in these models depends on the population response to income
changes. But income changes are only one of the determinants of population
growth and under South Asian conditions they are insignificant;[3] in any case this
response is only one among a series of forces making for or against stability,
just as the investment response is only one of many responses to an autonomous
rise in per capita incomes.[4] Nor is the *ceteris paribus* assumption justified.

---

[1] "Briefly, the mechanism is as follows: Any event that increases incomes will, at
first, also increase the rate of population growth. This, in turn, implies an increase in
the labor force, and both capital and land per worker are accordingly reduced. Furthermore, this tends to reduce income per capita, which depresses the 'induced' rate
of population growth, if not the actual rate. The end result may be the sort of fluctuations around an equilibrium subsistence income considered previously." (Leibenstein, *Economic Backwardness and Economic Growth*, p. 56.)

"This growth will occur for one of two reasons. Either the growth in incomes will
be transformed into consumption that is conducive to the reduction of mortality rates,
or there may be secular changes that lead to improved knowledge, sanitation, or other
public health measures, that in turn reduce mortality rates. In any event, the consequence of the operation of these forces will be an increase in the population size and,
assuming decreasing returns with respect to increases in labor, a consequent reduction
of per capita income. If the system is stable, the reductions in per capita incomes will
proceed apace until per capita income reaches a 'subsistence equilibrium level.' That
is to say, a level where the economy finds it possible just to replace those resources
that wear out during the period, and just to maintain the population. This, in brief, is a
description of a system that possesses a stable equilibrium with respect to average
income. The system permits the occurrence of outside events the initial effect of which
may be to increase resources per head, but eventually there is a return to the initial
equilibrium per capita income while other magnitudes remain at their expanded level."
(*Ibid.*, p. 20.)

[2] "This implies that unless the original increment in average income is large enough
the system cannot be unstable even under the favorable condition that the income
gain multiplier (M) is larger than the population multiplier (m). Furthermore, this
also implies that a small injection of new capital may fail to improve living conditions
in the long run, while a sufficiently large injection may succeed. Thus, if a program to
increase capital resources cannot be carried out on a sufficiently large scale it may
not be worth while to attempt to carry out such a program at all." (Harvey Leibenstein, *A Theory of Economic-Demographic Development*, Princeton University Press,
Princeton, N.J., 1954, p. 58.)

[3] Chapter 27, Sections 2, 7, 12, *et passim*.

[4] "We could, for example, have considered an X-function and a Z-function where
X represented those forces that were monotonic increasing functions of per capita in-

Neither the forces resisting development nor those reinforcing it are independent of each other. We therefore cannot call any one of them crucial. Since, as we shall see in Part II of this appendix, a series of retarding or reversing forces are related to each other in such a way that the removal of one affects some or all others, the social system does not permit simplification by singling out one crucial force reversing development because several forces interact. Even Leibenstein, who operates with several forces, tends to give principal stress to population responses.[1]

Our discussion of the Malthusian model has brought out the great variety of possibilities of interdependence. A number of forces may interact, each responding in an upward direction to an initial improvement, and yet the initial equilibrium may be stable. Alternatively, there may be forces, acting either independently or in response to the initial changes, that counteract the positive forces and restore equilibrium. The initial equilibrium may be stable, so that small variations will tend to return the system to its initial state, or unstable, so that small changes will move it further and further away. Theoretical models in which small changes give rise to self-correcting movements that restore equilibrium, while changes beyond a critical size lead to cumulative processes, must assume certain thresholds at which the degree of sensitivity changes or at which the strength of the counteracting forces is weakened or reversed. Theories of the "minimum critical effort" and the "big push" tend to be of this type. We shall discuss these theories as they relate to the development problems of South Asian countries in the following parts of this appendix.[2]

I I
Underdevelopment and Development

5 *Categories of Conditions*

We conceive of the situation in each South Asian country — as in any other country — as a *social system*. The system consists of a great number of *condi-*

---

come which, above some income level, tended to raise incomes further, and below some per capita income level tended to reduce them, while the Z forces reduced incomes, when incomes were above some specified level and raised them below that level. . . . *the main point, of course, is that these abstract and simple models enable us to see the process of economic change as one in which the outcome depends on a struggle between conflicting forces that operate simultaneously* . . ." (Leibenstein, *Economic Backwardness and Economic Growth*, p. 29.)

[1] *A Theory of Economic-Demographic Development*, p. 55, and *Economic Backwardness and Economic Growth*.

[2] Knut Wicksell's theory of the cumulative process that results from a deviation of the natural from the market rate of interest is another example of the application of the notion of circular causation. (Gunnar Myrdal, *Monetary Equilibrium*, William Hodge & Co., London, 1939, pp. 24 ff.) The writer's early attempt to use in a more systematic way the idea of circular causation in the study of underdevelopment and

tions that are causally interrelated, in that a change in one will cause changes in the others. We classify the conditions in six broad categories:

(1) output and incomes;
(2) conditions of production;
(3) levels of living;
(4) attitudes toward life and work;
(5) institutions;
(6) policies.

This structure of categories represents the conditions in a country viewed from the "economic" angle, which corresponds to the focus of the present study. The conditions in the first three categories represent broadly what is usually referred to as the "economic factors," while categories 4 and 5 represent the "non-economic" ones; category 6 is a mixture and is usually considered to belong to the "economic factors" when policies aim at inducing changes in conditions 1–3, but not otherwise. Often only categories 1 and 2 are considered in "economic" analysis. In the social system there is, however, no up and down, no primary and secondary, and economic conditions do not have precedence over the others. The demonstration and analysis of the interdependence pervading the system could just as well have been made from another angle, and the conditions classified in different categories and in a different order. Such classification would have covered the same social reality and would have had the same analytical content.

We shall consider here only categories 1–5, leaving category 6 for separate treatment in Parts III and IV of this appendix. The conditions in categories 1–5 are viewed as in different degrees "undesirable" from the point of view of *development*. The general problem of valuations will be discussed in Part III, but we can broadly say that judging conditions, and changes in conditions, from the viewpoint of development represents the application of the value premises of this study, discussed in Chapter 2. For the moment we are simply assuming that in the South Asian countries the various conditions can be categorically called *undesirable* because a one-way change in them is deemed desirable for engendering and sustaining development. The meaning of development will be clarified in Sections 6 and 7. A change of a condition in the direction of greater desirability from the development point of view will be called a change "upwards," and one in the opposite direction will be called a change "downwards." To begin with, we shall assume *uni-directional causal relationships* between the various conditions: a change in one condition will be assumed to tend to change the others in the same direction, upwards or downwards. In Section 11 we shall comment on exceptions to this rule.

We define the categories so that they refer to the national community as a whole or to any section, region, group, family, or individual — except the conditions in the fifth and sixth categories (institutions and policies), which can refer only to the national community or any of the sectional or spatially smaller communities. When no other sense is specified, we refer to the national community.

development, referred to in the second footnote to this appendix, was inspired by Wicksell; see *An American Dilemma*, pp. 1065 ff.

(1) *Output and incomes.* From an economic standpoint the most important general characteristic of the state of underdevelopment of the South Asian countries is low average labor productivity, and, consequently, a low national product per member of the labor force; the other side of this situation is a low national income per worker or per head of the population.[1] For reasons given in Section 7 below, this particular undesirable condition — low average labor productivity and low national income per head — can, with a number of qualifications, be taken as an approximate indication of all the others, that is, as an (imperfect) index of the level of underdevelopment in a country. It is not, however, a definition of "underdevelopment," nor is its upward change used as a definition of "development."

(2) *Conditions of production.* Together with low output per worker and low income per head another set of conditions affects the structure of the economy and the direction and intensity of economic activity, which are causes of low labor productivity and low income per head.

The industrial sector, and particularly organized large-scale industry, is small. In all other sectors, but especially in agriculture, crafts, and traditional industry, techniques of production are primitive and capital intensity is low. The savings/income ratio is low,[2] and therefore savings per member of the labor force and per head are lower still.[3] There is little enterprise, particularly in long-term productive investments. The overhead capital in the form of roads, railways, ports, power plants, and so forth, is inadequate. Labor utilization is low in regard to participation and duration (which together determine labor input), and labor efficiency.[4] This list can be enlarged and specified *ad libitum*.

These conditions are directly related to each other in the uni-directional way mentioned above. Thus the low savings ratio tends to keep down the formation of capital. Crude production techniques are partly the result of low capital intensity, insofar as more advanced techniques would require more capital per man. The same is true of the distribution of the labor force between the different sectors of the economy, and the relative size of these sectors: too many are occupied in activities requiring little or no capital, too few in those that require more capital and would raise output. Low labor input and low labor efficiency are in part a result of primitive techniques and lack of capital, wherever techniques employed and tools and machines available determine labor input and efficiency.

These conditions are, moreover, causes of the conditions in category 1 — low labor productivity and low incomes — while they are also, directly or indirectly,

[1] We abstract from differences in age and sex distribution and from differences in social customs with regard to work in different age and sex groups.

More generally, we abstract for the moment from the difficulties of aggregation in the underdeveloped countries of South Asia. See Section 23 below and Appendix 3, Section 5.

[2] For the difficulties of defining "savings" see Chapter 12, Section 2.

[3] The relationship is as follows:

$$\frac{\text{Savings}}{\text{Income}} = \frac{\text{Savings}}{\text{Labor Force}} \times \frac{\text{Labor Force}}{\text{Population}} \times \frac{\text{Population}}{\text{Income}}$$

[4] For a definition of these terms see Chapter 21, Section 15.

caused by them. Thus low incomes keep down total savings (even though the savings ratio in some income brackets is often remarkably high, compared with that in similar groups in rich countries) and lead to the undesirable effects mentioned above — low capital formation, poor techniques, low labor productivity.

(3) *Levels of living.* In the underdeveloped countries of South Asia levels of living tend to be low for the mass of the people and to manifest specific quantitative and qualitative deficiencies: insufficient food intake; bad housing conditions; inadequate public and private provision for hygiene and medical care; insufficient facilities for vocational and professional instruction and for training at all levels; and, more generally, insufficient educational and cultural facilities of all sorts.[1]

The low levels of living are caused mainly by the low levels of productivity and incomes. In the opposite direction the low levels of living cause low input and efficiency of labor, which in turn are among the causes of low incomes. This triangular causal relationship between productivity and incomes, levels of living, and labor input and efficiency is among the crucial determinants of underdevelopment.[2]

(4) *Attitudes toward life and work.* The prevailing attitudes and patterns of individual performance in life and at work are from the development point of view deficient in various respects: low levels of work discipline, punctuality, and orderliness; superstitious beliefs and irrational outlook; lack of alertness, adaptability, ambition, and general readiness for change and experiment; contempt for manual work; submissiveness to authority and exploitation; low aptitude for cooperation; low standards of personal hygiene; and so on.

To these attitudes should be added unreadiness for deliberate and sustained birth control. The steep and accelerating rise in population in these countries is a principal cause of poverty,[3] and birth control is the only means of checking this trend since we cannot wish to increase mortality or even check its continuing decline.[4]

All the other attitudes have indirectly the same effects by causing less favorable conditions of production under category 2, and by making the use of incomes for the achievement of the highest possible levels of living less effective. Thus low standards of personal hygiene are detrimental to health, and therefore to fitness for work and enterprise — apart from the ill health attributable to the lack of medical facilities.

In the opposite direction of causation, these undesirable attitudes and patterns of performance in life and at work are all, to some extent, a function of the low levels of living and thus, indirectly, of output and income, at the same time that they are a cause. Here is another causal relationship crucial for the explanation of underdevelopment.

[1] In this system of concepts low levels of health and literacy and of other intellectual aptitudes and capacities are not in themselves part of levels of living but the consequence of them and of conditions under categories 4 and 5.

[2] Section 21.

[3] See Chapter 28, Part I; and Section 10 below.

[4] Chapter 28, Section 9.

(5) *Institutions.*   The national community is also characterized by a number of institutional conditions unfavorable for economic development: notably a
land tenure system detrimental to agricultural advance; undeveloped institutions
for enterprise, employment, trade, and credit; deficiencies of national consolidation; imperfections in the authority of government agencies; instability
and low effectiveness in national politics; low standards of efficiency and integrity in public administration; ineffective organs for provincial and local self-
government; and a weak infrastructure of voluntary organizations – the institutional conditions which together constitute these national communities as "soft
states" in our terminology.[1] At the root of all these institutional debilities is a
low degree of popular participation and a rigid, inegalitarian social stratification.

All these institutional deficiencies are closely interrelated. So are attitudes
and institutions; attitudes generally support the institutions and at the same
time are supported by them. Through their effects on conditions in categories
2, 3, and 4 – conditions of production, levels of living, and attitudes toward
life and work – this whole set of unfavorable institutional conditions shares
responsibility for the low levels of productivity and low incomes and thus
also, indirectly, for the low levels of living. At the same time the low incomes
and the low levels of living and, in particular, the low levels of literacy and
education perpetuate the deficiencies in communal institutions.

*The preceding enumeration and comments are in the broadest terms our
"theory."* They are made to demonstrate in the abstract the mechanism of
causal interdependence of all the undesirable conditions in an underdeveloped
country. The analysis of this mechanism, to which this study hopes to contribute,
will have to do two things:

First, it must break up the broad categories, in order to make the list more
complete; define clearly and specify in greater detail the conditions for a fuller
analysis; and attempt to measure the conditions thus listed, defined, and specified.

Secondly, it must characterize the nature and measure the extent of their
interaction, that is, ascertain whether, and if so when, how, and by how much,
a change in one of the conditions causes any of the other conditions in the same
category or in other categories to change in the same direction.

(1)–(5) *"Economic factors" versus attitudes and institutions.* In general,
the causal connections between the conditions in the first three categories depend on the conditions in the "non-economic" categories 4 and 5. Many
economic models and the major part of the work on planning for development
in South Asia are based on certain assumptions usually left implicit, or abstract
and unclear. The three main ones are:

(a) That analysis can be safely concentrated on the interaction of the condi-
     tions in categories 1–3 and on those policies in 6 that are directed at in-
     ducing changes in conditions 1–3. Frequently even category 3 is left
     out of account.

(b) That the chain of causation between the conditions considered is not
     impeded by attitudes and institutions.

[1] Chapter 18, Sections 13 and 14 *et passim.*

(c) That the conditions under 4 and 5 (attitudes and institutions) are highly responsive to changes in 1–3 or even 1 and 2.

The last and basic assumption often amounts to an acceptance, indeed an amplification, of the Marxian hypothesis that the whole culture is a superstructure erected on the "modes of production" and thus simply a function of the "economic" conditions under 1 and 2. Hardly any attempt is made to test or prove this hypothesis, which is usually merely implicit in the analysis. Alternatively, various reservations and qualifications illustrated by selected examples are made in the text, which, however, do not materially affect the main line of reasoning and the inferences for policy drawn from it.[1]

In reality the attitudes and institutions are, as we shall point out, stubborn and not easily changed, least of all indirectly. Little reliance can be placed on the indirect effects of changes in categories 1–3 and still less in only 1 and 2. Attitudes and institutions represent heavy elements of social inertia that hamper and slow down the circular causation within the social system among the conditions in these categories. This, expressed in the most abstract terms, is the general reason for adopting what is customarily called an "institutional approach," which focusses the study of underdevelopment and development on attitudinal and institutional problems.[2] For the practice of planning, this implies the need for policies aimed at changing conditions under 4 and 5 directly and the futility of relying on the indirect effects of changes induced by conditions 1–3, or only 1 and 2.[3]

(6) *Policies.* On the assumption of complete *laissez faire*, that is, in the absence of policies, the social system would, as a result of primary changes and the interaction of all the conditions in categories 1–5, move in such a way that, depending on the initial situation and the coefficients of response to changes of the various conditions, there would be either an unchanged level of underdevelopment, which is to say stagnation, or else development to a higher level or a regression to a lower level. Policies, i.e., conditions in category 6, represent induced changes, applied to one or several of the conditions in categories 2–5. (Conditions under 1 cannot be influenced directly if we except pressure on other countries to give grants.) *Planning means coordination of policies in order to attain or speed up development.* Parts III and IV of this appendix will be devoted to the problem of plan-induced changes in the social system.

6 Conditions Differ but the Approach Is Generally Applicable

Conditions differ widely, of course, among the several countries in South Asia, as is pointed out in various parts of this study. Pakistan and India are the poorest. Average income is three and a half times as high in Malaya — and perhaps twice as high again in Singapore. The other countries fall between these two extremes. Health and educational facilities are usually better in the

---

[1] To this we shall return in Sections 14 and 19–21 and in Appendix 3, Section 3. See also Prologue, Sections 5–8.

[2] Prologue, Section 8, and below Sections 9, 19–21.

[3] See below, Sections 20 and 21, *et passim.*

less poor countries. Agricultural techniques, capitalization, and yields are much higher on the plantations, particularly the large ones, most of which are owned and managed by Europeans. Plantations are more prominent in the economies of Malaya, Ceylon, and Indonesia than in the other countries of the region. In Southeast Asia more land is available for new cultivation. Among the Chinese population in Malaya and in some of the other countries, there is abundant enterprise. Some peasants also respond more to changes in profitability within the framework of traditional agriculture. Serious under-nutrition is a general cause of low labor efficiency mainly in India and Pakistan, though qualitative deficiencies are present in all the other countries. India, on the other hand, is further along the road to an indigenous industrialization. National consolidation is more advanced in India and political life and administration are marked by higher levels of efficiency and honesty there than in most, if not all, of the other South Asian countries. On the other hand, India's social stratification is more inegalitarian and rigid. Natural population increase is still somewhat lower on the Indian subcontinent — because of lower survival rates, related to lower levels of income and of living, including public health facilities — than in most other South Asian countries, though very much higher than in the Western world. But the less favorable relationship of population to land and natural resources in India and Pakistan and the lower levels of income that make it more difficult to reach a higher savings quota may be more detrimental to development on the Indian subcontinent than comparative rates of population increase alone would suggest. This inference is strengthened when we take into account the probability or near certainty that India and Pakistan, with an already huge population base, will experience an increase in the rate of growth unless, or until, more effective policy measures are taken to check new births.

In measuring the levels of the various conditions subsumed under the first five main categories, we shall also find important regional and sectional differences within each country. Individual differences are, of course, even wider, depending mainly on the disposal of land and other wealth and, more generally, on the position of individual in the social structure, which determines not only their share of income, their levels of living, and, consequently, their health and education, but also their attitudes, and thus their behavior in regard to the conditions in category 2 and ultimately to all conditions in categories 1–5. But allowing for these differences between and within the several national communities, all the South Asian countries regard themselves as "underdeveloped."[1] This is important because the people's desire for development — or rather the desire of those who think, speak, decide, and act on their behalf — implies an interest in inducing changes in all the conditions enumerated in the preceding section — institutions, attitudes toward life and work, levels of living, conditions of production, and, consequently, productivity and incomes. Unlike the geographical location, climate, and natural resources of these countries, the unfavorable conditions enumerated in categories 1–5 are not fixed but can, in principle, be altered by policies.

They are all in that sense "social" conditions. The social sciences today do not

[1] Appendix 1.

reckon with inborn differences in capacities and aptitudes between the peoples in South Asia and those in the rich Western or Communist countries. Hereditary differences in physical and mental make-up tending toward a low level of development in the countries of this area cannot be excluded, of course, but they have not so far been demonstrated. On the evidence brought to light by recent research on group differences in inherited qualities, we may legitimately assume that, even if such differences exist, they cannot be large enough to contribute substantially to the prevalence of these undesirable conditions. The "development" at which every country in the region aims, and which, with varying effectiveness, it tries to promote by planning and state policies, is, indeed, defined as improvement in precisely those conditions in the social system that are not rigidly imposed by nature.

When conditions are characterized as in various respects undesirable for an underdeveloped country, this judgment is made not from the speculative and *a priori* point of view of some form of "welfare economics";[1] nor is it made in terms of some postulated absolute ethical norms. The conditions are deemed unfavorable simply from the point of view of the concrete development goals of the people of that country or, more precisely, of those who in that country decide policy. In particular, a moralistic attitude toward the conditions in our fourth and fifth categories — attitudes toward life and work and community institutions — has no place in an analysis such as this, concerned with causal relationships. For its major assumption, exemplified above and discussed further in the following sections, is mutual dependence through circular causation; this is also the main methodological hypothesis for the whole study. The deficiencies in attitudes and institutions are viewed as being caused by each other and by the deficiencies in (1) productivity and incomes, (2) conditions of production, and (3) levels of living; these in turn have resulted, in part, from the inherited framework of (4) attitudes and (5) institutions. Our analysis assumes that the people in these countries are not by nature different from those who have had a more fortunate economic fate; their circumstances are simply the result of different conditions of living and working both now and in the past.

Although our interest is focussed on the underdeveloped countries in the South Asian region, the interdependence of various conditions of life and work is, of course, a general characteristic of organized society and thus present in every national community, however highly developed. But a low level of development has, as we shall find, important consequences not only for the character but also for the strength of that interdependence.[2] Our assumption of an entire social system of interdependent conditions has, for this reason, much greater relevance in South Asia.

7 The Valuation of Changes in the Social System and the Index of Development

The uni-directional causal interdependence of the various undesirable conditions in our list, which we have assumed as a first approximation, implies that

[1] See Section 14 below and Prologue, Section 9.

[2] See below, Sections 19 and 20.

an upward change in any one of these conditions has, in addition to the "independent" value attached to it, an "instrumental" value, dependent on the effect of such a change on the upward movement of other conditions, and thus of the whole system. The "independent" valuation may in turn be instrumental to some values that lie outside the social system, or it may be desired for its own sake.

The independent value of a change is most apparent for the components of our third category: levels of living. Adequate food, better housing, improved facilities for health, education, and training, and general improvement of cultural facilities are all desirable in their own right and as means to the fuller development of the human personality, and are to that extent independent of their effects on other conditions and, in particular, on productivity and incomes. The independent positive valuation of an upward movement in conditions in the social system other than levels of living is less evident. In the traditional valuations in an underdeveloped country some of the upward changes in other conditions, and especially those in categories 2, 4, and 5, might even be negatively valued.[1] Insofar, however, as people in an underdeveloped country become more intensively interested in development, it can be seen that all conditions tend to acquire an independent valuation in line with the desire for development. The less desirable conditions for production and even attitudes and institutional conditions that are adverse to development are increasingly regarded as characteristics of backwardness and an independent value is attached to their improvement, in line with levels of living. This is a major effect of the spread of the modernization ideology. This tendency in an underdeveloped country to attach an independent positive valuation not only to development as a whole, but to each of the various changes in those interdependent conditions that are in line with development, gives more force to the urge for development itself.

Still more basic to the conception of development is, however, the notion of a causal interdependence of the various conditions and the implied notion that a change upwards in one of the less desirable conditions has an instrumental value because of its ability to cause upward changes in other conditions. It is this interdependence that makes it possible to regard those conditions as forming a "social system" and to define development as the movement upwards of that entire system. This definition of development – and the implied definition of underdevelopment – clearly suffers from vagueness, particularly when we want to specify a "rate of development." The vagueness stems from the lack of logical precision and homogeneity in the valuations. To bring to light this vagueness, by determining its basis and its limits, serves logical clarity.[2] Contrariwise, to define development more precisely than is justified is logically faulty and yields "persuasive definitions."

The indeterminacy in the concept becomes apparent when we attempt to measure it by an index. In the same way as the causal interrelationships of individual prices in a price system, also largely circular, allow the movement of that system as a whole to be represented by a price index so, subject to the

---

[1] Chapter 3, Section 1 *et passim.*

[2] Chapter 2, Section 2; and Appendix 1.

arbitrariness common to all indexes, the relative level of underdevelopment and the movement toward levels of conditions that are higher from a development point of view could, in principle, be represented by an index, calculated as an average of the levels of the various interrelated conditions at a point of time, weighted by the valuations attached to each component. In a sense, the idea of an index measuring the position, and the changes in position, of the social system as a whole is implicit in the thought of that system and in the application to that system of the dynamic conception of development.[1]

The weighting, however, is a much more complicated task. A change upwards in any of the several conditions in this system has, as was pointed out, two types of value: an independent value and an instrumental value depending on how much it causes other conditions to move. Higher levels of nutrition and housing, or improved health, educational, and cultural facilities, are of course important improvements in themselves; at the same time, they raise, in varying degree, labor input and efficiency and thus output. In the opposite direction, higher levels of efficiency, income, and output are instrumental in raising the level of living. *Mutatis mutandis* the same is true of improved attitudes and patterns of behavior in a great many respects, and of improved social institutions, such as, for instance, more effective and honest administrations or social orders free of caste distinctions. It is thus very difficult to arrive at an accurate basis for weighting the several conditions in the social system. Indeed, at the present stage of our knowledge of conditions in the South Asian countries and their interdependence it is impossible to attach weights with any degree of accuracy, for two reasons: uncertainty about and the heterogeneity of people's independent valuations of improvements of the several conditions, and lack of accurate knowledge of the actual conditions and the causal interrelationships that determine the instrumental value of an improvement in one of the conditions for improving, directly and indirectly, the others. Subject to this inescapable indeterminacy, *the movement of the whole social system upwards is what all of us in fact mean by development*. There is no escape from this, if we want to be "realistic."

In this situation, it is understandable and defensible that we turn to some *indication* of development that is easier to ascertain and measure than the ideal index. The rate of growth of the national product or income per head of the population is then a natural choice. Two general observations are pertinent. One concerns the reasons why — within wide margins of uncertainty — the increase in national income per head can serve as an indication of the movement of the entire social system. These reasons are, first of course, the basic interdependence of all conditions that makes it possible to conceive of them as constituting a social system; secondly, the dominant importance of people's incomes for their levels of living; thirdly, our assumption that levels of living are important, at least in the longer run, even for attitudes, patterns of behavior, and institutions; and, fourthly, our knowledge that if the latter conditions do not change or if they lag very much, this will show up by preventing productivity and incomes from rising substantially. The second observation is that "development" cannot be *defined* in terms of growth of national income

[1] Myrdal, *An American Dilemma*, p. 1068.

per head, but has to be defined as the upward movement of the entire social system. It might be argued that anyone is free to define his terms in any manner he wishes. But the difficulty with the term development is that we actually mean something much broader, as we easily discover if we watch our own inferences. The concept has also strong value connotations. We must avoid defining development in a way that would give rise to contradictions between our definition and the value implications the term carries in actual use.

A change in national income per head can thus never be used as more than a rough and ready *indicator* of that more complex change in the whole social system that we really want to record. This indicator is only a crude way of estimating development, not only for the well-known reasons that every index is necessarily arbitrary, that the statistical basis in an underdeveloped country, even for such basic magnitudes as production, income, and population, is inadequate, and that income distribution, the age and sex structure, leisure time, and so on, are neglected, but also for two more fundamental reasons: first, people's desires for development actually include the desire to improve many other conditions, which have independent as well as instrumental values for them; secondly, the interdependence of all conditions is not such that secondary changes in response to an initial impulse from income are always reinforcing;[1] and when they are, their size is not proportional in all sectors and for all groups and subgroups of conditions.

Still another note of caution should be sounded. The resort to a magnitude like the increase in income per head as an indicator of development should not be permitted to cause an undue concentration of interest on the more easily accessible "economic" conditions and in this way bias the choice of changes to be induced in the system, and thus of policies when planning for development. Undoubtedly, however, this "definition" of development and the concentration on the more easily measurable factors are partly responsible, in many countries, for turning planning in a more "materialistic" direction than would be rational from the point of view of people's actual valuations and of what we know about how "economic" conditions are, in fact, influenced by "non-economic" ones: this is recognized in a general way when it is said that in the final analysis "development is a human problem."[2]

The term "national income" or "product" is not in itself a very clear concept.[3] In the more than two hundred-year-old tradition of economic theory, the recognition that magnitudes like the rate of growth of national income per head are inadequate to account fully for our conception of development has, in principle, been allowed for in at least one respect, namely, by a general qualification for income distribution. We cannot abstract, however, from distribution, because size and distribution of the national income are logically inseparable.[4] Moreover, particularly in a changing society, the weights attached to the heterogeneous collection of goods and services that make up the "national income"

[1] See below, Section 11.

[2] See below, Sections 19 and 20.

[3] Chapter 11, Section 1.

[4] Gunnar Myrdal, *The Political Element in the Development of Economic Theory*, Routledge and Kegan Paul, London, 1953, pp. 129 ff.

depend on attitudes, behavior patterns, and institutions, which in turn change as a result of development. Thus the problem is not merely how to make the wants of different individuals commensurable, but also how to weight inter-temporally, for any one individual, his wants as they change in the process of development, and how to weight his wants against his valuations, which may be critical of the wants, and which also change as a result of the movement of the whole social system. Precisely the same logical difficulties that inter-personal comparisons present in a static society, and that have led to the attempt to distinguish between "real income" and "distribution," are created in conditions of development by inter-temporal comparisons — both between generations and within the life span of a single generation. But the difficulties go even deeper. Not only do tastes change with development, but the valuations attached to a system of tastes change also, and they change *as a result* of changes in other conditions in the system. Although aggregate income is valued according to tastes and/or valuations, its increase will change them. To judge the performance of the system by standards that are partly its own creation is therefore circular.

8   *Circular Causation and Cumulative Change*

Let us return to the basic concept of the social system. The underlying idea is that the several undesirable conditions, abstractly categorized in Section 5, "cause" each other, directly and indirectly. If these conditions for a country were to be completely listed and specified so as to serve ideally the purpose of intensive analysis, and if all the causal interrelationships were assessed correctly, we could give a full explanation in terms of causes and effects, why things are as they are at a particular point in time and why they change as they do, or why they do not change.

This is the sense in which, in regard to a stagnant society, we say that "a country is poor because it is poor." The movement of the system, if and when it moves, would then also be fully explained. Over a period of time a change in any one of the conditions will tend to change other conditions. The important thing is then that as the conditions have been defined and organized in our list in terms of their being undesirable from the point of view of the development goals, these secondary changes must generally go in the same direction as the primary changes. We abstract for the moment from exceptions to this general rule.[1] Each one of the secondary changes will then in its turn exert a tertiary influence on other conditions in the entire social system, including the condition that had experienced the primary change, and so on. If initially the system was in balance, the circular interdependence of the conditions in the social system would thus give rise to a cumulative process of change of that entire system, proceeding in the same direction as the primary change and affecting most or all conditions in the system. If, as is more probable, the system is not in balance but already changing in one direction or another, and if there is not one primary change but a number of simultaneous changes, the causal interdependence within the system would also make this more complex process cumulative.

The primary changes can come from outside the social system — for in-

[1] See Section 11.

stance, by the accident of a good or bad monsoon that affects crops, or of economic policy measures applied by foreign countries. Or they can be induced by policy measures (category 6) taken within the country itself and directed at improving one or several unfavorable conditions within the country. The primary changes can be once-for-all, or they can operate over a limited period of time, or permanently.

Prima facie this causal interdependence would seem to indicate a highly unstable social system. It is, of course, conceivable that at a particular point in time the various conditions should have attained precisely such levels as to represent a balance between the forces. This would imply a perpetuation of prevailing conditions from that point in time to the next. But, first, there would seem to be no reason to expect that, except by rare chance, a social system would ever fulfill the requirements of such balance. Secondly, the balance, if established, would be broken as soon as some outside event or some policy intervention at home moved one or several of the conditions up or down. Any such change in some conditions would tend to cause other conditions to move in the same direction, and these secondary changes would, in their turn, result in tertiary changes all around the system, and so on in a circular fashion. Normally, one might, on purely theoretical grounds, think that the social system would regularly be moving in one direction or another since impulses to change would be continually fed by circular causation with cumulative effects.

9   The Forces of Stagnation: (1) Time and Inertia

In sharp contrast to this expectation are not only the common experience of "low-level equilibrium" in underdeveloped countries and the serious obstacles to development policies, but more generally the astonishing stability of most social systems in history. Balance, far from being the fortuitous result of an unusual and obviously unstable combination of forces, seems to be the rule, not the rare exception. The great bulk of historical, anthropological, and sociological evidence and thought suggests that social stability and equilibrium is the norm and that all societies, and underdeveloped societies in particular, possess institutions of a strongly stabilizing character. In view of these findings the real mystery is how they can escape from equilibrium and can develop. The Western experience of scientific, technological, and economic advance may well be unique: a series of extraordinary circumstances seem to account for the cumulative process of development in Western history — even though the classical economists attempted to explain it by the removal of restraints and thus assumed a spontaneous tendency to develop. In this light the low-level equilibrium and the strong resistances to all attempts to overcome stagnation, characteristic of most underdeveloped countries, no longer appear puzzling. They can be explained by the forces that tend to perpetuate the *status quo* in the face of impulses to change it. This and the following two sections will be devoted to a preliminary analysis of these forces.

We should first note that the reactions of other conditions to a change in any one of them are seldom instantaneous but usually delayed, often for a considerable period. Sometimes there is no reaction in some of the conditions — and this becomes more important if it happens at an early stage, close to the initial change, so that circular causation via those conditions is stopped. A peasant who has the opportunity of cultivating more and better land or of adopting a technology that will raise yields on the land he already cultivates will not avail himself of these opportunities if he has no ambition to raise his level of living. The reaction of workers to higher wages, or of peasants to higher prices for their products, may be to work less; their incomes do not then increase (though their level of living does move up if leisure is considered a component of it). This type of behavior in pre-industrial Europe and in colonial territories has been given technical formulation in the backward-sloping supply curve.[1] Or institutional conditions, for instance in regard to land tenure, may be such that the peasant can have little rational inducement to exert himself.

The existence of genuine "backward-slopers" in South Asia has been questioned. It is clearly true that Indians and other Asians living outside their native countries often show "forward-sloping" reactions. It may be opportunities that are lacking, rather than the will to seize them, though the distinction is not always easy to draw. Nevertheless, there can be no doubt that in the traditional setting of South Asian societies (excepting to an extent the Chinese) many people are "survival-minded," striving for nothing other than to preserve their customary low levels of living. The very notion of a supply curve of effort is inappropriate, for it presupposes a calculation and weighing of alternatives, which is alien to a mentality whose aspirations are limited by custom and tradition, and it presupposes an institutional system in which efforts are matched by rewards. As always, attitudes and institutions support each other. Although it is uncertain how widespread and deep-seated survival-minded behavior is, it certainly is prevalent in many regions and strata in the South Asian countries. But even where people have followed traditional patterns, the introduction of higher monetary rewards may alter aspirations and reactions. Moreover, the introduction of cash payments, a direct attack on attitudes and institutions through such policies as land reform and the replacement of feudal by contractual relationships may change the way people respond to rewards. But such changes in attitudes and institutions may be difficult to engender or may take time to realize.[2]

Even apart from attitudes and institutions, reactions to changes may be delayed or altogether absent. An example is the direct relationship between levels of nutrition, the physiology and psychology of workers, and labor input and efficiency. A rise in nutritional levels should have some beneficial short-term effects on workers' health and willingness and ability to work, and thus on production and incomes. But the major effects may be delayed for years. Maximum improvement may not be realized until a new generation of workers, who have enjoyed improved nutrition from childhood, enters the labor force. And

---

[1] Chapter 21, Section 6.

It would follow, if workers did respond thus and the supply curve was symmetrical, that a *reduction* in wage rates or prices would be the measure appropriate to initiate development. Poll taxes imposed on poor indigenous peasants can be rationalized in this way.

[2] Cf. Part Five of this book on the problem of labor utilization.

these long-range effects may not occur at all if the rise in nutritional levels is only temporary. Circular causation that could give rise to a cumulative process will then be stopped. Similarly, a lowering of nutritional levels, if moderate and if people remain above starvation, may have only minor short-term effects on the quantity and efficiency of labor input, and more important ones only gradually; the full effects may not be felt until the next generation, and then only if the change has been a lasting one. The same is true for the effects of other changes in levels of living and, behind those, of changes in incomes as the main determinant of those levels.

But certainly the main resistance to change in the social system stems from attitudes and institutions (categories 4 and 5). They are part of an inherited culture and are not easily or rapidly moved in either direction. It will take time and endeavor for people to acquire discipline and habits of punctuality and cooperation, to want to improve their lot, to overcome their contempt for manual work, to become ready to experiment, and to take risks and accept change. And it will take time for the rigidities of an inegalitarian social stratification that supports these attitudes to begin to wear down in response to higher income levels, to more and better facilities for education, and to greater mobility, engendered by economic development. Again, a trend toward the improvement of defective community institutions — for example, increasing honesty and efficiency in the collective organizations for national government, or the spread and improvement of cooperatives and of local self-government — should normally be expected as a long-range effect of rising production, incomes, and levels of living and, in particular, of education, which should raise and improve popular participation. But all the existing community institutions, like the attitudes that are fostered within them and at the same time uphold them, are part of the wider cultural setting, and the results of gradual advances in these other respects may be insignificant for a long time. Even in the very long run, attitudes and community institutions may stay much the same, in spite of all efforts to raise educational levels, if the inegalitarian social stratification remains rigid and the national community remains a "soft state."[1]

So far as both attitudes and institutions are concerned, the most important immediate result of higher incomes and levels of living and of anything that more easily and rapidly follows such a general development, may be, and often is, to prepare the ground for, and make more effective, deliberate policy measures directed specifically at improving the attitudes and reforming the institutions themselves, if such policy measures are applied as additional induced changes. Even under the most favorable constellation of all conditions, policies designed to alter people's attitudes and performance and to construct more appropriate and effective community institutions will be difficult to apply and will take time to bear fruit.

The probability that a primary change may not push the system over the threshold into a cumulative process is greater if that change is once-for-all. But even if the primary change is sustained, the sensitivity of all other conditions to that primary change and the speed of their reaction will determine whether

[1] Chapter 18, Sections 13, 14, *et passim.*

a cumulative process will be set off, and will acquire momentum, or whether things will remain at the same level of stagnation or possibly move onto a slightly higher equilibrium. An illustration of such a sustained change would be the introduction of a system of compulsory primary education, which would make literate successive generations of children and eventually the whole population. This process has begun in all the countries of South Asia but has gone far only in Ceylon and Malaya. However, a rigid inegalitarian social structure may stubbornly resist improvements in popular education. The chain of causation from higher educational levels among a people to their readiness to press for and carry out a land reform may thus involve a very long and uncertain process; should a land reform be requisite for changing attitudes and substantially raising yields in agriculture, education will not, through this particular chain of causation, react back on productivity. And continuing poverty will, at the same time, mitigate the effectiveness of the primary efforts to raise educational levels.

A development start focussed on some of the conditions in category 2 — for example, efforts of the government to carry out a policy of planning for development by investments in the infrastructure and in new industries, perhaps promoted by aid and credits from the richer countries — will result fairly promptly in increasing output and incomes in those particular sectors of the economy. There should be "spread effects" to other sectors, but if attitudes and institutions do not respond, or respond only slowly, those spread effects will be weak or absent.[1] This is more likely to happen if the initial development starts are restricted to small sectors of the national economy and do not result in a large rise in levels of output and income outside those sectors. But even with a wider dispersal of development efforts and a wider impact on levels of living among people in all sectors — which would have to be within limits set by available domestic savings, foreign exchange, administrative resources, and so on — the inertia of attitudes and institutions may be formidable. The check to development impulses from this kind of inertia is one of the main reasons why a "take-off" may easily be abortive and not result in "self-sustained growth," to use the popular terms. It is just as true when the initial development starts are due to the accident of favorable circumstances as when they are induced by government policy.

We shall return to the practical planning problem in Part IV of this appendix when discussing the reasons for coordinating policies and generating a "balanced growth." At the present stage of the argument we note only that the request for "balance" in the development process has a much wider bearing than on planning in regard to sectors, localities, and the time sequence of investments and other economic development stimuli and restrictions. Planners are confronted with the problem of how to strengthen the generally weak and tardy effects on attitudes and institutions exerted by the development starts themselves and the more immediate induced changes in the incomes and levels of living of some portion of the population.

[1] See Chapter 24, Sections 7–9.

The general reason why this factor of inertia may prevent a development process from becoming self-sustained or, at least, delay this event is that circular causation will give rise to a cumulative movement only when, by the interaction of all conditions in the social system, a change in one of the conditions will ultimately be followed by a feed-back of secondary impulses to a further change of that particular condition big enough not only to sustain the primary change, but to push it further.[1] Mere mutual causation is not enough to create this process; otherwise the ubiquity of mutual causation would be inconsistent with the widely observed stability of social systems. The relationship between the size of the coefficients of response and the speed of the response will determine whether mutual causation results in stable, neutral, or unstable equilibrium. This means that the task of planning may be much more difficult; planning not only must set in motion initial and sustained impulses, but also has to try to alter the coefficients of response and speed up the responses if stability is to be transformed into a cumulative upward movement.

If this is not done, the social system will easily slip back to the earlier level or move only to a new low-equilibrium level. The development starts will remain "enclaves" as in colonial times. That there are "thresholds" to pass is a well-known fact in psychology as well as in physiology; in economic theory this thought is expressed by the concept of stability of equilibrium within limits and cumulative processes beyond them, so that the functional relationships of the interacting variables are not linear.

10 The Forces of Stagnation: (2) Independent Counteracting Changes

The likelihood that policy-induced changes of conditions will give rise to a cumulative process upwards of some considerable momentum is, of course, further reduced if there are other changes working simultaneously in the opposite direction.

All the South Asian countries are now, though in different ways and with different degrees of effectiveness, instigating development policies in many directions: they are investing in social and economic overhead facilities; initiating industries; introducing more rational techniques in agriculture and making available irrigation, fertilizers, and tools; instituting and revitalizing organizations for provincial and local self-government and cooperation; improving educational and health facilities, and so on. They are receiving grants, loans, and technical assistance from the more developed countries both in the Western and the Communist orbit to facilitate these development policies. By themselves these induced changes, if they are big enough to overcome the factor of inertia discussed in the last section, should be expected, through the interaction of all the conditions in the social system, to push that system over the threshold of low-level equilibrium and so engender a cumulative process of development; as these policies are being intensified, this process of develop-

[1] The writer has in earlier publications expressed himself with too little caution. I am grateful to Trevor Swan for having pointed this out; see p. 1844, footnote 1.

ment should gain momentum, the more so as in time even those conditions that are slow to react also begin to change. This expectation would be more likely to be fulfilled if the governments were wise and courageous enough to take action against rigid and inegalitarian social structures and all the other attitudes and institutions that are particularly stubborn and will, if unchanged, hamper severely, or even block, the upward circular process.

But working against this whole complex of development policies are not only the forces of inertia, which build up thresholds that must be passed in order to release and speed the upward cumulative process. In all these countries there are also a number of changes, occurring *independently and at the same time* as the application of development policies, some of which tend to drag the social system downwards. The most important of these countervailing changes is undoubtedly the population explosion.[1] In all South Asian countries the high and rising rate of population increase tends to influence incomes and levels of living in a downward direction.[2] Therefore, if it continues, the upward movement of the social system will be hampered and development slowed down. The obstacles mentioned in the last section will then exert greater force, locking the system into low-level equilibrium. In time, the rate of population growth may even become the dominant influence on the social system. A powerful intensification of development policies and of foreign aid may then be required merely to prevent stagnation or decline. In the end, if the population increase continues and accelerates, these efforts might turn out to be futile. The situation will be all the more serious if, as seems established,[3] such higher levels of living as can be expected in the foreseeable future do not result spontaneously in the spread of birth control and a substantial lowering of birth rates. This is the thought behind the insistence of demographers that, in the long run, if lower mortality is not followed by lower birth rates, mortality must rise again.

Another counteracting change is the deterioration in the trading position of most South Asian countries that has come about because of a slackening of the demand for their export products and a rise in their import needs.[4]

11   *The Forces of Stagnation: (3) Counteracting Changes Released by Development*

One of our assumptions has been that the causal interrelationships of all the conditions in the social system, as listed in our five categories, are such that a change in any one of them will tend to change the others in the same direction. It is for this reason that development efforts may through circular causation give rise to a cumulative upward process. Whether they do so or not, and if they do, how fast the cumulative process will move the social system upwards, depends then on a number of things listed in the two preceding sections: the magnitude and persistence of the development efforts; the direc-

[1] Chapter 27.
[2] Chapter 28, Part I.
[3] Chapter 27, Section 12.
[4] Chapter 13, Sections 1, 5, 12–15; Chapter 14, Section 4.

tion and speed of movement of the social system because of independent changes under way, some of which may be antithetical to development; and the size and rapidity of the response of the conditions in categories 4 and 5 — attitudes toward life and work and institutions — to changes in output, incomes, and levels of living. If in spite of considerable development efforts the cumulative upward process slows down or is altogether frustrated, so that the result is stagnation at the prevailing low level or slightly above it, this has to be explained either by the presence of counteracting changes (Section 10), or by the fact that some important conditions react so weakly or so slowly that the feedback of sustaining and spurring stimuli is absent or weak (Section 9), or by a combination of the two.

The basic assumption of uni-directional relationships within the entire social system is, on the whole, realistic, as our observations in Section 5 have indicated. Indeed, its realism and the opportunity this opens up of engendering development by planned policies form the basis for what hope there is that the underdeveloped countries in South Asia may succeed in lifting themselves out of underdevelopment. There are, however, exceptions to this general rule, when *the secondary changes instead move the system in the direction opposite to that of the policy-induced primary change.*

The classic example of an attempt to demonstrate the operation of a strong counteracting change resulting from development itself was the Malthusian theory of how a rise in income per head and levels of living induced population growth that wiped out that rise and returned the social system to its earlier stage of underdevelopment.[1] In our study of the population problems in South Asia, however, we have found the population increase to be a largely "autonomous" development, though the effects of rising levels of income per head and of living might lead to a minor rise in fertility and a perhaps somewhat larger decline in mortality.[2] There will certainly be a substantial decline in mortality in all South Asian countries, but this will not on the whole be caused by development there but by advances in medical science and technology and their progressive application in South Asia. The population outlook is very serious in South Asia, but for the most part it should be classified as a counteracting change, not released by, and dependent on, development itself but rather independent of it.[3]

It is not difficult, however, to imagine numerous counteracting changes resulting from development. The provision of irrigation works, for example, can lead to destruction of soils — if adequate attention is not given to drainage, and salination and waterlogging set in. The extension of cultivation in an area may lead to deforestation, dangerous for the climatic balance — if care is not exercised in choosing the new land for cultivation and reforestation is not carried out on other land. Schooling may have negative economic results if educational policy is not designed to prevent the newly educated from taking the attitude that they are too good to "soil their hands." Suffrage and greater

[1] Section 4 above.
[2] Chapter 27.
[3] Section 10.

political participation such as that provided by local self-government may strengthen the caste system by providing a new field for its operation if measures are not taken to stamp out caste feelings and the whole institutional structure that supports them. Government controls may foster increased corruption if vigilance is not preserved. New legislation that is not enforced may breed cynicism if administration of the laws is not strengthened.

We find in this book many instances in which circular causation has not, as we have assumed up to now, operated uni-directionally. In all, or most, cases where an induced or spontaneous change upwards in one or several conditions has given rise to downward changes in other conditions, more purposeful planning could and would have prevented this regression. Rarely are such secondary effects necessary if the planners are circumspect and the government is prepared to act with determination. As, moreover, such counteracting changes are exceptions, planning can proceed on the basis that circular causation has mostly uni-directional cumulative effects, though they may be delayed or completely obstructed by independently occurring contrary changes.

I I I

The "Ideal Plan" and Planning as a Practical Art

12   *Analysis in Terms of Ends*

Part II of this appendix was devoted to a causal analysis of the mechanism of underdevelopment and development in the South Asian countries. We focussed our attention on the undesirable conditions that constitute underdevelopment, and the connections between changes in these conditions. In this part and Part IV we shall consider the problem of planning for development. This means that we regard the social system from the point of view of the sixth category of the conditions listed in Section 5 — policies, and the coordination of policies through planning, aimed at development.

We assume a government that wants to promote development, defined along the lines laid down by the general value premises of this study.[1] The conditions listed under 1 to 5 offer opportunities for, and raise *obstacles* to, the realization of that desire. In the following, the term "obstacles" will refer more particularly to conditions in categories 4 and 5, that is, attitudes and institutions. The government is also constrained by various *inhibitions* from using all the means necessary to achieve development and from accepting fully its consequences.[2] The actual course of change in the social system is the result of the policies adopted by the government (category 6) and of all the other conditions (categories 1–5). Also, the causal connection between those latter conditions is influenced by the policy-induced changes.

[1] Section 7 above; Chapter 2, Section 4.

[2] The concepts "obstacles" and "inhibitions," and the abstraction from the complex reality they imply, are clarified in Chapter 2, Section 2.

The consideration of planning for development means that we shift from the theoretical to the practical plane.[1] We reason in terms of means and ends instead of causes and effects. As has been shown in various contexts in this study, the failure to distinguish clearly between analyses in causal and in final terms has led to confusion and unnecessary controversy. The confusion has been sustained by the heritage of teleological metaphysics — in which what is and what ought to be are equated. This confusion is inherent in the philosophies of natural law and utilitarianism, from which the social sciences evolved. It still permeates their framework of implicit valuations. This influence is particularly strong in economics. It is concealed by the "objectifying" definitions of concepts, which are the means of keeping the valuations hidden. These definitions are the teleological ballast that prevents the achievement of logical clarity and opens the door to biases.[2] In the following discussion, as in the whole study, we attempt to bring out carefully the value premises applied in both the theoretical and the practical analyses.[3]

13 The "Ideal Plan"

Behind the general discussion of planning there is, mostly implicit but sometimes explicit,[4] the concept of an ideal or optimal plan. If only we could take all relevant facts into consideration, it is thought, we could formulate and execute a plan that would engender development more effectively than any other set of policies.

Let us, in the light of the foregoing discussion of underdevelopment and development, consider what this notion of an optimal plan implies. It presupposes, first, knowledge of relevant conditions and their causal connections. Their initial magnitudes would have to be estimated and also their coefficients of change. These coefficients would have to be complex because they would vary with the direction, size, and speed of the change, and according to whether it occurs autonomously or in response to changes in any one of the other conditions — or a combination of several; the coefficients based on changes in several conditions could not be obtained by simple summation. Having gathered knowledge of the conditions and their relationships, we would then require a set of value premises for planning, sufficiently specific to solve the problem of optimization. In principle, the ideal plan would be concerned with the execution of the set of policy-induced changes in conditions that would move the social system upwards most effectively. To determine that set and thus the plan, we would have to attach definite independent valuations to the changes in conditions that, directly and/or indirectly, are the result of the execution of the plan. These independent valuations may themselves be instrumental to some ends that lie outside the plan, or they may be

[1] See Prologue, Section 9, footnote 2, p. 32, for definitions of the terms "theoretical" and "practical."

[2] Prologue, Section 9; below, Section 14.

[3] Chapter 2, Section 4.

[4] See, for instance, Jan Tinbergen, *The Design of Development*, Johns Hopkins Press, Baltimore, 1958, pp. 36 ff.

final valuations attached to the resulting conditions for their own sake. Because of circular causation between changes in conditions, the particular changes directly induced by the policy measures that constitute the plan have, from the planners' point of view, also instrumental value in furthering the objectives of the plan either directly or indirectly. But only a few of the changes in conditions can be considered by the planners as having *only* instrumental value. Most either have, or will acquire, independent values *also*.

By following out this scheme we would then be able to say which policies, inducing changes directly in certain conditions and indirectly in others, would result in an optimal upward movement of the social system, given our knowledge of conditions and their causal connections and given a set of value premises, specified sufficiently to allow the formulation of the ideal plan as inferences from this knowledge and the postulated value premises.

There is no need to stress the impossibility of gaining even a fraction of that full knowledge of conditions and their causal connections. Some of the significant data needed are among the most inaccessible social relationships, still largely unknown even in Western countries, where social research flourishes. Even if the set of value premises needed for planning could be thought of in terms of a volitional *a priori*,[1] their application would depend on our knowledge of conditions and their relationships, because changes in conditions would have to be considered in terms not only of their independent but also of their instrumental value. Moreover, not only the conditions but also the causal connections between them will change, both unintentionally, because of the movement of the social system as a result of all sorts of impulses to change, and intentionally, as a result of policies directed at changing not only conditions but also their interrelationships. The plan and its execution thus alter the material that was assumed to be given. Obstacles to, and thus opportunities for, development will be different at a future time as a result of development. And in drawing inferences from the value premises the instrumental value of various changes will then also alter.

What we have stressed so far is the impossibility of laying the basis for planning on a complete knowledge of the *facts and the relationships between the facts*. This in itself should not, however, invalidate the notion of an ideal or an optimal plan. To approximate and simplify is legitimate in all scientific endeavor and this principle applies fully to planning for development. But two reservations should be stressed. First, our knowledge of facts is exceedingly meager in South Asia. Rationally this should inspire a much greater humility than is usually demonstrated by the plan-makers and the economists who speculate about planning. Secondly, levels of living, attitudes, and institutions (categories 3–5) are of primary importance for the development effects of any induced change in incomes and production and in conditions of production (categories 1 and 2). This should exclude models of planning that do not take these conditions into account; to this we shall come back in Sections 19–21 and Appendix 3.

But in addition to the *empirical* difficulties of ascertaining the relevant facts

[1] The difficulty on that score will be commented on later in this section.

and the relationships between them, there are *logical* difficulties. They relate to the introduction of the value premises. The broad value premises, accounted for in Chapter 2 (Section 4) — the modernization ideals — which represent *the viewpoint from which we study the problem* of the South Asian countries, can only be presented with considerable vagueness.[1] Nevertheless, they permit us without much ambiguity to classify conditions and their changes as broadly "desirable" or "undesirable" from a development point of view and to define "development."[2] They also permit us to draw certain general conclusions about planning, which amounts to sketching a theory of planning.[3] But for solving the problem of producing a definite plan in a particular country at a particular time they are entirely inadequate. For one thing, they are not specific enough. A more serious difficulty is that a plan has to be produced in terms of the actual *valuations of the government* that is responsible for the plan. A plan is fundamentally a political program.[4] Even if those valuations are in broad agreement with our chosen value premises, actual planning requires a greater degree of specificity; moreover, on many points the more specific valuations of the government would be different from the value premises of our study.[5] *The specific, relevant value premises for constructing the plan cannot be separated from the social system of which even the government is a part.* Moreover, that social system and the valuations implied in the attitudes of the people and the government are changing as a consequence of development itself and of planning for development.

To begin with, people's actual valuations implied by the attitudes in category 4, fortified by the institutions in category 5, represent *obstacles* to planning and development. These obstacles are revealed by the study of conditions and their interrelationships. They are part of what the government must want to change by planning. For the assumption of all planning is that there is a government bent on development and thus also on changing the valuations in the country. These obstacles will, however, remain a serious limitation to planning, and to the freedom to apply the modernization ideals in actual policies. For no government is entirely free to follow its own subjective valuations, independent of the reactions of people in different localities, occupations, and social strata — though the power structure gives some governments more freedom than others. These obstacles raise no logical difficulty. In principle, they are no different from climatic or other obstacles that planning has to take into account.

But in addition to these obstacles there are what we have called the *inhibitions* working on the minds of those whom we designate vaguely as the government. Those responsible for directing the work of planning and devising and implementing the plan are, of course, never wholly disinterested and socially

[1] Chapter 2, Section 3 *et passim*. Logical clarity requires that this be pointed out.

[2] Section 5 above.

[3] Part IV of this appendix.

[4] Section 15 below.

[5] The application of a certain set of value premises in the study does not assume that they are actually applied in government policies; see Chapter 2, Section 3, and Postscript, Section 2.

detached; they are themselves part of the social system that is to be reformed, as are the planners and the rest of the articulate citizenry. They have their own economic and social interests, and share, to a greater or lesser extent, the popular attitudes that constitute the obstacles to planning. They also have political interests and want to maintain and increase their own power. All this tends to influence and limit their vision.[1] The remarkable thing about the spread of the desire for planning[2] and development among the articulate members of the South Asian national communities is not that they are unable to free themselves entirely from these attitudes or to act with complete disinterest, but that they can detach themselves at all from the prevailing attitudes in their societies and that they show any desire to change them.

The valuations relevant for planning are thus rooted in the actual conditions in category 4, which are fortified by the conditions in category 5, and cannot be separated even analytically from the empirical reality of the conditions prevailing in the social system. The very application of planning, however imperfect, *tends to change these valuations,* normally by reducing the limitation on planning imposed by the inhibitions of officials. This happens along several lines of causation. Although it is impossible, logically, to derive valuations from facts, psychologically people do rationalize their valuations in certain beliefs about reality. They think that they derive their valuations from what they believe they know. This is, in principle, as true of Westerners as of South Asians. They are mistaken, but undoubtedly there is a relationship between valuations and beliefs. As fuller knowledge modifies people's beliefs, valuations that do not accord with the new beliefs are deprived of support. Their "opinions," which are a blend of valuations and beliefs, change and the implicit valuations change with them.[3]

The planning process itself will help to rationalize the valuations toward greater conformity with the modernization ideals, the first of which is rationality.[4] The collection and analysis of data concerning conditions and their relationships, the political process of discussion, decision-taking, and decision-enforcing, and the education and propaganda that enter into the formulation and implementation of the plan will so change both the beliefs and the valuations

[1] "The image projected is that of a farseeing ruling group bringing about change in a reluctant traditional society. Obviously, this is an oversimplification. The ruling groups are themselves part and parcel of the traditional society, share a great part of its emotional and cultural climate and have, in addition, their own particular prejudices and interests. These factors affect the formulation of the programs as well as their implementation. Political considerations color every situation; sometimes they dominate it. . . . Consequently, an interpretation and understanding of the various elements in the program, from the political point of view, are essential for evaluation both of the structure of the program and of the manner of its implementation." (D. R. Gadgil, "The Importance of Evaluation for Development Planning, With Special Reference to Land Reform," in Foreword to Erich H. Jacoby, *Evaluation of Agrarian Structures and Agrarian Reform Programs,* Food and Agicultural Studies, No. 69, FAO, Rome, 1966, pp. 10–11.)

[2] Chapter 15.

[3] Myrdal, *An American Dilemma,* Appendix 1, "A Methodological Note on Valuations and Beliefs," pp. 1027 ff.

[4] Chapter 2, Section 4.

attached to means and ends in planning. This happens to both the government and the people and should tend to reduce the inhibitions among the former and the obstacles among the latter. More specifically, as we pointed out in Section 7, the attention drawn to development as an end will tend to incline people increasingly to attach a positive independent value, not only to rise in levels of living — itself a novel valuation to many people in a backward, stagnating country — but to a change upwards in all other conditions in the social system, including attitudes and institutions. This is what is implied in the spread of the modernization ideals. This aspect of planning for development has, more particularly, the effect of broadening the limits for planning set by inhibitions and will gradually also begin to break down those attitudes among the people which are obstacles for planning.

In the course of planning also, upward changes in conditions acquire instrumental value because people realize that such changes will push up other conditions too. From one point of view, development from a traditional to a modern economy is largely (though not entirely) the creation and expansion of a sphere of instrumental valuations where previously only independent valuations reigned. It thus leads to a widening of choice. To the primitive tribesman, the question "how many fishhooks is a banana worth?" is irrelevant. This widening of choice is not directly the result of greater opportunities but of changing valuations, although the opportunities may induce a change in the valuations, and stems from an increasing understanding of circular causation and greater readiness to regard changes as means to further ends. It would occur, for example, if certain trades or economic activities were detached from caste and evaluated according to their financial rewards; if the intrinsic dignity or stigma of certain jobs were transformed into differential compensation; if the taboos on work by Moslem and Hindu women in the upper strata were replaced by calculation of the advantages of leisure compared with work; if sacred cows, literal and figurative, were made into veal and beef.[1]

Indeed, unless an area of instrumental valuations can be mapped out, the whole discussion of the optimal plan is pointless. Considered, calculated, rational choice assumes either that some events have no value in themselves or that whatever independent value they have is not absolute but can be compensated for by the achievement of rival objectives. In a world where nothing has a price, there can be no optimal plan and, indeed, no planning whatsoever. For what can then be compared are only total sequences, and even such a comparison would assume a highly developed capacity for surveying reality and evaluating it. In stagnant societies, bound by tradition and by attitudes and institutions supported by a host of superstitious beliefs, the arena of means and commensurable ends is very narrow and in many fields totally absent, whereas developed countries, whether of the Western or the Communist type, have been able to rationalize beliefs and thereby also attitudes and institutions

---

[1] It is clear that development will inevitably reduce the range of choice for some, while also widening it for others. But this change in the range of opportunities available must be distinguished from the values attached to the choices. Although some previously instrumental values may acquire independent value, the normal course of the transition from a traditional to an economically progressing society will be the reverse. The notion of "rationality" implies the existence of a sphere of instrumental values.

— that is, the whole mode of thinking, desiring, living, and working — so that inhibitions to development, and also obstacles, have been largely removed.

The point in this context, however, is not only that planning assumes that at least the people in power — whom we have called the government — have gone some way toward overcoming inhibitions and freeing choices, a process the people at large are induced to follow, but also that planning and development, once started, will by themselves tend to change valuations by further breaking down both inhibitions and obstacles created by traditional attitudes and institutions. The spread of the idea of planning among the articulate layers of an underdeveloped, stagnant society demarcates the beginning of this process. Any attempt at planning will, in the first instance, affect those engaged in planning. The examples chosen above show, however, that this process cannot be expected to be very rapid, particularly when there are no policies specifically directed at changing attitudes and institutions but reliance is placed on the indirect effects of changes in other conditions, in the first instance, those of 1 and 2, to accomplish this result.[1]

Returning to the problem of an ideal or optimal plan, we conclude that since (1) the value premises for planning are not given *a priori*, since (2) we are not confronted with a satisfactory causal analysis of conditions, and since (3) there is change within the two spheres and interdependence within and between them, the optimal plan should be regarded as *a steadily forward-moving pattern of policies*, which has continually to be modified in the light of newly emerging events, changing causal connections, and changing valuations among the rulers as well as the ruled. The programs of the planners and the prognoses of the social researchers are not two distinct areas, superimposed on each other. The programs — intentionally and unintentionally — affect and alter the prognoses, and the prognoses in turn alter and modify the programs.

Looked at in this way, the optimal or ideal plan appears as a misleading abstraction, not only because it is impractical, but because it assumes two sets of static structures — one causal, the other final — where in reality there is change, interdependence, and interaction. The exploration of the facts alters the valuations and, since causal connections were constructed on the assumption of given valuations, alters the causal connections. *The plan is itself an evolving process. Planning cannot aim at an optimum, but at improvements.* It is guided by vision, but the vision is open-ended and flexible, not closed and rigid. It contains a rough perception of the connections between conditions prevailing over a period of time and the possibilities of moving, through rationally coordinated policies, in the direction of development.

14   A Note on the Tendency to "Objectify" Valuations and Its Relation to Model-Building

In the foregoing section it was taken for granted that, logically, there are no objective values, only subjective valuations. Valuations and beliefs are social facts that can be studied; between them there are psychological causal rela-

---

[1] To this problem and the related problem of revaluation or evaluation we come back in Sections 19 and 20.

tionships that can be analyzed. Beliefs can, of course, also be scrutinized from
the point of view of being more or less correct. But the valuations themselves
are not true or false, right or wrong.

Almost every social scientist would probably agree with this view when
stated in general terms. But the practice of social scientists, and of economists
in particular, contrasts sharply with this profession of agreement. The practice
in economic research is related to a specific conception of the importance of
the distinction between "economic" and "non-economic" factors, which broadly
corresponds to the conditions in our categories 1–3 (or primarily 1 and 2) on
the one hand and 4–5 on the other. In the next part of this appendix and in
other contexts we criticize this practice. In the Prologue we suggested that it
reflects a bias, opportune to economists in the West as well as in South Asia,[1]
and to intellectuals generally, whether of a conservative or radical bent.

The application by economists of this approach to the study of South Asia
has three main explanations. In the first place, institutions and attitudes play a
different part in Western countries, and their neglect in economic analysis there
is less damaging. In South Asia, however, the interdependence of "economic"
and "non-economic" factors is much more intensive and consequential. We shall
return to this topic in the next part of this appendix.[2] Here we shall merely
note that it is understandable that when economists after the Second World
War hurriedly turned to the study of the development of the underdeveloped
countries in South Asia they used the tools they were accustomed to using.[3]
The second reason is that "economic" facts are felt to be more easily accessible. They have been the object of more intensive observation and analysis than
other social facts. We have found, in the course of our study, that even this
knowledge is extremely thin in South Asia, partly because the collection and
analysis of data are guided by inadequate Western concepts. Nevertheless,
more is undoubtedly known about "economic" facts than about most other
social facts. The third reason, related to the other two, is the mistaken idea
that "economic" quantities are more "objective" because they can be reduced
to a common denominator and expressed in monetary terms. It is now generally
recognized that this procedure presupposes a whole set of more or less unrealistic assumptions, depending on the purpose for which the aggregation is
used. For purposes of allocation of resources, the use of prices assumes not
only fairly "rational" behavior and perfect competition, but also constant unit
costs and the absence of external effects on the side of production not reflected in costs or prices. For purposes of estimating levels of living, it assumes
a special psychology of consumers and the absence of external effects on the
side of consumption, and so on. But, in spite of numerous qualifications, costs
and prices can under certain conditions be used as indicators of forgone alternatives, whether in consumption or production. The "veil of money" can thus
be pierced, it is held, and costs and prices can be taken to stand for the more
ultimate facts of physical resources and of sacrifices and benefits.

The conclusion from these considerations has been that planners should thus

[1] Prologue, Section 6. Cf. Chapter 21, Section 9.

[2] Sections 20 and 21; cf. Appendix 3, Section 3 *et passim.*

[3] Prologue, Sections 2 and 5.

be provided with a simple criterion for the determination of the relative profitability of allocating scarce resources between competing uses. The implication
is that decisions guided by costs and prices are "objective," in contrast to decisions about alternatives that do not have a market value — a metaphysical
notion that opens the door to several biases.[1] On the one hand there are "productive investments," guided by "objective" criteria; on the other hand there
are policy decisions where alternatives have to be evaluated "independently,"
according to "political" considerations supposed not to be "objective."[2] Simi-

[1] Prologue, Section 9; Appendix 3.

[2] Cf. the following statement in a United Nations document: "In view of the complexities and uncertainties surrounding the role of social factors in economic development, including the difficulties of measurement, it is not surprising that economic
planners should be discouraged from trying to handle such factors in economic
analyses and programming." (United Nations, ECAFE, "Co-ordination of Economic
and Social Programmes," *Economic Development and Planning in Asia and the Far
East,* in *Economic Bulletin for Asia and the Far East,* Vol. X, No. 3, Dec., 1959, p. 28.)
    Even if their importance is acknowledged, the social aspects tend, in practice, to be
excluded and regarded as alien to "rigorous analysis." Thus Tinbergen at one point
notes that education is a "very important condition for development" but disavows
the consideration of it as a part of "economic policy." (*The Design of Development,*
p. 5.) At another point (p. 30) he writes: "To compare the advantages of an electricity plant with those of . . . a school will always be difficult, but at least it can be made
clear what increase in material production is sacrificed if a school . . . is built." But the
inability to calculate the returns of the school does not put it beyond the scope of economic policy. Looked at the other way, the returns of the electricity plant could be
regarded as the increase in material production sacrificed by not building the school,
and thus the opportunity cost of the electricity plant cannot be calculated. Choices
cannot be arbitrarily limited in this way.
    Lacking the tools for a broader analysis, the economist is tempted to confine himself
to a few selected economic variables that are familiar, manageable, and measurable,
and to spend his time studying the relationships of these variables to each other as in
formal "models," excluding consideration of other variables that may affect them or
be affected by them. (See Section 19 and Appendix 3.)
    The United Nations document cited above continues with the following quotation
from Kuznets: ". . . ever since the middle of the nineteenth century demography and
population theory have been excluded from the corpus of orthodox economics, and
only in the two most recent decades have economists been turning in haste to relearn
something about demographic processes; just as demographers are beginning to recognize the dire consequences of their neglect of economics. The situation with respect to
history of science and technology and the understanding of what moves it is even
sadder, and our ignorance of these key processes in economic growth is truly ap-
palling. Nor need I add a similar comment about the clearly increased importance of
political and sociopsychological factors in the understanding of the economic growth
of nations; or the helplessness of a mere economist when he observes, when he can
observe, results of economic growth obviously ascribable to political factors and
forces whose nature he cannot understand adequately. The outcome is either withdrawal into the refuge of mathematical models operating with a few variables, or
amateurish cogitations on a vast theme. One has the advantage of formal elegance,
and the other, that of at least calling attention to the wider array of factors that have
to be taken into account; but neither outcome is satisfactory." (Simon Kuznets,
"Notes on the Study of Economic Growth," *Items,* Social Science Research Council,
XII, No. 2, June, 1959, p. 15, quoted in ECAFE, *Economic Development and Planning
in Asia and the Far East,* in *Economic Bulletin for Asia and the Far East,* Vol. X, No.
3, December, 1959, p. 28.) On recent attempts to include "investment in man" in the
capital/output models, see Chapter 29, Sections 4–7.

larly, considerations regarding the distribution of the national product have since the time of John Stuart Mill usually been excluded from the "objective" sphere of planning and left to be decided by "independent" "political" judgment. The economist, attempting to confine himself to "objective" facts, considers it safer to refrain from pronouncing on these "political" matters. These distinctions reinforce the irrational hold of Western models over the analysis of the problems of South Asia, on which we shall comment below in several sections and to which we shall devote Appendix 3.

This line of reasoning would thus define "economic" planning as an "objective" procedure, while the planning in all other fields would be "political." It would, more particularly, draw a line of demarcation between "directly productive" investments and so-called "social" investments and redistributional reforms. Several variations of this thought, implicit in much of contemporary economic discussion and elaborated in the theoretical systems referred to as "welfare economics," are in fact merely variations and amplifications of Mill's theme of a logical difference between, on the one hand, the sphere of production and exchange, where objective economic laws rule, and, on the other, the sphere of distribution where political judgment has to be exercised. Long ago, however, it was shown that such a distinction is logically untenable and the whole attempt metaphysical.[1]

More specifically, even if we could abstract from all "non-economic" factors — a procedure that on logical grounds is not permitted — planning could not rationally be based on the existing price relationships. This would hold true even if markets were perfect in the technical sense. Even then the price relationships would first have to be changed by deliberate interventions in such a way as to give incentives to public and private enterprises in line with the actual goals of development planning — or such changes would have to be calculated and corresponding corrections carried out before price relationships could give an adequate basis for planning.[2] In the underdeveloped countries of South Asia actual costs and prices provide an even less legitimate "objective" basis for planning. A very large part of economic activity is non-monetized and outside all markets in the ordinary sense of the term. Where markets exist they are usually far from perfect; immense internal differences are evident in the capital and labor markets, for instance. It is, moreover, an institutional fact that people do not calculate their inputs and outputs rationalistically as is customary in the Western countries. As stimuli for changes in demand and supply the cost and price relationships are not effective in the same way, or to nearly the same degree, as in Western countries.

More fundamentally, however, this way of formulating optimal policies does not become more "objective" and is not liberated from its dependence on concrete value premises because markets, money, costs, and prices are used as criteria of allocation.[3] This holds true generally, but especially in underde-

[1] Myrdal, *The Political Element in the Development of Economic Theory*, pp. 114 ff. *et passim*.

[2] A critique of the theory of "accounting prices" is presented in Appendix 5.

[3] Appendix 5, Section 1.

veloped countries with their distorted price relationships, imperfect markets, and ineffective price incentives in many fields.

The traditional method of distinguishing between "economic" and "non-economic" factors, "objective" and "political" decisions, "quantitative" and "qualitative" determinants, and similar dichotomies has molded thought on planning. We shall return to it in various contexts. Section 22 below on physical versus financial planning takes up the relationship between the "veil" of magnitudes expressed in monetary terms and the "real" physical quantities behind it. Appendix 3 on models in development planning is devoted to a more detailed criticism of the type of thinking inspired by the tendency to select and objectify certain relationships and relegate others to a "political," "non-economic," "exogenous" limbo. Appendix 3 should be regarded as a continuation of this section that has been separated from the main text for reasons of exposition and length.

15   *The Plan as a Political Program*

The valuations relevant to planning are determined by the political process taken in its widest meaning. The people who act in this process can have a more or less comprehensive and correct knowledge of the complex reality that is evaluated. It is the purpose of rational planning to improve the basis of this knowledge and to use it for political action. But, in the final instance, planning is no substitute for policy-making. On the contrary, its value premises must come from and by the political process. In planning, value premises cannot be simple and general; they must be as specific and complex as the valuations that determine, and become determined by, the political process.

To work out a policy for husbandry in India without taking into account the common aversion to "cow slaughter" is, of course, impossible. This aversion represents an obstacle to government action. The planners may simply regard it as brute fact, like hurricanes and floods; but it may be part of their own valuations. If it is, it is then not only an obstacle but also an inhibition. In most cases policies run up against the need to change institutions that are supported by attitudes and by strong vested interests. An agricultural policy cannot be framed without specific premises covering the changes in land ownership and tenancy that the government will find both feasible and desirable in view of the actual power situation in a country. Similarly, the level and distribution of taxation, which is such an important complex of variables in planning, cannot be determined for the practical purposes of producing a plan by the intellectual exercise of drawing conclusions from the facts; it must result from a political decision by a government whose members have certain attitudes and are limited and conditioned in their actions by the structure of power relations and the attitudes and institutions in their country.

All planning thus implies political choices. The choices do not concern only broad and abstract goals. *They relate to all stages in the process of planning and to each specific step implied in planning.* Means have to be evaluated as well as the goals they are designed to serve. As the formulation and execution of the plan proceeds, beliefs and valuations are modified, not merely by those immanent changes that stem from the emergence of new facts and the clarification and modification of valuations, but also by those changes that result from the changing distribution of power and influence among individuals, departments, social strata, and political parties.[1] *A plan for development is thus in essence a political program,* and we are likely to be seriously confused if we do not keep this clearly in mind. (From the opposite point of view, it would, of course, be rational if every political program were as much a considered plan as the politicians are capable of making it; but this inference does not concern us in the present context.) In the normal course of state planning, the plan is the program of public policies of the national government, though conceivably an opposition party — where an opposition is permitted, as in India — or, indeed, anyone whose views differed from those of the party in power, might work out a national plan.

That a plan can have no existence except as a political program is evident on logical grounds. The point also has practical importance, for it implies that planning cannot be carried out as an isolated technical exercise but requires political decisions on public policies. In its final form the plan is a coordinated system of such policy decisions as have emerged by a long sequence of discrete and preliminary political decisions. For, as the work on planning proceeds, political decisions have to be taken continually. The technical work on a plan has only one purpose: to enable these political decisions to be taken on more rational lines and with a fuller understanding of the facts. No work, even on the details of a plan, can be undertaken and brought to a successful conclusion, except on the basis of seriatim political decisions. *Plan-making, therefore, is itself a part of the political process in a country.*

If India has advanced much further in its economic planning than other underdeveloped countries, this is largely because planners there have recognized from the beginning that planning must be backed and carried out by the gov-

---

[1] This is why, for logical reasons, the value premises cannot be separated from the facts; see above, Section 13. The following quotation is an example of a mistaken conception of planning:

"The theoretical reason for a statement of objectives is that it defines ends from which choice criteria can be derived. In this way, value judgements can be made by responsible leaders *at the beginning* of the planning operation and the remainder of the planning work can be turned into *purely technical process of deducing and applying criteria* that select the set of actions which will best serve the stated objectives. If more than one objective is stated, it is necessary also to state the limits which each imposes on the others so that unambiguous criteria can be deduced. *Logical separation* of the activity of making value judgments from the activity of choosing particular courses of action, which is attained in economic theory by taking the preference function as given, was not attained in the actual planning procedure of the [Pakistan Planning] Commission. In the first place, the Commission was never able to present, much less was it able to expect agreement on, an unambiguous statement of objectives." To illustrate the difficulty the writer quotes from the Planning Commission's *Revised Draft Frame* a passage reading in part: "'. . . We are . . . of the view that the maximization of national income should be the overriding objective. The other objectives, to the extent that these conflict with it, must be subordinated to it.'" (Fred C. Shorter, "Planning Procedures in Pakistan," *Pakistan Development Review*, Vol. 1, No. 2, Autumn, 1961, pp. 8–9. Italics added.) Cf. the present writer's "Ends and Means in Political Economy," translated and republished in *Value in Social Theory*, pp. 206 ff., from *Zeitschrift für Nationalökonomie*, Vol. IV, No. 3, 1933.

ernment, in contact with the people, through whatever of its organs, in all sectors and at all levels, it can cause to function effectively. And the plan is in the end sanctioned in the regular manner by parliament. It follows from the fact that planning is political programming that, like all other political organs in a country, the planning organs, if they are to cope successfully with their task, become *largely negotiating and almost diplomatic agencies of the government,* and that only a small part of their activity is devoted to scientific study. This is, of course, what has happened to the Indian Planning Commission. As such it is a healthy development, and, indeed, necessary if planning is to be more than an intellectual exercise. The Indian Planning Commission certainly needs to conduct more and better economic research and analysis; in particular, it needs to devote more effort to the collection of better statistics. But this should not be done at the expense of its political functions. For it is these political functions that give practical importance to its scientific analysis. Practically as well as logically they form the basis for all its technical considerations.[1]

In those countries of South Asia where planning has been only loosely connected with the government it has not gone far or deep, even as a technical exercise. The main reason is that these countries do not yet have strong and unified governments with sufficient authority, stability, and singleness of purpose among their individual members to fulfill the functions of government planning.[2] Ambitious work on plans has been initiated from time to time in all of the countries under discussion. Special organs for state planning have often been set up, and they have produced studies and reports. But this work has not gone far or had much impact on policy-making. Planning has been frustrated and has never reached the operational stage. It has not been integrated into the political process. This was the situation even in Pakistan until the military takeover in 1958 and the formation of a consolidated government, in this case a more authoritarian one.

When there is no government able or willing to integrate planning into its functions — that is, to take decisions continually as the work on planning proceeds and to use the eventual plan as its program for policies — the temptation is particularly strong to overstress the technical and "objective" character of planning and sometimes to employ experts from abroad. The purpose is not to help the government to make up its mind rationally on the major economic problems of the country in a continual and systematic way on the basis of expert knowledge of the facts — which is what planning is and the only thing it can be — but to give the impression that planning is going on when it is not. The public is deluded into thinking that experts, given time to apply the skills of their craft, will fashion a plan for the country — as if it were a question of ordering a golden Buddha for a temple. This has, for instance, been the situa-

---

[1] "The collection and analysis of data certainly is one important aspect of planning . . . ; but democratic planning, at least, takes place within a political environment that impinges on the process of decision-making at many points." (Edward S. Mason, *Economic Planning in Underdeveloped Areas: Government and Business,* Fordham University Press, New York, 1958, p. 66.)

[2] Chapter 15, Section 7.

tion in Ceylon.[1] The other side of the coin is that lack of government influence often gives the experts a freer hand to produce a "plan" — one that will not work, however, unless a new government comes to power that is prepared to back it. For this to occur the experts must have correctly anticipated what the new government would be willing and able to do within the power constellation in the country.

The habit of working with irrationally simplified economic "models" has facilitated evasion of responsibility. The models are constructed on the pattern of the "ideal plan" and suffer from the false separation of ends from means, of "economic" from "non-economic" factors, and of "objective" from "political" decisions. As a result of these misleading divisions, a spurious simplicity is given to the plan, which is presented as the solution to a technical problem. Attention is diverted from the lack of adequate knowledge, from the absence of specified and relevant valuations, and from the power realities and the moral, psychological, and political stresses and strains, while the soothing and elegant functional relationships between a few "economic" variables set the mind and the will at rest. We have seen how this leads to the systematic introduction of bias.[2]

The idea that all one has to do is to draw up an ideal plan, with a vision of goals and an exposition of means to achieve them, derives its force both from liberal rationalists steeped in the doctrine of the harmony of interests and from technocrats who regard people and social organizations simply as cogs in a machine. Utopian anarchism and ruthless autocracy here converge in their conclusions and planning practices. In fact, it is instead *part of the function of the plan to assist in striking compromises and bargains between conflicting interests and to construct a framework within which conflicts of convictions and interests can be thrashed out.*[3] Neither the assumption of harmony nor that of the application of absolute authority wherever conflict arises is warranted. The idea underlying both is that political choices have objective solutions, and this is deeply rooted both in the liberal harmony doctrine and in totalitarian ideology. In fact political choices are the result of a great number of different factors and forces: they are limited by social facts, though these facts are not unalterable themselves; they are constrained by vested interests, though these can be weakened; and they are guided by the moral and political convictions and the interests of the politicians themselves, though these can be changed by, among other things, inculcating more rational beliefs. For this reason, the political process of planning cannot be neatly, clearly, and briefly demonstrated by singling out one or a few of these forces. Neither a technocratic model, nor one based on a harmony of interests, nor one allocating to the po-

---

[1] At least until recently. The new government after the election in early 1965 decided to accept responsibility for a more serious planning effort; see Chapter 9, Section 4.

[2] Section 14. See also Prologue, Section 6; Chapter 21, Part II *et passim*.

[3] Chapter 15, Section 8.

litical authority the function of reconciling clashing interests, can do justice to the complexity of the facts and their interactions.

16   *Planning as a Practical Art*

The idea of an ideal plan is ever present, but the reality of effective planning can only take the shape indicated at the end of Section 13: a moving design of a society in which conditions shall, sooner or later, be improved.

"Objectives" or "main goals" that are broadly in line with the modernization ideals are usually stated in the introduction to the plans. But little effort is made to clarify their relationship to the actual policy prescriptions in the plan. This is natural and, indeed, necessary, because the planners for good reasons are not inclined, or not permitted, to make explicit the inhibitions of the government to implement these ideals, and because it is felt that it would be awkward in a political document to enlarge upon the other limitations of planning, which consist in the obstacles raised by the attitudes of the people and the institutions supporting these attitudes. The stated objectives and goals thus appear as conventional and stereotyped rationalizations without relation to those valuations according to which the government is actually prepared to act. Often they serve as tranquillizers offered to the intellectuals and radicals. They belong to the dreamworld of ideals that have little relation to the immediate and practical work of constructing the plan. For the political process, however, it is not unimportant that the modernization ideals have been given that expression and that significance.[1]

Within the vague vision of a moving design for improving conditions in a country, the actual plan cannot spring simply from an attempt to solve the problem of how to promote development in this sense. At an early stage of the work on the plan a choice has to be made of certain main features. This choice must be guided by a broad conception of the current attributes of the country: its natural resources and its people, its trading position in the world, and so on. It must conform to the major ambitions and valuations of the government, including the inhibitions of the governors; and it must permit a working compromise between the various social and political forces — pressures, vested interests, ideals, and the heavy obstacles in prevailing attitudes and institutions with which the government has to cope in order to remain in power and be effective. But there is at bottom an institutional and a volitional element in all planning.

The procedure in a planning agency has perhaps its closest analogy in an architect's preparation of a sketch of a public building for a city council. He takes into account the purpose of the building and the financial resources available for constructing it; the nature of the ground at his disposal; and the inclinations of the people he serves, which are partly influenced, as he is himself, by the fashions of the day, though he knows that his ideas are ahead of theirs and he wants to "sell" them as many new ideas as he dares without risking a falling out with them. Taking all these considerations into account, he applies his artistic imagination and his professional skill and accomplishes a sketch that will be

[1] Part IV. Cf. Chapter 3, Section 1.

as good as he can make it. If he gets it approved, he then produces the work drafts. The planning part of his work is to coordinate the elements and fit them together. There must be a roof, staircases, doors, and windows. The space should be utilized with economy. Being of the modern functional school (we assume), he will attempt to present both his sketch and his later drafts as rational responses to given requirements. This is partly true but mainly a trick of the functional school.

Similarly, once the crucial choice of the main features of the plan is made and this choice has been presented to the government in power and to other interest groups, including possibly the entire articulate part of the general public, the planners can go on to elaborate it in greater detail. As this work proceeds, more specific data are assembled and further research is done, always in the directions indicated by the sketch of the main features. In this process, these will themselves be modified, and new features will be added. Generally, the plan has to be made internally consistent. If steel plants are to be set up, coal, electric power, and transport have to be provided. Various difficulties — factual and political — will have to be taken into account. Much discussion and persuasion will take place. Generally, the makers of the plan will be much less free to move within the valuations and power relationships than the architect when designing a building. The plan, as it gradually takes shape and is finally accepted, will differ from the original sketch. But the importance of the sketch and the initial choice of the main features should not be missed. It has conditioned and given direction to the later work. What is thus partly a work of art will finally be presented as much as possible as the rational and objective conclusions from certain facts and from the general will to development as expressed in certain broad goals that will be given prominence at the head of the document in which the plan is presented. As we saw in the last section, political considerations, which are much more specific than and differ from those broad goals, have been important both in producing the original sketch and in amplifying it. In the end the plan has to fit the country's actual circumstances and at the same time be both politically acceptable and practical.

This characterization of how a plan comes into being and what it is should not be taken as a criticism: the knowledge of the facts is scanty; the valuations are not available *a priori* as an explicit and comprehensive system or list of value premises, but have to be ascertained as the work proceeds, by direct confrontation with the existing and relevant power structure in a country; and this structure itself is changing in this very process. This is, therefore, in fact the only way of making a realistic plan. There is scope and need for ideals and desires and for imaginative thinking, and at the same time it is necessary to face the actual material conditions in the country, and to seek political moorings.

As the plan takes its final shape, having passed various political hurdles and having been put to some extent into operation, it will have created conditions for further work on planning in the next period. Changing conditions, experience gained, and the lack of correspondence between the plan and its fulfillment will make alterations necessary in the plan even during the plan period, but the pattern of working with a plan covering several years will tend to make for major revisions and reconsiderations only between plans. We shall return to this problem in Section 25.

17 The Effects of Planning on Planning

We have seen in this part that if a plan is to be more than an intellectual exercise or a showpiece, it must meet certain conditions:

(a) It will have to be a political program, determined by, paying attention to, and itself altering, actual power relationships, obstacles (presented by the attitudes and institutions of the people), and inhibitions (of the planners themselves). While the plan therefore aims at changing the social system, it must itself be seen as part and parcel of the process of that change. Although (i) scientific analysis and (ii) clarity of objectives are essential for an effective plan, the interaction between the two must also be fully allowed for. (Section 15.)

(b) The relationship between scientific diagnosis and prognosis, on the one hand, and the political program on the other, is not static, but itself subject to change as a result of the progress of the plan and its implementation. Initially an intuitive vision, inadequately supported by comprehensive analysis, the plan develops — through pressures, stresses, and tensions, successes, failures, and compromises, through the growth of experience and knowledge — toward a more concrete design. (Section 16.)

(c) This does not mean that planning is not a rational activity. On the contrary, to postulate an "optimal" plan in which an "objective" set of functional relationships is confronted with an independent set of abstract objectives, and to proceed on the maxim "give me your ends and I'll churn out the means" is itself irrational. For if irrationalities are to be reduced they have first to be acknowledged and brought to light, not neglected or denied. (Sections 12 and 13.) We have seen that effective planning will, in various ways, tend to correct irrational beliefs and modify valuations previously based on those irrational beliefs in the direction of greater rationality, and so reduce obstacles and inhibitions to planning and development. Although there is no inevitability about this, and although some changes will be in the opposite direction (Sections 10 and 11), there is a presumption that fuller knowledge of the facts, clarification of issues, experience of change, and the encroachment of a growing sphere of instrumental values upon a declining area of taboos and superstitions will enlarge the area of rationality. Planning of this kind represents, in view of the initial situation of the South Asian countries, a truly heroic effort.

(d) Just as, according to the argument in (c), the area of irrationality is reduced as the plan is developed and executed, so, according to the argument in (b), the area of vague vision is narrowed down. Neither area can ever be assumed to be eliminated entirely: to believe that it can is to fall victim to the illusion of "optimal" planning in which unadulterated teleology confronts purely objective causality. (Section 13.) The more particular the project, the easier it will be to clarify the issues by specifying the relationship between analysis and policy, fitting the means to the ends, and treating the problem as a technical one. But even particular projects will have wider repercussions. Decisions regarding these wider issues, and the broad structure of the plan generally, will tend to be guided longer by the vaguer intuitions that inspire and pervade the process of planning. Nevertheless, technical considerations of efficiency will spread from projects to sectors and from sectors to the whole society, as a result of better collection of data, fuller knowledge, wider experience, and more accurate analysis. Thus social technology will gradually encroach upon intuition and vision.[1]

All this applies not only to "economic" planning, but to all social policy efforts. Detailed calculations for facilities required to train skilled personnel in new industries can be made. The need for doctors and nurses for new hospitals and other health projects, and for teachers for new educational institutions, can be specified. Such concrete planning problems are almost entirely of a "technological" nature. But the ultimate decision as to the rate and direction of efforts to promote health and education and their place in relation to other objectives in the plan, and the estimate of their effects on other items in the plan, are bound to remain the result partly of intuition and partly of the buffeting of pressure groups, interest groups, and different opinions within the government and outside it.

Similarly, even in India, and not least there, where the state governments are well organized and exert a powerful influence on the central government, decisions about, for instance, the location of large investment projects will be the result of the intuition and imagination of the planners and of political bargaining. This is natural and inevitable, and should not be deplored as irrational from the point of view of "optimal" planning.[2] It would be impossible to evolve

[1] Speaking about the second Indian plan, Edward Mason makes the following comment: "There appears to have been no analysis either inside or outside the Planning Commission of the question whether the proposed investment was a better or more efficient way of attaining the output and employment targets of the Plan than some alternative pattern of investment. Nor, outside the field of irrigation, is there any evidence that the calculation of prospective rates of return on proposed projects was considered to be a necessary function of the Planning Commission." (Mason, *Economic Planning in Underdeveloped Areas: Government and Business*, p. 79.)

D. R. Gadgil's judgment about the Indian plan is fair: "Was anything done in the formation of the Second Five-Year Plan which made a striking departure from the earlier practice? There were, no doubt, a number of papers produced by statisticians and some even by economists. It does not appear that they affected materially the structure of the Plan. Ultimately, given the policy biases which had been evolved, the Plan frame was based on common sense projections out of rough available data in various directions. It was always known that there had never been any real technical examination of the individual projections." (D. R. Gadgil, "Prospects for the Second Five-Year Plan," *India Quarterly*, January–March, 1957, p. 11.)

"Within the limits imposed by these political and administrative considerations, there still remains a large and important field for economic calculation. The problems of economic calculation center around considerations of efficiency and consistency." (Mason, *Economic Planning in Underdeveloped Areas: Government and Business*, p. 69.)

[2] "Indian planning pays a great deal of attention to a 'proper' distribution of public investment among the various states. And in Pakistan a politically acceptable allocation of development funds between the East and West wings is the first prerequisite of planning. This means that the development planner is concerned rather with the problems of 'sub-optimization' than with the *optimum optimorum* from the point of

a policy of "optimal" location that would, in a power vacuum, weigh the advantages of regional equality, of wider regional dispersion, and of *creating* external economies in stagnating areas against the advantages of *reaping* external economies from areas that already have flourishing growing points; or weigh the benefits of exploiting *existing* markets against those of creating *new* markets; or weigh the drawbacks of higher costs and waste from putting up plants in stagnating places against the disadvantages of forming or strengthening congested enclaves of privilege. Intuition and bargaining must go hand in hand. But as planning proceeds, more serious study can and will be devoted to the direct and indirect consequences of various policies of location. These will affect in turn the content of planning and the valuations that guide government policy.

From these points of view, the process of planning can be regarded as a "learning process" in which intuition is transformed into hunches and hunches into knowledge, political pressures into technical considerations, wholly independent into partly instrumental valuations, and in which the obstacles presented by social inertia and vested interests, the inhibitions of the planners, and the area of genuine ignorance and uncertainty are gradually reduced. Numerous other illustrations could be cited of areas in which successful planning will tend to increase rationality, such as the issue of concentration versus dispersal of efforts, many small versus a few large community development schemes, urban versus rural development, large-scale versus small-scale industry. In all these matters, the planners will begin by "feeling their way," but will gradually be able to prepare the ground for more rational decisions, through the broadening of information and the weakening of obstacles and inhibitions. "Weights" determined by intuition and political pressures will be replaced by "weights" based on calculations of secondary economic and non-economic effects. What begins as a game of blindman's buff will end as an attempt to piece together a jigsaw puzzle.

IV

Elements in a Theory of Planning for Development

The abstract analysis, in Part II of this appendix, of conditions in the social system and their causal interrelationships could be carried out, up to a point, without specific value premises; that is, with merely a general indication as to which conditions are undesirable for development and the desirable direction

---

view of national development." . . . "As I have pointed out, political considerations in Pakistan direct a relatively equal division of public development expenditures between the two provinces — regardless of the location of economic opportunities and administrative capacities." (Mason, *ibid.,* pp. 67, 74.) The point is that, from a wider point of view, so-called "sub-optimization" may be more realistic and, indeed, more efficient than some narrowly defined, imagined "optimization."

of change. In Section 5 we argued that such an analysis can derive from a broad conception of the modernization ideals, which constitute the general value premises of this study. Some important conclusions about rational planning can also be drawn from our knowledge of the interdependence of the conditions for development and these general value premises, without a deeper examination of the more specific valuations that are relevant in a particular country at a particular time. In this part we shall consider some of these conclusions, which should be the building bricks of a theory of planning for development.

18   The Rationale of the "Big Push"

One of these conclusions concerns the rationale of the "big push." The government of an underdeveloped country has many good reasons for pushing development as hard as it can. One reason is simply to achieve higher levels of development. There is, however, the additional fact that unless the push is hard enough, no development will occur. In the absence of what Leibenstein calls a "critical minimum effort," attempts to develop will fail.[1] Efforts beyond this minimum will tend to yield increasing returns.

The same notion is vaguely present in the popular metaphor of a "take-off" and in the formulas, recurrent in the plans and in discussions of the plans, that the aim is to reach as soon as possible a state of "self-generating" or "self-sustained" growth.[2] The precise idea underlying these expressions is not clear. Presumably it is not that development beyond the critical minimum effort will occur automatically, without any further planning and government policies. If the implication is rather that further growth can take place without reliance on non-commercial foreign loans and gifts,[3] there ought to be some indication of the numerous other conditions and policies in a country on which such a desired autonomy depends. Much also depends on the commercial and foreign exchange policies pursued by other countries, even their domestic policies and their rates of growth, and, more generally, on structural changes in world demand and supply. These conditions, which are beyond the control of an individual underdeveloped country, will make a big difference in its ability simultaneously to service past debts and pay its way internationally as development proceeds.

In spite of this lack of precision, the idea of a critical minimum effort suggests that one or a whole series of thresholds have to be passed before the

[1] *Economic Backwardness and Economic Growth*, p. 96 *et passim*.

[2] "If a self-generating economy is to be achieved within a reasonable time, the proposed increase in national income is the minimum required during the Second Plan period." (Pakistan, Government of, Planning Commission, *Outline of the Second Five Year Plan* (1960–65), Karachi, January, 1960, p. 2.)

[3] "The Third Plan was conceived as 'the first stage of a decade or more of intensive development leading to a self-reliant and self-generating economy.' The perspective was that 'progressively external aid will form a diminishing proportion of the total investment, and by the end of the Fifth Plan the economy will be strong enough to develop at a satisfactory pace without being dependent on external assistance outside the normal inflow of foreign capital.'" (India, Government of, *The Fourth Five Year Plan: A Draft Outline*, New Delhi, 1966, p. 2.)

cumulative process gets under way at all. In Sections 9–11 we discussed some of the forces, either independent of or themselves released by development, that will slow down, halt, or even reverse the upward movement. In particular, we noted the role that population growth and an unfavorable trading position play in this process. The strength of the feedback and its direction as well may thus crucially depend on the size of the initial stimulus and the speed of its application.

The discussion of the necessity for a "big push" is regularly directed to "economic" factors. Numerous illustrations are cited of the hoped-for gains after the point of minimum effort. The explanations turn essentially on external economies, discontinuities, indivisibilities, complementarities, imperfections, and asymmetries. The arguments from external economies stress that there are numerous occasions when the total gains from an investment greatly exceed the direct returns to the investor. Both existing enterprises and new ones gain from the action, without the agent being able to charge others fully for these gains. The investment may therefore not be undertaken, unless policies rectify the discrepancy between the gains to those who do not pay for them and the profits to the investors. When the act of investment is undertaken, it leads to more development than cost and profit calculations for the individual enterprise would indicate. The training of workers and personnel by a firm that may lose them later is a favorite example. Even this could be viewed as a special case of an indivisibility, for training cannot be conducted in small parcels. Other indivisibilities arise from the technical need to add to productive capacity, to demand, and to investments in blocks of a minimum size, the benefits of which accrue largely to others.[1] Other traditional examples are the need for social overhead capital (power, transport, housing, and so on) and for mutually supporting or "balanced" demand.[2]

But the idea can be extended to other areas, such as the ability to learn by one's own and others' experience, to gain confidence, to benefit from example by imitation. Not only technological complementarities exist between different investment projects, but also attitudinal and institutional complementarities and indivisibilities. As soon as the argument turns to external economies, it is, indeed, not possible to distinguish clearly between "economic" and "non-economic" forces. And the general case for the big push is based on the interrelationship of all conditions in the social system, not only those in our categories 1 and 2. The big push must jerk the system out of the grip of the forces of stagnation. In addition to inertia (Section 9), there are forces, both independent of development (Section 10) and caused by it (Section 11), that impede or reverse progress. Unless conditions are changed by specific, powerful,

---

[1] "A minimum quantum of investment is a necessary (though not sufficient) condition of success. This is in a nutshell the contention of the theory of the big push." (P. N. Rosenstein-Rodan, "Notes on the Theory of the 'Big Push,'" *Economic Development for Latin America*, Howard S. Ellis, ed., Macmillan, London, 1961, p. 1.) Ragnar Nurkse wants "a frontal attack . . . a wave of capital investments in a number of industries" to assure what he describes as "balanced growth"; see Section 24 below. (*Problems of Capital Formation in Underdeveloped Countries*, p. 13.)

[2] Section 24.

and coordinated efforts,[1] they will not change at all or will change too slowly or perhaps even in the wrong direction, and thereby either bring the development process to a halt or reverse it. Even if the process is not reversed and some upward movement is created, all that may be achieved is a somewhat higher level of equilibrium.

The development efforts will therefore not pay off until, through the mechanism of circular causation, there is a *substantial positive feedback* from those conditions that were not initially lifted by these efforts to those that were. A cumulative process will then be started. The "gains" to development derived from the feedback can then either take the place of some of the efforts or, if those are continued, can reinforce them. These gains will tend to be larger, the greater the momentum that the process of development has gathered. At the start, big efforts are needed to set the process in motion. Thereafter, the planners can relax or they can harvest proportionately ever larger and quicker yields from sustained efforts.[2] It is for this reason that *underdeveloped countries cannot rely on a "gradualist" approach* and that a growing number of economists have come to support the "big plan." Backwardness and poverty naturally make it difficult for a country to mobilize enough resources for a big plan, but they are precisely the reason why the plan has to be big in order to be effective.[3] From one point of view, the very idea that planning is needed to start development, and that market forces by themselves cannot do it, implies the thesis of the big push.

The thesis of the big push, as commonly advanced, has two aspects: the *size* of the initial efforts and the *speed* with which they are applied. In connection with the big push, other types of concentration are often proposed, such as concentration in *space*, or on *large-scale projects*, or on *capital-intensive techniques*. A large effort per unit of time — say the year or the planning period — highly concentrated on a few sectors and on a few regions, using capital-intensive techniques would combine several of these aspects. These other types of concentration, however, raise quite different questions, the answers to which are not necessarily the same as that with respect to size and speed.

[1] Section 19.

[2] "After all, it is an elementary principle that if a certain mass has to be moved against a certain friction, a strong enough force has to be applied to start with although once the mass has been set in motion, relatively less force may be required to keep it moving. If, therefore, any backward agricultural area has to be developed, the first impact of the agricultural extension service must be very intensive, although once the process of development has started, the size of the staff can be reduced." (Sen, "The Strategy for Agricultural Development," p. 14.)

[3] This dilemma has, for instance, been a main source of controversy about Indian planning from the time of the preparation of the Second Plan. The anti-gradualist approach is illustrated by the following quotation: "One might also glean from Indian experience a warning against gradualism. In terms of the resources in sight in 1956, the second Plan was of course fairly ambitious; in terms of what is needed to bring appreciable changes in productivity and to alter fundamentally the prognosis for future growth, however, it was clearly too modest. And if even this plan is abandoned for lack of resources, it may turn out that India will have missed her 'optimum moment' for generating a take-off." (Higgins, *Economic Development*, p. 730.)

An example of the debate about concentrated versus dispersed effort is centered on India's community development program.[1] The attempt to spread community development and agricultural extension work over the 500,000 villages of the country has been criticized on the ground that this dispersal of effort would fail, in our terminology, to initiate circular causation, with cumulative effects, anywhere. The "push" would not be "big" enough. It is argued that concentration on a few villages or districts where opportunities are most favorable would yield greater all-round benefits in the end than dispersal of efforts at the start. On the other side it is argued that the entire countryside must be prepared for development if rural India is to emerge from backwardness. Concentration on industry, particularly heavy industry, has likewise been propounded as the only course by which an underdeveloped country can be set firmly on the road to development.[2] Opponents of this policy argue that it would merely create small enclaves in an otherwise backward and stagnant economy. The proponents of concentration have to rely on spread effects for their policies to be effective; but spread effects are themselves a function of the level of development and are generally weak in South Asia.[3]

No *abstract* solution to *these* dilemmas is possible. Everything depends on the strength and direction of the series of repercussions, and they will vary from country to country, period to period, and project to project. Moreover, these repercussions can themselves be altered by policies. The practical problem whether to concentrate or disperse in space, or with respect to industries or sectors, must be posed in more concrete terms to be meaningful. It has, however, this relationship to the problem of the big push, so far as concerns the size and speed of the development efforts: the bigger the efforts are in a given period of time, the greater the possibilities of combining a certain concentration in regard to space, industries, and sectors, giving higher immediate yields, with widely dispersed efforts to lift general levels, partly by increasing the spread effects.[4]

[1] Chapter 18, Section 8; Chapter 26, Sections 10 and 19.

[2] Chapter 17, Section 8; Chapter 24, Sections 1, 3, *et passim*.

[3] Chapter 24, Sections 7–9.

[4] The dilemma of concentration versus dispersion is related to the controversy over unbalanced versus balanced growth, which we shall review in Section 24.

Generally, Western writers have an exaggerated belief in the ability of the underdeveloped countries in South Asia to begin to develop once a strong enough spurt has given the lead; this unfounded optimism is connected with a lack of faith, which may instead be well founded, in their ability to carry out effectively a great number of policies at the same time.

J. K. Galbraith argues against "the inclusion of all good things in the Plan" and gives an example of the usefulness of concentration: "In the late eighteenth and early nineteenth centuries the accessible agricultural area of the United States — that between the Appalachian Plateau and the sea — was relatively small and there were occasional food shortages in the sense that grain had to be imported from Europe. The solution was to drive a canal to provide access to the abundant and rich lands of the Ohio Valley. No other way of increasing production was so important; it was obviously worthwhile at this stage of development to concentrate on this one thing alone. This in effect was done. After the Erie Canal was opened in the eighteen-twenties food became abundant and cheap along the eastern seaboard. Had a modern agricultural mission set about increasing food production in the early nineteenth century, and in

19   *The Need to Coordinate All Policies*

Planning for development must aim, as we have said, at jerking the entire social system out of its low-level equilibrium and setting off a cumulative process upwards. *There is economy in the big push.* Smaller efforts mean waste. The effectiveness of the push depends, of course, not only on the size of the efforts but also on their timing and direction. Much will depend on which conditions are changed, by how much and how rapidly. We cannot rely on circular causation to see to it that the impulses that the plan has imparted to a few conditions will be propagated throughout the social system. Yet this is necessary for acceleration. Even if those impulses were sufficiently strong to spread widely, development would be slower than if change had been induced directly in many other conditions *at the same time* and efforts had been *coordinated.*

Coordination of policies should not, however, stop short at "economic" policies, for there are many causal sequences outside the "economic" field that would hamper development in the absence of policies acting on them either directly or indirectly through other changes large enough to transform their braking power into a motive force. As was observed in Sections 9–11, numerous forces hamper or reverse the process of cumulative development, either by reacting too weakly or too slowly or by acting against it. We may therefore conclude from our general knowledge of conditions in South Asia and their causal interrelationships not only that the efforts have to be larger than a critical minimum, but also that *they must be directed simultaneously at a great number of conditions, concentrated within a short period of time, and applied in a rationally coordinated way.*

The effects of any given policy will depend on the policies simultaneously pursued in other areas. Government policies can never be planned in isolation. In no field, therefore, can targets be set up and policy means chosen independently of what is done, or not done, in other fields. National planning implies

---

light of modern technology and organization, it would have urged the establishment of experiment stations, proposed an extension service, suggested the development and adoption of new varieties of grain, advocated supervised credit, proposed more attention to marketing services, and quite possibly have used the occasion to stress the importance of starting work in home economics, farm management, rural health and rural sociology. The canal would have been only one among all of these good ideas and would probably not have got built. And all the rest being of far less immediate effect, the food imports would have continued. At a later stage it is worthwhile in a country such as the United States to devote itself to ways by which central opportunities are exploited. It is not a pattern to be applied to countries where concentration on essentials is still the urgent requirement." (J. K. Galbraith, mimeographed and undated note on Pakistan's Second Plan Outline, pp. 17 ff.) See also the same author's *Economic Development,* Harvard University Press, Cambridge, Mass., 1964, pp. 58 and 74.

Galbraith's moral may not be applicable to South Asia. Even were there similar big ventures to be undertaken, their spread effects would be unlike those that followed upon the opening of the Erie Canal. Actually, the United States government did a number of other things at the same time it built the canal, including some of those mentioned by Galbraith as in his view having lower priority.

the comprehensive and coordinated execution of a program of state intervention in all fields of social and economic life, based on the available knowledge of the conditions and their interrelationships, and aimed at the acceleration of development (Appendix 3, Section 6 *et passim*).[1]

Still another conclusion can be drawn from our general knowledge of the causal interrelationships of conditions in an underdeveloped country, without introducing more specific value premises than those contained in the modernization ideals: The need for a set of policies on a broad front, in which all state intervention is coordinated, *is very much greater in underdeveloped than in developed countries.*[2]

There are several reasons for this difference. First, both the rewards of success and the penalties of failure are greater in an underdeveloped than in a developed country. The poorer a country and the greater the danger that it may not be able to lift itself beyond the thresholds to cumulative development, the more imperative that whatever efforts it makes and whatever scarce resources it scrapes together be used with maximum efficiency. It cannot afford waste.[3] Secondly, in underdeveloped countries attitudes and institutions are

---

[1] We do not mean attaining "maximum" development in any simple sense. If development has any costs, and it obviously does, maximum development regardless of costs cannot be the aim of the planners. Beyond a certain point, the sacrifices imposed by raising the rate of development further will appear excessive. These constraints depend not only on physical facts such as the extent to which consumption can be kept down without impairing people's willingness and ability to work, but also on moral and political value judgments. The simple quantitative connotations of "maximum" ignore this. Moreover, even apart from physical and valuational constraints, "maximum" is ambiguous, because it leaves the time distribution of development open. Which is "bigger": 10 percent more next year and thereafter staying put; or no more for ten years and thereafter a permanent annual increase of 60 percent; or a continuous annual increase of 2 percent? Inter-temporal value judgments are required to give meaning to a "maximum" rate of development. We reject the term "optimum" because it conceals behind a pseudo-objective idea a multiplicity of valuations. "Maximum desirable" or "as fast as is possible and desirable" are empty, evasive phrases.

The "maximum" thesis has occasionally been defended by making two assumptions: first, that there is a maximum rate at which the economy can absorb the bundle of coordinated policies and beyond which yield becomes negative; second, that gains short of this maximum rate are so great that they compensate for any sacrifices. The limits to this maximum rate are set by resources available for investment, attitudes, institutions, health, administration, and so on. This view implies the assumption that the ability and willingness to apply policies are not themselves constraints. (See Otto Eckstein, "Capital Theory and Some Theoretical Problems in Development Planning," *American Economic Review, Papers and Proceedings,* Vol. LI, No. 2, May, 1961, p. 94.)

[2] The dilemma is that, while the *need* to coordinate is much greater in underdeveloped countries than in advanced countries, the *ability* and *willingness* to do so are much less. That the need is greater we argue in some detail below in this appendix. That the ability to coordinate and even the willingness to do so are frequently less is apparent in many contexts in our study. Without this important proviso, the present discussion of the limitations of comprehensive planning in South Asian countries may appear unduly naive.

[3] "The smaller the resources and the more formidable and complex the problems, the greater the need for planning in order to achieve maximum results in the shortest

normally much less favorable to the spread of development impulses than in highly developed countries. In the latter a long process of adjustment toward rationality has already taken place. It has resulted in attitudes, patterns of behavior, and institutions sanctioned by laws and regulations, collective agreements, customs, and accepted ideas, disseminated by education, and permeating social intercourse generally. These forces provide for the regulated but free propagation of impulses from one field of activity and one location to others. In underdeveloped countries, on the other hand, the "spread effects" meet with stronger resistance, and attitudes and institutions may check or even counteract the impulses for development.

An illustration of the need for reforming attitudes and institutions is provided by our study of labor utilization in Part Five of this book. We find that the modern Western concepts of "unemployment" and "disguised unemployment" — in South Asia translated, or rather transformed, into "underemployment" — do not apply to the greater part of the population of working age — the "labor force" — in South Asian countries.[1] These concepts imply that there is a fluid labor market, that idleness within regulated working hours is normally involuntary, that inability to work can be clearly distinguished from unwillingness to work, and that the differences in the quality of labor input, which is to say its intensity and efficiency, can be disregarded. In the West these assumptions and, consequently, these concepts are meaningful. Attitudes there fit an analysis in the simple aggregative terms of employment and unemployment. For particular occupations, working hours and working conditions have been standardized, and differences in the quality of labor input either are not very important or can be reduced to a common scale. With few exceptions, a man without a job can be assumed to seek work, so that a sufficient rise in the demand for labor will create "full employment."

In the South Asian countries the situation is entirely different. Increasing the demand for labor, or creating opportunities for productive work by the self-employed, will by itself not lead to a better utilization of the labor force or will do so only to a minor extent. Such measures have to be supplemented by policies directed not only at investment and expansion of labor demand but also at changing organizations and habits, attitudes and institutions, and religious beliefs and social valuations. The presence or absence of such policies is crucial to the productivity of investments, a situation for which there is no parallel in the West. On the other hand, properly selected and directed investments are often an indispensable condition for implementing policies intended to improve attitudes and institutions. The exclusion of "non-economic" factors from the ordinary models used in economic analysis and planning has led to a serious distortion of the concepts used in relation to labor utilization.

20 *The Neglect of Attitudes and Institutions*

In the writings on development problems of underdeveloped countries, it is a commonplace to acknowledge that a close relationship exists between the ef-

---

time." (Pakistan, Government of, National Planning Board, *The First Five Year Plan 1955–60*, Karachi, 1958, pp. 59–60.)

[1] Chapter 21, Part II; Appendix 6.

fectiveness of development policies in the economic field and prevailing attitudes and institutions.[1] But it is fair to say that almost all economic studies of these problems, whether by South Asian or foreign economists, imply an almost complete neglect of this relationship and its consequences. In particular, all the development plans suffer structurally from this defect.[2] Prejudices derived from Western and "Marxist" thinking — which on this as on so many other points converge — and given support by vested interests or inhibitions in policy formation, blur economists' broader insights into South Asian conditions and confine their range of vision to "economic" factors.

In the Prologue (Section 6) and in many other contexts[3] we characterized

---

[1] "Prices do not respond to changing relative scarcities, or entrepreneurs do not respond to changing prices, or immobilities of resources are such as to prevent necessary movements of factors, or some other characteristic of the general social milieu interferes with the economic process working in such a manner as to generate continuing economic growth. It is apparent that such barriers must be eliminated before a society can play host to the kind of cumulative developmental process with which advanced countries have become familiar." (Gustav Ranis, "Economic Development: A Suggested Approach," *Kyklos*, Vol. XII, Fasc. 3, 1959, p. 440.)

"Sustained growth requires a considerable transformation in the educative process. . . . that is, it requires drastic changes in the mores, habits, and traditions of the populace. But the educative process and the consequent mores and traditions are so fundamental to the life of the society, and so pervasive in the day-to-day life of the community, especially within the family group, that it is almost unthinkable that these should respond drastically to small stimulants or shocks." (Leibenstein, *Economic Backwardness and Economic Growth*, pp. 35–36.) The writer gives "a partial list of the attitudes that it would be desirable to develop in order to promote economic growth" (p. 109): "(1) Western 'market' incentives, that is, a strong profit incentive, an eagerness to maximize money incomes, etc., (2) a willingness to accept entrepreneurial risks, (3) an eagerness to be trained for industrial and 'dirty' jobs rather than white collar jobs or those that have cultural prestige value, and (4) an eagerness to engage in and promote scientific and technical progress rather than devotion to an honorifically valued 'cultural' education. In sum, it is necessary to create an outlook in which success is gauged by market performance and in which rational, rather than conventional or traditional, considerations are the determinants of action." This list, as we find in the present study, is a very partial one.

"Development is not governed in any country by economic forces alone, and the more backward the country the more this is true. The key to development lies in men's minds, in the institutions in which their thinking finds expression and in the play of opportunity on ideas and institutions." (A. K. Cairncross, "International Trade and Economic Development," *Economica*, Vol. XXVIII, No. 109, February, 1961, p. 250.)

Everett Hagen correctly appraises the significance economists attach to these factors. He notes that "A number of economists who are students of economic growth make generous reference to the importance of noneconomic factors" and then — citing Kaldor, Leibenstein, Rostow, Lewis, Nurkse, Eckaus, Hirschman, and Mason and referring in general to "virtually all of the writers of texts on economic development" — he adds that "many of these treat these factors much as Mark Twain accused everyone of treating the weather. Having mentioned noneconomic factors, they then proceed to ignore them and discuss development as though only economic factors bring it about. The others (including present company) in essence say, 'change in noneconomic factors must be taken into account, but I don't know what causes it.'" (Everett E. Hagen, "Turning Parameters into Variables in the Theory of Economic Growth," *American Economic Review, Papers and Proceedings*, Vol. I, No. 2, May, 1960, pp. 624–625.)

[2] Appendix 4.

[3] For instance, Chapter 21, Section 9.

this approach as biased and discussed the social forces that have led to it. The economic models[1] to which we repeatedly refer are symptomatic of this bias. Even when the plans express a wider conception of the problem of planning and devote much space to proposals for changing non-economic factors, they still have at their core an investment program in which output is treated as a function of capital input, usually in terms of physical investment.[2] When, as in the treatment of labor utilization, the facts seem to underscore the necessity of altering attitudes and institutions, it is minimized by the use of the concepts of employment, unemployment, and disguised unemployment or underemployment — relevant and realistic in the West but not in South Asia.

This narrow approach to planning in the underdeveloped countries of South Asia implies one or both of two assumptions:
  (1) that development efforts directed at raising output by investment will induce changes favorable to development in all other conditions;
  (2) that efforts to change the non-economic conditions directly are difficult, impossible, or ruled out.

The first assumption has a long and honorable history. Adam Smith and the classical economists laid great stress on such non-economic factors as rationality, enterprise, efficiency, mobility, skills, education, and honest government, as pre-conditions of production. But they tended to regard their improvement as inevitable. They had, indeed, good reason for such optimism with respect to the countries with which they were concerned. Moreover, their liberal philosophy, inspired by a very different experience from that of the South Asian countries, made them hostile to state intervention. In their view, development — including reforms of attitudes and institutions — would result from giving free rein to individual initative and market forces. Marx — no more a planner than his predecessors[3] — also thought in teleological terms and regarded the realization of his ideals as the inevitable outcome of a historical process. Planning against the process was futile, planning for it unnecessary. His view of the entire culture — with well-known reservations — as a superstructure of the "modes of production" reflects an extreme optimism about the spread of impulses from the "modes of production," and particularly from industrialization, to cultural and social attitudes and institutions.[4]

The majority of contemporary Western economists, with a few notable exceptions, *are* planners, at least with regard to the underdeveloped countries. But influenced by Marx to a degree they are rarely aware of, they usually make the first assumption that economic advance will have strong and rapid repercussions on attitudes and institutions, especially on those important for development.[5] Without this assumption, one cannot make sense of the numer-

---

[1] Appendix 3.

[2] Appendix 4.

[3] See in Section 3 above.

[4] Prologue, Section 6; Chapter 5, Section 4.

[5] The present-day Communist doctrine is well expressed by Oskar Lange: "What is the essential of planning economic development? I would say that the essential consists in assuring an amount of productive investment which is sufficient to provide for a rise of national income substantially in excess of the rise in population, so that per

ous models and plans produced for the underdeveloped countries of South Asia. It has become almost a cliché in the region to say that the political revolution must be followed by a social revolution in order to permit an economic

---

capita national income increases. *The strategic factor is investment, or more precisely productive investment.* Consequently the problem of development planning is one of assuring that there be sufficient productive investment, and then of directing that productive investment into such channels as will provide for the most rapid growth of the productive power of national economy.

"These are the essential tasks of development planning. The problems which planning faces can be divided into two categories. One is the mobilization of resources for purposes of productive investment, the other is the direction of the investment into proper channels. These are the essential problems implied in planning." (Oskar Lange, *Economic Development, Planning and International Cooperation,* Central Bank of Egypt, Cairo, 1961, p. 10. Italics added.)

Shonfield and Hoselitz state the most common Western assumptions:

"Implicit in our whole approach is the decision to try and push economic development by purely economic means. We permit ourselves to hope that certain kinds of economic change will have political consequences; the ideology of the West is Marxist enough for that. We expect that the new middle classes will, once they are large and rich enough, eventually overthrow the corrupt government to which we are giving economic assistance today. But we are not going to do anything directly to bring that government down." (Andrew Shonfield, *The Attack on World Poverty,* Chatto & Windus Ltd., London, 1960, pp. 17–18.)

"As concerns present instances of economic development, it is quite proper to regard such factors as accumulation of (or mobilization of accumulated) capital, planned introduction of new skills and new work techniques as the primary variables, and to regard adjustments in the social structure as positive, negative or neutral 'responses' to these 'stimuli.' In other words, the governments of underdeveloped countries are resolved to plan for economic development and to carry out these plans to the extent of their abilities. The impact of social and cultural factors consists thus not in determining whether or not, or even in what form, economic growth is to take place, but how easily and smoothly the objectives of a development plan can be attained and what costs — not all of which are strictly measurable in terms of money or other resources — are involved in reaching the goals." (Bert F. Hoselitz, "Social Structure and Economic Growth," *Economia Internazionale,* Vol. VI, No. 3, Chamber of Commerce, Industry, and Agriculture, Genoa, 1953, p. 18.)

Nehru observes the similarity between the "Marxist" and the Western approach and attributes it to the rationalism of science: ". . . broadly speaking, planning for industrial development is generally accepted as a matter of mathematical formula. It is extraordinary how both Soviet and American experts agree on this. If a Russian planner comes here, studies our projects and advises us, it is really extraordinary how his conclusions are in agreement with those of — say, an American expert. It has been quite astonishing for me to come across this type of agreement from planners belonging to two different and contradictory political and economic systems. You see, they happen to be men of science, planners, experts, who approach our problems from purely a scientific point of view. Once they do so, they forget about ideologies and all that, and they agree, broadly, that given certain pre-conditions of development, industrialization and all that, certain exact conclusions follow almost as a matter of course. Of course, I am not talking of non-scientific people, like the American businessman, for example, who will talk about private enterprise and all that, or the Soviet politicians who will press Communist or Marxist solutions. They always do so. But the moment the scientist or technologist comes on the scene, be he Russian or American, the conclusions are the same for the simple reason that planning and development today are almost a matter of mathematics." (R. K. Karanjia, *The Mind of Mr. Nehru,* Allen & Unwin Ltd., London, 1960, pp. 50–51.)

revolution. But despite this stereotyped declaration, practice suggests that social changes are expected to follow in the wake of economic changes, inasmuch
as only an economic revolution, or in other words economic development, is in
fact attempted.

The first assumption of the inevitability of sufficiently strong and rapid, indirectly induced changes of attitudes and institutions is related to the second
assumption of the difficulty or impossibility of directly inducing changes, for
acceptance of the second assumption demands acceptance of the first if planners are to maintain faith in the usefulness of Western-type economic models.
The second assumption, though usually implicit, is occasionally made explicit.[1]
Unfortunately, the evidence, as set forth in the present study, suggests that
whereas the first assumption is glaringly untrue, particularly in the larger and
poorer countries of South Asia where the accelerating increase in population
adversely affects both economic and social conditions, the second assumption
may well be true.

As we point out in various contexts in this study, "economic" policies are
undoubtedly easier to carry out than are social policies that challenge vested
interests, violate deep-seated inhibitions, offend cherished traditions and beliefs, and work against the heavy weight of social inertia. If, however, development policies are, for these reasons among others, mainly directed at economic
development in the narrow sense, they will prove less than effective. Tibor
Mende has made this point well:

. . . no country has seen a frontal attack on all the major problems at the same time. I
should like to remark here that I am absolutely convinced that, sociologically speaking,
one of the reasons for the communists' success wherever they are active is that they go
on attacking all the major problems simultaneously. In an inert society where the de-
formations of the past have accumulated, you are exactly in the same situation as the
man who cuts a clearing in the jungle, if you go on attacking one problem; that clearing will not resist the jungle when it grows back, it will disappear. Either you go at it
seriously or better you don't touch it, because you will be disillusioned. I think this is
what has been happening in Southeast Asia. They have attacked one problem at a time;
I am not condemning them for it, because after all they had no personnel, they had no
capital, and it was very difficult to be more general. But anyway I think it is important
to realize that to create the general dynamism which makes people work wonders —
you see sometimes in these communist countries that people do extraordinary things
which statistically speaking are not expected of them — it is necessary that they go on
attacking all the problems simultaneously and generate this almost superhuman en-

[1] "Underlying these remarks is the assumption that desired patterns of fertility, desired attitudes toward thrift and investment, desired rates of savings, and desired
changes in and stimuli to the growth agents, and, most important, desired changes in
mores and traditions that underlie these changes cannot be achieved easily by direct
methods, . . . Belief in the efficacy of direct action in establishing desired attitudes, traditions, and behavior patterns seems to be somewhat similar to advocating direct action in fostering the spirit of optimism during periods of economic depression. Our
present knowledge of social psychology does not suggest that very much can be hoped
for in this direction at present. Of course, we cannot foresee the future, and future
socio-psychological discoveries may possibly change all this." (Leibenstein, *Economic
Backwardness and Economic Growth*, pp. 258–259, f.n. 6.)

thusiasm which makes people do extraordinary things. This has not been attempted anywhere in Southeast Asia.[1]

To Mende's observations about the policies of the Communist countries one may add that the Communists themselves have obviously not relied on Marx's optimistic hypothesis of the rapid and effective spread of impulses from the economic sphere to the "superstructure" but have directly intervened to change social conditions, while, as always, preserving Marx's doctrine in reinterpreted form. In the first place, they have used the government to reshape society, instead of letting society, changed by the modes of production, determine the government.[2] They have thus created something very different from Marx's dream of the "realm of liberty" that would replace the "kingdom of necessity" and in which, after the collapse of the capitalist system, the state would "wither away" and the government of men would give way to the "administration of things." The adjustment of the doctrine was clearly marked by Lenin's famous assertion that "Communism is *Soviet power* plus electricity" (italics added), although it is doubtful whether Lenin foresaw the amount and duration of the compulsion that would be used.[3] This adjustment of the doctrine

---

[1] Tibor Mende, "Southeast Asia and Japan," *Bulletin of the International House of Japan, Inc.*, Winter, 1959, No. 3, p. 26. When he speaks of Southeast Asia, Mende is referring to what in this book is called South Asia.

[2] As Edward Mason has noted: "The critical question confronting research on the role of government in economic development is the extent to which government can shape, or is inevitably shaped by, the society of which it is a part. To a generation deeply influenced by Marx, society, or rather basic economic and social change, was the shaper and government very much a strictly determined product. And indeed in the society that Marx described and analyzed — the society of Western Europe, and particularly Britain — government was shaped by the society. As George Unwin put it, 'The main feature of British history since the seventeenth century has been the remoulding of a State by a powerful Society.' (George Unwin, *Studies in Economic History*, London, 1927, p. 28.) But the political descendants of Marx have demonstrated in no uncertain manner that the state, appropriately equipped with instruments of authority, including terror, can go a long way in reshaping the surrounding society." (Edward S. Mason, "The Role of Government in Economic Development," *American Economic Review, Papers and Proceedings*, Vol. L, No. 2, May, 1960, p. 636.)

"The cardinal advantage of communist economic planning is that it can and does think consistently in these terms; for the communist, once he has consolidated his regime politically, has both the power and the will to impose on the community the physical distribution and utilisation of men and materials that his calculations show to be necessary for the attainment of his objectives. He need have no regard for immediate sectional interests, whether of landlords or capitalists, peasants or proletarians, and can act with a ruthlessness tempered only by the need to avoid provoking rebellion and to maintain producers' morale — in both of which tasks he is notably assisted by his monopoly of the means of propaganda. Non-communist governments cannot use similar methods, and consequently are unable to plan the economy in so comprehensive a manner." (A. H. Hanson, *Public Enterprise and Economic Development*, Routledge and Kegan Paul Ltd., London, 1959, pp. 98–99.)

[3] Sarvepalli Radhakrishnan, on returning from his ambassadorship in Moscow, told the present writer of a conversation he had had with Stalin, in which the latter had said that he foresaw, and hoped for, much more individual liberty once economic development had been pressed forward so much that further development would be compatible with it; but he meant that in the initial stages the planned development in the Soviet Union required the harsher rule.

may have been motivated by another circumstance that conflicted with Marx's forecast: the fact that the revolution occurred first in an underdeveloped country. In both respects revolutionaries like Bakunin, who saw the importance of changing attitudes, and who predicted the arrival of the revolution in countries like Russia, showed deeper insight and more accurate vision.

As is brought out in the fourth part of this book, the South Asian countries do not want to follow the Communist line of development. They aim at "democratic planning." In Chapter 18, Sections 13 and 14, on the "soft state," and elsewhere, we have argued that the term "democratic planning" has been used to justify a very serious lack of determination and ability to apply compulsion in order to enforce existing laws and regulations and to enact and enforce new ones. The dictum of the highly respected American jurist Learned Hand that "law is violence" would not appeal to, or be understood by, the greater part of the South Asian intellectual elite. The governments of these countries have been much more reluctant to promulgate and enforce obligations than have the rich democratic welfare states of the West, which do not regard the use of force for social ends as a retreat from democracy.

This reluctance not only helps to explain the relative absence of successful development in South Asia but can itself be explained by the status of underdevelopment. The "soft state" falls under the heading of our fourth, fifth, and sixth categories of undesirable conditions — attitudes, institutions, and policies — and is one of the main characteristics of underdevelopment. It derives historically from feudal or pre-feudal traditions, and was in many ways reinforced by the reaction against the colonial regimes and by the liberation movements they bred. But in the present era, the soft state does little to remove, and in fact helps to create, almost insurmountable obstacles and inhibitions to planning. By preventing vigorous attacks on all those conditions that lie outside the narrowly defined economic sphere, it impedes economic development. In this situation, *planning that is based on simple economic models and neglects non-economic forces serves as an opportune rationalization.* Necessity, especially political necessity, is made a virtue when it is lightheartedly assumed that investment will by itself engender development. To buttress this rationalization analogies are claimed to exist between conditions in South Asia and conditions in advanced countries, either as they now exist or as they did exist when these countries approached a period of rapid development.[1]

But the prospects of breaking down the barriers to development in the South Asian countries would be quite different if in a country like India, for example, the government were really determined to change the prevailing attitudes and institutions and had the courage to take the necessary steps and accept their consequences. These would include the effective abolition of caste, prescribed by the constitution, and measures, accepted in principle, that would increase mobility and equality, such as effective land reform and tenancy legislation; a rational policy for husbandry, even if it required the killing of many half-starved cows; eradication of corruption at all levels; enforcement of tax laws; effective taxation on income from land; a forceful attack on the problem of the "educated unemployed" and their refusal to do manual work —

[1] The differences in "initial conditions" are played down; see Chapter 14.

in general, enactment and enforcement, not only of fiscal, but also of all other obligations on people that are required for development. It would mean mobilizing the underutilized agricultural labor for permanent improvements in agricultural production and creation of social capital; a large-scale and effectively carried out campaign to spread birth control; and so on.

In many respects *a large and rapid change of attitudes and institutions is not more difficult than a series of small and gradual changes* — just as a plunge into cold water is less painful than slow submersion. Whatever resistance is called forth by any one gradual step forward will usually be more effectively mustered against the next step, whereas there is less chance for resistance when the change is rapid and multiple. This is particularly true if the small changes are attempted half-heartedly and if reliance is placed either on the indirect effects induced by economic changes or on exhortations and empty threats; in these circumstances the forces of resistance may be encouraged. Worse still is the practice, common in South Asia, of pronouncing or even legislating large-scale reforms and not implementing them. Such behavior breeds cynicism and contempt, and makes subsequent reforms more difficult.[1] All this having been said, it is admittedly very difficult to carry out reforms that offend against established institutions and attitudes, especially since those in power, responsible for reforms, often share these attitudes and have a stake in preserving the institutions through which they are molded; in other words, they suffer from what we have called inhibitions. To a varying extent this is as true, or almost as true, of the dictatorships in the region as it is of those governments that come to power through elections. Against this background the concentration in South Asia of planning on the narrow front of investment and production, expressed in the economic models and in the structure of the plans, becomes understandable.

As we noted, at the more general level of discussion the desirability of attacking on a broad front is generally recognized; but the gap between profession of principle and actual practice remains wide. The plans often include policies in many non-economic spheres, but the actual proposals are much more limited, and usually more lenient toward prevailing attitudes and institutions, than rational considerations of a high rate of development warrant.[2] One

[1] The problem referred to in this paragraph is a crucial one. Social anthropologists, interested in the potential dynamics of stagnant communities in the dichotomy of revolution or evolution, could make path-breaking contributions to the theory of planning for development. Cf. J. D. N. Verslays, "Social Factors in Asian Rural Development," *Pacific Affairs,* Vol. XXX, No. 2, June, 1957, pp. 161–162.

[2] The plans regularly contain general statements about the necessity to change the general social framework.

The Second Five Year Plan of India, for example, made it clear that "the task before an underdeveloped country is not merely to get better results within the existing framework of economic and social institutions but to mould and refashion these so that they contribute effectively to the realization of wider and deeper social values." (India, Government of, Planning Commission, *Second Five Year Plan,* New Delhi, 1956, p. 22.)

". . . the Philippine three-year programme of economic and social development also felt the need not to upset unduly existing non-economic value patterns, but, if this

influence in the direction of a wider approach in India is the Gandhian ideology;[1] similar ideas exist in other countries. They have not been very powerful, however, partly because planning and modernization represent a conscious break with these ideologies, and partly because they have urged voluntary changes in attitudes and institutions and opposed any form of external compulsion.

But it is not only the discussion inspired by Gandhian ideologies that has stressed the understanding of development and planning for development in terms of simultaneous changes in a multitude of conditions, both economic and non-economic. Writers unaffected by indigenous South Asian ideologies, and firmly in the tradition of the Western ideals of modernization, have also emphasized this need.[2] It has been summed up in the commonplace observation

---

was necessary, to plan for desirable changes in the political and social institutions." (Philippines, Government of, National Economic Council, *Three-Year Programme of Economic and Social Development (FY 1959/60 to FY 1961/62)*, Manila, 1959, p. 12.)

The plans of Ceylon and Pakistan ". . . view social development as a positive instrument for economic progress." (United Nations, ECAFE, "Experience of ECAFE Countries with Social Development Programmes," *Economic Development and Planning in Asia and the Far East, Economic Bulletin for Asia and the Far East*, Vol. X, No. 3, December, 1959, p. 10.)

The rationalization of the lack of determination to undertake any vigorous reforms of the social framework is put in terms of the need not to upset "the existing value system," to have a "smooth transition," to avoid or compensate for "traumatic disturbances," and, ultimately, the determination to remain within the bounds of "democratic planning," working with the means of "persuasion and not compulsion." These reservations point to important political inhibitions and obstacles, generally making these countries what we have called "soft states." Cf. Chapter 3, Section 8.

[1] "Whereas the modern concept of planning refers mainly to economic planning, Gandhian planning was concerned with the overall, balanced development of society, with special emphasis on the spiritual and moral development of the individual." (T. K. N. Unnithan, *Gandhi and Free India, a Socio-Economic Study*, J. B. Wolters, Groningen, Netherlands, 1956, p. 116.)

[2] "Technically, the essence of the problem of growth is that all parameters become variables. Any theory of growth which places great reliance on a few simple relationships does not deserve serious consideration as an explanation of so vastly interdependent a phenomenon. The classical view that economic growth would be engendered 'if only' restraints were removed and the contemporary view 'if only' several prerequisites were met, are oversimplifications which are not applicable to newly developing countries." (J. M. Letiche, "The Relevance of Classical and Contemporary Theories of Growth to Economic Development," *American Economic Review, Papers and Proceedings*, Vol. XLIX, No. 2, May, 1959, p. 492.)

". . . it will be argued in this paper that development is not a mere matter of funnelling technical knowledge or capital but that it involves people. People co-operate in institutions such as schools and banks and factories, and what takes time in the creation of these is not the construction of the edifices, but the training and motivating of the participants. Development requires that people be in some ways changed, and by the recognition of this we bring history back into the picture. Events force us to believe that development is more than the sum of simple technology, simple economics, and simple management." (Keyfitz, *Canadian Journal of Economics and Political Science*, Vol. XXV, No. 1, February, 1959, p. 36.)

"It is the conjuncture of forces causing economic growth that is important, and no one of them alone will have the same effect as it does in conjunction with others. The

that development is a "human" problem and planning means "changing men."

If intellectual conflict is not more apparent, this is largely because a division of responsibility has led some to speculate in general terms and others to build models and conduct technical discussions; often the second group maintains the appearance of sophistication by indicating an awareness of the broader perspective without, however, letting this interfere with their work.[1]

21 Levels of Living

In the last section we argued that in planning for growth in the advanced Western countries there may be good reasons for neglecting the fourth and fifth categories of conditions — attitudes and institutions[2] — but that these reasons do not hold for planning for development in South Asia. In this section we shall attempt to show that the same is true of the third category, levels of living.

In poor countries a change in the levels of living affects the contribution men make to production. We define levels of living in a broad sense, including health and educational facilities and cultural activities as well as nutrition and housing. By human productivity we refer not only to the quantity, intensity, regularity, skill, and general efficiency of labor inputs, but also to enterprise and other aptitudes and dispositions that, when improved, tend to raise production; in the following discussion we shall for simplicity's sake refer to all of them as labor input and efficiency. In rich countries, a rise in levels of living has either no effect, or a very much smaller effect, on human productivity. People normally consume enough — occasionally and in some respects perhaps too much — to maintain an optimal level of labor input and labor efficiency. Higher consumption would not raise labor input and efficiency, nor would lower consumption,

---

system is bound to be rather complicated; it is doubtful whether the method of 'successive approximations' will give the right answers. Dealing with the whole system at once enormously increases the intellectual difficulty of handling the problem." (Higgins, *Economic Development*, p. 415.)

[1] For instance, Jan Tinbergen warns that the "importance [of training and education] should not be overlooked," but he keeps them out of his analysis because "these activities are not as a rule considered a part of economic policy," a statement that implies all the metaphysical notions mentioned in Section 14 above. (Tinbergen, *The Design of Development*, p. 5.) Ragnar Nurkse, among others, more humbly explains that he is not taking up "matters relating to cultural, social and demographic conditions, partly because of the great diversity of those conditions . . . but mainly because of [his] lack of knowledge in these fields," which leaves open the question, how he then can come to such definite conclusions. (*Problems of Capital Formation in Underdeveloped Countries*, p. 2.)

As Everett E. Hagen observes: "Almost every economic analyst studying economic development agreed that some other factors are of importance. However, when an economist presented [his] analysis he often ignored other factors, because he claimed no competence with respect to them. And of course *ignoring them when making prescriptions is equivalent to assigning them zero importance*." ("The Role of Different Sciences in the Teaching Curricula of the Institutes," paper given at Tavistock Institute of Human Relations, roneod, London, no date, p. 3. Italics added.)

[2] We are aware that this concession is far too generous; a more institutional approach is needed even in the Western countries. However, our study is not concerned with this problem.

within practical limits, reduce them. Hence there is, in rich countries, a fairly clear line of demarcation, both for the community and for the individual, between that part of income which is consumed and that part which is saved. Saving, like income, is a composite term and covers, for the present purpose, all those activities which, *by reducing present consumption below what it would otherwise be,* raise future income above what it would otherwise be. It can take the form of the creation of productive assets different from consumption goods, such as fixed equipment, or it can take the form of using consumption goods, such as seedcorn, to increase productivity directly. Workers have to be fed while they are not adding to current consumption or simple "waiting" has to be done. The common feature is that saving is done with the intention of raising future production and income above what they would be if no saving had occurred, and the intention will be realized only if, and insofar as, direct investment is carried out. Although there are types of expenditure that, though not consumption, do not, and are not intended to, raise future production (e.g., military expenditure), by and large the distinction between consumption and saving or investment corresponds in rich countries to the distinction between non-productive and productive expenditure.

It follows that in the rich countries analysis of and policies affecting levels of consumption can be neglected when growth and development are considered, except insofar as they determine the resources set aside as savings and thus available for investment. A model for growth can be confined to the use of such concepts as savings, investment, employment, production, and price formation, which form the basic tools of economic analysis and policy.

Before turning to the theoretical implications of this difference between rich and poor countries, let us consider the components of the level of living briefly. In the rich countries, standards of nutrition are generally so high that a rise in the quantity or an improvement in the quality of food intake has no effect on labor productivity. They may, indeed, lower it. This is not so in any South Asian country.[1] For a large part of the population of India and Pakistan, and a smaller part of the population in the other South Asian countries, even the calorie intake is inadequate to maintain optimal levels of health, energy, and labor input and efficiency. Qualitative deficiencies and dietary imbalance, particularly shortages of protein, vitamins, and essential minerals, are even more widespread. Both undernutrition and malnutrition impair the energy of a large part of the population of these countries, and decrease labor input and efficiency. The same is true for housing, sanitation, and health facilities in general. In the rich countries the standards are such that higher expenditure has little effect on labor input and efficiency. Again this is not so in the countries of South Asia. The impact is greatest in the poorest countries, Pakistan and India. Even though mortality rates have fallen rapidly, high morbidity rates and the frequency of illnesses that lower stamina and energy, and reduce resistance to disease, have large effects on productivity.[2]

[1] Chapter 12, Section 4; Chapter 30, Section 11.
[2] Chapter 30, Sections 1 and 11.

Similarly, the level of elementary education has in the West for a very long time been so high that further advances have no great and immediate effect on the ability to work and the efficiency of the labor force.[1] Low levels of labor input and efficiency in all the South Asian countries, on the other hand, are partly the result of the low levels of elementary education. Industry there is starved for literate workers who can understand a complicated production process and follow written instructions and drafts. Agriculture and crafts would greatly profit if more people could read simple books and professional and trade journals, and if they could write, calculate, and keep accounts. The persistence of primitive techniques and the difficulty of introducing improvements through extension work and other methods are largely due to the low levels of elementary education. So is the resistance to the organization of co-operatives from which the bulk of the population, not only the better situated, could benefit. The absence of a rational credit system and the importance of the moneylender can be attributed in part to the same cause. If, on the one hand, there is a dearth of usefully educated, there are, on the other hand, the "educated unemployed." Schools turn out graduates who are neither fit nor willing to become semi-skilled and skilled artisans, fitters, electricians, mechanics, or even bookkeepers. Not just more but a different kind of education is needed, along with a change in attitudes, so that the "educated" will not shun manual work. Effective government policies along these lines are a precondition for a rapid advance in almost every direction.

These differences have important implications for planning. Although it makes sense in the rich countries to think of economic development in terms of savings, investment, employment, and output, and to disregard levels of living, except insofar as consumption decreases that part of income which could be saved, the situation in the underdeveloped countries is quite different. For the broad masses there, *an increase in consumption raises productivity, with variations according to the direction and composition of the increase.* This is another fundamental difference that renders Western concepts and theories inapplicable to the problem of development in South Asia.

To this must be added a further complication. Whereas in the rich countries of the West the expansion of certain policy measures directed toward higher levels of living, such as improved health services, has now become essentially a technical problem that can be treated in isolation, except for the question whether it is to be a public or private responsibility, *in the South Asian countries all policies affecting levels of living are interdependent.* The reason again is that these levels are so low. Western thinking applied to South Asian problems is bound to yield false conclusions. In South Asia health is closely connected with nutrition, housing, and education. Whereas the general level of education is such in the rich countries that popular attitudes present no serious obstacle to implementing health policies, or at any rate none that cannot be

---

[1] The situation is different for higher education and professional and technical training, but this is not commonly regarded as consumption or included in the level of living, but, quite properly, is considered investment, even if this is not yet fully recognized in national accounting.

For substantiation of what follows in this paragraph, see Chapters 32 and 33.

removed by an appeal to good sense, the obstacles presented by illiterate and tradition-bound communities are larger and much harder to overcome. Implementation of health measures there depends on raising the general level of education and changing fundamental beliefs.[1]

We have reached two conclusions for the underdeveloped countries in South Asia: first, it is not possible to deal with specific components of the level of living as technical problems, isolated from other components. They are all closely interrelated. Secondly, measures that increase production and productivity cannot be separated from measures that raise certain kinds of consumption. It follows that development policies, if they are to be effective, must be coordinated over a much wider range of activities, including some that are components of the level of living insofar as they raise production. As we have indicated, this conclusion has important corollaries for the adequacy of certain concepts and theories to development and planning for development.

To raise levels of nutrition, housing, and sanitation, to improve medical facilities for prevention and cure, to provide elementary education — these are objectives to which all communities attach independent value, for they enable people to lead a better and fuller life. They are an important reason why the underdeveloped countries of South Asia desire development, and in particular why they want higher production and incomes. In this they do not differ from the developed countries.[2] In addition, however, the underdeveloped countries should attach instrumental value to raising levels of living, for labor input and efficiency can thereby be increased. Raising one component of these levels has instrumental value in raising others, and raising all components increases productivity. The cumulative effects on productivity are thus both direct and indirect. In the developed countries consumption has either no instrumental value or a very much smaller one. There, raising levels of living is desirable only because of the independent value attached to consumption. This is not because of a particular value premise — for instance, the notion of the classical writers that we produce only in order to consume — but because of certain biological, physiological, psychological, and social facts. Living levels in rich countries are so high that changes, within practical limits, affect productivity little if at all.

Obviously, if consumption were substantially reduced, productivity would suffer even in the rich countries. We may speculate about a minimum consumption level necessary to preserve optimal productivity, and such speculation has been reflected in some of the arguments in the theory of public finance for basic allowances before taxable income is assessed. We may further speculate about a level of consumption at which the cost of a marginal increase is exactly equal to its marginal value productivity. This would presumably be the optimal consumption level from the point of view of a calculating slave-owner

---

[1] Chapter 30.

[2] Thus there is, for example, no limit to the expenditure that all countries may want to devote to prolonging lives and to eliminating disease, and even the richest are nowhere near these ultimate objectives. Indeed, solving one set of problems often raises many new ones.

or horse breeder. But such speculations about the minimum level of consumption that it is necessary or advantageous to maintain – and that, it could be argued, should be included in calculating the gross costs of production – have little practical relevance for the rich countries, except as motivation for an already existing system of income redistribution through social security and other policy measures financed by taxation. Consumption is so high that none of the policies for raising levels of living actually under consideration would affect productivity very much. In any case the difference in degree is so great that it amounts to a totally different type of problem.

This is the reason why saving in the sense of non-consumed income, which *ex post* is identical with investment, has a fairly clear meaning in the rich countries, and why aggregate output can be viewed as a function of the increase in the stock of accumulated capital. In the underdeveloped countries, where "under-consumption" on a vast scale is normal, the basic distinction between investment and consumption does not hold, and reasoning based on it is irrelevant and invalid. Higher consumption forms "investment" – that is, raises production – and *at the same time* remains consumption.

The productivity of this "investment" in the form of consumption varies with the amount of additional consumption, its duration, its direction, its composition, and its rate of change in time.[1] Extra savings in the sense of lowered consumption, imposed on people with depressed levels of consumption, would thus be a form of "disinvestment" in the wider sense. Even if, in a particular case, an investment in productive physical capital appeared so profitable that the government felt justified in reducing food consumption to enable the investment to take place, the depressing effect on labor productivity should be deducted in the calculations. For this type of calculation, models that work with savings (in the sense of non-consumed income), investment, and capital/output ratios are useless. These models isolate the conditions under categories 1 and 2 in Section 5 from those in category 3; as we saw in the previous section, they also neglect attitudes and institutions in categories 4 and 5 when they use notions such as employment, unemployment, and underemployment. More generally, approaches, concepts, models, and theories that fit conditions and policies in the West lose relevance when applied to the underdeveloped countries in the region because they are not adequate to reality.

It should be noted that the savings-investment-output models cannot be salvaged simply by the inclusion of productive consumption in the definition of investment. As we shall see in Appendix 4 on the structure of the plans, this is often attempted by including in the "development expenditures" of the plans an assortment of public expenditures that normally appear in the current account as public consumption.[2] The inclusion or exclusion of a particular item of expenditure of this type in the development budget is entirely arbitrary –

---

[1] Thus better feeding of workers has direct and rapid effects on productivity, better feeding of children has delayed effects, and better feeding of old people has no effects. Again, feeding has different effects from housing and clothing. Some part of better feeding contributes to the slow building up of strength and vigor and resistance to disease, while another part enables the worker to work harder almost immediately.

[2] Appendix 4, Section 3.

unless the *whole* budget is renamed "development budget." In addition, no attempt is made, or can be made, to redefine on the same principle that part of private expenditure on consumption that would on the same grounds have to be treated as "savings" and "investment." The composite figures for "private and public savings," which are so glibly used in scientific as well as popular discussion of development and planning for development in these countries, are, quite apart from their exceedingly weak statistical origins, arbitrary and unclear.

Since "underconsumption" in the underdeveloped countries in the region is, as we have noted, ubiquitous and relates to all major items of expenditure on nutrition, housing, health, and education, it is impossible to distinguish between that part which is productive and that part which is strictly consumption. In fact, for the overwhelming majority of people in these countries almost all consumption is, *at the margin*, lower than that required for optimum productivity. Almost every increase in workers' consumption raises productivity. Almost all consumption is *simultaneously* productive, though in varying degree. From this follows the logical defect of the concept "investment in man," which has recently become popular among economists.[1]

It is interesting that "Marxists" usually do not challenge the Western approach. Marx himself called man "the most productive force of all"; in particular he regarded all acquisitions of skills as investment.[2] But his followers have largely forgotten this, and its neglect in recent "Marxist" theory has undoubtedly contributed to the ready acceptance in South Asia of the distinction between investment and consumption, and the largely unquestioned use of Western models in planning. If anything, the mainstream of "Marxist" theory is even more restrictive in defining investment merely in terms of physical capital accumulation. The South Asian practice of including in the development budget expenditures other than on physical capital has no foundation in this layer of "Marxist" thinking. The political practice of the Soviet Union, how-

[1] This problem is further discussed in Chapter 29; see also Appendix 3, Section 7.

As suggested in Section 12, it may in principle be possible to separate the productive part of marginal consumption from that part to which independent value only is attached. But independent value is, of course, also attached to the productive part. As long as some independent value is attached to consumption, the optimum productivity must be less than that for identical outlays in directions having only instrumental value.

[2] Occasionally Marx went even further and emphasized that all consumption has a productive aspect. This is partly a terminological or taxonomic problem, such as his insistence that a product only becomes a product ("as distinguished from a mere natural object") by being demanded for consumption; partly a matter of classifying consumption as a necessary condition for carrying on production. But he also wrote: "Consumption is directly also production, just as in nature the consumption of the elements and of chemical matter constitutes production of plants. It is clear that in nutrition, e.g., which is but one form of consumption, man produces his own body; but it is equally true of every kind of consumption, which goes to produce the human being in one way or another. [It is] consumptive production." (*A Contribution to the Critique of Political Economy*, New York, 1904, p. 277.) His insistence that this is true of *every* kind of consumption detracts from the value of his insight and merely leads him to conclude: "Hence, it is the simplest matter with a Hegelian to treat production and consumption as identical" (p. 282).

ever, did not conform to this "Marxist" theory that capital accumulation is the only source of higher productivity. In addition to their investment programs, the plans always contained sections devoted to huge expenditures on the creation of non-physical productive assets. It is now evident that the Soviet Union's high growth rates were largely due to this "investment in men," and that earlier underestimates by Western observers of Soviet growth rates were due to their neglect of these expenditures. It is fairly certain that "Marxist" theory and its influence on the manner of presenting the plans in the Soviet Union contributed to these mistaken estimates by Western economists.

Faced with the practical problem of mustering the resources for the huge investment in physical capital, the Soviet Union did not simply enforce high savings by reducing consumption all around. The government was able to free resources for investment by a consumption *squeeze,* while at the same time *twisting* and redirecting consumption in such a way as to combine suppression in some directions with rapid and substantial increases in others, as dictated by the requirements of growth. The Soviet planners could do this because they controlled all production and prices, and felt no inhibitions in supplementing price policies by direct controls. The task was, however, much simpler in the Soviet Union than it is now in the bigger and poorer countries of South Asia, because there was a considerable food surplus to start with. In spite of the many glaring shortcomings of Soviet agricultural policies, it was possible, by and large, to maintain a fairly adequate level of nutrition. With this as a base, the government attempted until fairly recently to save resources by severely restricting consumption of housing and clothing, while pressing on with education and health. Recognizing the differing effects on productivity of the various components of consumption, Soviet planners did not apply a simple formula of enforcing a savings ratio to secure expansion of planned physical investment. The savings *squeeze* was supported by a consumption *twist.*

The rich Western countries can, of course, afford to let consumption take its course because it is in all directions above the level where changes have much effect on productivity. The main problem of policy is then to achieve a level of savings equal to the desired level of investment, so as to obtain internal and external balance.[1] *The underdeveloped countries of South Asia, however, should accord consumption policies an integral and important role in their economic planning.* Their task should not be merely to compress consumption in order to achieve a certain savings ratio, as domestic and foreign experts usually assume. Since their levels of living are so low that reduced consumption in almost all directions lowers productivity and even the prevention of an increase in consumption is detrimental, they must weigh carefully the effects on productivity of changing the components of consumption, and must then attempt to steer consumption in the most productive directions.

They must, in other words, break with the Western policy of allowing the

[1] However, the Western governments usually use fiscal and other devices to check undesirable consumption, such as that of tobacco and alcohol, and to stimulate consumption that is considered desirable, such as education and health. But these policies, important as they are, do not form an integral part of their general economic policies, except insofar as they affect the relationship between aggregate savings and investment. They can be, and are in fact, pursued in isolation from economic policies.

free choice of consumers to be decisive. Otherwise they will not be able to provide the necessary conditions for raising production, including the provision of enough savings for desirable investment — and they will inflict undue suffering on their people. Those countries that, unlike the Communist countries, do not tightly control all production and prices, and that cannot use an apparatus of controls over consumption, are obviously at a disadvantage not only in squeezing consumption in general but also, and more important, in steering it into productive channels. They must nevertheless face the problem. Their taxation policy, for example, should be conceived in these broader terms.[1] They have to accomplish what the Soviet Union has done, though their methods may be different. Failure to do so will frustrate their hopes of development.

22 *Physical versus Financial Planning*

The reliance on Western concepts, theories, and models, which have to do with savings, investment, and output, invites the presentation of the plans in terms of financial aggregates. As is stressed in Appendix 4 on the structure of the plans, all the actual South Asian development plans are financial or, even more narrowly, fiscal plans. Though a fiscal plan is necessary to insure administrative efficiency and a wider financial plan may also have limited usefulness, neither of them, as Appendix 4 makes clear, can be *the* plan. A plan that conveys what it purports to convey must be based on some kind of physical planning in terms of input requirements and output expectations of physical factors, goods, and services in the various sectors of the economy.[2]

It has been argued that the setting of targets for specific categories of final output from specific investments and their coordination in order to minimize the risk of bottlenecks and excess capacity, although desirable in principle, is often not feasible because adequate statistical information is lacking.[3] If this is so, it is pertinent to ask how it is then possible to draw up a workable financial investment plan. One difference between financial and physical planning is

[1] Appendix 8, Section 8.

[2] The term "physical planning" is occasionally used to denote a particular *method of implementing* certain objectives in a plan. Thus licensing, rationing, and allocations are called "physical planning," and are contrasted with "market conforming" measures such as global monetary and fiscal measures. The expression is a legacy of wartime "planning" in the United Kingdom, which was concerned with mobilization for one over-riding objective — the war effort — and keeping all non-essential activities down to a minimum without too much inflation. But this usage gives rise to confusion. It is possible to have numerous physical controls without a plan of the physical quantities, and it is possible to have a physical plan implemented largely by policies that work through the pricing system. Indeed, it has been argued that one of the functions of "planning" is, or should be, to overcome distortions caused by the use of administrative "physical" controls — which would lead to the paradoxical conclusion that the purpose of planning is to eliminate the results of planning. As we point out in Chapter 19, all the South Asian countries rely heavily on physical or direct controls (in our terminology discretionary controls), but they do little physical planning in the substantive sense.

[3] See, for example, United Nations, ECAFE, *Economic Development and Planning in Asia and the Far East, Economic Bulletin for Asia and the Far East,* Vol. VI, No. 3, November, 1955, Bangkok, 1955, pp. 7 ff.

simply that the latter cannot help revealing the weak factual information on which the plan is based, while the former often serves the function of concealing it. This is not to deny that every government must plan investments and their coordination as best it can, even though it cannot draw on adequate information and must rely largely on guesses. The point is that these guesses and estimates must, in the final analysis, relate to concrete physical items and their changes. The fiscal-financial plan can be at best only a superstructure, built on the basis of a physical plan.

Let us begin by considering public investment in a particular sector. In planning it, specific investment projects will be scrutinized. The different departments regularly draw up a "shopping list" of projects, which clearly must be done in physical terms. It is, of course, true that the pruning of these proposals, carried out by the departments, the treasury, and the planning agency, will often be discussed in financial terms. The fact that there are limitations of supplies will play an important part. The plan will ultimately present the agreed projects in financial terms, but behind these, giving them meaning and substance, must be the physical objectives.[1] As a country advances in effective planning, its financial plan becomes more firmly anchored to detailed physical plans. These may appear in appendices or remain in the files of the government. It is the details of physical planning that make the difference between planning in the clouds and planning on a firm foundation.

There are serious obstacles to the coordination of the physical investment projects. The departments and the agencies working under them, on whose information and judgment the planners must rely, often have little interest in, or competence for, the required coordination. Competent officials are scarce and the initial "shopping list" has probably not been worked out in sufficient detail and with sufficient accuracy to make physical coordination possible. The decision to spend a certain sum on a public investment project will then mark the beginning, instead of the end, of the determination of its physical equivalent

[1] The Ceylon Ten Year Plan makes it clear that the basis for planning is physical planning. "The Plan as a whole was drawn up primarily but not wholly in physical terms. This was done partly because financial processes are secondary to the physical, partly because the nature and magnitude of the financial problem can only be assessed in the light of the particular pattern of resource distribution which results from the process of planning in real terms. The essential point, from a financial point of view, is that the process of growth requires a relative shift in the use of resources from consumption purposes to those of investment. Of the increase in income generated during growth a higher proportion has to be devoted to investment than that which was obtained at the beginning of the period. In physical terms this means that external earnings have to be devoted to the purchase of machinery, building materials and raw materials rather than to the purchase of finished consumer goods and foodstuffs, and that an increased proportion of domestic output is required to provide food, clothing and shelter for the workers who are engaged in producing and erecting physical capital equipment and structures, which, in the short period, do not add to the current flow of consumer goods. The financial problem inherent in this process is how to ensure that a proportion of present incomes and a proportion of the increased incomes accruing during the process of growth are made available for engaging persons on construction work and for purchasing capital equipment." (Ceylon, Government of, National Planning Council, *The Ten Year Plan*, Colombo, 1959, p. 107.)

and the desired coordination with other projects, which is the essence of planning. If then, as is normally the case, the financial calculations have been excessively optimistic, shortages will later further curtail the physical scope of the projects or delay their completion. These reductions will then often be concealed from general inspection by inflated figures in plan evaluations made in financial terms. The fear of future inflation may again necessitate additional financial cuts in the budget; these cuts will further reduce whatever physical coordination there may initially have been in the plan.

One reason why this type of planning, and the ever-present specter of inflation, are so detrimental to the physical coordination of public investments is the concentration of the planners' and the government's interest on the scarcity of financial resources. It distracts attention from the scarcity of agents of production such as skilled labor, managers, technicians, and administrators, and from underutilization of completed projects as a result of deficient demand. These bottlenecks are much more serious in the underdeveloped countries of South Asia than in industrially and commercially advanced countries. Consequently, financial magnitudes are much less capable of reflecting the physical reality behind them, and any deficiency in accurate and detailed physical planning is much more damaging.

The result of inadequate physical planning behind the financial plan is waste. Inflation or the fear of inflation erodes the already imperfect edifice of initial planning. The resulting waste takes various forms. Projects started are not completed or are carried out in an inferior way, or completions are delayed. This has repercussions on the rest of the economy. The structure is out of joint, and even completed and successful investments will not be fully utilized. Thus the construction of a main road without the implementation of a plan for the construction of side roads to the villages, related to how and by whom these should be used and what should be carried on them, carries the risk that these side roads will not be built, or built only in part and/or in the wrong places, so that the investment in the main road will not yield the best returns. The same is true of an irrigation system that lacks the implementation of a plan for smaller canals to and from the fields, related to what crops should be watered and how the peasants should be persuaded to use the system.[1] It is often easier

---

[1] "This is the problem of the alleged current non-full utilization of irrigation resources. It is obvious that in case full utilization of water resources provided by a work of irrigation is sought early, much more action must be planned and executed than the mere construction of the irrigation work. This planning in advance includes the supply of water to the ultimate user in the field, proposals for the pattern of future land utilization with rotations of crops and appropriate tested varieties established for use in particular circumstances, the technical training of the cultivator in the adoption of the new programmes, and the supply to him of credit, materials, etc. required for them. It involves also the planning and construction, together with the new works of a system of transportation, of market centres, processing plants and other equipment which go with the new crops and production patterns. Of recent years, considerable interest is being shown by those in charge of irrigation works in assessment of economic benefits of the future or of economic performance of the past. In relation to this I would advocate that the approach be not confined to merely economic calculations. In relation to all future programmes, for example, it appears to me necessary to undertake full planning by joint expertise of engineers, agronomists, economists and others, of the region that is being commanded by new irrigation works. Such an effort at pre-

to provide new industries with markets — by import restrictions — so that their capacity is fully utilized, than to plan for the full utilization of overhead investments such as roads and irrigation. But even for new industries absence of the required complementary inputs, especially transport, power, and raw materials, may make for waste and underutilization.

A public investment plan in fiscal and financial terms is nevertheless fairly easily anchored to calculations of necessary physical *inputs*, though it may have to include precarious estimates of the increase in the output of other major industries required, and the repercussions on output in other sectors of the economy. But real and coordinated planning of the *output* of major products as well as inputs is a much more intricate task. Instead of one balance in terms of money spent on the project, a separate balance for each product is required, time lags have to be estimated for the various investments, and the calculations have to embrace the private sector.

So far we have been thinking only of conventional physical investment. This, however, forms only a small part of the changes in the social system that have to be induced in order to engender development. With regard to all other policies, a financial plan is still more vacuous. A budget figure for the cost of setting up birth control clinics has, for instance, little significance beyond stating the fact that a certain public policy entails certain charges on the budget. These charges are only a minor consideration compared with the obstacles and inhibitions this policy has to overcome that cannot be expressed in financial terms. An effective literacy campaign implies expenditures for teachers; it also requires certain amounts of printed material and, consequently, the construction of paper, pulp, and printing industries or the use of foreign exchange. But its value in engendering development and raising production is not closely related to these expenditures even when they are properly calculated. Other important reforms might not, at least directly, involve any financial costs at all. The effects of such policies will depend on how they are interrelated. Some, of course, will be related to investment in the conventional sense, others not. The point is that costs in terms of money or even in terms of physical resources are an entirely inadequate index of what development is attempted and what can be expected to be accomplished.[1]

We may sum up this section by stressing again that *all effective planning is physical planning*. Financial and fiscal planning is at best a reflection of physical planning. Physical planning is exceedingly difficult, and rough estimates and guesses are necessary, particularly in countries with an extreme scarcity of knowledge of the relevant facts. The practice of presenting the plan as a financial or fiscal plan has several flaws. First, it tacitly assumes that finance is the

---

paring an optimum plan for use of water and land resources in the region will bring to surface all the problems involved in the development process, and the resulting quicker and fuller utilization of new irrigation resources will amply repay the expenditure and effort put in." (D. R. Gadgil, "Technical Address, Planning for Agricultural Development in India," at the Thirteenth Annual Conference of the Indian Society of Agricultural Statistics, Poona, January 8, 1960, pp. 14–15.)

[1] Appendix 4, Section 2.

only bottleneck and that physical resources flow smoothly, at constant unit costs, in the direction indicated by money expenditure. Secondly, even if the financial or fiscal plan is given the more modest role of merely reflecting an underlying plan that coordinates physical magnitudes, it is impossible to avoid the implicit assumption that all of the obstacles to development can be overcome by a sufficient expenditure of physical resources and that, even where non-physical obstacles exist, the effectiveness of policies to remove them is related to resources used up in the process. Neither assumption is justified in the countries of South Asia. Money expenditures are not unequivocally related to physical resources, nor are physical resources alone related to the policies required for development. Thirdly, it gives an entirely false impression of the planning actually done. Fourthly, it permits the entry of a set of systematic biases, supported by vested interests. These problems are discussed further in Appendix 4.

23 *The Danger of Inflation and the Notion of a Ceiling*

The presentation of a financial plan not properly supported by physical planning is, from one point of view, an extreme case of misplaced aggregation.[1] The present section is intended to illustrate the problem of financial versus physical planning from this particular point of view. The planners in the South Asian countries are aware of serious limitations to their efforts to engender and accelerate development. Because the influence of Western models leads them to concentrate on expenditure and, in particular, on investment, the limitations to their planning efforts are seen primarily to concern these two quantities. This implies an aggregation that permits the planners to envisage an over-all ceiling for public expenditure on investment above which no further increase in output can occur. The result of further increase in expenditure is inflation.

The Western approach has two variants, very broadly definable as the quantity theory approach and the Keynesian and post-Keynesian approach. The first attributes price rises to an excessive supply of means of payment, the second to an excess of investment over saving and/or excessive rises in money costs. The first approach is typified by the very structure of the plans in the countries of South Asia and will be discussed in some detail in Appendix 4; this structure is fiscal with a loosely attached financial superstructure in terms of national accounting. There is an underlying idea of a "balanced" public budget being "neutral" to the economy, though a certain amount of "deficit finance" may be allowed to accommodate the supply of means of payment to the growth and the increasing monetization of the economy.[2] It is astonishing how much of the discussion of economic development in these countries is carried on, even by economists, in terms of this simple and otherwise discarded quantity theory. Inflation is regularly attributed to too much deficit finance, implying the creation of excessive means of payment.

But often this approach is combined, not always very clearly, with the second approach, inspired by the present-day analysis of inflation in Western

[1] Appendix 3, Section 5.
[2] Appendix 4, Section 4.

countries. This rests on a Keynesian analysis of excess demand and usually in-
corporates elements of cost-push analysis as well.[1] Unlike the first, the second
approach allows for the existence of unemployed and underutilized productive resources, for the effects of changes in interest rates and other credit conditions, and generally for the motivation of expenditure flows and the way by
which money and credit are introduced into the economy. But it is also aggregative and envisages a ceiling to aggregate demand in real terms that is set by
aggregate supply. If aggregate money demand rises above this limit, expenditure plans cannot be realized and prices rise or shortages occur; the result is
inflation. This approach can also be formulated in terms of savings and investment. Investment generates demand for consumption goods without adding to
currently available consumption goods, while *ex ante* savings are that part of
expected income not used for consumption. If planned investment exceeds *ex
ante* savings, plus net capital inflow from abroad, aggregate demand runs into
the ceiling; prices rise and the gap between aggregate money demand and
real supply, or between *ex ante* savings and *ex ante* investment, is eliminated
ex post, either by "forced savings," i.e., an unplanned reduction in consumption,
or by unplanned disinvestment (e.g., running down of inventories) or by a curtailment of fixed investment. The price rises and shortages of such an inflationary process are usually considered to be undesirable, and much thought and
effort are devoted to keeping investment down to *ex ante* savings.

There are a number of difficulties in using even this second and more sophisticated approach for the analysis of inflation. Some of these difficulties are
present even in developed countries. Thus (1) the absolutely fluid markets,
(2) the complete internal exchangeability and mobility within the two juxtaposed magnitudes supply and demand, and (3) the absence of any cost-push
element that makes it possible to assume that price rises do not appear below
full employment, are assumptions not warranted even in developed countries.
Particularly in regard to the first two conditions the difficulties with the Keynesian approach are very much greater in South Asia. In addition, there are
also the following difficulties in using the "modern" approach to inflation.

(1) Higher employment — not to speak of "full employment" — is usually
not attainable as a result simply of raising demand, particularly not in the short
run relevant to an analysis of the problem of inflation. These countries are "low-
elasticity economies"; and this applies particularly to the labor factor. Labor is
far from homogeneous; idleness is not "unemployment" in the Western sense of
the term.[2] The discussion of inflation has to be conducted on the assumption that
there is "unemployment" and "underemployment" in large sectors of the economy even at the ceiling where inflation becomes rampant,[3] and the further

[1] This type of analysis was developed earlier by Knut Wicksell and his Swedish followers; see Myrdal, *Monetary Equilibrium,* Introduction.

[2] Chapter 21, Part II.

[3] In Chapter 21 and Appendix 6, where we discuss the problem of labor utilization in the South Asian countries, we show that the concepts of "unemployment" and
"underemployment" are not adequate to reality in the South Asian countries. Low participation ratios, partial or total idleness, and low labor efficiency are, however, realities.

assumption that labor supply responds rather weakly, or not at all, to a rise in the demand for labor.

(2) Although South Asia has little that resembles a "labor market," policy measures to change institutions and attitudes in order to increase labor utilization are likely to be more effective when there is a shortage of labor in some sectors. The proviso must be added that even then the effects of such policy efforts will not be large in the short run.

(3) We have stressed that in South Asia much consumption is productive.[1] Increased supplies of certain consumption goods and services can thus increase labor utilization — labor input and labor efficiency — by improving health and physical and mental vigor and reducing apathy. In such a situation a reduction in "savings" unaccompanied by an equivalent reduction in "investment" would be less inflationary than in the Western countries; this amounts to raising the ceiling.

(4) Also, some of any extra money income earned will be going, or may be diverted by policy measures, into "innocuous demands," such as demands for entertainment and transport, where existing production facilities can be strained a bit further. The opportunity to raise production by a selective encouragement of expenditure is likely to be greater in South Asia where there is much underutilization of resources.

(5) The Keynesian analysis assumes that for a considerable time investment does not yield any addition to the flow of consumption goods. Hence increasing attempted savings and investment equally does not raise the ceiling now, but merely reallocates resources. But in fact some forms of investment raise without much delay the supply of consumer goods. Ships bought from abroad can be used immediately for catching more fish, if extra fishermen are available. This is probably more important in South Asia than in the West; here again, as when consumption is raised without reducing investment, the ceiling can be pushed up. Even in Western countries the ceiling is not such a definite limit as is often assumed. In South Asia there are additional reasons to suppose that it can be raised, particularly if the appropriate policies are pursued.

(6) The concern with avoiding inflation has a justified source in the concern with the balance of payments. But as long as controls are maintained on imports and as long as exports do not suffer, a moderate inflation may do little damage and may do some good, particularly as compared with a situation in which potential production is sacrificed for the sake of price stability. A good deal of dual morality prevails on this issue in the South Asian countries, as, indeed, also in the Western countries. Although it is rarely said in the plans, almost everyone says unofficially, and many say officially, that some inflation is inevitable in a country attempting development; some even say it is healthy and desirable.[2]

[1] Section 21 above.

[2] "But provided the increase is not substantial and is limited to about seven to eight percent during a period of five years and provided also the prices of food and other essential consumption goods are not permitted to rise too much, a slightly increasing price level is on the whole desirable. It would give resilience to the economy; it would keep profits at a reasonable level and thereby act as a spur to further savings and production. It would neutralise the inefficiency of the public and private sectors to some

More fundamentally, however, the whole notion of a single ceiling must be called into question when applied to the South Asian countries. This notion presupposes an inverted L-shaped aggregate supply curve: short-run supply is highly elastic up to total capacity and full manpower utilization (a distinction is not always drawn between these two aggregates) and thereafter almost totally inelastic. This in turn assumes fluid markets, mobility and flexibility of resources, and a response mechanism by which the composition of production is rapidly adapted to demands. Only then does aggregation make sense.[1] A country with ample foreign exchange reserves and credit lines to draw upon could always use imports to correct maladjustments of domestic production, and supply elasticities would thereby be increased. This is approximately true of many developed Western countries and was so even in their early development stage, but it is not true of the underdeveloped countries of South Asia. Here immobilities, inflexibilities, indivisibilities, imperfections, monopoly elements, and weak or nonexistent response mechanisms fragment the market into a great number of separate demands and supplies with little hope for substitution on the side of either consumption or production.[2] The concept of a "ceiling" can hardly be used for something that is compressible, can be pushed up to a different extent in different places, is craggy and of uneven height, and is called into existence as well as conjured away by elevators in other parts of the building.

Considerations such as these lead to the third approach, sometimes called "structural" or "structuralistic." It rejects the notion of a ceiling, a general price level, and analysis in terms of aggregate demand and supply, and stresses the

---

extent." (P. S. Lokanathan, "Pricing Policy," in India, Government of, Ministry of Information and Broadcasting, *Problems in the Third Plan — A Critical Miscellany*, New Delhi, 1961, p. 75.) "Finally, there can be no disguising the fact that inflation will continue to beset the Indian economy for several years. It is an inevitable accompaniment of the process of rapid development. The country must accept the consequences of some inflationary pressures and develop [a] certain degree of inflation tolerance." (*Ibid.*, p. 79.)

In the same publication Nehru says: "It is true that in a developing economy there is bound to be inflation. In fact, some inflation is good; it is itself a sign of development. We need not be frightened by that. But if it goes beyond that measure, then it is obviously harmful." (The Prime Minister [Nehru], "Strategy of the Third Plan," in *ibid.*, p. 40.)

In recent years prices have begun to rise very much more rapidly in India under the influence of the wars and crop failures (Chapter 7, Section 4; and Postscript, Section 1), and these arguments in favor of a moderate inflation have lost their relevance, as they did, of course, in unfortunate Indonesia long ago (Chapter 9, Section 10).

[1] Appendix 3, Section 5.

[2] "Perhaps the chief difference between under-developed and advanced countries in this connexion can be summed up by saying that in advanced countries the elasticity of supply is high. A given stimulus to expansion is less liable to run up against obstacles, indeed, it will be argued that bottlenecks present a desirable stimulus to further growth. The whole industrial hinterland, with a supply of skilled labour, a tradition of law and order and efficient administration, financial institutions and a population conditioned to systematic change and innovation can be drawn upon, if required. This explains why a Tennessee Valley Authority is more successful than a Helmand River Development scheme. It is the old story that nothing succeeds like success." (Streeten, *Economic Integration, Aspects and Problems*, p. 59.)

fragmentation, the disequilibria, and the lack of balance between supplies and demands in different sectors of the economy and between different groups in the community. The main criticisms of the notion of a ceiling implied in this approach are these:

(1) It suggests a global limitation, whereas limitations in fact are diverse and specific.

(2) It suggests an insuperable limitation whereas particular limitations can often be overcome, particularly if policy measures are applied to this purpose.

(3) It thus suggests an absolute limitation, whereas limitations are relative to the composition of demand and supply, to the technical methods adopted, and to the policies pursued.

(4) It focusses on the limitation of physical resources, whereas the real obstacles often consist in administrative or managerial ability and in attitudes and institutions in the form of inhibitions on the part of the planners and obstacles on the part of those planned for.

It is a truism to say that there are supply limitations and supply inelasticities: that we cannot have everything. But it does not follow that this situation can be relevantly characterized by saying that a ceiling sets the inflation barrier. The typical situation in the underdeveloped countries of South Asia is substantial underutilization of both capital and labor side by side with shortages and bottlenecks. It is questionable whether the terms "inflation" and "deflation" can be applied to such a situation. If we mean by "inflation" a tendency for prices to rise and shortages, rationing, and queues to appear, clearly there is inflation. If we mean by "deflation" capacity and manpower not fully used, equally clearly there is "deflation." There is also large-scale underutilization of a particular type of labor in some sectors and localities and in others scarcity of some other type of labor or even of the same type. Looking at the national economy as a whole, we would thus have to acknowledge "inflation" to coexist with "deflation," a "ceiling" to coexist with unused resources.

Since we have already seen that the notions of "aggregate demand" and "aggregate supply" cannot be applied to these countries, the inflationary symptoms we observe cannot be attributed to either demand-pull or cost-push or a combination of both. For the reasons we gave in showing the limitation of the Keynesian approach, the tendencies to inflation as they appear in the underdeveloped countries of South Asia are related to "bottlenecks." This more realistic "structural" approach takes into account the gross imperfections of markets, the fragmentation of the economy into non-competing sectional or spatial groups, and, indeed, the relative or absolute absence in large parts of the economy of the type of rational motivation that Western theory assumes.[1]

[1] The following remarks have merely the negative purpose of illustrating abstractly one set of reasons why we cannot work with a single ceiling for the whole economy. In the South Asian countries there are not two homogeneous sectors, as we assume, but a great number of largely unrelated sectors. The argument thus holds *a fortiori.*

We consider an economy consisting of two sectors: Agriculture (A) and Manufacturing Industry (M). As a result of development and industrialization, incomes, demands, and supplies rise. However, workers in M and A together want to buy more A products than are available and less M products than M capacity can supply. Modern technology in the M sector imposes new habits, new responses, and new meth-

Mechanism of Underdevelopment and Development   1928

According to this more realistic approach, the bottlenecks may, in a sense, have been caused by development policies, as those are applied to the situation described above in an underdeveloped country; the inflationary tendencies that appear are, indeed, often called "development inflation." Different types of bottlenecks will be accompanied by different types of price rigidities, different supply elasticities, different response mechanisms, different degrees of substitutability on the part of the purchaser, and different distributional effects. Such bottlenecks will appear not only in agriculture but also outside it, and in particular, in electricity, fuel, imported raw materials, transport, repair facili-

---

ods of work, and runs into fewer obstacles. Hence productive capacity in M rises more rapidly. In the A sector, habits, traditions, and institutions are hardened and the introduction of improved methods means not only learning but also unlearning, not only doing but also undoing. Hence A supplies lag behind M supplies. It is quite possible that total demand and supply are "balanced" in a sense (or, if deflationary policies are pursued, that demand is deficient). But demand and supply are not balanced in each sector separately. Demand exceeds supply in A, and falls short in M.

In the theoretical model usually applied in Western countries, either of several of the following would happen:

(1) Prices of M products fall and prices of A products rise; this will tend to reduce the demand for A products and increase the demand for M products among members of a fairly homogeneous population buying both;

(2) Unemployment rises in the M sector and a labor shortage occurs in the A sector;

(3) For either of the previous reasons resources move out of M and into A, thus raising the supply of A products and reducing that of M products. The balance between total supply and total demand will thus tend to be restored.

On the whole, this will not happen in the underdeveloped countries in South Asia. In one respect, however, they resemble advanced countries: industrial prices will tend to be inflexible downwards. This is due to lack of competition, whether caused by monopolistic organization of the M sector or by government regulations or labor union resistance to a reduction of wages. As a result of increased demand for A products, A prices will tend to rise but M prices will not tend to fall. In spite of underutilization of labor in the M sector as well as the A sector and rising prices in the A sector, resources are not transferred. The "general price level" rises (M prices stay put, A prices rise) and underutilization of labor continues. According to where we look we can diagnose the situation in terms of either inflation or deflation.

The A sector is peculiar not only because demand for its products is rapidly increasing but also because in the short run supplies are very slow to respond to price rises unaccompanied by other reforms (such as induced changes of attitudes and institutions). Indeed, the A sector may reduce its supply to the M sector when A prices rise, both because A producers retain more A goods for themselves and because they can now afford to work and produce less. This response will aggravate the price increase. If the government pursues Keynesian expansionist policies, this will feed the inflation without increasing labor utilization (in A). If it deflates, it will decrease labor utilization (in M) without necessarily stopping inflation (in A). A different therapy, based on a different diagnosis than the one based on the Keynesian approach, is indicated.

To fit this model more closely to the Indian situation in recent years we should assume a serious shortfall of production in the A sector; this would intensify the tendency toward imbalance between demand and supply in that sector; at the same time, shortage of foreign exchange, created by the need for increased import of foods, could cause a decrease of supply in the M sector due to scarcity of imported raw materials, spare parts, and other production necessities. There is, however, no assurance that supplies in the two sectors would decrease in a parallel way; besides, the demands have very different price and income elasticities.

ties, and credit facilities. This terminology should not lead to complete fatalism, however. To some extent, "development inflation" is not inevitable but can be counteracted, though less by general anti-inflationary policies than by specific controls based on effective physical planning, which should mainly aim at overcoming bottlenecks.[1]

When facing "structural inflation," planners should both do and avoid doing certain things.

(1) They should avoid trying to cut demand for the bottleneck products by cutting total demand, thus reducing production unnecessarily and slowing down development.

(2) They must, instead, attempt to raise the supply of the bottleneck items.. This may sometimes be done by permitting their prices to rise — though not necessarily to the equilibrium level — and bigger profits to be made in their production; entrepreneurial responses may have to be created, as well as used. This is particularly true as in South Asia very high rates of return can ordinarily be enjoyed by lending money and by speculation. But outside a small modernized industrial sector, price rises by themselves are not likely to bring about the required responses and adjustments. Other measures have to be taken, perhaps along with the creation of price incentives. In the case of food, price rises are often not sensible because of lack of response (or even perverse response) of supply and lack of substitutability of demand both for any given consumer and between consumers.[2]

(3) Another aspect of promoting higher production of the bottleneck item is to encourage mobility of factors and, more generally, to raise labor utilization by inducing changes in attitudes and institutions.

(4) Sometimes demand may have to be diverted from the bottleneck item

[1] One may ask at this point what precisely is meant by a "bottleneck" and, more particularly, by a "series of bottlenecks." Are we not simply concerned with various degrees of scarcity, which could and should show up in a price rise of the bottleneck item? The answer is that in the economies of South Asia price rises, particularly if they occur in isolation without other policies, do not tend to allocate the scarce commodity while the scarcity lasts, nor do they tend to remove the scarcity. Simply defined, a "bottleneck" would exist where the price that would equate demand to supply is substantially higher than production costs. In a system where attitudes and institutions are adapted to economic incentives, resources would move into the production of the bottleneck item. In the countries of South Asia a high price by itself does not normally induce additional supply and may even reduce supply. Even where resources are attracted, smaller price rises than "equilibrium" calls for may be more effective in encouraging supplies than large price rises. On the side of demand, a high price has in advanced economies the policy function of allocating the scarce item where it is most needed and enforcing economy in its use there. In the countries of South Asia, not only is ability to purchase a less adequate test of need, but the price rise, particularly if it is large, may spark other price increases, in which case it cannot fulfill its allocative function. Thus price increases that, in a different institutional setting, would be confined to a few items and carry their cure with them, will in an underdeveloped country tend to spread to other items and to be self-defeating. None of this implies that price policies do not have an important part to play in an integrated and coordinated set of policies. Cf. the discussion of devaluation and the need for import controls, Appendix 8, Part I.

[2] Chapter 26, Section 4 *et passim*.

toward products and services where surplus capacity of plant and equipment exists or where production can be increased quickly by turning to the use of somewhat obsolete equipment.

(5) Planners must attempt to confine the price increases to those sectors where they promote growth, or at least do little harm (most often the industrial sector), and prevent them from spilling over into the sectors where they would penalize the poor and have little effect upon supply. Within the sector where inflationary price rises are permitted, the profits made should be used to mobilize savings through direct and indirect taxation and through redistribution toward income receivers with high savings propensities.

(6) Planners must attempt to anticipate *future* bottlenecks and direct their planning at breaking them.

The success of the planners in avoiding damaging inflation and wasted capacity will depend on their success in working out the *direction, composition,* and *phasing* of supplies and demands — that is, on physical planning — rather than on their success in keeping within an aggregate ceiling. The implementation of more detailed physical plans will often require the use of price policies (1 and 5 above). India's Third Five Year Plan mentions a rise in prices charged by certain public enterprises as a method of mopping up purchasing power and also says that "it is particularly important to avert an adventitious or haphazard rise in prices."[1] This principle could be carried much further and prices could be allowed to rise, sometimes substantially, in some carefully chosen areas while prices in other areas were strictly controlled. If experience comes to determine expectations in accordance with such policies, the cumulative momentum would also be taken out of the inflationary process and runaway inflation avoided.

In several sectoral divisions that are particularly important for an analysis of supply limitations, the assumption of a high degree of substitutability and aggregation is particularly dangerous.

(1) Internal and external resources are often subject to entirely different rules. Foreign exchange can be used to buy substitutes for almost any home product. But domestic resources can much less easily be used to increase exports or substitute for imports. Hence traditional foreign-trade multiplier analysis cannot be used. A cut in imports, traditionally assumed to be inflationary, may cause severe unemployment if the import items cut are indispensable raw materials or pieces of equipment for which there are no domestic substitutes; while a rise in imports may start an inflationary process by stimulating complementary spending. A rise in export earnings may have hardly any domestic effects if foreign companies are the main beneficiaries, whereas a decline in export earnings which affects many exporters of primary products will impose the need for domestic structural changes that can easily touch off an inflationary process. A deflation of internal demands, at any rate below a critical level, may not reduce imports, which may in any case be controlled, nor increase exports because it will not increase the supply of exportable products; even besides this, exports may be limited by low foreign demand and tight

[1] India, Government of, Planning Commission, *Third Five Year Plan, A Draft Outline,* New Delhi, June, 1960, p. 15.

foreign restrictions. On the other hand, excessively high domestic demand may encourage people to circumvent import controls, may suck some exportables into the domestic market, and/or may raise production costs so that traditional exports are outpriced in the export market.

(2) The most important distinction for domestic consumption must be drawn between a rise in prices of essential goods, consumed by the mass of the people, like food-grains and simple textiles, and a rise in the prices of luxuries and semi-luxuries, consumed by the small middle class. India's Second Five Year Plan makes this quite clear:

. . . but a policy of "playing safe" is not always conducive to development. A measure of risk has to be undertaken, and the most effective insurance against this risk is command over reserve stocks of food grains — and a few other essential commodities — which can be used to augment the supplies in the market as and when necessary. Prices of food and cloth occupy a strategic position in the Indian economy, and a sharp rise in these prices has to be prevented by the use of all available devices. So long as these prices can be maintained at reasonable levels, the cost of living of the large bulk of the population can be kept under control. Increases in prices of other commodities would be a matter of comparative unimportance . . . [1]

The reasoning behind this approach is as follows. Excess demand for items other than necessities, whether it manifests itself in shortages or price rises, does not matter and may even be beneficial. In the former case, if there are shortages, unsatisfied buyers may save rather than buy more food, or they may make fuller use of facilities already available. If prices of non-necessities rise to the full extent, some additional production may be forthcoming and income will be redistributed toward private and public savers as long as money wages are kept under control. We assume then that import controls should prevent the extra demand from drawing in more imports; special devices such as tax reclamation could be used to prevent it from frustrating exports. It may not always be easy to prevent domestic inflation from harming the balance of payments and this may constitute the main limitation of the policy outlined above. A spilling over into the market for food-grains and other necessities will be easier to prevent because of low substitutability. Price control of necessities will thus be easier to administer.

Admittedly, such a policy by its nature cannot make a large contribution to forced savings, because mass consumption goods are protected against price rises. There is also the socio-political problem that the politicians who decide upon, and the officials who would have to administer, such a policy are members of the class that would be its chief victim: their money incomes will tend to be fixed while the prices of the goods they buy will rise.

---

[1] India, *Second Five Year Plan*, p. 86. Cf. Appendix 4, Section 5.
"The prices of luxury articles going up does not make very much difference, but price rise in essential goods does. The question of control of prices really applies to the essential commodities . . . In other words, a kind of selective control may become necessary." (The Prime Minister [Nehru], "Strategy of the Third Plan," in India, *Problems in the Third Plan — A Critical Miscellany*, p. 40.)
What has actually happened in India in recent years, on the contrary, has been that food prices have been allowed to rise very fast and substantially, while prices of less essential goods have often been more steady.

(3) The aggregate savings/income ratio conceals important differences between advanced Western countries and the underdeveloped countries of
South Asia. The savings of the rich may finance the consumption of the poor in
return for the transfer of land to moneylenders. Some savings go into hoards
of precious metals and ornaments. The channeling of savings into productive
assets is very imperfect. This is reflected in the wide divergence between rates
of return in different lines. We have already seen that some reductions in
consumption also entail reductions in production.

We may conclude this section by stating the obvious fact that there is a point
at which a further rise in investments will raise a number of prices. Indeed, the
low supply elasticities and bottlenecks will make this point come much sooner
than it would in a corresponding situation in developed countries. But this very
fact suggests that the limitation is not that of a single ceiling, but of a large
number of specific physical supply limitations and other, non-physical obstacles
that make themselves felt as development proceeds.

If the concept of a ceiling is used simply as a reminder that resources, including skills, administrative talent, and foreign exchange, are scarce and that
attitudes and institutions adapted to development are absent, it is innocuous
enough. But if it diverts attention from the fact that numerous demands run
for different reasons into limitations of numerous supplies and that it is the task
of planning to reconcile these and to anticipate and break specific bottlenecks
at the proper time, it is misleading.

24 Balanced versus Unbalanced Growth

In recent years there has been a lively controversy between two schools of
economists, one urging balanced growth, the other unbalanced growth. In the
preceding sections we presented many observations and arguments by pro-
tagonists of both schools relating to various points dealt with in other contexts
in this study. But the main controversy respecting balanced versus unbalanced
growth has little relevance for the problem central to this appendix: how South
Asian countries should plan development. *Both doctrines are essentially beside
the point.* The purpose of this section is merely to demonstrate this negative
proposition.

We might first note in passing that both schools move largely within the limitation of the modern Western approach. In their models they neither pay much
attention to the needs for induced changes in attitudes[1] and institutions, nor do

[1] Hirschman's stress on *decisions* implies, however, a shift of emphasis, though very
partial, toward attitudes, which he does not, as is usual in models developed by
others, assume to be constant or automatically adjusted to precisely the required extent. This is undoubtedly an advance, though a limited one because Hirschman confines himself largely to *investment* decisions. Even if we disregard the broad category
of attitudes of the masses of peasants and workers and confine ourselves to those of the
upper strata, which we must remember decide and implement development policies,
there are other decisions of great importance, as Walinsky has pointed out.
  "Hirschman, on the other hand, might find it more difficult to support, by reference
to the Burmese experience, his thesis that development strategy should be directed at
maximizing investment (which he equates with development) decisions. Decision-

they observe the productive effects of consumption in very poor countries. In other words, they apply the customary reasoning in terms of savings, employment, investment, and output, and they focus their interest on physical investments, primarily in large-scale industry and public utilities, which in the ordinary way they assume to be the vehicles for development; all observations outside this framework are marginal and inconsequential for the conclusions they draw. Rather than repeat our criticism of this general approach, we shall in this section accept the assumptions implicit in it and confine ourselves to an immanent criticism of the two schools of thought.

We turn first to the role of supply limitations and supply inelasticities in the controversy regarding balanced versus unbalanced growth. Surprisingly enough neither school pays much attention to the presence of a ceiling and, consequently, the danger of inflation if investment is pushed beyond this limit — or rather, as we argued in the preceding section, the limit set by a great number of specific, successive physical bottlenecks and other obstacles to rising production. Nurkse explicitly confined his discussion to the demand side. He assumed supplies to be available and asked what investment would have to be like in order to justify them. He made the reservation:

There is no suggestion here that, by taking care of the demand side alone, any country could, as it were, lift itself up by its bootstraps. We have been considering one particular facet of our subject. The more fundamental difficulties that lie on the supply side have so far been kept off-stage for the sake of orderly discussion.[1]

Nevertheless, Nurkse's main stress is on markets as the principal limitation on growth, not on supplies. We might observe already at this stage of our immanent criticism that if the creation of complementary markets as an inducement to invest were really the crucial development problem, it should ordinarily be fairly easy to solve. Final markets can be created by import restrictions and, though less easily, by export expansion.[2] If Nurkse stresses markets as the main

making was indeed a critical factor in this experience. But the decisions which were most needed and most lacking were not investment decisions, but administrative, managerial and policy decisions." (Louis J. Walinsky, *Economic Development in Burma 1951–1960*, Twentieth Century Fund, New York, 1962, p. 593.)

It should be added that sometimes Hirschman has a somewhat wider concept in mind, as is shown by his use of the terms "development decisions" and "developmental tasks." (Albert O. Hirschman, *The Strategy of Economic Development*, Yale University Press, New Haven, 1958, p. 25.)

[1] Nurkse, *Problems of Capital Formation in Underdeveloped Countries*, pp. 30–31.

[2] Nurkse's main line of reasoning relates to final goods and principally to consumer goods. As far as intermediate markets are concerned, Nurkse came out in favor of unbalanced growth (vertical imbalance) in his second Istanbul lecture. (Ragnar Nurkse, *Equilibrium and Growth in the World Economy*, Harvard University Press, Cambridge, Mass., 1961, pp. 259–278.) Social overhead investment provides the conditions and inducements for consequential direct productive investment. As for horizontal balance, he believed that the case "rests on the need for a 'balanced diet' ":

"The difficulty caused by the small size of the market relates to individual investment incentives in any single line of production taken by itself. At least in principle, the difficulty vanishes in the case of a more or less synchronized application of capital to a wide range of different industries. Here is an escape from the deadlock; here the

limitation on growth, the other doctrine, particularly in Hirschman's version, stresses investment decisions. The implication of Hirschman's theory is also that supplies will be forthcoming with relative ease if only the lack of decision-taking can be overcome. It should readily be admitted that lack of entrepreneurs willing and able to venture into long-term investments is a serious obstacle to development in most South Asian countries — though to a differing degree — but there are also supply limitations and they are not overcome by "unbalanced" decision-taking.

The tendency of both schools — and particularly of the adherents of the doctrine of unbalanced growth — to *underplay supply limitations* diverts attention from the fact that planning must be directed as much at *restricting* investments, production, and supplies in certain directions as at *expanding* them in others. The policy package in rational planning presupposes a *choice* of allocating limited supplies — that is, supplies growing at a limited rate, and in response to certain stimuli — to the most important uses, combined with the creation of stimuli to decisions *of all kinds* (not only investment decisions). Supply limitations are considerably less important in advanced industrial countries now, and they were also less important in the early developing phase of many now advanced countries such as Sweden or the regions of recent settlement. These countries had almost unlimited access to capital at low interest rates, a reserve of literate and skilled labor, and plentiful natural resources. Again, certain underdeveloped regions in advanced countries (Southern Italy, the South of the United States) can draw on supplies from the other regions in the country but lack development decisions. The models developed in the controversy between the two schools and, in particular, by Hirschman seem to have drawn on this kind of experience in "ceilingless economies"; to a limited degree the analogy may be relevant to some South American countries like Argentina, but not to the entirely different problems of South Asia. The two important differences between, on the one hand, the advanced countries now and in their early development phase, and, on the other hand, the underdeveloped countries of South Asia are (1) that investments in advanced countries can more often be treated as marginal than those in underdeveloped countries and (2) that advanced countries are, and were, high supply-elasticity economies with responses and institutions already adapted to economic growth.

The absence in both doctrines of a proper consideration of supply limita-

---

result is an over-all enlargement of the market. People working with more and better tools in a number of complementary projects become each others' customers. Most industries catering for mass consumption are complementary in the sense that they provide a market for, and thus support, each other. This basic complementarity stems, in the last analysis, from the diversity of human wants. The case for 'balanced growth' rests on the need for a 'balanced diet.'" (Nurkse, *Problems of Capital Formation in Underdeveloped Countries*, p. 11.)

He later drew a distinction between balanced growth as a method and as an outcome or objective. (*Equilibrium and Growth in the World Economy*, p. 279.) What remains of the doctrine is the emphasis on the complementarity of markets for final goods as an ultimate objective for investment incentives. But the absence of markets is not normally a serious obstacle to development; even where it is, it is by no means the main obstacle nor one that will always yield to balanced growth.

tions and supply inelasticities, which tends to make them irrelevant to the study of development problems in South Asia, should be viewed in connection with another common feature that is *prima facie* equally astonishing. *Neither school has related its theses to planning;* this relationship has been left in the air. They have not made clear whether they are arguing a principle to be followed when working out a plan or whether they are thinking of a development that takes place without planning or, alternatively, one that takes place with only an initial impulse of planning in the form of an investment project and thereafter takes its own course with market forces responding to demand and supply.

Both schools are unclear and, occasionally, hesitant on this point, though they generally seem to think in terms of one or the other of the latter alternatives. Thus Nurkse, in arguing balanced growth, seems to have been thinking primarily of a private enterprise economy without much comprehensive planning.[1] It is, he argued, private investment that needs market inducements from the demand side. As we pointed out above, demand can fairly easily be created by import restrictions (and, though with greater difficulties, export promotion); balanced growth would thus appear not to need comprehensive planning. In any case, Nurkse did not explain how his limited desideratum of balanced growth of different industries reached by an adjustment of demands should be fitted into the type of comprehensive planning that is the declared policy in all South Asian countries and that has a strong rationale in their actual situation.[2] Neither does the doctrine of unbalanced growth as propounded by Hirschman require *initial* and still less *continued* planning. In any case, it is not his main purpose to lay the theoretical foundations for comprehensive planning.[3]

In planning for development supply limitations *have* to be taken into consideration. The planners must therefore *choose* between possible investments; they must induce restrictions as well as expansion. In a sense much wider than Nurkse's they must aspire to *balanced growth*, where the balance is concerned

---

[1] Nurkse, *Equilibrium and Growth in the World Economy*, pp. 249–250, 280.

[2] Chapter 15, Section 3.

[3] The role of the state in Hirschman's theory is both to induce and to repair disequilibria. Thus state action becomes a dependent as well as an independent variable. (Hirschman, *The Strategy of Economic Development*, pp. 65, 202.) This is, by itself, a realistic observation (see Section 13 above) and should not be lost sight of; in particular, Hirschman's discussion of forward and backward linkages — part of what we discuss as "spread effects" — is provocative and fruitful: it brings out the previously neglected possible effects of one investment on investment at earlier and later stages of production. But the doctrine underplays obstacles (also resistances in attitudes) called into being by imbalance. Shortages create vested interests; they give rise to monopoly gains; entrepreneurs may get their fingers burned by malinvestments and may get frightened by the growth of competition. The business attitudes and institutions evolving through development will arouse opposition and hostility. Once again, the absence from the models of this type of reaction is more appropriate for Western countries and is at the same time opportune for the planners in South Asia. But the basic weakness of the doctrine is the neglect of the supply limitations, which is related to the unclarified relationship to planning.

with increasing certain supplies as much as, or even more than, with catering to demand. When the plan calls for investment in a steel plant, the planners must prepare for its operation by providing for supplies of raw materials, power, and transport. It would be wasteful to wait for them to be produced as a result of the linkage effect of the initial investment in the steel plant. Planning means coordination of policies — and, indeed, coordination over a much wider field than that of physical investment in modern industry and public utilities to which our immanent criticism of the two schools in this section is limited.

At the same time it is *inevitable* that most, or all, of the investments decided on in a plan will be *unbalanced* in the sense that they provide more supply than can be taken up instantaneously by demand. They are usually lumpy. For technical reasons — and also because planning should have a long-time perspective — investments in industrial plants and equipment and those in the basic infrastructure have to consist of large indivisible units. Adjustments required by development in an underdeveloped country cannot be made in infinitesimally small steps,[1] least of all in the sectors we are discussing in this section. In addition, there are rigidities and very sluggish responses not only on the demand side but also on the side of supplies. There will be difficulties in meeting many urgent requirements, whether of products, raw materials, or power and transport facilities, as well as in finding markets permitting full utilization of the main investment. Too much faith cannot in such situations be put in market forces.

This is indeed one of the principal reasons for planning. But even with the best planning there will not be balanced growth (in the wider sense). That investment has to be unbalanced, does not mean, however, that this is a desideratum.[2] Whatever the planners can do by means of coordinating investments, and

---

[1] The concept "marginal," which has played such an important part in neo-classical Western economic theory, is largely out of place in the discussion of South Asian conditions, and remarkably enough, particularly so in the "modern" or "organized" sector. In the Western countries a new profitable investment project is (and was) normally small relative to the size of existing capital equipment (however measured), relative to new investment, and relative to the hinterland of facilities on which it draws. In underdeveloped countries indivisibilities are more prominent and marginal adjustments rarer for at least four reasons. First, insofar as economic development is directed at industrialization, this normally implies an increase in the number of big and indivisible units. Secondly, both the existing stock of equipment and the additions to it are small compared with those in advanced countries with comparable populations. Since plant and equipment often have to be of a minimum size for technical reasons, the addition of a plant or a piece of equipment constitutes a greater proportion both of the stock of capital and of total investment. Thirdly, the basic infrastructure of industry (power, steel, transport, housing, government buildings) consists of large indivisible units. Fourthly, complementarities between enterprises and activities are likely to be more important in the meager economies of underdeveloped countries, so that a given investment is more likely to require complementary and supplementary investments in other industries.

[2] There is a danger that planners will turn necessity into virtue, as the following euphemistic passage from India's Second Five Year Plan shows: "There cannot be a complete balance between developments in each five year plan; to some extent, a measure of imbalance — seeming over-expansion in some lines and under-expansion in

all other policies to avoid imbalance — and insure full servicing and full capacity utilization of their investments as soon as possible — means greater economy. A degree of imbalance is unavoidable, but balanced growth — in the wider sense — is obviously what the planners will try to aim for, though they will not achieve it.

In a situation where some imbalance is *inevitable* but where the planners have to do their best to keep the imbalance to a *minimum,* the admonitions of the Hirschman school to seek imbalance are obviously inappropriate.[1] Although nobody really has said "create an imbalance and this will call forth responses that will engender development," it is a fact that a favorable connotation has been affixed to investments being unbalanced. This has been possible because of two closely interrelated, usually only implicit, assumptions — that supply limitations can be disregarded and that there is no effective planning.

25   *The Continuity of Planning*

Most of the plans contain declarations that planning must be a continuing activity and that flexibility is therefore essential. Adaptation must be made to unforeseen events, and new opportunities must be seized as they present themselves.[2] Subject to these reservations, the planning agencies have, however, produced plans for fixed periods of three, four, five, or ten years. Within these periods the governments are supposed to fulfill the plan objectives. In some cases, a long-term plan is made spanning several plan periods. In India this is called perspective planning.

A plan for a fixed future period is obviously essential when planning is started. It has also the advantages of simplicity and of encouraging the govern-

---

others — may facilitate more rapid and better-balanced development over a period. Considerations of this kind apply particularly to sectors like development of power, transport and basic industries where investments are by nature 'lumpy.'" (India, *Second Five Year Plan,* p. 17.)

[1] ". . . to those not readily enchanted by the paradoxical, the Hirschman strategy may seem to resemble that incorporated in such statements as 'The most efficient way to walk a tightrope is to advance, swaying precariously first to one side and then to the other,' or 'To teach your child to conduct himself safely in traffic, set him off to cross Times Square against the traffic light.'" (Walinsky, *Economic Development in Burma 1951–1960,* p. 594.)

[2] "Through careful annual planning, it should be possible not only to implement the Five Year Plan with greater flexibility, introducing such changes as may be called for by current developments in the economy, but also continuously to correct targets and estimates in the Five Year Plan and take a forward view of the growth of the economy and of favourable technological and economic possibilities." (India, *Fourth Five Year Plan: A Draft Outline,* p. 156.)

"Because planning is a projection of programmes over a number of years, its process must necessarily contain a substantial element of flexibility." (Pakistan, *Outline of the Second Five Year Plan (1960–65),* p. iii.)

"Moreover the Plan, even after adjustments and improvements, must not be taken as representing a once and for all statement. Periodical revisions over time are of special importance. Such revisions must take into account changes in internal and external circumstances and actual experiences in respect of performance." (Ceylon, *The Ten Year Plan,* pp. 55–56.)

ment and the people to move along the chosen track and to resist the temptation to backslide. But against this, it has grave disadvantages. Administratively, it means that an additional rigidity is superimposed on a system already teeming with rigidities. Necessary or desirable adjustments to unforeseen changes or corrections of errors may not be made, and the adaptations that are made will tend to occur abruptly between plan periods.[1] Psychologically, too, the compulsion to revise the plan downward when no formal provision for this is made can have demoralizing effects. This is illustrated by the experience in India after 1957, when those in authority issued contradictory statements and were even tempted into pious falsification of the facts. This tended to spread confusion, cynicism, and defeatism in business, in the administration, and among the public. More flexible planning could have prevented some of the miscalculations of foreign exchange requirements and some of the faults in the handling of import licenses in the beginning of this period.

On the other hand, when things turn out better than anticipated, a plan for a fixed period strengthens the inhibitions against stepping up efforts. If India's Second Plan illustrates the dangers of events turning out less favorably than planned, its First Plan illustrates the dangers of their turning out better. In the beginning of the 1950's India could have more than fulfilled the plan in view of the good monsoons, her underutilized industrial capacity, and her strong balance of payments position. Tax efforts also could have been raised and the five-year targets could perhaps have been hit within three or four years, had there been more built-in flexibility. It is therefore arguable that, in addition to the administrative merits, there are also psychological merits in a rolling plan, which would elicit on balance greater and more persistent efforts by compelling the government to raise or lower its sights.

The South Asian countries borrowed their pattern from the Soviet Union, as the East European Communist countries had done. Planning over several years had been popularized and adopted in specific fields by certain Western countries, but it was undoubtedly more appropriate for the Soviet Union. Foreign economic relations there are less important. They are, moreover, regulated by state monopoly and can thus be fitted into a plan more easily. Domestic activity also is more fully controlled by the state. In spite of this, as we have seen in the post-war era, other Communist countries, more vulnerable to unforeseen changes abroad, and the Soviet Union itself occasionally, have had to change a plan in midstream.

The question therefore arises whether the countries in the region should not adopt a more flexible planning system, at least after they have once got started during an experimental period. This applies particularly to the provision of opportunities for adaptive responses to changes in their trading position

[1] ". . . one of the disadvantages of a plan limited by a definite time-period is this lack of flexibility. Too many things are so neatly tied in that a basic change can only be made when a new plan is drawn up, and even then, past commitments are likely to limit the area of manoeuverability. A lack of flexibility is also the necessary price enforced upon a plan which starts with a process of capital formation in projects with long-gestation periods. Giving them up half-way through is often less economic than either not having tl em at all or completing them." (United Nations, ECAFE, *Economic Survey of Asia and the Far East, 1961*, Bangkok, 1962, p. 86, f.n. 41.)

as a result of changes in world markets. There is a particular danger here that an already inflexible economy may be burdened with yet another element of inflexibility. As we have seen in our criticism of the ideal plan, the purpose of planning is the rational adjustment of means to ends in the light of changing circumstances, including new experiences and new ideas generated in the process of planning and plan implementation. It is not to put the economy into a straitjacket but to increase flexibility and thus liberate efforts for progress, so that favorable opportunities can be seized and pitfalls avoided. Thus the required curtailments during India's Second Plan, as well as the possible increases during the First Plan, were made more difficult or prevented because of the fixed planning period.

Not only for the sake of greater flexibility, but also for a clearer perspective and a better view of the priorities, a "rolling plan" would have advantages. Every year three new plans should be made and acted upon.[1]

First, there should be a plan for the current year. It should include the annual budget as well as a carefully worked out foreign exchange budget. Fixed five-year plans cannot relate these matters closely to economic planning. The annual plan should lay down economic policies for the public sector and, as far as it can be controlled, for the private sector. Secondly, there should be a

---

[1] The same proposal is made by Ragnar Frisch:

"Whatever method is used for the elaboration of a plan, it is not possible in the changing world of today to publish at a given date a plan for any five years, with much detail and *petrify* it, trying to follow this petrified pattern for the five years. Planning is a continuous process. At intervals, most conveniently perhaps every year, the whole problem should be reconsidered in great perspective taking account of new information, improved data and improved analyses. At each such round certain commitments will have been made that cannot be changed, while others are such that they may be modified in the light of the new information and analyses. A technique for such periodic revision should be worked out and incorporated as an essential part of the planning machinery.

"At each revision it will be well to look into the future a number of years which is determined by the *nature of the factual circumstances* and not determined by the formal question of how many years 'are left' out of some five years whose beginning was conventionally fixed at some date in the past. If five years is deemed to be a suitable horizon, this number of years may be applied at each of the yearly revisions. In a sense one would then always be working in the beginning of a five-year period." (Ragnar Frisch, "The Methodology of Planning in an Underdeveloped Country," roneod, undated, p. 3.)

Ceylon's plan advocates a "rolling plan": "Reference should be made in this connection to the concept of a 'Rolling Plan.' In terms of such a concept a forward perspective would at all times be maintained. Actual programmes would then continue to remain within the context of a long term perspective. It would be desirable to adopt such an approach in Ceylon." (Ceylon, *The Ten Year Plan*, p. 56.)

Professor P. C. Mahalanobis had early developed this view in connection with the formulation of the Draft Plan-frame to the Second Plan: "Planning must be flexible and continuous. There should be a general frame-work for five years; and detailed annual plans should be prepared every year. Targets, projects and policies must be continually re-assessed and reformulated in the light of new experience. Also, we must always keep in view the growth of the economy over a long period of 10 or 15 or 20 years, so that a balance can be secured between short-term and long-term objectives." ("Approach to Planning in India," radio lecture, September 11, 1955, p. 7.)

Mechanism of Underdevelopment and Development   1940

plan for a number of years — three, four, or five — which, however, should be changed each year. In this plan, targets and techniques should be laid down. As in the annual plan, price relationships and price policies and all other controls[1] should find their place. Thirdly, every year a perspective plan for ten, fifteen, twenty, or even more years should be presented, in which the broader goals are stated and the outlines of future development are forecast. The annual one-year plan should be fitted into the same year's new three-, four-, or five-year plan, and both should be framed in the light of the perspective plan.

This system of rolling planning would not increase the work by much, for the plans of earlier years would provide the basis for the succeeding plans. Moreover, some of the required alterations and adaptations would, in any case, have to be made. To some extent any planning inevitably involves rolling planning. The difference is that formal expression would be given to this, and the effectiveness and rationality of planning would be thereby increased.

There remains the question whether — and if so, how and to what extent — parliaments and governments could and should make decisions that are binding, within limits, on themselves and future parliaments and governments. But this question is not answered by fixed period planning. Both systems of planning raise the problem to what extent future parliaments and governments can be committed to specific undertakings made to public corporations and other decision centers inside or outside the administration.

[1] Chapter 19, Sections 1 and 2.

ECONOMIC MODELS AND

THEIR USEFULNESS FOR

PLANNING IN SOUTH ASIA

---

1 Introduction

Social scientists are in an unusual position in that the objects of their studies and their own activities are within the same context. For these studies are themselves socially conditioned activities. Social scientists should therefore have a head start over other investigators. Yet the traditions, habits, and biases of economists, rooted in the philosophies of natural law and utilitarianism and reinforced by their ambition to be "scientific," are such that they have preferred to remain unaware of this. They have continually tried to lift their investigations out of the social context into a supposedly "objective" realm, from which other socially determined relationships are surveyed — as from an Archimedean point, from which the earth, on which we all still stand at the time of writing, is lifted. This attempt makes economists naively innocent of their own social determinants.[1]

This unawareness is reflected in their separation of "economic" from "noneconomic" factors and their identification of the former with "objective" and the latter with "political" or "moral" issues.[2] Behind this separation is the thought, to some extent correct, that the "economic" facts are more accessible to investigation. "Economic" quantities can, moreover, be expressed in monetary terms and made commensurable, at least in market economies. But the idea that commensurability in this sense renders the analysis "objective" is wrong. The distinction between "objective" choices guided by criteria of "yield" and "subjective" choices guided by morality or politics is a deeply metaphysical one that leads to the false belief that economic recommendations

---

[1] For a fuller development of the discussion in this and the next few paragraphs, see Prologue; Appendix 2, Sections 12–14 and 19–20, *et passim* in the several chapters of this book.

[2] Appendix 2, Section 14.

can be made without commitment to value judgments. Another thought basic to the separation of "economic" from "non-economic" factors is the assumption — largely correct for Western countries — that people's attitudes and their social institutions have been rationalized and standardized and are therefore either adapted or adaptable to economic progress. Abstracting from them is therefore legitimate for many problems in the West.[1] The same assumption cannot, however, be made about attitudes and institutions in South Asia. Western theories provide a convenient escape from the fact that attempts to change attitudes and institutions in that part of the world ordinarily meet with strong opposition from vested interests and with other obstacles and inhibitions.

This whole way of reasoning is particularly damaging in the analysis of development problems in underdeveloped countries like those in South Asia, not only for the reasons suggested but for others set forth in Appendix 2 and elsewhere in this book.[2] The fact that it is less damaging in the analysis of the problems of the Western countries provides part of the explanation for its tenacious hold in the West and the ease of its transfer to the analysis of South Asian problems. Another part of the explanation is that reasoning of this type meets the needs for rationalization of both conservatives and radicals, Western and South Asian.[3] Marx made a conscious break with this type of reasoning, characterized by the isolation of "economic" from "non-economic" factors. But he, and even more his followers, who established "Marxism,"[4] fell into the opposite error of assuming that the required adjustments in the parameters — attitudes and institutions — occur inevitably and rather rapidly. This assumption helped make it possible for Marx to root his "economic" reasoning in the classical traditions of political economy. The more recent formalization of "Marxist" models and their "tightening up" have tended to bring the "Marxist" and the Western type of model-thinking closer together.[5]

Economic models have come to stereotype this whole way of thinking, which we have called the Western or modern approach,[6] and in turn have strongly influenced the plans and the discussion of planning for development in the South Asian countries. As is shown in various contexts in this book, this

[1] Appendix 2, Sections 19 and 20.

[2] See also Myrdal, "'Value-loaded' Concepts," in Hugo Hegeland, ed., *Money, Growth, and Methodology and Other Essays in Honor of Johan Åkerman*, Glerup, Lund, 1961, pp. 282 ff.

[3] Prologue, Section 6.

[4] "Marxism" is not used as a technical term in the present book, because it means different things to different people. The quotation marks are also useful for distinguishing "Marxism" from Marx's own views. See Chapter 15, p. 726, footnote 1.

[5] Prologue, Sections 5–6; Appendix 2, Section 20 *et passim*.

[6] This approach, with its escape from the need to change institutional and cultural obstacles to development, was not followed in either theory or practice in Germany (where Friedrich List criticized classical economics on historical and institutional grounds) or Japan, which embarked on development in the nineteenth century. These countries proceeded straight to the reform of attitudes and institutions, recognizing that these were the strategic points and expecting economics to follow. One may speculate what fate would have befallen them if they had had the advice of modern economists, though it must be admitted that even nowadays practice is often somewhat better than economic theology would lead one to expect.

particular type of model-thinking has systematically biased the planners' view of reality in a way that suits the convenience and vested interests of conservatives and radicals alike. The present appendix will elaborate the theoretical criticism of this approach offered in Appendix 2 and in other contexts of the study.[1]

The economic models used in planning can be critically examined in two distinct ways. They can be studied as manifestations of certain habits of thought and social pressures that result in biases. As such, the investigation is part of the sociology of knowledge,[2] and is treated more fully in the Prologue and elsewhere in this book. In this appendix our criticism is directed at the method and content of these models and their claims to scope, validity, and relevance. In Part I our criticism is transcendental and concerns the assumptions, made explicitly and implicitly; these assumptions are examined in terms of the logic of their adequacy to reality. In Part II we proceed to an immanent criticism of these models, accepting the assumptions but examining their precise meaning, the validity of the inferences, and the consistency of the models.[3] In Part III we draw some conclusions.

I

The Models

2   *General Characteristics of the Models*

Models in their pure form are not expected to provide full explanations or correct predictions. According to our definition of "theory,"[4] they are different from "theories" in at least three important respects. First, they deliberately deal with only a few selected relationships. Secondly, they purport to be,

---

[1] This appendix is the work of Professor Paul P. Streeten.

[2] "Sociology of knowledge" is perhaps too narrow a term. Since knowledge is by definition true belief, held with certainty and on good grounds, it would, strictly interpreted, exclude the sociology of uncertain opinion, whether true or false, of confident false belief, and of true belief held on insufficient grounds. But we intend the expression to cover all these things.

[3] Transcendental and immanent criticism cannot be sharply distinguished. To criticize abstraction from a variable that is in fact subject to larger changes than the variable analyzed is transcendental criticism. To criticize abstraction from a variable whose change is logically implied in the assumptions of a model is immanent criticism. But, for certain purposes, change that is logically implied can nevertheless be regarded as inessential. The question whether the change is indeed essential is therefore partly one of transcendental and partly one of immanent criticism. Thus many models abstract from the passage of time, without denying that all events must occur in time. But if the passage of time can be shown to change crucially certain factors assumed to be constant, a criticism that points this out is partly transcendental, partly immanent.

[4] Preface; Prologue, Section 7.

Economic Models and Their Usefulness for Planning 1944

but are not always, closed systems, in which, granted the premises, the conclusions necessarily follow. "There is no place in the model for, and no function to be served by, vagueness, maybe's or approximations."[1] Thirdly, the relationships are formulated in such a way as to be, at least in principle, and at least ordinally, quantifiable.

To observe that models are *selective, abstract and logically complete,* and *quantifiable* is to expose their limitations: they are not comprehensive but partial; they can be quite irrelevant; and they tend to neglect those factors that, at least so far, have proved difficult to quantify.[2] They are often expressed in the language of mathematics or symbolic logic, because this medium makes it easier to discover inconsistencies. But it also facilitates the neglect of relevance and realism, and ambiguities enter by reason of the various possible empirical interpretations of the logically formulated premises. When the models are "applied," their selective and therefore arbitrary nature is usually forgotten. More important, these models frequently pass under false pretenses, inasmuch as some of the assumptions that are essential if the models are to be rigorous are not stated; often the model-builders are not even aware of them. This bent is encouraged by ignorance of the history of economic thought[3] and naiveté about, and contempt for, the sociology of knowledge. The result is that, contrary to the intentions and pretensions of their authors, the models often have only the appearance of logical consistency, rigor, and precision, covering up what in reality is gross looseness in thinking (Prologue, Section 8). We shall make some further general observations on the "realism" of models in Section 8.

The discussion in this part of the appendix will keep in the forefront, as an archetype of model-thinking, one type of model that dominates the literature and the plans. This is the Harrod-Domar model and its numerous variations. In this, the strategic variables that are selected are aggregates such as employment, investment, and output. But instead of the neo-classical assumption of perfect substitutability of capital for labor, the starting point is the assumption of fixed technical or behavioral coefficients, so that aggregate output is related to the stock of capital by the capital/output ratio, otherwise known as the capital coefficient. This is the salient feature added by the Harrod-Domar model to the Keynesian short-period theory of employment. The crucial role, in economic theory and planning, of the "capital/output ratio" is well brought out in an article by an Indian writer:

[1] Milton Friedman, *Essays in Positive Economics,* University of Chicago Press, Chicago, Ill., 1953, p. 24.

[2] We do not accept the common idea that there is scope for what is sometimes loosely called qualitative reasoning in economics or other social sciences. In principle, everything can be measured; all research should be directed to this end. The fact that it cannot be accomplished immediately should not excuse loose thinking and conceptual laxity. See Prologue, Section 8.

[3] It is, for instance, a remarkable fact that in the recent revival of "welfare economics," which has resulted in a flow of books and articles, particularly in America and England, and has influenced the models criticized in this appendix and elsewhere in this book, there has been little evidence of awareness of the intensive discussions of the same problems in the golden age of welfare theory — in the writings of J. S. Mill, Edgeworth, and Sidgwick, for example. See Appendix 7, p. 2063, footnote 1.

Economic Models and Their Usefulness for Planning 1945

If there is one concept that has dominated recent discussions on growth theory and development planning, it is that of the capital-output ratio, or the capital-coefficient as it is sometimes called. It has been extensively used in various growth models, e.g., those of Harrod, Domar, Kaldor, and Mahalanobis, and it has also helped the formulation of our First and Second Five Year Plans.[1]

Another approach, less pertinent to problems of economic planning in South Asia, uses a Cobb-Douglas production function of the form $Y = aK^\beta L^\alpha$ where K and L are the quantities of capital and labor, respectively, and a, α, β are assumed constants, where $(\alpha + \beta)$ may equal, exceed, or be less than 1, according to whether constant, increasing, or decreasing returns to scale are assumed. In this kind of approach there are also certain difficulties, such as how to treat changes in the *quality* of capital and labor, how to incorporate *changes* in knowledge and the passage of *time*, and how to determine the magnitude of the *constants*. The capital/output ratio in this formulation is not a determining variable, but a resultant of the changes in K and L as well as in α and β. While one can therefore easily deduce average and marginal capital/output ratios from the production function, these are endogenous variables, not determinants as they are in the Harrod-Domar analysis.[2] Since the plans are concerned pri-

[1] Pankaj Kumar Sen, "Use of the Capital-Output Ratio in Economic Planning," *The Indian Economic Review*, Vol. V, No. 1, February, 1960, p. 23. See also the report of a group of experts: "After estimating the current rate of savings, the *crucial* question will be what amount of net national output can be expected from the investment to be made on the basis of the estimated savings. A number of studies have been made on the amount of capital required to increase output by one unit per annum in each sector of economy and for a national economy as a whole. This amount is called the 'capital-output ratio,' or 'capital coefficient.'" (United Nations, *Programming Techniques for Economic Development: With special reference to Asia and the Far East*, Report by a group of experts, Bangkok, 1960, pp. 10–11.)

And: "The rate of economic growth may be analytically considered as being a function of two factors, (a) the rate of capital formation and (b) the capital/output ratio; accordingly development policies may be described as aiming to increase the former, reduce the latter, or do both." (U. N., ECAFE, "Economic Development and Planning in Asia and the Far East," *Economic Bulletin for Asia and the Far East*, Vol. VI, No. 3, November, 1955, Bangkok, 1955, pp. 25–26.)

Lewis's book *The Theory of Economic Growth*, especially the chapter on capital, illustrates the central position of this concept together with that of the savings ratio: "The central problem in the theory of economic growth is to understand the process by which a community is converted from being a 5 percent to a 12 percent saver — with all the changes in attitudes, in institutions and in techniques which accompany this conversion." (W. Arthur Lewis, *The Theory of Economic Growth*, Allen & Unwin Ltd., London, 1955, pp. 225–226.) This is based on a required growth rate for national income of approximately 3 percent and a capital/output ratio of approximately 4.

[2] In an article entitled "The Production Function in Allocation and Growth: A Synthesis" (*American Economic Review*, Vol. LII, No. 5, December, 1962, pp. 995–1022), Marvin Frankel shows how, mathematically, a micro-economic Cobb-Douglas function for each individual firm can be combined with a macro-economic Harrod-Domar function. Production in the enterprise is governed by a function of the form $P_i = aHK^\beta{}_iL^\alpha{}_i$ where H is called the "development modifier," a parameter for the enterprise but a dependent variable if all enterprises expand together. If $H = \left(\dfrac{K}{L}\right)^\gamma$ the aggregate production function is $P = a\left(\dfrac{K}{L}\right)^\gamma K^\beta L^\alpha$; and if $\gamma = \alpha$ and $(\alpha + \beta) = 1$, it reduces to $P = aK$, the Harrod-Domar relation. In terms of our Figure 2

marily with the capital/output ratio as a strategic relationship in determining the rate of growth, we can in our discussion largely ignore the Cobb-Douglas production function. Some of the criticisms, both of the assumptions (advanced in this part of the appendix) and of the internal consistency of the model (discussed in Part II), would, however, apply to any of the traditional notions of a "production function."[1]

These concepts and models play a considerably smaller role in practice, of course, than in theoretical discussions. For a number of reasons, good and bad, planning goes its own way while economic theory is paid lip service. Nevertheless, whatever actions are taken, they must be the worse for having an irrelevant and logically inconsistent theory to guide them. Moreover, these concepts and models represent an approach, and one that molds the entire structure of the plans whether or not the models are formally applied.

We criticize in the following sections four principal ways in which errors enter into model analysis. They are revealed by four closely interrelated assumptions, usually not made explicit. These assumptions are: (1) that certain parameters, which are tacitly assumed to be fully adapted to the development process, will stay constant or, alternatively, that they will be automatically adapted to the extent required; (2) that the number of strategic variables can be narrowed down to a single one; (3) that very dissimilar items can be analyzed in terms of a single category; and (4) that certain sequences can be isolated and analyzed without regard to their relationship to other sequences. After discussing these four assumptions, we attempt to sketch briefly the requirements that should be met by models used in analyzing the problems under consideration. The critical discussion therefore proceeds under the following headings:

Adapted *Ceteris Paribus* or Automatic *Mutatis Mutandis*
One-Factor Analysis
Misplaced Aggregation
Illegitimate Isolation

3 Adapted Ceteris Paribus or Automatic Mutatis Mutandis

The distinction in economics between variables and constants and between independent and dependent variables is dictated in part by the problem under consideration and by the focus of interest as determined by more or less implicit valuations, in part by convenience, and in part by habits of thought. Arbitrariness enters when economists relegate to the category of constants or independent variables those conditions that appear to be more resistant to

---

(Section 14 below), each individual enterprise believes it moves along a diminishing returns curve, but if all grow together they move up the straight line.

[1] After a brief discussion of the use of this type of production function in *forecasting* (not planning) growth in *advanced countries* (not in underdeveloped countries, where statistics are vastly inferior), Otto Eckstein concludes: "Since aggregate production functions so far have not yielded reliable estimates of the relationship between investment and growth, one must try other methods." ("Capital Theory and Some Theoretical Problems in Development Planning," *American Economic Review, Papers and Proceedings*, LI, No. 2, May, 1961, p. 98.)

quantification than are the conditions they are accustomed to quantify. In the more formalized models the assumption is usually that the conditions from which the analysis abstracts remain *constant*.

Even conditions sometimes counted as "economic" may be excluded from analysis by the static assumption of *ceteris paribus*. Thus through the whole neo-classical period and until recently "the state of the arts" was assumed in theoretical analysis to remain unchanged, and this assumption is implied even today in most capital/output models. It should be stressed that, quite apart from their alleged resistance to quantification, such conditions as "technical knowledge" and its commercial and industrial application are difficult to assimilate in a model. Knowledge, though clearly not available in superabundance, is not scarce in the sense that the more we use of it in one direction, the less is left for use in another. Knowledge is substitutable for other factors insofar as an improvement in technique enables the same product to be produced with less land, labor, or capital; but the costs of the improvement fall under those of either labor (specially trained employees) or capital (purchase of patents or setting up of research laboratories). Knowledge can be lost, but its technological and commercial application is not reversible, and its accumulation is not systematically related to expenditure on its acquisition.

The assumption that "the state of the arts" is constant is particularly inappropriate in the underdeveloped countries of South Asia, because the application and adaptation there of the higher technology from the developed countries is generally held to be a most important instrument of development. But the higher technology is obviously not a "free good" for the underdeveloped countries to draw on; it has to be acquired and adapted, and this involves costs.[1] Recent attempts to measure the "productivity" of expenditure to acquire and adapt knowledge — success in which would make it possible to include "the state of the arts" among the dependent variables — have not been satisfactory in explaining development; their logic is dubious and the results are inconclusive.[2]

Levels of living are another set of conditions usually considered as "economic" and nevertheless left out. Their exclusion from the models as determining variables may be valid in developed countries, where there is no feedback from a change in levels of living to the input and quality of labor and to output. This assumption is not justified in South Asia, as we show in Appendix 2, Section 21.

In addition to the conditions conventionally regarded as "economic," it is characteristic of model-thinking that the "non-economic" conditions, which we call attitudes and institutions,[3] are assumed to be both constant (often an ex-

[1] Chapter 14, Section 6.

[2] Section 7 below; also Chapter 29.

In Chapter 14, Section 8, we point out that, as a matter of fact, scientific and technological advance as now directed makes development for the underdeveloped countries in South Asia more difficult. This causal relationship is, of course, entirely beyond the grasp of an analysis in terms of models; this helps explain why it has been commonly overlooked in the discussion of development.

[3] Appendix 2, Section 5.

plicit assumption) and fully adapted to the development process (usually implicit). This assumption may be fairly realistic for developed countries, but, as we illustrated in Appendix 2, Sections 9 and 20, it is quite unrealistic for the underdeveloped countries of South Asia, where attitudes and institutions are mainly responsible for the inertia in the social system that hampers and sometimes blocks economic development. The trouble with the assumption that attitudes and institutions are fully adapted so as to permit a smooth development process is not only that it is implicit but also that it is entirely indeterminate. Even if it were brought out into the open, it could not be tested by observation, for the same events can be interpreted as denoting either low "economic" returns to "adapted" conditions or (potentially) high returns if "non-adapted" conditions were to become adapted.[1]

The implied assumption, moreover, invites a gliding from *ceteris paribus* to automatic *mutatis mutandis,* that is, to an assumption that attitudes and institutions, though not fully *adapted* to the development process under consideration, are *adaptable* without intentional and direct policies.[2] The gliding may occur under the pressure of an uneasy awareness that the "non-economic" conditions cannot be assumed to be constant and fully adapted. It is then assumed that the *adaptation will be induced automatically,* so that the process analyzed in the model will not be impeded or blocked. In other words, conditions for smooth development are either assumed in a *ceteris paribus* clause or it is assumed that they will be created automatically. Thus, for instance, it is assumed that people either want to work, whether equipment is available or not (*ceteris paribus*), or that they will be automatically *induced* to want to work as a result of the provision of equipment. In either case, the assumption is logically indeterminate and invalidates all reasoning in terms of "economic" variables. It is usually connected with an unrealistic ("Marxist") view of the ability of "economic" changes to bring about changes in attitudes and institutions, and to do so rapidly; see Appendix 2, Section 20.

We thus conclude that neither of the two assumptions — adapted *ceteris paribus* or automatic *mutatis mutandis* — makes possible a realistic analysis of the development process in a South Asian country. Both, singly or in combination, create logical difficulties.[3] If this is not apparent to the producers and consumers of the models and of less formal analyses using the same approach, it is because the whole area lies in the deep shadow of implicit reasoning. In this shadow, conceptual confusion and biased opportunism can sprout freely while the reasoning on which the light is focussed looks precise, rigorous, and consistent.

[1] Thus unwillingness to use irrigation water can be interpreted as a sign that the "capital/output ratio" of the irrigation works is high, if land ownership and peasant incentives are assumed to be adapted; the capital/output ratio would be lower if institutional and attitudinal reforms were thought to lead to fuller use.

[2] See the quotation from Arthur Lewis on p. 1945, footnote 1.

[3] The automatic *mutatis mutandis* assumption, unless much more carefully spelled out than has been done anywhere, harbors the added logical difficulty that if any "economic" action yields the predicted result because unanalyzed conditions are assumed to vary to the required extent, there is no operational work to be done by analysis.

4 One-Factor Analysis

The procedure of assuming either adapted *ceteris paribus* or automatic *mutatis mutandis* or a combination of the two is further simplified in the models most frequently used by concentration on a *single* productive factor — usually capital. Capital as the strategic variable is then juxtaposed to output as the dependent one.

This approach is in the tradition of neo-classical and, indeed, classical economics. Of the three conventional factor groups, "land" is defined as the "original and indestructible powers of the soil" and is therefore by definition of little interest for economic policy. Improvements — plowing, irrigation, drainage, fertilizing, etc. — are treated as investment. Labor is not "man-made" in the economically relevant sense, and its supply is influenced by "non-economic" conditions.[1] Capital is man-made and can be augmented; it is regarded as easily quantifiable and can thus be neatly fitted into models; it can be treated as having purely instrumental value. In view of the history of economic thinking and the various biases discussed in other contexts in this book, the tendency to single out capital as the main strategic variable of development is easily understandable.

This tendency has culminated in the capital/output model. Designed originally by Harrod as a theoretical tool in dealing with the problem of stagnation and instability in advanced industrial countries and showing the required rate of growth of income if investment is to be justified, this model or some variation of it was applied to the utterly different problems of underdeveloped countries, to show the required investment if income is to grow at a desired rate. It came to determine the very structure of the plans.[2]

According to classical and neo-classical economic theory, an increase in the use of capital per head, with no increase in technical knowledge, will sooner or later yield diminishing marginal returns. In Marx's theory, the increasing organic composition of capital can be interpreted as implying a rise in the capital/output ratio. Attempts to test these theories statistically some ten to fifteen years ago indicated, however, that output has grown roughly in proportion to capital input in advanced industrial countries over several decades. These studies seemed to substantiate the theory of a constant capital/output ratio,[3]

---

[1] In Section 7 we discuss the recent attempts to deal with "investment in man" in the same way as investment in physical capital.

[2] Appendix 4.

Numerous qualifications have always been made. Enterprise, management, technical know-how, education, and research have been stressed as important sources of development. But these factors are soon forgotten or are singled out, isolated, and, like capital, treated as homogeneous inputs to which output responds, while other factors are assumed to remain constant. See below Section 7.

[3] Insofar as capital is valued by capitalizing profits at a constant interest rate, the constancy of the capital/output ratio is based on circular reasoning. Thus if the share of profits in the national income is one quarter, and if profits are capitalized at 5 percent (10 percent), the stock of capital will always be five (two and a half) times the annual income, regardless of technological change. $\dfrac{K}{Y} = \dfrac{P}{Y} \cdot \dfrac{K}{P} = \dfrac{P}{Y.r}$, if K is the stock of capital, P annual profits, Y national income, r the rate of profit. By using a con-

although it was, of course, recognized that the ratio varied greatly between industries and sectors, and over short periods under the influence of wars, trade cycles, and so on.

The statistical discovery, by itself, established no explanation of the causal relationship between capital growth and income growth. It might be that the growth of income, caused by changes in other conditions, resulted in a certain rate of capital accumulation; or that both capital growth and income growth were the results of a third set of changes. On the other hand, the Harrod-Domar model alone could not have been used for development planning if the value of the capital coefficient had been believed to vary considerably and unpredictably. But the model and the statistical discovery supported each other, and the newly won confidence in the concept of a constant capital/output ratio inspired its use for the development plans in underdeveloped countries.[1]

The relationship between the one-factor analysis in the typical model and the implicit and indeterminate assumptions dealt with in the preceding section is that these assumptions become necessary when output is made a function of the one factor, capital. In any model relating output to variations in capital it must be assumed that all other conditions either are fully adapted or are adaptable through investment. As we proceed, we shall see a number of other ways in which the various assumptions are related to each other.

---

stant r for discounting the profit stream, $\frac{K}{Y}$ will be constant as long as $\frac{P}{Y}$ is constant. Careful calculations must be made, of course, to attempt to get an independent valuation of capital.

Moreover, even quite small variations in the capital/output ratio make large and cumulative differences in output after some time. The allegedly narrow range of the coefficient can therefore give rise to misleading conclusions.

[1] A few quotations can be given to illustrate this confidence. Thus, after a word of caution about statistical difficulties, Tinbergen writes: "For a given or desired increase in production *the necessary investments can be calculated* by multiplication with the coefficient. It is to be hoped that *further research will narrow down the margins of error of such calculations* which, for the time being, are still considerable." (Jan Tinbergen, *The Design of Development*, Johns Hopkins Press, Baltimore, 1958, p. 75. Italics added.)

And earlier in the same work (p. 13, again with italics added): "One vital problem may now be considered: will savings plus estimated capital imports be sufficient to raise the national capital to the extent required to attain the assumed national income? The relationships which are relevant to this question have been dealt with in a concise and simple way by the introduction of the so-called 'capital coefficient.' *Experience shows* that, at least for countries, the ratio between investments and the resulting increase in net national income varies less than was long believed. Something can be said about its order of magnitude, although the margin of uncertainty is still fairly high. Or, to put it in a different way: there appears to be a fairly constant ratio between a country's wealth and its income per annum."

From a United Nations report: "*Available data clearly show* that for a number of countries, e.g., the Federal Republic of Germany, Japan, Norway, the United Kingdom and the United States, the capital-output ratio for a national economy as a whole remains stable over somewhat longer periods at a level of 3 to 4. . . . Even though there are variations, it is perhaps one of the most useful parameters with a fair degree of stability." (U. N., *Programming Techniques for Economic Development: With special reference to Asia and the Far East*, p. 11. Italics added.)

5 Misplaced Aggregation

It is generally recognized that, in principle, quantification of changes in heterogeneous aggregates is arbitrary. If the number of some items in a collection of different items increases while the number of other items falls, nothing meaningful can be said about the change in the total unless a system of weights is adopted to reduce heterogeneity to homogeneity. The use of index numbers for measuring changes in total production is justified for advanced industrial countries, as long as the index numbers do not pretend to a greater precision than they have. The reason why this is so is to be found in the mobility of factors and the substitutability of both factors and products in advanced countries. This flexibility is in turn the result of certain technological, institutional, and attitudinal facts, such as the spread of engineering knowledge, organized and fluid markets, and economic calculation and motivation.

The situation in the underdeveloped countries of South Asia is very different. There prices do not respond to demand and supply; factors of production, including entrepreneurship, are more often specific and respond sluggishly if at all to economic incentives. Market imperfections, ignorance, and irrationality are the rule. There is much less diversification. Indivisibilities abound. Mobility is absent or tardy, and complementarities are ubiquitous and strong. The use of aggregates in such economies conceals more than it reveals.[1] It may be justifiable to add swords and plowshares at their production costs in an advanced country, and quite meaningless in an underdeveloped country. If there is excess demand in one sector and excess supply in another, but the supply in one cannot be used to meet the demand in the other, there is no sense in talking of aggregate demand or aggregate supply.

The objections to aggregation apply to most of the concepts that are the economist's stock in trade in the analysis of developed economies: "labor," "national income," "inflation," "the price level," "savings," "productivity," "unemployment." The use of investment and output aggregates for development plans presupposes that a homogeneous, adequately trained, willing labor force is available and will quickly become employed if capital equipment and effective demand are provided. That this type of aggregation is misplaced in South Asia has been pointed out in Appendix 2. In some cases the very concepts used — for instance, "unemployment" and "underemployment" — are logically faulty and not adequate to reality in South Asia.[2]

The foregoing critical observations apply to models and to less formal analyses in which these concepts are used. Such analyses are normally elaborations and refinements of the simple master model, in which output is a function of capital input. Here we have only two aggregations. All other influences, whether of other productive factors or of other "economic" conditions or of "non-economic" conditions, are ignored on the ground of either the adapted *ceteris paribus* or the automatic *mutatis mutandis* assumption, or some unspecified combination of the two. But neither "output" nor "capital" can properly be aggregated into a single category. Both certain facts — such as rigidity, immobility, differences in responses, indivisibilities, and interdependencies —

[1] Appendix 2, Section 23.
[2] See Chapter 21, Part II, and Appendix 6.

Economic Models and Their Usefulness for Planning   1952

and certain valuations — such as the desire to spread benefits and avoid increasing inequalities — make aggregation inappropriate. The so-called direct investments in agriculture and in other unorganized sectors cannot be satisfactorily measured in monetary terms, and even if they could, they could not be added to investments in the organized sectors.

In order to get the model to move, a third aggregate — savings — is introduced. "Income" is split into "consumption" and "savings" and the addition to the stock of capital is "investment." We have seen elsewhere that the rationale for the distinction between consumption and saving is absent in South Asia.[1] In addition, "savings" is itself a misplaced aggregation.[2] The development effects of "savings" made available through foreign exchange are quite different from the effects of internal abstention from consumption, and the effects of internal savings differ according to where they occur and what other measures are in effect.

In addition to the empirical and statistical problem of collecting the relevant data for aggregation, the objections to aggregation are twofold. First, misplaced aggregation occurs when an activity is inappropriately categorized. The aggregation that results might be appropriate for advanced countries, but not for underdeveloped ones. Secondly, the category must be defined specifically as it applies to a situation of underdevelopment. Thus the distinction between "consumption" (income minus savings) and "investment" is a matter of definition that can result in misplaced aggregation. If investment is defined as "abstaining for the sake of higher consumption later," the first objection may rise. But if investment is defined as any input that yields higher output later, whether it involves "abstaining" or not, the second problem arises. The error then is not a conceptual one but merely a failure to group under "investment" certain activities that, in advanced countries, are defined as "consumption." The point is not that all forms of aggregation are unjustifiable, but that the criterion of appropriate aggregation must be whether the differences between the items that are grouped together are irrelevant to the investigation.

In its simplest form the capital/output model contains only one sector. If such massive aggregation can be justified at all, it can be justified only for a developed economy with a high degree of mobility, flexibility, and adaptability.[3] To meet the obvious difficulties of misplaced aggregation, the construction of models of two or more sectors is attempted with increasing frequency. These attempts are useful primarily for the negative purpose of showing the limitations of the one-sector models. This negative function is important, however, since it has not been possible to dislodge the strong grip on mental habits of certain models, merely by noting facts that contradict them.[4] Beyond that, they are not especially useful. The aggregates in two-sector models are far too

[1] Appendix 2, Section 21.

[2] Cf. Chapter 12, Sections 1 and 2.

[3] The fact that the classical writers and Marx displayed a greater interest in intersectoral relations than is customary in Keynesian analysis reflects the higher stage of development reached by the economies analyzed by the Keynesians.

[4] Cf. Part II, Section 15.

broad for these models to lead to a better understanding of South Asian reality. Even if the sectors are well chosen, the fragmentation of the economies is too great and the misplaced aggregation within each sector is excessive. Moreover, the greater complexity in sectoral breakdown often results in over-simplification in other respects; in the assumption, for example, that all machines are made by hand or last forever, or that only one final product is produced. Such over-simplifications may of course be justified to clarify certain points but without a much more detailed breakdown they do not contribute much to an understanding of the development process.

In the attempt to reduce the complexity of concrete detail to a single-sector abstraction the baby is thrown out with the bath water. The same may be said with almost equal force of the two- or three-sector abstractions, particularly when the additional sectors are achieved by over-simplification in other respects. For in the discussion of savings, investment, consumption, and inflation, the *direction* and *composition* of government policies and their effects are relevant, not some spurious totals. It is much more important, for example, to know *who* consumes and *what* he consumes than to know changes in aggregate consumption; to know *where* investment occurs and *what* supplementary and complementary actions are taken than to know how much is added to total capital when we consider the capital/output ratio; to know *where* supply bottlenecks occur than to postulate a general ceiling when we analyze inflation; to consider *which* imports are affected than to apply multiplier analysis when we analyze the effects of a devaluation on internal activity. The objection to aggregation is not the over-simplification as such, but the abstraction from the very facts that matter most.

Misplaced aggregation is a more general fault than one-factor analysis. It is possible, indeed quite common, to construct multi-factor models in which the aggregates, though functionally related, are inappropriately aggregated. But one-factor analysis, and, in particular, the aggregation and juxtaposition of output and capital input, are outstanding examples of misplaced aggregation. Without the device of misplaced aggregation there would be no one-factor analysis. Both the *ceteris paribus* and *mutatis mutandis* assumptions imply aggregation of "economic" and "non-economic" conditions; and within the "economic" conditions, aggregation of both those that do not change, or change for reasons not considered in the model, and those whose change is a function of the variables. All these misplaced aggregations are logically connected with illegitimate separations, to which we turn in the next section.

6 Illegitimate Isolation

The assumption in constructing economic models, that it is possible and useful to isolate certain variables and concentrate on them without regard to their inseparability from variables that are left out of consideration, is in one sense the reverse of misplaced aggregation and in another its complement. To construct models on such an assumption is like judging a violin concert by the number and quality of violins without regard to the skill of the violinists. Violins, however fine, cannot produce a melody without skilled violinists, nor can violinists without violins. The appropriate unit is violin plus violinist, and to talk of a violin/melody ratio is to commit both the fallacies, misplaced aggregation and illegitimate isolation.

Misplaced aggregation and illegitimate isolation go hand in hand when differentiated items are aggregated and the components are separated from their supplementary and complementary conditions. In the capital/output model all forms of capital are aggregated and each piece of construction and equipment is isolated from (a) its specific relation to other pieces of construction and equipment; (b) other influences, such as levels of living (including facilities for acquiring skills), human attitudes, and social institutions; and (c) policies directed at other conditions. Yet all three factors crucially affect the contribution to output of the particular piece of investment.

Illegitimate isolation is a specific manifestation of the assumption that all other conditions remain constant and adapted to development. For if conditions are assumed to be constant whose change is either necessary to the required results or makes an important difference in their direction, speed, and size, there has been illegitimate abstraction. If automatic *mutatis mutandis* is relied on, so that it is assumed that these other conditions will change but in such a way that they will always be automatically adapted, there is no isolation. But, as we have seen, this assumption must be questioned on both empirical and logical grounds. Empirically we know that in the South Asian countries conditions are not automatically adapted in the required fashion. Logically, the specific contribution of the variables under consideration remains indeterminate if we always keep in the pack a joker that can take all tricks. If we have an unspecified combination of the two assumptions, both illegitimate isolation and indeterminacy are present. It is the purpose of both the *ceteris paribus* and the *mutatis mutandis* assumptions to isolate the study of the causal relationship between capital input and aggregate output. As we have stressed in various contexts, this approach introduces the bias that capital is the only, or the main, source of development in the underdeveloped countries of South Asia. The separation of capital from certain components in the level of living that affect labor input and labor efficiency, and from attitudes and institutions crucial for effective capital use, is one of the main forms of illegitimate isolation.[1]

The effects of plant and equipment on output depend not only on where and how the investment occurs (as explained in Section 5 above) but also on what other policies that affect levels of living, attitudes, and institutions are pursued. In the South Asian countries the two last-named conditions cannot be regarded either as already adapted to development or as automatically adaptable through investment. The effects of a development plan with a given amount of investment will differ greatly according to what policies with regard to attitudes and institutions are pursued in conjunction with the investment.[2]

Moreover, illegitimate isolation is implicit in aggregation if the complementarities between the components of the aggregate are ignored. The output effects of one investment project depend on other investment projects that are

[1] Appendix 2, Sections 20 and 21.
[2] Appendix 2, Section 19.

embarked on either simultaneously or in sequence as phases of a coordinated program. In an economy where each project is infinitesimally small and can profit from adapted attitudes and institutions, aggregation irrespective of composition may be legitimate. But in the South Asian countries investment projects are large, in relation to both the existing stock of that type of capital and annual additions to it.[1] The resulting output varies sharply according to the availability of complementary supplies, such as appropriate construction elsewhere and other pieces of equipment, and the existence of appropriate demand. It is then entirely misleading to treat "capital" as a homogeneous quantity. It is a heterogeneous collection of specific bits and pieces that have to be fitted together.

Much investment, particularly public investment — in highways, power stations, ports, railways, workers' houses — provides opportunities and possibly incentives for consequential output-generating investment. This, indeed, is one of the reasons for carrying out public investment, which often seems unlikely to recover its costs by profits. But many forms of private investment are also of this nature. The short-term and sectoral capital/output ratio of a given project may be high, but the long-term ratio may be much lower, if it can be calculated at all. It will depend on fuller utilization of the project's own capacity and the capacities of other already existing enterprises and also on the seizure of consequential investment opportunities and the output generation to which these give rise.[2] If, on the other hand, it turns out that operating, maintenance, and supervision costs are unexpectedly high or that the expected complementary investment is not forthcoming, the long-term ratio, which includes external effects on other projects, will be high or may rise. Certain projects, such as improvements in cultivation methods, may themselves require little capital, but may require complementary investment in transport, power, storage, and other facilities. In either case, it is certainly misleading to pay attention only to the initial investment and its direct effects.

If a series of investment projects are interrelated, either sectorally or temporally, each depending on the others for its success, the very notion of a capital/output ratio for any one of them in isolation becomes as meaningless as the question, What is the contribution of the first violin to the Ninth Symphony?[3] It is the composition and the relationship of the parts that matter in appraising the result. Misplaced aggregation and illegitimate isolation conceal this. The problem is like that of putting the pieces of a jigsaw puzzle together. It is the placement of the pieces in relation to each other that matters, not the display of any single piece (illegitimate isolation), nor the counting of the total number of pieces thrown together at random (misplaced aggregation).

If changes in attitudes and institutions are taken into account in appraising

[1] Appendix 2, Section 23.

[2] Changes in utilization are discussed in Section 18 below. The creation of investment opportunities falls outside the scope of the normal assumptions and embraces variables normally assumed constant and adapted or adaptable.

[3] Except in a situation of general equilibrium, in which a capital/output ratio can be attributed to each industry on the assumption that the required adjustments are made in all other industries.

capital projects, some projects are seen to be more productive than others not only, and often not primarily, because of their physical effectiveness but also because of their impact on decision-taking, incentives to entrepreneurial or political action, attitudes toward work and venture, and the formation, reform, or destruction of habits, traditions, customs, and aspirations of workers and entrepreneurs. The application of improved techniques is in many ways related to investment. Improving levels of living, particularly levels of nutrition, health, and education, will raise output. The conclusion is that unless supplementary and consequential actions are taken on a wide front, an investment project may misfire; and in spite of a positive direct flow of production from it, the ratio — including effects on other projects and enterprises and, often, private and public actions — may rise to infinity or become negative for capital increases.[1] The success and effectiveness of investment in contributing to the growth of output depend not only on its being an addition to an aggregate "stock of capital" but on its direction (neglected by aggregation), its composition, and the present and future complementary policies with which it is packaged (neglected by isolation).

Rational planning in South Asia has to be a coordinated system of policies directed at a very large number of conditions that must be changed in order to engender development.[2] The approach to planning represented by the capital/output model tends to conceal this fact and provides no useful theoretical framework for this type of planning. As we show in Appendix 4, the structure of the plans in South Asia has been determined by this model to the detriment of planning in the region.

7   A Note on "Investment in Man"

Experts in health and education have long been aware that expenditure to improve the quality of the population may often be more important for development than physical investment. The failure of recent generations of economists to respond to this type of argument until recently is explained by their habitual ways of thought. For one thing, the argument cuts across the traditional distinction between investment and consumption. Consumption has an instrumental as well as an independent value, particularly in the underdeveloped countries of South Asia. Economists have tended to ignore its instrumental value.[3] Moreover, programs to improve the quality of the population have effects that are widely diffused, spread over a long time, and not easily measurable — a characteristic which has been regarded as justifying their exclusion from "economic policy."[4]

---

[1] It should be noted that not all negative *ex post* incremental "capital/output ratios" indicate waste. It may be sensible to modernize and re-equip an industry, the demand for whose product is falling. Capital expenditure may reduce costs per unit of output, while output is reduced. Simple-minded students of the capital/output ratio might conclude that output could be raised by reducing the stock of capital. See Section 14 below.

[2] Appendix 2, Sections 2 and 19.

[3] Appendix 2, Section 21.

[4] Appendix 2, Section 14.

This is not, however, a good reason for neglect. Widely diffused effects may be more important than highly concentrated ones. Long-term effects may be much greater than immediate ones. And effects that are difficult to measure may be greater than the more easily quantifiable effects of a physical investment.

As we see in Chapter 29, the challenge of estimating the returns on expenditures in certain of these "non-economic" directions has been accepted in recent years, but misplaced aggregation and illegitimate isolation are catching. The very same mistakes have been made that have vitiated the use of the capital/output ratio, both in analysis and in planning. New models have been constructed. Most of these have attempted to isolate the contributions to growth made by expenditures on education, but some have also included health and other factors previously rejected as "non-economic." The starting point has usually been the addition of a term to the Cobb-Douglas production function, making it $Y = aK^\alpha L^\beta H^\gamma$, where Y is national income, K capital, L labor, and H a ragbag term for "human factor," including "improved knowledge," better organization, economies of scale, and so on; a, α, β, and γ are constants; and $\alpha + \beta = 1$. Thus whatever is not caught in variations of K and L is attributed to H. "Improvement in knowledge" is another name for what has been called the "coefficient of our ignorance."[1] Whatever the value of these models for advanced Western countries and however welcome their attempt to get away from concentration on physical investment, their application to the problems of underdeveloped countries has bred confusion.[2]

In brief, the reasoning behind these new models is that the increased use of one factor of production while others, including "knowledge," are kept constant will yield diminishing marginal returns. If the expansion of land, labor, and capital does not account for the whole increase in national product over several decades, the remainder must be due to "investment in human resources," often loosely identified with "education." In another approach, attempts have been made to estimate the relationship between the higher earnings of the educated and expenditures on their education. These approaches have seemed to show that the returns on this type of "investment" exceed substantially the returns on physical investment. This has led to the political conclusion that

---

[1] Cf. T. Balogh and P. P. Streeten, "The Coefficient of Ignorance," *Bulletin of the Oxford University Institute of Statistics*, Vol. 25, No. 2, May, 1963. The phrase "measure of our ignorance" is Moses Abramovitz's.

Edward F. Denison in his much-quoted book, *The Sources of Economic Growth in the United States and the Alternatives Before Us* (Committee for Economic Development, Supplementary Paper No. 13, 1962), assumes simultaneously a linear homogeneous production function and perfect competition in order to use average returns per unit of a factor as a measure of its marginal value product and attributes a substantial proportion of "residual" growth to economies of scale. It is not clear how, on these apparently inconsistent assumptions, factor incomes and factor shares are determined.

[2] For a good, brief discussion of these attempts, see John Vaizey, *The Economics of Education*, Faber and Faber, London, 1962, Chapter III. For excellent criticisms of the application of this type of analysis to underdeveloped countries, see T. Balogh, "Balance in Education Planning," *The Times Educational Supplement*, June 8, 1962, p. 1179, and "Misconceived Education Programmes in Africa," *Universities Quarterly*, 1962.

planners in underdeveloped countries should give higher priority to expenditures on education and on other means of improving knowledge; this political conclusion is believed to have quantitative precision.[1]

The pitfalls and fallacies in this chain of reasoning are too numerous to be discussed here in detail.[2] In the models of an aggregate production function, a relationship, based on static assumptions, is *assumed* between capital, labor, and output. Then it is seen that the *observed* historical relationship in *advanced countries* diverges widely from the assumed relationship, and it is *postulated* that the difference is due to the improved productive quality of the human factor, uncritically identified as "improvement in knowledge." This conclusion is then transferred bodily to the totally different technical, historical, cultural, religious, institutional, and political setting of the *underdeveloped* countries. The fallacies of both illegitimate isolation and misplaced aggregation are committed. Even if improved knowledge were a necessary condition for growth in production, it might yield output in conjunction with machines, or if exploited in specific ways, or if combined with other policies, but not in isolation. Nor is all education equally productive. The teaching of Sanskrit has different results from the teaching of land cultivation. The teaching of bookkeeping may increase the efficiency of manual labor; the teaching of certain religions may reduce it. Isolation of "education" ignores the importance of coordinating policies; aggregating "education" obscures the type of education required for development. The error of misplaced aggregation is then compounded by lumping everything into a single financial magnitude.

Similar objections can be made to the attempts to calculate the returns from education on the basis of the higher earnings of the educated than of the uneducated. Most of the data on which the models are based are American. They do not provide evidence as to whether expenditures on education are the cause or the effect of superior incomes. Even if we could assume education to be a condition of higher earnings, the models do not demonstrate whether it is a sufficient or a necessary condition of growth,[3] and they do not separate monopolistic and other forces that are correlated with but not caused by education and also influence differential earnings. Moreover, the calculations based on these data ignore both the indirect (financial and non-financial) returns to

[1] Thus at a conference of the United Nations Association in Cambridge Malcolm S. Adiseshiah, UNESCO's Acting Director-General, said: "So my thesis is that accelerated economic growth is, to a large degree, a function of adequate and commensurate development of human resources. . . . the expenditure in formal education, in training, in mass media and in research and development leads to increased returns both to the individual and to the community. . . . The return from education over a 12-year period to the individual, expressed in terms of the relation between the amount invested by him and/or his parents and his higher earnings in the future, can be averaged at 16 percent gross or, if allowance is made for income forgone while at school or college, the net average would be 11 percent. Similarly, a two-year training course increases future earnings by around 6 percent gross or 3 percent net." (Malcolm S. Adiseshiah, *War on Want*, Pergamon Press, 1962.)

[2] See Chapter 29 and the comprehensive analysis of health and educational conditions and policies in the following four chapters.

[3] Industrialization in Britain preceded general compulsory education.

the uneducated and the direct (non-financial) returns to the educated. On the other hand, they emphasize "income forgone during study," which constitutes a large proportion of the costs of investment in education. But they do not estimate either the income forgone by other groups in society (housewives, voluntary workers, and those — such as university teachers — who accept lower incomes than they could get in other occupations) or the non-financial benefits enjoyed during education. Since the lifetime earnings span of the educated is quite different from that of the uneducated, earnings today must be calculated as returns from education in the 1920's. To conclude from such a calculation anything about today's returns is like comparing a crystal radio set with Telstar.

Assuming that the ratio of returns to costs of education reflected something significant, it would be rash to attribute it to education alone. There is a high correlation between expenditures on education and income and wealth of parents; ability, intelligence, and motivation; educational opportunities, such as urban residence and proximity to educational centers; access to well-paid jobs through family and other connections. Any one of these factors could, by itself or in conjunction with any of the others, account for the superior earnings.[1] Monopolistic elements enter not only into the differences in advantages enjoyed by the children of wealthy and of poor parents, but also into the differences in the rewards reaped from an education. How much of the earnings of lawyers and doctors is due to "investment in men" and how much to restrictive practices under the guise of requirements for qualification? The higher earnings are, in large part, not a return on education but a monopoly rent on (1) the scarcity of parents who can afford to educate their children well and (2) the scarcity of newcomers permitted in a profession whose members have a financial interest in maintaining scarcity.

Anyone using these models to calculate the returns from education in the underdeveloped countries of South Asia would discover that the rates of return are even higher than in advanced countries. But this would mean only that pay scales in the civil service, in universities, in the professions, and in business management are governed by traditional standards, or influenced by international scales and by natural or artificial restrictions. It would provide no clue to the "true" profitability, from the planner's viewpoint, of "investment in man."

The approach embodied in these models, though logically weak, not only appeals to the snobbery and flatters the self-esteem of the educated (who carry out these calculations that seemingly justify existing income differentials) but also buttresses vested interests. The measures required to make expenditure on technical and agricultural education effective would be painful, would violate vested interests, and would run into numerous inhibitions and obstacles. What a relief to the educated and privileged, then, to be served by the econometricians with a neat model, one that, conveniently for them, makes a statistical residual into the engine of development and transforms ignorance

[1] Denison's cursory manner of dealing with these factors contrasts with his detailed and ingenious measurements. He simply assumes that 60 percent of the observed difference in incomes is due to differences in schooling and the remaining 40 percent to other factors. See *The Sources of Economic Growth in the United States and the Alternatives Before Us*, p. 69.

into "knowledge" and privilege into excellence. Instead of having to specify *which types of education combined with what other measures* (such as investment in improved methods of cultivation and provision of the right equipment) are needed to create skills and the ability and willingness to work efficiently, instead of having to work out in detail the *complementary policies* necessary to reform attitudes and institutions (land reform, credit, civil service), they have only to single out one item as the necessary and sufficient condition, as the strategic variable of development. But the wrong kind of education, or the right kind without the required complementary actions, can check or reverse the process of development. An intelligentsia left in idleness and largely unemployable can be a source of reactionary, rather than economic, activity; young people brought up to despise manual work can reinforce the resistance to development; education that drains off talent from the land reinforces the stagnation of the villages; an excess of would-be bureaucrats seeking civil service employment aggravates the shortage of technologists. Aggregation of all "investment in human capital" and its separation from "investment in physical capital" obscures the complementary nature of some subgroups of the two and permits intellectual escape from unpleasant social and political problems.[1]

A third type of model uses the manpower planning approach.[2] These models are formally identical with capital/output models, with fixed coefficients and several sectors, applied to educational planning. Just as it is assumed that one type of capital good can create either consumption goods or another type of capital good, so it is assumed that people with a certain level of education will contribute to production or train others to do so. Fixed coefficients are assumed between development and the number of people educated, between the number educated at universities and the number required for secondary education, and so on. In addition to these artificially assumed relationships there are a large number of implicit assumptions behind the linear equations. Since most of the criticisms of the capital/output ratio apply also to these structurally identical models of manpower planning, no special attention will be paid to the latter type of models. All one has to do to understand their deficiencies is to read for "capital input" in the criticism of the capital/output ratios "input of people educated for a given number of years."

The use of financial terms to express misplaced aggregates further obscures the distortions they give rise to and the importance of coordinated complementary policies. Although an understanding of the potential contribution of consumption to development is a step forward, the manner in which educational expenditure has in fact been handled has led to new confusions and served ancient biases. Having stressed the productivity of one component of "consumption" — educational facilities — the logical next step is to include expendi-

[1] Chapter 29, Section 5.

[2] Cf. H. Correa, *The Economics of Human Resources*, Netherlands Economic Institute, 1962, Chapter XIV; H. Correa and J. Tinbergen, "Quantitative Adaptation of Education to Accelerated Growth," *Kyklos*, Vol. XV, 1962, pp. 776–786; and J. Tinbergen, "A Planning Model of Education Requirements for Economic Development," in *The Residual Factor and Economic Growth*, Study Group in the Economics of Education, O.E.C.D., Paris, 1964.

ture on health, nutrition, and, indeed, *all* consumption. The term "investment in man" can easily be extended to embrace all forms of consumption that may in one way or another contribute to or be necessary conditions of production. Since all expenditure then becomes "investment," either in physical or in human "capital," all expenditure becomes productive, and the inclusion of all of it can be justified. But the real problems have been evaded: What kind of physical and human investment is needed and in conjunction with what other "investment" and "consumption," supported by what other policies? What types of expenditure should be curtailed? These are the important questions: questions of the "twist" — increasing some activities while cutting down others — and of coordination.[1]

We may soon see new types of models — for calculating the returns yielded by expenditure on research and development, on training in management and administration, perhaps even on psychological treatment to transform tradition-bound into achievement-motivated personalities. But the results will be useless or worse if crucial distinctions are blurred by aggregation, crucial connections severed by isolation, historical and geographical differences neglected, and excessive stress placed on financial flows.

8   *The Problems of the "Realism" of Models*

Much of the foregoing criticism of economic models may be described as "institutional."[2] Like the rest of this book, it has reference primarily to South Asia. Whether and to what extent our strictures apply also to the use of these models in advanced countries does not concern us here. We have demonstrated, however, in several places that for advanced countries the usual aggregations are less misleading, because demand and supply and prices and costs respond to rational calculations; similarly, isolation is justifiable because it can be assumed that attitudes and institutions are such that the concepts "employment," "investment," "income" or "output," "saving," "consumption," and "general price level" are meaningful. "Economic" and "non-economic" conditions are much more closely and strongly related in the South Asian countries than in the industrial countries of the West.[3] In the latter, the creation of employment opportunities can be treated in isolation, because there are men able and willing to work and because work is organized in the standard week and for standard performance.[4] Health policies, education, and nutrition can be considered in isolation.[5] Since the effects on productivity may not be marked, the distinction between consumption and investment, and the separation of the accumulation of capital from the social framework may be justified.[6]

Some of the concepts used in the models under consideration may be of limited use even in underdeveloped countries. Thus the capital/output ratio may

[1] Chapter 29, Section 6; Appendix 2, Section 21.

[2] Prologue, Section 8.

[3] Appendix 2, Section 20.

[4] Appendix 2, Section 20.

[5] Appendix 2, Section 21.

[6] Appendix 2, Section 21.

be technologically relevant to a specific project; benefit/cost ratios may be calculable for particular public works, schools, or hospitals; and some economic models may find a useful application in the management of firms.[1] Generally, however, the application to the underdeveloped countries of South Asia of concepts that may be appropriate to developed countries leads to what philosophers call "category mistakes" — ascribing to one category attributes appropriate to another. "How tall is an hour?" or "Do material objects really exist?" represent category mistakes. A question may be appropriate in some circumstances but not in others. Thus it makes sense to ask, when in Stockholm, "Where is the University of Stockholm?" but it does not to ask in Oxford, "Where is the University of Oxford?" Similarly, to treat an economy in which many sectors must be distinguished as if it contained only one sector is a category mistake. The questions "Has national income per head risen?" or "Has unemployment declined?" can be as meaningless in the South Asian environment as "What sex has your family?"

But it may be asked: "If you want to scrap the only models we have for analyzing the development problems of South Asia, what do you propose to put in their place?" Planners need to know not only what type of analysis is wrong but also what type is correct.[2]

One reply to this question is that a bad guide is not necessarily better than none: bad guides not only mislead but also give false confidence. It may be safer to do without a model than to use a biased and faulty one. Moreover, the criticism of certain models in this appendix and elsewhere in this book is not directed against the use of all models in economic analysis and policy-making. Models are essential aids to clear thinking. Indeed, all thinking in terms of systematic functional relationships between variables is model-building and model-using. Anyone attempting to trace and compare the effects of various policies in underdeveloped countries is using some model, though he may be as unaware of it as Monsieur Jourdain was that for more than forty years he had been speaking prose.

The first virtue of models is that they can make explicit and rigorous what might otherwise remain implicit, vague, and self-contradictory.[3] Even if a model is totally unrealistic, it may have therapeutic value. Since ordinary thinking too often proceeds by fairly simple rules of thumb and uni-causal explanations, and rarely ascends to a complex system of interdependent relationships, model-thinking may serve as a kind of thought-therapy, loosening the cramped intellectual muscles, demonstrating the falsity or doubtfulness of generalizations, and suggesting the possibility of an interdependence previously excluded. The most justifiable claims for the use of economic models are the modest ones that they are cures for excessive rigidity of thought and exercises

[1] ". . . as Professor Dorfman has shown, there are some formal similarities between the management of water storage reservoirs and some chapters in classical capital theory . . . [and] some notions of the wage-fund doctrine [may be] useful in administering foreign aid under P.L. 480." (Eckstein, *American Economic Review, Papers and Proceedings,* Vol. LI, No. 2, May, 1961, p. 101.)

[2] Prologue, Section 8.

[3] The models must, of course, be properly formulated. In Section 2 we noted the common failure to state all premises explicitly and define them clearly.

in searching for interdependent relationships. But one can make more lofty claims for their use. Progress in the study of underdevelopment, development, and planning for development in South Asia will depend on the successful formulation of the relationships between meaningful conditions for development and on quantifiable knowledge about these conditions and the coefficients of interdependence. The whole of Part II of Appendix 2 is an attempt to sketch a model intended to throw light on the problems of underdevelopment, development, and planning for development in the South Asian countries. In surveying their political development in Chapters 7–9 we search for the explanatory mechanisms.[1] Our technical terms "obstacles" and "inhibitions" relate to an abstract but, we believe, relevant distinction between the masses and a ruling group; the ruling group is the subject of policy, the masses are its object.[2] When studying the excessive use of discretionary operational controls in South Asian countries, again we inquire into the underlying mechanisms of the relationship between various controls and collusion of interests.[3]

Models are useful, however, only if they focus analysis on relationships that are important for understanding reality and strategic for purposes of policy. Otherwise, instead of serving as thought-therapy and as guides to the formulation of relevant questions, they themselves cramp the mind; rigor petrifies into rigidity. Broadly speaking, this is our accusation against the model-thinking that has been applied to economic planning in South Asia and is reflected in the structure of the plans.[4]

Models should be judged by their *relevance* to the problems under investigation, their logical *consistency*, their *adequacy* to reality, including their *correspondence* to observable facts. They should not be judged by their comprehensiveness, their faithful reflection of numerous features of reality, their inclusion of all concrete details. To formulate a truly comprehensive model, including all relationships, would be neither possible nor useful. It would be like attempting to map a landscape in full scale and detail. Modern techniques of electronic computing permit the inclusion of an increasing number of variables and relationships, but compared with the richness and variety of "reality" these variables and relationships must inevitably be highly abstract and selective. These will be virtues rather than faults, however, if the abstraction and selection are made according to the criteria we have set forth.

What is or is not adequate to reality depends on the purpose and indicated coverage of the model. Indeed, to the student the only meaning of "reality" is that of a testing ground where observations, organized by theory, can be

---

[1] Chapter 7, Section 5.

[2] Chapter 3, Section 1.

[3] Chapter 19, Sections 6 and 7; and Appendix 8.

[4] It is true that if one traces model-thinking through the three Indian plans, the development is from a crude capital/output model to a multi-sector model and, indeed, toward a flexible treatment almost liberated from a single, simple economic model. But this is not the effect of the model initially used, but rather of the pressure of experience in observation and action. More important, the capital/output model represents an *approach* that has determined the structure of the plans, including India's most recent plan, with results damaging to planning; see Appendix 4.

seen to fit or not fit the theory. For what constitutes reality is determined by how we arrange experience,[1] and models are ways of arranging selected features of experience. A full explanation would require enumeration of all the necessary and sufficient conditions of development. In view of the paucity of data and the complexity of the situation, this is rarely possible. Models may therefore be confined to the formulation of sufficient conditions until new evidence proves the provisional explanation incorrect. This implies that for any given situation a large number of models is initially possible. The number can be reduced with the accumulation of evidence inconsistent with some of the models. The models using capital/output ratios, employment, savings, aggregate output, educational expenditure, and so on, could therefore have helped to isolate *sufficient* conditions of development, had it not been for their logical defects. It is improbable that we shall have in the near future a theory stating as fully as we want the necessary and sufficient conditions of development. Meanwhile, we should welcome testable hypotheses.

In what sense, then, should a model be "realistic"? In the first place, the categories must relate to observable facts; the questions asked must have discoverable empirical answers; the filing system must contain headings with empirical counterparts.[2] Secondly, a model must be realistic in the sense that its "territorial" claims, that is, the coverage indicated, must be warranted. There has been some discussion as to whether the "assumptions" must be tested for realism or only the "indirect implications" and predictions. One difficulty of this dichotomy, postulated by Milton Friedman, is that it is not exhaustive.[3] Models may serve humbler purposes than to yield correct predictions. They may take the form of prognoses or of qualified or hypothetical arguments. They

---

[1] Prologue, Section 7.

[2] Milton Friedman requires of the "language" of theories that it should "serve as a filing system for organizing empirical material and facilitating our understanding of it; and the criteria by which it is to be judged are those appropriate to a filing system. Are the categories clearly and precisely defined? Are they exhaustive? Do we know where to file each individual item, or is there considerable ambiguity? Is the system of headings and subheadings so designed that we can quickly find an item we want, or must we hunt from place to place? Are the items we shall want to consider jointly filed together? Does the filing system avoid elaborate cross-references?" (*Essays in Positive Economics*, p. 7.) It can be seen that many concepts used in the models criticized do not meet these criteria.

[3] See his *Essays in Positive Economics*, Part I. Although models need not and cannot be entirely "realistic," we do not accept Friedman's general analysis of this question. In order to draw clearly the distinction between (1) comprehensiveness, concreteness, and enumeration of conditions that are *both* necessary *and* sufficient and (2) correspondence to observable facts, we term the latter "adequacy to reality." A model must be selective and abstract and may be confined to formulating sufficient conditions, but its assumptions must not contradict relevant observations. The distinction drawn by Friedman between direct implications, which need not (should not?) be realistic, and indirect implications or predictions, which must be refutable, is arbitrary and therefore untenable. To speak of the "realism" of assumptions in contrast to that of predictions is to commit a category mistake. "Reality" is the testing ground of the theories taken as a whole. Moreover, "predictions" is too narrow an interpretation of the implications of a theory.

may be "ideal types" not intended to apply to any actual situation. Yet models that Friedman would discard, since there is nothing to test them against, may be useful. Their value is in their formulation of "iffy" and "as iffy" statements; and it would be a mistake to replace them by categorical assumptions from which implications are derived and tested by actual events.

When observations relevant to the questions raised by the model do not agree with its assumptions, relationships, prognoses, or predictions, the model has to be discarded and replaced by a better fitting one, or its claims as to coverage have to be reduced. But perfectly useful models may never be testable by their predictions, simply because they do not predict. The progress of knowledge is the interaction between observations relating to any part of the model and adjustment of the model.[1]

If models are to be usable, then, their minimum requirements are:
(1) The concepts used must be (a) clear and meaningful and (b) must have a meaningful empirical counterpart.
(2) All necessary assumptions must be stated explicitly and
(3) must be logically consistent with each other, so that valid conclusions will follow from them.
(4) The assumptions must be "adequate to reality," in the sense that they should not be contradicted by observations, and dependent variables must not be assumed to be independent and vice versa. But the models should be abstract and selective in order to highlight the relevant features. Whether or not a model is "realistic" is determined not by "gazing at reality" but by assessing its relevance to the questions asked and the purpose for which it is to be used. What is "adequate to reality" for one purpose may not be for another.
(5) The model as a whole must be refutable by empirical evidence.
(6) The model may be confined, at least initially, to the formulation of sufficient conditions (rather than the more ambitious necessary and sufficient conditions) until new evidence proves them to be incorrect.
(7) A model is a systematically related set of questions addressed to the observable data. In that sense it thus becomes a "theory" in our terminology.[2] It is an invitation to classify the data in a certain way. The categories "true-false" are therefore too restrictive. Such categories as "useful-useless," "complete-incomplete," "valid-invalid" are more applicable. The empirical link is provided by testing the "assumptions," which for that purpose must be made explicit, and specifying the model's scope and limitations. Its abstract and partial character delimits (deliberately) the area of applicability. Unlike the rigorous and ab-

[1] Prologue, Section 7.
The corresponding process in the sphere of valuations is moral criticism and self-criticism in the light of discovered inconsistencies and lack of correspondence of beliefs (upon which valuations are based) to facts. The two spheres overlap because the search for knowledge itself has positive value in our society. See Gunnar Myrdal, *An American Dilemma*, Harper and Bros., New York, 1944, Appendix 1, "Note on Valuations and Beliefs," pp. 1027 ff.

[2] Preface; Prologue, Section 7.

stract character of the model itself, these "territorial claims" will inevitably be concrete, imprecise, and vague. Thus analysis in terms of a capital/output ratio may be appropriate for advanced economies, or for some of them, or for particular sectors, or for particular engineering processes even in underdeveloped countries.

(8) If the model is applied to areas outside the "territory claimed," estimates of the excluded relationships must be added. In particular, estimates of the "non-economic" conditions in the social system and of their *modus operandi* must be made before policy conclusions can be drawn. In this way, the model becomes a broader *theory*.

Conditions (1) to (5) apply to all models, but (6), (7), and (8) apply with special force to models designed for use in underdeveloped countries for the reasons already mentioned — condition (6) because of the complexity of the material and the paucity of the evidence in those countries, and conditions (7) and (8) because attitudes in underdeveloped countries are less rational and institutions less subservient to economic activity. Thus our objection to the use of certain economic models is not that they abstract — all thought is abstraction — but that they abstract illegitimately; not that they separate, but that they separate inseparables; not that they aggregate, but that their aggregation destroys crucial divisions. The objection is that they assume as independent what is dependent and as given what has to be created; and that they are applied directly to country-wide planning in the underdeveloped countries of Asia without proper allowance for the forces excluded from the model — that is, their territorial claims are excessive.

Whether a model is worth constructing and elaborating will depend on whether the parameters and variables can be defined with sufficient precision and whether there is any hope of estimating the numerical relationships among them. Since our findings tend to be negative on this score, we have stopped short of intensive model-building. We know, however, what sort of models would be useful in analyzing the development problems of South Asia. A multi-sector model would be preferable to a one-sector model, but the number of sectors would depend on the information available. Given adequate information, an input-output model of the Leontief type would be preferable to a Keynesian model. A model incorporating inter-regional flows would be preferable to a one-region model. A model envisaging both cumulative movements and stable equilibria would be more helpful than one assuming stable equilibria only; one that successfully quantified relevant variations in behavior, institutions, and attitudes would be better than one that assumed them to be constant and adapted or automatically adjusted; one that allowed for the passage of time and that differentiated between a sum of independent decisions and a joint collective decision would be better than a timeless, atomistic one.

The main aggregate concepts used in models of the type we criticize in this appendix are largely inapplicable in an analysis of South Asian conditions. The regional setting is such that national output, or income, and savings lose much of their meaning;[1] levels of living cannot be usefully represented by aggregate consumption defined as the income that is not saved, but have to be

[1] Chapter 11, Section 1; Chapter 12, Section 1.

specified by reference to physical items.[1] The lack or gross imperfection of markets makes it impossible to analyze "inflation" in terms of a general rise in prices and a "ceiling."[2] Even if the economy is broken down into a traditional and a modernized sector, there remain very large diversities[3] that frustrate any attempt to work out a neat sector model that is in any degree useful for the analysis of reality; the same holds true if the economy is simply split into an agricultural and a manufacturing sector. In the process of criticizing the aggregate Western concepts of employment, unemployment, and underemployment we are led to rely on the simple, behavioristic concepts: participation in the active labor force, duration of work, and efficiency of work.[4] Education and health in South Asia become under our scrutiny very complex phenomena[5] that cannot be comprehended if the discussion is in terms of levels;[6] still less can their "improvement" be analyzed in terms of inputs of financial resources.

These are the directions of analysis to which we have been driven in our search for knowledge. When we have discarded the generalizations contained in the prevalent model-thinking and in the financial core of the plans, this is not because we are opposed to generalizations. While, from the point of view of prevalent models, our approach may seem to imply mainly disaggregation and subdivision, it is not our intention to restrict analysis to more limited concepts, though we do want to replace ragbag terms that do not correspond to anything in reality. As theoretical analysis focussed on the facts and empirical observation guided by this analysis advance, we may come to construct new theoretical "boxes" that are so fashioned that they can be filled by observable data. We may, indeed, look forward to the reformulation of broader aggregates, to new boxes that will differ from the old. Some of the new categories will cut across the old ones. Thus when we examine the forces determining labor utilization (instead of "employment"), we will discover that certain forms of education improve the quality of work and its efficiency, and also the duration of work through improved hygiene and sanitation and attitudes toward work. Capital equipment may improve the duration of work and its efficiency (the machines enforcing discipline). Instead of separating equipment from labor and aggregating each, we may arrive at a new abstraction in which skill and knowledge are infused through the introduction of equipment.[7] We may

---

[1] Chapter 12, Section 3.

[2] Appendix 2, Section 23.

[3] Chapters 22 and 23.

[4] Chapter 21, Part III.

[5] Chapters 30–33.

[6] Chapter 29, Section 1.

[7] An interesting attempt to construct a model in which changes in productivity are embodied in new investment was made by Robert M. Solow in "Technical Progress, Capital Formation and Economic Growth," *American Economic Review, Papers and Proceedings*, Vol. LII, No. 2, May, 1962, pp. 76–86. N. Kaldor has also proposed a model of this type in *Review of Economic Studies*, June, 1962. In the same issue Kenneth Arrow has elaborated a model in which people "learn by doing."

These models are the exact opposite of the models discussed in Section 7. In those, advances in knowledge occur independently of capital accumulation; in these, capital

dissolve the long-standing consumption-investment dichotomy by finding that consumption affects labor participation, duration, and efficiency. In particular, we shall want to introduce time as a significant variable, for much of orthodox economics is timeless.[1] However, as far as the conceptual structure is concerned, in many areas we have not yet moved beyond disaggregation, an exercise performed to clear the stage for new and more adequate formulations of theory.

II

An Immanent Critique of the "Capital/Output Ratio" and Its Application to Development Planning[2]

9 *Introduction*

As we have seen, the capital/output ratio plays a crucial role in the development plans of underdeveloped countries and, explicitly and implicitly, in thinking about planning.[3] A critical analysis of this concept would examine:

(a) its meaning and measurement;

(b) its use in planning or in providing explanations, prognoses, or predictions of development;

(c) the meaning and validity of its use as a criterion for the allocation of capital, as exemplified by the phrases: "minimize the capital/output ratio," "maximize the reciprocal of the *social* marginal capital/output ratio," or "allow for the fact that the capital/output and the savings ratios are interdependent."

The discussion in Part II of this appendix is concerned with (a) and (b), but has implications for (c). It should be read in conjunction with Part I, particularly Section 6 on "Illegitimate Isolation," which is a *transcendental* criticism of the basic assumptions of the capital/output ratio. Part II is largely an *immanent* criticism; here we accept the framework of the concept and its use in planning models and consider particular ambiguities, inconsistencies, and diffi-

---

accumulation is a vehicle carrying improvements into the economy. In those models, most things can be done without capital; in these, everything is either infused through capital or depends on the provision of equipment.

[1] For examples of how "static comparisons" distort the analysis, see Appendix 6, Section 8, and Appendix 7, Section 1.

[2] O. Braun, W. Eltis, K. Griffin, G. Mathur, S. R. Merrett, J. M. Montias, G. Ohlin, L. Pasinetti and A. K. Sen contributed very helpful comments to earlier drafts of this part.

[3] See Sections 2 and 6 above and Appendix 4.

culties within this framework.[1] Section 23 of this appendix compares briefly the different ways in which the concept is used in the plans and its estimated values. The uselessness of this concept is confirmed by the large differences between anticipated and actual coefficients and between the coefficients in different countries and at different times. Because of the widespread use of the capital/output ratio and its strong grip on habits of thinking in the field of development planning, we consider a detailed immanent criticism justified, in spite of the transcendental criticisms advanced earlier. Experience shows that exposure of the inadequacy of the assumptions on which a model is based is rarely convincing. Facts rarely refute theories. The transcendental criticism therefore has to be complemented by criticism that accepts the assumptions and exposes logical difficulties and weaknesses within the model.[2]

In Part I we criticized (a) the selection of one type of expenditure — expenditure on physical capital — while ignoring other types of expenditure and policy (not necessarily involving expenditure) and (b) the lumping together of two aggregates, "capital" and "output." The fallacies of this approach are that it assigns the role of sufficient condition to what may or may not be a necessary condition (illegitimate isolation) and that it aggregates where separation is required (misplaced aggregation).

Despite the ambiguities and confusions to which the use of these procedures has given rise, let us now assume, for the sake of the argument in this part, that they are legitimate. We therefore assume that attitudes, institutions, and policies are constant, that changes in levels of living have no effect on output, and that secondary *dynamic* effects on other investments can be ignored. Aside from these assumptions, both the theoretical master model and the assumption of a constant ratio have certain faults that make them particularly misleading when applied to the problems of development in underdeveloped countries.

10   *The Master Model*[3]

> Let Y   be income (or output),
>   S   savings and
>   I   investment.

---

[1] To illustrate the distinction: Hirschman-type "linkages" — that is, the effects of one type of investment on investment at earlier and later stages of production — are excluded from the analysis in this section, because it is normally (though wrongly) assumed that investment incentives do not have to be specially created. (See Section 3 above.) Investment policy aimed at changing attitudes falls outside the scope of capital/output models. On the other hand, the effects on output of changes in the utilization of existing capacity fall under what are considered to be "economic" considerations and are therefore within the scope of this part.

[2] The same argument defends our detailed discussion of the concept and theory of "underemployment" in Appendix 6.

[3] A clear statement of the assumption of a constant capital/output ratio can be found in Gustav Cassel's *Theoretische Sozialökonomie*, published in 1922. The quotation following is from the English translation by Joseph McCabe:

"The meaning of the continuous formation of capital is seen most clearly in the evenly progressive economy. This may now be defined in more general terms than in

Economic Models and Their Usefulness for Planning   1970

Define

$$s = \frac{S}{Y} \quad \text{(the savings ratio)}$$

$$k = \frac{I}{\Delta Y} \quad \text{(the } ceteris\ paribus \text{ investment/incremental output or the incremental capital/output ratio)}$$

$$g = \frac{\Delta Y}{Y} \quad \text{(the rate of growth of income or output)}$$

Then, if the incremental capital/output ratio, k, is assumed to be constant[1] and if

---

the preceding chapter. In the monetary economy economic progress, assuming unaltered prices, can be measured by the increase of the abstract total capital, and may be regarded as uniform when this capital increases annually by a definite and invariable percentage. Let us call this capital C, and suppose that C increases annually by p percent, p being constant. This increase of capital is, as we have seen, only possible on condition that there is a certain amount of saving. Let us call the annual income I, and suppose that annually the proportion $1/s$ — in absolute amount I/s — is saved. We will call this quotient which arithmetically expresses the community's thrift, the 'degree of saving.' Clearly $\dfrac{I}{s} = \dfrac{p}{100}$ C, and consequently $I = \dfrac{sp}{100}$ C. If we further suppose that the degree of saving $1/s$, or the relative saving of the community, is constant, which clearly harmonises best with our assumption of an even development, we find that the total income is in an invariable ratio to the total capital. From this we get the important principle that in the evenly progressive economy *the income increases in the same percentage as the capital.* This principle is approximately correct for every economy if we take long periods into consideration. It is only during periods of transition that there will be any material difference in the rate of increase of capital and income. This result is important because it affords us standing ground for a critical examination of statistical data as to the increase of income and capital. We find also that it is possible to estimate the income of an evenly progressive exchange economy by multiplying the capital by the product of the percentage of increase and the reciprocal value of the degree of saving. This should be borne in mind in statistical calculations and estimates.

"If we assume, for instance, that the percentage of progress is equal to 3, and that, therefore, the Capital (C) increases annually by 0·03 C, and further suppose that one-fifth of the annual income is saved, the income is, according to what we have said, equal to 15 percent of the capital. These figures must be about right in the case of Sweden, where the national wealth and national income in 1908 were estimated at about 14,000,000,000 and 2,100,000,000 kronor. An official commission of national defence, in fact, estimated the annual percentage of increase of the national wealth during the period 1885–1908 at 3.18 percent. Such figures can, of course, never be precise, but the figure given must be a fairly correct estimate.

"For the countries of Western Europe we may assume for modern times (before the [First World] War) that the normal advance was about 3 percent. Although the figure is only approximate, it is as well to have some standing ground for comparisons, and to be reminded that on the whole, and for long periods, the increase of both capital and income must be indicated by the same figure." (Gustav Cassel, *The Theory of Social Economy,* translated by Joseph McCabe, Vol. I, T. Fisher Unwin Ltd., London, 1923, pp. 62–63.)

[1] One could, alternatively, assume that the marginal capital/labor ratio $\left(c = \dfrac{I}{\Delta L} \right)$ is fixed and k the dependent variable. If $w = \dfrac{\Delta Y}{\Delta L}$ is defined as the marginal productivity of labor, $\dfrac{I}{\Delta Y} = \dfrac{c}{w}$ and $g = \dfrac{s.w}{c}$.

savings equal investment (either as an *ex post* identity or as an equilibrium condition), it follows that

$$\frac{\Delta Y}{Y} = \frac{\Delta Y}{I} \quad \frac{S}{Y} \tag{1}$$

or

$$g = \frac{s}{k} \tag{2}$$

Alternatively, we may assume that output per worker is growing at an annual percentage rate, p, and that the labor force increases by r percent per annum. Full employment of the labor force will then require that aggregate demand grow at an annual rate of p + r.

If both assumptions are made simultaneously (and if the Δs become infinitesimally small), full employment of both the labor force and the capital stock will require that these growth rates be identical, i.e.,

$$g = \frac{s}{k} = p + r \tag{3}$$

Should this condition not be fulfilled, the full employment of labor or the full utilization of the stock of capital, or both, will be impossible. On certain assumptions about the investment function, such models can illustrate a state in which chronic inflation is accompanied by growing unemployment.

11 *Definitions*

The following definitions will help to clarify the subsequent discussion.

1. *Marginal, incremental, and average capital/output ratio.* The marginal capital/output ratio is the *infinitesimal*, the incremental the *non-infinitesimal*, addition to capital divided by the addition to income over a given period. The average capital/output ratio is the *total* stock of capital divided by *total* income per unit of time.

2. *Ceteris paribus, historical, and projected capital/output ratio.* The *ceteris paribus* ratio is the ratio of capital to output based on the assumption that other productive factors and all other conditions, such as knowledge, tastes, attitudes, and institutions, remain unchanged and that changes in levels of living have no effect on output. Historical ratios are derived from observed past changes in capital and in income. Projected ratios are derived from projected changes in the labor force and in other resources and, possibly, improvements in knowledge.

3. *Net v. gross capital/output ratio.* The net ratio excludes depreciation from output. Depreciation can be calculated either as the loss of *productive capacity* due to the wearing out of existing capital, or as the *cost* incurred in replacing it. With technical progress the two measures will diverge.[1]

4. *Project, sectoral, and global capital/output ratio.* The differences in these ratios depend on the extent to which the project under consideration (i) inflicts

---

[1] With technical progress in the machine-making sector, the same *cost* (however measured) as that incurred for the original machine will provide *capacity* for greater output. Measuring capital in terms of its output capacity would normally give a different result from measuring it in terms of the *inputs* required to reproduce it.

costs on or (ii) yields benefits to other enterprises not included in the project. The ratio for a given type of project is likely to vary from place to place, from time to time, and according to what other projects are executed and what other products are produced.[1]

5. *Short-term v. long-term capital/output ratio.* The distinction here is based on the length of time over which costs and yields are considered, and the weights attached to net output at different times.[2]

6. *Ceteris paribus v. mutatis mutandis capital/output ratio.* The *ceteris paribus* ratio assumes all other plant and equipment, technical knowledge, tastes, attitudes toward savings, work, and venture, and institutions to be constant and adapted to output increases. The *mutatis mutandis* ratio, if it could be calculated, would take into account changes in these conditions induced by the investment.[3]

7. *Current v. technological capital/output ratio.* The technological ratio is dictated by the capacity of completed projects to yield output (assuming a normal degree of utilization). It differs from the ratio of work currently under construction to output when starts differ from completions.

8. *Incremental v. decremental capital/output ratio.* The ratio will normally differ according to whether capital is increased or reduced.

9. *Aggregate (or country-wide) v. sectoral capital/output ratio.* The aggregate ratio is an average of all sectoral capital/output ratios, with sector outputs as weights. It can be an average of the average ratios or of the marginal ratios.

10. *Ex ante v. ex post capital/output ratio.* The former is the planned, intended, or expected ratio, the latter is simply an observed statistical residual.

11. *Investment/marginal output ratio v. investment per time-unit/marginal output ratio.* The former disregards the length of time over which capital is added to the existing stock, the latter takes it into account.

Some relations to familiar concepts are: Keynes's *marginal efficiency of capital,* like Fisher's rate of return over cost, is the reciprocal of the *ex ante ceteris paribus* marginal gross project ratio, if a constant flow of output per unit of time is assumed.[4] The Pigovian *social marginal efficiency of capital* is the reciprocal of the *ceteris paribus* marginal global net ratio, except that some costs and

---

[1] This distinction, if applied to the *ceteris paribus* ratio, would correspond to Pigou's distinction between social and private marginal net product, were it not for the fact that not all costs and benefits can be "brought in relation to the measuring rod of money." It should be noted that the *global* ratio, as here defined, is *not* the country-wide or aggregate ratio, but the ratio relating to the sector or the project, with allowance for external effects.

[2] Since the capital/output ratio is the ratio of a stock to a flow, it has a time dimension. Hence the oddity of calling a "ratio" short- or long-term.

[3] There would exist not one but a very large number of *mutatis mutandis* ratios, depending on the history of the economy, the impact of the investment and its repercussions, and the type of disturbance created. It is not a usable concept, but its function is to point up what we would have to know in order to use it. The ratio that we can know is useless, the one that would be useful we cannot know.

[4] Note also Wicksell's natural rate of interest; see Gunnar Myrdal, *Monetary Equilibrium,* William Hodge & Co., London, 1939, Chapter IV.

benefits may resist being "brought into relation with the measuring rod of money."

12 Problems of Measurement

The question of the measurement of "capital" and "output" raises a large number of very difficult problems, touched on only briefly here, partly because, insofar as they are relevant to the problems of this book, we discuss them in other places and partly because the theoretical aspects of the definition and measurement of "capital" have been widely discussed recently.

The question concerns us at two levels: at the statistical and empirical level and at the level of logic and definition. As for the first problem, we show in Appendix 4 how planned public "development expenditure," not all of it investment in the normal sense, and estimated private investment are lumped together to arrive at capital input. In addition, there is the question of the correct valuation of capital and output in economies where restrictions and direct controls are ubiquitous. Currency and trade restrictions and licensing and allocation prevent prices from equalizing demand and supply. To assert that actual prices are largely arbitrary is not to indicate that "equilibrium" prices, could they be ascertained, would necessarily be adequate measures for evaluating capital and output.[1] In some instances the discrepancy is obvious. With currency and exchange restrictions, the contribution of exports to development may exceed their market prices and the capital/output ratio in export industries is thus smaller than weighting by market prices would indicate. On the other hand, if imported capital equipment is used in the export industries, the higher valuation appropriate for export-output enters into the numerator as well as the denominator of the capital/output ratio and to that extent cancels out. Similar considerations apply to all inputs and outputs whose market prices are kept low by government policies.

As for the second problem — that of logic and definition — we showed in Part I of this appendix that the specificity, heterogeneity, complementarity, and indivisibility of capital in South Asia make aggregation impossible. Here we shall only enumerate some of the general problems that arise in the measurement of capital.

If there are several items on each side of the capital/output ratio, and if these do not change in the same proportion, we are faced not only with the problem of index numbers, including the indeterminacy introduced by price changes in the planning period and by different income distributions, but with all the difficulties peculiar to the measurement of capital that arise from the fact that:

(a) capital lasts, but does not last forever;
(b) it takes time to construct;
(c) its quality changes as improvements are incorporated;
(d) replacement and improvement are not distinct acts;
(e) it is utilized to varying degrees at different times;

[1] For a discussion of accounting prices, see Appendix 5.

(f) anything that changes the relative prices of capital goods and consumer goods, or of different goods generally, whether from the demand side or the supply side, will alter the capital/output ratio, even without any change in physical capital, physical output, or technology. In particular, changes in real wages, in the rate of interest, and in the prices of imports will change the capital/output ratio, even though neither the composition of investment nor techniques have changed.

When the productivity of newly constructed capital goods changes, the question arises whether the capital goods should be measured in terms of output or of input. Measurement in terms of output is useless for our purpose, for it would make the capital/output ratio a tautological constant. The difficulty with the input measure, on the other hand, is that despite the increase in the productivity of these capital goods, the value of the resources used in their production may not have changed.

Furthermore, there is the problem of rents and quasi-rents, which arises in connection with the use of scarce inputs in conjunction with capital. Consider two projects with identical initial capital costs. One uses an input that is scarce (from a planning point of view), such as a scarce foreign exchange component or a scarce type of skill, while the other uses labor and raw materials in more plentiful supply. Should rents and quasi-rents be included in valuing output, a procedure that would give a lower capital/output ratio for the first than for the second project? Or should rents and quasi-rents, and thus the opportunity costs of using complementary factors, be excluded in valuing output? The problem is not only the accurate evaluation of rents and quasi-rents, but whether to include them at all. For many large public sector projects, moreover, opportunity costs will not be reflected in any prices, for there are no other "bidders." Should capital/output ratios reflect not only the opportunities forgone now but also those forgone later?

13   Confusion Between the Average and the Incremental Capital/Output Ratio

Some writers calculate the prevailing average capital/output ratio in advanced countries and extrapolate it to predict the marginal productivity of capital (whatever this may mean) in underdeveloped countries. Quite apart from other problems, the fallacy in this argument is the confusion of the average capital/output ratio OA/AB (=BD/CD) with the incremental ratio BD/ED (Figure 1), assuming with traditional theory that OBE is the function relating capital to total product, all other things remaining equal, and BD the (non-infinitesimal) investment.[1] The marginal ratio BD/FD lies between the other two.

14   Confusion Between Theoretical, Ceteris Paribus, and Historical Statistical Ratios

Here, the average capital/output ratio is calculated for certain years in the past. Since the ratio is found to be fairly constant over long periods, it is con-

[1] See, for example, A. Shonfield, *British Economic Policy since the War*, Penguin Books Ltd., Harmondsworth, 1958, p. 109, and *The Economist*, March 26, 1960,

cluded that the marginal and the incremental ratios, being identical with the average, can be extrapolated for increases in capital.

But this statistical time series can give no clue to the relevant incremental capital/output ratio. First, even assuming that we were concerned with a single functional relationship, as in Figure 3, the fact that a ratio is constant for three observed points does not necessarily mean that it will remain constant for smaller or larger increases in capital. But, more important, both labor and capital have in the past improved and increased, so that the *ceteris paribus* productivity curve has shifted upward (Figure 2). Secondly, the data collected incorporate the effects of economic progress and of improvements in technical knowledge, which are at least partly autonomous and would have occurred even without additional labor and capital.[1] Hence productivity would rise in any case, though at a limited rate, and a large addition to capital cannot be relied on to raise total output proportionately.[2] The slope of a *ceteris paribus* curve might decline steeply. Yet it is the avowed purpose of the plans to raise the savings and investment ratios.

The difficulty with historical observations is that they cannot tell us whether the situation we are facing is like the one in Figure 2 or 3 or 4.[3] The absurdity of the procedure is brought out clearly if we assume observations as in Figure 5. Technical progress, combined with a substitution of other factors of production for capital, has led to changes from position 1 to position 2 to position 3. A

---

quoted in Colin Clark, *Growthmanship*, Institute of Economic Affairs, London, 1961, p. 18.

[1] If the curves in Figure 2 represent upward shifts resulting from improved equipment, they assume perfect adaptation of the whole stock of capital to the new knowledge. In fact, there will always be "old" pieces coexisting with improved ones and the productivity of capital will thus depend on its age composition. The curve relating output to an increase in investment will therefore be steeper than the total adaptation curve for the old equipment, but less steep than the straight line. If the marginal productivity of the new equipment is the same as it would be if the whole stock consisted of new equipment, it will have the same slope as the curve showing full adaptation to the new equipment, which lies vertically above it. Thus, starting at the point of intersection of curve 2 with the straight line, it would show the same slope as curve 3 vertically above it and would lie between the line going through 2 and the straight line.

[2] Several studies have attempted to show that "technical progress" has been responsible for 80 to 90 percent of the growth of output per unit of labor, and capital for only 10 to 20 percent. But since "technical progress" is a catchall for economies of scale, external economies, improved health, education and skill of the labor force, better management, changes in the composition of output, and other improvements, as well as for technical progress in the strict sense, Moses Abramovitz's term "measure of our ignorance" or Evsey Domar's "residual" would be more appropriate. Cf. E. Domar, "On the Measurement of Technological Change," *Economic Journal*, December, 1961. Others, including Kaldor and Solow, have abandoned the notion of a "real" stock of capital, measured in physical terms, and have combined technical progress and changes in the "stock" of capital, thus abandoning the distinction between movements along, and shifts of, the production function. Marvin Franklin has shown how a microeconomic Cobb-Douglas type of production function can be combined with a macroeconomic Harrod-Domar model, so that, in our Figure 2, each firm believes it is moving along a curve of diminishing returns, whereas all are moving together up the straight line. See footnote 2, p. 1945, in Part I of this appendix.

[3] Cf. T. Balogh and P. P. Streeten, "Domestic versus Foreign Investment," *Bulletin of the Oxford University Institute of Statistics*, Vol. 22, No. 3, August, 1960.

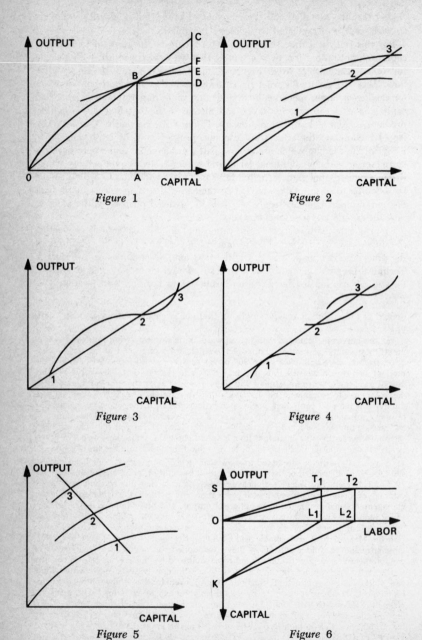

Figure 1

Figure 2

Figure 3

Figure 4

Figure 5

Figure 6

capital/output ratio deduced from a line drawn between them appears to be negative, suggesting that by reducing the stock of capital, output can be increased!

The capital/output ratios used in development planning do, however, assume a certain rate of increase in the labor force and are therefore not to be interpreted as *ceteris paribus* ratios. If there are no obstacles and inhibitions to the employment of extra labor other than the absence of capital, if both the ratio of men to machines in the production of all products *and* the product mix are rigidly fixed, and if all other factors of production are in abundant supply, then the extra capital needed to equip a given percentage increase in workers employed can be calculated. But no conclusion can be drawn from this ratio as to the additional capital that would be required to equip each worker so as to raise output and income per head. Yet these two distinct notions are not ordinarily separated.[1]

15 *The Pattern of Investment and Different Techniques*

The aggregate (or country-wide) incremental capital/output ratio is the average of the sectoral ratios, weighted by the output increases, assuming techniques in each sector to be rigidly fixed. If an investment of £100 is divided equally between two sectors, one of which has a capital/output ratio of 5 and the other of 2, total extra output will be $10 + 25$, and the total ratio will be $100/35 = 5$ times $10/35 + 2$ times $25/35 = 2.8$. In general, if there are several sectors with capital/output ratios of k_1, k_2, k_3, etc., respectively, and if the share of each sector in total output is λ_1, λ_2, λ_3, etc., then the average aggregate ratio will be $\lambda_1 k_1 + \lambda_2 k_2 + \lambda_3 k_3 + \ldots = k$.

A constant aggregate ratio therefore presupposes that, for given sectoral ks, the distribution of investment between sectors will remain the same. Such an assumption is quite unwarranted, as changes in the pattern of investment are bound to occur, whether because of changes in income elasticities of demand or in tastes or because of general policy decisions. If the constancy of the aggregate ratio is the result of offsetting trends in the sectoral ratios, its significance is greatly reduced. On the other hand, since the weights are the shares

---

[1] "More generally, to raise income per head by 3 percent a year requires an investment program of at least 2 and perhaps 4 times $(x+3)$ percent of national income, where x is the rate of increase in population." (Tinbergen, *The Design of Development*, p. 14.) This is based on the view that "It would seem often safe to assume that for development programs a capital coefficient of 4 is needed, but we will also consider the consequences of lower values, even down to 2" (p. 13). And: "Any reduction in percentage population increase means a two- to four-fold reduction in the rate of savings needed to achieve a given rise in the standard of living" (p. 15). "Suppose that the expected population increase is 1.5 percent a year, the saving ratio 6 percent, and the capital-output ratio 4. This will leave the standard of living unchanged, and represents the minimum rate of investment . . . If the *per capita* national income must increase by, say, 2 percent a year, the national income must increase by $1.5 + 2.0 = 3.5$ percent every year. This means that, with the same capital-output ratio, the savings ratio must be increased from 0.06 to 0.14, requiring a considerable adjustment in policy measures." (U. N., *Programming Techniques for Economic Development: With special reference to Asia and the Far East*, p. 12.) Cf. Appendix 7, Section 2.

Economic Models and Their Usefulness for Planning 1978

in *output increases* and not the shares in *investment,* exceptionally high capital/ output ratios in certain sectors do not affect the total ratio very much, if these sectors account for only small increases in output.[1] Assume, for example, that an economy with a capital/output ratio of 2 decides to allocate half its total investment to a project with a capital/output ratio of 50. Its country-wide ratio will not rise to 26 but only to 3.8.

Attempts have been made to formulate multi-sector models with different capital/output ratios in each sector. Perhaps the most influential of these are Mahalanobis's two-sector and four-sector models.[2] These models have been criticized both on empirical grounds — that the sectors do not correspond to "fillable boxes" — and on logical grounds. Mahalanobis assumes that investment is distributed between two sectors, consumer goods (e.g., looms) and capital goods (e.g., machine tools). We thus have two capital/output ratios: the investment/extra consumer goods ratio and the investment/extra capital goods ratio. The former is assumed to be lower than the latter, but the *rate of growth* of investment depends now on the rate of growth of output in the "capital goods" sector and thus on the allocation of investment between the two sectors. There is an implicit assumption that foreign exchange resources for importing capital goods are strictly limited, so that "foreign trade productivity" is zero. Thus *the proportion of total investment allocated to the capital goods* sector (together with its capital/output ratio) becomes the crucial variable determining the long-term rate of growth of consumption goods.

This model has been criticized from various points of view.[3] It has been argued that no empirical meaning can be given to the distribution of investments between the two sectors, since most industries supply products to both. The model has also been criticized for implicit and unwarranted assumptions about exports; for neglecting supply limitations other than capital goods; for ignoring depreciation, raw materials, and all intermediate goods; for confusing a tech-

---

[1] Cf. W. B. Reddaway, "Some Observations on the Capital-Output Ratio," Reddaway, ed., *The Development of the Indian Economy,* Allen & Unwin Ltd., London, 1962, p. 209. The appropriate average is the harmonic mean, defined as the reciprocal of the arithmetic mean of the reciprocals of the capital/output ratios. Thus in the above example k $= \dfrac{1}{1/2.1/2 + 1/5.1/2} = \dfrac{1}{14/40} = 2.8$. The arithmetic mean would be $\dfrac{5+2}{2} = 3.5$. In other words, the correct average is the reciprocal of the average output/capital ratio, namely, $\dfrac{10}{50} \cdot \dfrac{1}{2} + \dfrac{25}{50} \cdot \dfrac{1}{2} = \dfrac{35}{100}$, the reciprocal of which is 2.8.

[2] P. C. Mahalanobis, "Some Observations on the Process of Growth of National Income," *Sankhyā,* Vol. 12, Part 4, September, 1953, and "The Approach of Operational Research to Planning in India," *Sankhyā,* Vol. 16, Parts 1 and 2, December, 1955.

[3] See, for example, Shigeto Tsuru, "The Applicability and Limitations of Economic Development Theory," *The Indian Economic Journal,* April, 1962; K. N. Raj, "Growth Models and Indian Planning, *The Indian Economic Review,* February, 1961; K. N. Raj and A. K. Sen, "Alternative Patterns of Growth under Conditions of Stagnant Export Earnings," *Oxford Economic Papers,* Vol. 13, No. 1, February, 1961; the contributions in *Oxford Economic Papers,* Vol. 14, No. 1, February, 1962, and the reply by Raj and Sen, *ibid.,* June, 1962. See also Evsey D. Domar, "A Soviet Model of Growth," Essay IX in *Essays in the Theory of Economic Growth,* Oxford University Press, New York, 1957, which discusses the very similar model of the Soviet economist Feldman.

Economic Models and Their Usefulness for Planning

nological capital coefficient with an economic choice as to how much of the product of the capital goods sector should be used for investment; for treating the productivity of investment and the capital/labor ratio as independent; for inadequately considering the relation of demand to supply; for assuming labor/capital ratios to be constant; for neglecting the benefits to development that arise from expanding some types of consumption; and for not distinguishing between capital goods in general, machine-making goods and heavy and basic industries. When all criticisms are taken into account, certain valid conclusions remain. In the absence of all other limitations on production, if there is a machine that can either reproduce itself or produce other kinds of products, the production of other kinds of products can be raised at some later date by a greater allocation of capital now to the reproduction of the machine.[1] Alternatively, if other limitations on production are postulated, the tautological prop-

---

[1] K_c The stock of capital that produces consumption goods

K_m The stock of capital that produces machines
A machine can either reproduce itself or produce a machine that makes consumption goods. Machines live forever.

I Investment, i.e., additions to the stock of capital

C Consumption goods

k $= \dfrac{K_c}{C} = \dfrac{K_m}{I}$ The capital/output ratio k is the same in each sector and the average is equal to the marginal.

p The proportion of investment I allocated to K_m

(1) $K_m = I.k$

(2) $K_c = C.k$

(3) $\Delta K_m = \dfrac{p.K_m}{K}$ i.e., the part of investment allocated to making more machines

(4) $\Delta K_c = \dfrac{(1-p)K_m}{K}$ The remainder of investment increases the stock of machines making consumption goods.

(5) $\dfrac{\Delta K_m}{K_m} = \dfrac{p}{k}$ dividing 3 by 1

(6) $\dfrac{\Delta K_c}{K_c} = \dfrac{(1-p)K_m}{k\,K_c}$ dividing 4 by 2

Hence, the smaller p and the larger $\dfrac{K_m}{K_c}$, the greater the rate of increase of machines making consumption goods. But the larger p is *now*, the larger $\dfrac{K_m}{K_c}$ will be *later*. If $p = \dfrac{K_m}{K_m+K_c}$, i.e., if the proportion of machines allocated to making machines is the same as the ratio of the stock of machine-making machines to the machines, $\dfrac{\Delta K_m}{K_m} = \dfrac{\Delta K_c}{K_c}$. If $p > \dfrac{K_m}{K_m+K_c}$ the rate of growth of consumption will be smaller than the rate of growth of investment and vice versa.

If we assume that all machines can produce either consumption goods or more machines, K_m and K_c then stand for the number of machines producing more machines and for those making consumption goods, respectively. And p then reduces to the marginal propensity to save, and the growth rate depends only on the savings ratio and the capital/output ratio.

Oscar Braun of the University of Buenos Aires assisted in formulating this note.

osition is left that if the growth of an economy is limited by a bottleneck in the production of capital goods (however defined), removal of this bottleneck will accelerate growth. In India's First Plan, emphasis was placed on the marginal propensity to save. It has been healthy to distribute the emphasis among other constraints, such as availability of capital goods, and to show that these may prevent the savings potential from materializing. To raise the investment/income ratio is obviously not enough. Decisions will also have to be taken as to how the investment is to be *distributed* among different activities. Not only the aggregate of savings but also its distribution is important. But any bottleneck — skilled labor, administrative ability, foreign exchange — could be selected as a constraint and the proportion of expenditure (or effort) devoted to reducing this constraint could be made the determinant of development.

But Professor Mahalanobis and some of his predecessors and followers have advocated more "roundabout" methods of increasing production, in the sense of increasing the allocation of investment to the capital goods sector. These methods are vulnerable to a criticism that Wicksell advanced against Böhm-Bawerk.[1] The features criticized are not identical, for more "roundaboutness" is not the same as increased allocation to the capital goods sector, and Wicksell's lengthening leads to a once-for-all increase in income later, whereas reallocation leads to a permanently increased flow. But the parallel brings out the assumptions about Pareto optimality.

To translate Wicksell's bewilderment into the language of the Mahalanobis model, one may begin by asking: if it is the distribution of investment between machines and machines making machines that is the key to rapid growth, why not invest in machines making machines making machines and achieve a still higher rate of growth, and so on? It is irrelevant in the present context to reply that time preference is not zero and that there are political difficulties in the way of such postponement. The present question focusses on the technical possibilities, and Wicksell's reply was that

. . . technically advantageous roundabout methods of production are profitable only to a limited extent economically. If by sacrificing 50 crowns or 50 labour units now I can receive in return 100 from a one-year production process, but 150 from a two-year one, then it is obvious that I ought to choose the *one*-year alternative, even if I intend to wait two years for my returns, because by repeating the one-year production process the next year on double the scale (since I then have 100 crowns or labour units at my disposal), I will obtain 200 at the end of the second year instead of 150. In other words, if a successive lengthening of the production process is also to be economically profitable, the product must increase at a more than geometric rate of progression, as time is increasing at an arithmetic rate. In general this can only be so to a limited ex-

---

[1] Wicksell, too, found the problem a tricky one. He writes: "The *technical* superiority of present goods (including present productive forces) over those of the future is probably the part of . . . [Böhm-Bawerk's] reasoning which has set his readers pondering most, at least it has been so for me. I do not know how many times I have returned to this point without being clear *why* it was that Böhm-Bawerk's treatment did not satisfy me, until, particularly by reading Bortkiewicz's criticism ('Der Kardinalfehler Böhm-Bawerks,' *Schmollers Jahrbuch*, Bd XXX), I think I definitely found the solution." (Knut Wicksell, *Selected Papers on Economic Theory*, Allen & Unwin Ltd., London, 1958, p. 182.)

tent through newly occurring changes. (If the sacrifice necessary to obtain the same product had been 75 crowns instead of 50, the two-year production process would have been the more profitable, because it would have led to a doubling of the capital, whereas two successive one-year productions would have given an increase in the ratio $\frac{3}{4} \cdot \frac{3}{4} = 9 : 16$).[1]

In the language of the Indian plan, Wicksell's criticism can be stated thus: plowing back seeds (presumably consumption goods) *may* yield the same future results and leave more to be eaten now than constructing machine tools to make steel mills to make fertilizer plants to make fertilizers to produce more seeds. Methods of production that are "inefficient" in the Pareto sense must be ruled out. That is, if by adopting some other method of production, output at one time could be increased without reducing output at any other time, the present method is unambiguously inefficient. If for an infinite time-horizon we substitute a flow of output to the horizon plus a final capital stock, the criterion for inefficiency is that output could be increased at some time without decreasing it at any other and without decreasing the amount of any item in the final capital stock. It is frequently assumed in the discussion that all methods of production using more and more capital goods are "efficient" in the sense of not being unambiguously inefficient. But only after it has been determined what are "efficient" methods can it be asked which of these efficient methods should be adopted in view of technological limitations, the need to enforce savings, and the political value judgments about time.

The Mahalanobis model also adds a constraint set by savings.[2] If it is assumed that savings can be raised only by introducing capital-intensive methods of production, then emphasis on heavy industry and capital goods becomes a means of enforcing savings. In terms of the Harrod-Domar model, in which the growth rate (g) equals the savings/income ratio (s) divided by the capital/output ratio (k), s becomes a function of k, and k is a function of the distribution of investment: by changing the direction of investment we can increase the average k, thereby raising s more than proportionately and thus raising the growth rate g. But before choosing this method of increasing g we should be certain that there are no ways of reducing k that would reduce s less than proportionately.

So far we have discussed the distribution of investment between sectors, assuming techniques in each sector to be given. But if it is assumed that one sector supplies inputs to another, a change in sector composition of investment is the same as a change in the technique of producing the final output. Within each sector, techniques of production can often be varied, so that more or less capital can be used per unit of output, with less or more of other factors. Since $k = \frac{c}{w}$ (p. 1970, note 1), any non-proportional change in c and w will affect k. All ks can be assumed to be constant only if the neo-classical assumption of substitutability is replaced by the assumption of complete fixity of coefficients,

[1] *Ibid.*, p. 183.
[2] Chapter 24, Section 3.

so that the marginal productivity of labor is zero.[1] Many writers assert that the marginal productivity of labor in many areas in South Asia is in fact zero. If no other inputs were required, we could then postulate constant returns to capital. But the latter assumption is not justified and we criticize the former in detail elsewhere.[2] The allocation between labor and capital will depend, among other things, on time preference, on relative factor prices, and, if there is disequilibrium, on availabilities. Any change in prices and availabilities will therefore tend to affect the capital/output ratio.

We have discussed and criticized a number of different models in this section. First, we criticized models that neglect differences in sectoral coefficients, pointing out that the average capital/output ratio is a weighted average of sectoral ratios. Secondly, we discussed a two-sector model in which one sector produces machines and the other consumption goods. We showed that in this type of model a technological restraint on the growth rate is added to the savings restraint. We also showed that the proportion of income saved is not the only consideration; how these savings are allocated between the two sectors is also important. Thirdly, we mentioned a quasi-political constraint on the savings ratio that makes it dependent on the capital coefficient. The introduction of realistic constraints on the growth rate other than low aggregate savings ratios and high aggregate capital/output ratios is useful — more, however, to show the limitations of accepted models than to illuminate new relationships.[3] Fourthly, we discussed models in which an increasing amount of capital is used in combination with limited supplies of other factors. The two-sector model can be of this type, if it can be assumed that the machine-making sector works with a constant labor force. But the assumption of fixed coefficients is inappropriate if the ratio of capital to other factors can be varied.

We may conclude that, far from being constant, the capital/output ratio will depend on the size of additional output, on income and price elasticities of demand for and supply of products and factors, and on political choices.[4]

[1] This is illustrated in Figure 6. OK is the amount of capital invested. If the capital/labor ratio falls from OK/OL_1 to OK/OL_2, the capital/output ratio OK/L_1T_1 will remain constant only if the curve relating output to labor inputs is horizontal, i.e., if the marginal productivity of labor is zero. Yet this appears to be the assumption of the Mahalanobis model. See Tsuru's article, "The Applicability and Limitations of Economic Development Theory," *The Indian Economic Journal*, April, 1962, p. 375. Mahalanobis is quoted: "Let us suppose that the values of all θ's [the marginal and average productivity of labor] are doubled but β's [the marginal productivity of capital] remain the same, . . ." ("The Approach of Operational Research to Planning in India," *Sankhyā*, Vol. 16, Parts 1 and 2, December, 1955, p. 43.)

[2] Appendix 21, Section 14; Chapter 6, Sections 6 and 7.

[3] As was pointed out in Section 5, the main function of some models is to demonstrate the inadequacy or falsity of another model, for one cannot easily dislodge a theory from the minds of its supporters by facts but only by another theory.

[4] A further difficulty, discussed in Section 6 and Section 18, is that capital/output ratios of particular projects, industries, and even sectors are not independent. Capital requirements for a given output depend partly on what other outputs are produced.

16 *Irreversibility*

Using additional capital always means doing things in a different way, often a new way, and this in turn implies learning, acquiring skills, and, as we saw in Part I, perhaps changing a way of life. The capital/output ratio depends on the direction of the change and on past peak output, so that the ratio would not always be the same for an increase in capital as for a reduction. A reduction in capital would not cause a commensurate reduction in output — a fact of special importance in underdeveloped countries, where the initial level of skills is low. This point is entirely separate from the more familiar one that the lumpiness of capital equipment makes a perfect adaptation of the capital stock to a changing output flow impossible and that the durability of capital equipment introduces asymmetry into the capital/output ratio: because, once full capacity is reached, increases in output require increases in the capital stock, while decreases in output will not be accompanied by a corresponding scrapping of capital equipment. The present criticism concerns the notion of reversibility, even if perfect adaptation of the capital stock were assumed. Movements along the "production function" inevitably, because of the effects of learning, involve shifts of the so-called function. Increases in capital and improvements in knowledge cannot be separated. This is why attempts to separate productivity increases due to capital accumulation from those due to improvements in knowledge are particularly misleading for underdeveloped countries. It also points to one of the dangers of extrapolating the capital/output ratio observed in times of post-war recovery or reconstruction to long-term development. The coefficient may be very low as income rises to the pre-war level, but it will be higher when income rises beyond that level. Similar considerations make it impossible to apply ratios derived from increases in capital to a sectoral decline in capital.

The notion of a stable capital input/output relationship, which is the pillar of thinking about planning, rests on a tacit assumption that such a relationship is independent of time. A hypothetical functional input/output relationship must assume that each point has existed in the past and that all other variables, particularly expectations, have become fully adjusted. It is logically impossible to transfer reasoning applicable to a hypothetical function, all points of which have a full equilibrium history behind them, to an actual movement in the real world. For such a movement is bound to involve a shift of the whole function that destroys its stability.[1]

17 *The Role of Time*

The capital/output ratio is clearly not in the same family as other "great ratios" — the savings/income, the consumption/income, or the investment/income ratios, for example. These are ratios between flows and therefore have no time dimension. The capital/output ratio, as normally defined, on the other hand, is

---

[1] This kind of objection applies, of course, to numerous functional relationships in economic theory in which the roles of time, memory, expectations, and other factors are not specified. But this is not our concern here.

a ratio between a stock and a flow, and therefore has a time dimension. We must specify whether we have in mind one year, or the period of the plan, or some other time span. So much is generally recognized. But it is not equally recognized that the ratio cannot be treated as if it were independent of the period of accumulation of the additional capital stock to which the incremental output flow is related. Time distribution is relevant for several reasons.

(i) Consider a specific project representing a given addition to the capital stock. Much depends on whether the construction period of this project is spread over one year, two years, or five. The shorter the period, the more likely it is that shortages will develop, which will be reflected in rising costs, bottlenecks, hurried improvisations, and substitution of inferior materials or expensive imports. Construction is therefore likely to be less efficient if compressed in time, though the project will, of course, yield output sooner. (The resulting shortages in *other* enterprises are discussed below in Section 18.)

(ii) Differences in construction periods for projects with the same capital input clearly affect the aggregate capital/output ratio when the mixture of projects in the plan changes.

(iii) The fact that construction takes time means that there is a lag between capital expenditure and increases in output.[1] This lag can be assumed to be constant if (1) the construction period for each project, (2) the composition of investment with respect to projects of different construction periods, and (3) the proportionate rate of change of investment per unit of time remain constant.[2]

In a lagged system

$$\frac{I_t}{\Delta Y_t} = \frac{I_t}{B_{(t-1)} \cdot \frac{\Delta Y_t}{B_{(t-1)}}} = \frac{I_t}{B_{(t-1)}} \cdot \frac{B_{(t-1)}}{\Delta Y_t} = \frac{I_t}{B_{(t-1)}} \cdot k = f.k$$

where l is the average construction period and B is projects started, k is the technological incremental capital/output ratio, that is, the ratio between extra *completed* machines and extra output at time t, at a constant degree of capacity utilization. $\frac{I_t}{B_{(t-1)}} = f$ is the coefficient by which k has to be multiplied in order to get the ratio of current total investment to current extra output. From this it can be seen that (1) if investment grows at a constant percentage rate, $B_{(t-1)}$ will grow at the same rate and the lagged coefficient will be constant. The lagged ratio will be greater than the technological ratio, if $I_t > B_{(t-1)}$; (2) if the percentage rate of growth of investment rises, the lagged ratio also rises: if the percentage rate of growth of investment declines, the lagged ratio also declines. This may be illustrated by a simple table. Assume a two-year construction period, a capital/output ratio of 2, and a uniform spread of starts through the year.

[1] There are also lags between the initiation of inquiries or applications and final decisions, and between the latter and the start of expenditure, particularly if waiting for replies to applications for import licences is involved.

[2] Reddaway deals with this problem in "Importance of Time Lags for Economic Planning," *The Development of the Indian Economy*, Appendix A.

Economic Models and Their Usefulness for Planning   1985

Year	Starts (B)	Completions	ΔY_t	Under construction at end of year	I_t§ (approx.)	$\frac{I_t}{\Delta Y_t}$	k	$\frac{I_t}{B_{(t-1)}}=f$
0	1	0	0	1	¼		2	
1	2	0	0	3	1¼		2	
2	4	1	½	6	2½	5	2	2½
3	8	2	1	12	5	5	2	2½
4	16	4	2	24	10	5	2	2½
5	32	8	4	48	20	5	2	2½

§ Investment is equal to ¼ of the starts in the same year plus ¾ of the starts in the previous year. See Reddaway, "Importance of Time Lags for Economic Planning," *The Development of the Indian Economy*, p. 196.

It is difficult to estimate the average lag for a growing economy; the longer the lag, the higher the ratio will tend to be.

(iv) Any given addition to capital equipment can result in a variety of different time distributions of final output; sometimes the pattern of output will show large initial yields followed by small yields, sometimes the reverse. If the stream of returns has an irregular time pattern, the capital/output ratio will not be clearly defined. Either the irregular flow has to be discounted at the "social rate of time discount" and this discounted value compared with the capital cost, or the rate that equates the discounted value to the capital cost has to be determined and compared with the "social rate of time discount." Once the "social rate of time discount" and the composition of final output are determined, it may be argued that it would be wise to minimize the capital/output ratio, when "output" stands for the current discounted value of a given composition of commodities. But it would be foolish to deduce from this that a lower capital/output ratio would be preferable if it could be achieved only through a different time distribution or a different composition of future output. The desirability of low capital/output ratios implies neither that the Indians should not produce capital-intensive producer goods nor that they should go in for mass barbering. A reduction in the ratio bought at the expense either of lower future output or of more useful commodities requiring a higher ratio of capital to output is not necessarily a blessing. India's First Plan has been criticized on these grounds. Indonesia's 1956–60 plan also falls into this trap.

A particular problem of choice arises if two investments that cost the same and yield the same flow of *net* output have different durability and therefore differ in their flow of *gross* output. The investment with a shorter life will yield greater annual depreciation allowances that can be reinvested in better equipment. Because of this advantage it may be that projects with a small *net* output are preferable to those with a large net output, if the larger *gross* output of the former affords sufficient advantages in flexibility of reinvestment. Formally, the same flexibility of reinvestment can be achieved by reducing the larger net output of longer-lived projects by an appropriate addition to depreciation due to obsolescence. But since the size of the additional allowance cannot be known before the event, the point remains valid, and will be applicable particularly to situations in which a country's investment ratio is increased. For then the average age of the capital stock will be reduced and so will the flexibility permitted by replacement. Countries stepping up their investment ratio will have to pay particular attention to this distinction between net and gross ratios.

(v) Indivisibilities and variations in the degree of utilization of existing and completed capacity constitute other reasons why the time distribution of output enters into the calculation of the capital/output ratio. These are discussed in Section 18 below.

In the calculation of the capital/output ratio, as normally defined in the plans, neither the time rate at which capital is accumulated nor the period of time over which the increment in output is spread is considered.[1] Clearly, annual ratios are not very meaningful, for construction periods are often much longer than a year. Even the period of a whole plan is too short for the bulk of the projects. But if one were to consider decades or even longer stretches, the *ceteris paribus* assumption would lose all plausibility, especially since the very aim of the plan is to make "other things" *un*equal.

18   *Capacity Utilization*

Changes in the degree of utilization of existing capital equipment upset the technological capital/output ratio. Output can rise without any investment if capacity is more fully utilized, and capacity can rise without any extra output if investment leads to reduced utilization because it deprives other sectors of either inputs or demand. Special difficulties arise in the application of the "capital/output ratio" to underdeveloped countries. The assumption of perfect divisibility of investment projects is particularly inappropriate in these countries, where projects are often large.[2] Indivisibilities are more prominent than in advanced countries and marginalist reasoning is therefore less applicable for several reasons. First, it is important to build ahead of the expected growth in demand.[3] Secondly, since new plants and equipment in underdeveloped countries are often necessarily large, investment in them is high in relation to both the stock of existing capital and total new investment. Thirdly, economic development is directed at industrialization, a goal that normally results in an increase in the proportion of a nation's capital tied up in indivisible manufacturing units. Fourthly, much of the necessary social overhead capital and the basic structure of industry (power, steel, transport, housing, government buildings) consists of large indivisible units. Fifthly, a given investment is more likely to require complementary and supplementary investments in the meager economies of underdeveloped countries. For example, a new textile mill requires more cotton, fuel, and transport services, and the whole investment

---

[1] As defined in equilibrium theory, including equilibrium growth, this question does not, of course, arise.

[2] Cf. Part I, Section 6; and Appendix 2, Section 23.

[3] See paragraph (i) (a) below.

complex, if it is to be successful, will tend to be a large indivisible lump.[1] Thus the application of constant capital/output ratios may be upset both because of the indivisibility of the investment project under consideration and because of the indivisibilities in the rest of the economy.

(i) *Project Capital/Output Ratio.* If the project itself is lumpy, an incremental capital/output ratio calculated from small additions is clearly irrelevant, and extrapolations from periods or countries characterized by less lumpy projects are misleading. The ratio will depend on (a) the size of the addition to capital and (b) the degree of its utilization. Small additions, taking the form of extensions of existing plant, sometimes yield a large amount of extra output per unit of capital, whereas the extra output per unit of investment of large additions, involving the construction of new plants, may be considerably less.[2] On the other hand, extensions may involve disturbance and interruption of current production (see (a) below), whereas new plants, particularly if fully utilized soon after completion, may yield more extra output.

Furthermore, utilization of capacity often increases only gradually. Surplus capacity may be created deliberately, under certain circumstances:

(a) If long-run costs are declining, even if demand is expected to remain constant and there are no indivisibilities, it pays to build a plant larger than that which is optimally adapted to the desired output, and to underutilize it, for the unit costs of production of the optimum plant would be higher than the unit costs of the same output produced by the larger plant. If demand is expected to increase, initial construction of excess capacity may be desirable, even if it results in greater production costs of current output. The amount of excess capacity will depend on a number of considerations. For ex-

---

[1] We have discussed these points in different contexts in Part I and in Appendix 2, Sections 22–24. They are mentioned here in order to bring out clearly why indivisibilities are much more important in underdeveloped countries than in advanced countries. The importance of indivisibility, in turn, is that for a given amount of investment the amount of extra output can vary over a wide range.

Against the view that the process of development ties up capital in lumpy, indivisible units, it could be argued, transcending the framework of the model, that development aims at increasing transferability of factors and flexibility generally. The education of workers, the provision of transport and housing, the improvement of the means of communication, the increasing share of "basic" industries whose products can be used in many different lines, and increased earnings of foreign exchange, all tend to reduce the proportion of national capital tied up in specific production units. A steel plant is technically large, but since there are numerous demands for steel, it is less likely to suffer from underutilization because demand is deficient than, say, a shoe factory of comparable size.

[2] George Rosen found in all cases that the marginal capital/output ratio for extensions of existing plant was lower than for new plant. Cf. George Rosen, *Industrial Change in India,* Free Press, Glencoe, Ill., 1958, Chapter 5.

There are several reasons why the ratio will be higher for large changes. The ratio will tend to be higher for large increments because increasing amounts of capital will be needed to break bottlenecks. In Section 14 we suggested that small additions can incorporate technical knowledge that has accumulated independently over time. In Section 17 (iii) we showed that the higher the ratio of investment to completions, the higher the capital/output ratio. But this is a problem of increasing the rate of investment, not of maintaining it at a high rate. Finally, large additions may require more complementary changes (e.g., more social overhead investment) than small changes.

ample, planners will have to consider the future costs of expanding and rebuilding equipment and of interrupting production while expansion is under way. Such costs can be avoided if the initial outlay, instead of being adapted to current demand, is geared to future, larger demand. The choice is between three possibilities: (1) optimum plant for the anticipated output and an additional plant when demand increases; (2) excess capacity to accommodate a future rise in demand; (3) a plant that is not perfectly adapted to produce the anticipated output, but that can be expanded without excessive disruption of the production process. A political inter temporal value judgment will be required in weighing the desirability of achieving future cost reductions at the expense of higher current costs.

(b) A temporary labor reserve may be available to build a project before it is needed, as in the Ceylon plan.

(c) Technical indivisibilities may be important. Investments in transport, except in industrially developed, congested areas, are not fully utilized until long after their completion. This is also true of investments in electric power in remote, poor regions and of irrigation schemes in sparsely inhabited districts to which settlers move only reluctantly.

(d) Electric power plants and irrigation and transport projects may provide not only opportunities but also incentives to further development and may therefore contribute to increasing the rate of growth of output.[1] The Tennessee Valley Authority is perhaps the best-known scheme of this kind, though the assumption of its transferability has not been justified.

Excess capacity is, of course, often inadvertently created through miscalculation of demand or supplies, obsolescence, foreign exchange shortages, changes in domestic or foreign policies, or other unforeseen circumstances. The capital/output ratio in the organized industrial and mining sector in India was exceptionally high in the late 1950's and early 1960's, largely as a result of errors and unexpected changes.

(ii) *Ceteris Paribus Global Capital/Output Ratio.* If indivisibilities are characteristic of the economy, the capital/output ratio may differ substantially[2] according to the *direction* of investment, and the *global* capital/output ratio[3] may differ substantially from the capital/output ratio of an individual *project*. The global ratio will be lower than the project ratio if the project breaks a bottleneck, thus enabling other sectors to make fuller use of their existing capacity. The repair of a bridge bringing back into use an important traffic line, for example, will reduce the global capital/output ratio. The global ratio may be higher than the project ratio if the project creates excess capacity in other sectors by depriving them of resources or demand. For example, the replacement of handloom weavers by a modern textile mill deprives other sectors of demand. The erection of the steelworks in India's Second Plan caused a shortage of railway capacity and thus deprived other sectors of transport facilities and supplies.

The interdependence of several projects, some of them indivisible, can per-

---

[1] This point is discussed in Section 6, "Illegitimate Isolation."

[2] For a definition see Section 11, paragraph 4.

[3] For a definition see p. 1971.

haps be seen most clearly when considered in terms of the criteria by which a large firm judges the profitability of its investments.[1] Business firms do not necessarily invest in those projects that promise the highest direct yield, for they realize that some low-yield projects may be necessary prerequisites to subsequent high-yield projects. Long-term expansion of basic capacity or the promotion of improved working conditions and workers' welfare schemes may involve high costs in terms of forgone opportunities for profitable expansion of manufacturing capacity, but in combination with later contingent investment, the high expenditures may prove wise. If these projects were carried out by different firms or by different sectors (for example, public versus private sector) the resulting gains would appear as external economies. Investments with a high project capital/output ratio may pave the way for high-yield projects later.

Thus we have seen that the direction of investment is of crucial importance and that the secondary consequences of the investment may be more important than the primary. There are several more fundamental reasons for this than those discussed here (see Section 6 above). The inability to add to, or subtract from, investment projects in relatively small doses in underdeveloped countries is one of them.

19 Market Imperfections

It is well known that rates of profit vary greatly among firms, industries, and sectors in underdeveloped countries:[2] 100 percent or more can be earned on loans to peasants and 10 percent on investment in mining. Imperfections in the capital market — ignorance, monopoly, deliberate restrictions, weak incentives, and lack of organized trading — are responsible for this. These imperfections are significant in the present context for two reasons:

(i) If there is neither interdependence nor indivisibility and there is a fairly perfect internal capital market, the rate of profit will be roughly the same for projects of similar risk. For a given share of profits in domestic product, this could be accepted as an indication that the marginal productivity of capital, and therefore its reciprocal, the *ceteris paribus* marginal capital/output ratio, is roughly the same for different projects. But the absence of a functioning capital market renders the aggregate marginal capital/output ratio (calculated as a weighted average of projects with widely different ratios) useless, both for evaluating a specific project and for making or criticizing a plan.[3] Once

---

[1] As Göran Ohlin pointed out in commenting on a draft of this section, the problems of planners are often analogous to those of private investors. The principles expounded by Western management and business economists may be better guides than those of the pure economists who might advocate equating marginal returns. To assume independence where interdependence in fact prevails is a professional weakness. But the problems faced by planners are old ones that have been present, though perhaps in different contexts, since economic activity began.

[2] See "Gross Margins in Indian Industry," *Monthly Abstract of Statistics*, New Delhi Vol. 14, No. 1, January, 1961.

[3] The objection to the use of a marginal ratio, which is the average of different project ratios, for accounting purposes is subject to the same criticism that Böhm-Bawerk directed against Marx's use of the notion of an "average" in his formulation of

again it is the *direction* rather than some aggregate *amount* of investment that matters. Redirection of a given amount of resources for investment may have more spectacular results than increasing the resources.

(ii) So far, we have assumed the imperfections to be given. But an important objective of capital expenditure is to *alter* and *reduce* these imperfections. An investment that breaks or weakens a foreign or a domestic monopoly will be much more productive than one that adds to output in an already fiercely competitive industry. Changing the degree of monopoly in an economy changes the degree of utilization of existing equipment and the *rate* and *direction* at which equipment is added in different sectors. But it also changes relative prices and therefore the relative weights of different products and the relative price levels of capital and consumer goods.[1]

20 Investment in Working Capital

Discussion of the capital/output ratio tends to be focussed on investment in fixed capital equipment; little attention is paid to investment in working capital (inventories and work-in-progress). Thus the capital/output ratios for certain projects — railways, canals, telephones, telegraphs, and warehouses, for example — may be exaggerated unless the reduction in inventories and work-in-progress made possible by these projects is taken into account. Amartya Kumar Sen has found that if working capital is included, the capital/output ratios for cotton weaving in India and for the cottage hand-spinning wheel (the *ambar-charkha*) are considerably higher than is commonly supposed.[2] But fixed-capital-intensive projects, such as the construction of a steel plant, also often require large additions to working capital, and confining consideration to fixed capital results in an understatement of the capital/output ratio.

As one would expect, the ratio of working capital to output changes as development proceeds, though it is not clear whether it declines, as is commonly assumed. First there is the change in the composition of output. Because agricultural output is produced at one time of the year and consumed evenly over the whole year, larger inventories of agricultural products than of manufactured products are required (though not necessarily in the agricultural sector). Hence, as the composition of demand changes from the predominantly agricultural to a greater emphasis on manufactured products, even if the propor-

---

the law of value: "We might just as well try in this way to prove the proposition that animals of all kinds, elephants and May-flies included, have the same length of life; for while it is true that elephants live on an average one hundred years and May-flies only a single day, yet between these two quantities we can strike an average of fifty years. By as much time as elephants live longer than the flies, the flies live shorter than the elephants. The deviations from this average 'mutually cancel each other,' and consequently on the whole and on the average the law that all kinds of animals have the same length of life is established!" (Eugen Böhm-Bawerk, *Karl Marx and the Close of His System*, translated by Alice M. Macdonald, T. Fisher Unwin Ltd., London, 1898, p. 79.)

[1] Section 12(f).

[2] Amartya Kumar Sen, *Choice of Techniques*, Basil Blackwell, Oxford, 1960, Appendix C, pp. 110–113, and Appendix D, p. 118, f.n. 7.

tion of each type of product required for inventories is constant, the average proportion of inventories in the economy will decline. On the other hand, requirements for working capital depend not only on technical factors, such as production lags, but also on institutional factors, such as the system of payments.[1] In a peasant society the lag between wage payments to labor and the arrival of the product of labor is absent, and work-in-progress is thus an unimportant factor. Peasants must, of course, eat to survive, but additional effort does not elicit immediate additional remuneration, as it might if wages were paid by an employer. Only when the extra crop is harvested are the extra efforts rewarded. This involves large economies in incremental work-in-progress if the peasant sector is important to the economy. It is often argued that the wage sector in both agriculture and manufacturing industry expands with development. If this argument is accepted, this economy in work-in-progress in the agricultural sector disappears, and additional hours worked call for an immediate increase in the demand for wage goods. For this reason, the shift from household-based production to wage labor in both agriculture and manufacturing will tend to raise the requirements for work-in-progress. Furthermore, if harder work requires more consumption of food, the requirement for an increased stock of food will also raise working capital. It is therefore not clear that the shift from a household-based to a wage-based economy, if it occurs, reduces the need for working capital.

Secondly, the increase in the size of the manufacturing firm will make internal economies in inventory possible. Thirdly, enterprises will enjoy external economies in the form of more efficient and cheaper transport facilities, a higher degree of specialization, fuller utilization of waste products, and greater skill in avoiding waste, all of which will greatly reduce the inventory/output ratio. Possibly the most important effect of the construction of railways and roads is the substantial saving in inventories.

21 Work Shifts

Certain types of reorganization, such as the introduction of additional work shifts, have very low incremental capital/output ratios, which may in extreme cases fall to zero.[2] Assuming that the additional shift requires no additional investment, and that labor and material are abundant, two distinct benefits accrue from it.[3] First, assuming that all depreciation is user cost, so that doubling

---

[1] A. K. Sen, "Working Capital in the Indian Economy: A Conceptual Framework and Some Estimates," Chapter 6, pp. 128–131, in *Pricing and Fiscal Policies, A Study in Method*, P. N. Rosenstein-Rodan, ed., Allen and Unwin Ltd., 1964; *Studies in the Economic Development of India*, No. 3, Center for International Studies, Massachusetts Institute of Technology.

[2] Multiple work shifts are, of course, a particular means of fuller utilization of capacity, discussed in Section 18 above. The subject is treated separately because, unlike a simple increase in the supply of some input or in the demand for the output, multiple work shifts appear to involve more deep-seated changes in organization, attitudes, and policies.

[3] Cf. P. K. Sen, "Use of the Capital-Output Ratio in Economic Planning," *The Indian Economic Review*, Vol. V, No. 1, February, 1960.

the use of machinery leads to twice the depreciation, the capital/output ratio will be halved. If Y_g is income gross of depreciation, and d is depreciation,

for one shift: $\dfrac{I}{\Delta Y_g - d} = k_1$

for two shifts: $\dfrac{I}{2\Delta Y_g - 2d} = k_2$

therefore: $k_2 = \dfrac{k_1}{2}$

If no additional wear and tear is inflicted by the second shift, a further gain accrues:

$$\frac{I}{2\Delta Y_g - d} \text{ which is smaller than } \frac{k}{2}.$$

Normally, however, depreciation will rise but not double. If the non-user cost element in depreciation is n, the ratio for two shifts will be

$$\frac{I}{2\Delta Y_g - (2d - n)} \text{ where } n < d.$$

On the other hand, the widespread resistance to this apparently obvious and simple solution of the problem of capital scarcity suggests that there may be serious obstacles to the introduction of multiple shifts. An interesting paper by David Granick[1] makes the point that, though the Russians had enthusiasm for three-shift, seven-day work weeks in the early 1930's, they had to revert to the single shifts general in Western Europe.[2] His explanation is that multi-shift operations require better work organization than was possible, tighter scheduling, and fewer bottlenecks. Flexibility was enhanced by working general equipment on one shift and only equipment that might cause bottlenecks on more. Flow-production of a limited number of products makes smaller demands on the labor force. Also, working single shifts requires lower skills, because there is more time to repair damaged machinery and less need for careful timing of processes. Single shifts are therefore more effective for training large numbers of "raw farm youths." Although the physical output was less than it would have been from multiple shifts, the principal gain was in training an industrial labor force.[3]

There are means other than multiple work shifts that management and organization can use to reduce the capital/output ratio. Instruction in better care and maintenance of machinery to prolong its life reduces the net capital/output ratio without any investment. The steady introduction of small, often routine,

[1] "On Patterns of Technological Choice in Soviet Industry," *American Economic Review, Papers and Proceedings*, LII, No. 2, May, 1962, pp. 149–157.

[2] "Even today, the United States is most exceptional among capitalist industrialized countries in the extent to which it employs multishift operation in industries other than those where technical requirements force its adoption." (*Ibid.*, p. 152.)

[3] Granick adds that multiple work shifts encourage irresponsibility by individual workers in the care of their equipment since they do not bear sole responsibility for it. This argument is more important for a raw labor force than for one with a tradition of pride. Finally, he stresses that an increase in the number of industrial workers is an ideological aim of Soviet planning, irrespective of economic efficiency.

improvements in machines, and the skills acquired from experience in working them, reduce the capital/output ratio without a spectacular rise in investment and even without marked organizational changes. Some improvements yield very high returns up to a point, but none beyond. Extrapolations from periods in which temporary effects of innovations have been experienced can therefore be misleading. Increased output in agriculture often depends more on improved techniques (fertilizers, seeds, pesticides, rotation) than on substantial investment.

III

Concluding Observations

22 *Summary, Conclusions, and the Impossibility of Salvage*

In Part I of this appendix we criticized the separation of items of capital expenditure from complementary items and from levels of living, attitudes, institutions, and policies that crucially affect output. We also criticized the aggregation of these capital items into a category called "capital." We showed how the model-builders and others either do not attempt to justify separation and aggregation at all, or attempt to justify them by assuming that conditions excluded from the models are adapted or are adaptable to the development process without specific, direct, coordinated action. In Part II we accepted the *ceteris paribus* assumptions of adapted attitudes and institutions and the absence of effects of levels of living, and the abstraction from the coordination of policies attacking conditions on a wide front. We subjected the concept capital/output ratio to a criticism on its own terms.

But the distinction between the two types of criticism is to some extent artificial. A distinction cannot always be clearly drawn between assumptions that are logically valid but unrealistic and assumptions that are logically faulty. If the criticism is made that the introduction of a piece of equipment adds to the skills of the workers as they learn how to use it, thus gradually reducing the capital/output ratio, it can be regarded as pointing up the unrealism in assuming "given skills and responses" or the logical invalidity in ignoring the influence of the passage of time. Changes in work shifts were discussed in our immanent criticism in Part II, but the discussion of these and other changes in organization and management could be regarded as questioning the assumption of "given organization." Similarly, model-builders and model-users might be quite ready to incorporate in their models the effects on the capital/output ratio of changes in expenditure on education, health, nutrition, housing, and other "consumption" items. Indeed, this addition is vaguely accepted by including in the development budget, along with public investment, additions to (but not the total of) certain types of expenditure on these items. As we show elsewhere, however, this procedure is not logically defensible.[1]

[1] Appendix 4, Section 3.

Not only certain forms of public expenditure for what is normally regarded as "consumption," but private consumption expenditure, too, may affect the capital/output ratio, and it may be held that allowance for this could, in principle, be made in the model. First of all, improvements in nutrition increase both the ability to work and, by reducing apathy, the willingness to work. Secondly, certain incentive goods (e.g., bicycles), introduced at strategic points, increase the desire of workers for consumer goods and make them work harder to obtain them. If one is inclined to think in terms of supply curves, these incentive goods can be said to twist the backward-sloping supply curve forward.[1] Resultant increases in output may occur without any investment, but could be attributed to fuller utilization of *human* capital, just as fuller utilization of physical capacity might result in increased output without added investment.

Furthermore, for the calculation of an aggregate capital/output ratio it is important to know not only the effects on output in the organized sector of the economy but also what happens in the traditional sector. Part of the problem is that changes may occur in the traditional sector that raise output but could not be classified as "investment," even if the statistics were available. Also, the effects of investment in the organized sector depend partly on spread effects and backwash effects in the traditional sector — unrecorded direct changes in output and repercussions on levels of living, attitudes, and institutions that only indirectly affect output. The problem is that these effects do not appear in any accounts anywhere. Nevertheless, investment in the organized sector affects directly and indirectly both the demand for the products of, and the supply of raw materials and labor in, the traditional sector.

Finally, government policies affect the capital/output ratio, both by giving rise to problems of correct valuation[2] and by affecting the degree of capacity utilization, investment incentives, and other conditions.

In view of such considerations, it may be asked whether the capital/output ratio could be modified by adding the influences of these various factors and thus making it more adequate to the reality studied. An interesting attempt to refine the capital/output ratio in this way has been made by W. B. Reddaway.[3] In order to illustrate why this kind of attempt must fail, let us follow his refinement with a few small modifications and extensions.

We begin by considering the capital/output ratio at *sector level*. This allows for the fact that there are wide variations in the sectoral capital/output ratios, that the aggregate ratio is affected by the composition of investment and output, and that, unless further refined, the sum of the weighted sectors cannot take into account the interdependence of sectoral ratios. In spite of these limitations, it may be argued, the formula indicates the questions we need to ask and the information we need to collect, and we should therefore attempt to separate various influences affecting investment and changes in output for each separate sector.

[1] Gustav Ranis, "Economic Development: A Suggested Approach," *Kyklos*, Vol. XII, 1959, Fasc. 3, p. 444.

[2] Section 12.

[3] "Some Observations on the Capital-Output Ratio," *The Development of the Indian Economy*, Appendix C.

Investment in a specified period in a particular sector will consist of I, plus any capital expenditure designed to save labor and other scarce resources without increasing output (M for "modernization").

As for the increase of output in a particular sector between two specified dates, we may distinguish between the following influences:

(1) $\frac{I}{fk}$, the increase in output resulting from I, given the technological capital/output ratio k and the coefficient f expressing the lag of completions behind starts. Thus if the technological capital/output ratio $= 2$ and $f = 6$, a current annual investment outlay of 12 will yield extra output in the same year of 1.[1] There are difficulties about f. If growth does not proceed geometrically, f has to be replaced by a term in the numerator that indicates the lag between expenditure on construction and completions.

(2) An increase due to better methods applied to old plant, involving little or no capital expenditure (T for technical progress not embodied in capital).

(3) Increases (or decreases) due to fuller (or lower) utilization of old plant, as a reflection of changes in demand (called U).

(4) Changes due to better management and organization, as, for example, more work shifts (called S).

(5) Changes due to weather (W).

(6) Changes due to improvements in attitudes and responses, better nutrition, education, training, health, etc. (A).

(7) Changes due to improved institutions (N).

(8) Changes due to revisions in domestic and foreign policies, as, for example, changes in the terms of trade (P).

One might then attempt to construct a modified formula for a sectoral capital/output ratio of the kind

$$\lambda_1 \frac{I + M}{\frac{I}{fk} + T + U + S + W + A + N + P}$$

where λ_1 is the sector's share in total extra output. And one could get a coefficient for the whole economy by adding the coefficients of all sectors weighted by their share in extra output.

Those who believe in the usefulness for planning of a technological capital/output ratio implicitly assume that $f = 1$ and that all terms except I are negligible. Once the other influences are recognized, it would be possible to maintain a modified capital/output ratio (no longer equal to the technological ratio k), if the other terms were (a) fairly stable and (b) independent of each other.

There are, however, difficulties in attempting even to attach a meaning to the now emaciated technological capital/output ratio k. It assumes a large number of conditions to be independently determined, including the number of shifts, the degree of capacity utilization, labor supply and other inputs, attitudes, institutions, and policies. If any of these is itself affected by investment, the assumption is unwarranted. In the service sector, increases in output can vary widely for a given investment; it is not possible to speak of a technologi-

[1] See Section 17, iii.

cally "fixed" ratio. Even in the industrial sector there are numerous difficulties — discussed in previous sections — such as differences between increases and decreases, differences according to whether existing facilities are expanded or new ones are built and how big the new or expanded facilities are.

Few other conditions can be assumed to be stable or independent of each other. The purpose of the development effort is precisely to change some of them drastically (for example, to raise f, T, and S). And scarcely any one of them is a wholly independent variable. Many depend on historical factors. All are asymmetrical for upward and downward moves. And the valuation of output and of its flow in time involves political judgments. Labor-saving installations M depend partly on the rate of growth of demand and thus on I; T depends on I + M, for knowledge is acquired in the process of capital accumulation; $\frac{I}{fk}$ depends on the size of I, and so on.

Then there is the problem of combining the sectoral ratios into an aggregate ratio. We can allow for greater or smaller capacity utilization in any one sector as if it were an exogenous influence, but without further complicating the formula we cannot allow for the fact that changes in investment and/or output in one sector affect capacity utilization in another. Similar interdependence applies also to other conditions. Nor would the problem be solved if allowance were made for simple interdependence. The size of aggregate investment and the timing of sectoral investment will make important differences in the degree and form of interdependence.

In the light of these difficulties and ambiguities, it is apparent that the "capital/output ratio" can be of no assistance to the planner in deciding where, when, how, and how much to invest. In particular, the illegitimate isolation of a set of conditions and their misplaced aggregation neglect the importance of complementary policies and of all types of external economies and diseconomies. The concept can be used neither to calculate investment requirements for given output increments nor to estimate additional output from given investment. If sectoral capital/output ratios were meaningful and calculable, aggregate ratios would be unnecessary; if sectoral ratios are not known, aggregate ratios cannot be known. The ratio is thus either unnecessary or impossible to calculate.

When a factor — in our case capital — is singled out as the generator, or as a strategic instrument of growth, it is implicitly assumed that this factor can be used to overcome every other impediment. Thus a shortage of skilled labor, of administrative talent, or of foreign exchange must be capable of yielding to a sufficient application of capital. We showed in our transcendental criticism in Part I that this assumption is not justified. Complementarities between specific pieces of capital, between capital and other factors, and between investment and other policies may be so strong that substitutability is ruled out. The very concept of contrasting "capital" with "labor" on the one hand, and "investment" with "consumption" on the other, abstracts from the relevant relationships and cuts across the relevant dividing lines.

But in Part II we accepted the proposition that more capital per unit of output can surmount the impediments to a higher growth rate that are represented by shortages of natural resources and managerial skills, and pressure of time. Given these impediments, we may ask, what is the minimum amount of capital required to generate a million units of additional output, defined as a combination of outputs at base year prices or some set of shadow prices determined by the planners. We assume a choice of techniques for calculating each of the various outputs, the sum of which constitutes additional output. Granted the assumptions about substitutability and assuming we have all the required knowledge, we can discover the minimum capital requirements. Suppose these are two million units. We then have an incremental capital/output ratio of 2. But what will the capital requirements be if the desired increment in output for the same period is doubled? Clearly, this problem cannot be solved in the same way as the first one. Insofar as capital can be substituted for resources that are becoming increasingly scarce and have to be used less intensively, the use of capital will have to be more intensive, and the new capital requirements will thus be larger than 2.

Even on the assumptions implicit in the model, then, the capital coefficient can have no use. On the other hand, if we possessed all the required microeconomic information, the aggregate ratio would be unnecessary. The capital/output model is thus either useless or unnecessary.

Until more useful concepts are available, it would therefore seem more sensible to specify as best we can the anticipated effects — immediate and long-run, direct and indirect, primary and secondary — of each project than to conceal a host of suppressed valuations, ambiguous observations, and defective analyses under the blanket expression "capital/output ratio."[1] It may be said of the efforts made in this appendix to reach this conclusion: *parturiunt montes, nascetur ridiculus mus.* But a tiny real mouse may be better than a mythological beast, however elegant and splendid.

23   A Note on the Capital/Output Ratios in the Plans

The purpose of this note is to document very briefly what we say in the first two parts of this appendix and in Appendix 4 about the use of the "capital/output ratio" in the plans and to illustrate the arbitrariness of the concept and its uselessness for planning. Use of the "capital/output ratio" in the develop-

[1] W. B. Reddaway states his conclusions admirably:
"For my own part I would hesitate to do more than put tentative questions, which would not necessarily be couched in terms of capital-output ratios. 'Do you really think that better methods in agriculture will produce such rapid results? Will you *both* have so much fertilizer available in the time *and* induce the peasants to use it?' 'Have you allowed enough for the teething troubles of new industrial plants, as well as the period of construction?' 'Is it not likely that *both* investment *and* the increase in output will be lower, through administrative delays, difficulties over sites, etc.?'
"This sort of approach seems to me to get down to examining the real reasons why output will rise, which are not confined to the increase in the capital supply. . . . discussions about the capital-output ratio, and assumptions made about it by model-builders, seem in danger of diverting attention from other factors." ("Some Observations on the Capital-Output Ratio," *The Development of the Indian Economy,* p. 212.)

ment plans takes various forms. It is not always clear in the plans whether planned investment or planned output increases come first. Some plans project a "hoped-for" level of national income at the end of five years, and then decide how much investment is "needed" to obtain it. Others apparently start with how much investment they can undertake and project the income from this.[1] The first two Pakistan plans and the plans for the Philippines and Thailand appear to estimate output increases and probable investment independently, without using the "capital/output ratio" at all.

India's First Plan begins with a discussion of the "needed" rate of net investment. After looking at the situation in developed or rapidly developing economies, such as Hungary, Poland, Norway, Finland, Japan, the U.S.S.R., the United Kingdom, and the United States, the plan concludes that "in underdeveloped countries with low standards of living and rapidly increasing population, a rate of growth commensurate with needs cannot be achieved until the rate of capital formation comes up to around 20 percent of the national income."[2] Thus "the question is in what manner and how quickly the rate of capital formation in India can be stepped up, consistently with other objectives, from about 5 percent of the national income to, say, about 20 percent."[3]

[1] Soviet planning in the past appears to have been based on the implicit assumption that the capital/output ratio must be raised in order to achieve rapid growth. The plans provided for a faster growth of capital goods than of consumption goods. This is, theoretically, compatible with a constant or even a declining capital/output ratio. The share of gross investment in gross national product can rise, while the rate of growth and the capital/output ratio are constant. This is so because a larger share of gross investment may mean a shorter average life of capital. This means that a higher proportion of workers are equipped with new capital, and since output per worker is higher with new than with old capital, average labor productivity will rise. Although in the transition period from the longer to the shorter life the rate of growth of output rises, once the capital stock is fully adjusted to the shorter life the rate of growth (at higher levels of output) will return to its initial level. Thus, after a period of adjustment, the faster growth of capital goods than of consumption goods will be accompanied by a higher proportion of gross investment to gross national product and a constant capital/output ratio.

Moreover, in the Soviet Union, the capital/output ratios could have remained constant in spite of increasing *capital/labor* ratios, if labor productivity had grown at the same rate as the capital/labor ratio. Stakhanovism, incentives to peasants, and massive effort in health and education show that much was done to raise labor productivity. But it seems improbable that the effectiveness of "investment in labor" equalled that of investment in equipment. More recently planning in the U.S.S.R. and in China has placed less stress on raising capital intensity. In the Soviet Union the importance of reducing the capital/output ratio by various methods has been emphasized. In China, labor-intensive techniques and social change have been stressed in contrast to capital intensity and industrialization. Inefficiency in the form of unintended excess capacity and unnecessarily high inventories because of inefficient distribution also make for a high, and if increasing, for a rising capital/output ratio.

N. M. Kaplan and R. H. Moorsteen reach the "highly tentative and provisional" conclusion for the Soviet Union that "The ratio of capital to output has increased . . . monotonically and substantially over the observed years from 1927/28 through 1950, but the change is ambiguous . . . through 1957." ("An Index of Soviet Industrial Output," *American Economic Review*, Vol. L, No. 3, June, 1960, p. 317.)

[2] India, Government of, Planning Commission, *The First Five Year Plan*, New Delhi, 1953, p. 14.

[3] *Ibid.*, p. 17.

The rate at which development can proceed is deemed to depend on (1) the rate of population growth and (2) the increase in national income likely to "follow a given increase in the capital stock."[1] These two factors determine how much of the additions to national income can be added to the stock of capital.

After this emphasis on the aggregate capital/output ratio, it is acknowledged that "There is no unique capital-output ratio applicable to all countries at all times. Much depends not only on the stage of economic development reached but also on the precise forms of further expansion."[2]

On certain key assumptions:

(a) population growth = 1.25 percent per annum

(b) marginal capital/output ratio = 3.1 (with a time lag of 2 years)

(c) average savings/income ratio (1968–69 onwards) = 20 percent (initial, i.e., 1950–51, average ratio = 5 percent); marginal savings ratio from 1956 to 1957 = 50 percent

it is estimated that "*per capita* incomes can be doubled by about 1977, *i.e.*, in about twenty-seven years."[3] It is clear that this estimate is based on the experience of Japan. "In Japan, with the population growing at an average annual rate of about 1¼ percent, *per capita* income is estimated to have been doubled between 1878 and 1912; it was doubled again between 1913 and 1938."[4] Thus Japan achieved a doubling of national income over successive periods of thirty-four and twenty-five years, respectively, with a rate of population growth identical with that assumed in India's First Plan. But the First Plan estimates that Japan's investment rate fluctuated between 12 and 17 percent from 1900 to 1929,[5] and uses a capital/output ratio appropriate to "some of the relatively more developed countries of the world."[6]

Japan's achievement seems to represent the Indian goal, and the First Plan is based on assumptions that generally fit the Japanese experience. The "needed" rate of investment postulated is comparable to that of Japan's second period, while the rate of population growth is taken as equal to Japan's. The capital/output ratio, however, is nearer to the United States and the United Kingdom experience.

In the Second Plan most of the assumptions were revised:[7]

(a) The rate of population growth was kept at 12.75 percent per decade for 1951–60, but raised to 13.3 percent for 1961–70 and 14 percent for 1971–80. (This would have resulted in a population of 408 million in 1960–61; it was in fact 438 million at the beginning of 1961 and is now over 500 million.)

[1] *Ibid.,* p. 18.

[2] *Ibid.*

[3] *Ibid.,* pp. 20–21.

[4] *Ibid.,* p. 14.

[5] *Ibid.,* p. 13. However, the Second Plan states that in Japan the net investment rate averaged 16 to 20 percent between 1913 and 1939. (India, Government of, Planning Commission, *Second Five Year Plan,* New Delhi, 1956, p. 10.)

[6] India, *The First Five Year Plan,* p. 19.

[7] India, *Second Five Year Plan,* pp. 8–10.

(b) The incremental capital/output ratio was revised downward in the light of experience in the first quinquennium but was assumed to be rising. The values established were: 2.3 for the Second Plan, 2.6 for the Third, 3.4 for the Fourth, and 3.7 for the Fifth Plan. Numerous qualifications to a simple use of the capital/output ratio were mentioned, including good monsoons, full utilization of capacity, technical advance, efficiency in handling new investment, quality of managerial and organizational skill, coordination of programs, avoidance of business cycles, composition of investment. It is also pointed out that non-monetized investment had not been included in capital inputs.[1]

(c) The estimated rate at which savings and investment could be increased was lowered. The ratio was now assumed to go up from 7 percent of national income in 1955–56 to about 11 percent in 1960–61, 14 percent in 1965–66, 16 percent by 1970–71, and 17 percent by 1975–76. From this it was concluded that *"per capita* incomes would be doubled by 1973–74."[2]

In the Introduction to the Second Five Year Plan it was stated that Professor Mahalanobis's work determined the basic approach. His model, as we have said, departs from the Harrod-Domar model.[3] There can be no doubt that the Mahalanobis model strongly influenced the Second Five Year Plan. It served a useful purpose in deflecting emphasis from the savings ratio and in stressing other limitations, such as lack of foreign exchange and the inadequate share of a *given* savings ratio being allocated to investment goods, and in suggesting, if only implicitly, a possible interdependence between the savings ratio and the capital/output ratio. Insofar as it loosened the grip of the crude capital/output model it presented a move toward flexibility, though the particular division into sectors was a move away from rather than toward reality and operational meaning.

In the Third Plan the capital/output ratio as an explicitly formulated concept was dropped altogether. But there is still evidence of a prior determination of output growth, implying a certain rate of "needed" investment. The aim, as stated in the Draft Outline, is "to secure during the third plan a rise in national income of over 5 percent per annum."[4] "For achieving a cumulative rate of growth of over 5 percent per annum, it will be necessary to undertake net investment to the extent of more than 14 percent of the national income as compared to the present level of about 11.5 percent."[5] The needed investment is, however, analyzed on a sectoral basis in the Third Plan. Nevertheless, there is a tendency to neglect some of the problems we have discussed in this part, and one gets the impression that the output projection is little more than *past* growth rates slightly raised.

[1] *Ibid.,* pp. 9, 10.

[2] *Ibid.,* pp. 10, 11.

[3] Mahalanobis, "Some Observations on the Process of Growth of National Income," *Sankhyā,* Vol. 12, Part 4, September, 1953, and "The Approach of Operational Research to Planning in India," *Sankhyā,* Vol. 16, Parts 1 and 2, December, 1955. See above, Section 15.

[4] India, Government of, Planning Commission, *Third Five Year Plan, A Draft Outline,* New Delhi, June, 1960, p. 11; cf. India, Government of, Planning Commission, *Third Five Year Plan,* New Delhi, 1961, p. 48.

[5] India, *Third Five Year Plan,* p. 51.

The plans in India and elsewhere do not always show that much detailed analysis goes on behind the scenes. Although attempts have been made — at least in India and Pakistan — to get away from aggregate capital/output ratios and to undertake project planning, some of the objections discussed apply, as we have seen, also to project and sector ratios. And these attempts apply only to the public sector. A common method is to start with an aggregate capital/output ratio, stipulate a certain amount of public investment and a certain rate of income growth, and then derive the required private investment as a residual. However sensible this approach to public investment may be, the plan is vitiated by the lack of control over the private sector. There is a slide from "needed" to "planned" to "projected" investment, creating the illusion that the private and the public sector have been treated symmetrically.[1]

Most of the plans use the country-wide incremental capital/output ratio as a rough guide to the amount of investment required in order to achieve the rise in national income that is planned or expected or hoped for — it is not always clear which of these is being estimated. The importance attached to this ratio justifies the presentation of a table showing the explicitly or implicitly assumed (*ex ante*) and the actual (*ex post*) ratios. According to Table 1, there are wide divergences not only between the countries of the region (ranging from an assumed low of 1.26 for the Philippines to an actual high of nearly 5 for Pakistan) but also between the assumed and the actual ratios where they have been calculated, as for India and Pakistan. Such variations reflect more the weaknesses of the concept as a tool of planning and forecasting than any fundamental differences between the economies or in the degree of success in planning.

It should be noted that even quite small errors in the calculation of the capital/output ratio have large effects. Thus if a coefficient of 3.1 is used when it is in fact 3.2, additional output will have been overestimated by more than 3 percent; and if 3 is used when 4 is correct, the overestimation is one third for the first year and more later.

We present the figures as an illustration of the argument in the preceding parts of this appendix, and not as constituting valuable evidence in their own right. The following points are worth noting:

1. *Climate.* In India the low actual ratio in the First Plan was the result of favorable monsoons in the last two years of the plan period, whereas in Pakistan poor weather was responsible for the high actual ratios at the end of the First Plan.

2. *Gestation Period.* Only India's First Plan makes an explicit assumption about this. The others generally ignore it. Yet many projects will not yield output until some time after the normal planning period. Problems of phasing seem generally to be ignored.

3. *Working Capital.* Its treatment is quite inconsistent and obscure. Some plans do not say whether it is included or not (Burma I, Thailand, South Vietnam, and Indonesia). Some exclude it explicitly (Burma II, p. 36; Philippines, pp. 14–15). India's First Plan is vague and has no provision for working capital.

[1] Appendix 4, Section 1.

Table 1

IMPLIED AND ACTUAL INCREMENTAL CAPITAL/OUTPUT RATIOS

Country	Plan	Plan Period	Output Concept	Investment Concept	Incremental Capital/ Output Ratio (I: Implied; A: Actual)
Pakistan	I	April 1955– March 1960	NNP fc	Gross	(I) 3.51
					(A) 4.42
					(A) 4.90
	II	June 1960– July 1965	GNP fc	Gross	(I) 3.69
India	I	April 1951– March 1956	NNP fc	Net	(I) 3.00
					(A) 1.83
	II	April 1956– March 1961	NNP fc	Net	(I) 2.31
					(A) 3.12
	III	April 1961– March 1966	NNP fc	Net	(I) 2.31
Indonesia		Jan. 1956– Dec. 1960	NNP fc	Net	(I) 2.10
Burma	I	Oct. 1956– Sept. 1960	GDP mp	Gross	(I) 3.69
					(A) 3.26
	II	Oct. 1961– Sept. 1965	GDP mp	Net	(I) 3.10
South Vietnam		Jan. 1957– Jan. 1961	GDP mp	Net	(I) 2.00
Philippines		Jan. 1957– Dec. 1961	GDP mp	Net	(I) 1.26
Thailand		Jan. 1961– Sept. 1966	GDP mp	Gross	(no estimate priv. inv.)
Ceylon		Jan. 1959– Dec. 1968	GDP fc	Gross	(I) 2.85
			NNP fc		(I) 2.30
Malaya	II	Jan. 1961– Dec. 1965	GNP mp	Gross	(I) 3.84

Note: The incremental capital/output ratio is defined as "investment" divided by the increase in national income over the plan period.

GDP = gross domestic product
GNP = gross national product
NNP = net national product
fc = at factor cost   mp = at market prices

(*Notes continued on following page*)

Notes to Table 1 continued

Pakistan: The First Five Year Plan says: "We do not know what the incremental capital-output ratio in Pakistan is, nor is it useful to attempt to apply ratios calculated from the very different experience of other countries." (*The First Five Year Plan 1955–60*, p. 67.) The two estimates of the capital/output ratio in the First Plan reflect the two separate figures given for "total development expenditure." No explanation for the difference is given. (Pakistan, Government of, Planning Commission, *The Second Five Year Plan* (*1960–1965*), Karachi, 1960: at p. 3, Rs. 9,715 million; at p. 28, Rs. 10,780 million.) Since the investment figures are in current prices and GNP figures in constant prices, we deflated the former by national income deflators. (Institute of Development Economics, Monographs in the Economics of Development, No. 4, *A Measure of Inflation in Pakistan 1951–60*, March, 1961, Karachi, p. 21.)

India: In the First Five Year Plan the capital/output ratio was taken as 3, *with a time lag of 2 years between the increase in investment and the increase in output.* (*Second Five Year Plan*, p. 8.) Unadjusted, the capital/output ratio would have been 3.5–3.6. Apparently no such time lag is assumed in the Second Plan, which gives the capital/output ratio as 2.3. (*Ibid.*, p. 9.) The Third Plan provides for a rise in national income of Rs. 4,500 crores and investment of Rs. 10,400 crores in 1960–61 prices, which yields a marginal capital/output ratio of 2.31. (*Third Five Year Plan*, p. 28.)

Indonesia: The Indonesian plan says: "It must be emphasized that the marginal capital-output ratio of approximately 2 applies only to the First-Year [sic] Plan (1956–1960) . . . , after which it will rise to 4." (Indonesia, Government of, State Planning Bureau, *Broad Outlines of the Five-Year Development Plan 1956–60*, Djakarta, 1958, mimeographed, p. 3.)

Burma: Reckoned at the current prices assumed in the First Plan, the anticipated capital/output ratio would be 3.69; reckoned at constant prices (according to another plan assumption), the ratio would be 3.28. The Second Plan says: "Net investment requirements during the Plan period are worked out . . . assuming a gestation period of one year, and marginal capital-output ratios of 3:1 and 2.9:1." (Burma, Government of, Ministry of National Planning, *Second Four Year Plan for the Union of Burma 1961–62 to 1964–65*, A Draft Outline, Rangoon, 1961, p. 26.) Of the two, the Second Plan prefers the latter: "If a marginal capital-output of 2.9:1 is accepted for the Plan period, total net investment in 1959–60 prices required to produce a 5 percent growth in three years within the Plan period (1962–63, 1963–64 and 1964–65) and one year outside (1965–66) would be K 96.0 crores, K 100.8 crores, K 105.9 crores and K 111.3 crores respectively for the four plan years. . . ." (*Ibid.*, p. 27.) The plan does not "include any provision for employment of the presently unemployed . . . [nor does it] contemplate any more modern and therefore more productive methods of production than exist at present." (*Ibid.*, p. 31.)

Ceylon: The Ten Year Plan gives capital/output ratios for different sectors of the economy. These "have been computed by dividing the respective amounts of expansion investment (viz. investment which increases gross domestic product as distinct from replacement investment which is required for maintaining the existing level of gross domestic product) by the corresponding increase in gross domestic product." (*The Ten Year Plan*, pp. 80–81.) For the economy as a whole, the capital/output ratio thus defined – gross investment, including non-monetized investment, minus depreciation divided by increase in gross domestic product – is 2.6. (*Ibid.*, p. 110.) The ratios in the table relate gross investment to GNP and net investment to NNP at factor cost. It seems that the sectoral ratios have not been used for planning purposes. After a discussion of the advantages and disadvantages of investing in industries with high and low capital/output ratios, the plan says that "a compromise has been adopted and provisions have been made for an expansion of sectors with a low as well as high capital output ratio." (*Ibid.*, p. 82.)

Malaya: The Second Plan explicitly assumes "a ratio of investment to output of about 4:1 which is about one-third higher than similar ratios in many other countries." (*Second Five Year Plan 1961–1965*, p. 24.) The length of time required for investments to mature is given as the reason for this difference; otherwise it appears that no use has been made of the concept in the plan.

The Second and Third Plans provide for increases in inventories, but the Second Plan does not say whether public investment includes working capital; it assumes working capital to be 6.5 percent of total net investment. The Third Plan includes an estimate of Rs. 200 crores for investment in inventories in the public sector (total investment 6,300 crores) and Rs. 600 crores for this purpose in the private sector (total investment 4,100 crores).[1] A. K. Sen, however, estimates that the working capital requirements for just the five sectors he considers will be well above Rs. 1,800 crores — considerably more than twice the amount actually provided for. The requirements of manufacturing alone will be considerably greater than the total provided for in the Third Plan.[2]

4. *Municipal Overhead Capital.* This is an important component of capital expenditure, particularly when development is attempted. Although sewage, water, gas, and municipal housing absorb scarce resources, the plans do not always clearly account for them.

5. *Private Investment.* Since only public investment is under the direct control of the governments, it is not always clear how the aggregate ratio, which includes private investment, is calculated. One method, as we have seen, is to start with an aggregate ratio, stipulate public investment and a certain rate of income growth, and then derive the required private investment as a residual. The distinction between "required," "hoped-for," and "planned" investment is not clear. Alternatively, one starts with public investment, adds to this guesses about private investment and output growth, and then derives the capital/output ratio as a residual.[3]

6. *Non-monetized Investment.* This is particularly difficult to estimate. Pakistan's First Plan says it "may be of the order of 1,500 to 2,000 million . . . rupees during the Plan period,"[4] but no estimate is given in the plan and no indication of what significance such an estimate can have. Pakistan's Second Plan does not even mention it. The Ceylon plan, however, includes it as a big item (Rs. 855 million out of total gross investment of Rs. 13,600 million).[5]

[1] India, *Third Five Year Plan*, p. 59.

[2] A. K. Sen, "Working Capital in the Indian Economy: A Conceptual Framework and Some Estimates," Chapter 6, p. 146 in Rosenstein-Rodan, ed., *Pricing and Fiscal Policies, A Study in Method.*

[3] For example, this appears to be the procedure employed in the Second Plan of Malaya. (Malaya, Government of the Federation of, *Second Five Year Plan 1961–1965*, Kuala Lumpur, 1961, pp. 22–25.)

[4] Pakistan, Government of, National Planning Board, *The First Five Year Plan 1955–60*, Karachi, 1957, p. 16.

[5] Ceylon, Government of, National Planning Council, *The Ten Year Plan*, Colombo, 1959, p. 78.

THE STRUCTURE OF THE PLANS

---

1   *The Fiscal Budget as Development Plan*

In all the South Asian countries the plans for development are prescribed in *financial* terms. Development is understood to mean a rise in *aggregate output or income* (and, more pertinently, in income per head of the population), as defined in terms of national accounting, and *investment* is granted the strategic role in engendering development. Implicitly or explicitly, the relationship between total investment and aggregate output is determined by an incremental *aggregate capital/output ratio*. But the core of the plans is regularly that much smaller part of the economy which is accounted for in a *fiscal* budget. With the development process hinging on investment, this fiscal plan becomes essentially a *development budget*, embracing developmental expenditures that can be classified as investments or quasi-investments. We shall try to demonstrate in this appendix why this structure is not the most appropriate one for the development plans of the South Asian countries.

Every government obviously must have a fiscal budget in order to register its plans and decisions about public expenditures and their financing to assist in determining whether or not these plans and decisions are being carried out. A fiscal budget is needed also as an accounting device for the purposes of orderly administration and effective management. And it seems eminently sensible for governments to work out fiscal plans with a longer time perspective than a fiscal year. Even if development planning were carried out and presented in an entirely different framework — say in terms of volume and composition of output and changes in specific outputs (which would most closely correspond to the definition of development in terms of national accounting) or in terms of the utilization of available manpower — a fiscal budget would have to be appended as a safeguard since one of the first conditions for development in the South Asian countries is improvement of government and administration.

Actions and decisions in the public finance field, moreover, will have effects on the economy as a whole. Fiscal budgeting focussed on investment is in line with planning policy in the Soviet Union, its five-year plans having served as models for South Asian plans. It should be noted, however, that in the Soviet

Union the public sector comprises, with only minor exceptions, the entire economy and, in particular, almost all investments and their sources of finance. Even in Western "free enterprise" economies the budget covers a much larger proportion of all economic activities than do the development-oriented budget plans of the underdeveloped countries of South Asia.

As there has always been a fiscal budget of some sort, which it is obviously in the interest of good government to preserve and improve, the wider financial estimates, taking in the large private sector, become viewed as an extension, intended to complete the plan.[1] But in view of the general principles underlying the plans and the definition of development as increases in national output or income, it would seem more rational (subject to the reservations noted in Appendix 2, Section 7) for the planners to come to grips with the national economy as a whole and attempt to analyze the size and composition of aggregate output, the inputs, outputs, and value added in the several sectors, and how these sectoral magnitudes might change in response to future developments and policies. Such an analysis would yield a matrix for that rational coordination of policies which is the essence of planning. It would demand, and indeed largely consist in, planning in physical terms for the economy as a whole. We have seen, in Chapter 11 (Section 1), on how shaky a statistical basis such exercises in national accounting would rest in all of the South Asian countries. Except for small "organized" sectors, calculation of the size and composition of past and present input and, especially, output has to be very largely guesswork, to say nothing of estimates for the future with or without allowance for the effects of development policies.

In this situation the fiscal budget provides a refuge. Meaningful estimates of inputs and outputs, both actual and planned, can be ascertained in the public sector — though they seldom are with any thoroughness. Moreover, the public policies represent the dynamic element in the economy. But it is the potential future behavior of the entire economy, including the much larger private sector, that determines what changes can be planned or accomplished. And so we are brought back to national accounting — which, as we have seen, cannot provide an answer founded on any satisfactory input-output analysis. Aggregate output has then to be "estimated" in some way.

[1] Ceylon's Ten Year Plan, for example, states: "It is important that the Ten Year Plan be of an overall and exhaustive nature. The programmes and plans that have been prepared in the past have been of direct relevance only to the public sector. Such partial programmes serve the purpose of emphasizing specific measures to be taken by Government. They constitute an important initial stage in planning. But partial plans do not provide an adequate picture of the full impact of a development effort. This is particularly true in respect of such factors as national income, investment rates, balance of payments, employment levels, and so on. The Plan presented here is an overall Plan. It has been drawn up in terms of both the public and the private sectors and covers the course of development over the economy as a whole." (Ceylon, Government of, National Planning Council, *The Ten Year Plan*, Colombo, 1959, p. 54.)

And farther on (p. 76): "The programmes for the private sector are of a different nature. They are essentially . . . estimates of the performance which can be expected from this sector given the conditions and opportunities that would prevail over the 10-year period."

It is at this point that the strategic role assigned to investment becomes important: it seems to offer a short-cut from the public policies that make up the plan to their accomplishment in terms of development defined as a rise in aggregate output. The emphasis on investment as the determinant of aggregate output is in accordance with what in this study is called the modern approach. It has its roots in both classical and neo-classical economics but has been given its "purest" formulation in models of the type criticized in Appendix 2 (Sections 14, 19–21) and Appendix 3; as noted there, the strategic role of investment, even when not made explicit, has determined the very structure of the plans. The planned rate of increase in output becomes related to the planned investment by means of an aggregate capital/output ratio.

Although the two terms in this ratio must naturally relate to the economy as a whole, the development plans remain essentially, and sometimes exclusively, fiscal budgets for public investment. Estimates of private investment are then loosely attached and a financial superstructure is erected for the whole economy, based on a capital/output ratio. With loose and circular definitions permitting much sliding from "planned" to "needed" to "projected" and back again, the illusion is fostered that the private and public sectors have been treated symmetrically. One procedure is to postulate a target rise in aggregate output, plan a public investment program, and assume a capital/output ratio; the "needed" private investment — in monetary terms — then appears as a residual. Alternatively, an estimate of a rise in output is derived from an assumed capital/output ratio.[1]

This approach has logical weaknesses that are detrimental to the rationality of planning. There are in South Asia numerous inhibitions and obstacles to development other than inadequate investment, and policies directed at removing them have crucial effects on the growth of different outputs and thus on development.[2] Moreover, neither outputs nor investments in the region can be meaningfully aggregated in monetary terms. For these reasons, any attempt to look at output as a function of investment — or of public investment alone — is invalid. The approach involves both illegitimate isolation and misplaced aggregation;[3] it deflects attention from crucial relationships. Thus the presentation of a plan in financial terms, though it may give the appearance of completeness and internal consistency, invites superficiality through neglect of physical planning. Targets of inputs and outputs are sometimes spelled out concretely, some-

---

[1] Even in India, where planning is more advanced than in other countries, an expected rate of increase in output is presented as a consequence of aggregate investment, without detailed analysis and as a result of the crudest guesswork. It is noteworthy, however, that in tacit recognition of this deficiency the Third Plan makes no explicit reference to a global capital/output ratio. (The ratio quoted in Appendix 3, Table 1 was calculated by us for purposes of comparison.) The Indian Planning Commission itself — though seldom the commentators at home and abroad — has also been rather cautious in evaluating performance in aggregate terms; it has more and more refrained from talking about plan fulfillment in terms of a rise in aggregate output or, even more so, of a realized capital/output ratio.

[2] Appendix 2, Sections 9–11, 19–21.

[3] Appendix 3, Part I.

times not. Aggregate input and output are broken down for some sectors, and estimated targets are in some cases projected for production and employment. Certain main objectives or general goals of development have been laid down, but with no, or very little, relationship to the actual policies contained in the plan. Some of these problems, discussed in the text, will be touched on in this appendix as we examine the general financial and fiscal framework of the plans and the presentation of the plans within this framework.

2   General Biases Fostered by the Structure of the Plans

All national planning tends to lead to "introversion." Without exception the South Asian plans have been nationalistic, particularly in their comparative lack of interest in promotion of exports. "The emphasis of a planned system is inevitably on the home market since only this can be controlled."[1] This nationalistic bias, inherent in all state planning, can operate with less restraint in the absence of intensive analysis of economic development in the matrix of national accounting; it would be more readily exposed by a form of planning that went beyond the fiscal budget. As such planning is not very feasible, it is important to be watchful for the nationalistic bias.

The selection of public investment as the strategic means of promoting development may be expected to lead to the favoring of public over private investment. Obstacles and inhibitions to raising funds for public investment may, however, more than counteract this bias.

We have pointed out that financial planning invites superficiality.[2] An apparently coherent, closed, and complete plan can be presented within this framework without serious consideration of the primary requirements of planning: the introduction of vigorous measures to improve statistics, the scrutiny of the physical realities underlying the financial aggregates, the physical planning based on this analysis, and the rational coordination of all policies essential to the fulfillment of the plan.[3] In short, the financial structure makes it possible to have a plan without planning, to create an appearance without reality.

It is a central theme of this study that the dominant — and in the models and the broad approach to planning, the exclusive — role given to investment as the determinant of development is not a valid assumption, particularly in the underdeveloped South Asian countries. But supposing, for present purposes, that it is possible to think in terms of aggregates such as output or income, savings, investment, and production, and to disregard the absence of a statistical basis for an intensive input-output analysis of these magnitudes, let us consider merely how investment in the private sector is related to the policies implied in the plan. The rise in output sought is dependent on both public and private investment. We assume that the aim of planning must be to control private investment in such a way as to use fully and distribute as desired the

[1] J. B. Condliffe, "Exports in the Third Plan," *A.I.C.C. Economic Review*, August 22, 1960, p. 71.

[2] Appendix 2, Section 22.

[3] Appendix 2, Sections 19, 22.

resources available after the demands raised by public investment have been deducted.[1] It is clear that this control over private investment cannot be exercised merely by public investment. From the point of view of planning, private investment is logically a function of public investment *and of numerous other government policies,* both inducements and restrictions.

In a general way this is recognized in the plans.[2] Yet they remain essentially, and sometimes exclusively, fiscal budgets for public investment. It is this approach that makes it possible to avoid planning of the whole system of operational controls[3] that are needed for plan fulfillment. This is one of the most important biases introduced by planning from the investment angle. Indeed, it is characteristic of all the plans in the countries of South Asia that they are not "operational." They give little or no indication of the controls that the government must apply to internal and external trade, the capital and credit market, foreign exchange, prices, and so on. Because attention is focussed on investment expenditures, even the public budget, which is the hard core of the plans, becomes directed mainly toward accounting for public expenditures; little attention is paid to planning taxes and other policy measures to finance the expenditures. These measures are among the levers of policy we designate as operational controls. As our analysis of the problem of operational controls in Chapter 19 (Section 7) discloses, powerful vested interests are well served by the failure to consider such controls and how they might be coordinated with each other and integrated in the plans.

There are, in addition, permanent alterations in the institutional framework of society that can be brought about by legislation, regulation, and changes in administrative practice. These may be of paramount importance for both the momentum and the direction of development.[4] Like the operational controls,

[1] "Since the performance of the private sector can be closely influenced by governmental policies and measures, it is implicit that government policy would be directed towards bringing forth this performance." (Ceylon, *The Ten Year Plan,* p. 76.)

"The scope of our planning is limited, in the first instance, to the public sector and to such developments in the private sector as follow directly from the investments in the public sector, or, on the whole, are more amenable to planning and control. With the data available, we have tried to view as far as possible the repercussions of the plans for these sectors on other sectors of the economy, and on the development of the system as a whole, but it must be emphasized that the scope for precision in this respect is, at this stage of our work, strictly limited." (India, Government of, Planning Commission, *The First Five Year Plan — A Draft Outline,* New Delhi, July, 1951, p. 3.)

[2] Chapter 19, Section 2.

[3] In this study we use the term "operational controls" to cover both "negative controls" and "positive controls." For definitions of these terms, see Chapter 19, Section 1.

[4] Thus the United Nations in "Findings of the Working Party on Economic Development and Planning (Fifth Session)" reports:

"The Working Party found that certain social measures, not necessarily calling for considerable expenditures, had to be implemented to lay the foundation for both economic and social development in the future. Generally speaking, such measures should seek to create an appropriate social setting designed to foster rapid economic development. Certain types of measures, including regulations for the protection of industrial workers and for proper labour-management relations, because of their low economic cost as compared with their social advantages, could be given high priority in social development programmes. Adjustment in certain elements of the social system could

some of them would perhaps require additional public expenditure on administration; others, on the contrary, might help to simplify administration sufficiently to save public expenditure. Far-reaching institutional reforms, such as land reform and tenancy legislation, normally require many supplementary measures, which might or might not entail large public expenditures. But the plan, presented as a fiscal budget, does not provide a rational basis for coordinating such measures. Their relation to the fiscal budget is incidental; when reforms of this kind are broached in the documents presenting the plans — as they are, for instance, in the Indian and Pakistan plans — they appear in chapters or sections loosely appended, while the center of interest is the fiscal structure, with its discussion of public expenditures of the investment type. Only these appear as commitments and are regularly examined in the evaluation reports. Undoubtedly, this encourages planning that favors groups with an interest in opposing major and effective changes in the institutional *status quo*.

In addition to the operational controls necessary to implement the plan and broader policies aimed at institutional reform, another important problem of planning tends to be obscured by the emphasis on investment expenditures, or what can be called such. The effectiveness of most development policy measures, including investment expenditures, depends on the weakening or removal of other limitations to development, such as shortages of competent administrative personnel, lack of responsiveness of professional groups, and resistance of vested interests to the endeavors of the planners and the government. Expenditure for development cannot rationally be separated from policies for removing these other limitations. To do so implies illegitimate isolation.

The appropriateness of using a fiscal budget as the basis for choosing and coordinating policies is further reduced by the fact that the results of policy measures are not directly related to the cost of carrying them out. When expenditure is not the only, or not the crucial, limitation to development, it does not make sense to optimize benefits by attempting to equate the marginal yield of public expenditures in different directions. If, for example, the efforts to set up family planning clinics in India should have the effect of spreading birth control among the masses, these efforts would, on the margin as well as in the aggregate, have an impact on development quite out of proportion to their cost in public expenditure.[1] Budget considerations could never be a valid reason

---

aid in the gradual modification of traditional patterns of cultural value-systems. Incentives for economic activity could be provided by the elimination of some of the rigidity imposed by the traditional structure of society. Agrarian reforms, transforming tenants into peasant proprietors, or at least regulating rents and fixing contractually the rights of tenants, might reduce apathy, and thus spur agricultural production and raise levels of living in the countryside. The institutional changes called for also included the establishment of a legal framework and especially of efficient state machinery which would enforce law and order, and take a determined lead in the development process. The nature of the state, i.e., the orientation of its leading groups, would definitely influence development patterns. All these transformations might often be the source of many hardships." (United Nations, ECAFE, *Economic Development and Planning in Asia and the Far East, Economic Bulletin for Asia and the Far East,* Vol. X, No. 3, December, 1959, p. 55.)

[1] Chapter 28, Part I.

for limiting these efforts. There are, however, numerous other limiting factors (reviewed in Chapter 28, Part IV, including inhibitions on the part of the government to giving its wholehearted support to the spread of birth control. To varying degrees, the same is true of a wide range of other policies.[1] Public expenditures often yield pecuniary and non-pecuniary benefits (external economies) that greatly exceed the returns directly attributable to the project. This is true even in the narrowly interpreted field of "productive investment."

In short, because the development results of specific policies are so loosely related to the expenditure that shows up in the fiscal budget, and because they depend on the effects of other, complementary policies that may have no, or only incidental, budgetary implications, the budget has little bearing on a properly planned allocation of efforts and resources for development, even of investments. The fact that any planning must include a fiscal budget, if only for orderly government and administration, does not mean that the fiscal plan can represent *the* development plan: it cannot be the framework for a rational consideration and coordination of policies.

In India as well as in Ceylon and the other countries, the unwarranted stress on expenditure has given rise to the curious phenomenon that the public debate about all development policies, even those outside the narrowly economic field, is almost always carried on in terms of how much should be spent to apply the policies. Plan fulfillment is similarly discussed in terms of how far various authorities have succeeded in spending the money allotted to them, not in terms of overcoming the real limiting factors in operation of the policies nor of the real accomplishments. This is not, of course, the fault of fiscal budgeting as such, but of implying that budgeting is planning. Nehru pointed out this fallacy:

We have often talked about how much money has been spent or why it has not been spent. It has always struck me that we are looking at things in a very imperfect way; the question is what has been done, not how much money has been spent. Maybe the quantum of money spent is an indication of what ought to have been done, or might have been done, but the real thing is what actually has been done. This business of appraisal is therefore of the utmost importance.[2]

---

[1] This is occasionally admitted, at least implicitly. Shrinan Narayan, a member of India's Planning Commission, speaking to a meeting of State Agricultural Ministers, stated that if, as the Third Plan proceeded, it was found that additional resources were necessary for achieving the targets of agricultural production set out in it, these funds would be provided through the annual plans. He continued: "If the State Governments can undertake larger programmes for minor irrigation and soil conservation, the corresponding financial resources will be forthcoming." (*The Overseas Hindustan Times*, September 7, 1961.)

[2] The Prime Minister [Nehru], "Strategy of the Third Plan," in India, Government of, Ministry of Information and Broadcasting, *Problems in the Third Plan — A Critical Miscellany*, New Delhi, January, 1961, p. 45.

In a similar vein is the following, from an American publication: "Praise or criticism by upper authority has come to be excessively based on mechanical results. The heights or depths of this phase have been reached by the upside-down fiscal criterion that is now constantly applied. How much money have you spent? Why haven't you spent it

(*Footnote continued on following page*)

The practice of letting the fiscal budget represent the plan and, more particularly, the stress on planned expenditure and the evaluation of plan fulfillment by the amount of money spent have some unfortunate effects even on the use of the budget as a means of realizing effectiveness in administration. As one writer has observed:

A chief evil of the present system is that about the only systematic attention given to expenditures is the negative attention of a review designed to effect economy. Only at year's end is there a hurried calculation of how far short the programs have fallen and a somewhat feverish effort to get expenditures up to target. Far too little is known about expenditures; too little and too imprecise planning is done to make expenditures actually equate with program. To remedy this situation requires close, continuing study of expenditures, careful and frequently modified projection of expenditures, and changes in action indicated by those projections. The Ministry of Finance needs to shift more of its attention to better budgeting and away from detailed expenditures control after budgeting.[1]

To sum up the main points made in this section:

(1) Although the fiscal budget has its place in the efficient auditing of public expenditure, it is largely irrelevant as an indicator of what has been done, is intended to be done, or should be done. It tells nothing about the necessary operational controls (negative and positive) for the private sector or the manner in which institutions impeding development are to be reformed. Yet if these are not part of the plan, the outcome of investments budgeted under various headings may bear no relation to the intended results.

(2) The effectiveness of a given amount of public expenditure will differ according to the purpose for which it is spent and will depend on factors having little or nothing to do with the amount of money spent or the physical resources used up. There are several reasons for this. One is that various types of expenditure result in external economies; that is, a public expenditure may not yield profit to the public authority except indirectly through higher tax receipts from higher incomes, and/or it may render other undertakings profitable though it is not.

(3) Complementarity is another reason for the differing effects of the expenditure of a given amount of public money. Complementary action comprises not merely other economic measures but also the removal of limitations that have only a tenuous relationship to expenditure. Peasants must be persuaded to use irrigation water, women to use birth control clinics. The need to scrutinize expenditure in one direction for the complementary and supplemen-

---

faster? Will you spend it all by such a date? The results of this are a false set of values. The assumption is incorrectly made that money spent is equivalent to good work achieved, when equally often better quantity and quality can be achieved for less money. More money often produces helterskelter attitudes and activities that are the negation of sound planning and development." (Albert Mayer and Associates in collaboration with McKim Marriott and Richard L. Park, *Pilot Project, India, The Story of Rural Development at Etawah, Uttar Pradesh,* University of California Press, Berkeley and Los Angeles, 1958, p. 318.)

[1] Paul H. Appleby, *Re-examination of India's Administrative System,* Government of India Press, New Delhi, 1956, p. 34.

tary policies in other directions remains even if there are no external economies and no inefficiencies.

(4) A given expenditure may also differ in effectiveness because of inefficiency and waste. This point is related to the previous one, for any expenditure that requires other policy measures to support it becomes wasteful if these are not carried out or are carried out badly, but it is really a separate point. An "efficiency audit" can exercise very little control over the efficiency, in the wider sense, of expenditure: in particular, it can censure excessive expenditure, but it does not normally censure omission of expenditure or inadequate expenditure, or omission of actions not involving expenditure. The same sum of money spent on a road that is built of the right materials, properly supervised while being constructed, and maintained afterward will, of course, have other results than if the wrong materials are used, with inadequate supervision during and no maintenance after construction. But the cost of maintaining the road will also depend on what policies are pursued to put rubber tires on ox carts.

(5) The assumptions underlying the identification of the fiscal budget with the plan are:

(a) that the only limitation to the achievement of development objectives is scarcity of physical resources; or if there are other limitations, that a sufficient application of physical resources can always be substituted for other measures (in fact, attitudes, incentives, institutions, and policies themselves constitute limitations and their reform must complement application of physical resources);

(b) that these physical resources can be aggregated and evaluated in terms of money;

(c) that a given sum of money, irrespective of how, where, and in conjunction with what other policies it is spent, represents somehow the same "effort";

(d) that the private sector is subject to the same influences and controls as the public sector.

None of these assumptions is justified.

3 *The Arbitrary Definition of the Development Budget*

Does a fiscal budget, even though it is not a real plan, at least clarify the financial limitations to development? Before taking up this question, we must discuss the definition of the development budget. We aim at an immanent criticism and shall therefore accept the Western framework of concepts, including the aggregates "consumption," "savings," and "investment," but only in order to isolate the problem under consideration.

The dividing line in the total fiscal budget between the current and the development budget is drawn on the basis of a mixture of several logically unrelated considerations, some of which are: whether a particular expenditure is to be recurrent or one-time; whether it is new or customary, and if the latter, whether it involves a large increase; whether it raises the level of a particular public activity; whether or not the results will be incorporated in some type of physical installation; whether it will yield a monetary return to the exchequer, and if so, whether this return will be sufficiently large to make the undertaking self-liquidating, or whether it will instead, or simultaneously, result in external economies or provide free public services; whether its intended effects will be spread over a long or a short period. Underlying all these considerations and to some extent motivating them is the vague idea that the current budget should reflect "consumption," enjoyed collectively by the citizens and provided collectively for them, while the development budget should reflect "capital formation." The development budget of the South Asian countries thus has its ideological origin in the capital budget, discussed in the literature on public finance since the Cameralists and used in some Western countries in modern times, particularly where the state built railways. It seemed natural to finance such large-scale investments by issues in the capital market, as private corporations do, rather than by taxation. The absence of the concept or the practice of a capital budget in Britain and the United States is partly due to the fact that in these countries railways and other public utilities were largely left to private enterprise.

The capital budget when narrowly conceived was restricted to investments that yielded to the exchequer sufficient returns to cover interest charges, amortization of the capital invested, and running costs. Public expenditures that met these conditions could, according to fiscal convention, be financed by loans. Where this budget structure was most rigorously thought through — as, for instance, in Sweden and Denmark — that portion of an investment which was not expected to be covered by receipts was financed by taxes in the current budget. Thus if the receipts of new railways constructed in order to promote development in an underdeveloped section of the country or for strategic reasons were not expected to cover fully capital charges in addition to running costs, they were, to the extent they were expected to fall short, treated as current expenditures. The *raison d'être* of the separate capital budget was thus to provide a category of public expenditures that, without violating the traditional canons of "sound finance," would not have to be met out of taxation because it was self-liquidating. These canons were drawn up in analogy to the prudent management of an individual or a firm. The analogy was more justified when the public household comprised only a small part of the national economy, so that the effects of the former on the latter could be disregarded, both in theory and in practice.[1]

The concept of the development budget in the South Asian countries can be regarded as the result of a gradual widening of the scope of this type of capital budget, defined by the prudent conventions of "sound finance." The first and most natural step was to include expenditures embodied in physical installations as a whole in public investment, even if their returns were not expected to meet capital charges fully and they would thus be only partially self-liquidating, as is the case with many ports, power stations, and irrigation works. The next step was to include with public investments in the development budget all expenditures for durable physical installations, even those not ex-

[1] Gunnar Myrdal, *Beyond the Welfare State,* Yale University Press, New Haven, 1960, pp. 69–72.

pected to yield any return but intended solely to provide external economies and free public services, such as non-toll roads. Most governments, however, have hesitated to include expenditures on public buildings or defense. There is no logical explanation for this hesitation, but we should remember that the whole problem is one of fiscal conventions, not of logic or economics.

Once expenditures for projects yielding no direct return to the exchequer were accepted as part of the development budget, it was a natural next step to drop altogether the requirement that expenditures included should be embodied in physical installations. Thus expenditures on improved education and health, on agricultural extension schemes to raise technological performance in agriculture, and on teaching, training, demonstration, and subsidies to stimulate advances in industry, especially small-scale and cottage industry, can all be included in the development budget. And once this step is taken, why should not all expenditure for community development be included? These steps are taken more easily when a new type of expenditure is incurred or when a substantial increase is made in an old type, previously in the current budget. The questions then arise whether, to what extent, and when recurring expenditures for maintaining the new activity or the higher level of activity, once the goal specified in the development budget has been achieved (for example, a program of education or agricultural extension work), should be transferred to the current budget. The plans do not solve these questions uniformly.

The deeper explanation of the arbitrariness of the definition of a development budget is, of course, that few public expenditures can be characterized as pure "consumption" or pure "investment." They are almost all costs incurred jointly for "consumption" *and* "production," that is, "investment." This is particularly true in poor countries, where a rise in living levels can normally be expected to raise labor input and labor efficiency.[1] To raise certain components in the level of living — such as education, health, and, in the poorest countries, food — is particularly effective in this regard.[2] It follows that the definition of the development budget must be more arbitrary in the underdeveloped countries in South Asia than in the developed countries in the West. No clear-cut, logical distinction can be drawn between public consumption and public investment, because, to begin with, consumption is normally much more productive in underdeveloped than in developed countries. If a dividing line is nonetheless drawn, it must be recognized that it is drawn arbitrarily, according to tradition, convenience, and the political interests of the government.

Certain obvious interests of the South Asian governments tend to make them extend the share of the total budget devoted to the development budget. One is the desire to increase public expenditure substantially in various directions in order to encourage development. However, they feel inhibitions and

---

[1] Appendix 2, Section 21.

[2] Certain expenditures, of course, are largely wasted, such as the construction of ostentatious government offices, luxury houses for officials, or extravagance of official representatives at home or abroad. Unfortunately, public expenditures of these types are large in all the South Asian countries. But waste is waste, whether it is reckoned as consumption or productive investment; from the point of view of rational planning, it has no legitimate place in either the current or the development budget.

encounter obstacles to the imposition of higher taxes. In this dilemma, the lingering association with the capital budget of the notion that it is "sound finance" to relieve the taxpayer of the obligation of paying for profitable public investments constitutes an escape, though not a very logical one. Also, the greater the scope given to the development budget, the easier it will be to "balance" what remains in the current budget. It may even be possible to show a "surplus" on current account that can be called "public savings" and carried over to help finance development expenditure. Thus the respectability of "sound finance" is gained for the development budget at higher levels of public expenditure while the levels of taxation are kept low. Furthermore, the more inclusive the development budget, the more the government can impress its own people and other nations with a really big development effort. Appeals for foreign loans and grants will seem reasonable and modest if the foreign contribution sought is a small share of total development outlays.

The distinction between the current and the development budget is thus based on administrative and legal conventions, modified in an opportunistic direction by political interests and pressures, and *is entirely arbitrary;* it is therefore inadequate to the needs of economic analysis and planning. There is no rational basis for regarding this arbitrary distinction as demarcating "public consumption" and "public investment." It is thus also inappropriate to add "public consumption" to "private consumption" and "public investment" to "private investment." By the approach to planning in South Asia commented on in Section 1 — according to which aggregate investment, the capital/output ratio, and aggregate output are interrelated — the latter manipulation, in particular, is necessary to close and complete the plan. But since private investment is normally defined as expenditure for the creation of income-earning assets, usually consisting of physical goods, while a broader definition is used for public investment, this is a clear example of misplaced aggregation. If we were then to enlarge the scope of "private investment" so as to include expenditure on certain items of productive consumption, such as food consumption of the masses of people and education of all, we could perhaps make public and private investment somewhat more comparable. But then, when calculating their returns, we would not be able to account fully for external economies created by all investments, both private and public, and we would have moved farther from the clear-cut distinction between consumption and savings that is characteristic of Western analysis but inapplicable to South Asian countries.

Because the meaning of these concepts must be arbitrary when they are applied to the underdeveloped countries of South Asia, analysis in terms of the rate of total savings and investment, the relationship between the two and the proportions of investment and savings that originate in the public and private sectors, and so on, provides a shaky foundation for development plans and leads to inferences that are invalid or untrue.[1] Not only the analyses in the plans but

---

[1] There is also a good deal of arbitrariness in the treatment by private firms of current and capital accounts, even in the West. They show the same bias in favor of putting physical structures that endure on the capital account while treating as current expenditures outlays on research, advertising, and training — which yield returns just as do plant and machinery even though they do not show up in physical structures.

the entire literature on the plans, whether it originates in South Asia or in the Western countries, is adversely affected by this lack of logic.

4 "Balanced Budget" and "Deficit Financing"

So far we have discussed only the expenditure aspects of the development budgets. According to established conventions of "sound finance" the fiscal budget should be "balanced." This does not mean, tautologically, that all actual expenditures must be paid for somehow, but that they must be financed in a particular way, by specific types of public intakes, deemed appropriate from the point of view of the canons of "sound finance." According to the Anglo-Saxon tradition, which makes no distinction between a current and a capital budget, balancing the budget means that all expenditure should be covered by taxes. But with the introduction of a capital budget it became acceptable to finance capital expenditures by borrowing in the capital market — in competition with private borrowers.[1]

The doctrine of the capital budget has been applied to the development budget in the South Asian countries with certain modifications. The current budget is supposed to be balanced by taxes and receipts from public enterprises, in full accordance with fiscal conventions. Perhaps because the development budget is ordinarily broader than a capital budget proper, since it contains expenditures for "investments" that are not self-liquidating, it is characteristic of planning in the region to attempt to have the current budget contain a surplus, a "government saving" to be transferred to the development budget as a contribution toward financing it. No clear rule is laid down as to the size of this surplus, and the attempt is not always successful, in spite of the enlargement of the development budget commented on in the preceding section. More importantly, however, it is generally assumed that the capital budget need not be fully balanced by that surplus and by government borrowing. This is interpreted as a permission to "underbalance" the development budget, or to "balance" it by "deficit financing."[2] Since it is assumed that the current budget will be balanced by taxes — and perhaps will even render a surplus for the development budget — the "underbalancing" or the "deficit financing" is applicable to the total budget as well. There are other ways of describing the method, but they are differences in terminology only, not in substance.

The introduction of a deficit into the budget represents from this point of view of principles the most conspicuous innovation made in South Asia to the established code of "sound finance" inherited from the doctrine of the capital budget. The reasoning behind this adjustment of the doctrine is that a certain amount of deficit financing will not interfere with — indeed, is necessary to the maintenance of — the "neutrality" of the exchequer in its relationship to the private sector. It is assumed that when the development budget — and

[1] Sales of public assets are financial receipts in the capital budget in the same way as purchases are expenditures.

[2] "The major sources of such financing are government saving, government borrowing from the private sector, external assistance and *deficit finance*." (United Nations, ECAFE, *Economic Bulletin for Asia and the Far East*, Vol. XII, No. 3, December, 1961, p. 13. Italics added.)

thus the total budget — relies for its "balance" not only on the current account surplus, loans in the capital market, and net sales of assets but also on deficit financing, the public expenditure is financed to the extent of the deficit by the banking system, which creates additional means of payment. This is assumed not to infringe on the private sector nor to detract from the budget's "neutrality" if the additional means of payment are matched by increased requirements for means of payment resulting from the growth of the economy and its rising degree of monetization. If, however, deficit financing goes beyond this point, inflationary pressures can be expected. Thus the relationship between a balanced budget and deficit financing becomes the central consideration in estimating the effects of government policies on monetary stability.[1]

This line of reasoning is here presented in a streamlined and simplified form. The method of dividing the total budget into a current and a development budget and the definitions of balanced budget and deficit financing vary from

---

[1] A few quotations, chosen at random, may illustrate the idea of deficit financing.

"As all the above methods of financing government development expenditures have their limitations in practice, it is natural for governments to resort to borrowing from the central bank. This is deficit finance in its true sense. (It should be noted, however, that government borrowing from commercial banks will have the same effect as borrowing from the central bank to the extent that commercial banks sell their holdings of government securities to the central bank.) As far as inflationary impact is concerned, the main difference between taxation and genuine borrowing from the private sector on the one hand, and borrowing from the central bank on the other, is that the former represents transfer of purchasing power, whether active or idle, from the private sector to the government, while the latter involves the creation of new purchasing power, with its possible secondary wave of credit expansion." (Shu Chin Yang, "Deficit Financing for Development and Its Inflationary Impact" — with special reference to Southeast Asian countries, *Ekonomi dan Keuangan Indonesia*, May/June 1959, p. 179.)

"The term is used here to mean any government spending in excess of current revenues that has the effect of increasing total outlay in the community." (Raja J. Chelliah, *Fiscal Policy in Underdeveloped Countries*, Allen & Unwin Ltd., London, 1960, p. 30, f.n. 1.)

". . . in defining what type of financing constitutes deficit financing, the criterion should, by and large, be whether or not the transaction in question tends to increase money supply. . . . The only practical course is to adopt a convenient convention which under prevailing practices gives as near an approximation to the purpose in hand as possible. In India, where the normal practice is not to rely on the central bank for subscription to new issues of long-term securities and where short-term debt of the government is largely held by the central bank, a deficit measured in terms of withdrawals of cash balances and net increases in floating debt gives on the whole, a reasonably reliable indication of the impact of the budget on money supply." (India, Government of, Planning Commission, *Second Five Year Plan*, New Delhi, 1956, pp. 83–84.)

"The method used in the second Five-Year Plan of Pakistan may serve as an example. The plan pointed out that the increase in money supply which is consistent with price stability depends on (i) an increase in national output, (ii) an increase in the monetization of the non-monetized sector, and (iii) an increased demand for cash balance by individuals and firms. The safety limit of the increase in the money supply thus estimated applies to the whole economy; the government's non-inflationary deficit financing has to be arrived at by subtracting from the total the likely monetary expansion in the private sector." (United Nations, *Economic Bulletin for Asia and the Far East*, Vol. XII, No. 3, December, 1961, p. 17.)

country to country and from plan to plan and regularly contain a considerable amount of logical confusion. Similarly, the reasons given for the different practices vary. This is not surprising, because the idea of the capital budget — of which the development budget is a variation — has never been very clear in the Anglo-Saxon tradition, or, for that matter, in the Dutch and French traditions, in which the South Asian countries move. In the following discussion we shall, however, adhere to the main line of the motivation of deficit financing sketched above, without criticizing the conceptual muddle in the plans and in the discussion of the plans and of planning generally. This will suffice because our thesis is the negative one that there is no reason to expect a fiscal budget, however balanced, to be "neutral," and that, therefore, any approach using the concepts "balanced budget" and "deficit financing" is invalid. The financial effects of the public policies set forth in the budget cannot be analyzed in this way. The amount of deficit financing, even when balanced against the expected increase in the needs for means of payment, is not a useful tool for estimating these financial effects. It does not measure even approximately the financial effects of the activities of the public sector.

Although the crude quantity theory of money has been generally discarded, the old idea that a balanced budget is a neutral budget (or that the budget is neutral when a deficit corresponds to an increased need for means of payment) recurs, even in the West. This idea is not confined to popular and political debates. National accounting statistics and budget figures of public receipts and expenditure are often based on this idea and are used to support arguments derived from it. In South Asia the economic analysis and the evaluation of the plans are regularly based on this type of reasoning, since the entire structure of the plans is built on a "balanced" fiscal budget, "balanced" ordinarily including some deficit financing. In particular, the discussions of inflation in South Asian countries, by Western as well as South Asian writers, are almost always conducted in terms of balanced budgets and deficit financing. Were it not for these facts, even a brief critical analysis would seem unnecessary.

The valid part of the doctrine is the tautological truth that in a closed economy public investment must be matched either by public or by voluntary private (individual or company) savings out of income, or, finally, by "forced savings" resulting from inflation. Granted, for the sake of argument, the usefulness of the aggregate notion of savings and investment, these sources exhaust, logically, the sources of financing investment. But the error lies in identifying these sources with particular methods of financing. Thus public savings are identified with surpluses on the "current" budget; private savings drawn on for balancing the budget are identified with taxes and long-term loans in the capital market; and the additional "savings" accruing from greater need of means of payment because of the growth of the economy and of monetization are identified with the non-inflationary part of deficit financing.

These identifications are quite improper, for (a) not all taxes reduce current private expenditure, nor do the same taxes imposed on different people or different companies reduce it equally; (b) not all loans to the government reduce private borrowing and investment; (c) the creation of new means of payment has no connection with savings out of new incomes. Furthermore, (d) not all current government expenditure adds, or adds equally, to current demand, and (e) not all public development expenditure increases net investment. On the one hand, a balanced budget or even a surplus is no guarantee against inflationary financing; on the other hand, even a substantial budget deficit may have no inflationary effects. The former will be the case if, for instance, tax payments and government loans do not restrict private spending sufficiently to match government expenditure. The latter will, for instance, be the case if the public expenditure, financed partly by the creation of new money, is directed into lines where the use of surplus capacity and surplus manpower makes possible a rise in production and incomes and thus, or in other ways, generates voluntary savings. These examples do not exhaust the possibilities of a lack of identification between balance and neutrality of the budget. We shall also have to consider the operational controls other than taxation.

5 The Irrationality of Analysis Based on Budget Balance and Deficit Financing

Accepting for the moment the notion that money creation by the central bank beyond the growth of national product and of increased monetization is inflationary, there are a number of *inconsistencies and difficulties* in the use of "deficit financing." In many cases, the central bank, or the government through the central bank, furnishes various financing agencies with funds, which are put at the disposal of private businesses to finance their investment. If, as often happens, these transactions are not fully accounted for in the budget, the amount of deficit financing is understated. Furthermore, there is always a good deal of fund-utilization or, alternatively, fund-formation. Money previously accumulated but not currently appropriated is used up, and currently appropriated money accumulates unspent. This should be added to, or subtracted from, the amount of deficit financing. It is expenditure flows, and not appropriations, that are relevant. Then, a spending agency may finance its expenditure by unloading government bonds on a government agency. Yet this will not appear as deficit financing. The government or the central bank may indeed purchase bonds or promissory bills anywhere in the open market, not confining itself to the spending agencies, and the receipts of the sellers should be counted as sources of deficit financing, if used to finance additional expenditure. It is not clear, however, from this analysis how any funding or unfunding of the floating debt should be treated. Since such operations do not alter the total amount of money available, they are presumably regarded as "neutral," yet they clearly are not. It makes a substantial difference who takes up or unloads what kinds of securities — whether it is government departments and agencies or private companies. Public investment may be financed by the sale of long-term securities, but if these are taken up by other government departments, whose expenditure is not affected, this would presumably constitute deficit financing, whereas if they are taken up by the public the effect would be "neutral." It is particularly difficult to see how estimates of such open-market operations and their effects over the ensuing four or five years could be calculated. Perhaps there is a tacit assumption that such operations would cancel each other out in the long run, but such an assumption is inappropriate.

In the following analysis we abstract from these and similar ambiguities in accounting; we assume, in other words, that, somehow, the fiscal budget reflects scrupulously the ideas of budget balance and deficit financing. This assumption must be borne in mind as one of the reasons, in addition to those discussed below, why the concept "deficit financing," when used as it is normally used, contains much logical confusion.

We shall first examine the effects of deficit financing in a *closed economy*. The view that too little taxation or inadequate mobilization of net savings in the capital market to cover government expenditure causes domestic inflation or adds to planned inflationary pressures is subject to a basic criticism. The effects of the fiscal budget — particularly a change in its size and composition — on demand and supply will depend on the direction of the various items of expenditure, the incidence of the taxes, and the sources of the loans that together constitute the budget and determine the "deficit financing." It is therefore meaningless to aggregate these effects into a single net difference and attach economic importance to that difference.

Let us first consider the effects on *demand*. Neither all taxes nor all debts incurred by the government reduce demand. When they do, the reduction is related to their incidence. Some taxes are paid out of savings, and some government borrowing does not reduce private expenditure. It follows that a given sum of money raised through taxation or government borrowing may have quite different effects on private expenditure according to where the money originates, how it is raised, and to what expectations these fiscal operations give rise. Similarly, not all public expenditure adds to current demand the full amount of the expenditure. It may replace private expenditure and induce the public to save more. On the other hand, it may stimulate private expenditure with multiplier effects. Again, the effects depend on the type of expenditure, its direction, timing, and distribution.

Moreover, inflation in the South Asian countries cannot be analyzed in terms of aggregate demand, aggregate supply, and a "general" price level.[1] Changes in prices of different products have entirely different effects on both demand and supply. The assumptions of a high degree of substitutability between different products consumed and between products consumed by different groups of consumers, and between consumption and production, which underlie analysis in terms of a "general price level," are not warranted. Index numbers constructed by conventional aggregation and weighting methods can give entirely misleading impressions. Laspeyres and Paasche indexes may give contradictory results. In any case, market prices do not express correctly valuations put on different items by planners, and "accounting prices" do not help.[2] Absence of substitutability makes aggregation illegitimate. Thus taxation and other policies that curtail the demand for food-grains and a few other essentials have an entirely different impact from policies reducing expenditures on other items. And an "inflation" that raises the price of food-grains slightly while keeping other prices stable has a totally different significance from an "inflation" that

[1] Appendix 2, Section 23.
[2] Appendix 5.

raises the prices of other items substantially while keeping the prices of food-grains stable.[1]

Turning now to the effects on *supply*, we must note that a given amount of government expenditure will result in different amounts of additional supplies according to its direction and support by other policies. Insofar as additional supplies materialize, directly or indirectly, the timing will vary from project to project. The concepts of the "balanced budget" and of "deficit financing" are based on an aggregation of expenditures without regard for the character, amount, and timing of the supplies elicited by them. Once again, the assumption of homogeneity is unjustified.[2]

How expenditure on a public project affects the "neutrality" of public policy thus depends on whether the additional incomes generated are matched by additional final goods and services, on what proportion of these incomes are saved and taxed, on what products the remainder of these incomes are spent, and on how responsive the supply of these products is to additional demand. Thus, if the expenditure is matched by final supplies and if the people earn-

[1] Appendix 2, Section 23.

"The best defence against inflation is, in a sense, to keep clear of it, but a policy of 'playing safe' is not always conducive to development. A measure of risk has to be undertaken, and the most effective insurance against this risk is command over reserve stocks of food grains — and a few other essential commodities — which can be used to augment the supplies in the market as and when necessary. Prices of food and cloth occupy a strategic position in the Indian economy, and a sharp rise in these prices has to be prevented by the use of all available devices. So long as these prices can be maintained at reasonable levels, the cost of living of the large bulk of the population can be kept under control. Increases in prices of other commodities would be a matter of comparative unimportance, although any excessive rise in prices anywhere in the system does carry the danger of a drawing away of resources into low-priority uses. Corrective action can, however, take care of such a situation. A further defence against inflation is discriminating but prompt use of the instrument of taxation to prevent excessive increases in consumption in certain lines and to mop up the excess profits or windfall gains that deficit financing tends to generate. Finally, physical controls, including rationing and allocations, can be used to prevent consumption from increasing beyond a particular level and for economising scarce materials or scarce productive resources. But experience of the past suggests that physical controls, especially on essential and staple consumer goods, are not a device that can be relied upon to function effectively or equitably for any great length of time. This makes it all the more necessary to utilise to the full all the other available safeguards and correctives, for a curtailment of the plan itself can, in the nature of things, be thought of only in a situation of extreme difficulty." (India, *Second Five Year Plan*, pp. 86–87.)

"The prices of luxury articles going up does not make very much difference, but price rise in essential goods does. The question of control of prices really applies to the essential commodities." (The Prime Minister [Nehru], India, *Problems in the Third Plan — A Critical Miscellany*, p. 40.)

[2] "Some schemes of investment that seem to be clearly indispensable to improvements in the long run, such as electrical installations, take a long time to yield any fruit and meanwhile the workers engaged on these have to be supplied. The secret of non-inflationary development is to allocate the right amount of quick-yielding, capital-saving investment to the consumption good sector (especially agriculture) to generate a sufficient surplus to support the necessary large schemes. It is in this kind of analysis, rather than in the mystifications of 'deficit finance,' that the clue to inflation is to be found." (Joan Robinson, *Economic Philosophy*, C. A. Watts & Co. Ltd., London, 1962, p. 120.)

ing the extra incomes spend them entirely on the extra supplies, it can be seen immediately that the monetary impact is "neutral"; if, instead, extra supplies exceed extra incomes, but incomes are spent on other goods in inelastic supply, the impact can be inflationary, and so on. Public expenditure on additional railway traffic in an underutilized state-owned railway system, even though deficit-financed, need have no inflationary impact. The same expenditure on extra food will have inflationary effects, even if covered by extra taxation that reduces spending on motor cars.

In addition to internal inflation, the budget deficit, accompanied by too large expenditures, is also thought to affect demand for foreign products in an *open economy*. It is thus assumed that deficit financing increases the excess of foreign expenditure over foreign receipts, causing a drain on — or, if the inflation is planned, adding to the planned reduction of — foreign exchange reserves. There is no justification, however, for lumping together in a single indicator — the deficit — the domestic effects on demand (and supply) and the effects on demand for foreign products and, consequently, on the foreign balance (as is done in a Keynesian model for an open economy in which exports are added to domestic investment and contrasted with imports and domestic savings). In the countries of South Asia the effects on the balance of payments have quite different policy implications from the effects on internal prices, and they should therefore not be lumped into a single indicator, as is done when we reason in terms of deficit financing. The effects on the balance of payments will depend on the extent to which the additional supplies generated by the "inflationary" government expenditure substitute for imports or add to exports, and the extent to which different spenders demand goods and services of varying import content. A reduction in internal demand or an increase in domestic supply would not automatically yield foreign exchange, even if supplemented by other policies. Supplementary policies, such as export drives, may involve costs and absorb domestic resources. A deterioration of the terms of trade, which reduces the foreign exchange gains, may have to be accepted. Resources may become unemployed or employed less efficiently, instead of exported, and internal price rises may wipe out gains from extra exports or import substitution. The presentation of the plan in terms of a development budget in general, and the impact of "deficit financing" on the balance of payments in particular, tend to obscure these manifold possibilities.

There is, finally, the question of *operational controls*.[1] They can be used in various combinations to ensure that a budget consisting of expenditures, taxes, loans, and deficit financing — which without these controls would create excess demand for foreign exchange and internal inflation — is rendered "neutral" in the sense that balance is preserved between demand and supply, both in the aggregate and in particular markets. A system of higher interest rates and credit restrictions or such controls as licensing, rationing, and raw material allocation could, in principle, achieve this. Such balance is consistent with a budget deficit of any size, given sufficiently stringent controls. On the other

[1] Chapter 19 and Appendix 8.

hand, a development budget showing a large surplus can be inflationary if operational controls are lax and inducements are offered to spending. The monetary impact of the budget cannot be isolated from other policy measures. The size of the deficit is not, in itself, an index of the distance of a budget from "neutrality."

It may be objected that the use of operational controls to check domestic inflation and a drain on foreign exchange reserves does not restore "balance" but merely "suppresses inflation." On this line of reasoning, "balance" is endowed with a complex of tacit valuations, in this case the absence of operational controls — all those controls that prevent price increases without adding to government revenue or to the profits of public enterprises and that do not reduce government expenditure, so that the deficit remains unaffected. But a definition of "balance" that includes absence of controls in this sense obscures the rational discussion of policy. Instead of turning our attention to the merits and demerits of particular policies directed at achieving "balance," in the sense of absence of price increases, we are invited to argue whether "balance," in the value-loaded sense, actually exists.[1] This becomes particularly misleading if controls serve purposes other than the control of inflation and the balance of payments, as they almost inevitably must. Thus controls of luxury building may be intended to bring about a more equitable income distribution and also to control inflation. Similarly, control of luxury imports is intended to promote equality and help stabilize the balance of payments. Is their presence then compatible with "neutrality" and "balance"? This type of metaphysical question is inevitable unless one eliminates all spurious valuations derived from the definition of "balance" and discusses, on the basis of explicit value premises, the merits and defects of particular measures designed to prevent price increases and foreign exchange losses.[2]

Reasoning in fiscal terms, the legacy of outmoded Soviet and Western ways of thinking is particularly unsuited to South Asian problems, since the fiscal budget is a small part of the total economy in the underdeveloped countries of South Asia. This is quite different from the rich countries of the West and from the Soviet Union, where the fiscal budget covers much more of the economy and where much tighter controls are exercised over internal prices and foreign transactions.

[1] The argument clearly does not imply that the system of operational controls used in South Asia is either very effective or desirable. But the desirability and efficacy of controls should be discussed on their merits and not concealed by a definition of "balance." See Chapter 19 and Appendix 8.

[2] The problem is analogous to that of the definition of "equilibrium" in international trade, which one school of thought tries to define in terms of absence of trade restrictions, absence of unemployment, absence of "disequilibriating capital movements," as well as absence of cumulative drain of reserves. This type of definition prevents a rational discussion of the respective merits of different policies to prevent drain, by lumping all policies except exchange rate variations into the definition of "equilibrium." The invisible hand works by a sleight-of-hand. (Cf. Paul Streeten, "Elasticity Optimism and Pessimism in International Trade," *Economia Internazionale,* Vol. VII, No. 1, Geneva, 1954, p. 5.)

We may conclude that the size of the deficit does not provide a yardstick for measuring the effects of the budget on inflation and/or on the balance of payments, mainly for the following reasons:

(i) Expenditures, taxes, and loans vary and have varying effects on the timing, direction, and size of demand and supply in different domestic markets and also on all of these factors in relation to foreign transactions; simple aggregation is therefore misplaced.

(ii) The effects of the budget cannot be separated from the effects of a number of other policies that do not appear in the budget; this would imply illegitimate isolation.

(iii) The budget covers only a small part of the whole economy, and therefore many important areas are left in the dark.

6 No Short-Cut Possible

There is no short-cut to an analysis of these economic effects of public expenditure, taxes, and loans. Certainly the fiscal budget does not provide one. *We cannot escape from an analysis of the effects of specific expenditures, taxes, and loans in the setting of the actual conditions of the particular country under study and of all the operational controls it applies and the institutional reforms it inaugurates.* Admittedly the inferences drawn from such an analysis are bound to be exceedingly vague and uncertain when statistics are as poor as those of the South Asian countries. It can generally be assumed, however, that new public expenditures, whether in the current or the development budget, if not matched by additional current supplies, will tend to increase inflationary pressures, and that new taxes and government loans newly raised on the capital market will tend to reduce demand somewhere and to some extent. It may be further assumed that, as is typical of poor countries attempting development, the budget will raise demand more than immediately available supply, even in the absence of deficit financing. The tendency, commented on in Chapter 19 (Section 6), to keep to a minimum a number of important controls that determine costs,[1] in order to foster private enterprise, will make this result even more likely.

It is therefore natural that the treasury — the government's financial conscience — will be inclined to ask the theoretically nonsensical question, "Where does the money come from?" Because of analogies between the public budget and individual spending and earning, the question has the appearance of good sense and is generally "understood." Since there are always strong pressures for increasing expenditures in numerous ways, on the one hand, and, on the other, against raising taxes or tightening credit, the treasury will regularly try to stretch the time-honored and respectable conventions of "sound finance" to meet these pressures (see above in Section 3). It does so both by enlarging the development budget and by permitting as much deficit financing as it believes is consistent with budgetary "neutrality," on the argument that the economy is growing and increasingly monetized. However, such behavior will prevent neither inflation nor a drain on foreign exchange reserves. If, in addition, non-

[1] Appendix 8.

discretionary operational controls, operating through changes in the price system, are weak and ineffective, a large number of discretionary controls will then be clamped on,[1] while monetary balance will nevertheless remain precarious. The fiscal reasoning presented by the treasury and reflected in the budget, which is part of the plan, is *political bargaining*. As analysis it is useless. A proper inquiry must not even begin with this type of reasoning but must be carried out in entirely different terms.

The demonstration in Sections 3–5 that the definition of "public investment" is arbitrary and that the concepts "balanced budget" and "deficit financing" are useless for planning is worked out in theoretical terms, although with the actual plans and the discussions and practices in South Asian countries in mind. We have in passing referred to the fact that the terminology used in the plans varies a great deal and is full of ambiguities. In the course of our study we prepared a lengthy analysis of how such concepts as current, capital, and development expenditure and deficit financing are in fact used in the plans, but abstained from publishing it here, because the only additional inference that can be drawn from that semantic analysis is that there is great ambiguity and confusion in the use of these concepts. This additional inference is not very important, since our conclusion is that the concepts, even if clear and consistently used, could not form the basis of a realistic analysis of the impact of the public budget on a country's economic development.

7 The Iceberg

The argument so far can be briefly summarized.

(1) The common assumption in development planning is that the additional national product is related to the value of physical investment by the incremental capital/output ratio. Although in the context of national accounting this ratio is, at best, nothing more than a tautological identity, it tends to bias thinking by making investment the strategic variable, and in the models and the approach to planning, the exclusive one.

(2) Once the use of the capital/output concept is established, there is a transition from total investment, via public investment, to public development expenditure, and thus to the development budget. The definition of this budget is arbitrary, determined by convention and the pressure of political interests; it is useless as a concept in theoretical analysis. Aggregate investment – using this definition of public investment – is for the same reason not a valid concept – this aside from the misplaced aggregation it implies. The questions how this budget is financed, and whether it is "balanced," in one sense or another, are irrelevant, as are the general questions as to what fiscal measures should be taken to hit the growth targets and what are the real limitations of development, and the particular question, what are the financial limitations to development. Once again, the emphasis on the fiscal structure introduces biases into thinking, by (a) concealing specific problems of sectoral limitations behind inappropriate aggregates, (b) ignoring the operational controls, and (c) neglecting all economic and non-economic activity relevant to development out-

[1] See Chapter 19, Section 5.

side the budget, or only incidentally related to it. All three biases tend to strengthen the bias discussed under (1), that is, the emphasis on investment, and in particular public investment, as the key that opens the door to development.

(3) This discussion is not intended to imply that a fiscal budget is unimportant or that it should not be audited as carefully as possible. The point is that it must not be confused with *the plan*, nor can it contain the plan. Awareness of this point is occasionally evident in the discussions of the plans, but it is not carried sufficiently far and does not, in any case, affect the general approach in terms of budget balancing and deficit financing.

It should be stressed, however, that a good deal of physical analysis is being done, and it is this that in the end can make planning in South Asia a force for rationality by accomplishing a coordination of policies. Such analysis is mostly fragmentary, but in India each new plan has been based on more intensive calculations of physical quantities, and a trend in the same direction is beginning to be noticeable in the Philippines, Pakistan, Ceylon, and some other countries. Unless this fact is borne in mind, unfair conclusions might be drawn from the criticism in the preceding sections. To begin with, inputs and sometimes outputs are often calculated for public investments. Targets in physical terms for investment and production in various branches of the private sector are worked out. Employment targets are similarly stated, though usually founded on very inadequate analysis. An approach to manpower planning is occasionally envisaged. Estimates of the requirements of personnel and other inputs are usually made for the planned public health and educational policies, though as yet hardly any calculations are attempted of the returns on this policy in physical terms, either in the short or the long run. But much of the crucial discussion between the ministries of health and education and the treasury, for example, or within the planning agency, is undoubtedly conducted in realistic physical terms and not simply in fiscal terms. In these fields, as in others, memoranda are drafted, committees deliberate and issue reports, witnesses are called, investigations are conducted, and special chapters and sections are written about specific and real problems.

Underlying the financial and fiscal plans are thus bits and pieces of physical planning. Otherwise there would be no planning at all in real terms.[1] As planning improves, these bits and pieces become more numerous, the analysis more intensive, the inputs and outputs more accurately assessed, and the policies more effectively coordinated for different sectors. The results appear in separate chapters or sections of the plans — on the various industries, on land reform, administration, education, health, and so on. Operational controls, too, are dealt with, though usually in a cursory way and without intensive analysis. But the unfortunate thing is that little coordination is attempted — except the illusory and misleading kind in terms of the fiscal budget and of a financial superstructure resting on a single precarious pedestal, the capital/output ratio, if on anything at all.

Planning in the South Asian countries can thus be compared to an iceberg,

[1] Appendix 2, Section 22.

most of which is under water; it is this submerged portion that can be called planning in a real sense. The fact that the small visible part is so strongly molded by the fiscal budget is unfortunate because it confuses public, official, and scholarly thinking on these matters. It is particularly unfortunate that the wider ramifications of effective planning are not fully brought out, because, as we saw in Appendix 2, Sections 19–21, the reasons for coordinating all policies are more urgent in the underdeveloped countries of South Asia than in the West. The practice of attaching primary interest to the invalid financial and, narrower still, fiscal planning is supported by strong vested interests that are apt to make their own use of the biases encouraged by this structure of the plans.

8 A Note on Budget Reform

The principles that should guide the formulation of the fiscal budget can be summed up as follows:

(1) The primary purpose of a budget is to enforce economy in the use of public funds and efficiency and honesty in their administration, to serve as a check against waste and prevent unnecessary expenditures. But it is easier to hold people responsible for what they have done wastefully than for what they have failed to do. A system of controls should be devised that penalizes omissions as well as commissions.

(2) The budget can never be a plan. Public expenditure is a necessary condition for many activities, but seldom a sufficient condition; its size has only an incidental relation to development policies. Its permissive character should not be elevated to a motive force and the other conditions that have to be fulfilled to carry out a plan should not be obscured.

(3) The budget should be so organized that it helps, or at least does not hinder, clear thinking. This means that distinctions must be made between regularly recurrent and periodic expenditures, between expenditures yielding a commercial return on costs and those that yield benefits for which no charges are or can be made; between estimates, appropriations, and actual expenditure, and so on.

(4) The division into a current and development budget is, however, arbitrary and misleading. All expenditure items should be judged by their contribution to development, directly or indirectly, in the short run or in the long run, and in conjunction with or as substitutes for other measures.

(5) All items of expenditure and receipt should be judged by how they affect demand and supply of particular products and services and particular sectors at different times.

9 Concluding Note

This appendix was originally intended to be merely the theoretical introduction to a comparative analysis of the South Asian plans. Two more parts were to follow: one an analysis of the conceptual framework of the different plans and the other an analysis of the actual plans and their fulfillment. The last was to be the main contribution, and much effort was spent in clarifying the concepts used in the plans and revising and adjusting the figures, so that they expressed the intentions of the planners, were consistent with each other, and were comparable for consecutive plans in any one country and for plans in different countries.

In the end, we decided not to publish the bulky tables that were the result of our labor. Even in their adjusted form, the figures were arbitrary and their probable errors so large that their inclusion in this study did not seem justifiable. The other part, the critical analysis of the conceptual framework of the plans, was intended mainly to be instrumental to the work in the final part. It also illustrated the great ambiguity and confusion of this conceptual framework. However, as we explained in Section 6, it was not needed for the theoretical criticism of the structure of the plans; and since it too was very bulky, we decided against publishing it.

Chapter 19

OPERATIONAL CONTROLS OVER THE PRIVATE SECTOR

In Appendix 4 we point out that the development plans of the South Asian countries are constructed as financial plans and that in essence they have the still narrower scope of fiscal plans, focussed on public expenditure and, in particular, public investment. We there discuss in some detail the shortcomings of that approach to planning, noting that there is little real coordination of public policies, even as to investment in plants for the production of material goods.[1] In regard to other policies it is true that the plans often give considerable attention to legislative and administrative measures intended to bring about alterations in the attitudinal and institutional framework of society — improvement of administrative services, land reform, various projects for community organization through "democratic planning," the spread of birth control among the masses — and to policies designed to improve education and health, and so on. However, since these reforms are only incidentally related to public expenditure, they are not really integrated into the body of the plans.[2] These types of long-range policy measures are dealt with in other chapters of this book.

[1] See also Appendix 2, Section 22.
[2] Appendix 4, Section 2.

In addition there is a whole system of what we shall call "operational controls" over the private sector. Within that system we include all the short-range policy measures applied by governments to influence people's economic behavior in some particular respect. Even though similarities exist, operational controls are different from long-range reforms in that they are meant to be flexible and continually adjusted to meet variations in economic conditions. They are the levers of policy, the manipulation of which is needed to ensure that development proceeds from month to month and year to year as closely in line with the targets of the plans as is feasible in a context of change. In this chapter we shall present an analysis of operational controls, viewed as tools of short-term policy. The more substantive problems of planning in the South Asian countries will be taken up in the next part of the book.

1   The Problem

While policies intended to induce fundamental alterations in institutions and attitudes are often discussed at length in the plans, operational controls, and the way in which they should be handled, are usually not discussed at all. Little attention is paid to such vital matters as government policies in regard to interest rates and other credit conditions in the money and capital markets, the prices charged for services and products provided in the public sector, the licensing of various activities conducted by private enterprise, price controls and rationing in various markets, and import and exchange controls. Even the methods of financing public expenditure, including the types and rates of taxation to be employed, are often left open. In particular, the plans are silent on the crucial problem of how to achieve a rational coordination of controls so that *together* they direct development toward plan fulfillment.

This means that the plans are not "operational." From another point of view, it indicates that implementing measures are not really planned in advance, but are improvised in an *ad hoc* fashion.[1] In the words of Benjamin Higgins:

The main evidence of failure to complete the planning process is the absence of firm recommendations in the Plan for the policy measures and regulations needed to implement it. Statement of targets and broad outlines of the sources of finance are not enough in what is still overwhelmingly a free private enterprise economy.[2]

[1] "Both import and export licensing have throughout the plan decade been controlled ad hoc, and have never been . . . formulated in relation to long term planning." (D. R. Gadgil, "An Approach to Indian Planning," *Economic Weekly*, July, 1961, p. 1131.)

[2] Benjamin Higgins, *Economic Development,* Norton, New York, 1959, p. 729.

The planners and government officials may feel that they need a free hand and that they will have it if they keep the planning of operational controls to themselves. The writer has occasionally met this argument in discussing the subject with officials in India. But even in India, where planning generally has achieved a much higher level of sophistication than in the other countries in South Asia, the plain fact is that in most fields there is little or nothing "planned" to disclose.

Neither are operational controls very prominent in the public discussion of planning; as is true of the plans themselves, this is concerned mainly with aggregates and proportions of aggregates of investment and production in various fields and their effects on other aggregates and proportions, particularly national income *in toto* and per head, savings, marginal savings, investment, and employment. Even scientific studies of the economic problems in South Asia have to an astonishing extent by-passed the problem of operational controls and their coordination. Facts about the controls and their application are not systematically recorded and it is very difficult to acquire any reliable and comprehensive knowledge about them. They are, in any case, not analyzed as a system in the sense that the several controls are seen to be interchangeable or that one type of control makes other controls necessary. From the point of view of planning, the problem should always be viewed as the total impact on development of the various controls applied.

Operational controls can be classified in two broad groups: *positive* and *negative*. The positive controls are aimed at stimulating, encouraging, facilitating, and inducing production or consumption, generally or in a special sector. In regard to enterprise, investment, and production, the positive controls include educational campaigns aimed at clarifying the business situation and encouraging investment, the provision of technical assistance, subsidies, tax holidays, and credits on easy terms, the setting of low prices on products and services from the public sector, and foreign exchange and import controls, which provide not only low-cost foreign exchange for some enterprises (in case the demand for foreign exchange exceeds the supply) but also, along with customs barriers, protection against foreign competition. The negative controls, on the contrary, are meant to prevent or limit production or consumption by means of bullying, administrative restrictions on capital issues, investment, and production, the denial of foreign exchange, the rationing of consumer goods, and the imposition of excise duties, or the raising of various costs by other means.

Although in common usage the word "controls" has a negative connotation, for want of a better term we have adhered to it to describe all operational state intervention in the private sector. A more material qualification to be borne in mind is that controls may often be negative and positive at the same time. For instance, when the state prevents or restricts the import of goods by means of exchange rationing, this is a negative control from the standpoint of some importers but a positive control for others; more generally it is a positive control so far as domestic producers of competing products are concerned. When using this terminology it is therefore necessary to be clear as to the specific economic activity in regard to which a particular control is postulated to have positive or negative effects.

Another distinction between controls over the private sector, whether of the positive or negative type, relates to the way they are applied. If their application involves an individual decision by an administrative authority with power to act at its own discretion, they are considered to be *discretionary*. If the application follows automatically from the laying down of a definite rule, or from induced changes in prices, the imposition of tariff duties or excise duties, or the giving of subsidies to a particular branch of industry without the possibility of discrimination in favor of particular firms, the controls are presumed to be *non-discretionary*.[1] In regard to all controls except those non-discretionary ones that work through induced changes in prices, there are wide differences in the *degree* of administrative discretion, depending on how firm and specific the governing directives are and how literally they are observed. In the extreme case, when the rule laid down for administrative action is so clear and specific that there is no room for discretion, and this rule is strictly adhered to, the control is deemed to be non-discretionary, even though it is carried out by administrative decision. But that case is rare in South Asia. Whenever administration gets its fingers into the pie there will be opportunities for discretion and, consequently, discrimination.

Distinguishing between types of controls according to whether they are non-discretionary or discretionary does not imply that the one is more in accord with a *laissez-faire* philosophy than the other. Independent of the type of controls utilized, the practice of planning economic development represents an entirely different economic policy from that of leaving the course of events to be determined by the price mechanism as it operates under the influence of market forces.[2] Even though the greater use of price policies implies a higher degree of "automatism" — in the sense that people's economic behavior is guided by relative rates of costs and

---

[1] The distinction between discretionary and non-discretionary controls is, on the whole, identical with that between "direct" or "physical" controls and "indirect" controls, as described in the literature. But a legislative or administrative act forbidding a certain activity altogether, if it is enforced, or the provision of a service, for instance a road, free of charge to everybody is certainly "direct" in the ordinary sense of the word but it is also non-individualized and automatically applied, which makes it non-discretionary in our terminology.

[2] "Development policy therefore should include an elaborate system of stimuli and deterrents intended to provide some guidance to private activity." (Jan Tinbergen, *The Design of Development*, Johns Hopkins Press, Baltimore, 1958, p. 50.)

returns rather than administrative discretion — this assumes that the price mechanism has first been adjusted so that it provides the specific inducements and inhibitions that are "correct" in view of the goals and targets in the plan. On this point there is great confusion in the plans and in the economic literature and we have devoted Appendix 5 to an attempt at clarifying the issue.

A main thesis of the present chapter is that, in comparison with the developed Western countries, the countries in South Asia — with some considerable differences, as we shall note — are relying very heavily on administrative discretionary controls as opposed to automatically applied, non-discretionary controls. The contrast would be at least as great, if not greater, if the comparison were made in terms of the conditions that prevailed when the Western nations were in the early stages of industrialization. This development gained momentum early in the liberal interlude between Mercantilism and the modern welfare state and was concomitant with a decrease of controls, particularly those of the administrative discretionary type. The scarcity in South Asia of administrative personnel with both competence and integrity should make discretionary policies all the more difficult to execute with reasonable effectiveness and reliance on them more hazardous, even morally. With this consideration in mind, the discussion in this chapter will be based on the derived value premise that, on the whole, it would be desirable if non-discretionary controls were used to the maximum extent possible. The rationale of this value premise is, at the same time, partly a result of our analysis.[1]

2   In the Plans

We have already pointed to the cavalier way in which operational controls are dealt with in the plans. When the subject is not altogether omitted from consideration, it is treated from the standpoint of conditions in the organized sector of the economy, though this is usually not explicitly stated. In principle, non-discretionary policies, and, in particular, those utilizing the price mechanism, are regularly given preference. Thus the classic Draft Outline of India's First Five Year Plan contains a general recommendation for using price policy as a means of implementing the plan:

For the fulfilment of the objectives defined in the Plan, it is necessary to have a price policy which secures an allocation of resources in conformity with these objectives. In the private sector, decisions are made in the light of prevailing prices and expectations as to their future trend. Unless the alignment of prices favours the use of resources along the lines indicated by the targets worked out

[1] Chapter 2, Sections 3 and 4.

for this sector, there is likelihood of a serious discrepancy between the results expected and the actual achievements. A change in price relationships in one line has its repercussions on the distribution of resources in several other lines. In the absence, therefore, of an effective policy aimed at maintaining an appropriate structure of prices, planning in respect of the private sector cannot succeed.[1]

This statement, which implies the use of what we, in Appendix 5 (Section 4), call "correct" or "planned" prices, is complemented by an equally clear statement, spelling out abstractly the implications of price controls in regard to relations with foreign markets:

While planning does not mean either a complete insulation of the economy from trends abroad or a complete control over all spheres of economic activity, it does imply a price policy which will enable the fulfilment of the targets laid down and, at the same time, maintain a certain balance between the various classes of the community. To this end, it is necessary to reduce, as far as possible, the impact of foreign prices on the domestic level of incomes and distribution of resources. Already, export duties are being levied as part of the general anti-inflationary policy, but under rapidly changing international conditions, there is need for constant adjustments in coverage and rates of levy. If the proceeds of export duties which are in the nature of a windfall are used to subsidise the imports of essential commodities, it would be possible to protect the domestic price and cost structure more effectively.[2]

It is recognized that it will also be necessary to establish a system of discretionary negative controls (usually referred to in the plans simply as "controls"): "This [system] will comprise (a) capital issues control, (b) licensing of new enterprises and of large extensions of existing ones, (c) foreign exchange allocations, and import and export controls, and (d) price and physical controls."[3] About the scope and operation of these controls little is said, except that "In the planning, administration and periodical reviews of these controls, the machinery for consultation and co-operation with the private sector will have an effective share."[4] However, one very important guideline, which as we shall find is very imperfectly observed in practice, is laid down:

The point to stress here is that each control has to be viewed as part of a system and it must be operated so as to contribute effectively to the fulfilment of the twofold aim behind the system, *viz.*, the containment of inflationary pressures

[1] India, Government of, Planning Commission, *First Five Year Plan, A Draft Outline*, July, 1951, p. 26.
[2] *Ibid.*, p. 33.
[3] *Ibid.*, p. 26.
[4] *Ibid.*

and the maintenance of relative prices at a level designed to secure the achievement of the targets defined in the Plan.[1]

Later Indian plan documents have not improved on these statements of principles. There has been a growing tendency in the plans, as well as in public debate, to avoid any discussion of relative prices and to define price policies mainly as policies aimed at preventing an inflationary rise in the price level.[2] The issue both in the plans and in public discussion has been the choice between a system of administrative discretionary controls and those non-discretionary controls affecting the whole economy that are commonly referred to as fiscal and monetary policies.[3] This implies that the problem of price relations and their control has been relegated to obscurity.

Pakistan's First Five Year Plan states bluntly that "Administrative and social conditions are not favourable for the successful operation of physical [i.e., discretionary] controls, and we do not in general favour them."[4] After this declaration of principle the plan continues:

It will, however, clearly be necessary to continue the controls on imports, foreign exchange, new industrial enterprises and capital issues . . . Direct physical controls may be needed to meet shortages of important commodities . . . In particular, price controls and rationing may become necessary when essential supplies are short and the ordinary price mechanism threatens to cause serious hardships to the more vulnerable elements of the community.

[1] *Ibid.,* p. 33.

[2] Nevertheless, the Second Five Year Plan contains the following statements:
"Given an appropriate structure of relative prices, which Government can and has to control and influence, the desired allocation of resources in the private sector can be induced." (India, Government of, Planning Commission, *Second Five Year Plan,* New Delhi, 1956, p. 29.)
"Simultaneously [with public investments], over a large field of economic activity the role of economic policy in a mixed economy is to influence the course of private investment through appropriate changes in relative prices and profitability." (*Ibid.,* p. 38.)

[3] "There are, broadly speaking, two types of techniques through which the objectives in view have to be attained. Firstly, there is the overall regulation of economic activity through fiscal and monetary policy, and, secondly, there are devices like export and import controls, licensing of industries or trades, price controls and allocations which influence and regulate economic activity in particular sectors or sub-sectors of the economy. There has been of late a good deal of discussion as to whether planning should confine itself to the former type of control or whether it should extend to the latter type also. Overall fiscal and monetary discipline, it would appear, can go a long way towards regulating the ebb and flow of economic activity, and differential taxation can assist in channeling resources at the margin in certain directions. There is little doubt, however, that a comprehensive plan which aims at raising the investment in the economy substantially and has a definite order of priorities in view cannot be seen through on the basis merely of overall fiscal and monetary control. The second type of controls mentioned above is thus inescapable." (*Ibid.*)

[4] Pakistan, Government of, National Planning Board, *The First Five Year Plan 1955–60,* Karachi, December, 1957, p. 88.

Pakistan's Second Five Year Plan also contains some courageous statements about "a broad area which can best be left to regulation through
the mechanism of the market," and goes on:

Even where controls are necessary, taxes and subsidies [controls of the non-
discretionary type] may frequently be preferable to direct [discretionary] controls as an instrument to influence the uses to which existing resources are put,
the pattern of production and consumption, and the direction of new investment.
Direct controls are not only inefficient in many cases; they also place an additional burden on the scarce administrative talent of the country, which might be
better employed on development. . . . Once the principle is accepted that prices
should be used primarily as a regulatory device, there appears to be no need for
the many specific controls in various sectors of the economy. A judicious system
of taxes and subsidies can be used to promote a rational allocation of resources.[1]

Similar statements in favor of automatically applied non-discretionary
controls, usually involving the price mechanism, can be found in most of
the other South Asian plans. Practice, however, is very different. One often
feels that the planners regard the use of administrative, discretionary controls as standard procedure, indeed as the very essence of planning, at
least in their present stage of planning economic policies. They are wary of
other types of controls:

To what extent interest rates and price adjustment could be employed as instruments of economic policy are questions of frequent debate but, without going
into detail, it may be stated that on the whole, in the use of these instruments of
economic policy, *the approach has been one of caution.* It is expected, however, that as planning becomes more comprehensive and its scope increases,
indirect methods and controls [that is, non-discretionary controls] will gain in
preponderance.[2]

In regard to the choice between non-discretionary and discretionary
controls the same ambivalence and lack of clarity on the level of principle is apparent in the positions taken by economists. It is not difficult to
find clear statements in favor of a policy of working through non-discretionary controls.

In so far as the private sector is an important part of a mixed economy, prices
should be used both for purposes of regulating allocation of scarce material as

---

[1] Pakistan, Government of, Planning Commission, *Outline of the Second Five Year
Plan* (1960–65), Karachi, January, 1960, pp. 25, 26, 28.

"The creative energies of the people can be best harnessed to the needs of development if policies of economic liberalism are pursued." (Pakistan, Government of, Planning Commission, *The Second Five Year Plan* (1960–65), Karachi, June, 1960, Preface.)

The formulations indicate that the authors of the plans have not had clearly in mind
the fundamental distinction made at the beginning of Appendix 5.

[2] India, Government of, Planning Commission, *The Planning Process*, Delhi, October, 1963, p. 10. Italics added.

well as of discouraging consumption of a kind not really essential during the initial periods of economic development. Prices have a very important function as instruments of economic policy, whether in a socialist society or a mixed society such as ours: and unless there is integrated and purposive price policy it would be very difficult to get the best out of a mixed economy in terms of economic development and also get it moving in the direction of a socialist society. Hence the great importance of a proper price policy.[1]

But as the few economists who express a critical attitude toward planning direct much of their ire at state interference of the discretionary type, opposition to such policies by economists who endorse planning tends to be subdued. One gets the feeling that South Asian economists and politicians of a more radical bent look upon the willingness of a government to employ discretionary controls as a particularly "socialist" trait. This confusion is reflected by many Western writers who find in the plethora of administrative discretionary controls in South Asia an indication of a socialist or even a "Marxist" turn of mind.[2] Business circles keep up a running fire of criticism against the government for interference in business, but this criticism is queerly subdued and very apparently not meant to be taken too seriously. The explanation for this is that, as we shall find in Section 7, the interests of business and particularly big business are, on the whole, greatly favored in the system of discretionary controls that is actually applied.

One concept that has cropped up in recent years in the theoretical discussion of planning in South Asia, though not, as far as we know, to an appreciable extent in the actual work on planning, that of "accountancy"

---

[1] V. K. R. V. Rao, "Prices, Incomes, Wages and Profits in a Socialist Society," in *All India Congress Committee, Planning Sub-Committee, Ooty Seminar May 30– June 5, 1959 (Papers Discussed)*, New Delhi, 1959, pp. 176–177.

Communist economists advising the non-Communist underdeveloped countries often take a similar view: "With regard to the private sector, the plan has not the power of a directive, but is a desire expressed which must be followed by creating such incentives as will induce private producers to do exactly the things which are required from them in the plan. It is quite clear and does not require further explanation that with regard to the private sector the price system, including interest rates, is an important incentive serving to induce the private sector to do things required from it in the plan. But also in the public sector the need for incentive exists. It is not sufficient just to address administrative directives to public agencies and public enterprises. In addition to that it is necessary to create such economic incentives that the public agencies, enterprises, etc. find it in the interest of their management and their employees to do the things which are required from them in the plan. This again requires a proper price system." (Oskar Lange, *Economic Development, Planning and International Cooperation*, Central Bank of Egypt, Cairo, 1961, pp. 16–17.)

[2] "The more Marxist the values of the group in power in any country, the more likely they are to choose a system of planning and direct controls. In theory it is possible for socialists to utilize the market mechanism to allocate resources, but in practice socialists think in terms of some degree of physical controls and direct planning, at least for 'essential' sectors." (H. T. Patrick and Peter Schran, *Economic Contrasts: China, India, and Japan*, Center Paper No. 24, Yale University, New Haven, 1963, p. 170.)

or "shadow" prices, will be kept outside the discussion in this chapter for reasons set forth in Appendix 5. When we talk about induced changes in prices as an instrument of policy, we mean actually realized changes (sometimes in conjunction with various other non-discretionary controls like duties and taxes, which have the same effect on costs and returns as induced changes in prices). In theory the introduction of accounting prices should make it possible to exert part of the directive influence of price policies without altering actual prices in the market.[1]

3 In Agriculture

The preponderance of administrative controls of an individualized, discretionary type in South Asian countries should be viewed against the background of the area's history and the legacy of that history in the form of economic and social institutions. If first we turn to agriculture,[2] where by far the largest part of the population wins its livelihood as it always has done, we find that the productivity of labor and land is low and techniques are primitive. Social and economic relations are largely determined by tradition-bound attitudes and institutions. In particular, most economic transactions do not take place in markets within the meaning of Western economic theory, still less in nationally coordinated and fairly perfect markets. The policies of the colonial governments had many very important effects on agriculture in the South Asian countries, as will be shown in Chapter 22; but they did not Westernize this sector in any respects pertinent to the problems dealt with in this chapter. The situation in agriculture and in rural areas generally, therefore, did not give the national governments, as they emerged in the new era of independence, much scope to use automatically applied non-discretionary controls, least of all those intended to work through induced changes in prices.

Another heritage is an authoritarian tradition that was strengthened by colonial rule. Such "integrated" local communities as existed in pre-colonial times had been static rather than "self-reforming,"[3] and colonial governments were quite content to adapt themselves to this circumstance. In the type of authoritarian society that prevailed, the masses of people were accustomed to rely on the higher-ups to organize and direct their activities. On the other hand, they very often exhibited a sullen attitude of non-obedience. People were accustomed to being ordered about, but also to getting away with as much as possible. The only way to overcome such lawlessness — which usually manifests itself in a casual and amorphous way rather than in organized rebellion — is by exhortations, threats or

[1] Appendix 5, Section 5.
[2] Not including the plantations, which we invariably count among the industries.
[3] Chapter 18, Sections 5 and 14.

appeals, punitive action, educational efforts, and other individualized and discretionary controls. It is characteristic of an authoritarian society, however, that the people in command — whether officials or those who because of their social and economic position hold power in the villages and districts — become accustomed to indulge the people's resistance to a punctual and efficient fulfillment of duties.

Western colonial officials and other West Europeans in the colonies were, from the beginning, conditioned to regard the villagers and the bulk of the indigenous population as disorderly, lazy, and unambitious children whom they had to look after,[1] and nothing in their "experience" was of a nature to change their attitude. The colonial government's interference in the life and work of the people in the rural districts was limited also by the *laissez-faire* precept that they should not attempt to meddle too much in social and religious matters. Within this limitation and the limitation of available personnel and funds, ordering people about and, to an extent, assuming paternalistic responsibility for their welfare was the natural role of colonial officials. Administrative discretionary control was exercised directly by these officials assisted by a hierarchy, broadening toward its base, of indigenous officials or trusted feudal chiefs, whose authority was enhanced by their relation to the colonial governments.

This type of regulatory activity symbolized the possession of power and authority. To step into the shoes of the colonial rulers and do the things they had done must have been a natural ambition for native politicians and officials, and the people probably expected that they would do just that. To many, both high and low, "independence" meant doing those things that earlier were the monopoly of the foreign rulers. The increase in bureaucrats and bureaucracy in all these countries, particularly at the lower levels, has certainly been due in part to the desire of persons in the educated class to accede to positions of authority and privilege.[2] The struggle for and winning of independence meant a strengthening of one characteristic of this traditional and authoritarian society and the bending of the controls in one specific direction. The states that the new governments took over were "soft states," as we pointed out in the last sections of the previous chapter, and this was particularly the case in rural areas and in regard to agriculture. In the present context the implication is that the independent governments found themselves even more constrained than the colonial governments to use positive controls and to avoid negative controls.

[1] Certain stereotyped notions about the South Asian peoples, and the opportunistic role of those stereotypes as rationalizations in colonial times, are discussed in Chapter 21, Section 6.

[2] The development of Thailand, which had retained its political independence, has been no different, except that perhaps Thai officialdom has been even more prone to employ discretionary controls.

However, one very big difference was involved in the coming to power of native political leaders in the former colonies. They, as well as the whole intellectual elite in the area, were committed to push for fundamental change. They were ideologically against the *laissez-faire* tactics of the colonial regimes. They wanted planned development and were anxious to institute needed reforms. They also wanted democracy, not least at the local level. They wanted to create for the first time a "self-reforming" society in South Asia. The outcome of this new ideological bent was the attempt to spread, through cooperation and self-government, the notion of "democratic planning," which we analyzed in the preceding chapter. In view of the conditions that existed in rural districts and, in particular, the "soft-state" attitudes and the social facts in which they were embedded, the governments felt compelled to exert an increased influence on community life but at the same time to confine themselves to positive administrative and discretionary controls; they did not attempt, and did not want to attempt, to lay down specific duties for the villagers. The organizations for cooperation and self-government discussed in Chapter 18 became, in fact, instruments for offering positive inducements, ranging from information, instruction, and advice to subsidies of all sorts; negative controls were shunned.

In the preceding portion of this section we have tried to explain in causal terms how operational controls developed in South Asia. But in many ways the causes enumerated serve to build up a rationale for the use of the type of policies which we have seen are being applied. Thus in agriculture the relative avoidance of non-discretionary controls, especially those that depend on the manipulation of prices, and the reliance instead on discretionary controls to implement policy, is justified by two complexes of facts. The first is the absence of anything like perfect markets; many transactions are not of the market type at all. The other and more basic one is that price incentives are weak. Few people calculate in terms of costs and returns, and if they do, their economic behavior is not primarily determined by such calculations.[1] The masses of the people are

[1] P. K. Mukherjee reminds us how the pioneering economist in India, M. G. Ranade, shortly after the turn of the century, summed up the position of India in regard to the ordinary assumptions of Western economic theory: "With us an average individual man is, to a large extent, the very antipodes of the economical man. The family and the Caste are more powerful than the individual in determining his position in life. Self-interest in the shape of desire of wealth is not absent but it is not the only nor principal motor. . . . Custom and State regulation are far more powerful than Competition, and Status more decisive than Contract. Neither Capital nor Labour is mobile . . . Wages and Profits are fixed . . . Population follows its own law — being cut down by disease and famine; while production is almost stationary the bumper harvest of one year being needed to provide against the uncertainties of alternate bad seasons. *In a society so constituted, the tendencies assumed as axiomatic, are not only inoperative but are actually deflected from their proper direction.*"
Mukherjee adds that while half a century has seen some changes Ranade's "descrip-

"survival-minded," to the extent of calling forth the old image of a backward sloping supply curve. Tradition is also an important influence on behavior. In Chapters 21 and 22 we shall analyze in detail how these attitudes are conditioned by the institutional system of land ownership and other realities in the South Asian situation.

A few generalizations will illustrate the unsuitability of the market mechanism as an instrument for automatic and non-discretionary controls of the price policy type. First, in India the bulk of the marketable surplus of agricultural produce is not provided by a market process but is exacted as tribute from sharecroppers and other peasants by the landlords and moneylenders on whom they depend. Only above the level of the great majority of agriculturalists is there anything like a real market. Secondly, what in rural districts corresponds to a capital market is still predominantly the unorganized, individual transactions between a peasant and a moneylender. The situation is further complicated by the fact that the peasant's transactions with his landlord, the buyer of his produce (if he has any surplus for sale), the provider of merchandise for his farm or household, and "middlemen" generally, often involve elements of credit at rates of interest that are determined mainly by tradition and the power situation. Furthermore, they are difficult to ascertain; nothing is more apparent than the great difficulty of producing reliable estimates of prevailing interest rates outside the narrow confines of the organized credit market. Such estimates as have been made point to an extraordinary dispersion of interest rates, even locally. Using the Western term "market" to characterize the aggregate of the diverse credit relations in the rural sections of South Asia is obviously foolish. Thirdly, the labor "market" in agriculture is similarly compartmentalized; indeed, the relationship between employer and employee is often a highly individual one, the extreme case being that of "attached labor."

In India, Burma, and the Philippines attempts have been made to legislate general minimum wages for agricultural laborers and most countries in South Asia have tried to maximize interest rates and even tenancy rates. The fact that markets, where they exist at all, are very compartmentalized and imperfect has, of course, tended to nullify such attempts at regulatory intervention. The weakness of local administration and the opposition of officials who side with vested interests against this course of action also contribute to nullifying the practical results of this type of legislation. Attempts to regulate the prices of agricultural products have usually been designed to prevent increases in the living costs of the non-agricultural part of the population or, as in Burma, as a form of taxation. Sometimes,

---

tion of an Indian rural economy remains true to a great extent even at the present moment." (M. G. Ranade, *Essays on Indian Economics*, Madras, 1906, pp. 10–11, quoted in P. K. Mukherjee, *Economic Surveys in Under-developed Countries*, Asia Publishing House, Bombay, 1959, p. 27.)

however, price regulations have been used in order to re-direct production. Such price policies aimed at plan fulfillment, which, apart from middlemen of various types, only concern that minority of agriculturalists who have anything to sell in the market, have been more successful, though not always or unreservedly so; controls aimed at keeping down prices have been less successful.[1]

The whole program surveyed in the preceding chapter on democratic planning has as one of its major aims the rationalization of the attitudes and behavior patterns of the agricultural population, which should make price incentives more effective and create national markets. One branch of the cooperative movement is directed toward creating a market where peasants can both sell produce and buy commodities for their farms and households. The credit cooperatives are, of course, designed to systematize, as well as subsidize, the supply of credits available to agriculturalists. The planners also hope to make people more rational and market-oriented by mitigating the conventions of caste and overcoming other social and economic rigidities, by breaking down social taboos against manual work, and, more generally, by making the younger generation more mobile and more alert to blind alleys. The building up of the school system and the improvement of transport and communications should also work in this direction.

While all these policies involve mainly positive and discretionary controls, their success in a later stage of development would create a greater opportunity for the use of non-discretionary controls of both a positive and a negative nature. Also, if the effectiveness and honesty of administration on the local level could be raised, this should, in time, make it possible to enforce more negative controls, even of a non-discretionary type. If villagers could be charged with more duties toward the community, the outcome might be the inculcation of greater discipline, which is a necessary condition for success in planning for development. The South Asian countries would then be less accurately described as "soft states." There are, however, strong vested interests in the positive and discretion-

---

[1] A former Indian minister of finance explains: "I am myself a believer in the value and the need for integrated control, but my sad experience is that in our country our mechanism of control has completely failed. We talk of a controlled price. Let us take . . . any foodgrains; except the growers of food, it is my belief that not more than 10% of our people really get the foodgrains at controlled price. Probably 10% is an overestimate. The rest really buy in the black market. Today we have got in our country an inflation which is not reflected in the index figures that we have published. The index figures are published on the basis of our controlled prices. But if an index figure was prepared today at the black market price at which people have to buy these essential foodstuffs, you will find the index figure will be absolutely alarming. What is the use of keeping up this show of control then when you really cannot manage?" (C. D. Deshmukh, *Economic Developments in India 1946–1956*, Asia Publishing House, Bombay, July, 1957, p. 52.) See Chapter 26, Section 4.

ary policies now in use. This, and the lack of progress achieved with those policies aimed at rationalizing behavior and enforcing more discipline, has had the general effect of muting, even in public discussion, the expression of the need for a re-direction of controls.

We must also stress the fact that some of the discretionary positive controls applied must be expected to diminish the effectiveness and integrity of the administration; this development makes it more difficult to move later to non-discretionary controls, especially negative ones. The subsidies distributed to the rural population in India consist of literally hundreds of thousands of small grants or cheap loans, aimed at giving greater effect to the other positive and discretionary controls mentioned. They are for the construction of irrigation canals, the digging of wells and tanks, the repairing of roads and houses, the building of schools, and the provision of other community amenities, and to make more attractive the offers of fertilizers, improved seeds, and herds — indeed, for doing thousands of things that will contribute to the uplift of the villagers and the improvement of their economy. All the subsidies, including the credits, are channelled as far as possible through cooperatives and local community authorities. An additional function of the subsidies is, in fact, to make such collective organizations more appealing to the villagers and thus more effective.

Even if the network of organs for cooperation and for local and provincial self-government were to be spread much more widely and tightly, and were to work more effectively, these positive administrative controls would in the main have to be handled by local officials. The volume of administrative work involved in a scheme like the Indian one is immense, and the democratic processes involved in cooperatives and panchayats do not make the administrative task simpler, but often the opposite,[1] at least in the short run. What is done on the local level must, in turn, be controlled; rules for administrative discretionary intervention must be laid down. It is inevitable that the paper-shuffling necessitated by dispersed and individualized positive discretionary controls will be multiplied by the need to supervise the controllers and the controllers of the controllers. On the other hand, attempts to lay down blanket rules and enforce them often lead to policies less well adjusted to the local situation. This is another dilemma in democratic planning to be added to those analyzed in Chapter 18. Rigidity, red tape, and bureaucracy easily become the *signum* of planning and reform.

South Asia's administrative resources are weak to begin with, although the Philippines, India and Ceylon are much better equipped than Indonesia and Burma. Undoubtedly, the large and growing volume of positive discretionary controls, which call for ever more discriminatory decisions,

[1] Chapter 18, Section 10.

is an influence tending to lower the standards of administrative efficiency and honesty in South Asian countries. Ineptitude and corruption, in turn, are apt to poison the spirit of the movement to promote democratic planning through local participation in organs for cooperation and self-government. This is a true dilemma that cannot possibly be solved in an ideal way. It may be true that "The injection of planning into a society living in the twilight between feudalism and capitalism cannot but result in additional corruption, larger and more artful evasions of the law, and more brazen abuses of authority."[1] But under the existing conditions the alternative is to leave things pretty much as they are. When attitudes and institutions are archaic — and price incentives are weak, and markets lacking or grossly imperfect — and more fundamental institutional reforms are excluded for political reasons, little can be done in pursuance of a development policy by means of price policies and other automatically applied, non-discretionary controls; negative controls are unworkable as they lack political and psychological authority.

Conditions and policies in agriculture are dealt with in more substantive terms in other chapters of this book. In this section we have merely attempted to characterize, in abstract and summary fashion, the mechanism by which operational controls in agriculture have been confined almost entirely to positive, administrative and discretionary measures. Very much the same pattern holds true for crafts and small-scale industry, particularly in rural areas but also in cities.

4 In the Organized Sector: The Institutional and Ideological Framework

There are in South Asia establishments in private industry, commerce, and finance that form what is commonly referred to as the "organized" or the "modernized" sector of the economy. Within that sector, goods and services are produced for a national and, occasionally, an international market; there economic behavior is supposed to be rational in the sense that it is based on calculations of costs and revenues and directed at maximizing net returns. The distinction between organized and unorganized economic activity has become a standard conception in all discussion about planning for development, especially in India where the organized sector is fairly large and quite modern in the above sense. To quote Raja J. Chelliah:

There is a curious mixture of the modern and the primitive in the economy of India. . . . The organized sector is very similar in many respects to an advanced

---

[1] P. A. Baran, "On the Political Economy of Backwardness," in A. N. Agarwala and S. P. Singh, eds., *The Economics of Underdeveloped Areas*, Oxford University Press, London, 1959, p. 89.

economy. It is responsive to economic stimuli. By contrast, the unorganized sector is tradition-bound and backward, and a considerable part of it is outside the monetary system. It must be remembered that subsistence agriculture and self-consumption still are very much the rule in the rural sector.[1]

As we mentioned, what little discussion there is about operational controls in the plans and in the literature concerns almost entirely the organized sector of the economy, though usually this is not clearly stated. Even though the traditional sector is far larger in all the South Asian countries, the organized sector is particularly important from a planning point of view, as enlarging it and, eventually, causing the traditional sector to adopt its more rational patterns of economic behavior is a main sightline for planning in the region.

In Chapter 23 we point out that in South Asia large-scale industry and the organized sector generally have retained many characteristics of the traditional society. Ownership and management show pre-capitalistic traits of paternalism and nepotism. Loyalties to caste, family, and ethnic group play a considerable role; "connections" are extremely important. Only with reservations, therefore, can it be asserted that the enterprises in the organized sector are directed according to a rational consideration of price stimuli as they affect costs and returns; even the foreign-owned plantations, mines, and other industrial or commercial enterprises have quasi-feudal peculiarities as compared with enterprises in the developed Western countries. Some of these non-capitalistic traits are undoubtedly due to the type of operational controls exerted by the states in South Asia (see below). More fundamentally, however, both the character of the enterprises in the organized private sector and the nature of state controls have to be explained in terms of the region's historical legacy of institutions and attitudes.

There are gross imperfections and maladjustments in the markets in which the enterprises in the organized sector buy and sell. This situation is only partly a reflection of the conditions mentioned in the previous paragraph. A more important consideration is that the organized areas exist as enclaves in a much larger "unorganized" economy, which is for the most part backward and static. To begin with, their demand for labor, as also for managers and technicians, does not operate in markets that show much resemblance to the corresponding markets in Western countries; the same often holds true of the demand for the supplies needed for production. The markets for finished products are also often imperfect in various ways and degrees. The attempt to give a stagnant society dynamism by promoting the advance of its organized sectors, including large-scale industry, creates imbalances — bottlenecks on the one hand and

---

[1] Raja J. Chelliah, *Fiscal Policy in Underdeveloped Countries*, Allen & Unwin Ltd., London, 1960, p. 28.

unutilized capacities on the other — because both supply and demand are highly inelastic[1] as compared with the situation in the Western world.

With these reservations, it is nevertheless in regard to the organized sector that price policies and other non-discretionary controls could be expected to be most effective, and we would assume that planners and governments would use this opportunity to the utmost since it would minimize the need for state intervention of the discretionary type to attain the targets of the plans. As we pointed out in Section 2, this approach to the problem of how to control and direct private business would conform to certain general statements of principles in the plans and the literature. The fact is, however, that even in regard to the organized part of the private sector resort is had to administrative discretionary controls to an extraordinary extent.

One further observation is appropriate at this stage of our analysis of the South Asian pattern of operational controls. With the advent of the Second World War all the Western countries found it necessary to rapidly re-allocate a large part of their productive resources in order to fulfill expanding new needs, the satisfaction of which did not contribute to meeting normal investment and consumption demands. At the same time, and partly for this reason, the international flow of goods and services was disrupted. The resulting combination of bottlenecks and unused capacities presented Western governments with the practical problem of how to adjust the economy to military needs and the needs of the civilian population. The necessary adjustment could not be expected to occur through the operation of market forces, even were costs and returns reconditioned by non-discretionary controls. For social reasons the governing authorities had to freeze many prices and then, partly in order to back up this price control, they had to resort to the rationing and allocation of goods. Thus they rapidly found themselves equipped with a whole system of "direct" or "physical" controls, many of which were necessarily of a discretionary type. As colonial powers, they introduced such controls in their territories. In fact, the independent governments that came to power in South Asia after the Second World War often inherited most of their discretionary controls; in any case, the Western wartime controls provided a model for them to copy and develop further.

The need for direct controls, often of a discretionary nature, in the developed Western countries was temporary, and they were gradually abolished as normal peacetime conditions were restored. In the low-elasticity economies of South Asia the need is much greater and more enduring; even in the organized sectors, market conditions are such that the governments must regularly apply discretionary controls to a much

[1] Appendix 2, Section 23 *et passim*.

greater extent than the Western countries found necessary even in war-time. This analogy points, however, to a rationale for the control system applied in South Asia. The basic reasons are the region's poverty and underdevelopment — which is reflected in the traditional, less than market-oriented character of business enterprises in an economy where bottlenecks and surpluses are more normal than a balance between demand and supply[1] — and its interest in engendering and directing development.

A great number of the shortages now existing in the organized sector could be overcome by imports. This implies that a scarcity of foreign exchange is in many respects the "master bottleneck." This scarcity cannot be overcome to any substantial extent by price policies or other non-discretionary controls. A country in India's or Pakistan's position would need exchange and import controls even if its currency were devalued;[2] in the next section we shall explain why such controls, in turn, necessitate discretionary investment controls of various types. Only if more foreign exchange were available or if import needs were reduced by slowing down development would the need for administrative discretionary controls decrease substantially. The differences among the South Asian countries as regards their resort to these controls — stretching from India and Pakistan at one extreme to Malaya at the other — are explained largely by the relative scarcity of foreign exchange and the relative intensity of their development efforts.

If the character of economic activity, even in the modernized sectors, goes a long way toward explaining the extraordinary extent to which South Asian countries have adopted administrative discretionary controls, there is no doubt that this development is also in line with the authoritarian and patriarchal tradition we have already touched on. It is more natural in South Asia than in the Western world for government to supervise and direct the conduct of private business. From colonial times politicians and civil servants inherited their role as guardians of the people and the superior status that went with it. Combined with these inherited attitudes is a mistrust of capitalism and business people, which often gives a peculiar coloring to the new ideology of planning for development.[3]

5 *Negative Discretionary Controls*

In India, new security issues of companies are controlled by the government under the Capital Issues (Control) Act (1947). Under the Industries (Development and Regulations) Act (1951, amended 1953 and

[1] Appendix 2, Section 23.
[2] Appendix 8, Part I.
This is not, by itself, an argument against devaluation; see Appendix 8, Section 1.
[3] Chapter 15, Section 4; Chapter 16, Section 4; Chapter 17, Section 1 *et passim*.

1956) a government license is required for all new major undertakings in the industrial field, including any substantial extension of existing plants, or change in their location or in the articles manufactured. A license may specify conditions regarding location, minimum size, and so on. In addition, the government is given the power to investigate the conduct of any industrial enterprise, to issue directives where its records do not seem satisfactory, and, if the directives are not followed, to substitute a new management or even to take it under its own management. To quote the official rules:

This [supervisory power] includes the control of prices, the licensing of distribution, transport, disposal, acquisition, possession, use or consumption; the prohibition of withholding from sale; the compulsory selling of stocks; the regulation or prohibition of commercial and financial transactions in relation to the article concerned.[1]

The Essential Commodities Act (1955) empowers the Indian government to control, regulate, or prohibit the production, distribution, transport, trade, consumption, or storage of a large number of commodities — all foodstuffs, all principal raw materials, important industrial components, and all iron and steel products — to prescribe their prices, and even to take over stocks on conditions it itself sets. A regular duty of the Indian Tariff Commission is to fix the prices of the products of protected industries so as to limit profits to 8–12 percent of invested capital; with regard to a "representative" firm, the law states only that the practice is to "select units of average size from different centres."[2] The State Trading Corporation has been given a monopoly on the import — and sometimes, as in the case of cement, the acquisition from Indian manufacturers as well — and distribution of a number of important commodities with the object of ensuring a "fair distribution at reasonable prices." As in all other South Asian countries that import food-grains, these imports are a state monopoly; the government disposes of them through channels and at prices which it decides on. Wages and labor costs are government controlled by procedures determined by legislative and administrative acts.[3]

Under the Imports and Exports (Control) Act (1947), the government established controls over imports and exports, though it is mainly only in regard to the former that they are used with any strictness. Except for certain articles, the import of which is prohibited, and a few articles placed under open general license, all private imports are subject to indi-

---

[1] India, Government of, *The Registration and Licensing of Industrial Undertakings Rules, 1952 (as modified up to the 1st March, 1957)*, New Delhi, 1957.

[2] India, Government of, *Report of the Fiscal Commission 1949–50*, Vol. I, New Delhi, 1950, p. 173. In addition the Commission shall supervise all protected industries, implying a great number of discretionary powers besides fixing the rates of custom protection and prices.

[3] Chapter 18, Section 11.

vidual licenses. The reason is, of course, the great scarcity of foreign exchange. In general, essential commodities such as foodstuffs, capital goods, and industrial raw materials are given priority; most other imports are severely limited or prohibited. As the conduct of most individual enterprises and the starting of new ones almost always depends on the entrepreneur's ability to import machines and other production necessities, import and exchange controls are the most necessary and most effective of the whole range of government controls over the modernized sector of the private economy. Because of the scarcity of foreign exchange, the government is compelled to decline many individual requests or to curtail them severely. In practice, the granting of import licenses has to be coordinated closely with the control of capital issues and the licensing of new undertakings or the extension of existing plants.[1]

The consequence of these and other many-faceted and often overlapping negative discretionary controls is not merely that, as in Western countries, private business must operate within a framework set by public laws and regulations. The fact is that *no major and, indeed, few minor business decisions can be taken except with the prior permission of the administrative authorities or at the risk of subsequent government disapproval.*[2] This implies that "private" business in India is something entirely different from what it normally is in the Western countries, a point that will be further developed in Section 7. As one Indian commentator puts it:

It is the Plan which lays down which are the industries to be developed and to what extent, and it is made incumbent on the authorities to make the necessary resources available so that expansion of the private sector, as planned, can be achieved. The means by which the targets can be achieved have also to be provided for — so the complicated mechanism of control on capital issues, the State-sponsored investment corporations, import licenses for capital equipment, allocation of maintenance imports and scarce materials.[3]

This statement gives, however, a false impression of the importance of the plans in determining the negative discretionary controls employed. As we mentioned, the plans do not contain any specific directives for the use of operational controls. The legislative acts authorizing the government to institute discretionary controls and the additional rules issued from time

---

[1] Appendix 8, Section 2.

[2] "The official is frequently compelled by law to make the businessman's decision for him on where he should locate his plant, for instance, or on what is a reasonable rate of return on his capital, or on how rapidly he should take on local managers, or even on whether he should be permitted to invest in a particular direction at all. These are obviously decisions the official is not well qualified to make. The decisions, therefore, are for the businessman, quite unpredictable; he does not know on what basis they will be made, all that he knows is that his own basis of decision, profit, is one the average official disclaims." (Maurice Zinkin, *Development for Free Asia*, Chatto & Windus, London, 1956, p. 12.)

[3] *Economic Weekly*, December 21, 1963, p. 2059.

to time by the government or the administrative authorities give only the vaguest and most general instructions as to their use and these are often confusing and occasionally contradictory.

It must be noted that all of the negative discretionary controls authorized are never utilized to the full. If they were, no part of the organized sector could be called "private" in any meaningful sense. The legislative structure referred to represents partly only the delimitation of a wide area within which the government has discretionary power to act, if the need arises. But import and exchange controls have to be applied and with great restrictiveness, and this necessitates the licensing of new industrial undertakings and the exercise of price and market controls. From time to time the scope of those controls that are actually employed is altered by governmental or administrative decision, as are the ways in which they are utilized. Often the need is stressed for greater efficiency and the speedier processing of applications. But as competent administrators are extremely scarce, and in the majority of cases a great number of considerations — often involving separate administrative authorities, as in the licensing of new undertakings — must be taken into account before a decision can be made, there is a narrow limit to what can be accomplished in this direction.[1]

In this section we have focussed our attention on India. In Pakistan, despite repeated assertions in the plans and by government spokesmen that administrative discretionary controls should be relaxed and more reliance placed on the price mechanism, the situation is broadly similar to that in India. Ceylon has been moving in the same direction and this trend has accelerated as the economic situation has become more strained under the influence of population increase among other factors. A continuation of this development will be all the more likely if Ceylon's industrial development proceeds more satisfactorily, thus increasing the need for imported goods. Burma and Indonesia have been pushed ever farther in the direction of administrative discretionary controls by the radical bent of their political development and the civil wars that have marked their recent history; at the same time civil strife has tended to decrease the effectiveness of all government controls. Malaya, the Philippines, and Thailand have relatively few negative discretionary controls, though their positive controls, for instance the granting of tax exemptions to new undertakings, are to an unusual extent a matter for political and administrative

[1] For an account of all the administrative hurdles an industrialist must pass when he wants to set up a new industrial plant, see a brilliant anonymous article, "Government Procedures and Industrial Development," *Economic Weekly*, Annual Number, February, 1964, pp. 265ff. In the article, it is also pointed out how the developed countries' practice of giving tied loans and grants complicates the administrative tangle and increases the paper work. Cf. also A. C. Chhatrapati, "Planning Through Red Tape," *Economic Weekly*, Special Number, July, 1961, pp. 1171ff.

discretion. It should be noted that in all of Southeast Asia, as in Ceylon, discretionary regulations, particularly those pertaining to internal and external trade, have been adopted partly because of the desire to discriminate in favor of majority groups as against ethnic minorities and foreigners.[1] This aim could not be pursued by means of non-discretionary controls.

6   *The Cumulative Tendency*

In a system of operational controls of the Indian type, the application of one set of controls has a tendency to make necessary the application of others. As we have already pointed out, the scarcity of foreign exchange and the resort to import and exchange controls make the licensing of new undertakings or additions to old ones a matter of urgent necessity.[2] To make fixed prices effective, allocation and rationing are needed; often more far-reaching intervention on the supply side is also required.[3] There is thus a self-perpetuating and expansionary tendency in every system of negative discretionary controls, especially when the economy is suffering from a shortage of domestic supplies and foreign exchange.

Of even greater and more general importance in increasing the need for compensatory negative controls is the system of positive controls applied. All economic planning in South Asia starts out from the idea that development should be pushed. More particularly, it is felt that private enterprise and, specifically, investment in production is in need of promotion and stimulation. This view is commonly held even in India, where the growth of the public sector is a prominent goal in planning.[4] We also find that state undertakings in basic industry and public utilities have the effect, usually intended, of improving conditions for private business.[5]

In addition, a great number of other policies have the object of encouraging investment in the private sector. A major consideration in fixing the prices of goods and services produced in the public sector has been that they should be kept low to encourage private enterprise. Rates of interest in the organized credit market are also held down, partly for this reason, and special credit institutions are created that often provide commercial establishments with credit at less than market rates. Various

---

[1] Chapter 17, Sections 1 and 11–14.

[2] Appendix 8, Section 2.

[3] The implication of an official determination to solve India's severe food crisis in 1964 is well developed in D. R. Gadgil, "Price Policy for Foodgrains," *Economic Weekly*, September, 1964, pp. 1561ff.

[4] As Burma, Indonesia, and Ceylon move in a more radical direction, they may increasingly come to regard private enterprise in the organized sector as undesirable; see Chapter 17, Sections 11–13.

[5] Chapter 17, Section 8.

tax exemptions are given to encourage new business ventures, and the laxity of tax administration works in the same direction. In addition to ordinary customs tariffs, import and exchange controls discriminate against foreign competition and thus permit industries working for the home market to charge higher prices. Moreover, when exchange rates are fixed so low that demand exceeds supply, every enterprise that gets an import license and foreign exchange receives a *de facto* subsidy.[1] The policies enumerated in this paragraph are discussed in Appendix 8.

The above is a summary statement of the various devices whereby costs are decreased and/or returns are increased for enterprises in the private sector. The "too low" cost price established for capital and foreign exchange also tends to spur public investment. In particular, the low rate of interest makes investments with a long gestation period — for instance, investments in large-scale irrigation — seem more profitable than they really are. Such investments have the consequence of decreasing the capital available for private investment and thus lowering the "ceiling" where they have to be curtailed by discretionary negative controls.

Even though the initial notion that there is too little private enterprise and that it needs to be encouraged is correct, it has actually been encouraged to the extent that it has had to be curbed by discretionary controls, as supplies, particularly of foreign exchange, are not inexhaustible but very limited, the more so since low rates of interest have spurred public investment in certain directions. To begin with, many of the positive operational controls, through which private enterprise is encouraged, cannot be permitted to be non-discretionary. Administrative discretion must be exercised to determine who shall be serviced by the public sector and who shall receive loans at special rates of interest from finance corporations and, of course, who shall be allotted foreign exchange. But in addition there will be an increased need for the whole paraphernalia of negative discretionary controls outlined in the previous section, and for a more restrictive use of them. In the process of promoting and curtailing business, the government and the administration become directly involved in all phases of private enterprise. In the language of a plan document:

The State can assist in the fulfilment of the programmes in this [private] sector, partly by *cutting out* undesirable investment — through capital issues control, control over exports and imports and licensing of industries; partly through tax adjustments and *concessions* and in part by way of selective financial *assistance* through the various corporations which have been set up for the purpose. The

[1] "It is common knowledge that each license fetches anything between 100 per cent to 500 per cent of its face-value if sold." (India, Government of, Ministry of Home Affairs, *Report of the Committee on Prevention of Corruption*, New Delhi, 1964, p. 18; cf. p. 251.)

progress of investment in the private sector has to be constantly watched even as that in the public sector and the necessary adjustments in policy have to be made from time to time.[1]

An odd situation is thus created. While everybody talks about the necessity of encouraging private enterprise, and while a great number of controls are instituted with this end in view, *most officials have to devote most of their time and energy to limiting or stopping enterprise.* This is like driving a car with the accelerator pushed to the floor but the brakes on. The need for a wide range of negative discretionary controls and for placing so many of the positive controls on a discretionary basis is to a large extent the result of applying excessive positive operational controls. With somewhat less encouragement, there would be less need for curtailment. The important point to stress is that encouraging private enterprise beyond practical limits makes necessary a gargantuan bureaucratic system of administrative discretionary controls to harness it.

At this point we have to recall the reasons spelled out in Section 4 why the South Asian countries are compelled to use discretionary controls over the organized private sector on a scale unmatched by the Western countries even in wartime. This analogy suggests that in some cases the government has reason to apply controls working in conflict with one another. However, the principle often stated in the plans, that the controls should be coordinated (Section 2), would imply that those cases should be held to a minimum. The abolition or relaxation of some positive controls would make it possible to reduce the role of administrative discretion and would render some negative controls less necessary. The widespread existence of conflicting controls has thus the implication that there is need of *more* controls and that a *larger* part of them must be of a discretionary type than would otherwise be necessary. This is particularly unfortunate from a development point of view, as one of the most serious bottlenecks in the South Asian countries is the lack of administrators of competence and integrity.[2]

---

[1] India, *Second Five Year Plan*, 1956, p. 93. Italics added.

[2] "The Government embarked upon rapid schemes of economic development. At the same time it increased the number and scope of [discretionary] controls. Along with an increase in the number and nature of the Government's functions there should have been correspondingly an increase in the efficiency of the machinery of administration. On the other hand, on account of the departure of a number of experienced civilian personnel and on account of the relatively inferior quality of the new personnel that were recruited, and also on account of the lack of understanding on the part of the administrative personnel of the significance of the new functions which devolved upon them, the degree of administrative competence was not equal to the new task imposed upon them. This, along with the prevalence of the atmosphere which was psychologically conducive to short and quick gains, led to an increase in the amount of corruption. In spite of the good intentions underlying the control mechanism, the working of controls was far from efficient." (C. N. Vakil and P. R. Brah-

The situation we have described, where controls regularly work in conflict with one another and have a tendency to breed additional controls, is undoubtedly in large part due to a lack of coordination, that is, to a deficiency in planning. As we pointed out in Section 1, the plans are not operational; they are worked out in aggregate, financial, and fiscal terms and are silent on the system of operational controls to be applied. The natural tendency of the planners and still more of the executors of the plans to set their sights high, but not provide enough non-discretionary restraints to achieve their objective leads to a system of controls full of internal conflicts with the result that it becomes necessary to increase the volume of controls and make them discretionary.[1]

7   The Play of Interests

It would be a great mistake to explain the multiplicity of discretionary controls in South Asia only by reference to the factors we have so far analyzed: the institutional and ideological legacy and the nature of economic activity in South Asian countries (Section 4), and the cumulative tendency inherent in existing systems of operational controls (Section 6). We must perfect our institutional model of the mechanism leading to an overgrowth of administrative discretionary controls by taking into account the play of interests involved. Directing our attention to the organized sector of the economy as before, we have next to note that one major effect of the combination of conflicting controls outlined in the last section must be *extraordinarily high profits for those private enterprises that succeed in running the gauntlet of discretionary positive and negative controls.* From a planning point of view, such profits are "unnecessarily" high, in the sense that they are not needed in order to call forth the desired volume of investment and enterprise; they are a consequence of the price system's not being conditioned to give entrepreneurs the induce-

mananda, *Planning for a Shortage Economy, The Indian Experiment,* Vora & Co., Bombay, 1952, pp. 22–23.)

The shortage of administrators is even more pronounced in most of the other South Asian countries.

[1] "By applying contemporary growth models and drawing up plans for development solely in terms of the broad economic aggregates, many of these countries have encountered serious difficulties. They have nearly always turned out to be overambitious plans which they were unable to implement. This has impeded the development of relevant pricing mechanisms for their environment — especially in the market for capital. The governments have therefore been compelled to use inefficient direct controls to an ever increasing extent; and this has led to greater and greater ineffective bureaucracy dealing with bigger and bigger monopolized industry." (J. M. Letiche, "The Relevance of Classical and Contemporary Theories of Growth to Economic Development," *American Economic Review,* Vol. XLIX, No. 2, May, 1959, pp. 491–492.)

ments that are "correct" from the standpoint of plan fulfillment.[1] These
"too high" profits are, moreover, not very effectively soaked up by taxation; even when marginal tax rates are very high, South Asian tax laws
contain convenient loopholes, and large-scale tax evasion is the rule.[2]

Extremely high profits would exist even though investment and enterprise were so severely limited by administrative discretionary controls
that demands for foreign exchange and other production necessities did
not exceed supplies — that is, if the development in any particular sub-
sector of the organized sector were brought into "balance." Any laxity in
the administration of the negative discretionary controls will generally
make it necessary to apply these controls more severely in the future,
though perhaps in other subsectors. In the foreign exchange sector such
a tightening of the reins will come about more or less automatically. If
permission is given for more investment and enterprise than can be serviced by domestic supplies, the result may be price increases and, perhaps,
a general inflation. This will then often be used as an argument for
stronger efforts to keep down cost prices for which the government is
responsible and maintain an "overvalued" currency. Such efforts will tend
to increase the pressure on supplies still further and to enhance the need
for negative discretionary controls, while at the same time *raising the
rates of profit still higher* for those enterprises that succeed in obtaining
the licenses and the foreign exchange.

To the officials entrusted with handling the levers of positive and negative discretionary controls, and the politicians behind them, a natural
rationalization of this state of affairs is that the country no longer adheres
to a *laissez-faire* policy, but believes in government intervention in order
to spur and direct development. The point is not well taken, however, as
a better coordinated system of controls — where positive controls did not
breed negative controls to the same extent and there was less need for
administrative discretionary intervention generally — would be more rational from the planning point of view. But the practices characterized

[1] "The private capitalist who makes out a case to start an industry and succeeds in
obtaining a licence for the same, is in effect obtaining a monopoly in the country with
reference to this product." (C. N. Vakil, "The Industrial Revolution in India,"
Walchand Memorial Lectures, Bhagwat Mouj Printing Bureau, Bombay, 1961, p. 9.)

[2] Appendix 8, Section 9.
The planners are not unaware of this situation. Asoka Mehta explains: "The private
sector really gets away with incentives and concessions. . . . For instance, while it
[government policy] accepts that producers and traders have made large incomes
from price rises and imports and that sale of foreign goods has brought large gains to
certain people, it has failed to mop up these gains. . . . If the States are reluctant to
touch the rural vested interests the Centre is not willing to hurt the vested interest in
industry and trade. . . . Agriculturists, specially in the top and middle echelons, who
have benefited considerably as the result of development, have been relatively under-
taxed for political and other non-economic reasons, while in some States industrial
magnates have been granted undeserved concessions in the form of lower power
tariffs, etc., at the State expense." (Asoka Mehta, "The Fourth Five-Year Plan,"
Link, August 15, 1965, p. 48.)

above are in accord with the authoritarian and paternalistic legacy referred to in Section 4. And certainly they give a wealth of power to officials and politicians, and power is always sweet; we shall have some further comments on this point below.

To businessmen who must find a path through the jungle of administrative discretionary controls,[1] the situation may seem more complicated. On the one hand, they are tempted to complain about the heavily bureaucratic regulation of private enterprise, and they are encouraged to take this line by Western business ideology. Outcries against government interference and regimentation will always be raised when businessmen meet in their associations, but no observer can fail to note that the complaints in this case are rather weak and halfhearted. There are several explanations for the muted character of business criticism. For one thing, private entrepreneurs have become so accustomed to the situation that they take it as much for granted as the climate, the observed caste rules, and many other conditions of life. Also, the officials in charge of the discretionary controls are so powerful that the individual private entrepreneur is seldom tempted to challenge the system; since he knows that he will repeatedly have to seek their favor, he is even loath to protest a particular decision.[2] But the main consideration is, of course, that the stakes are high enough to make all the inconveniences worthwhile. The extraordinarily high profits, which are a result of the South Asian pattern of conflicting operational controls, mean that all those who can hope to pass the controls have a powerful vested interest in the continuation of that pattern.[3] Our next question, therefore, is who can entertain such hopes.

[1] "Entrepreneurship consists very largely of working round the government regulatory mechanisms." (K. Mukerj, "Allocative Efficiency of Controls in Indian Planning," *Economic Weekly*, February, 1964, p. 261.)

[2] The present writer has often heard that argument advanced in private conversation with businessmen in India. In a letter to the writer, a young Indian businessman explained: "Rightly or wrongly, they fear that to do so [that is, come out in open criticism] would put them in a bad way for future applications for licences, or that their contracts with the government might run into difficulties or, more still, that revenge on them might be taken by having their income tax returns re-examined."

Said one member of a seminar in New Delhi: "Personally I would not wait for the industrialists — I know how timid and demoralised they are, how in a controlled economy they have to worry about their own permits and their own licences and how little many of them seem to care about the way of life in which they profess to believe." (M. R. Masani, in *Afro-Asian Attitudes*, Selections from Proceedings of Rhodes Seminar by Ayo Ogunsheye *et al.*, Congress for Cultural Freedom, New Delhi, 1961, p. 75.)

[3] A member of the Indian Planning Commission, T. N. Singh, observed: "There is a great deal of hue and cry for doing away with controls. . . . I can only say that I have hardly met an industrialist who really wants to do away with all controls. Our industries have up to now grown in a sheltered market because of controls. And most manufacturers seem to prefer sheltered markets." (T. N. Singh, "Strategy for a Self-Reliant Economy," *A.I.C.C. Economic Review*, August 15, 1963, pp. 62–63.)

We should first note that any system of administrative discretionary controls must tend to favor those who are already active in a field where permission of some sort is needed to continue or to expand production. Giving special consideration to interests already in the field represents one of the few "objective" criteria for administrative action that can be invoked. From the point of view of the government it also often stands out as the best way of maintaining production and, in case of a desired expansion, of making investment as productive as possible. Those who already are "in business" are also better informed and have established relations with the key officials. The tie between the government and existing firms is naturally strengthened when the administration seeks cooperation and advice from established enterprises or their trade associations.[1] Those established enterprises best equipped to give advice are mostly the big ones. Also, it is easier for an overburdened administration to deal with a few large concerns than with a number of small firms.

All this tends to restrict competition, favor monopoly and oligopoly, and pamper vested interests. True, the plans and the rules laid down for granting various authorizations, as well as the discussions centering around the plans and the controls, regularly give expression to the view that newcomers and small businessmen should be granted preference in order to counteract the tendency toward a concentration of power.[2] But it is common knowledge that the trend has been, and is, in the opposite

[1] "Through regulation and financial aid India is attempting to merge the goals, methods, and even the personnel of public and private enterprise. The new financial institutions bring together representatives of big business and the government. Business representatives are sitting with technical experts and government officials on development councils which have been set up to plan expansion in certain key industries. Prominent businessmen are also members of such tripartite boards as the Labor Panel to the Planning Commission and the Central Advisory Council of Industries designed to implement and to obtain acceptance for the mixed-economy type of planning. Outstanding business leaders along with civil servants serve on the boards of the new State Bank of India (formerly the Imperial Bank with twenty-two per cent of the nation's banking assets), the now nationalized Reserve Bank of India, the Industrial Finance Corporation, the National Industrial Development Corporation, and the Industrial Credit and Investment Corporation to which the government as well as private industry and foreign capital have contributed. Businessmen and civil servants are directors of the new nationalized industrial corporations such as National Air Services, Sindri Fertilizer, Hindustan Cables, government shipyards, steel mills, and so on. Private businessmen are a distinct minority on these boards but they are there." (H. B. Lamb, "Business Organizations and Leadership in India Today," in Richard L. Park and Irene Tinker, eds., *Leadership and Political Institutions in India*, Princeton University Press, Princeton, 1959, p. 265.)

[2] "The trend in a socialist economy is in favour of minimising the emergence of new large-scale enterprise in the private sector. . . . Preference will ordinarily be given to new entrants when considering proposals for the establishment or the expansion of an industry. It will also be necessary to examine the monopolistic practices that may have developed in the private sector." (All India Congress Committee, Planning

direction.[1] The Committee on Distribution of Income and Levels of Living, under the chairmanship of Professor P. C. Mahalanobis, recently issued a report[2] in which this trend was analyzed. The report finds evidence that "the working of the planned economy has contributed to [the] growth of big companies in India."[3] The latter are favored by the financial institutions that give long- and medium-term credits, often at bargain rates; they are in a better position to get permission for new capital issues and to borrow from the banking system; and they can better take advantage of tax concessions and rebates.[4] They have almost a monopoly on joint ventures with foreign firms that provide a flow of investment funds and technical know-how from abroad.[5] Also, established businesses and, in particular, large-scale enterprises control the businessmen's organizations and dominate "business opinion"; often they own newspapers.[6] Fi-

---

Sub-Committee, *Report of the Ooty Seminar* (May 30–June 5, 1959), New Delhi, September, 1959, p. 20.)

"Licensing policies should be so operated as to facilitate the entry of new firms, promote medium and small enterprises and exercise due vigilance in regard to the expansion of large businesses." (India, Government of, Ministry of Information and Broadcasting, *Problems in the Third Plan: A Critical Miscellany*, New Delhi, 1961, p. 11.)

Even more recently the same principle has been laid down. "The Dhebar Committee has now recommended that the Government should take a decision 'not to issue any licences for new projects to existing large industrial concentrations.'" (*Economic Weekly*, May 16, 1964, p. 831.) "Steps must also be taken to reduce concentration of economic power and resort to monopolistic practices, while simultaneously extending the field for new comers and fresh talent in all fields." (India, Government of, Planning Commission, *The Fourth Five Year Plan: A Draft Outline*, New Delhi, 1966, p. 29.)

[1] Chapter 16, Section 6.

"The plan helps the continuance of present trends of concentration of economic power and the continued increase in the riches of those classes and regions who are already comparatively the richer." (D. R. Gadgil, *Economic Policy and Development*, Gokhale Institute of Politics and Economics, Publication No. 30, Sangam Press Ltd., Poona, 1955, p. 140.)

[2] India, Government of, Planning Commission, *Report of the Committee on Distribution of Income and Levels of Living*, Part I, New Delhi, February, 1964, Chapter 4.

[3] *Ibid.*, p. 30; cf. p. 53.

[4] *Ibid.*, pp. 30ff.

[5] *Ibid.*, p. 50.

[6] "Economic power is exercised not only through control over production, investment, employment, purchases, sales and prices but also through control over mass media of communication. Of these, newspapers are the most important and constitute a powerful ancillary to sectoral and group interests. It is not, therefore, a matter for surprise that there is so much inter-linking between newspapers and big business in this country, with newspapers controlled to a substantial extent by selected industrial houses directly through ownership as well as indirectly through membership of their boards of directors. In addition, of course, there is the indirect control exercised through expenditure on advertisement which has been growing apace during the Plan periods. In a study of concentration of economic power in India, one must take into account this link between industry and newspapers which exists in our country to a much larger extent than is found in any of the other democratic countries in the world." (*Ibid.*, pp. 51–52.)

nally, although the report does not go into that wider problem, they are favored when it comes to obtaining all the numerous licenses and permits that are required for investment and enterprise in India. The report mentions the various measures taken "for encouraging the growth of new entrepreneurs and small industry," but concludes that they have not been effective in reversing the trend toward a concentration of economic power.[1]

In the present context this means that established businesses and, in particular, large-scale enterprises are greatly favored by the system of operational controls applied in India. A major explanation of this practice, which is in direct contradiction to stated policy goals, is, of course, that in the specific case a big firm that is already in business offers better prospects for development.[2] If we assume the control system as given, administrative officials may have perfectly valid reasons for giving preference to big firms and, more generally, to firms already in business. These reasons would work themselves out as forces determining the trend even were more scope given to non-discretionary controls, and they would influence the administrative decisions to be taken in a system with fewer discretionary controls. The point here is that the present system tends to give big established firms additional oligopoly power by placing obstacles in the way of the birth of new firms or the expansion of small firms. According to a United Nations analysis:

The small business units and the newcomers in enterprise are particularly hindered and discouraged by the multiplicity of controls, for their economic power is so weak that they can hardly deal effectively with the control authorities and cope with the delays and red tape involved. On the other hand, existing large enterprises enjoy a comfortable semimonopoly position under the protection of controls and make easy profits through access to the scarce factors made available to them cheaply. There is hardly any incentive for them to improve productivity or operating efficiency.[3]

It is apparent that big business concerns have good reason to support the prevailing system of conflicting and discretionary operational controls. The solid basis for that vested interest is the oligopoly power and the extremely high profits the system affords them. Important businessmen find it very much worth their while to break their way through the jungle of administrative discretionary controls, planted to keep the

---

[1] *Ibid.*, p. 54.

[2] "It must be pointed out, however, that the growth of big business as such, though indicating the presence of economic concentration 'does not necessarily mean the deliberate adoption of an anti-social policy. There is such a thing as the economy of scale which works in favour of big business, on purely economic grounds; and economic considerations are certainly relevant especially in the context of our scarce resources and the imperative need for our making the most economic utilisation of these resources." (*Ibid.*, p. 35.)

[3] United Nations, Economic Commission for Asia and the Far East, *Economic Bulletin for Asia and the Far East*, Vol. XII, No. 3, December, 1961, p. 7.

volume of investment and enterprise down to the level where demands can be satisfied by supplies. For whenever they succeed in getting a permit, a license, a loan, or an allocation of foreign exchange, they get a gift. As the system operates, they are the ones who have the best chances of getting the paper slips that are worth money. It is natural that they should become weary of the mesh of bureaucracy they have to cope with and that they occasionally complain. But, though it is never spelled out, they must be aware of the fact that the overgrowth of administrative discretionary controls is an effect of, and a condition for, the low cost-prices and the lack of competition that ensure them of very high profits.

That the officials and politicians who operate the controls also have a vested interest in their preservation and further proliferation is even more obvious. We have already pointed to the power they acquire by virtue of the fact that so many controls are discretionary.[1] This power is the greater as the controls are not integrated in the plans and the directives governing their use tend to be vague; application is a matter of administrative judgment. As we have also pointed out, there will often be good reasons to decide in favor of established, large-scale firms, so they can preserve a good conscience.

But in a setting where caste, family, economic and social status, and, more generally, "connections" traditionally mean so much, the risk of collusion is great — and it extends from the upper strata in the capitals down to the villagers. The result is often plain corruption. Indeed, the prevalence of discretionary controls invites dishonesty. A report of a United States Economic Survey Team states:

It should . . . be recognized that the operation of direct controls invests power in administrative officials to grant licenses, to overlook violations of regulations, and to do other favors for people who . . . find such special dispensations valuable and can afford to pay much for them. These controls therefore add greatly to the incentives for, and the rewards of graft and corruption. The problem of graft is the Siamese twin of direct controls.[2]

Quite apart from any moral considerations, corruption puts sand in the economic machinery; it is a force slowing down development.[3] The crucial

[1] The President of the International Finance Corporation, speaking to the 1961 meeting of the Board of Governors, testified in cautious words: "Even limited experience in dealing with officials in some countries reveals that they are largely influenced by what will give them the greatest personal power and rewards. The greater the control in government hands, the more personally lucrative can be the exercise of such control." (Address by Robert L. Garner at the 1961 meeting of the Board of Governors, *International Finance Corporation Bulletin,* Vienna, September 21, 1961, p. 10.)

[2] United States, Government of, Economic Survey Team to Indonesia, *Indonesia Perspective and Proposals for United States Economic Aid,* Yale University Southeast Asia Studies, New Haven, 1963, p. 110.

[3] Chapter 20, Section 5.

role of South Asia's system of discretionary controls in undermining morality should not be underestimated. When during and after the war Western countries had to rely on a plethora of discretionary controls, black markets proliferated and corruption spread in spite of their very superior administrative machinery and personnel. There is circular causation with cumulative effects in the sense that a corrupt body of administrators and politicians will have an interest in preserving and building up discretionary controls that give them the opportunity to enrich themselves.

The problem of corruption in South Asia will be taken up in the next chapter.

8 The Illiberal State

Many of the countries in South Asia are eager to be regarded as "socialist." In Chapter 17 (Sections 3 and 13) we explained that this designation is not very accurate if it implies the existence of a large number of state undertakings. Many Western and South Asian observers find that these countries' reliance on operational controls of an administrative discretionary type imposes a "socialist" pattern on the economy. This must likewise be considered a misnomer for a system of policies that broadly tends to give oligopoly power and very high profits to established big business. But terminology apart, there is no doubt that the type of operational controls applied in South Asian countries constitutes one of the most important differences between them and the developed Western countries, both as the latter are now and as they were at an earlier stage of industrialization. As one analyst says: "The combination of these measures [of discretionary operational controls] varies from country to country, but they proliferate in most underdeveloped areas to an extent unknown in early nineteenth-century development."[1]

In the West, the liberal interlude between the Mercantilist era and the modern democratic welfare state left a legacy, which in a sense can be characterized as the quest for a rule of law rather than of persons, and that ideological heritage has taken deep root in the cultural ethos of the Western world. In that sense the welfare state is still "liberal"; the volume of state intervention has been rising, but apart from wartime emergencies it has generally not been of the discretionary type. Adjustment of the price mechanism has been the preferred method of dealing with economic problems. Thus when agriculture has needed assistance, the government has improved the incomes of farmers, or lowered their costs of production by means of a change in the relevant prices or by some other equally non-discretionary measure. Private or public charity and individualized poor

---

[1] Edward S. Mason, *Economic Planning in Underdeveloped Areas: Government and Business*, Fordham University Press, New York, 1958, p. 10.

law assistance, inherited from the pre-liberal era, have been transformed into a system wherein the needy are legally entitled to receive social insurance payments according to fixed standards valid for the whole national community. The goal of social security legislation was not only to provide income for individuals and families when their earnings fell off; equally important was the substitution of general rules for arbitrary, discretionary paternalism. In the same way, bargaining among the organizations within the institutional infrastructure shows a tendency to become nation-wide and to result in settlements regulating various matters in a manner that is equal for all.

Through a long political process, the price mechanism in the Western world has increasingly become the servant of the policy inclinations of the people, as these are expressed through democratic institutions. And the conditions under which that mechanism operates are continually changed to fit those inclinations better in a changing world. In this process the state has come to exert an ever greater influence on the course of events — a far greater one than in the South Asian countries, which are all "functioning anarchies," to use a term Galbraith has coined for India, one of the more firmly ruled countries in the region. But this influence is brought to bear by means of price policies and other non-discretionary controls. When Western governments in time of war or other emergency situations have had to resort to administrative discretionary controls on a large scale, this has usually been regarded as an unfortunate development, to be reversed as rapidly as possible. The total volume of state intervention has been increasing, but not the volume of discretionary controls.[1]

The South Asian system of controls over private enterprise shows, of course, still less similarity with the policies of Communist countries, which do not have a private sector of any importance to deal with. Again we face the fact that the South Asian countries are a third world of planning.

The analysis in this chapter has been based on the value premise that operational controls should to the maximum extent possible be of a non-discretionary type. This value premise is derived from the modernization ideals;[2] it represents one of the points where, in their own interest, the South Asian countries should try to be more like the Western countries — if they do not opt instead for nationalizing the private sector and becoming like the Communist countries. It must be pointed out, however, that a change in this direction can hardly be expected. The South Asian coun-

[1] The writer expects that as the institutional infrastructure grows and becomes more effective, the state as such will be in a position to actually decrease its controls and particularly those controls that still are of a discretionary type; see Gunnar Myrdal, *Beyond the Welfare State*, Yale University Press, New Haven, 1960, pp. 92ff. Discretionary controls over industry and economic life generally are less prevalent in a country like Sweden than in the United States.

[2] Chapter 2, Sections 3 and 4.

tries' reliance on discretionary controls is in part firmly rooted in necessity. In agriculture and crafts the fragmentation or even absence of markets and the lack of, or distortion of, response to price incentives make non-discretionary controls relatively ineffective (Section 3 above). The same is true to some extent even of the organized sector of the economy (Section 4). Even less than the Western economies in the emergency conditions of war can the low-elasticity economies of South Asia be regulated exclusively by non-discretionary means.

Nevertheless, it should not be necessary to have so many discretionary controls. If the operational controls were better planned and coordinated there would be greater scope for non-discretionary controls and, in particular, it would be possible to avoid those controls that are the result of indefensible conflicts of policy (Section 6). Also, much of what the state is doing to make people more rational and mobile will tend to make non-discretionary controls more effective.

There are, however, strong forces working to preserve and strengthen the structure of discretionary controls. One such force is the ideological and attitudinal legacy of authoritarianism and paternalism (Section 4). Another force working in the same direction is the vested interest of administrators, politicians, and big businessmen (Section 7). Everything considered, it is difficult to be very optimistic about the future.

The analysis in this chapter of the institutional mechanism that explains the type of operational controls adhered to in South Asia has had to be of a very general nature. In no other major field of South Asian economic policy is there such a lack not only of scientific analysis but of systematic and specific knowledge of the empirical facts. The operational controls are not planned, they are clearly not coordinated, and the manner of their application is usually not disclosed in any detail. What we have tried to do is to put together a "theory" that will provide a logically coordinated system of questions for further research.

See the complete work for Chapter 20.

A NOTE ON "ACCOUNTING PRICES" AND THE ROLE OF THE PRICE MECHANISM IN PLANNING FOR DEVELOPMENT

1 *Introduction*

Albert O. Hirschman pinpointed a major difference of opinion in regard to economic policies in the underdeveloped countries when he observed that "The economic profession comes very close to having its own two-party system: one party extols, the other criticizes the price system."[1] Unfortunately, the dispute rests on confused notions, and this confusion is apparent in the literature and in the plans insofar as they touch on the problem.[2] The mix-up goes back to the very basis of economic thinking; given the naïveté in regard to the problems of the philosophy of knowledge prevailing in the profession, which we referred to in the Prologue, most economists are probably not even aware of their lack of clarity.

Two quite different propositions are confounded:
  (1) that *prices* — either those prevailing now, or expected in the future, or hypothetical prices arrived at by assuming equilibrium between demand and supply (see below, Section 3) — are "correct" and thus provide *objective criteria* for planning; and
  (2) that *price policies* — that is, measures designed to maintain prices as they are or to change them in a desired way — can be *instrumental* in planning.

The first proposition implies that the price system itself contains *norms*, which determine *rational ends* not only for individuals (according to the usual assumptions employed for economic analysis in theoretical terms, prices always

---

[1] Albert O. Hirschman, "Primary Production and Substitutes: Should Technological Progress Be Policed," *Kyklos*, Vol. XII, Fasc. 3, 1959, p. 354.

[2] Chapter 19, Section 2.

provide such guidance, by definition as it were; see Section 2 below) but also for the community of individuals, that is, the state. The norms are *in principle* those implicit in the doctrine of interest harmony and *laissez faire*. When current prices are recognized to be incorrect, in the sense that under their influence the interests of the individual and the state do not converge, this is thought to be a consequence of market imperfections (the problems of external economies and diseconomies are usually forgotten). The state must then adopt policies aimed at realizing free and perfect markets.

Since the time of John Stuart Mill, a general reservation relating to the distribution of income and wealth has commonly been added. However, this reservation is often forgotten as the analysis proceeds, and the same is true of the reservation about market imperfections. This first proposition then tends to be in practice a defense of the more vulgar incarnation of *laissez faire*, that is, non-interference with price and market systems as they currently exist even though they have not been reconstructed to fit the abstract ideal implicit in the doctrine.

The second proposition sees in prices and in the price system, not norms and ends, but *means* for state policy. The criteria for their utilization must be established in some other way; they are not implicit in the price system itself. This does not exclude the possibility that some current prices, or the prices that would come into being in a freer and more perfect market, may be considered correct if they are the best means for the state policy actually pursued. But this is not self-evident. It must result from weighing the consequences of those prices and other prices in terms of how well they support the government's plans for development.

On logical grounds the first proposition can be proved categorically false.[1] Prices, like all other elements on the economic scene, are current facts, or expected future facts, or hypothetical facts that would occur on certain abstract assumptions; they do not themselves contain any norms for planning policies. The opposite opinion is deeply rooted in the old metaphysical harmony doctrine. Its reflection in modern times serves, as it always has, as a rationalization for a political bias toward non-intervention; in other words, it provides an "objective" foundation for that bias, so that it need not be formulated as an explicit valuation. The very idea of planning for development is contrary to the proposition that prices have normative significance. Economic planning is political programming and its criteria must be certain valuations regarding means and ends emerging from the political process.[2]

It would, on logical grounds, be impossible to find in the price system objective criteria for planning even if, as an attitudinal and institutional fact, price incentives were effective — that is, if all the participants in economic life were guided in their activities by an endeavor to minimize costs and maximize net returns — and if there were markets and those markets were perfect. The fact that in large sections of the South Asian economy price incentives are very far from effective and markets are largely nonexistent or very imperfect should

[1] Gunnar Myrdal, *The Political Element in the Development of Economic Theory*, Routledge & Kegan Paul Ltd., London, 1953; and *Value in Social Theory*, Harper, New York, 1959.

[2] Appendix 2, Parts III and IV.

make it even more impossible to think of the price system as providing a norm for planning.

The second proposition, on the other hand, is both sensible and highly relevant to the discussion of economic planning in South Asia. In Chapter 19 we reached the conclusion that the governments in the South Asian countries would be wise to make more and better use of the price and market mechanism in their planning. Even if under existing conditions they cannot reach plan fulfillment merely by employing price policies and other automatically functioning operational controls, they should use these controls as much as possible, in order to minimize the need for administrative discretionary controls and in order to make such controls, when applied, less inimical to the goals of planning, less expensive in terms of administrative personnel, and less conducive to corrupt practices. This argument is founded, not on any assumed sanctity of the price system, but on an analysis of the practical effects of following alternative policy lines.

2   The Significance of Prices for Individual Planning

Markets do exist in certain sections of the South Asian economy, though they are often isolated from other markets and internally compartmentalized and imperfect. In these sections, the entrepreneurs act with the motive of minimizing costs and maximizing net returns, although other considerations may carry more weight than is customary in the developed Western countries. Prices thus are significant in determining the behavior of the individual company, and hence the development of the national economy.

Whether the individual entrepreneur will choose to remain in an old line of trade and production; whether he will want to contract or expand his activities in this line; whether instead, or at the same time, he will move into a new line; what products or services, and in what proportions, he will plan to place on the market; how he will combine different factors of production, and what techniques he will apply — the decision in every case will be based on the businessman's calculations of costs and returns in terms of the present and anticipated prices of products and services and factors of production in the markets where he operates.

When public investments are made, the normal procedure in all South Asian countries is to turn over the construction work to private contractors. In their own interest, these contractors must similarly draw up their plans on the basis of actual and expected prices. Even state entrepreneurial activities, which constitute the public sector, are assumed to be managed as "economically" as possible. In practice this means that efforts are made to minimize the costs of providing the required goods and services by making rational calculations based on prevailing and expected factor and material prices.[1]

---

[1] Often the costs, assumed to be minimized in this way, are given normative importance in assessing the returns that are considered "normal" and "correct" for public enterprises. These public businesses are frequently required to fix the prices at which they sell their products and services at the cost, or cost-plus-normal-profit, level even when they are in a position to charge more. This, however, is not a valid theoretical inference; such enterprises could be run "economically" on the cost side regardless of the prices they charge; see Appendix 8, Section 10.

These remarks refer to the modernized sectors of the economy. But insofar as there are markets, though local, compartmentalized, and imperfect, and some degree of monetization, prices are important in the traditional sectors, too, particularly when it comes to directing the production of different goods. In all planning for development, efforts are made to increase the mobility of labor and capital, widen the monetized market economy, and rationalize attitudes toward work so that price incentives will have more influence on people's behavior.

For the sake of simplicity, we shall focus our attention on the entrepreneurs in the modernized sectors. When stressing the significance of prices in determining their behavior, and thus the actual development of the national economy, we must add certain qualifications. What happens in the organized sectors depends in various ways on the whole attitudinal and institutional situation. First, it must be remembered that factor costs there — especially wages and interest rates — diverge substantially from prices in the rest of the economy. Costs in the organized sectors are determined very largely by the government, often by administrative discretionary measures. Also, in other respects, the behavior of individual entrepreneurs is restrained and directed by operational controls of the kind usually referred to as "direct" because they do not operate via induced changes in prices. It is only within the limitations set by these controls that prices become significant for entrepreneurial behavior.

To South Asian governments, the general justification for applying administrative controls of the discretionary type, such as licensing, must be that market prices are not "correct" — that is to say they do not by themselves spur entrepreneurs to act in accordance with the goals and targets of the plan. No doubt, conditions in the underdeveloped countries in South Asia are such that nondiscriminatory price policies alone — including not only induced changes in prices but also generally applied subsidies of various sorts, excise taxes, customs duties, etc. — would not be sufficient to steer the national economy, or even the organized sectors of it, in a way that would assure the desired pattern of development. Some other controls will normally be necessary, though for various practical reasons it would certainly be advisable to keep them to a minimum and make the greatest possible use of the price mechanism, adjusted as necessary to make certain that entrepreneurial behavior will conform to the plan.

3 "Accounting Prices"

It is against this background that we must judge the proposals made in the literature that the planners work with what are called "accounting prices" or "shadow prices."[1] The general idea behind these proposals is that actual prices are inappropriate and that corrected prices should be used in planning. Unfortunately, these concepts have been caught up in the general confusion referred to in Section 1 above.

Jan Tinbergen, the most prominent representative of this way of thinking,

---

[1] Not to be confused with the use of the term "shadow prices" in linear programming; see, for instance, Robert Dorfman, Paul A. Samuelson, and Robert M. Solow, *Linear Programming and Economic Analysis*, McGraw-Hill, New York, 1958.

defines accounting prices as those that correspond to *"intrinsic values."*[1] "Intrinsic value" is in turn defined as the price that would equate the supply and demand for a particular factor or good, if full *"equilibrium"* prevailed. Equilibrium presupposes a perfect *national* market for that factor or good. Indeed, though Tinbergen does not say so, it is clear from the context of his remarks that he must assume equilibrium in perfect national markets for *all* factors and goods; otherwise it is difficult to see how the price of one factor or good could come to correspond to its "intrinsic value." In other words, since an equilibrium price in one sector depends on equilibrium prices in other sectors, the determination of the "intrinsic value" of a factor or good implies knowledge of the *full equilibrium matrix for the entire national economy.* This knowledge has to be acquired in countries that according to Tinbergen are characterized by "fundamental disequilibria." The proposed solution is an all-or-nothing solution and is no help to piecemeal planning.

Leaving aside all questions pertaining to the practical application of this model — to which we shall return in the last section — and keeping the discussion entirely on the level of principles, the concept is *indeterminate.* The prices that would prevail under the assumed relationship of demand to supply depend on the existing social institutions. Without a further definition of those institutions — as they actually are and as they would have to change in order to be compatible with full equilibrium in all markets — accounting prices are not ascertainable. Specifically, it is part of the institutional situation in all the South Asian countries that the governing authorities are now pursuing policies that affect a wide range of economic activities. Thus the accounting prices for building materials will differ according to whether or not private building is restricted. Or, to take a broader example, the accounting prices for land will depend on government policies with regard to land reform and the opening up of new land for cultivation; indeed, on agricultural policy in general. But since this policy helps to determine accounting prices, to argue that these prices can guide policy is *circular reasoning.*

The orthodox *laissez-faire* solution to that logical difficulty would be to assume a free market economy (see Section 1) when ascertaining accounting prices. Planning would then be directed exclusively toward the establishment of "intrinsic values" in the specific sense of the prices that would prevail in a perfect equilibrium matrix *in the absence of all other policies.* But this is not what Tinbergen has in mind. He is not arguing for *laissez faire* but is trying to guide planning of a type that sets up specific objectives. Even apart from the contradiction involved in guiding policy by means of "intrinsic values" that themselves depend on policy, the attempt to abstract from the institutional framework when dealing with a national economy is not logically defensible — particularly when the realization of the equilibrium conditions would require sweeping changes in that framework, which is itself the main reason why the countries concerned suffer from "fundamental disequilibria." So there is no escape from the indeterminateness — or, in regard to policies, the circularity — pointed out above.

Then comes the question: equilibrium *at what time?* One possibility might

[1] *The Design of Development,* Johns Hopkins Press, Baltimore, 1958, pp. 39ff. *et passim.*

seem to be to define the concept as a static and timeless one, relating to *present* scarcities. But this would make it meaningless. For it is obvious that no such equation between demand and supply could conceivably come about except as the end result of a development in time. Tinbergen evidently conceives his "intrinsic values" as the result of a *development in time*, though he does not specify the development and the time period other than by assuming that "the investment patterns under discussion were actually carried out."[1] Now, however, it is clear that the developments in this time period will include many policy measures besides those directed toward the "realization of the (planned) investment pattern." In addition there will be a number of changes that are not planned and cannot be forecast. A development *in abstracto* — comprising merely the realization of a given investment pattern and the attainment of equilibrium between demand and supply — is unthinkable. It must be assumed that the equilibrium price will vary, depending on the character of this development and its outcome; the concept is thus *indeterminate* for this reason as well as for those previously outlined.

Moreover, there is no reason to believe that the equalization of supply and demand will take place within the time period required for the realization of the present investment pattern; indeed, it is not certain that there will be any development along the former line while the latter development takes place. It is therefore probably correct to assume that Tinbergen made the concession to time and dynamics in time merely to account for the results of the presently planned investments on relative scarcities in the calculation of the "intrinsic values." If this is an accurate assumption, Tinbergen's concept is *basically static and timeless*, relating to present scarcities, plus the anticipated effects of presently planned investments. This construct, like all so-called "static comparisons,"[2] is meaningless, as we pointed out in the last paragraph.

Apart from these logical defects, all of which are decisive, and assuming that equilibrium prices could be ascertained, the question remains why they should represent "intrinsic values," which, unlike actual prices, are *correct* and provide *objective criteria for planning*. Tinbergen and the other writers of this school *do not even raise this question;* they take a positive answer for granted — which shows that their thinking is under the spell of the time-honored proposition that prices have normative significance, with the equally time-honored reservation that perfect competition exists (Section 1 above).

Tinbergen is frank to admit that there are *practical difficulties* in the way of ascertaining "intrinsic values" and applying them to countries with such "fundamental disequilibria" as exist in South Asia.[3] That the whole conception is

---

[1] *Ibid.*, p. 39.

"The realization of the investment pattern will itself influence these values [the "intrinsic values"], but only after some time, since investment processes are essentially time-consuming."

[2] In relation to the concept "underemployment," this is demonstrated in Appendix 6, Section 8, and referred to in several contexts; in relation to population optimism, it is demonstrated in Appendix 7, Section 1.

[3] *The Design of Development*, pp. 39 ff. *et passim*.

"It may be repeated that even if it is not possible to make any sensible estimate of an accounting price, it may be useful to make a set of alternative calculations using plain guesses for the accounting prices." (*Ibid.*, p. 86.)

wildly *unrealistic* and gives no theoretical basis for practical conclusions is, however, related to the definition itself. This is why a logical criticism is pertinent.

4 "Correct Prices" in Terms of Planning

In our discussion of operational controls in South Asian countries in Chapter 19 we reach the conclusion that it would contribute to successful planning in the region if the governments concerned did not resort to administrative discretionary controls to the extent that they do, but relied more on price policies and other automatically functioning controls. Our reasons for this conclusion are not based on metaphysical notions like that of "intrinsic value." They are instead founded on a consideration of the relative merits of the two types of policy with respect to administrative overhead, effectiveness, possible corruption, and the contribution made to the efficiency of both state planning and the conduct of private and public enterprise. Although we point out that under prevailing conditions in South Asia exclusive reliance cannot be placed on automatic controls, we believe that it is wholesome to try to maintain prices at the "correct" level with fewer administrative discretionary controls.

In defining "correct" or, rather, "planned" prices, we do not abstract from actual attitudinal and institutional conditions, nor from operational controls other than those specific ones that may be rendered unnecessary, more effective, and less costly by altering prices. Nor is the concept thought of in timeless and static terms; it is related to a definite — usually short — future period, the planning period. We assume that the planned prices may be different at a later stage of development; indeed, they might be thought of as changing during the planning period.

Our definition of planned prices is simple: they are those *prices that, under all existing conditions including the full range of government policies, would give entrepreneurs and, more generally, producers, traders, consumers, and savers incentives to act according to a particular development plan.* By relating the concept of correct prices to an actual plan in the given situation of a particular country at a particular time, we have stripped it down to its realistic and concrete kernel, and freed it from metaphysics. Our correct prices have no direct connection with any vision of over-all "equilibrium." If, in the actual development, certain planned prices prove not to provide the correct inducement for plan fulfillment, these prices will have to be further adjusted in the light of experience.

Actually, of course, none of the countries of South Asia has so intimate a knowledge of the mutual responses between prices, demand, and supply as to enable it to ascertain what specific prices and price movements would be most appropriate for plan fulfillment. But all these countries decide on and attempt to implement a plethora of economic policies, which they try to see as part of a development plan. They all have a vision of development goals. Indeed, they fix guidelines that indicate how entrepreneurs, workers, consumers, savers, and so on should or should not act if their goals are to be attained. Basic to the targets of the plans are forecasts and projections, which must be built on some notion of how people are influenced in their economic behavior by, among other things, prices. Even if no formal plan is drawn up, the same considerations will apply as soon as a country's various policies are conceived of as parts of a whole. There must be a coordination of policy measures that will ensure that prices will provide the right inducements and checks; otherwise there is an inner contradiction in the plan and its fulfillment cannot be expected.

5   The Practical Application of "Accounting Prices"

In the above discussion of the prices that in a given setting are correct from the viewpoint of plan fulfillment, it is assumed that these planned prices will be established through price policies (including other automatically functioning controls, like non-discriminatory subsidies or taxes). In the discussion of accounting prices, there is considerable ambivalence on this point.

"Accounting prices" are often thought of as merely a device for politicians and economists when they work out their plans; it is not necessarily assumed that these prices will be established in the market. In a mixed economy, however, it can hardly be expected that private entrepreneurs will make their calculations without reference to actual prices – though they may be induced by discretionary controls to act in a way different from what these calculations would indicate. It must be extremely difficult to get even public enterprises to base their calculations on hypothetical prices, rather than on the prices that actually determine their costs and returns. We find, therefore, that the proponents of accounting prices often urge that they be translated into actual prices through price policies.[1]

But this recommendation is not generally followed out. It is perhaps natural that the whole matter should be left undecided and vague, since accounting prices are utterly unreal and otherworldly in concept, particularly in underdeveloped countries like those in South Asia and as it is recognized that they cannot be definitely ascertained. In regard to labor, it is felt that an attempt to bring wages down to the level of their "intrinsic" value would cause unbearable hardship and endanger social peace.[2] The underlying thought is often the mistaken notion that the marginal productivity of labor is zero.[3] But even if social reasons preclude establishing accounting wages in the labor market, they should not prevent the raising of interest rates in the organized capital market

---

[1] "Private investors, however, can and will do so [behave as the accounting prices would require them to] only if accounting prices can be made a reality to them. This may be done by certain types of subsidy and certain types of taxing, tending to stimulate the use of abundant, and to discourage use of scarce, factors." (*Ibid.*, p. 41.)

"Loans to be made by the government to either lower authorities, or government enterprises, or even private enterprises, might be made at a rate higher than the moderate rates at which the government itself borrows, on the principle that the accounting price of capital justifies such a differential." (*Ibid.*, p. 54.)

[2] "Making wages equal to their intrinsic value would mean imposing on the workers a level substantially lower than presently prevails and having the revolution right now." (*Ibid.*, p. 40.)

[3] "It will be possible to take this price [the accounting price of unskilled labor] as equal to zero in a good number of cases." (*Ibid.*, p. 86.)

For a criticism of this view, see Chapter 21, Section 14; Appendix 6, Sections 6–7; and Chapter 26, Section 3 *et passim.*

or rates of foreign exchange to their accounting values. The more fundamental reason why the concept of accounting prices is not applied in practice is the one developed in Section 3: the whole idea that an underdeveloped national economy of the South Asian type, with recognized "fundamental disequilibria," can be projected in an abstract and timeless way to an imagined situation — unchanged except for the realization of a now planned investment pattern — of perfect and general equilibrium[1] is so utterly unrealistic as to have no value either for the explanation of facts or the determination of policies.

It cannot be denied that speculation in terms of accounting prices or shadow prices relates to real and important problems raised by the attempts to plan for development in the underdeveloped countries in South Asia. Most certainly there is, for instance, a vast underutilization of the labor force in agriculture and elsewhere in the economies of the region; similarly, in the organized sector there is a greater scarcity of capital, and particularly foreign exchange, than is indicated by their prices. We devote many chapters of this book to establishing and analyzing these facts and to drawing the policy inferences that follow from them and from our explicitly stated value premises. These facts and policy inferences should be taken into account when deciding on institutional reforms and price policies and other operational controls. Planning should reflect the political choices of the planners and, behind them, the government; it should be founded on as much factual knowledge as is attainable, including that pertaining to the responses of people to prices and price changes.

The abstract and metaphysical concept of accounting prices cannot help to solve the theoretical and practical problems facing South Asian planners. It stands out as a typical example of the pseudo-knowledge, given a learned and occasionally mathematical form, that unfortunately has formed a major part of the contribution of Western economics to the important tasks of ascertaining the facts in underdeveloped countries and creating a framework for policies designed to engender and direct development.

---

[1] "They [accounting prices] are the prices at which supply is just sufficient to satisfy demand; they represent the value of the marginal product to be obtained with their aid, since projects showing no surplus above the cost, at accounting prices, of the factors used, will be on the margin between acceptance and rejection." (*Ibid.*, p. 40.)

A NOTE ON POSITIVE

OPERATIONAL CONTROLS

This appendix deals with the major positive operational controls over the private organized sectors of the South Asian economies:[1] cheap rates of foreign exchange and protection from foreign competition by import restrictions, low rates of interest, low prices for services and goods from the public sector, and low effective taxation of profits. A general proposition basic to our analysis, which either is self-evident or will be shown to be true, is that in South Asia rates of foreign exchange, rates of interest, prices of services and goods from the public sector, and rates of taxation can be determined by government decree and can be kept low — if sufficiently strong negative controls are applied. A guiding principle, founded on our value premises[2] — particularly those of rationality and planning — is that all operational controls, positive and negative, discretionary and non-discretionary, should be viewed as a system, where one control necessitates, or can replace, other controls; together, all the operational controls have as their purpose to maintain a situation where, so far as possible, demands are satisfied by supplies, while the economy is progressing according to plan. In dealing with the problem of coordination, which in this field as in others is the essence of planning, we assume as a derived value premise that discretionary controls should be kept to a minimum.[3]

In Chapter 19 (Section 6), we developed the thought that the governments in South Asia, by managing their positive controls in such a way as to keep costs "too" low and returns "too" high, create a situation where they have to employ "too many" and "too restrictive" negative controls and give both positive and negative controls "too much" of a discretionary character in order to restrict demands to the level of supplies. Because profits in the sphere of enterprise and investments then became "unnecessarily high," there are strong vested interests behind this procedure.[4] The policy of *simultaneously* stimulating

---

[1] For a definition of operational controls of various types, see Chapter 19, Section 1.

[2] Chapter 2, Sections 3 and 4.

[3] Chapter 2, Section 4; Chapter 19, Section 1.

[4] Chapter 19, Section 7.

and curtailing business has tended to escape the criticism it deserves because the individual controls have not ordinarily been viewed as constituting a system or requiring coordination for maximum effectiveness with a minimum of discretionary intervention. Operational controls and, in particular, the problem of their coordination have been neglected in the plans as well as in the discussion they provoke, and this is why the plans are not operational.[1]

The treatment of positive controls in this appendix will be schematic. It will be narrowly focussed on their tendency to increase the need for negative controls and to give both positive and negative controls a discretionary character. We shall begin with an analysis of the problems raised by the scarcity of foreign exchange that in a sense represents the "master bottleneck."[2] We shall concentrate on India and Pakistan.

I

The Foreign Exchange Front

1   *Reasons For or Against Devaluation*

Import controls are, of course, primarily negative controls.[3] India and Pakistan have been for many years in a position where, in spite of an increasing volume of grants and loans from developed countries, they have had to prevent or severely limit all imports except essential consumer goods and development goods. In regard to food they have become increasingly dependent on imports, though up to now most of these have not been paid for on commercial terms but financed under the United States P.L. 480 program. Foreign exchange is so tight that they have from time to time been compelled to curtail even development imports, in particular imports of raw materials, spare parts, and other items necessary for the full utilization of plants.[4]

It is natural to view India's and Pakistan's need for very tight import controls as evidence that their national currencies are considerably "overvalued." A practical corollary is often the policy advice that they should depreciate their currencies to a rate where there would be equilibrium between the demand and supply of foreign exchange without import controls. Devaluation is thus seen as a policy substitute for restricting imports by "artificial" means. We shall criticize this view below; it is another example of the careless application of

---

[1] Chapter 19, Sections 1 and 2; Appendix 4, Section 2.

[2] Chapter 19, Section 6.

[3] Chapter 19, Section 1; and Section 2 below.

[4] Burma and Indonesia are, of course, in a similar situation and Ceylon has been rapidly moving toward it. The Philippines also has severe exchange difficulties. Thailand and, in particular, Malaya — like Ceylon a little more than a decade ago — are for the time being in a much less tight situation in regard to foreign exchange. Thailand's import restrictions have been negligible, while Malaya has imposed limited restrictions on account of being a member of the sterling area, not because it lacked exchange.

economic concepts and models that may be fairly realistic in Western countries[1] but are not descriptive of conditions in South Asia, which leads to false conclusions.

Some of the arguments propounded against devaluation are not valid. Although they cannot provide a justification for present policies, they have been among the reasons given for adherence to them or have at least served as rationalizations for national policy interests and various vested interests (see below). One such irrational view, often stated in official as well as non-official publications in South Asia, is the thought that maintaining a low value on foreign exchange can promote economic development by holding down the cost of development goods.[2] But from a national planning standpoint, these goods are not cheaper. For similar reasons the common argument that devaluation would increase the burden of foreign debt is mistaken. The same criticism holds true of the argument that maintaining the value of the national currency holds down the price of food, which is a major item in consumer budgets. Food costs for the consumers, but not for the national economy, could, of course, be kept down equally well by a straight subsidy, as Ceylon's experience illustrates.

Another "reason" for resisting devaluation that is hardly rational in the ordinary case refers to the violent changes that occur annually in the availability and need for foreign exchange.[3] The demand for many of South Asia's exports is not responsive to price changes,[4] but fluctuates widely in the short run with even minor changes in economic activity in the developed countries. The supply may also fluctuate but it is not elastic with respect to prices in the short run.[5] Agricultural yields are dependent on the vagaries of the monsoons; they

[1] Even in the Western countries the approach signified by reference to the concepts "overvaluation" and "undervaluation" is often not very realistic. However, that is not part of our problem in this study.

[2] Two examples may be cited. One is chosen from Pakistan's First Five Year Plan: "The process of industrialisation was encouraged by the adoption of appropriate measures and policies in the commercial field. The rupee was not devalued when the sterling and a number of other currencies were devalued in September 1949. This held down the rupee costs of industrial machinery." (Pakistan, Government of, National Planning Board, *The First Five Year Plan 1955–60*, Karachi, December, 1957, p. 179.)

The same view was taken by the secretariat of ECAFE, when, among other things, it mentioned "the need to keep the cost of imported development goods low" as constituting "a strong argument for the maintenance of an overvalued currency." (United Nations, ECAFE, *Economic Bulletin for Asia and the Far East*, November, 1956, p. 57.)

[3] Some years ago, when India and Pakistan still harbored memories of the considerable reserves of foreign exchange they had after the Second World War, these violent changes gave support to the idea that their exchange difficulties were only temporary.

[4] This is especially true since, with the exception of rice in Burma and Thailand and cotton textiles in India and Pakistan, there is virtually no internal consumption of the main export products in this category. See Appendix 15.

[5] For a closer examination of the export and import situation hinted at here and in the following paragraphs, see Chapter 13.

vary from year to year, affecting import needs as well as exportable surpluses.

It is apparent that short-run exigencies cannot be met satisfactorily by frequent alterations in the exchange rate; also, floating exchange rates would conflict with the requirement of stability in international business relations and undermine confidence in the national currency (see below). But this cannot be deemed an argument against establishing a lower value for the currency if the expectation is that that rate would be maintained for a reasonable length of time.

The relative price inelasticity of the supply of export goods even in the longer run constitutes, however, a valid reason why devaluation would not be much of a remedy for a South Asian country's exchange difficulties. The supply of the region's traditional exports is particularly inelastic. Technological innovations can, in many cases, help substantially to increase the output of these products; the results obtained by replanting with high-yield rubber trees and tea bushes in Malaya and Ceylon are an example. The experience of these two countries also indicates how this can be accomplished without lowering the exchange rate.[1] An attempt to increase the export of other products, mainly in the field of manufactures, would meet with great difficulties,[2] which would not be substantially alleviated by lowering the value of the national currency. (This judgment will subsequently be qualified.) India and Pakistan have reduced imports to essential consumption goods and development goods and this total cannot be allowed to shrink, whatever the exchange rate is. In the final analysis, then, it is the low level of their exports and the difficulties in the way of raising it at any rate of exchange — together with their great poverty and their desire to plan for development — that compel India and other South Asian countries to take steps to preserve foreign exchange for imports of essential consumer and development goods.

The fact that devaluation cannot be expected to improve the foreign exchange situation much, if at all, should lead the analyst to adopt a near-neutral position in regard to devaluation. This observation gives relevance to the further fact that in every country there is a prestige value attached to preserving as far as possible the exchange value of the currency. It is felt to testify to the strength of the government and the monetary authorities as well as to the soundness and stability of the economy. There is undoubtedly an irrational overtone in this argument, but it also has an element of rationality. Once a change in the currency *status quo* were permitted, it might be more difficult to maintain "confidence in the currency." Price increases might cause people to buy in advance, and delay selling, and generally increase speculation and hoarding. An added incentive would be given for hoarding (and smuggling) gold and foreign exchange and for capital flight. Under the pressure of speculative behavior, prices might well spiral upward, ultimately forcing the government to further currency devaluation. The likelihood of such developments

[1] Principally by using revenues from export taxes to subsidize replanting. In this appendix, as in Chapter 19, we are simplifying our task by largely ignoring operational controls over exports, mainly taxes and/or subsidies. For reasons partly suggested in the text, they are much less important than import controls.

[2] Chapter 13, Sections 12 and 14.

would, of course, be minimized if the devaluation were decided on in an orderly manner and at a time when prices were stable, and the government thereafter kept a tight rein on prices at home and foreign exchange transactions, including capital transfers.

Since devaluation cannot — either in the short or the long run — be expected to stimulate a very considerable increase in export volume, it cannot free countries like India and Pakistan from the necessity of preventing or severely limiting imports other than those of essential consumer goods and development goods. *Devaluation is not an alternative to import controls.* Indeed, if "overvaluation" is defined in relation to that lower international value of the national currency which would make import controls unnecessary, it should be frankly recognized that the concept is not applicable to these countries. The use of the terms "overvaluation" and "undervaluation" in reference to their currency — which is universal among both the proponents and opponents of devaluation — implies a biased and misleading view of their exchange situation.[1] The removal or substantial relaxation of import controls would without any doubt result in an increase in less essential imports, independent of the rate of exchange. Since foreign exchange reserves are scanty and, more important, the imports that are now permitted could not, or should not, be allowed to decrease, this would throw the balance of payments out of gear in short order and give rise to a cumulative process of speculation, inflation, and continued devaluation during which not only would any planned development come to a halt but broad strata of the population would suffer deprivation and even starvation.

The practical problem is not the choice between devaluation and import controls, as is too often assumed in discussions of these problems, occasionally in South Asia but more frequently in the Western countries. The realistic questions are, first, what sort of import controls should be applied and, second, whether with the recommended controls on the whole in force there would still be a case for a devaluation. The former problem will be discussed in the next section. In regard to the latter question there are a number of considerations, all of which argue for keeping the international value of the national currency of countries in the situation of India and Pakistan low. For one, if foreign currency were made more expensive there would be somewhat less eagerness to obtain it, which would make exchange controls easier to enforce.[2] Where import per-

---

[1] It is difficult to find an alternative definition of these terms. The difference between the official and the black-market rate of exchange is determined also by the strictness of the controls in force and can hardly say much about the exchange rate in the absence of controls. The concept of "purchasing power parity" is particularly inapplicable to underdeveloped countries because of problems connected with the "bundle of goods" used to weight the index. Even if restricted to "international goods" it could not define "overvaluation" and "undervaluation," since the need to resrict imports, whatever the exchange rate, means that the prices of goods that are imported are higher in countries like India and Pakistan than they are abroad. The terms "overvaluation" and "undervaluation" are not used in this study.

[2] "It is the undervaluation of foreign exchange, as much as anything in the licensing system itself, which is responsible for making the system so difficult to administer." (Syed Nawab Haider Naqvi, "Import Licensing in Pakistan," *Pakistan Development Review*, Karachi, Vol. IV, No. 1, Spring, 1964, p. 68.)

missions are not subject to some form of taxation, a license would be somewhat less of a windfall gain.[1] There would be a somewhat stronger incentive for private entrepreneurs, particularly in the industrial area, to venture into production for the export market. This effect would probably be minor, as import controls would still afford strong protection to production for the home market, and thus make it a lucrative field for enterprise,[2] but the possibility of marginal effect on exports should not be overlooked.

2 Import Controls as Negative Operational Controls

Whatever the exchange rate, if India or Pakistan left its import composition to be determined by demand in relation to prices set outside its boundaries, it would be giving up one of the most important tools in its planning armory. The imports that are now prevented or curtailed would increase so much that not enough foreign exchange would be left for the import of essential consumer goods, not to mention development goods. With the prevailing economic stratification in these countries, it could be expected that the demand not only for "luxury" imports but for all less essential imports would show a particularly high degree of response to an opening up of the market for foreign exchange. *That minimum of planning needed to design import controls to prevent such a disastrous development is simply a necessity.[3] Foreign exchange difficulties are not a temporary exigency but a normal and permanent condition in very poor countries, pressing economic development to the limit set by all the attendant circumstances.* The severity of the import controls that are needed will depend on, besides the exchange rate, all the economic policies pursued by the government and, particularly, all the other positive and negative controls in force. In the field of enterprise and investment low rates of interest, low prices on goods and services from the public sector, low rates of taxation, and laxity in the assessment and collection of taxes, as well as generous tax exemptions, etc., will tend to increase demands all around, including the demand for imported goods, while severe negative controls of types other than import controls will decrease demands. While stressing this general setting, we shall focus our attention in this section on the consequences of choosing one or another type of import controls.

These controls will under all circumstances have to be selective and discriminatory in regard to the nature and quantity of goods to be imported. If it is the government's intention to allow certain imports in certain quantities, it would seem that the government is still free to choose between non-discretionary and discretionary controls to realize that intention. The choice of the

---

[1] Section 3, below.

[2] "Why should producers in developing countries exert themselves to sell in unsheltered markets abroad at low prices when they can sell at high prices at home?" (Isaiah Frank, "Aid, Trade and Economic Development: Issues Before the U. N. Conference," *Foreign Affairs*, Vol. 42, No. 2, January, 1964, p. 218.) See Chapter 13, Section 17, and Chapter 24, Section 2.

[3] As we have pointed out, that *necessary* minimum of planning of import controls is discussed in the plans only in very general terms; see Chapter 19, Sections 1 and 2.

former type of import controls implies that the import permission (and the permission to acquire and use foreign exchange) will be determined by the price mechanism, though the costs of imported goods of various kinds must first be raised in order to hold imports down to the desired level. The use of discretionary import controls assumes, instead, that licenses to use foreign exchange to import a certain quantity of a particular commodity will be issued to individual persons or firms depending on an administrative assessment of the merits of their application.

Examples of non-discretionary import controls are customs tariffs, multiple exchanges rates, exchange taxes and import surcharges of a selective nature, and the auctioning to the highest bidder of important licenses for specified quantities of selected categories of goods. The last type of import control has hardly ever been used in South Asia, though it has sometimes been discussed. Customs tariffs were generally low in all South Asian countries in the colonial era, though they have risen in recent years. This reflects the fact that initially, as now, there was little industry to protect and the metropolitan powers followed a policy of keeping colonial markets open for the products of their own industry. Multiple exchange rates, exchange taxes, and import surcharges have been used in some Southeast Asian countries from time to time, though not in India and Pakistan.[1] In the latter countries the main devices for controlling imports have been discretionary import and exchange controls.[2]

The reasons for resorting to a system of individual licenses are obvious. The selective rise in import costs that could be accomplished by non-discretionary means would not curb imports to the extent necessary in countries like India and Pakistan, unless they were made prohibitory or very severe, and this is considered impractical. It is also felt that where the situation is as tight as it is in India and Pakistan, every single import — outside of a very few items needed for development, for instance raw materials, which might be left to open licensing — must be carefully examined from the point of view of its priority. It might be thought that discretionary controls, at least over imports of producer goods, could be exercised in an indirect way by restricting capital issues, investment, and enterprise.[3] However, because of the general deficiencies of all controls in these "soft states" and the prevalence of corruption,[4] such indirect discre-

---

[1] See "The Application of Multiple Exchange Rates in Selected Asian Countries," *Economic Bulletin for Asia and the Far East,* November, 1954; "Foreign Trade, Exchange and Investment Policy," *ibid.,* November, 1956; and Shu-Chin Yang, *A Multiple Exchange Rate System: An Appraisal of Thailand's Experience 1946–1955,* University of Wisconsin Press, Madison, 1957.
The so-called "exchange retention" scheme in Pakistan and similar policies in India, whereby exporters are subsidized by being given more or less free use of part of their earned foreign exchange for import purposes, amount in essence to a limited application of a form of multiple exchange rates.

[2] In cases where the import of a certain commodity is absolutely prohibited, naturally the control is non-discretionary. The discussion in the text concerns imports that are not prohibited.
Discretionary import controls, often in combination with non-discretionary controls, have also been used in other South Asian countries.

[3] Chapter 19, Section 5.
[4] Chapter 20, Section 3.

tionary controls, even when used in conjunction with stringent non-discretionary import controls, probably would not be sufficient to accomplish the task. The discretionary import controls are combined with a whole system of other negative discretionary controls to provide a double check.[1]

3 Import Controls as Positive Controls

When primarily negative discretionary import controls also operate as powerful positive controls, this is due to two circumstances. One is that, in the scarcity situation that exists, import licenses have a value and represent a gift to the persons or firms that receive them. By keeping down costs of capital investment and production, the licensing system helps to create a high — from a planning point of view, an "unnecessarily" high — level of profit in the enterprise sphere.[2] It also constitutes a moral hazard that leads to the spread of corruption.[3] If the licenses can be sold, they often bring a price that is one hundred percent or more of the import cost. The attempts made in India and Pakistan as well as in other South Asian countries to control the prices of imported commodities directly by fixing a maximum profit margin on the landed costs cannot eliminate these windfall gains when the importer uses the commodities himself. In regard to traders they have been found to be ineffective, at least in the long run. Moreover, even if effective, such price control only implies a transfer of the gains to a middleman or, under the best of conditions, to an ultimate buyer who is using the commodities in his own plant.

The logical remedy would, of course, be for the government to charge a price for import licenses corresponding to their value on the market. This could be done, at least in part, by complementing the discretionary import controls by non-discretionary controls: customs tariffs, multiple exchange rates, or exchange taxes. In addition to preventing profiteering, this would also provide handsome revenue to governments having serious difficulties in making their tax policies effective.[4] One simple way of expropriating the windfall gains resulting from discretionary controls would be for a state agency to monopolize imports and charge higher prices when reselling them to users. Even where, as in India, there is some monopolistic state trading, it is not conducted on this basis, though that has sometimes been suggested.[5]

[1] Chapter 19, Section 5.

[2] Chapter 19, Section 7.

[3] Chapter 20, Sections 3 and 4.

[4] Exchange taxes and import surcharges applied in the Philippines during 1951–52 yielded about 25 percent of the total government revenue; as applied in Indonesia in 1952–53 these levies contributed about 40 percent. In Thailand, government profits from multiple exchange rate administration amounted to 10–18 percent of total government revenue during 1949–53. See "The Application of Multiple Exchange Rates in Selected Asian Countries," *Economic Bulletin for Asia and the Far East*, November, 1954, pp. 19ff.; and Shu-Chin Yang, *A Multiple Exchange Rate System: An Appraisal of Thailand's Experience 1946–1955*, p. 79 *et passim*.

[5] "To-day, due to import control and the large unsatisfied demand for imports that accompanies it, very large profits are being made by the traders in imports and there is no reason why this by-product of planned economic development should be left to be enjoyed, by private individuals. State trading could also be extended to some of the

One reason why little or next to nothing is done in India and Pakistan to expropriate the windfall gains resulting from discretionary import controls is the simple idea that private enterprise and investment should be encouraged.[1] As the incidence of the gains is very unequal and, from a planning point of view, entirely irrational (they will tend to be biggest where the controls are most severe, which ordinarily means where the government does not want to encourage enterprise), this does not constitute a very valid argument for the present policy line. Another defense is the widespread idea that charging higher prices for imported commodities would increase the costs of production and might be inflationary.[2] On a deeper level the present system of import controls, of course, reflects the vested interests involved and the tendency toward collusion among politicians, officials, and business people.[3]

The second way in which import controls become positive controls is that they serve to protect home producers from foreign competition. In this respect there is no difference between discretionary and non-discretionary controls, except the quantitative one that the former, if strictly applied, may provide almost total protection, while the protective effects of non-discretionary controls presumably are more limited.[4] An underdeveloped country certainly needs protection for its infant industries, and the holding down of imports by controls expeditiously creates domestic markets for the expansion of home industry. Quite aside from the classic infant industry argument, the chronic underutilization of labor provides grounds for protection. However, since import controls were adopted for foreign exchange reasons, they were not considered from a protectionist point of view when they were introduced. In other words, *the protective effects are incidental, not planned.* There is therefore no reason to expect that they would correspond to the genuine and rational needs for protection from the planning standpoint. Certainly import controls ordinarily give a greater — often a much greater — degree of protection than the planners and the government would find justified, if protection were the primary

---

more secure and stable exports; this would not only lead to the accrual to Government of the profit from such export trade, but it would also enable Government to exercise a more effective control over the leakages in foreign exchange receipts that are inherent in its being left in the hands of private trade." (V. K. R. V. Rao, "Approach to the Third Five-Year Plan in the Light of the Country's March towards a Socialist Society," *Ooty Seminar*, May 30–June 5, 1959, p. 33.)

[1] Chapter 19, Section 6.

[2] J. Bhagwati correctly refutes this idea as applied to one particular method of expropriating windfall gains: "It is sometimes argued that the system of exchange auctions would have inflationary effects. By this, it is meant that the domestic price level would rise. This argument, however, appears to be specious. The current method of import restrictions already raises the price level of the imported goods, except in the few instances of effective price control, and exchange auctions need not have any different overall effect on this price level." (J. Bhagwati, "Indian Balance of Payments Policy and Exchange Auctions," *Oxford Economic Papers*, Vol. 14, February, 1962, p. 64.)

[3] Chapter 19, Section 7.

[4] This is the other side of the need to use discretionary controls when the exchange situation is very tight; see the preceding section.

motive for introducing this type of regulation. The prices to which they give rise cannot be regarded as either "correct" or "planned."[1]

As a rule, profits of industries enjoying "unplanned" protection are "unnecessarily" high from the planning point of view. Under the system of discretionary import controls applied in India and Pakistan profits are, as we have shown, "too high" because of the "too low" cost prices of imported producer goods to those getting licenses. But a much broader effect, favoring enterprises whether they are the recipients of import permits and foreign exchange or not, is that the sale prices of products domestically produced are "too high." If the domestic industries thus protected could expand rapidly under the stimulus of high profits and if there were effective competition, the "excess" profits due to the latter cause would be just a temporary phenomenon; if in addition those industries produced necessities or quasi-necessities, all would be well. This might be the situation, for instance, of the bicycle and sewing machine industries in India. But more generally, the biggest stimulus will not be given to those industries that the planners especially want to see expand. Instead, profits will be particularly high in the case of luxury goods or non-essential goods generally, the import of which is either prohibited or kept to a minimum. Nor is the industrialization effect likely to be rapid, particularly as in most cases it would require imports of producer goods that the country cannot permit. "Excess" profits under "unplanned" protection will therefore mount and become a permanent feature of economic life. The government will so be induced to check investment and production in undesired fields by negative discretionary controls of the type we discussed in Chapter 19 (Section 5); it will also often find reasons to try to fix product prices. This is one of the ways in which controls breed controls.

When a certain type of home production is not forbidden altogether, a rational device for deflating profits would be to supplement import controls by imposing internal excise duties on the domestic production of goods similar to the curtailed imports. They should be fixed at a rate that would neutralize so much of the protective effects of the import controls that the entrepreneurs would be given the "correct" degree of inducement for fulfilling the planners' intention. Such counteracting excise duties have rarely been imposed in any South Asian country and never in the systematic way which would mesh with planning.[2] The reason why so little thought has been given to this non-discretionary control is not the administrative difficulties involved — which, compared with many other controls actually applied, would generally not be overwhelm-

---

[1] Chapter 13, Section 17; Appendix 5, Section 4.

[2] The problem was touched on in the Draft Outline of the Indian Fourth Plan: "As the economy develops and becomes more diversified, a variety of new commodities will become available, not all of which will fall in the category of basic essentials. The market for many of these commodities within the country will be a protected one, so that such commodities are likely to command from the very start fairly high prices. Given this situation, it might be proper to subject them to an excise duty from the very beginning. Indeed, adoption of such a policy could also facilitate the direction of available domestic resources into the priority industries or activities." (India, Government of, Planning Commission, *The Fourth Five Year Plan: A Draft Outline*, New Delhi, 1966, p. 87.)

ing — but the established preference for discretionary controls. Unlike excise duties, discretionary measures serve the vested interests of big business, the politicians, and the administrators.[1]

The "too low" cost of foreign exchange and the "unplanned" protection over a much broader field implied in all import controls, when not counteracted by an expropriation of the windfall gains accruing to those who get the foreign exchange and excise duties levied on industries that receive the protection, should be viewed as an integral part of the whole system of "administered" low-cost and high-return policies applied in South Asia, which we shall analyze further in the following sections of this appendix. As supplies are limited in many sectors of the economy, negative controls become a virtual necessity and they are usually given a discretionary form. When the relative prices of factors and products are not brought in line with those that would give the "correct" inducements to private entrepreneurs, the government is compelled to supervise in considerable detail the manner in which businesses are run, despite the extreme scarcity of administrators competent to do this job.

II

Rates of Interest in the Organized Sector

Like exchange controls, the various rates of interest are primarily negative controls. They become positive controls, in our terminology, only when credit is granted at a price so low that selective credit controls and complementary negative controls of the type described in Chapter 19 (Section 5) are necessary in order to maintain whatever degree of balance between demand and supply on the credit market is deemed desirable and practical in the particular case. As with all other operational controls, the South Asian countries keep credit controls and, in particular, interest rates outside the purview of their plans.[2] It is a remarkable fact that, while the economic plans of all these countries center on capital investment, no consideration is given to the price of capital or to other controls over the disposition of capital.[3]

Our analysis of credit controls will be as schematic as our analysis of exchange controls in Part I of this appendix; it will be focussed on the relationship be-

[1] In Ceylon and the Southeast Asian countries they also facilitate discrimination against foreigners, in particular "Oriental aliens." See Chapter 17, Sections 5 and 11–14.

[2] Chapter 19, Sections 1 and 2.

[3] This omission is almost never noted in discussions of planning in South Asia. One exception is the following statement: "Monetary policy in India has slipped in a groove. . . . The advent of planning, instead of provoking new thinking, appears to have led to an abdication of monetary policy, it being tacitly assumed that investment decisions are related to physical needs as laid down under the plans and no longer subject to monetary policy." (P. B. M., "Interest Rate Policy," *The Economic Weekly*, November 7, 1959, p. 1497.)

tween these controls and all other controls in the organized economic sectors. For the most part, we shall limit our discussion to conditions in India and Pakistan. We shall assume that the organized capital market is a single unit, managed by the government. This simplification, which will not seriously invalidate our argument, implies that the government determines the policies of the central bank, and that the central bank, in turn, determines the policies of all other credit institutions — by its open-market operations, its willingness to extend credit to the banks, its rules regarding the cash reserves the banks must keep, and other devices, as needed. We shall not concern ourselves with the relationship among the different interest rates in the organized credit market, but shall confine ourselves to "the level of interest rates."

4 *An Insulated Market*

In India, or in Pakistan, the national credit market is, for all practical purposes, insulated from the credit markets of the rest of the world. Rather than an abstract assumption, this is a fairly accurate description of the existing situation.

It is true that foreign branch banks in the country, national commercial banks, and the central bank itself regularly engage in some short-term credit operations with banking institutions in Western financial centers, particularly London. There is, in particular, a competitive, international segment of the credit market which is dominated by credit conditions abroad. However, that segment is very small and very special, being for the most part limited to the financing of foreign trade. Neither the operations in this special segment of the credit market nor the transactions of foreign branch banks operating in the country imply any substantial flow of capital into the national capital market (or out of it, if the foreign exchange controls operate effectively to prevent such an occurrence). These short-term credit operations are therefore of no importance so far as the wider problem of the supply of capital in the country is concerned. At most, they may denote the presence of a revolving fund of credit from abroad, which the country has every reason to value.

Apart from the documents arising from foreign trade, which are self-liquidating within a foreseeably short period of time, the country has no securities to offer that might make foreign commercial credits possible. As a result, virtually no medium- and long-term credits are available on commercial terms. The short-term capital inflows in connection with imports of development goods and the short- and long-term capital inflows connected with direct investments are guided by the prospects for profit, and the profit rate demanded by the foreign businessman as a condition for investing is not governed by the interest rates in the national market. Grants and loans on a concessionary basis from foreign governments and from inter-governmental organizations do represent a substantial capital inflow, but their size and the conditions on which they are granted, including the rate of interest, if any, that must be paid, are not determined by the interest rates within the country. Private lending in connection with exports is similarly unaffected.

The insularity of the national credit market implies that the level of interest rates within the country can be determined without reference to the interest rates prevailing outside the country. Relations with credit markets abroad do not impose any limitation on the freedom of the government to set interest rates at home at the level it deems desirable from a planning point of view.

5 Scarcity of Capital and Low Rates of Interest

Underdeveloped countries like India and Pakistan are handicapped by a great scarcity of capital in comparison with the rich, developed countries, as witness the much lower share of capital as a factor in aggregate production, the small size of investment in relation to the national product, and the severe limitations on possible development imposed by the relative shortage of capital for investment purposes.

In view of this common observation, it is surprising that it is not regarded as paradoxical that interest rates in these countries' organized capital markets have been held at such relatively low levels. At the start of the independence era, both India and Pakistan had discount rates of 3 percent,[1] and other rates on their organized credit markets were correspondingly low. Since then the discount rates in these two countries have risen to 6 and 5 percent, respectively, and other interest rates have moved up in a generally parallel way. But they are still conspicuously low, and in fact not as high as the rates in many developed countries. Broadly speaking, interest rates have followed the general pattern that unfolded in the rich Western countries from the time of "easy credit" policies shortly after the Second World War to the era of more restrictive policies that superseded it.

To meet the need in the organized sectors for medium- and long-term credit, and occasional demands for equity capital, South Asian governments have set up a number of special development-financing institutions.[2] The rates of interest charged by these institutions have been relatively low because they have had available funds on special terms from foreign governments and inter-governmental organizations, and their home governments have borrowed for them or underwritten their bonds and have occasionally provided some interest-free capital. As a rule, these rates of interest have been regulated so that they bear some relation to the discount rate.

Generally speaking, in countries like India and Pakistan *the entrepreneurs in the organized sectors have had available from the banks and the specialized institutions just described short-, medium-, and long-term capital at interest rates that are about the same, if not lower than, those in rich, developed Western countries.*

The paradox of a great scarcity of capital and low interest rates has been made possible by two policy devices. First, "credit-worthiness" is not the only criterion used in weighing demands for credit; selective and discretionary controls are exercised in deciding who shall be financed and for what purpose. Secondly, exchange controls and the great number of discretionary negative controls described in Chapter 19 (Section 5) are used to limit production and investment. The tighter the discretionary negative controls over investment and

[1] The rate in Burma was 2 percent, in Ceylon 2½ percent, in Indonesia and Pakistan 3 percent, and in the Philippines as low as 1½ percent; Thailand was exceptional with a bank rate of 7 percent.

[2] Chapter 17, Section 4.

production, the less need there is for discretionary credit controls, and *vice versa*. The discretionary credit controls and the other negative controls have to be applied with more force, the lower the level of interest rates.

There is practically no public awareness in either India or Pakistan of this important relationship between low rates of interest and the need for negative discretionary controls of all sorts, nor is the point made in Western literature. The situation in the organized sector of the credit market is regularly treated in the conventional terms of supply and demand and the balance or lack of balance between them; policy is discussed in terms of the need for development[1] and the threat of inflation.[2] The two viewpoints are, of course, reconcilable — on the basis of an "equilibrium" concept (see the next section).

On the whole, the discussion in India and Pakistan, and in the rest of South Asia, has been dominated by the development argument and has been adverse to high interest rates on the ground that they are inappropriate in "developing countries."[3] The frequent references to, and comparisons with, events in the monetary and credit field in the Western countries disclose that little thought is given to the possibility of fundamental differences; the importance for policy of the fact that the national credit market is insulated from credit markets abroad is not noted.

6 Reasons for a Higher Level of Interest Rates

In Section 4 we showed that countries in the situation of India and Pakistan are free to determine their interest rates without reference to interest rates abroad. In Section 5 we noted that the low level of interest rates in these capital-

[1] "Monetary policy has to be devised in such a way that shortages of money funds as distinguished from deficiency of real resources do not hinder the process of development. General credit restraint in a developing economy is only a negative policy which dictates a line of 'Don'ts.' A positive monetary policy must provide incentives and prepare the ground enabling the commercial banks so that they can act positively in allocating credit judiciously to industries for productive purposes." (P. Nijhawan, "Price Level and the Monetary Policy of the Reserve Bank of India," *A.I.C.C. Economic Review*, October 22, 1960, p. 14.)

[2] "A rise in the bank rate serves as an anti-inflationary measure, thereby controlling rising prices, higher profits, and investment in capital goods." (R. N. Gupta, "The Change in Bank Rate in India — Why and What For?," *A.I.C.C. Economic Review*, January 26, 1963, p. 117.) Cf. Appendix 2, Section 23, for criticism of the concept "inflation."

[3] In a recent study of India's National Council of Applied Research (*Management of Public Debt in India*, New Delhi, 1965) a different position is taken. "One basic thesis is that the level of interest rates should be allowed to rise to reflect the relative scarcity of loanable funds in relation to demand" (p. 62). However, this conclusion is based on an analysis of public debt management and its economic effects. The authors make no mention of the relation between a low level of interest rates and the need for a multitude of discretionary negative controls over private enterprise and investment. There have always been a few economists who have argued that the level of interest rates was unrealistically low. See, for instance, a report on the annual conference of the Indian Economic Association in late 1963 in the *Economic Weekly* (January 11, 1964, pp. 49ff.). One participant, Dr. Raj Krishna, characterized the prevailing interest rates as "artificial" and "theological" and argued that they "distorted the choice of public and private investment projects as well as factor proportions." (pp. 49–51)

starved countries is possible only because of a superabundance of discretionary controls that limit the entrepreneur's ability to acquire capital and foreign exchange and his right to invest and produce. This implies that *"equilibrium" could also be attained and preserved at a considerably higher level of interest rates, if these controls were relaxed.* Indeed, the concept of "equilibrium" in the money, credit, or, more widely, capital market is meaningless, except when all controls other than the level of interest rates are taken as given. As this is not the assumption used in our analysis, the term will not be used.

As we pointed out, the relation between the level of interest rates and all other controls is not discussed or even, it would seem, given much conscious thought. Occasionally, however, one finds an oblique reference to it, as when a spokesman for the Indian Reserve Bank in defending the low level of interest rates was reported to have asked: "Since there are other measures to directly control and regulate investments, is there any point in trying to use the Bank rate for that purpose?"[1] This reflects the preference, in principle and in practice, for discretionary rather than non-discretionary controls which we noted in Chapter 19 (Section 2).[2] For reasons developed at some length in that chapter, we do not share this preference, but believe South Asian countries would be well advised to shift as much as possible away from discretionary controls to price policies and other non-discretionary controls. In regard to the credit market this would imply the establishment of a considerably higher level of interest rates and the dismantling of discretionary controls that became superfluous as a result of this move.

We noted as one of the adverse effects of reliance on discretionary controls the fact that the profits accruing to entrepreneurs who succeed in running the gauntlet of those controls are "too high" from a planning point of view, in the sense that they are higher than would be needed to call forth the investment and production activities that take place.[3] In this connection it is interesting to come upon the frequent assertion that "investment is insensitive to the interest rate."[4] In the present writer's discussions with planning officials in India and Pakistan he often encountered the argument that profits in big business, which dominates the organized market, are so high that a rise in interest costs would be absorbed without any appreciable change in investment propensities. These officials were thinking, however, of a rather small upward adjustment in interest levels, and not of the considerable rise that could and, as we see it, should be instituted. It must also be recalled that the level of interest rates is only one of the many positive controls that would have to be scaled down before discretionary controls could be dismantled. It may be true that a change, particu-

---

[1] "Monetary Policy," *The Economic Weekly*, January 4, 1964, p. 7.

[2] See in particular the quotation at page 908 from the Indian Planning Commission's 1963 publication entitled *The Planning Process*.

[3] Chapter 19, Section 7.

[4] This was reported in the *Economic Weekly* (January 4, 1964, p. 8) to be the view of the spokesman for the Indian Reserve Bank whom we quoted earlier.

"In a largely protective economy like ours, where profit expectations rule high, dear money loses importance as a deterrent to investors." ("How Positive Is Our Credit Policy?," *The Economic Weekly*, December 21, 1963, p. 2085.)

larly a small change, in one item would not make much difference, but a systematic and rather extensive change in all items would create a new situation.

We have so far discussed a substantial rise in the level of interest rates in terms of a "static comparison," which is not a realistic approach to the problem. There would be a period of transition, during which the rise in the level of interest rates would have to be matched by a more liberal handling of the discretionary controls in order to maintain the volume of enterprise and investment at the desired level; in the process, various measures would have to be taken in order to maintain liquidity in the banking system and in the economy as a whole. As our analysis is schematic, we shall pass over the problems encountered in moving from a lower to a higher level of interest rates. They are not major. In fact, the level of interest rates has been about doubled in less than two decades — in an unplanned way, rather thoughtlessly imitative of developments in the rich countries and, as there, motivated by the belief (false, it would appear) that such action would serve to check an inflationary process. There is no reason why the level of interest rates could not easily be doubled again, and why this could not be accomplished in an even shorter period, particularly if the change were planned as part of a general move from discretionary to non-discretionary controls.

The fact that big business has a strong vested interest in preserving the discretionary controls,[1] and in having an easy money and credit market serving the organized sector of the economy,[2] makes it unlikely that the level of interest rates will in a rational way be made a concern of the planners in these countries and that a systematic combination of changes, such as we have suggested, will be instituted. Another reason for a lack of optimism is the almost total absence, in both political and scientific discussions, of any reference to the relation between a low level of interest rates and the need for discretionary negative controls.

7 *Other Effects of a Higher Level of Interest Rates*

The introduction of a substantially higher level of interest rates would have other effects besides that just discussed. On balance, these effects are probably desirable from a planning point of view.

There would be changes in the relative prices of goods and services, the absolute change depending, in each case, on the extent to which capital was used in the production process, and changes also in the demand for factors of production. As a higher level of interest rates is more in harmony with the great

---

[1] Chapter 19, Section 7.

[2] Big business is prominently represented on the boards of banks and the special development finance institutions, and has close links with the central banks.

"When I asked Mr. Eugene Black why this was so he replied laconically, as if the answer were self-explanatory: 'But they're government banks.' In Asia the new investment institutions, which the World Bank has helped, are managed by representatives of private investors, even though most of the initial capital is provided out of public funds." (Andrew Shonfield, *The Attack on World Poverty*, Chatto & Windus, London, 1960, pp. 133–134.)

scarcity of capital in the South Asian economies, these adjustments would generally lead to a more rational allocation of resources.[1] More specifically, a higher level of interest charges would tend to induce greater economy in the use of capital in construction and in production processes, a desideratum in all the countries of the region.[2] If very capital-intensive public investment projects were reappraised in terms of a higher interest level, many of them would appear inadvisable (even taking into consideration external economies and other benefits not reflected in their cost/return accounts). In the case of projects that would still be carried out, the costs of the services or goods that constituted their end products would rise.[3]

On the whole, in the lively discussion that goes on today about the optimum technology in the public and private sectors, particularly with respect to capital and labor intensity in investment and production, no consideration is given to the level of interest rates and the possibility of changing that level. Recognition of the fact that factor costs influence investment decisions is explicit, however, in the suggestion that the use of "accounting prices" or "shadow prices" would lead to more rational production techniques and prevent the sinking of large amounts of capital in relatively unproductive investments in the public sector. Those who put forward this suggestion assume that the prevailing low level of interest rates is "unrealistic" in view of the scarcity of capital.[4] In Appendix 5 (Section 5) we pointed out that introducing accounting prices without changing actual prices is an impractical way of trying to change investment decisions. To the criticism we offered in that appendix we can now add that none of the proponents of accounting prices has observed the important relationship, stressed in the present discussion and in Chapter 19, between low rates of interest and the need for a plethora of discretionary controls.

Higher interest rates would bring about a decline in capital values. Flows of income from old investments would, however, be maintained — except that oligopolistic profits in big business would decline as such discretionary controls

---

[1] "A policy of low interest rates has been wasteful. It has encouraged the employment of production techniques which are incompatible with the factor proportions in this country. . . . Thus although capital is a very scarce factor in India, the economic planning proceeds on the false assumption that it is not." (India, *Management of Public Debt in India*, p. 66.) ". . . both the Government and the capitalists might economise capital and might choose an investment pattern that would produce more output per unit of capital than has been possible so far." (*Ibid.*, p. 68.)

[2] Chapter 24, Section 4; Chapter 26, Section 21.

[3] This would have consequences for the prices charged in the public sector; see Section 10.

[4] "In the present circumstances, the demand for capital surpasses its supply and it is one of the functions of the accounting rate to equilibrate them — at the same level of supply and hence of investment. Conversely, a lower accounting wage rate will stimulate the employment of labour, which at present is not fully utilized. The other functions of the accounting rates are to change the use made of the factors and better to adapt this use to the available supply. In industries where a choice can be made between more capital-intensive and more labour-intensive processes, more labour-intensive processes will be chosen, thus saving capital and reducing unemployment." (Jan Tinbergen, "Note for Professor Mahalanobis on the influence on the process of industrialization exerted by accounting interest rates and accounting wage rates," mimeographed, no place, no date, p. 7.) Cf. Appendix 5, Sections 3 and 5.

as were no longer needed were dismantled; to achieve that result is, indeed, a main reason for raising the level of interest rates. The fact that land values would decline must be regarded as a definite advantage, since this would increase the feasibility and reduce the cost of a large-scale change in the structure of land ownership and tenancy.[1]

In regard to future issues, the cost of debt service would rise, both on government bonds and on private bonds. The major portion of all government securities is held by government-owned agencies, and to that extent the higher level of interest rates would only bring about a change in accounting relationships within the public sector. Insofar as public and private bonds are held by private persons, the higher interest rates would tend to bolster the rentier class. This could be regarded as unfortunate, particularly in view of the laxity that exists in the assessment and collection of taxes (Section 9). However, as bonds can be registered, recipients of income from this source would be a very easy target for reforms aimed at making taxation more effective; income from loans in other forms would, as now, be more difficult to trace. In any case, the argument that rates of interest should be kept low because taxation is lax is hardly tenable if a country wishes to plan its development.

In regard to the supply of capital, there is first the advantage that much of the indigenous businessman's irrational resentment of the fact that foreign entrepreneurs require large profits as a condition for direct investment would dissipate if interest rates at home were higher. There is also the possibility that the private capital market abroad might to some extent be activated. Considering the widespread anxiety about the lack of rapid development in South Asia, some people in the West might be prepared to hold a portion of their funds in Indian or Pakistani securities if the yield were sufficient to compensate them for the risks involved. Meanwhile, there is no reason why foreign governments and inter-governmental agencies would raise the rates of interest they charge when awarding non-commercial credits, since these rates are not determined by interest rates in the recipient countries. There might, it is true, be reasons, some of them rational, why the South Asian countries would not be eager to have investment — either direct[2] or indirect — increase to a major extent; but if it did, the governments concerned would have no difficulty taking measures to stop an unwanted capital inflow.

There has been some discussion of the effect higher interest rates would have on savings. In general, it is recognized that if interest rates were higher, savings in these countries would tend to increase. Also, money would find its way into the credit market instead of being dissipated in speculation and hoarding (particularly of gold, which today is so prized that smuggling is very lucrative), conspicuous consumption, and conspicuous investments of all sorts, including the purchase of land (at inflated prices) and foreign securities. Insurance, especially life insurance, would be cheaper, and savings in this form should be stimulated accordingly. How important these wholesome effects on savings

[1] For a discussion of the many issues involved in land reform in the broader sense, see Chapter 26, Sections 12–17 and Part IV.

[2] Chapter 17, Section 9; Chapter 19, Section 7.

would be is, of course, impossible to gauge; it would depend, however, on how much the interest level was raised.

In every South Asian country the organized sector is only a small part of the economy, and our discussion above has no direct bearing on the credit market in the rural economy or on that in the larger part of the urban economy, which is dominated by small-scale industry, crafts, and retail trade, above the level of the destitute who are outside any organized form of economic activity. In both India and Pakistan endeavors have been made to meet those credit needs by making loans available cheaply through cooperatives and other public institutions.[1] Public lending to these sectors has generally involved more in the way of direct and indirect subsidies than the credit facilities provided by development institutions for investment in the modernized sector of these economies. This public activity has not, however, succeeded in satisfying more than a small part of the credit needs in the traditional sectors; moreover, contrary to the announced intent of its backers, it has, on the whole, benefitted mainly those who are more affluent, among them the old-time moneylenders, who still dominate the credit field and charge very high interest rates.

Thus, in spite of these efforts, the central bank has not gained effective control over the credit markets outside the organized sector of the economy. The explanation of this lies partly in the difficulty of building up efficient channels for the distribution of credit in the traditional sectors and partly in the expensiveness of the subsidized loans to the public credit sector. The way to gradually break down the dualism in the credit market would seem to be, first, to increase interest rates substantially in the organized market and, second, to decrease or eliminate the subsidies involved in public lending in the traditional sectors; requests for aid should be treated as a separate issue, and aid should not be made available to the upper strata, which now get most of the subsidized credits.

If credits in the traditional sectors were placed on a businesslike basis, so that the volume of credits could be expanded without cost to society, the state could more seriously compete with the usurious moneylenders, and average interest rates would eventually even be lowered. In any case, consideration for the traditional sectors cannot be invoked in defense of the low interest rates in the organized sector. It is worth noting that in Japan, where the rural and small-scale industrial sectors are much more integrated in the organized credit market (more than half of all agricultural credit is provided by financial institutions), interest differentials are much smaller: on the average, interest rates are lower in the traditional sectors, but considerably higher in the fully organized sector, than in India and Pakistan.

The analysis in Part II of this appendix has concerned India and Pakistan. With minor adjustments it is valid for Ceylon, and for Burma as well, provided that Burma retains any private organized economic sector. It could also apply to Indonesia, if internal order were restored sufficiently that a discussion in terms of markets had any relevance there. Of the other countries in South Asia, the Philippines most closely resembles India and Pakistan as far as monetary prob-

[1] Chapter 18, Section 8; Chapter 25, Sections 3–6; Chapter 26, Section 18.

lems are concerned. Malaya, which still has a positive trade balance, is in a good position to continue drawing on the British capital market, of which it is still almost a part; it also has access to the Chinese money market through the Chinese in Singapore and Hong Kong. The situation might change in Malaya, however, because of the very rapid population increase and the possibility that, for this and other reasons, the Malayan government might become more actively interested in pushing industrialization, a policy that requires considerable capital; changes in Malaya's foreign policy could also alter its present monetary situation.

III

Fiscal Controls

8 *Background Observations on Fiscal Systems in South Asia*

Insofar as we accept the evidence of the grossly deficient statistics available in most South Asian countries, tax revenues amount to a little more than 10 percent of national income. In Pakistan the ratio is somewhat lower than 10 percent, while in both Ceylon and Malaya it is around 20 percent. The higher ratios in Ceylon and Malaya are related to the fact that these countries are more prosperous than their neighbors,[1] and the further fact that their imports and exports, being relatively sizeable,[2] provide them with convenient "tax handles." The ratio of tax revenues to national income has remained fairly steady except in India, where it has doubled since the beginning of the 1950's, and Pakistan, the Philippines, and Thailand, where it has increased by perhaps a third, a fourth, and a fifth, respectively. In general, indirect taxes account for two-thirds to three-fourths or more of total tax revenue, the rest coming mainly from income and corporation taxes. Neither gift and inheritance taxes nor taxes on wealth and capital gains play any significant role in the South Asian countries.[3] The relation between total tax revenue and national income in the South Asian countries (except Ceylon and Malaya) corresponds to that which was customary in the Western countries in the beginning of this century, before the financing of major wars and rising expenditures for defense, education, health, and social security necessitated more vigorous tax policies. In the Western countries today, tax receipts amount to about 25 percent or more of national income.

In the discussion of fiscal problems in the region, it is usually assumed that taxes should be raised in order to decrease consumption and increase savings and, by implication, investment.[4] But savings and investment do not have the

---

[1] Chapter 11, Section 1.

[2] Chapter 13, Section 2.

[3] Statistics on the matters referred to in the text are given in "Tax Potential and Economic Growth in the Countries of the ECAFE Region," U. N., *Economic Bulletin for Asia and the Far East*, Vol. XVII, No. 2, September, 1966, pp. 29ff., and earlier ECAFE publications cited there.

[4] A typical statement is the following: ". . . economic development is, ultimately, a

all-important role in development that is assumed in the modern approach. Furthermore, the purpose of taxation and public expenditure, considered in conjunction, should be not simply to decrease consumption across the board but to decrease some consumption and increase other (private and public) consumption, while leaving room for physical investment.[1]

The common assertion that the purpose of raising taxes is to permit development without inflation is equally inadequate to reality in South Asia. In most of the poorer countries of the region, food production tends to lag behind increases in the demand for food, and foreign exchange is very scarce. Under these conditions, tax increases alone will not widen the scope for enterprise and investment; neither will they check an inflationary trend, unless the circumstances are exceptional.[2]

The paucity of tax revenues and the limited volume of public expenditure in the South Asian countries are often simply attributed to the low levels of income in these countries. However, in more sophisticated discussions it is pointed out that the distribution of income is very unequal and that a very large part of the national income — in the poorest countries probably a fifth or more — accrues in the form of rent on land and property and is spent mostly on luxuries or is not very wisely invested.[3] Under these conditions a progressive land tax would produce additional revenue with a minimum of sacrifice. It would also make land reforms more feasible by lowering land values and, if properly constructed, would raise productivity. But a tax of this nature would be resisted by the landholding classes, which are powerful everywhere in the region. It is the political influence of these classes that explains why land taxes, which in the colonial era often made up a very large part (in British India and some other countries the larger part) of all tax revenues, are now very low in all the South Asian countries. Modern income taxation had been introduced in South Asia in colonial times, mainly so that citizens of the metropolitan countries doing business in the colonies should not enjoy an unduly favorably position compared with their compatriots at home; other foreign or indigenous businessmen were taxed to

---

matter of capital formation. . . . [One of the] basic tasks of public finance in underdeveloped countries [is] to raise the rate of saving by restricting . . . consumption." (*Ibid.*, p. 29.)

Government "savings" as a percentage of government revenue have been decreasing in almost every South Asian country. (*Ibid.*, p. 48.) However, this conclusion is based on the division of the budget into a "running budget" and a "development budget," which is not rational; see Appendix 4, Section 3.

[1] Appendix 2, Section 21. This is a much more important consideration in the South Asian countries, where levels of nutrition, health, and education are low, than it is in the Western countries, where living levels are relatively high. "But for the most part, the mass of their people are living below the minimum of subsistence necessary for working efficiency. The problem can be stated in a straightforward manner in terms of the need to provide for an increase in necessary consumption while restraining unnecessary consumption." (Joan Robinson, *Economic Philosophy*, C. A. Watts & Co. Ltd., London, 1962, p. 117.)

[2] Inflation and the concept of a "ceiling" are discussed in Appendix 2, Section 23.

[3] See, for instance, Nicholas Kaldor, "Will Underdeveloped Countries Learn to Tax?" and other articles on the role of taxation in economic development, reprinted in his *Essays on Economic Policy*, Vol. I, Duckworth, London, 1964, especially pp. 256ff.

prevent them from having an "unfair" competitive advantage. In the independence era, tax rates have been raised considerably, with the result that now marginal rates in the highest brackets tend to be as high as, or higher than, those in the Western countries, although they are not effective for reasons we shall discuss in the next section.

Taxation on income has remained almost exclusively an upper-class burden in all the South Asian countries. In the two richest countries of the region, Malaya and Ceylon, two percent or more of all households are liable to income tax; elsewhere this proportion is only a fraction of one percent. And this is not the whole story. In most South Asian countries the tax rates are stiff in the highest income brackets but very moderate in the lower and middle brackets of taxpayers. This means that, theoretically at least, the larger part of the tax burden falls on a very small group in the assessed population, a group that in Ceylon and Southeast Asia is still largely made up of Westerners and Oriental aliens.

In the political discussion, the lenient treatment of people in the lower and middle income brackets has been defended on egalitarian grounds. This argument has little validity since all persons who are liable to income taxation belong to a very small upper class. As, however, persons who are in this class though not in its top echelon dominate the articulate strata of the population, attempts to increase the rate of taxation in the lower and middle brackets meet great political resistance. Any move to broaden the tax base by lowering the level at which personal incomes cease to be exempt would also pose serious administrative problems.[1]

These sketchy comments on the general fiscal structure and some of the main fiscal problems in the South Asian countries are meant only to set the stage for our attempt to explain how (1) low effective rates of income and corporation taxation and (2) low prices of services and goods from the public sector necessitate more discretionary negative controls than would be necessary at higher rates and prices. Even these two more specific problems will be given only a very schematic treatment. As in the two earlier parts of this appendix, we shall confine our analysis to organized sectors and deal mainly with India and Pakistan.

9 *Low Effective Rates of Direct Taxation*

Capitalist entrepreneurs in the organized sector make up a large part of that tiny minority who are liable to income and corporation taxes in South Asia; the owners of the big enterprises are prominent among those subject to very high tax rates. There are several reasons why such taxation is not effective where these individuals are concerned. First, powerful business lobbies are usually able to ensure that the tax laws contain a variety of loopholes and exemptions. This was glaringly demonstrated when the Indian government, on the advice of Professor Nicholas Kaldor, introduced new taxes on capital gains, wealth,

---

[1] In Ceylon hopes have been expressed to eventually have a "universal income tax." To this end, the exemption should be lowered by a series of steps. The administrative difficulties are recognized, but the advantage of "training [the citizens] in the responsibilities of citizenship . . . is a cost which the state should be prepared to meet." (Ceylon, Government of, National Planning Council, *The Ten Year Plan*, Colombo, 1959, pp. 117–118.)

personal expenditures, and gifts;[1] during the deliberations in parliament members of all parties manifested understanding amusement when one M.P. characterized the gift-tax law as "the gift-tax-exemption law." The legislation relating to more regular taxes on incomes of individuals and companies is similarly emasculated, though perhaps not to the same extent.[2] Even a cursory reading of tax laws in South Asia also reveals that they are more complicated, unclear, and ambiguous than necessary,[3] and it is difficult to avoid the suspicion that this circumstance is largely due to the machinations of powerful interested parties.

The tax laws being as they are, tax avoidance on a large scale is easy and natural. "It is common knowledge," says one author in the official Indian Congress economic journal, "how the business of advice on Income Tax matters has flourished during the last few years in this country. Perhaps the very phenomenal increase in the number of Income Tax practitioners is an index of the flourishing trade in tax evasion [should be tax avoidance]. . . . And the cleverest in the art . . . are the most successful in escaping the liabilities imposed by law."[4]

In addition to what we have called tax avoidance — that is, the practice of exploiting the loopholes and ambiguities in the tax laws — there is outright tax evasion. As early as 1951, the classic outline of the First Five Year Plan in India stressed the prevalence of this procedure:

It would appear that at present a large number of incomes in the higher income ranges escape the payment of income tax and super tax, and there is in these and in other ranges of income an understatement of incomes. There is considerable leakage on account of non-declaration of profits made in black markets.[5]

A year later C. N. Vakil and P. R. Brahmananda noted that "evasion of taxes [had] developed into a fine art and [had been] accepted as a common feature

[1] For Kaldor's own appraisal of the reform, see "Tax Reform in India," *Essays on Economic Policy*, Vol. I, pp. 216ff.

An Indian economist reflects: "Estate duty and taxes on gift, wealth and expenditure exist only in name. In the financial year 1964–65 the revenues estimated from these are estate duty Rs. 7.40 crores, gift tax Rs. 3.10 crores, wealth tax Rs. 10.20 crores, expenditure tax Rs. 1.55 crores — a total of Rs. 22.25 crores, about 1 per cent of the estimated tax revenue of the Government of India. We must stop caricature of these taxes. They must be made effective sources of revenue. It should be easy to make company taxation simple once personal taxation is made effective on a broad base." (Laksminarayan Sinha, *Capital and Employment: Problems of Developing Economy*, Mithila Mandal, Darbhanga, 1964, p. 94.)

[2] The authors of the Draft Outline of India's Fourth Plan revealed their awareness of the situation when they recommended "plugging the loopholes in the tax system that lead to legal avoidance of tax liability, and taking prompt action to close the new loopholes as they emerge," and "a closer look at the items allowed as deductions for taxable income, and especially the scale on which they are allowed, in order to prevent functionally avoidable lowering of tax receipts." (India, *The Fourth Five Year Plan: A Draft Outline*, p. 32.)

[3] "The complicated provisions of the direct taxes Acts, not all of which are easily intelligible, are responsible, to some extent, for tax avoidance and evasion." (India, Government of, *Report of the Direct Taxes Administration Enquiry Committee, 1958–59, Summary of Conclusions and Recommendations*, New Delhi, 1959, p. 22.)

[4] S. K. Goyal, "Some Aspects of the Budget 1963–64 — II," *A.I.C.C. Economic Review*, April 1, 1963, p. 29.

[5] India, Government of, Planning Commission, *The First Five Year Plan, Draft Outline*, New Delhi, July, 1951, p. 22.

of life."[1] Another one of India's most prominent economists, D. R. Gadgil, confirmed this judgment:

Reference may . . . be made to the extent to which tax evasion by industrialists and traders constitutes a major problem in India. . . . It has always been known that the financial communities in India had developed tax evasion into a fine art. The extent of evasion rose to new and great heights with increased taxation in recent years. . . .[2]

There is common agreement that since these statements were made both tax avoidance and tax evasion have assumed greater proportions in India. The former Attorney-General, M. C. Setalvad, recently stated that tax evasion "is not sectional or limited. . . . It is mass evasion of tax so far as the business community is concerned." He stressed particularly that "it was not only small traders and businessmen who did not pay up their dues to the state but that the big businessmen, the big industrialists and company directors also indulged in proportionately large evasions."[3] The same charge is made repeatedly in books and in articles in newspapers and periodicals.

In explaining the situation reference is often made to the lack of a "code of honesty, discipline and civic obligations. Tax evasion is only one aspect of the general absence of such a code in what is still an essentially pre-industrial society."[4] It is pointed out that in colonial times taxation was looked upon as an instrument of exploitation and that resistance to paying taxes was often part of the nationalist struggle for independence.[5] Although that day is long past, the idea that taxes should be paid according to the intention of the legislator has never become part of the mores of the business community. Tax offenders are seldom prosecuted;[6] when they are and are found guilty, the punishment is very mild and no publicity attends it.[7]

The very high tax rates in the upper income brackets make avoidance and evasion highly profitable. A Pakistan report on taxation indicates that these rates are the reason why so many individuals seek to circumvent the tax laws:

In the case of income-tax, the Government appears to have been caught in a vicious circle. It is fully aware of the magnitude of evasion not to mention avoidance through

[1] *Planning for a Shortage Economy: The Indian Experiment,* Vora & Co., Bombay, 1952, p. 1.

[2] *Economic Policy and Development (A Collection of Writings),* Gokhale Institute of Politics and Economics, Poona, 1955, p. 115.

[3] Reported in *Link,* November 29, 1964.

[4] Pranab Kumar Bardhan, "Tax Payer Psychosis in India," *The Economic Weekly,* March 10, 1962, p. 447.

[5] *Ibid.* See also R. N. Bhargava, *Indian Public Finances,* Allen & Unwin Ltd., London, 1962, pp. 49, 80, *et passim.*

[6] ". . . practically no prosecutions have been launched for the past several years." (India, Government of, *Report of the Direct Taxes Administration Enquiry Committee 1958–59, Summary of Conclusions and Recommendations,* p. 27.)

[7] ". . . evasion is encouraged by the mild punishment with which it is let off. The maximum penalty prescribed under Indian law is one and a half times the tax and even this is rarely imposed. The law permits prosecution, but the offences are usually compounded and the tax evader escapes publicity and prosecution. Tax evaders are not black listed and continue to maintain their position in the eyes of the public and the Government." (Bhargava, *Indian Public Finances,* p. 80.)

legal means, which has kept the receipts low. The low receipts do not permit the Government to reduce rates in high income brackets, as high rates are considered necessary to offset loss through evasion. High rates in turn provide the incentive to tax-payers in the maximum income bracket to evade taxes. Under the existing rates it pays a business-man in the high income brackets to spend liberally on the fees of lawyers, accountants and tax experts to find ways of reducing high tax liability.[1]

However, an Indian report disputes this: "While it cannot be denied that the higher the rate of tax, the greater will be the temptation for evasion and avoidance, the tax rates by themselves are not to blame for the large extent of evasion in the country."[2] Exorbitantly high marginal tax rates in the upper brackets make it plausible for the administration to try to work out a reasonable compromise with the taxpayer, a practice that, in turn, makes the taking of a bribe more natural.

The problems of increasing the number of officials concerned with tax assessment and tax payment, of raising their level of competence and their salaries, of increasing the penalties for tax evasion, etc., are continually discussed, but no decisive reforms have been carried out. Proposals to make tax returns and assessments public[3] and to publicize cases where penalties have been imposed,[4] have not been acted upon. Big businessmen have never supported such measures and it is a fair inference that they have a vested interest in the status quo.

The government's failure to come to grips with the problems of tax evasion and tax avoidance has serious implications. R. K. Hazari comments in the *Economic Weekly:* "So long as avoidance or evasion of taxes continue to be widespread, and what is worse, no social opprobrium attaches to such practices and known tax evaders are openly patronized by Government in various ways, the abuses of corporate management are bound to remain and continue to flourish."[5] In a leading article in the same publication, a broader view is taken:

For over a decade Government have permitted a colossal evasion of tax payments. In addition to bidding resources away from plan projects and in addition to feeding smuggling and black marketing, it has had another very unfortunate repercussion, viz. a far reaching withering of morals. They say it openly in industry and trade now that there is almost nothing and nobody that money cannot buy. In the face of the most shameless and impudent profiteering that is rampant in every facet of economic life, we cannot any longer look labour and the lower salaried classes in the face and ask for their best efforts and sacrifice for this generation and the next. On the subject of sacrifice, it is a matter of regret that we have failed to rouse the common men and women of the country in this entire process and to utilise the tremendous potential

[1] Pakistan, Government of, *Taxation Enquiry Committee Interim Report,* Karachi, 1959, p. 7. This statement of the problem was made when the military government was well in the saddle and had made an initial effort to strengthen the enforcement of the tax laws; see Chapter 8, Section 7.

[2] India, *Report of the Direct Taxes Administration Enquiry Committee 1958–59, Summary of Conclusions and Recommendations,* p. 22.

[3] India, Government of, *Report of the Committee on Prevention of Corruption,* New Delhi, 1964, pp. 49, 50.

[4] India, *Report of the Direct Taxes Administration Enquiry Committee 1958–59, Summary of Conclusions and Recommendations,* pp. 30–31.

[5] "The Corporate Sector," *The Economic Weekly,* April 15, 1961, p. 605.

which lies dormant in the four hundred and fifty millions who constitute India. An opportunity in centuries has been missed perhaps. Even a national emergency could not evoke the expected response.[1]

Several attempts have been made to estimate the amount of revenue lost through tax evasion in India. Kaldor estimated it to be about on a par with assessed income; official estimates put it much lower.[2] The statistical basis for any estimate of tax evasion is exceedingly weak. But there is no doubt that tax evasion has become a normal business routine. Therefore, if account is taken not only of tax evasion but also of tax avoidance, due to loopholes in the tax laws and their expert utilization, and tax arrears, which are large,[3] it seems probable that paid-in taxes in India amount to only a minor part of the taxes that the *bona fide* legislators felt should flow to the exchequer.

We have discussed the problems of tax avoidance and tax evasion as they exist in India and Pakistan. It is our judgment that the situation is similar in Ceylon. In Indonesia, Thailand, and, particularly, the Philippines it is probably even worse. It may be slightly better in Malaya where tax rates are lower and where a greater portion of the indigenous companies and individuals making up the organized sector belong to the Chinese minority. To what extent tax avoidance and tax evasion are practiced in Burma by those individuals and firms who are permitted to continue in private business seems uncertain.

It is in the general context of large-scale tax avoidance and evasion, which make tax rates largely ineffective, that we have to study the various tax exemptions provided to encourage industrial growth.

In India new enterprises are exempt from paying taxes on profits up to 6 percent during their first five years of life; recipients of dividends paid out of such profits enjoy a similar "tax holiday." Both new and existing enterprises are granted a "development rebate" for new plant and machinery expenditures and this, together with liberal depreciation allowances, means that they can deduct from income more than the amount of their actual investment. Certain expenses connected with the employment of foreign technicians are deductible for three years; expenditure on scientific research can be deducted in full. Many other tax exemptions intended to stimulate enterprise and investment are scattered throughout the tax system in India. To quote a statement directed to foreign investors:

The net result of all the deductions allowed is that in many cases of industrial companies, the tax is levied on an income much less than that indicated in the balance sheets of the companies. There are, indeed, cases where the balance sheets indicate profits, while for purposes of income-tax, there is not only no taxable profit, but indeed, a loss, which is allowed to be carried forward in subsequent years. This often happens in the ordinary course, without allowing for certain other special tax concessions which have been provided for the further encouragement of industrial investment.[4]

[1] *The Economic Weekly*, February 22, 1964, p. 409.

[2] Bhargava, *Indian Public Finances*, pp. 78ff.

[3] *Ibid.*, p. 86.

[4] A. K. Roy, *Position of Foreign Enterprises in the Indian Tax Structure*, Government

The other countries of South Asia also have tax exemption schemes. They are all broadly similar, although those in Malaya and the Philippines are more definitely directed toward encouraging "pioneering enterprises" in new fields that are deemed to be in the "public interest."

So far as we know, no one has ever asked whether enterprise and investment need encouragement in the form of tax exemptions; it is simply assumed that this is the case.[1] In fact, however, profits are so high that, as we pointed out in Chapter 19 (Sections 5 and 6), officials are mostly engaged in attempting to hold back investments so that demands can be met by available supplies. Their weapons are discretionary controls. Anyone seeking to found or enlarge an enterprise must apply to them for a variety of licenses and permits. Thus even in Indian and Pakistan, where most of the tax exemptions are provided under general rules in the tax laws, they come indirectly under discretionary controls, as no tax-exempt investment projects can materialize without licenses.

Directly, and indirectly by necessitating more discretionary negative controls, tax exemptions — operating in the general framework of large-scale tax avoidance and tax evasion — like the availability of cheap credit and foreign exchange and the protective wall around production for the home market created by the import restrictions, thus tend to make profits "unnecessarily" high. Less severe negative controls of a discretionary type would be needed if the tax laws were more effective and there were fewer tax exemptions of the type described.

10   *Low Prices on Goods and Services from the Public Sector*

The pricing of the goods and services provided by the state raises as many problems in the underdeveloped countries of South Asia as it does in the developed Western countries. In this section we will discuss only the pricing of those goods and services which enter into the cost of production and investment in the organized private sectors of the South Asian countries. Even that limited topic will be analyzed from one specific point of view, namely, the incentives to enterprise and investment that low prices can provide.

A main reason for state investments in power, transport, and other public utilities has been to promote private enterprise. Where, as in India and Pakistan, the state has also ventured into industry on a large scale, it has done so mainly in fields where for various reasons private industry could not be expected to take the initiative. Furthermore, it has taken this step mainly in order to make supplies of raw materials or capital goods available to private industry. In the Philippines the feeling has been that state industrial ventures were justified only

---

of India, Ministry of Finance, Department of Revenue, Directorate of Inspection (Income-Tax), reprinted from the Supplement to *Capital*, New Delhi, December 19, 1957, p. 6.

[1] "With the increase in rates of personal income-tax . . . , we are of the view that it would be necessary to afford specific incentives in the tax system to productive investment. . . . The increasing intensification of competition in the world market makes it all the more necessary that the capacity of Indian industry to finance development should be reinforced in a general way." (India, Government of, Ministry of Finance, *Report of the Taxation Enquiry Commission 1953–54*, Vol. II, New Delhi, 1955, p. 98.) Cf. *ibid.*, p. 19.

if they helped to provide incentives for private enterprise; the same thought has been prevalent everywhere in the region.[1]

In regard to the price policies of public enterprises, the discussion in the South Asian countries — like that in the Western countries — has not been very clear and conclusive. However, one theme has recurred: "If we want rapid economic development, the prices of producer goods [and services] should be kept low."[2] This notion does not give any very firm guidance to pricing policy, although it is usually assumed to justify even lower prices than would follow from the application of the time-honored doctrine of "no profit, no loss."[3]

There are two reasons why in practice this doctrine leads to a "subsidy"[4] for the purchasers of goods and services from the public sector: the fact that the capital invested has been acquired at an excessively low rate of interest (Part II), and the even more important fact that the profit rate is ordinarily calculated on the basis of the original capital investment rather than on the cost of replacing the plant and equipment involved, a quantity likely to be much higher when there has been a general rise in the price level. The doctrine leads to still lower prices when all of the external economies, "the final contribution to national income or national welfare," are counted in when figuring the rate of return, as is often urged.[5]

This doctrine is usually related to the liberal classical equilibrium theory. However, at least from Alfred Marshall on, it has been generally recognized that when the proportion of fixed costs to total costs is high, as in the case of roads and, indeed, most public utilities, it may be rational to charge relatively low prices or even to make goods and services available free of charge. It is sometimes argued, however, that public enterprises are more likely to be rationally and economically run if they are expected to "break even." But as the enterprises in question usually enjoy a degree of monopoly power, this argument is weak. A public enterprise could be inefficiently run and still break even, just as it could be efficiently run and fail to break even. In this context, efficiency is more a matter of holding down costs than of balancing receipts and expenditures. Efficiency in the management of public enterprises has to be secured by means other than free competition and the price mechanism.

Throughout most of the region goods and services from the public sector have been priced so low that the rates of return on capital invested have been lower than the ("too low") rates of interest prevailing on the capital market.[6] The general theory that public enterprises should price their goods and services in

[1] These matters are discussed in Chapter 17, Sections 6–10.

[2] N. K. Rothagi, "A Note on Price and Profit Policy in Indian Public Enterprises," *A.I.C.C. Economic Review,* February 7, 1961.

[3] This "break-even" doctrine — well known from discussion in the Western countries — sometimes carries the proviso that public enterprises, like private ones, should yield a "reasonable profit," at least in the long run.

[4] In this context, purchasers are "subsidized" when prices are lower than adherence to the doctrine would dictate, and "taxed" when prices are higher. These definitions have thus no greater validity than the doctrine itself.

[5] V. V. Ramanadham, *The Finances of Public Enterprises,* Asia Publishing House, London, 1963, p. 53.

[6] For India, see *ibid.,* pp. 4ff.

such a way as to provide incentives for industrial development is not the only reason for this state of affairs. Private industry has used its influence to keep prices down.[1] Also, as the Planning Commission has pointed out, the various states — which are responsible for the power plants — have established low electric power rates to attract industries away from their neighbors.[2] Considering the vested interests involved and the general inclination to believe that low prices are used to promote development, it is not difficult to understand why "administered prices" like those now under consideration have tended to lag behind the general run of prices during the current inflation.

More recently, a different doctrine has been enunciated, namely, that enterprises in the public sector should follow a price policy permitting a substantial accumulation of capital. Proponents have pointed out that self-financing out of profits has been a main element in the growth of private industry in both developed and underdeveloped countries. Reference is also made to the fact that state enterprises in the Soviet Union and other Communist countries are conducted so as to yield a "profit." As a higher price policy would facilitate the growth of enterprises in the public sector — by making them semi-independent of the credit market and taxation — it has often been called a "socialist" policy — although we might note that keeping prices low in order to promote the growth of private industry has also occasionally been described as "socialist."

R. K. R. V. Rao, one of the chief proponents of the new doctrine, states his views as follows:

Public enterprise must be carried on a profit-making basis, not only in the sense that public enterprise must yield an economic price in the terms described . . . but must also get for the community sufficient resources for financing a part of the investment and maintenance expenditure of Government. Increasingly, the share of the profits of public enterprises in financing the investment and maintenance expenditure of Government must keep on increasing. It is not only the expenditure on the public sector as such that will indicate the march of the economy towards its socialist goal. Even more important is the increasing role that the public sector must play for finding the

[1] For instance: "Not surprisingly, the suggestion that industrial power rates should be raised has been opposed by the Federation of Indian Chambers of Commerce and Industry which has advanced the argument that such a step would adversely affect industrial growth and raise industries costs." ("Higher Power Rates for Industry," *The Economic Weekly*, January 11, 1964, p. 46.) The situation was a little delicate as the World Bank, which had money invested in power projects, had taken an opposing position and spoken in line with the more recent doctrine we shall comment upon below: "The policy of low tariffs, and particularly for industrial users, . . . does make difficult the accumulation of funds for the further expansion of generating capacity" and is therefore "not a stimulus to growing investment and larger production"; the Bank had pointed out that, in the majority of cases, power costs were only a very minor fraction of the total production costs. The article reflects: "It is strange that the spokesmen of private industry, who swear by the World Bank Mission's report on other matters, find its recommendations on power rates unacceptable."

[2] "The proposal to raise power rates, particularly for industrial and commercial consumers . . . has raised a hornet's nest [at a meeting of state ministers of power and irrigation]. Several of the assembled Ministers protested that if power for industry was made costlier, the tempo of industrial development would be slowed down." (*Ibid.*, p. 45.)

resources needed for meeting both the maintenance and investment expenditure of Government. This involves a price and profit policy in regard to public enterprise which goes against accepted opinion so far in regard to public enterprise. The theory of "no profit, no loss" in public enterprises is particularly inconsistent with a socialist economy, and if pursued in a mixed economy it will hamper the evolution of the mixed economy into a socialist society. The sooner, therefore, this theory of "no profit, no loss" in public enterprise is given up and the policy accepted of having a price and profit policy for public enterprise such as will make the State increasingly reliant on its own resources (as distinguished from taxing the personal incomes of its citizens), the quicker will be the evolution of a socialist society.[1]

In India, the idea that government enterprises should be income-producing has now become the official doctrine. It was endorsed by the important Ooty Seminar.[2] The Planning Commission was for a time hesitant to take a stand, but in the Third Plan it came out strongly in favor of the new concept.[3] The Reserve Bank of India has also made plain its approval.[4] Turning from the general to the particular, government bodies have suggested that public enterprises in the public utility field raise their prices substantially.[5] The new idea has crept into studies of the ECAFE secretariat.[6] In Ceylon, the National Planning Council has accepted it in principle,[7] but has been quite inconsistent about applying it

[1] "Prices, Income, Wages and Profits in a Socialist Society," in All India Congress Committee, Planning Sub-Committee, *Ooty Seminar May 30–June 5, 1959 (Papers Discussed)*, New Delhi, 1959, p. 176.

[2] "The Seminar emphasized that the prices of goods and services produced in the public sector should not, by and large, be determined on the principles of 'no-profit, no-loss.' Public enterprises will have to serve as the main instruments for providing the State with the resources it requires for development. . . . Prices of commodities and services in the public sector should not only be sufficient to meet the cost of production but also include the following items, *viz.* depreciation, provision for expansion, contribution to tax revenues and capital formation. The share of the profits of public enterprises in financing the investment must keep on increasing. This cannot happen unless there is a radical change in popular opinion on the nature of the price policy to be followed in regard to the production of State enterprises." (*Ibid.*, pp. 31, 32.)

[3] The Commission urged profits large enough for "financing the expansive programmes of these [the public] enterprises." (India, Government of, Planning Commission, *Third Five Year Plan*, New Delhi, 1961, p. 97.)

[4] "Another source for mobilising savings is surpluses from public enterprises, which in a mixed economy have an important role to play in promoting development. . . . Self-financing has made an important contribution to industrial development in most countries and there is thus every reason to adopt this principle for public sector enterprises, when mobilisation of all possible savings is required to attain the maximum tempo of development without excessive inflationary stresses." (Reserve Bank of India, *Report of the Central Board of Directors for the Year Ended June 30, 1962*, August, 1962, p. 12.)

[5] For instance, to a profit level of "not less than 10%" in electric power enterprises. "This will, we hope, enable [the state boards] to put to reserve for further expansion enough of their current earnings to finance a substantial part of [the] expansion." (India, Government of, *Report on the Energy Survey of India Committee*, New Delhi, 1965, p. 158.)

[6] See, for instance, United Nations, ECAFE, *Economic Bulletin for Asia and the Far East*, Vol. XII, No. 3, December, 1961, p. 14.

[7] "It is particularly important . . . that these public enterprises set themselves the objective of earning adequate surpluses for further capital accumulation." (*Ceylon, The Ten Year Plan*, p. 53.)

in specific fields.[1] A belief in the merits of higher prices is also becoming prevalent in Pakistan. In the other South Asian countries, either the question is not discussed or the weight of opinion continues to favor low prices.[2]

Even in India, where "a clear decision has now been made in favour of substantial surplus accumulation" in public sector undertakings, profit rates remain very low.[3] The reasons are those already hinted at: the lingering idea that it is possible and desirable to give incentives to private enterprise by setting low prices on services and goods from the public sector; the opposition of private industry to higher prices, reflected also in the positions taken by the state governments; and the difficulty of raising administered prices in pace with the rise in the general price level.

The argument that private industry might not need the encouragement provided by low prices on services and goods from public enterprises has not been put forth, except occasionally as an afterthought.[4] It is sometimes pointed out that demand often exceeds supply,[5] so that recourse must be had to discretionary controls in the form of rationing. But it is seldom recognized that the low prices set on the services and goods the public sector supplies to industrial enterprises in the organized private sector represent a positive control that, along with other positive controls, such as low effective tax rates and special tax exemptions, cheap credits, cheap foreign exchange, and import controls serving to protect the home market, helps to make necessary the plethora of negative discretionary

---

[1] For instance, *ibid.*, pp. 419ff.

[2] In the Philippines, even the public trading agencies follow a low-price policy. "In India, the pricing policy of the State Trading Corporation is generally one of profit-making on a commercial basis; while in the Philippines, the pricing policies of state enterprises generally involve some element of subsidy to the consumer in that the prices fixed are lower than those which would have obtained had the transactions been undertaken by private traders." (United Nations, ECAFE, *State Trading in Countries of Asia and the Far East Region*, New York, 1964, p. 5.)

[3] Ramanadham, *The Finances of Public Enterprises*, pp. 24 and 4ff.

[4] "A higher price of electricity is likely to result more in a reduction of the large margin of profit of private enterprises than in a rise of prices of products of these enterprises. This is due to the fact that if there were any possibilities of charging higher prices for their goods, these enterprises would have already done so in view of the fact that there exists a considerable degree of monopolistic pressure in the economy." (A. Qayum, "Return on Capital in the Electric Industry," *The Economic Weekly*, November 25, 1961, p. 1770.)

In an article in the *Economic Weekly*, J. M. Healey argues that "A rise in freight charges [of Indian railways] would have increased the surplus earnings of railways and made a more substantial contribution towards [a] high level of fixed capital formation during this period." He then added the comment: "It would, of course, have raised costs for industry as a whole but there is little reason to believe that the growth of Indian manufacturing industry would have been seriously impeded by such a policy. Indian industry has largely served the domestic market and has been heavily protected against foreign competition by tariffs and stringent foreign exchange controls during this period. Domestic demand for manufactured goods has been buoyant and if prices of manufactured goods had been raised this would have had little effect on the cost of living index for working class families." ("An Analysis of Railway Costs and Prices," *The Economic Weekly*, January 4, 1964, p. 19.)

[5] "For much of the 1951–60 period the demand for wagons exceeded the supply of wagons . . ." (*Ibid.*, p. 19.)

controls discussed in Chapter 19 (Section 5). The simultaneous application of positive and negative discretionary controls is responsible for the "too high" level of profits. This being the case, private industry would have an interest in seeing that state enterprises adhere to a low price policy not only because it would keep down their costs but also because, in so doing, it would tend to increase the need for negative discretionary controls, as we indicated in Section 7 of Chapter 19.

Chapter 21

"UNEMPLOYMENT" AND

"UNDEREMPLOYMENT"

I

The Ideological Roots of the Prevalent
Approach to Economic Development

An extreme underutilization of labor is generally assumed to characterize South Asian countries. That there is fundamental truth in the assumption is suggested by the obvious fact that the average output of the labor force is very low. It is low partly because much of the labor force is idle, either completely or for a large part of the day, week, month, or year. But even when members of the labor force are at work, their productivity is usually low. This phenomenon can only be explained as the result of many conditions, among them low labor efficiency.

1   The Role of "Unemployment" and "Underemployment"
in the Prevalent Approach

In economic terminology, waste of labor is commonly discussed as "unemployment" and "underemployment." Together the unemployed and un-

deremployed in South Asia are assumed to constitute a reservoir of un-
tapped productive potential, the existence of which is conventionally
explained, in the first instance, by deficiency in effective demand for wage
employees or, in the case of those self-employed in agriculture or elsewhere in the economy, by the absence of opportunity for productive work.
This abstract approach, it should be noted, is based on a number of assumptions that are regularly left implicit:[1] it presupposes that "unemployment" and "underemployment" are "involuntary," that members of the
labor force who make little or no useful contribution to production do so
only for lack of a satisfactory alternative, and that once they are presented
with work opportunities, they will take them up. This line of reasoning is
premised on the existence of a fluid labor market and a rational outlook
toward life and work on the part of members of the labor force. While recognizing that considerable idleness is present — particularly in the slack
seasons in agriculture but also quite regularly in the whole economy — and
that some work is not very productive, this conventional approach also
fails to give systematic attention to the efficiency of labor when people are
in fact working.

In the mainstream of economic theory, unemployment and underemployment on a vast scale are regarded as a primary cause of poverty in the
South Asian countries. At the same time, the large volume of unutilized
labor possessed by these countries is thought to have a productive potential
capable of creating capital and increasing production, thereby making
possible higher levels of consumption — in short, a potential that can be
used to eliminate poverty. The supreme task of planning is thus to drain
this labor reservoir by creating work opportunities and by channelling the
unemployed and underemployed into productive work.

These thoughts form a *leitmotiv* in general discussions of economic problems in the South Asian countries, at popular, political, and scholarly
levels alike. Western statesmen and officials concur in these views in the
diagnoses of development problems they offer in inter-governmental organizations and elsewhere. Western economists dealing with South Asian
development problems also commonly apply this approach as a matter of
course. Nor is the Communist view basically different, despite contrasts
in the explanations offered and the specific policy measures favored. And,
both in the South Asian countries themselves and abroad, the notion of a
vast labor reservoir awaiting productive employment is generally shared
by Communists, leftist socialists, liberals, and conservatives of all shades.
It can thus be described as the conventional theory, but to avoid depreca-
tion by terminology, we refer to it as the "modern" theory or the "modern"
approach. While we shall focus our attention on the manner in which the
"modern" approach deals with the analysis of employment problems, this

[1] Section 10.

topic is but a species of a genus, namely, aggregative model-building of the Western type.[1]

From the beginning the plans regularly gave a prominent place to expressions of this common diagnosis of the economic situation and to assertions that the enlargement of work opportunities is one of the supreme tasks of planning. Typical is the statement in the Draft Outline of India's First Five Year Plan that "A development plan is essentially an effort to create conditions for full employment."[2] One of the broad goals included in the more recent Ceylon Ten Year Plan is to "bring about the relatively full utilization of manpower resources by the end of the ten year plan period."[3] Similar statements are made in official documents relating to economic planning published in other South Asian countries.[4]

Despite the emphasis on creation of employment opportunities, the more sophisticated plans, as worked out in detail, set employment targets that are surprisingly unambitious. As they usually do not aspire to do more than at most provide work opportunities for those expected to join the labor force during the plan period, these targets, even if fulfilled, can only check deterioration in the employment situation. In no other respect is preservation of the *status quo* an almost declared objective of planning. And, if the results are measured against the announced targets, it appears that those countries which have prepared detailed estimates have failed to reach even these modest goals. At a later point in the argument, we shall examine the reasons why planning in South Asia, contrary to the declared general objectives, has been so modest in its employment targets and why actual performance has been so disappointing.[5]

Promotion of "full" or "fuller" employment is, of course, only one of several general objectives set out in the plans, and the relative emphasis given

[1] Prologue, Section 5; Appendix 2, Part 4; Appendix 3 *et passim*.

[2] India, Government of, Planning Commission, *First Five Year Plan: A Draft Outline*, New Delhi, 1951, p. 19.
As early as 1944, the Bombay Plan, drawn up by the Bombay industrialists, stressed this point. "Of all the measures that we suggest for raising the general level of income in India, provision of fuller scope for employment is the most important. Provision of full employment for the working part of the population would no doubt present formidable difficulties, but, without it, the establishment of a decent standard of living would remain merely a pious hope." (Nabagopal Das, *Unemployment, Full Employment and India*, 3rd ed., Asia Publishing House, London, 1960, pp. 77–78.)

[3] Ceylon, Government of, National Planning Council, *The Ten-Year Plan*, Colombo, Ceylon, 1959, p. 86.

[4] See, for example, Pakistan, Government of, Planning Commission, *The Second Five Year Plan (1960–1965)*, Karachi, June, 1960, p. 370; Philippines, Government of, National Economic Council, *The Five-Year Economic and Social Development Program for FY 1957–1961*, Manila, January, 1957, mimeographed, p. 39; and Indonesia, Government of, State Planning Bureau, *Broad Outlines of the Five-Year Development Plan 1956–1960*, Djakarta, 1958, mimeographed, p. 143.

[5] See, in particular, Chapter 24, Sections 4–6.

to it has undergone some modification in the successive rounds of planning. "Fuller" employment figures less prominently, for example, in the Third and the Fourth than in the First Indian Plan. This shift is not unrelated to the point mentioned above — that, though employment targets have been low, performance has failed to live up to expectations.[1]

Nevertheless, the employment objectives of planning still command a great deal of attention. It is in this connection that two aspects of the modern approach converge. At one level, the employment aspect of planning fits into the Western theoretical models that buttress an aggregative approach to planning. At another — in the form of the concept of underemployment — it conveys the impression that the peculiar conditions of the region have been taken into account. We shall explore these points in detail in later sections of this chapter. Our first task, however, will be to attempt to explain why the obvious waste of labor in South Asian countries is conventionally approached through the Western (and Communist) concepts of employment, unemployment, and underemployment.

2   The Recent Origin of the Prevalent Approach

This stress on unemployment and underemployment and on the urgency of creating employment opportunities that forms the essence of the now conventional approach is mainly a post–Second World War phenomenon. In the earlier literature, the paramount concern was the persistent shortage of labor encountered by colonial governments and by private entrepreneurs. In perhaps no other respect has the modern discussion of economic problems in South Asia more sharply reversed that conducted in colonial times. The basic problem is now seen as one of providing work opportunities for the unemployed and underemployed masses, whereas not long ago it was viewed as one of attracting wage laborers in sufficient numbers.

It will be a main purpose of the first part of this chapter to explain in some detail how this dramatic reversal came about. In the broadest sense, it is clearly related to the vast political change that occurred when the South Asian countries gained their independence, and the power to determine their own approach to the problems of the day. They hoped to develop their economies through the instrumentality of planning.[2] They also aspired to become welfare states — or, more accurately, this was the

---

[1] It may be noted that commentators on the Indian Third Plan were particularly critical of its modest employment targets. The following observation typifies this line of criticism: "My main conclusion is that the [Indian Third] plan is insufficiently bold in its attack on underemployment." (I. M. D. Little, "A Critical Examination of India's Third Five-Year Plan," *Oxford Economic Papers*, Vol. 14, No. 1, February, 1962, p. 24.)

[2] Chapter 15.

aspiration of those who thought, spoke, and acted for them.[1] Under the impact of these political and ideological forces, it was natural for planners to regard idle or unproductive labor as, on the one hand, a curse and a cause of poverty and low living levels and, on the other, a potential resource for development. The practical problem was to devise ways to employ the labor force more fully. At the same time, population expansion — which has occurred at unprecedented and increasing rates in the past two decades — has cast the problem of work opportunities for the masses in a new light.

Influences from abroad have also given powerful support to this orientation of policy interest. In Western countries, the gradual change in the organization of the labor market and in the internal balance of political power between different social strata in the emerging democratic welfare states had tended, since about the beginning of the century, to shift the focus of public discussion, and of social and economic analysis, to the employment issue.[2] The consummation of this trend occurred at the end of the Second World War when, in all Western countries, full employment was declared a major goal of economic policy and a responsibility of governments.

At that time, the colonial power system in South Asia was crumbling and newly independent states were coming into being. An important by-product of this concurrence of events was that Western economists and their confreres in the South Asian countries — who were just as thoroughly steeped in the Western conceptions — took over the ultra-modern Western concept of unemployment in undiluted form and applied it in South Asia. To embrace the self-employed — particularly in rural areas — who formed the larger part of the labor force, they devised the concept of "underemployment." This notion is analogous to the notion of "disguised unemployment" developed in industrialized countries during the Great Depression to describe the status of workers who had been temporarily pushed into casual pursuits less remunerative than their regular occupations.[3]

Ideological winds from the Communist countries — where no employment problem was recognized to exist — could hardly counteract this influence from the West. The claim by Communist writers and propagan-

---

[1] Chapter 16.

[2] Section 8.

[3] Joan Robinson, who first worked out this concept, noted the possible relevance of "disguised unemployment" to hired agricultural workers in underdeveloped countries, though her first concern was with wasted skills, during depression, in highly developed economies. It is of some interest that the first sentence of her article reads: "An economy consisting of self-supporting families each working their own land must always enjoy full employment, since each individual is free to work as long as he considers the real reward he obtains a sufficient inducement for his efforts." (Joan Robinson, "Disguised Unemployment," *Economic Journal*, XLVI, No. 182, June, 1936, pp. 225–237.)

dists that capitalist countries had not solved, and could not solve, employment problems tended rather to strengthen the hold of the new Western orientation in South Asia. Least of all did it encourage scrutiny of the major assumption underlying Western concepts of unemployment and underemployment: that idleness, above the set standards of work, was involuntary and thus there was a reservoir of labor that could be tapped by increasing demand and augmenting opportunities for work; labor efficiency was disregarded.

Within this general framework a number of other ideological influences, to be described in the following sections and particularly in Section 9, had much the same effect.

3 *Colonial Labor Market Theory a Branch of Mercantilism*

As in many other fields,[1] economic thinking about the labor market in the colonies was originally of a Mercantile type. And, however much it was modified in more recent decades, it retained a great deal of this character to the very end. Analysis of the similarities between economic speculation in colonial times and Mercantilist thinking is a fruitful subject for detailed study. Here only some broad observations can be offered as hypotheses for further research.

The domestic economic policy of Mercantilists in sixteenth and seventeenth century Europe tended always to view the labor market from the perspective of employers. Though the details of Mercantilist policy differed in various parts of Europe and altered through time, a plentiful supply of cheap, docile, and disciplined labor was assumed to be in the public interest, in countries where this thinking held sway. Otherwise, the overriding objective of economic policy at the time — a favorable balance of payments and, with it, additional "national wealth" — could not be reached. A main purpose of the regulations of labor conditions established by state and municipal authorities was to assure employers of an adequate labor force available on favorable terms.[2]

This way of looking at things was entirely natural to a power structure that from a modern democratic point of view was severely biased. It fortified the privileges of cities against surrounding rural districts and, within the cities, advanced the interests of the rich merchants and manufacturers against those of the workers. Colonial government represented, in a sense, an extreme variant of such an inegalitarian power structure.

[1] Chapter 28, Section 6.

[2] As Furniss has observed, "The Mercantilist did not perceive that the poverty of the majority was incompatible with the wealth of the whole; quite the contrary: he came to believe that the majority must be kept in poverty in order that the whole might be rich." (Edgar S. Furniss, *The Position of the Labourer in a System of Nationalism*, Houghton Mifflin, New York, 1920, p. 7.)

The colonies were governed from faraway metropolitan capitals. The new entrepreneurs were also outsiders, mostly from the ruling country itself or from other European countries.

Later they were joined by non-European entrepreneurs, usually operating enterprises of smaller scale and utilizing less advanced techniques and capital equipment. In Southeast Asia these were mostly "Oriental aliens" — Chinese or Indians. But even in India, where they were of indigenous stock, though from small segregated castes or minority communities, such entrepreneurs tended to look at the labor market from the employers' point of view as Europeans did. Through the managing agency system and in other ways, they were closely linked with the top strata of European entrepreneurs.

It was also natural, as it was for merchants and manufacturers and Mercantilist theoreticians and politicians in Europe, for these entrepreneurs to feel that their interests coincided with economic progress for all. The Mercantilists were not simple and morally corrupt cynics, but men who argued and acted to advance what they conceived to be the common good, just as did the colonialists and business people who held power in South Asia in colonial times.[1]

When, in later times, colonial governments felt a stronger urge to promote improvements in the living conditions of the masses of dependent peoples, their basic approach was nevertheless that of outsiders.[2]

4   The Facts

Labor market policy in the colonies and the motivations behind it must be viewed against the background of prevailing power relations. The Mercantilist type of thinking could thrive because it corresponded to these

[1] J. S. Furnivall has noted that in the tropics, "Low wages seem to reduce the cost of production and, until recently, have been regarded as contributing to economic progress. In Java, up to the end of the nineteenth century, low wages were considered one of the chief assets of the country, and a source of its prosperity." (J. S. Furnivall, *Colonial Policy and Practice, A Comparative Study of Burma and Netherlands India*, Cambridge University Press, London, 1957, p. 351.) This is plain Mercantilism, given in the colonies a shelter where it could survive through the nineteenth century, entrenched by the peculiar power situation of colonialism.

[2] Many factors converged to support this trend toward a less exploitative policy. In the present context, it is perhaps worth noting that much of the urge to improve living conditions for the textile workers in India had its origin in the interest of the English textile industry in curbing what it considered to be unfair competition. This occasionally caused suspicion and resentment among Indian nationalists. (Cf. D. R. Gadgil, *The Industrial Evolution of India*, 4th ed., Oxford University Press, London, 1942, pp. 78 ff.; and Charles A. Myers, *Industrial Relations in India*, Asia Publishing House, Bombay, 1958, p. 101. See also Chapter 23, Section 3.) In the same way, modern income taxation in the colonies was introduced by the colonial governments mainly in order to keep their nationals (and other foreigners) from escaping the burden of taxation that gradually was placed on people at home. See Appendix 8, Section 8.

power relations. But European colonists found a tradition of unfree labor well established at the time they arrived in Asia. The forms ranged from outright slavery to the "attachment" of bonded workers, and differed from country to country.[1] A reshaping of the indigenous institutions was clearly necessary in order to accomplish some of the major economic objectives of European rule, for the traditional forms of compulsion were seldom ideally suited to promoting expansion of commercial production.

In pre-colonial times, the most widespread form of compulsory labor throughout much of South Asia gave the chief, the headman, or the feudal overlord the power to commandeer labor for part of the year, often for such purposes as building and maintaining roads and irrigation canals. This practice might now be described as a device for creating capital through the absorption of the underemployed in the agricultural labor force. Much of this inherited pattern was preserved in colonial times; and often it was intensified. The zamindars created by the British in parts of India often used compulsory labor to keep up roads and irrigation systems. Likewise, in Thailand, the modernization initiated during the reign of King Chulalongkorn toward the end of the nineteenth century was deemed to require the wholesale use of compulsory labor. In most or all of the South Asian colonies the same method was relied upon in varying degrees and in different forms to produce manpower for public works or their maintenance. But while compulsory labor applied in this manner served many worthwhile purposes, it seldom provided substantial increases in marketable agricultural surpluses. The Mercantilism of European rule sought commercial output from which profits could be earned. To achieve this objective, a different approach to the labor force was needed.

Commercial output suitable for sale in export markets could be obtained in a number of ways. The least complicated was to have the specialty products of South Asia voluntarily offered for sale by the indigenous population. This arrangement was not always dependable, however, nor was it a simple one to establish, except where the institutional structure had developed to the point that the feudal overlord, through his powers to collect tribute from the land, could organize the collection and transport of export products. Variations on this arrangement served reasonably well in the period when the interest of Europeans in the countries of the region was confined to the trading activities of the Chartered Companies, but were far from satisfactory when the demand for tropical specialty products grew and the production of new types of output was desired. Increasingly, the interest of Europeans shifted from that of purely commercial activity to the direct production of export commodities. Alternative arrangements then had to be devised.

One scheme was the *cultuurstel* system adopted by the Dutch in Java in

[1] On this historical background, see Bruno Lasker, *Human Bondage in Southeast Asia*, University of North Carolina Press, Chapel Hill, 1950.

the 1830's, whereby peasants were obliged to set aside one-fifth of their land for the production of specified crops such as coffee, sugar, tea, and tobacco. The output was either purchased by the government at a low price or claimed in kind as taxes. This system was, however, rather exceptional. Much more significant than any scheme that left the basic responsibility for the protection of commercial crops in the hands of individual peasant producers was the formation of plantations that were organized, financed, and directed by Europeans. This type of organization came to the forefront in the last half of the nineteenth century and introduced an important modification in the approach of colonial governments to the problems of labor supply. No longer did they think their only role was to keep peace and create conditions suitable for the successful conduct of international trading activity. Instead, governments began to intervene more directly in the organization of export production. They encouraged European capitalists to initiate production of exports and were expected, in turn, to help these enterprises obtain labor on satisfactory terms. Special measures would, of course, have been unnecessary if members of the indigenous population had come forward spontaneously to take up the opportunities offered by wage employment. But this they seldom did.

Thus it came to pass that the indigenous system of forced labor, which colonial rule inherited, was adapted to induce large-scale movements of labor. The inducement was often, particularly in earlier times, of a type that implied compulsion. And even when workers from distant places were recruited on a basis that preserved some elements of "voluntariness," the process of settling them down to steady work was accomplished in ways that severely restricted their freedom of movement. The plantations and mines in Ceylon and Malaya were manned in this fashion. The system of moving people around as indentured laborers was not new to the region, particularly not to India, but it was now set to function on a much larger scale and in a more organized form by governments and entrepreneurs.

These policies could easily be rationalized as necessary to accomplish economic development in the form sought by the colonizers. An important fact, on which we shall comment further in later chapters, was that it was hard to get even the poorest strata in the countryside to accept wage employment. Greater still were the difficulties in getting workers to settle down as wage earners on the plantations and in forging them into a steady and disciplined work force if they were not first forcibly uprooted, moved far away from their local moorings, and herded together in an alien environment. These aspects of the behavior of the indigenous population led a number of European employers to the conclusion that the natives were incorrigibly lazy and indifferent to opportunities to improve their real incomes. Their observations went a long way toward supporting belief in the "backward-sloping" supply curve.[1]

[1] Section 6.

But it must be remembered that this view of a limited labor supply, as taken by employers, had an important qualification implicitly attached to it. To the employer, labor scarcity meant that demand exceeded supply at a very low level of real wages. As in Mercantilist times in Europe, there was little enthusiasm in the colonies for experimenting with the wage scale to test responses. Indeed, there was never, even on the intellectual level, a discussion of using higher wages to induce workers to accept conditions of steady, disciplined work. It was also cheaper and simpler to seek out labor — usually from a considerable distance — that could be acquired at low wages. Organized recruiting had a further recommendation: workers, when far removed from their homes, were more amenable to discipline.[1]

The vested interest of employers in a cheap labor supply was often plainly demonstrated. In Burma, where new land for cultivation was readily available, the local peoples could not be persuaded to work at wage rates which imported Indians would accept. The large-scale dependence on Indians as common laborers and as lower, as well as higher, officials stemmed originally from the difficulty of recruiting Burmese labor for these tasks at prevailing wage levels. On this point a Mercantilist way of reasoning was most clearly apparent, for "the government subsidized the importation of Indian coolies with a view to bringing down the rate of wages."[2]

In Malaya, Indian and Chinese workers formed the wage labor force, the former serving the rubber estates and the latter manning the tin mines. In the early period of Dutch rule in Java, Chinese workers were imported in large numbers as coolies on tobacco plantations and also to serve as intermediaries between the government and the indigenous population.[3] Similarly, the successful operation of tea plantations in Ceylon depended on the large-scale importation of Tamil workers from Southern India.

In retrospect, one may be tempted to question whether it would not have been wise from the point of view of the employer, and particularly from that of the colonial government, to have adopted a policy of paying wages high enough to attract local workers. It may be asked whether a more cautious and understanding attitude on the part of European employers and

[1] This phenomenon was by no means unique to colonial employment practice in South Asia. Employers in Africa encountered similar difficulties in the first stages of colonial contact, and similar expedients were adopted. Colonial rulers in Africa, however, were much quicker to use devices such as the head tax to provide a negative inducement for wage employment. Even so, problems in recruiting a stable African labor force in volume remained, and organized recruiting of labor from remote areas was developed. Nor was recruiting confined to the African continent. Indentured workers from India were brought in to build the Uganda railway and to man the sugar estates in Natal.

[2] Furnivall, *Colonial Policy and Practice*, p. 351.

[3] W. F. Wertheim, *Indonesian Society in Transition*, W. van Hoeve Ltd., The Hague, 1956, pp. 57 and 67.

the colonial governments would not have overcome most of the resistance of local people to wage employment. But, first, it was not in their interest to pursue such a policy, at least as their interests were then conceived. The system in use also offered other advantages. Foreign laborers, isolated in unfamiliar surroundings, were more docile, more easily organized for effective work, and more permanently attached; the import of labor thus tended to minimize labor costs in this way, too. Secondly, and more pertinent to the present discussion, the difficulties in attracting local people to wage employment were serious — though again we must remember that the matter was never considered on any assumption other than an extremely low level of wages. And thirdly, no one who had any say in policy saw anything wrong in bringing in foreign labor.

The picture was less clear-cut on the Indian subcontinent. In places where a particularly rapid development in a new line of activity raised the long-term demand for regular labor, as for instance on the plantations in Kerala and Assam, or in the coal mines in Central and Eastern India, laborers were brought in from remote regions.[1] That, in India, resort to foreign labor — that is, labor from other colonies — was not taken is simply a reflection of the fact that India, being so large, included regions in which labor could be made plentifully available. Often tribal people were herded together and made to work under strict supervision at low rates of pay.[2]

[1] "The Assam plantations get their labour chiefly from distant Chota Nagpur; the Bengal peasant is attracted neither by these nor by jute mills but only moves in order to occupy the lands in the Assam Valleys. The coal mines do not prove attractive enough to the Chota Nagpur aboriginals and have to recruit a large proportion of their labourers from the districts of U.P. and Bihar. These same districts send labour in large numbers to Calcutta, Bombay and other parts of India, but not to any large extent to the tea plantations. One has again to distinguish between migrations from the different strata of the population. Numerically the most important migrations are always those of the labourers and the peasants, but the small trader and artisan migration may also assume quite considerable proportion and may be economically important. To the Gujarat peasant the conditions outside are nowhere attractive enough, but the small trader from the region has moved out in large numbers to Africa and to other regions of India itself." (D. R. Gadgil, *Economic Policy and Development* (*A Collection of Writings*), Gokhale Institute of Politics and Economics, Poona, 1955, pp. 26–27.)

[2] The plantation owner had the authority of government behind him in maintaining discipline over his workers. As noted by Surendra J. Patel: "When the plantations began to develop at the close of the first half of the nineteenth century, planters found it difficult to attract an adequate supply of cheap labour to the thinly populated and mostly malarious hill tracts of Assam. To help the plantation owners (who were mostly British) in their task of recruiting such a labour force from distant parts of India, the government granted them certain statutory rights regarding their employees. These rights empowered the owners to carry on the practice of indentured labour." (Surendra J. Patel, *Agricultural Labourers in Modern India and Pakistan,* Current Book House, Bombay, 1952, p. 133.)

"The general scheme," remarked the Royal Commission on Labour, "was that the labourer was bound by a contract to serve for a specified period on a garden to which he was recruited; if he failed to work without reasonable cause, or absconded, he could

From an economic and social point of view, those who were imported to work in mines and on plantations in India were equally, or almost, as foreign as the imported plantation workers in Ceylon and Malaya.

At the same time, it is striking that some very large undertakings, such as the construction of railways and public works in India after 1860, seldom suffered seriously from labor shortage, though wages rose conspicuously as the demand for labor increased.[1] This situation can be at least partly related to the recurrent droughts in Indian agriculture that made agricultural laborers "glad to have an opportunity of supplementing their earnings in the off-season in agriculture."[2] In the latter half of the nineteenth century, wage labor was already an important element in Indian agriculture and the effects of crop failures were almost immediately observable in the form of reduced opportunities for wage employment in agriculture. In addition, some village artisans, weavers in particular, felt the pinch of competition from foreign and, later, home-manufactured products and thus were more amenable to taking up wage employment. Money wage rates increased, but it is not clear that real wages rose correspondingly, as prices of food-grains rose also.

Labor difficulties apparently plagued most industrial enterprises but especially those requiring a labor force prepared to accept factory disciplines and acquire some degree of competence but not one large enough to justify the organized recruiting resorted to by large plantations and mines. The nascent textile industry in India had to struggle against a persistent scarcity of labor throughout a period of rapid growth up to the First World War and even beyond. This new industry was not prepared to provide attractive wages or conditions of employment. But these factors cannot fully explain the chronic labor shortage that the industry experienced. For, then as now, poverty and distress were great among the

---

be punished criminally and the planter had the right of arresting an absconder. The system of indenture did not solve the difficulties; it would be more accurate to say that it aggravated them." (Great Britain, India, Royal Commission on Labour, *Report,* 1931, p. 360.)

Recruitment of labor for Assam suffered "grave injury in the past owing to the system of penal contracts, and of private arrest." (*Ibid.,* p. 376.)

W. Nassau Lees, in his *Land and Labour of India,* gave a graphic picture of the way in which the contractors of labor recruited workers for plantations in Assam. He wrote: "False representation, corruption, and oppression of every and the worst description were used to swell the numbers of the contractors' recruits. The old and the decrepit, the young and the tender, the halt, the maimed and the blind — nay, even the infected, the diseased and the *dying* — were pressed into the service of the most degraded (the contractors of indentured labourers). With some truth it may be said that the horrors of the slave trade pale before the horrors of the coolie trade of Assam and Cachar in the years 1861–62." (W. Nassau Lees, *The Land and the Labour of India: A Resurvey,* London, 1867, pp. 203–205.)

Concerning labor conditions on plantations, cf. Chapter 23, Section 3.

[1] Gadgil, *The Industrial Evolution of India,* pp. 18 ff.

[2] *Ibid.,* p. 18.

poorer classes in the countryside — the landless laborers, the sharecroppers, and the workers in declining crafts. Moreover, the phenomenon now referred to as rural unemployment and underemployment cannot have been absent in those days.

Generalizing over a very wide area and a long period of time, several tentative conclusions appear to be legitimate. The available evidence indicates that, broadly speaking, the new enterprises that grew up in the colonial era — whether plantations, mines, or urban industries — were often troubled by labor shortage. In any event, the new industries did not ordinarily encounter an enormous labor surplus, pressing for employment. As seen from this angle, the countryside did not by itself generate a large supply of readily available labor waiting to be tapped.[1] The difficulties experienced in recruiting labor — as well as the view held by employers and governments that new enterprises offered progress to a backward economy — gave force and sanction to policies that we have characterized as a branch of Mercantilism. The approach of governments and employers had a "factual" background; to them it must have seemed to correspond to actual circumstances and to be founded on "experience." Ideologies, to those holding them, have always appeared to be simple, and indisputable, conclusions from obvious facts.

5   The Situation in Agriculture

The state of affairs in the rural economy in the South Asian countries — and the changes in it through time — is a matter largely for speculation. Virtually no empirical data exist that could throw light on trends in agricultural production and in output per head. The obvious inference is that with increasing population and little change in techniques, output per head was maintained by drawing fresh lands into production whenever physical circumstances permitted. But when this avenue of adjustment was

[1] "It has often been asserted (or at least assumed) that India has the advantage of an almost inexhaustible supply of cheap manual labour, suitable for industrial production. Such an assumption is directly opposed to the actual facts. Although wages are low, labour is dear, and although the population is redundant, the number of persons offering to undertake industrial work at a wage which the traffic can bear is strictly limited. . . . Indian agriculturalists and rural artisans are extremely reluctant to take up industrial life in the towns or in rural factories, even when they can thereby considerably increase their earnings. . . . This explains the apparent paradox of the scarcity of labour in India." (Vera Anstey, *The Economic Development of India*, 4th ed., Longmans, Green & Co. Ltd., London, 1952, pp. 228–229.)

Things are not everywhere entirely different even now. "The more difficult problem (in Ceylon) is that of obtaining labour for semi-skilled and unskilled industrial employment. The agricultural and familial type of social organization of today offers great resistance to factory work." (N. K. Sarkar, *The Demography of Ceylon*, Government Press, Colombo, 1957, p. 267.)

not open, or when it appeared unattractive, an increasing volume of under-utilized labor may have been bottled up in the rural areas. The latter inference was often drawn in colonial times, though the discussion was cast in terms of "overpopulation" rather than "unemployment" or "underemployment."[1] This conclusion was easy to reach from the demographic trend in those parts of the region, particularly Java and several districts in British India, in which there was little room to expand the area of cultivation.

Speaking very broadly about the South Asian region as a whole, it nevertheless appears to be a more valid generalization to say that, up till recent times, labor input in agriculture must have increased more or less *pari passu* with the growth of the agricultural labor force. Since levels of living did not fall catastrophically, some combination of three types of changes must have taken place: an increase in the cultivated area, intensification in tillage on land already cultivated, and improvement in agricultural techniques. Some slow improvement in agricultural methods did occur, particularly in connection with the extension of the irrigated area, but there is little to suggest that such improvement was more than sufficient to offset the decline in food output per unit of labor in agriculture that would otherwise have resulted from the expansion of cultivation — whether on the extensive or the intensive margin. All of these measures required a higher aggregate labor input — the latter probably increased at about the same rate as the labor force grew. This amounts to saying that rural underutilization of labor — what now is thought of as underemployment — might on the whole have remained fairly constant.[2]

[1] See Appendix 6, Section 3, and Chapter 28, Section 6. This terminology should not be surprising as the "unemployment" issue, and indeed the very use of the term "unemployment," is rather recent even in European countries; see below in Section 8. Overpopulation and interest in the man/land ratio generally is much older; it was prominent in Malthusian writing and even earlier. It should be noted, however, that when, as often, "overpopulation" was discussed in terms of increasing idleness, this was not strictly in the main line of the classical tradition, according to which the effect of population growth was a diminishing — marginal and consequently average — productivity of labor, assuming full and optimal employment.

[2] Chapter 10, Sections 5 and 6.

"The supposition that it [overpopulation] existed even earlier is not unwarranted. In 1802 the colonial official Nederburgh reported that 'Java was overcrowded with unemployed,' and this at a time when Java could not have had a population larger than 4 million. In 1816 Engelhard, a former director of the province of Java's North East Coast, remarked that in his time the rice fields were cultivated on rotation, because the 'population far exceeded the cultivation.' In the well known report of the Commissioner General Du Bus in 1827, the Javanese village is characterized in general by an excess of *budjangs* or *penumpangs*, i.e. persons who are not entitled to participate in sawah ownership." (J. M. van der Kroef, *Indonesia in the Modern World*, Vol. II, Masa Baru Ltd., Bandung, Indonesia, 1956, p. 67.)

"All this would seem to justify Boeke's pronouncement that 'Javanese village society has had for centuries and centuries an enormous population density and a population surplus; both these characteristics have nothing whatever to do with the absolute population figures.'" (*Ibid.*, p. 67, quoting from J. H. Boeke, *Ontwikkelingsgang en Toekomst van Bevolkings- en Ondernemingslandbouw in Nederlandsch-Indië*, Brill, Leiden, 1948, pp. 7, 57.)

However, there may have been some conspicuous and perhaps large-scale exceptions to this broad generalization in areas where the agricultural density rose beyond a point where, with only slowly improving techniques, additional labor input could add proportionally, or even significantly, to output.[1] The result must then have been considerably lower standards of living. Java is perhaps an example of this pattern.[2] Certain heavily populated districts in the Indian subcontinent and even some of the paddy districts in Ceylon may have been exceptions as well.

In stating these broad generalizations, we have disregarded the simultaneous modifications in social and economic stratification arising, in particular, from changes in the pattern of landholding. These changes, of course, are not unrelated to the growth in population, and in the more heavily populated regions it has usually been assumed that they tended to increase the proportion of the population forced to eke out an existence as landless laborers or on tiny plots for which they were obliged to pay exorbitant rents in kind (Chapter 22, Part I).

In addition, non-economic relationships, represented by the institutions of the joint family and "attached" labor, may have slowly loosened, following the gradual trend toward increased monetization and increased mobility. This phenomenon is also assumed to have ensured that the underutilization of labor and its economic consequences were most severe among the lower social and economic strata in the rural districts. The repercussions on the social dynamics of the villages will be discussed later in various contexts. Many writers have stressed the importance of these processes and have concluded that their effect must have been to transform a vast amount of underemployment into open unemployment — to use the terminology of the modern approach. This would happen even apart from the increase in the labor force, but would, of course, be spurred by it.[3] Other writers have instead stressed the great inertia of traditional agriculture and its insulation from all impulses for change. This

---

[1] See Chapter 26, Section 2, about the development of output per head of population in colonial time.

[2] Even this exception to our generalization is no more than a conjecture, like the generalization itself. There is no firm basis for asserting that with growing density average levels of living in the Javanese villages declined.

[3] "[When so regarded], the problem of employment in underdeveloped economies, it will be obvious, is essentially a problem which grows in size. For, with the progress of economic development and the consequent changes in physical and mental environment, the remnants of the older form of social organisation may be expected to release the surplus labour they still hold. In other words, it is of the essence of the process of economic change and growth that the supply of labour offering itself for employment at a wage in the open market will progressively increase, even without growth of population. It is no use claiming that unemployment has not increased, on the ground that a large part of it represents precisely this kind of conversion that is the crux of the problem of employment in a society in transition." (K. N. Raj, *Employment Aspects of Planning in Under-developed Economies*, National Bank of Egypt, Cairo, 1957, p. 6.)

view implies that the rural communities may have been left much as they were generations ago.[1] If, as we have suggested, the increase in food requirements brought about by population growth was, on the whole, met by a higher aggregate volume of work from the increased labor force while productivity remained fairly constant, then the notion that conditions did not change substantially appears more probable.[2]

Thus far we have considered labor conditions in the rural districts from a dynamic point of view corresponding to the speculation surrounding the effects of increased population pressure in colonial times. But quite apart from trends, vast underutilization of labor at any given moment must have been, and was, apparent to every intelligent observer. There was much idleness in the stagnant and traditional economy, particularly among self-sufficient agriculturalists and the landless laborers, who were an increasing part of the rural labor force and also among the village craftsmen and in the ordinary urban occupations. Indeed, even the enclave enterprises experienced difficulties in keeping their labor force working steadily, intensively, and effectively.

Following a traditional bent, conditioned by poverty itself, people tended to be idle for much of what would be a normal working day, month, or year from a Western point of view and from the point of view of entrepreneurs influenced by Western attitudes. Even when working, they worked less efficiently. Though the masses of people were very poor, they were apparently not eager to improve their lot by increasing their labor input in agriculture and still less by offering their labor for wage employment.

[1] P. K. Mukherjee, speaking about India, says: "The peasant's life and routine of labour are everywhere organized by custom and tradition." And: "Nearly a hundred years of industrialization in India has not basically changed the country's economic structure which is, even today, predominantly agricultural, and stagnant at a very low level of productivity. As far back as the beginning of the present century, students of Indian economics were stating in a stereotyped fashion that the self-sufficiency and subsistence type of economy has gradually become extinct and has given way to an interdependent, competitive type of economy having the cash-nexus as the principal generator of change. These students have not investigated the matter thoroughly, in order to prove their preconceived hypothesis with the help of quantitative data. And this explains the confusion still existing in their minds about the nature and extent of the transition from a vast and subsistence type of economy to a cash and commercial one." And he gives examples of contradicting statements, illustrating this confusion. (P. K. Mukherjee, *Economic Surveys in Under-Developed Countries, A Study in Methodology*, Asia Publishing House, Bombay, 1959, p. 24.)

[2] Many writers question whether much change is taking place even now. A progressive, high-quality Indian journal, *The Economic Weekly* (Vol. XVI, No. 8, February 22, 1964), states: "One . . . wonders if the planning efforts so far have really come to grips with the basic fatalism, inertia, and the unquestioning acceptance of a low standard of living which permeates the mentality of the bulk of population engaged in agriculture and, to some extent, perhaps in other occupations as well." For documentation of such a view, see Kusum Nair, *Blossoms in the Dust*, Duckworth, London, 1961, *passim*.

This was one side of the picture. The other side we have illustrated in the preceding section, viz., that there was an acutely felt labor shortage in the new dynamic sectors of the economy. Recruiters of labor for the enclave enterprises faced major practical problems that engaged the continuous attention of colonial administrators and the managers of enclave enterprises; and, as we saw, their difficulties were invoked to support unusual methods of labor recruitment.

6 The Colonial Explanations

There was thus a paradox to explain: the scarcity of labor in the midst of so obvious a labor surplus. A colonial theory aimed at explaining this phenomenon did emerge. It took various forms at different levels of sophistication; it remained vague; and in the later periods, it was seldom explicitly articulated.

Its main theme was that the natives' tendency toward idleness and inefficiency, and their reluctance to seek wage employment was "voluntary" in a sense, an expression of their wantlessness, very limited economic horizons, survival-mindedness, self-sufficiency, carefree disposition, and preference for a leisurely life. To explain this bent of mind, the idea emerged that South Asian peoples were differently constituted from those of European stock, in that they normally did not respond positively to opportunities for improving their incomes and living levels. Since economic incentives failed in their purpose, this belief provided a justification for the use of harsh methods in recruiting workers and keeping them at work.

In technical parlance, this attitude is nowadays usually expressed by way of the backward-sloping supply curve. In colonial times the main tenet behind this theoretical formulation was already familiar: that the quantity of labor supplied, and also the intensity of work performed, decrease in response to an increase in earnings per unit of labor input. And it was generalized to include self-employed workers: labor input and exertion in work decrease when productivity of labor increases. This theory of the survival-mindedness of working people was, as we should remember, also a theme of European Mercantilist thought about labor and was used by some writers to defend low wages combined with harsh regulations.[1]

[1] As E. Heckscher has noted: "According to the statements of many Mercantilist writers, the more people were paid, the less they worked." (E. Heckscher, *Mercantilism*, Allen and Unwin, London, 1935, p. 165.)

Fears that wealth would lead to idleness provided a rationale for excluding the masses from sharing in national prosperity. It was for this reason that "Out of every ten interferences with the relationship between employers and employed, at least nine were in the interests of the employers. The authorities prohibited workers' associations and strikes, but shut their eyes to similar action on the part of the employers." (*Ibid.*, p. 167.)

Many Mercantilist writers, including major ones like Defoe, Mandeville, Davenant, Cory, and Clark, were, however, on the side of labor against these regulations.

Fundamentally, the backward-sloping supply curve (or the less systematic earlier theory) was merely a sophisticated statement, and in some ways not a very coherent one, of the common belief among the colonizers that the natives would not respond to incentives to raise their levels of living.[1] As in Europe in pre-industrial times, this view was sometimes romanticized.[2] But basically it implied condescension toward the natives and depreciation of their aptitudes and their way of life. They were lazy and would not exert themselves more than was necessary to maintain the miserable levels of living they had known for ages. Offering them opportunities to raise those levels would not induce them to greater exertions; on

---

[1] This belief was a major factor, for example, in the decision of the Dutch to introduce the *cultuurstel* system in Java. As Wertheim has noted: "This measure had been preceded by vehement discussion on whether private entrepreneurs, if granted waste land for exploitation instead of private estates already cultivated, could obtain sufficient workers on a voluntary basis. As there was little confidence in this possibility, van den Bosch cut the Gordian knot. Since he rather doubted the advantages enjoyed by labourers under a system of private enterprise, he preferred compulsory labour provided that it was not controlled by individuals (as was the case with private estates) but by a modern state. Thus, the culture system came into being, which compelled the peasantry of vast areas on Java, and in a few regions of the Outer Islands as well, to cultivate, besides the usual food crops, commercial crops for export." (Wertheim, *Indonesian Society in Transition*, p. 237.)

Mukherjee quotes the Royal Commission on Agriculture as follows: "Since the Government of India passed, in 1858, from the hands of the East India Company to that of the Crown, there have been many developments, but the main characteristics of village life, are still those of the centuries anterior to British rule. . . . Even when the population of India was much less dense than it is today and the area available for cultivation per head was much greater, it does not appear that there was any considerable section of the community which attempted to add to its wealth by producing more than it required for its immediate needs." (Royal Commission on Agriculture, *Report*, Government Central Press, Bombay, 1928, pp. 5–6, quoted in Ramkrishna Mukherjee, *Dynamics of a Rural Society, A Study of the Economic Structure in Bengal Villages*, Akademie Verlag, Berlin, 1957, p. 57 f.n.)

[2] Some Indian patriotic writings speak sympathetically of the "frugal life of the villagers." For example, Mukherjee quotes Azizul Hugue, who as a leading figure in the Krishak Praja Party was closely connected with the problems of the Bengal peasantry in the nineteen-thirties:

"The needs of the Bengal peasantry are very modest and limited. A little food, some scanty clothing, a few crude utensils, a humble shelter, a few lean animals to plough with and the simplest instruments for tillage — these are what he needs [*sic*]. He lives on the land of his ancestors and he would be happy to die in the same open yard where all those who have gone before him breathed their last. He has no equipment in the shape of either education or knowledge to enable him to go out of his village to seek his living elsewhere. He loves his land, his family and his inefficient and uneconomic cattle." (Azizul Hugue, *Man Behind the Plough*, p. vi, quoted in *ibid.*, p. 55 f.n.)

Mukherjee himself puts the blame on the British. "But it should be evident from the foregoing analysis that the agrarian crisis in Bengal was neither due to the backwardness and indolent habit of the people nor could it be solved merely by a charitable disposition to the peasants. One may therefore conclude that this truth could be unravelled only by a study of the economic structure of the society which showed that the agrarian crisis was due to the colonial system imposed on the country and the role of the parasitic landowning class as an appendage to that system, whereby their profit-motive could find ample satisfaction while preserving the 'peasant' cultivation without any capital outlay in order to improve the state of the productive forces." (*Ibid.*, p. 57.)

the contrary, they would then decrease their efforts. The prevalence of these attitudes among the common people was plainly visible and could be taken as proved by "experience."

That the natives were constituted to react differently from Europeans was then commonly related to racial distinctions between the native stock and the white people in Europe. A closer reading of Mercantilist literature over the centuries would perhaps have raised some doubts about this interpretation, as similar attitudes had been ascribed to the lower strata in Europe in pre-industrial and pre-liberal times. But in the nineteenth century that literature was widely forgotten; when not completely buried, it survived only with respect to the Mercantilist views on international trade, bullion, governmental regulations of commerce and industry, etc.

Even among the unsophisticated, however, some facts — apart from racial differences — were also enlisted to account for the puzzling behavior of the natives. It was thus commonly observed that the hot and often damp climate made sustained hard work odious and laziness inviting.[1] Generally, climatic factors figured more prominently in the literature of colonial times than in modern discussion.[2]

Often it was also observed that undernutrition, and inferior levels of living generally, lowered stamina and ability to work and to work intensively. This element in the causation of attitudes could occasionally be given an optimistic slant, as it would imply — contrary to the assumption of the backward-sloping supply curve — that rising income would increase preparedness to work and to work with greater efficiency, at least in the somewhat longer run.[3] But as such a thought ran counter to the main doctrine,

[1] Chapter 14, Section 2, and Appendix 10.
The influence of climate was often related to the backward-sloping supply curve.

[2] Various attempts were made to tie the racial factor to the climatic and broadly geographical factor: "It is difficult to say what causes one race to progress and another to stagnate. The spiritual factor is decisive, but racial character is itself ultimately the outcome of geographical environment. Every particle of our bodies comes out of the ground, and Man is, as it were, only the most complex of the plants grown by the soil. Different earths and climates grow different men just as they grow different trees. There is little stimulus to action in lands which have so easy a climate that the earth, tickled with a hoe, laughs with a harvest. Above all, a race is heavily handicapped if for centuries a murderous sun beats down upon its head, and generation after generation is born with malaria in its blood to sap the will, to destroy one working day in three, and to shorten life by decades." (G. E. Harvey, Outline of Burmese History, Longmans, Green & Co. Ltd., Calcutta, 1947, pp. 88–89.)

[3] For example, Adam Smith in his criticism of the Mercantilists commented as follows on the effects of "plenty" (i.e., cheap food and thus higher real wages if the money wage remained unchanged): "That a little more plenty than ordinary may render some workmen idle, cannot well be doubted; but that it should have this effect upon the great part, or that men in general should work better when they are ill fed than when they are well fed, when they are disheartened than when they are in good spirits, seems not very probable." (Adam Smith, An Inquiry into the Nature and Causes of the Wealth of Nations, 5th ed., Methuen, London, 1934, p. 84.)

it was usually suppressed or embodied in incidental and rather oblique remarks.

Often attitudes toward work and employment were also related to various observable elements in the system of social relations. The many inhibitions to manual work imposed by social and religious customs and taboos were much commented on in colonial times. The resistance, prevalent even among the poorest, to a change-over from work in the traditional household pattern to wage labor for an employer, even when the latter promised a higher income than could be gained in the traditional occupation, was understood to be part of the same social setting. Rooted in the social stratification were also many impediments to labor mobility, as, for instance, the "attachment" of laborers to particular employers, often with a firmness amounting to virtual serfdom. As the colonial governments had adopted a *laissez-faire* attitude toward indigenous social organization and ways of life, influences of this sort on the natives' attitudes toward work could not be changed. Colonial rulers might be aware of the problem but, reluctant to risk the unrest that might follow from tampering with traditional institutions, they made no attempt to solve it.

On a higher level of sophistication, the colonial explanations thus amounted, in fact, to a whole theory, explaining in sociological terms the tendency to idleness and low labor efficiency. Occasionally aspects of this theory were worked out in more specific terms and supported by empirical evidence. Differences were thought to exist between groups of different ethnic origin. The Chinese, and outside India often also the Indians, were regarded as more energetic and diligent than the mass of native stock.[1] Individuals, or particular castes or communal groups, were supposed to be different in some ways or in some degree. Particular ethnic groups were considered to be more "martial" and useful as soldiers. All this was backed up by "experience." In their more popular versions the explanations were stamped into stereotypes that became a sort of folklore. At the bottom of this theory, whether at the popular or more sophisticated levels, was the racial inferiority doctrine.

These views — on various levels of sophistication — were common to for-

---

[1] Harry Williams, giving a planter's nostalgic view of old times in Ceylon, commends the Indian Tamils for their high efficiency and characterizes the Singhalese, by contrast, as too much attached to leisure and to the enjoyment of an easy climate to be attracted to work on the plantations:

"There are enough Sinhalese peasants in Ceylon to man the tea industry many times over, but unfortunately for the tea industry, the Sinhalese peasant is a gentleman with a philosophy of life that he is not prepared to barter for material prosperity. One other point which makes him unsuitable as a permanent worker on an estate is that he detests rain, the lowlander very much more so than the highlander. But the latter has never become reconciled to the subjection of his beautiful mountains to the needs of an alien agriculture. He stands aloof except when hunger calls, and few Kandiars work upon tea estates in a regular capacity." (Harry Williams, *Ceylon, Pearl of the East*, 5th ed., Robert Hale Ltd., London, 1956, p. 225.)

eign entrepreneurs, colonial officials, and also to the mainstream of writers on social and economic problems who worked in the setting of political and economic colonialism. To a large extent, these attitudes — even including the racial inferiority doctrine — were often shared by those few individuals of indigenous extraction who in later times rose to higher positions in government service or who occasionally succeeded in becoming modern, large-scale entrepreneurs. Even many of those who were lower officials or middlemen, particularly when they belonged to an ethnic minority differentiating them from the masses, held these beliefs.

Although now more or less completely suppressed and never expressed publicly except in highly euphemistic forms, such attitudes are still widely held by Europeans working in the South Asian countries and by many individuals of indigenous extraction in the upper strata, as the author has observed. This presents an important problem for systematic research, for beneath the conventional egalitarian doctrine of these countries — which is sanctioned by strong interests both foreign and domestic — there survives a whole undergrowth of attitudes reflecting what we have here called "the colonial theory."

7 The Opportunism of the Colonial Theory and the Protest Background of the Modern Approach

As we have noted, this theory is very much akin to a strand of Mercantilist attitudes toward the masses of people in Europe.[1] Even more generally, it is the type of theory regularly held by the higher strata about the lower social and economic strata in very inegalitarian societies. It has, *mutatis mutandis,* its close parallels in popular views toward women not so many years ago, toward recent immigrants, or toward Negroes in America.[2] In

---

[1] Even the racial inferiority doctrine, which was a basic element in the colonial theory on South Asian peoples, is not entirely an exception to this parallelism. In feudal times in Europe, the upper strata certainly felt themselves a different breed from the serfs, though the contrast was less sharply etched there than in South Asia. That this feeling was usually not expressed in biological and racial terms can largely be explained by the fact that the view which these terms denote may, in a sense, be regarded as a strange fruit of the Enlightenment and a result of the recognition of *Homo sapiens* as only a species of the animal world. See Gunnar Myrdal, *An American Dilemma,* Harper, New York, 1944, p. 89.

[2] See *ibid.,* Chapter 4, "Racial Beliefs," and Appendix 5, "A Parallel to the Negro Problem," *et passim.*

"The list of beliefs with specific purposes could be made much longer. The underlying hypothesis is this; that in analyzing the popular beliefs, we have to work as a detective reconstructing the solution of a crime from scattered evidence. For both the student of popular beliefs on the Negro and the detective, the guide to the explanation is given in the question: To whose good? Beliefs are opportune; they are in the service of interests. It is these general and specific rationalization needs which give the beliefs their pertinacity. They give to the stereotypes their emotional load, and their 'value' to the people who hold to them." (*Ibid.,* p. 108.)

earlier times, all these popular beliefs were expressed and expounded even in learned treatises. They were always founded on "experience" and not entirely without a semblance of reason.[1] Even the understanding, excusing, and romanticizing tendency, which occasionally breaks through, has its parallels in the views toward women, Negroes, and underprivileged social groups generally.

In colonial times, the theory sketched in the preceding section was, of course, opportune to the colonizers, as a theory implying inferiority of a lower group is always opportune to those at the top of society. It gave a rationalizing defense for the colonial power structure. The "white man's burden" was, in the final analysis, his duty to govern those who could not govern themselves. The racial inferiority doctrine, in particular, helps us to understand why colonial rulers often felt that nothing much could be done to raise the standards of the indigenous peoples, because their plight was the consequence of immutable biological facts. Explanations in terms of social conditions led to the same defeatist conclusions; the social environment was held to be outside the jurisdiction of the colonial governments. In turn, the more basic racial inferiority doctrine supported the established *laissez-faire* attitude in social matters.

All knowledge, like all ignorance, tends to be opportune and to advance the cause of special interests — as long as investigators fail to observe the necessity of working with specific and explicit value premises. There is a "convenience of ignorance"[2] that enters into our observations and inferences and tends to fit them into a conception of reality conforming to our interests. Recognition of this fact does not, of course, imply that all our observations and inferences are faulty, but it does mean that we should scrutinize them carefully.

The colonial theory was not flattering to the dependent peoples, and partly for this reason was suppressed in public discussion even in colonial times. It was expressed bluntly only when foreigners of the upper class were with their own kind, in their clubs, homes, and offices. Keeping views vague and muted — particularly when educated members of the indigenous groups were listening, and even when it could be assumed that, at bottom, they shared them — was part of the backward-leaning considerateness to which people brought up in the Western tradition were schooled.

---

[1] "It is obvious to the ordinary unsophisticated white man, from his experience, that the Negro is inferior. *And inferior the Negro really is;* so he shows up even under scientific study. . . . The Negro is judged to be fundamentally incorrigible and he is, therefore, kept in a slum existence which, in its turn, leaves the imprint upon his body and soul which makes it natural for the white man to believe in his inferiority. This is a vicious circle; it is, indeed, one of the chief examples of cumulative causation. . . . The Negro situation being what it is and the unsophisticated white man's mind working as it does, the white man can honestly think and say that his beliefs are founded upon close personal experience and hard facts." (*Ibid.*, pp. 97, 101, and 102.)

[2] *Ibid.*, pp. 40 ff. *et passim.*

This became even more of a policy when, in a later period, a nationalist movement arose that drew an important part of its emotional charge from the sensitivity of the educated and alert among the dependent peoples to the attitudes of their foreign masters.

The urge to social exclusiveness, as exemplified in the clubs and in the various etiquettes that minimized or frustrated direct and intimate social contacts, stems from this situation. Europeans needed organized forms of social life that would permit them to speak freely and react with candor. The educated and alert non-Europeans, who in any case were the only members of the dependent populace who could aspire to social relations with Europeans, were quite aware of European attitudes, and indeed often shared them, at least to some extent. Nevertheless, those views were still felt to be offensive. The educated South Asian, while disliking the exclusiveness of Europeans, was hardly eager to establish close social relationships with them — an ambivalent attitude toward the institutions of separateness, e.g., clubs for whites only, which is plainly visible even today.

One further ingredient of the popular theory about the distaste of natives for sustained and intensive work should be noted: the idea that the natives in their laziness and wantlessness were happy, perhaps more so than the Europeans whose ambitions drove them to exertions that often ended in frustration. The notion that the underprivileged are particularly happy is, as we know, an almost regular element in the rationalization of inequality by a privileged group; visions of the happy and carefree Negro, the happy and contented woman, the well-satisfied servant, etc., are paraded before us. Conversely, the higher status of an upper stratum is pictured as not merely an advantage, but a "burden" carried for the common good, and not without sacrifices. After all, it does not necessarily make one happy to have power and wealth. An underprivileged person may be happier in his humble circumstances. He may have a closer and more undisturbed relation to the fundamentals in life, to sex, religion, music, and myth, for instance.[1]

This thought received some backing from the anthropologists, who, particularly in the colonial period, were quite obviously experiencing a reaction against European ethnocentrism. In their traditionally static models they wanted to give sense, purpose, and value to the social organization of even the most primitive societies. The hypothesis that marked their approach, and toward which their conclusions also tended, was that all cultures are valuable. In effect, this approach viewed indigenous societies as living museum pieces with a purity and integrity not to be contaminated by insensitive outsiders. The important social process of change in these structures in response to contact with the outside world was for the most

[1] This is related to the theory of the "Asian values," which makes the Europeans generous in admitting and stressing that the Asians have a philosophy of high caliber, though different from their own. See Chapter 3, Section 5.

part neglected; when it was not, attention was usually focussed on its unfortunate disturbing effects.

It is hardly surprising that the modern approach to the problems of labor
utilization, which broke through after the Second World War when the
colonies became independent, was *a protest against the dominant theory
of the colonial period*. Indeed, the fact that the modern approach bears so
much the stamp of protest makes an understanding of the dominant ideas
of the earlier period important to the study of present-day South Asia.

Implicitly, colonial theory looked at conditions in South Asia from a
Western point of view and measured attitudes and performance there
against Western standards. Thus it derived its condescending, humiliating,
and offensive character. But in point of view and standards of judgment
applied, nothing fundamental distinguishes the older from the modern approach. Not only those South Asian intellectuals who identify themselves
with the Western world, but equally those more aggressive nationalists
who are positively anti-Western, *must apply Western standards of judgment when, and insofar as, they advocate modernization*.

The colonial theory, of course, was put forward to explain not only the
backwardness and poverty of the South Asian peoples but also the lack of
progress and, indeed, the apparent absence of great possibilities for progress. Those intellectuals in South Asia who now want to spur progress *are
thus tempted to discount all those components of colonial theory that
emphasized the impediments to it*. Broadly, this means a rejection of the
colonial view that people and conditions in South Asia are fundamentally
different from those in the Western world. The specific implications of this
approach for the modern theory of labor utilization will be taken up in
Section 9.

8   *Another Contrast*

To grasp fully the historical and ideological background of this new approach, we need to remind ourselves that this dramatic development of
ideas about labor problems in South Asia bears close parallel with the
transformation in thought about the same problems in Western countries.
In South Asia, however, the change in approach was more sudden and
drastic than in the West. In the Western countries, moreover, the shift in
ideological orientation was preceded by fundamental changes both in the
character and organization of the labor market and in the political power
relations of society. In the interests of realism, modifications in modes of
thought were then needed. The institutional and political changes that occurred in Western countries had, however, only very diminutive counterparts in South Asia.

It is apparent from the writings of contemporary Western economists that they are not always aware how recently interest in the employment problem became intense in Western countries. Nor do they always fully appreciate the relative novelty of the now commonly accepted view that unemployment, rather than an individual problem, is a national problem for which the state has the primary responsibility. As an Indian writer has pointed out, even the word "unemployment" did not come into common use until toward the end of the nineteenth century.[1] In the different institutional and political milieu of earlier times, unemployment was not a focus of interest, and no effort was made to estimate it, statistically or otherwise.[2]

Going still further back, unemployment could not be an appropriate term for describing idleness in feudal times. As Schumpeter noted: "In principle, mediaeval society provided a berth for everyone whom it recognised as a member: its structural design excluded unemployment. . . . In normal times, unemployment was small and confined to . . . beggars, vagrants and highwaymen. . . . Mass unemployment . . . was unknown to the middle ages."[3] It can be assumed with fair certainty that if modern economists attempted to examine labor utilization in feudal Europe with the conceptual apparatus now so boldly used in South Asia, they would soon be sharply censured by economic historians.

In this respect, not much was changed in the long era of Mercantilism, at least not in theory. The Mercantilists, as we pointed out, viewed the labor market almost entirely from the employers' point of view. Insuffi-

---

[1] Nabagopal Das, *Unemployment, Full Employment and India*, 3rd ed., Asia Publishing House, London, 1960, p. 2. He also points out: "In the 1911 edition of the Encyclopaedia Britannica, for example, unemployment was defined as 'a modern term for the state of being unemployed among the working classes.' Then it went on: 'It is more particularly within the nineteenth century that the problem of unemployment has become specially insistent, not by reason of its greater intensity, but because the greater facilities of publicity, the growth of industrial democracy, the more scientific methods applied to the solution of economic questions, the larger humanitarian spirit of the times, all demand that remedies differing considerably from those of the past should be tried.'" (*Encyclopaedia Britannica*, 1911 edition, quoted in *ibid.*, p. 3.)

As J. H. Clapham has observed: "Since the early 'eighties, Socialist propaganda and philanthropic solicitude had fastened on . . . unemployment [as a] cause of poverty and destitution." A footnote reads: "'Unemployment' is first recorded in The New English Dictionary from 1888, 'unemployed' as a noun from 1882." (J. H. Clapham, *An Economic History of Modern Britain*, Vol. III, Cambridge University Press, London, 1938, p. 419.)

The current *Oxford English Dictionary* reports "unemployment" as "in common use in 1895."

[2] Even in Marshall's *Principles*, the term "unemployment" does not appear until the fourth edition in 1898. The term is used in the fifth ed., 1907, and in subsequent ones. Even in the eighth edition, Marshall's treatment of the problem is circumspect: "There seems to be no good reason for *thinking* that *inconstancy of employment* is increasing *on the whole.*" (Alfred Marshall, Guillebaud (ed.), *Principles of Economics*, 8th ed., and 9th (Variorum) ed., Macmillan, London, 1961, p. 688. Italics added.)

[3] Joseph Schumpeter, *History of Economic Analysis*, Oxford University Press, New York, 1954, p. 270.

ciency of labor supply — not unemployment — was the practical problem to which they directed their attention, and public policy was framed to create a sufficient labor supply at low wages. Some of the laws, regulations, and administrative practices through which this policy was executed, and still more, the approaches embodied in them, survived far into the liberal era.[1] In Mercantilist times idleness was assumed to be due to a personal defect, and was often dealt with as a criminal offense.[2] Again, as we also pointed out, the explanations of a labor shortage amid a large amount of idleness were not very different in Europe from those advanced in the colonies. The backward-sloping supply curve, or the theory of minimum-subsistence mentality expressed by it, is a very old idea, first applied to the poor in Europe.

When, in the post-feudal era of European economic development some idleness emerged which could not be regarded as altogether "voluntary," efforts were made even during the Mercantilist period by the state and local authorities in some countries to create work or to ease the sufferings of those afflicted by what we should now call unemployment. The development of the English Poor Law system, going back to Elizabethan times, is the clearest case of a state attempt to alleviate post-feudal "unemployment."[3] In addition, as Schumpeter contends, the protectionist arguments of Petty and some other Mercantilist writers were expressly motivated by the desire to create employment,[4] even if the general line of reasoning still stressed the need to augment the wage labor force in order to speed development. But the break-up of feudalism often created distress among the landless and poor which led governments and local authorities, the Church

---

[1] For example, Swedish statistics about the situation in the agricultural labor market were until 1928 worked out in terms of labor supply, not unemployment. The questionnaires sent to the chairmen of the municipal councils in rural communities asked whether the labor supply was "good," "sufficient," or "insufficient" (in 1926, a question about unemployment among agricultural workers was added). "Good" meant more than ample, which surely must seem to us a strange way of looking at things. Actually, this view has been passé in Sweden since almost the beginning of the century, but the statistical bureaucracy had not caught up with the change in thought.

[2] In this period, a "defenseless person" — in Swedish terminology a person without *laga försvar* — i.e., a person without means and without the "protection" of being employed by somebody, could be taken by the police and put in the workhouse.

[3] G. D. H. Cole and R. Postgate, *The British People*, Knopf, New York, 1947, pp. 108 ff.

[4] "Protectionist legislation, motivated by the employment argument, is of course still older by at least a hundred years [than 1549] and is rarely absent from the more considerable books. Malyner, Misselden, Childs [who makes it (employment) his criterion of the advantage that accrues to the mother country from colonies], Barbon, Locke, Petty — all have it [the employment argument]. . . . Some of the 'Mercantilist' writers went to surprising, in fact to Keynesian, lengths [and] expressed themselves as if they thought that the national advantage to be reaped from foreign trade consisted solely in the employment it gave. . . . The employment argument was not only advanced *per se*, but also in its indirect form, *via* the stimulus which inflowing cash will give to business." (Schumpeter, *History of Economic Analysis*, p. 350.)

and private charitable organizations to come to their aid. The assistance, however, was meager and the limits of action narrow.

But such tendencies were on the whole exceptions. And at a later stage when the feudal employer-worker relations had been more completely dissolved, attitudes tended to move back toward the harsher variant of Mercantilist thinking. The influential groups were no longer the surviving feudal landlords, with a sneaking sympathy and feeling of responsibility for the ex-serfs and a contempt for the newly rich merchants; the new rulers were the merchants themselves. Their concern was with labor scarcity and availability, not with worklessness. Hence in England, Chadwick's Poor Law Amendment Act of 1834 was specifically aimed at augmenting labor supply by refusing outdoor relief and making workhouse conditions "less eligible than the most unpleasant means of earning a living outside."[1]

This general approach had the support of economic theorists in the classical tradition who had sharply criticized the administration of the Poor Laws — especially of the requirements of residence within a single parish to claim eligibility for assistance — because of its restrictive effects on the mobility and adaptability of the labor force. The reaction against even the minimal social security provisions of the pre-liberalistic era was thus backed by a "new" economic theory affiliated to a philosophy that was radical in all respects other than the economic one.[2]

This liberal economic theory, which in its classical and neo-classical versions remained the type of thinking that mainly rationalized and greatly influenced public policy until recent decades, was less purged of Mercantilist ideas in its approach to the labor market than in its approach to foreign trade and the regulation of internal production and commerce. It had, in its very structure, a built-in tendency to look upon idleness either as the result of a personal shortcoming — as the Mercantilists had been inclined to view it — or as the result of a temporary maladjustment within the economic system. In the latter case, involuntary idleness could occur, but it presented no problems that called for policy action. If left alone, the system was self-correcting, as J. B. Say's law had affirmed. No chronic mass unemployment was easily conceivable within the assumptions of the emerging classical theory, and worklessness was not much of a problem.[3]

Even business cycle theory, as it began to take shape in the latter part of the nineteenth century in reaction to the classical and neoclassical equilib-

[1] Cole and Postgate, *The British People*, p. 234.

[2] See Gunnar Myrdal, *The Political Element in the Development of Economic Theory*, Routledge & Kegan Paul, London, 1953, pp. 118 *et passim*.

[3] "Economic theory was, for a century, completely hoaxed by an utterly meaningless 'proof,' Say's 'Law,' according to which supply could not outrun demand. Unemployment could then be treated as a 'residual' problem, due solely to 'frictions' resisting the ideally smooth functioning of the economic system." (Thomas Balogh, *Unequal Partners, The Theoretical Framework*, Vol. I, Basil Blackwell, Oxford, 1963, p. 1.)

rium theory, did not place great emphasis on workers being out of jobs. This phenomenon was treated as a by-product of "industrial fluctuations" and generally regarded as a relatively unimportant variable, as it was assumed to be a rather passive consequence of cycles. When Gustav Cassel treated the employment factor in the fourth part of his *Sozial-oekonomie* (published in 1918, but finished before 1914), it was in the context of industrial fluctuations and again from the supply point of view; the existence of a labor reserve in agriculture permitted the boom to reach a higher level before it collapsed.[1]

After the trade union movement grew up, it became common within these traditions of thought to ascribe the inability of workers to find employment in a particular section of the economy to wage rate rigidities caused by monopolistic trade union practices. Even Marshall, who was far from being an uncritical advocate of "Manchester" *laissez-faire*, tended to choose his assumptions in such a way that involuntary unemployment was impossible, unless workers combined in trade unions to keep the price of labor above the level appropriate to demand.

We are here attempting to characterize the "established" line of economic thinking that corresponded with the interests felt by the dominant social and political strata in an age before the widening of suffrage and the growth of trade unionism. The congruence of these interests and the mold of economic thinking can hardly be accidental. Nevertheless, specific concern with unemployment was kept alive right through the nineteenth century by social workers and by radicals and socialists. The latter were gradually aided by the mounting volume of statistical material amassed, particularly in England, by government departments and by committee reports and social surveys, of which they made intensive use. To a large extent, they anticipated the modern Western approach to the employment problem.

This rising tide of empirical and theoretical inquiry on the employment problem was largely ignored, however, by economists in the classical line until the rise of working class pressure changed the balance of social and political power in Western countries. The trade union movements grew up and overcame the restrictions on their activity — and on their very existence at an earlier date — imposed by law, administration, and directly by employers. They began to keep records of their unemployed members and to press for policy measures to alleviate the distress of the unemployed. Simultaneously, the gradual widening of the franchise opened the channels of government to people who raised the issue in the parliaments. The "social question" rose to importance and it was defined as the labor question (*die Arbeiterfrage*); after the First World War the International Labor

[1] Gustav Cassel, *Theoretische Sozialoekonomie*, Leipzig, 1918; English translation by J. McCabe, *Theory of Social Economy*, T. Fisher Unwin, Ltd., London, 1923.

Organization was set up and provided an international forum for the rising trade union movement.

This was a prolonged and gradual process, starting around the turn of the century in the different European countries and proceeding at different speeds. In the beginning, the main pressure was for unemployment relief. Gradually the reformers raised their sights to demand that employment opportunities be created through public works, first at sub-market wages, but later market scales of pay were claimed. Still later the idea emerged that the entire complex of public policies should be molded to minimize — if not eliminate — unemployment. Meanwhile laws were requested and gradually introduced covering all sorts of labor conditions; together they strengthened the bargaining position of the trade unions. The process reached its culmination after the Second World War when, in all Western countries, including the United States, the state agreed that it was its responsibility to promote "full employment."

In this process the phenomenon of unemployment — which, as we have seen, had been ignored by the mainstream of nineteenth century economic thought — was brought to the foreground. Employment analysis has now taken a central position in modern economics. This development of approach and doctrine is commonly viewed, not least by economists, as an independent growth of theory climaxed by the "Keynesian revolution." But it should not be forgotten that the light was kept burning throughout the nineteenth century by a host of collectors and analysts of empirical data in the social survey tradition and by the more radically inclined theorists. Their work was largely ignored, however, by writers in the dominant tradition.

More importantly, the ultimate breakthrough of the new orientation in economics must realistically be viewed as a response by economists to the vast changes in the structure of the labor market and to equally important shifts in the political power balance of Western society. Trade unions are now bargaining on terms that, with the help of public policy measures, have been greatly adjusted in favor of the workers. Moreover, there is universal suffrage, permitting the lower-income brackets to share in political power. In this mighty process, books supported social changes that made the time ripe for other and more radical books. But books certainly did not provide all, or even the larger part, of the momentum in this process of social, political, and ideological change.[1]

9 *The Appeal of the Modern Approach in South Asia*

By the accidents of history, the unemployment issue came to the center of economic theory and planning in Western countries at about the same

---

[1] The fact that economics and social science generally trail behind political changes was noted in the Prologue, Section 2.

time that South Asian countries gained their independence and could begin to consider their development problems along lines of their own choosing. It was in this setting that a mode of thinking about economic policy quite recently adopted in the rich democratic welfare states was suddenly applied to problems of labor utilization in the economic discussion of planning in South Asia.

Amid the outburst of interest in the problems of underdevelopment, development, and planning for development in the region, Western writers were, of course, inclined almost mechanically to think in terms that to them were familiar.[1] Generally, they preserved great professional naiveté about the doctrinal history of their own mode of thought and, in particular, its moorings in quite recent institutional and political changes. They must also, of course, have sensed that the colonial rationalizations were out of date in the new political situation and, indeed, distasteful to those who thought and spoke for the liberated countries.

South Asian economists were under much the same influence, as they had been educated to think in Western terms. In addition, the emotional load carried by the modern approach in Western countries, through its close association with radicalism in matters of social policy, undoubtedly heightened its appeal to South Asian intellectuals.

But the modern approach had a broader appeal. Though its historical links with the radical tradition were close, it had now become the commonly shared and respectable approach in Western countries; indeed, it was conventional and official doctrine. One did not need to feel radical to accept it. On the other hand, the many South Asian intellectuals who preserved radical leanings, and even elements, or more, of "Marxist" ideology, could appropriate it with little hesitation. On this particular point, the basic conception of labor problems held by "Marxist" theoreticians was not fundamentally different from the modern Western view.

Most important, however, was the fact that adoption of the new Western approach gave wholesale release at one stroke from all the objectionable elements in a colonial theory which had emphasized the uniqueness of the attitudes and behavior patterns of South Asia's indigenous peoples. It was a relief to forget those matters. The new Western approach to the labor problem said nothing, of course, about race; in the rich democratic welfare states, as they now emerged, homogeneity in biological constitution was an axiom. In this respect the modern approach marked an advance in rationality, and was supported by the results of modern research. Even before independence, theories that were based on the assumed racial and biological inferiority of South Asian peoples had largely been driven underground. Nevertheless, a sort of basic conviction lingered in white people's minds, as did a vague suspicion among many of the indigenous

[1] Prologue, Section 5.

people that there might be something in these allegations.[1] But such attitudes can no longer be part of a theory, whether on the scientific or the popular level, purporting to explain aptitudes and abilities of the people in South Asia. Equality in inherited mental traits between groups of people is now taken for granted and never challenged.

Dissimilarities in behavior and attitudes could still be explained by differences in environmental circumstances. On this point, the modern approach displays its character of protest mainly by ignoring the issue. Environmental factors, which, as was shown in Section 6, had been brought in as elements of the colonial theory, were now thrown out of consideration almost completely. This tendency is particularly strong in economic discussion that is guided by model-building, and it is reflected in the plans.[2] When they are dealt with by sociologists and other practitioners of what are sometimes called the behavioral sciences or by persons working on practical problems of land reform, community development, family planning, education, and so on, environmental factors are seldom coordinated with the broad economic theories and plans but live a life apart, in special books and articles and in separate chapters of the plans.[3] Some of these factors are given surprisingly little attention, even by experts who work close to the raw realities. Seldom — and never effectively — is their influence discussed in a way that would challenge economic theories and their implicit assumptions.[4]

In Western countries, abstraction from the physical environment is seldom detrimental. Differences in climate, for example, have never been of major economic significance in the temperate zones. In South Asia's colonial period, however, climate held an important place in economic and social speculation and had been relied upon to explain part of the tendency to idleness and low labor efficiency displayed by the population. Nowadays it is almost entirely left out of account.

As we have noted,[5] climate is hardly considered in modern economic literature on underdevelopment, development, and planning for development. One can read any number of books and articles on these topics without finding even a hint that South Asian climates are very different from those in Western Europe and that this fact has economic and social consequences. And practically no research, either in South Asian or in Western countries, has been directed to establishing the influence of climate on economic life in the region or to the possibilities for controlling this influ-

---

[1] An analogy to women's and Negroes' mental aptitudes and abilities is here again appropriate. Even if as a result of the popularization of the findings of research, it is widely accepted and proclaimed that there can be no appreciable differences, not only the males and the whites but also women and Negroes retain doubt in their minds; the old prejudices linger on and can be found as hidden mental reservations.

[2] Appendix 2, Section 14; Appendix 3.

[3] Prologue, Section 8; Appendix 2, Section 20; Appendix 4, Section 2 *et passim*.

[4] Prologue, Section 8.

[5] Chapter 14, Section 2.

ence. The writings in Communist countries are similarly biased. This by-passing of the physical environment is clearly a flight from reality.

In yet another respect, the analogy to Western conditions implied in the modern approach assisted escapism. Modern Western economic literature has given little attention to nutrition and levels of living and their relationship to labor input and labor efficiency. This omission can largely be justified by the high income levels attained in the West, combined with social security legislation and other redistributional reforms. But in South Asia, such props to nutritional and other standards are absent.[1] Nevertheless, when nutrition or levels of living more generally are considered in South Asia, they are, as in the West, usually considered only from the point of view of people's welfare, and not their ability and preparedness to work or their diligence and efficiency when working. The same has been the case in regard to health and educational facilities. In very recent years some economists have become interested in "investment in man," but this "investment" has been put on a par with physical investment in the aggregative capital/output models, and this "newest" approach has not even given rise to a realistic statement of the problems of health and education.[2]

Also aiding the escape from South Asian reality have been a number of institutional facts in Western countries that influence attitudes toward work and lend a fair degree of realism to the modern approach there. In Western countries, the labor force is differentiated and compartmentalized by skills, and within each compartment it works under fairly standardized norms. Also the length of the working day, and the number of working days in a year, are fixed by collective agreements or legislation. Save for the exceptional asocial cases, those who are without work can be assumed to want a job under these standardized conditions.

Generally, workers and all others have come to think rationally, weighing costs and incomes. As for the self-employed and entrepreneurs, they are not far removed from the old concept of the "economic man." This is not a matter of economic theory; it is the actual outcome of attitudinal and institutional conditions which have increasingly come to prevail. With the growth of rationalism in outlook of all people and the increased fluidity of markets, employment is the normal thing in Western countries, and unemployment, when it occurs, can generally be considered to be involuntary.

Unemployment in the Western countries is understood as a situation in which a person has no job but is seeking one, or at least wants one, at the going wage. There is also "disguised unemployment," which occurs when

---

[1] Appendix 2, Section 21.

In the statistics on unemployment and underemployment deficiencies in nutrition, health, and education are occasionally referred to as causes of idleness but economists have not been inspired to discuss seriously the problems involved and their relevance for the concepts used and the theories expounded.

[2] Chapter 29.

a worker, particularly in a situation of large-scale unemployment, has found temporary refuge in a line of work less productive and less remunerative than his normal occupation. Disguised unemployment has, however, usually been insignificant, especially in the post-war years when "full employment" has not only become the commonly accepted policy goal, but has also largely been realized in Western countries. Those who are normally self-employed in Western countries can, under existing conditions, be assumed to earn incomes which, everything taken into account, are high enough to compete with the incomes they might obtain by working for others. There is thus an economic reason why this group abstains from entering the wage labor market.

Unemployment — plus a fringe of disguised unemployment that occasionally can be of some importance but is distinguishable from regular self-employment — can therefore be measured in quantitative terms. Under the assumptions of rationalistic attitudes, standardized working conditions, and fluidity of markets — assumptions that for Western countries are highly realistic — aggregation of the number of unemployed in different skill and occupational groupings makes sense, as does the aggregation of such magnitudes as savings, investment, and output.[1] From a planning point of view the unemployed and the disguised unemployed represent a "labor reserve." This reserve can be regarded as a "readily available labor supply" that only waits for work opportunities to be absorbed into productive work. The labor reserve can, consequently, be mobilized by measures that bring about an increase in aggregate demand, supplemented, when necessary, by measures to retrain and resettle part of the labor force.

In Part II of this chapter we shall comment further on why the assumptions underlying the modern approach are inappropriate in South Asian conditions and why the concepts and theories worked out within this scheme are not valid in South Asia. In the present context, however, we should note that the planning problem in South Asia would be greatly simplified if we could regard the idle labor there as a reserve of unemployed constituting a readily available labor supply which could be tapped primarily by enlarging the scope of work opportunities. It would be further simplified if we could legitimately disregard a qualitative dimension of labor input, i.e., labor efficiency. Both these possibilities are plainly unrealistic.

The problem is made still more complex by the fact that the very existence of much idle labor in South Asia has instilled an attitude resistant to measures which might raise labor efficiency. In some quarters, efficiency is regarded as detrimental to employment.[2] The tendency — which is implied in the modern approach and colors all aspects of plan-making — to place

[1] Appendix 2, Section 20 *et passim.*

[2] "There is a generic confusion running through current Indian economic commentary concerning the relationship of labour productivity improvement to employment and

the main responsibility for the waste of labor on the lack of complementary factors of production, and particularly on the insufficiency of capital, also provides an escape from many awkward problems.

Another important fact is the existence of widespread unemployment and fear of unemployment among the educated class in the South Asian countries.[1] Institutional conditions in the labor market affecting this group bear a recognizable resemblance to Western patterns. Members of the educated class, who provide and articulate the ideologies and theories, have naturally been tempted to generalize their employment conditions and their fear of unemployment to their view of the entire society.[2]

A further confusion in thought about the employment problem stems from awareness of the accelerated rate of population growth in the postcolonial era. As we shall show in a later chapter,[3] its implications for employment are not the most crucial aspect of population growth. At least within the perspective of the nearest decades — which is the perspective of all planning — its significance has been incorrectly assessed. Nevertheless, the population specter is commonly seen mainly as signifying a need to provide employment for a rapidly increasing labor force.

II

The Inadequacy of the Modern
Approach in South Asia

In the first part of this chapter we have attempted to trace the intellectual ancestry of the modern approach to the underutilization of labor in terms of the concepts of employment, unemployment, and underemploy-

---

to the efficiency of land-use and capital-use. One hears that because labour is abundant, raising labour productivity is far less important than boosting output per acre in agriculture and per unit of capital in industry. From many discussions of the employment problem it would be easy to gather that an upward trend in output per manhour is positively antisocial; that its overriding effect is simply to kill off jobs." (John P. Lewis, *India's Rural Development Gap*, roneod, undated (probably 1959), p. 18.)

[1] Chapter 23, Section 6.

[2] "Because he has usually been educated in a town and his experience of the countryside is mainly confined to going back to his ancestral village on holiday or to collect his rents — he is often a small landholder — his immense goodwill for the villager is not always matched by an equally profound knowledge of the villager's circumstances: he exaggerates, for example, the importance of rural underemployment and the willingness of the villager to fill such spare time as he may have with subsidiary handicrafts. He attributes to the villager, indeed, his own terrible fear of unemployment. . . . In consequence, the Indian intellectual's fear of unemployment distorts Indian policy even more than the British coalminer's fears have distorted British policy." (Maurice Zinkin, *Development for Free Asia*, Chatto & Windus, London, 1956, pp. 239–240.)

[3] Chapter 28, Sections 3 and 13; cf. Appendix 7, Section 1.

ment. We have indicated the strength of its appeal to the planners in South Asia and have noted the elements of opportunism on all sides in its ready incorporation into the master model of concepts upon which planning in the region is built. That ideas should be opportune does not mean that they are wrong, but it does suggest that they should be examined with unusual care.

In Part II of this chapter, we shall address ourselves to the question of the appropriateness of this modern approach for the present environment of the South Asian countries. According to regular methodological rules, two criteria are normally used in evaluating the validity and relevance of theoretical constructions in economics: first, their adequacy from the point of view of analyzing reality; and second, their logical consistency.

We should, moreover, take note of a powerful factor that causes economists in the Western tradition to adopt constructions that are unreal and logically inconsistent — that is, their disposition to avoid political value premises by presenting concepts and theories that purport to be purely "objective." These claims to purely detached objectivity cannot be sustained. We stress again a point made in the Prologue (Section 9) and in Chapter 2 (Section 2): value premises are inescapable in social research and a *wertfrei* social science is unthinkable. Value premises necessarily affect the choice and definition of concepts, and thus the theoretical framework of research as well as the practical and political conclusions drawn from the facts obtained. This is not widely understood, and most economists in the Western tradition live in a philosophical muddle about what they are doing in their research. This confusion about premises is as we shall see, one of the major explanations for the lack of logical consistency. It is revealed when we insist on a third criterion: that we explicitly identify all value premises entering into our analysis and acknowledge their presence in research.

On all three counts, we shall find the modern approach to be deficient as a guide to an understanding of the present realities and future possibilities of South Asian economies. In the following sections we shall set out our main reasons for rejecting the modern approach to labor utilization problems in South Asia, and at the beginning of Part III of this chapter we shall outline an approach that we believe to meet these three criteria more satisfactorily.

10   The Basic Presuppositions of the Modern Approach

The modern approach sketched in Section 1 implies a number of assumptions about economic and social facts that, for reasons touched upon in the first part of this chapter, are fairly realistic in the Western world. Three of these assumptions are immediately apparent:

(1) that labor input can be discussed primarily as a quantity with little specific attention to a qualitative dimension, i.e., labor efficiency;

(2) that a low aggregate labor input, i.e., idleness, can be treated as "involuntary"; and

(3) that, therefore, idle labor represented by "unemployment" and "underemployment" constitutes a "readily available labor supply" in the sense that the provision of work opportunities is the main condition necessary for the elimination of idleness.

In turn, these assumptions, implicit in the modern approach, presume an abstraction from most of the peculiar and closely interrelated environmental conditions of South Asian countries — whether physical, technical, institutional, or broadly attitudinal — and, in particular, from:

(a) climatic factors;

(b) low nutritional and health levels;

(c) institutional conditions;

(d) attitudes that are molded by institutions and, in turn, reinforce them;

(e) the relative immobility of labor and the great imperfection of all markets and of the labor market in particular resulting from (a) through (d) above, but especially from (c) and (d).

In the general mold of thought shaping the theoretical economic discussion and reflected in the plans, it is further assumed:

(4) that in the economic discussion political, administrative, and organizational problems can largely be bypassed; and

(5) that the general explanation for the failure of idle labor to be absorbed in work opportunities lies in deficient supplies of complementary factors of production, mainly land and capital.

As land and other complementary factors, such as managers, technicians, and skilled workers, are limited in quantity and an increase in their supply calls for investment, the explanation of the large-scale involuntary idleness — that is, in the terms of the modern approach, unemployment and underemployment — can thus be reduced to:

(6) an insufficiency of capital from internal savings and foreign capital inflow.

The remedy implied is a heavier volume of capital input in the economy and a link is thereby established with the various economic models relating capital input to increases in aggregate output.[1]

With the assumptions noted above, the elements of the modern approach can be fitted into a coherent system of thinking. In South Asia, the Western

[1] Appendix 2, Section 14 *et passim*, and Appendix 3.

This is in the classical line: ". . . to say there is a great abundance of labour, is to say that there is not adequate capital to employ it." (David Ricardo, *Notes on Malthus' Principles of Political Economy*, Sraffa ed., Cambridge University Press, Cambridge, 1951, p. 241.)

When the "human factor" and, more particularly, the productivity of education was rediscovered, that factor was translated into "investment in man" and included in model thinking (see Chapter 29, Sections 4 and 5, and Appendix 3, Section 7).

model in terms simply of employment and unemployment is supplemented by an appendage, which is thought to bring it into closer touch with conditions in the region — a theory of underemployment, particularly among the self-employed members of the economy, whether in agriculture or elsewhere. One implication of this doctrine and of the other assumptions made is that:

(7) the unemployed and underemployed together can be viewed as constituting not only a labor reserve, but at the same time a savings reserve. To the extent that they can be set to work without increasing aggregate consumption, and the costs arising from their employment — such as those for capital equipment — can be held down, the aggregate volume of investment can be increased without making claims on the organized capital market.[1]

The modern approach is here sketched in a highly simplified relief that does not do justice to the insights into South Asian reality which appear as occasional qualifications and reservations in the voluminous literature. The important point, however, is that despite these qualifications and reservations — which are sometimes given great stress in introductions and whole chapters — this broad approach guides the economic discussion, the definitions of terms in the collection and analysis of statistical data, and the construction of the development plans.

11 Lack of Realism

A moment's reflection shows that these basic assumptions are badly tailored to a South Asian environment. The difficulties do not arise solely from the fact that the modern approach abstracts from some elements of South Asian reality. No theoretical system can possibly embrace all the complexities of social reality, nor should it attempt to do so. What is important is that the basic assumptions underlying the modern approach abstract from the crucial dimensions of the reality to be studied. South Asian societies have not experienced the processes of economic advance and of standardization, integration, and rationalization that have made these assumptions useful in the West as starting points in aggregative economic analysis.

[1] "In any analysis of the potential capital resources of an under-developed country, primary consideration is usually given to resources of monetary or commodity nature. One important source — labour — is generally neglected. It is not unusual that potential of unutilised surplus labour is regarded as a burden because it consumes without producing. It is now generally recognised that mobilisation of unutilised manpower can make a considerable contribution to the investment effort. We should utilise the energies of the surplus manpower which hitherto consumed without producing." (All India Congress Committee, Congress Planning Sub-Committee, *Report of the Ooty Seminar*, May 30–June 5, 1959, All India Congress Committee, New Delhi, September, 1959, p. 26.)

While the economic discussion, the gathering of statistics on unemployment and underemployment, and the plan-making continue along the path of the modern approach, the inadequacy of this procedure in South Asia has been stressed by individual authors. An Indian economist who has devoted much work to the problem of labor utilization in his country and is seeking a new approach, K. N. Raj, sums up his views in the following way:

The forms of social organisation, in a country like India, range from the most modern in the large cities, in which unemployment is as open and manifest as anywhere else in the world, to the most primitive tribal forms, in relation to which all the concepts of employment and unemployment that we use make no meaning at all. The concepts of manpower surpluses and of disguised unemployment, though useful for certain purposes, blur these important differences and conceal dimensions which are vital in formulating an approach to the problem.[1]

Another who has called attention to the inadequacy of Western concepts is P. C. Mahalanobis, who, as the founder and chief of the Indian Statistical Institute and in other capacities, has had a major responsibility for some of the most important attempts to throw light on the problem of labor utilization through statistical inquiries. He has said:

I should explain that there are great difficulties in adopting in India the concept of "unemployment" used in the advanced countries of the world, where practically all gainfully employed persons receive wages and salaries or have earnings in money (except for time spent by members of a family on their own household work). It is, therefore, possible to specify in an objective manner whether a person is gainfully occupied or is out of work. There are, of course, technical difficulties of standardising the definition of unemployment even in the advanced countries, but these are not very serious. In an underdeveloped country like India, on the other hand, there is inevitably a great deal of ambiguity in defining unemployment in an objective manner. . . . In fact, only about 13 million persons, who work under Government and public authorities or in private organised large scale enterprises, have employment of the type usual in the advanced countries. . . . The technical concept of "unemployment" can be strictly used only in the case of these 13 million persons (out of a total labour force of 160 million), but it is not applicable to the remaining 147 million who work in household or small scale enterprise.[2]

Mahalanobis, nevertheless, reaches an estimate of the magnitude of unemployment in India that corresponds to unemployment in the Western sense. He also explains that in the sample surveys of the Indian Statistical Institute, to which he refers in the passage quoted, it has been found necessary "to consider how many persons *have to* sit idle a part or most of the time for lack of work and other economic reasons."[3] The implied

[1] Raj, *Employment Aspects of Planning*, p. 7.

[2] P. C. Mahalanobis, "Science and National Planning," *Sankhyā, The Indian Journal of Statistics*, Vol. 2 ℭ, Parts 1 & 2, September, 1958, pp. 77–78.

[3] Italics added. The estimates Mahalanobis presents will be referred to in Appendix 16.

assumption is that the idleness of workers, not only in the minute organized labor market — where according to his assumption, the concept of unemployment has a fairly clear meaning even in India[1] — but also in the much larger field of unorganized industry, trade, and, above all, agriculture, is really involuntary, in the technical sense that a supply of labor awaits work opportunities and will spring forward to grasp them.

In order to highlight the unrealistic nature of this assumption in South Asia, it will be convenient to distinguish between two interpretations of labor underutilization: one in terms of the "readily available labor supply"; the other, the "labor reserve." The former concept denotes the amount of labor input in ready supply in excess of that taken up by demand for wage employees or in work opportunities for the self-employed; the latter concept should be understood as the unutilized labor potential available to planners seeking to increase labor utilization.

In Western countries, the readily available labor supply and the labor reserve at the disposal of planners usually amount to about the same thing: the number of unemployed plus occasionally a fringe of disguised unemployed. This reserve can be mobilized by increasing the demand for labor — a maneuver which can be executed with relative ease, primarily through expansion of aggregate demand for goods and services. We do not wish to minimize the extent to which aggregative solutions, even in the most advanced economies, may be insufficient to deal with the sticky problems of persistent unemployment in certain localities and among certain groups. Nevertheless, there is a significant contrast between such conditions in the West and those typically found in South Asia.

In South Asia, the readily available labor supply represents only a very small proportion of the real waste of labor. A massive waste of labor — whether because labor is not utilized at all, or is utilized for only parts of the year, month, week, and day, or is utilized in an almost useless way, that is, at a very low level of productivity — is one of the obvious facts of economic life in the region. In the present context, the important point is that little of this slack in the labor force can be taken up by turning on the tap of aggregate demand. Underutilization of labor vastly exceeds the supply that could be mobilized by expansion in monetary demand.

Instead, the bulk of the labor force is embedded in a climatic, social, cultural, and institutional matrix that not only tends to perpetuate present low levels of labor utilization, but also resists rapid and immediate adaptation to novel and unfamiliar ways of living and working. Idleness and low labor efficiency depend upon institutions, custom and tradition, attitudes toward work and leisure — including taboos and inhibitions related to status and to the participation of women in work. Moreover, the relevant

---

[1] We shall question the validity of the unemployment doctrine even in this segment of the labor market; see Chapter 24, Sections 10 and 11. Cf. Chapter 23, Section 3 and Part II *passim*.

attitudes are set in a framework of institutions, and the relationship between attitudes and institutions is mutually reinforcing.

Within this institutional framework, part of the labor force that is wholly or partly idle or engaged in unproductive work is excluded from the pool of the readily available labor supply for reasons that cannot even be thought of in terms of the rationalistic conceptions of voluntariness or involuntariness. And even those members of the labor force who could be assumed to want to work or to work more and with a higher efficiency if the opportunity were offered may — because of economic and social attachments supported by custom and tradition or because of climatic conditions or bad health — be prevented from working or from working during certain periods of the year, or from working with other than certain employers or associates, or from working in other localities. In addition, they may be conditioned to working very short hours and with low efficiency. The detailed reasoning supporting these conclusions will be presented in the following chapters.

When one probes into what is known about the facts, the rationalistic assumptions applicable to Western countries and uncritically transferred to the study of South Asian countries break down entirely. The labor supply which is actually and readily available in the technical meaning of economic analysis, and which, therefore, can be mobilized by creating additional opportunities in the wage labor market and in the large sectors where labor is self-employed, turns out to be very much smaller than is usually assumed in discussions — whether popular, political, or scientific — that are dominated by what we have called the modern approach.

Within the framework of that approach, the readily available labor supply has been grossly exaggerated. This phenomenon can largely be explained by the historical and ideological moorings of modern Western theory, which we have tried to lay bare in the preceding part of this chapter. It reflects the fact that at the back of the minds of those who take part in this discussion lies a notion that basically there is very little difference between the labor reserve and a readily available labor supply. In Western countries, the consequences of neglect of the distinction between the two concepts are not dangerous, because the Western institutional environment, for all practical purposes, tends to minimize the discrepancies between them. This is not the case, however, in South Asia.

In this connection we may note another difference. In Western countries, the practical aim of policy has increasingly become "full employment"; unemployment, when it occurs, is viewed as an anomaly, calling for policy correctives. With a labor market characterized by a high degree of mobility and adaptability in these countries, the unemployment problem can be dealt with, at least as a working approximation, in terms of the broad aggregates which play such a significant part in macro-economic analysis of the problem of short-period economic stabilization. But in South Asia the character of underutilization of labor is different and the problem is a long-term one; "full employment" is a distant goal and not one which can be reached via aggregative measures which leave attitudes and institutions unchanged. The limited scope of organized markets, among other things, makes aggregative measurement of the underutilization of labor far less possible.

12 The Policy Assumption Implicit in the Concept of a "Labor Reserve" in South Asia

When we use the concept of a readily available labor supply, we are asking a rather straightforward question: how much labor input would appear in response to an increase in demand for labor both in the wage labor market and in the sectors dominated by the self-employed? Essentially, we are interested in establishing a behavioral fact, based on the attitudes of members of the labor force and quite independent of the norms of outside observers. But even this apparently simple question does not permit a completely straightforward answer in South Asia. Workers themselves, on whose response the answer depends, may have difficulty in even imagining such a changed state of affairs: one in which they would find it attractive to take up new work, or work for longer periods, or work with greater intensity.

When we turn our attention to the labor reserve at the disposal of the planner, the problem becomes even more complex in South Asia. Here we are attempting to grasp the waste of labor from the point of view of an outsider concerned with reducing that waste. The labor reserve in his conception is the additional labor supply and input he would have at his disposal after having set various policy measures in motion — policy measures which would, both directly and indirectly, produce a variety of effects, including some changes in the attitudes of members of the labor force and in the institutions conditioning their attitudes and behavior. The standards of behavior he works with are thus different from those manifested and observable in the present behavior of the labor force. The concept of a labor reserve becomes therefore a highly hypothetical magnitude, dependent upon the direction and intensity of the planned policy measures.

The planner's ideas of what a fuller utilization of the labor force should imply for the length of the working day and the number of working days per month and year, the participation of members of various social strata and of women and children, and the intensity of effort in work, as well as his ideas about the types of policy measures he is prepared to use in order to increase labor utilization, are normative in nature and thus political. That he proceeds in this way is entirely legitimate. Because he sets improvement as his target, he cannot regard the *status quo* as his norm. Central to the very idea of planning for improved labor utilization is the fact that individuals must be induced to change their traditional attitudes toward employment and work, both directly — by education, propaganda, leadership, regulations, and compulsion — and indirectly, by creating better working conditions through such means as increasing capital investments, improving production techniques, and reforming the institutional framework in regard to ownership of land.

In these dynamic policy terms, the labor supply and the labor input, and the duration and efficiency of work are themselves functions of the policy measures intended to be carried into effect. Indeed, even when the planner moves to mobilize the actually available labor surplus, or part of it, by simply increasing labor demand and work opportunities, he is setting in motion forces that induce change. Even if limited in scope, such efforts to increase work opportunities will tend to change many conditions of life and work and, indirectly as well as directly, alter the attitudes of the labor force and thereby generally increase the size of the readily available labor supply. Even then the readily available labor supply is not identical with the labor reserve that can be made available through the intelligent execution of planning policies.

Every attempt to look upon the underutilized labor in South Asian countries as a labor reserve implies by logical necessity a policy assumption. The magnitude of the labor reserve is a function of the policy measures assumed to be applied. It cannot be defined — and thereafter ascertained empirically and measured — in an "objective" way as merely related to facts and independent of policy assumptions.[1]

[1] This has been recognized by N. V. Sovani in his criticism of the static concept of underemployment — see Section 14 — though he does not press the argument to its logical conclusions: "A removable surplus does not exist as such but has to be created by some reorganisation, small or large, in the production unit concerned. It is always potential and its realisation or emergence is contingent on reorganisation. It follows that the extent of the reorganisation determines the extent of the removable surplus. As such a removable surplus is not to be measured, but estimated with reference to the reorganisation or change contemplated and specified, according as the change or reorganisation is small or large the estimate of the removable surplus may be termed static or dynamic. To emphasise the fact that the removable surplus is embedded in change, it would perhaps make for clarity to describe it always as dynamic." (N. V. Sovani, "Underemployment, Removable Surplus and the Saving Fund," *Artha Vijñāna*, Vol. 1, No. 1, March, 1959, p. 24.)

"Because in the general discussion the change is not specified concretely, the fact that the estimate of the removable surplus population is determined by that change is not realised. . . . Any estimate of the removable surplus is really inherent in the assumptions one makes regarding the existing situation and the change in it. A removable population surplus is not something which absolutely and independently exists but is what we create even theoretically by assuming certain specified changes. Any estimate of it is governed by its assumptions and there can be many estimates of it in any particular context which are all equally valid under their own assumptions." (*Ibid.*, p. 25.)

Also, K. N. Raj remarks: "An estimate of the potential labour surplus can have no

The question to which research should be directed is the functional relationship between, on the one hand, alternative sets of feasible policy measures and, on the other hand, changes in the supply of labor on the wage labor market and in the labor input among the self-employed, as well as changes in labor efficiency for both categories of workers. In general terms the more far-reaching and effective are the planned policy measures and the more sharply they are focussed on the specific objectives of increasing the available labor supply and input and of raising labor efficiency, the larger we should expect the labor reserve to be.

The thesis we here expound — and which in Section 14 will be buttressed by a critique of a different theory contained in the modern approach and posed in static and "objective" terms — is this: that, under South Asian conditions, the labor reserve, for logical as well as for practical reasons, must be conceived in dynamic and policy-determined terms. Even conceptually, this becomes an involved matter. The planner's reserve cannot refer simply to a single moment in time but must assume a time span during which the policy-induced changes can take effect and produce secondary adjustments. In addition, the natural increase in the labor force during that period must be drawn into the analysis. Further, sensible policy cannot be directed solely toward increasing aggregate labor input; it must also aim at improving labor efficiency. The labor reserve will thus have to be defined in terms of both qualitative and quantitative changes in labor input.

The complications do not end there. Some changes — notably those involving capital input, technology, the institutional framework, and labor efficiency — have complex effects in that they may partly decrease requirements for labor input, thus releasing labor in some sections of the economy; they do not simply expand opportunities for productive work. As an ultimate goal, the planner and policy-maker must aim, however, to absorb the total labor reserve by utilizing the labor force fully at higher levels of labor efficiency and still higher levels of labor productivity. The concept of a labor reserve is thus a "middle term," indicating the difference in labor utilization between the present situation and an envisioned state attainable through policy measures that are feasible, though not as yet applied. Viewed in this sense, it is clear that the labor reserve available to the plan-

---

meaning, however, except in a clearly-defined context. The nature of the sanctions behind the norms fixed for hours of work, the political and social forces set in motion to draw out both male and female labour, and the precise changes in organisation and technique that are considered feasible at a given moment of time can each make a considerable difference to the surplus that actually emerges. When there is a variety of alternatives in regard to these measures, any estimate can obviously appear as good as any other and may, therefore, in fact, serve no better purpose than merely impressing, with an astronomical figure, the amount of labour that could be secured for development purposes in an apparently over-populated country." (K. N. Raj, "Employment and Unemployment in the Indian Economy: Problems of Classification, Measurement and Policy," *Economic Development and Cultural Change*, Vol. III, No. 1, October, 1958.)

ner and policy-maker in South Asian countries is very much bigger than the readily available labor supply.

In Western countries, labor is scarce and cannot be wasted. Non-utilization is therefore exceptional. Unemployment is normally involuntary (except for asocial persons) and labor performance is standardized in the several sectors and occupations, as to training, skill, and efficiency and as to number of working hours during the week and working weeks during the year. And, in the institutional and attitudinal setting of Western countries, the self-employed largely work according to the same standards and, even more significantly, strive to improve their position, calculating costs and profits in a rational way. These are the reasons why unemployment, and disguised unemployment, to the extent that they exist, provide a rough measure of the labor reserve the policy-maker can reckon on.

It is pertinent to note that, during the time of mass unemployment in the years of the Great Depression, there was concern in all Western countries about the "unemployables," those persons who were believed to be unwilling to work or incapable of meeting normal standards of punctuality, diligence, and skill. Such persons were then often supposed to represent a very considerable part of the mass of unemployed. This group of seeming unemployables was clearly an effect of unemployment itself, as was demonstrated when they were rapidly sucked into the production process as soon as the demand for labor increased — though probably with some lowering of efficiency standards here and there, at least temporarily.

It is open to speculation whether, had demand for labor remained low for several decades, Western countries would not gradually have approached the South Asian situation of a large gap between the readily available labor surplus and the labor reserve viewed from a policy perspective.[1] The existence of such a gap would have necessitated defining and measuring the labor reserve in terms of policy assumptions more complex than the straightforward view held in the Western countries that unemployment is undesirable and should be eliminated.[2]

[1] It is interesting that concern about the unemployables and, more broadly, "structural unemployment" re-emerged to some extent in the discussion of unemployment problems in the United States in the late 1950's and early 1960's, after a decade of relative stagnation in the American economy; cf. the author's *Challenge to Affluence*, Pantheon, New York, 1963.

[2] The reservation should be made that this simple value premise when dealing with the unemployment problem is not the only one even in Western countries. In Sweden, which is one of the full-employment or "over-full-employment" economies, the major emphasis in unemployment policy has for several years been placed on identifying industrial enterprises whose competitive ability is lagging, and the particular localities where unemployment is appearing in spite of the brisk overall demand for labor. Policy measures are taken to move workers to the expanding industries now hampered by labor shortage, to subsidize their movements from the distressed areas, and to retrain them with new skills. In the United States, which is not a full-employment economy (see footnote above), interest in a similar policy has recently emerged. If America should

13   Attempts to Use a Dynamic and Policy-Determined Concept of the Labor Reserve

What is sometimes called "potential unemployment"[1] comes nearest to a definition of the labor reserve available to the planner and policy-maker that, in a rational way, is determined by a policy premise. The policy premise is usually stated rather loosely, however, in terms of improved techniques, and sometimes in terms of changes in the size of farm holdings. As a matter of fact, very little study has been devoted to the functional relationship between policy measures and the aggregate utilization of labor that we have named as the main problem for economic analysis.

The thought is present, however, in comparisons between high-productivity Western countries and the South Asian countries, as, for instance, in attempts to calculate how much larger the output of Indian agriculture could be — even with a much smaller labor force — if only capital inputs, production techniques, and institutional arrangements were the same as those in the United States or Europe. Such statements can convey some impression of the contrasts between conditions in India and those in other parts of the world. But they provide no aid to practical planning and policy-making in India, as they assume demographic, social, and economic conditions totally alien to those that must be dealt with.

The literature is replete with unworldly statements about how much labor could be saved while yields were increased in peasant farming in South Asian countries and how much labor could be saved in many other occupations if production were rationalized. There is nothing wrong with the general drift of such assertions, and the consciousness of their essential truth is the intellectual force behind the efforts at planning and policy-making in these countries. But unless they are supplemented by specification of the particular policy measures required in the actual circumstances of a South Asian country, they are not helpful and lack clear meaning.

One inquiry into the labor reserve in agriculture that is rationally conceived in dynamic and political terms, and attempts to lay down definite policy assumptions applicable in a realistic situation, is Tarlok Singh's book *Poverty and Social Change: A Study in the Economic Reorganisation of Indian Rural Society*.[2] Based on field studies in the early 1940's, it was written well before independence. Its philosophy and practical recom-

---

become a steadily progressive full-employment economy, nevertheless it would continue to need such a policy; even in an expanding economy, there are always industries, individual enterprises, and localities, perhaps whole districts, which tend to become unemployment pockets.

[1] See Chiang Hsieh, "Underemployment in Asia," *International Labour Review*, Vol. LXV, January–June, 1952.

[2] Published by Longmans, Green & Co. Ltd., London, 1945.

mendations, which emerged from progressive thinking about India's situation, have had considerable influence on the policy of the Congress Party and the government. Nevertheless, this pioneering attempt to define a rural labor reserve in policy terms has not been followed up very effectively.

Tarlok Singh wants "to transform the peasant economy by a process of peaceful but rapid change,"[1] more specifically, by bringing agriculture under "joint village management." This would be "a system in which the claims of ownership are respected, but owners pool their land for the purpose of management."[2] The rationalization of agriculture through cooperative farming would mean a reduction in the number of workers who could be employed in cultivation. He tries to estimate "the surplus which will be thrown up as a result of the rationalization of agriculture"[3] and which must be given non-agricultural employment, either in the cities or in the villages. Taking into consideration "other occupations as well, the best conjecture which we can make is that in British India alone" – thus excluding the princely states – "in the course of the next decade, we must create *new employment* in towns and in villages so as to be able to absorb 21 and 22 million male adult workers."[4]

It is true that various links between Tarlok Singh's deductions and the facts he observed can be criticized. For obvious reasons the materials available now, twenty years after his study was undertaken, would also make it possible to improve on his calculations. He should have been more specific about the time period involved and should have taken into account the expected increase in the labor force. Further, his neglect – in line with the modern approach – of questions of labor efficiency and of the involuntariness of idleness diminishes the realism of his study. He falls into wishful thinking in his confidence, which he has largely retained, that joint village management – based principally on a system of cooperative farming that preserves most of the present distribution of ownership of land and offers no cure for the landlessness of a large part of the agricultural population – will more or less automatically eliminate the evils of economic and social inequality.[5] It is a hope that lacks foundation. He does not analyze the problem whether, how, and to what extent, the labor "released" from agriculture can be given employment.

[1] Singh, *Poverty and Social Change*, p. 8.

[2] *Ibid.*, p. 57. The problem of cooperative farming will be treated in Chapter 26, Section 17.

[3] *Ibid.*, p. 10.

[4] *Ibid.*, p. 11.

[5] "When the village begins to function effectively as an economic unit in agriculture and in relation to industry, the present division into more or less fixed groups will tend to be modified, and all sections of the community including the depressed classes may hope to achieve equal opportunity and equal freedom. Thus, in attacking the rural problem at the root, we shall strive not only for freedom from poverty, but also for freedom from social injustice and indeed for freedom from those other evils which are fed in turn by poverty and social injustice." (*Ibid.*, p. 8.)

"The programme of reorganisation which we have set forth in the preceding chap-

But his fundamental approach to the problem of estimating the labor reserve in Indian agriculture is the correct one. He attempts to study the actual circumstances; he not only defines a general policy goal but also spells out the specific measures to be applied; he then investigates their effects on labor demand and compares these estimates with the labor force available in different parts of the country. His concept of a labor reserve is thus dynamic and political, as, for logical reasons, it must be.

14   The Static "Objective" Concept of Underemployment

In general those who subscribe to the modern approach, instead of following Tarlok Singh's early and pioneering study, have tried to define the labor reserve in static terms, as existing at a point of time, and unrelated to any policy assumptions. In regard to the workers in the wage labor market the usual procedure has been to accept as the labor reserve the readily available labor supply as manifested by workers who seek, but fail to find, employment. But the major effort in this line of reasoning has been to define and measure the amount of surplus labor bottled up among the self-employed workers in peasant farming and in other family enterprises, consisting of workers who are wholly or partly idle or who work at a very low level of productivity.

This attempt, as has already been noted, is undoubtedly inspired by a feeling that the modern approach needs to be adjusted to the very different circumstances of South Asia and other underdeveloped countries. Carrying out an analogy to the unemployment discussion in the Western countries, this surplus is often called "disguised unemployment" or, more frequently, "underemployment," though there are many other synonyms.[1] In the present discussion, we shall refer to it as "underemployment."

Though there are many variations on this theme, the basic idea behind the "underemployment" approach to the definition and measurement of the labor reserve is a static one: it assumes that under unchanged conditions of capital input, production techniques, and institutional framework, and with only minor changes in the organization of work, the same aggregate produce could be obtained even if a part of the labor force was re-

---

ters will lead to important changes in social structure and economic life. When techniques change and a large number of new occupations come into existence, the significance of caste of hereditary status in old occupations will be free from any such link. It may also be anticipated that the sort of hierarchy which now marks the social economy of peasant villages will tend to disappear, although for various reasons, leaders and organisers will, for a considerable period, come largely from the ranks of peasant owners. On the whole we have reasons to expect a steady decrease in inequality among workers. Difference in income and status will tend to be due, less to accidents of birth and caste, and more to skill, education and achievement." (*Ibid.*, p. 170.) See Chapter 26, Section 20.

[1] In Appendix 6, an immanent criticism is made of this concept and the implicit theory contained within it.

moved. This static definition of underemployment, of course, requires judgment according to an external set of norms. In some cases, the standards applied have been based on performance on farms where labor is utilized more intensively;[1] in other cases it has been assumed that a cer-

---

[1] Thus, B. Datra assumes the work done in double-crop areas as the standard full-time work for a cultivator. According to his estimates, only about 16 percent of the Indian cultivated area is cropped twice; he reaches, under a number of other assumptions, the conclusion that 28 percent of the labor force is wasted. See B. Datra, *The Economics of Industrialisation*, The World Press, Calcutta, 1952. Moti Lal Gupta observes that this is not a quite correct procedure. It gives too low a figure as there is also underemployment on the farms practicing double-cropping, because even there the farms are too small and the man/land ratio too high. (Moti Lal Gupta, *Problems of Unemployment in India*, Nederlandsche Economische Hoogeschool te Rotterdam, 1955, p. 25.)

Two estimates of underemployment in Indian agriculture may be mentioned here for illustrative purposes. One is reported on in an Evaluation Report of Community Development. The study was carried out for 13 community blocks, 1959–60. In the study it was found that "the groups," i.e., cultivators, artisans, and laborers, "lost about 3 to 6 per cent of the available time because of sickness and another 1 to 3 per cent on account of weather, i.e. in the aggregate 5 per cent to 8 per cent are lost for reasons unconnected with the employment situation. Of the 92 to 94 days out of every 100 days available for gainful work, the cultivators find employment for 69 days in the busy and 58 days in the slack seasons. Taking the busy and slack together, cultivators and artisans are unemployed for 30 per cent of the total man-days and agricultural labourers for 35 per cent. . . . Chronic or perennial unemployment is . . . twice as large in magnitude as the extra seasonal unemployment among cultivators and agricultural labourers and three times or so among artisans." (India, Government of, Department of Community Development, *The Seventh Evaluation Report on Community Development and Some Allied Fields*, Vol. 1, New Delhi, April, 1960, pp. 124 ff.)

So far this is an attempt to measure idleness pure and simple. It corresponds — except perhaps for the open unemployment in terms of labor offered on the labor market for which there is no effective demand — to the ordinary definition of underemployment. In addition, the study defines "disguised unemployment" as the difference between the number of man-days of labor ostensibly put in on the farms and the number required. Assuming "existing conditions of the farm economy," and taking into account the cropping pattern and the proportion of the area which is irrigated, the study adopts as a standard the number actually employed by the farms in the top quartile in each category of farms, assuming that their workers are "fully" employed. The conclusion is: "Judged by the standard adopted, half the man-days ostensibly spent on the farms can be considered unwanted. That is to say, if other farms in each cell could emulate the top quartile, about half the man-days of work now put in can be dispensed with and made available for other purposes. The degree of disguised unemployment does not vary much between the two seasons, the busy and the slack." (*Ibid.*, pp. 124 ff.)

The number offering themselves for wage employment had risen from the 34.3 percent recorded in a study undertaken in 1954 to 41.1 percent, while in both studies the agricultural workers were only 12 percent.

S. S. Gill, on the basis of farm management surveys for two districts in the Punjab pertaining to the year 1954–55, found by a detailed comparison between labor utilization on farms of different size that "28 per cent of the total permanent farm labour force on the farms . . . is surplus, though 'underemployment' varies with the size of farm. It is as high as 62 per cent on the smallest size-groups — 0.5 [acres] and 10 per cent in the fourth size-group — 20–50 [acres]." (S. S. Gill, "Unemployment and Underemployment of Permanent Farm Workers," *Artha Vijñāna*, Vol. 2, No. 4, December, 1960, pp. 259, 260.)

He adds: "The estimate of the surplus given above will remain a mere theoretical and statistical category, if no change in farmwork organisation is envisaged. Its realisation, however, is feasible by the enlargement of the operational size of the holdings of

tain number of hours or days of work per year correspond to full employment.[1] Sometimes it is not made clear what standards have been applied and whether static conditions are assumed to be fully preserved.[2]

This way of thinking is in line with the tradition in the social sciences,
especially in economics, to "objectify" concepts and to reach politically
meaningful conclusions without a value premise.[3] In regard to labor utilization in the South Asian countries, the temptation to adopt this procedure
is strong for two reasons. On the one hand, there actually is, by any relevant valuation, a tremendous waste of labor. A strong urge is thus felt to
express this waste in quantitative terms. On the other hand, the cure for
underutilization of labor touches explosive issues, about which there can
be no unanimity in the countries concerned. Discussions about the incidence of taxation, land and tenancy reform, and compulsory work arrangements, for example, are obviously highly charged with vested interests and
emotions. The doctrine we criticize represents an attempt to be "scholarly"
in the time-honored way by a maneuver that is logically impossible: by defining and measuring the waste of labor while remaining innocent of how
anything can be done about it.

Applying an external set of standards is, as pointed out in Section 12,
quite legitimate and, indeed, logically imperative in a discussion of policy and its effects. But it is more difficult to understand how external norms
can be made compatible with a non-political, "static" analysis. As a matter
of fact, when scrutinized further, this line of analysis is static, not only in
regard to its assumptions about capital input, production techniques, and
the institutional framework, but also with respect to aggregate production,

---

the smaller cultivators to the level of about 30 acres (the average size of holding in the
fourth size-group). This can be achieved, without affecting any change in property
rights, etc., by some sort of co-operation amongst the small cultivators through joint
field-operations, central aid teams or such other forms of co-operative farming." (*Ibid.*,
p. 260.)

[1] Colin Clark, for example, has assumed that 2,500 hours per year should be the
standard for full employment in Pakistan agriculture. (Colin Clark, cited in J. Russell
Andrus and Azizali F. Mohammed, *The Economy of Pakistan*, Oxford University Press,
London, 1958, pp. 26–27.)

[2] A work by W. A. Lewis provides an example: "Disguised unemployment in agriculture is difficult to measure. It depends upon the level of technique, upon the capital in
use, and upon the nature of the crop. In India it is thought that, with the bullocks and
ploughs in common use, a hundred acres in grain can provide employment for perhaps
fifteen persons 'gainfully occupied' in agriculture; whereas the average number 'gainfully occupied' in India per hundred acres is about thirty. Allowing for the fact that
some of India's agriculture is more intensive than grain, Indian economists estimate
conservatively that a quarter of the rural population is surplus, in the sense that its removal from the land would make no difference to agricultural output." (William
Arthur Lewis, *Aspects of Industrialisation*, National Bank of Egypt, Fiftieth Anniversary Commemoration Lectures, Cairo, 1953, p. 8.)

[3] Prologue, Section 9, and Appendix 2, Section 14 *et passim*.

which is assumed to be unchanged. This technique is not "true statics" but "comparative statics," for the volume of underemployment is treated as the difference between two situations separated by a timeless and abstract, though very great, change: the "removal" of a large part of the labor force in the course of which, according to one of the static assumptions, aggregate output remains the same. In Appendix 6 it is shown why this reasoning is logically untenable and why the resulting figures for underemployment are arbitrary and, in fact, without meaning. A labor reserve cannot be defined without specifying a time span during which definite policy measures are applied to a concrete situation.

We have thus far criticized the concept and theory of underemployment from the point of view of logical consistency. Putting the observations of the facts in this theoretical Procrustean bed also leads, however, to gross distortions of reality. These are largely the distortions common to all theories that are based on the modern approach. The intensity of labor input is regularly disregarded, and all idleness is assumed to be involuntary. The latter assumption has, as we have seen, been used in a very specific sense to imply that the same aggregate labor input — producing an unchanged aggregate output under conditions that are static in all the respects mentioned — will be provided by a smaller labor force, once enough workers have been removed to eliminate the phenomenon of underemployment.

One could express this, perhaps, by stating that the labor supply is assumed to be almost infinitely "elastic," in the sense that if the aggregate labor force is reduced, the labor input of those who remain in agriculture instantaneously rises sufficiently to fill the gap. At the same time, this way of reasoning implies that labor requirements in agriculture are highly inflexible and rather rigidly determined by the land area and soil conditions, together with other geographical features and with the factors kept constant in the comparison, e.g., capital input, production techniques, and the institutional framework.

This latter assumption of fixed labor requirements in agriculture also emerges in an assertion, regularly made in the discussion of underemployment, that the existence of underemployment means that the marginal productivity of labor is zero or even negative.[1] In this respect, there is a logical contradiction in the assumptions implicit in the modern approach.

The two assumptions — that labor supply is highly "elastic" but labor requirements are fixed to constant production — are unrealistic. Contrary assertions about both labor supply and labor requirements would come nearer the truth.

---

[1] See Appendix 6, Sections 6 and 7, in which we show that this (untenable) assumption is not necessary. Why it has been used is not difficult to understand; it helps to make more credible the further assumption that all idleness is involuntary, as a larger labor input would be useless.

Consider first the labor requirements per unit of land.[1] Even within a given cropping pattern and with known production techniques, possibilities for varying the labor intensity of cultivation are great almost anywhere in South Asia. This is demonstrated by the huge differences in the labor intensity of paddy production in various parts of the region, and also by the historical trend — for instance, the extension of cultivation from lower to higher lands in Java during a period of population increase.[2] Similarly, the extent of irrigation, the irrigation methods used, and the degree to which existing irrigation facilities are utilized can vary widely in response to changes in the input of labor. And, of course, the cropping pattern can be changed, especially by adding more labor-intensive products — such as sugar, jute, potatoes, and new horticultural crops — to the usual subsistence crops. To this should be added the fact that in South Asia, generally speaking, yields per hectare are mostly very low outside the plantation sector.[3] There is no doubt that, even under the assumptions made in the theory of underemployment about unchanged institutional framework, capital equipment, and techniques, the yield can almost everywhere be raised by an increased labor input.

In other words, far from being determined rigidly by natural conditions, the amount of labor applied to a unit of land is highly variable even when the man/land ratio is high. Nor is there a low ceiling on the amount of useful work to which spare hours could be put in raising the productive value of cattle, in cultivating fish in the ponds, in planting trees, and in making and improving tools, houses, roads, furniture, etc., without assuming any new technical knowledge.[4] And, of course, idle hours could be used for study or for acquiring skills.

Turning to the other side of the picture, the idea that idleness or very unproductive employment implies a pressure for work, that is, a high "elasticity" of labor supply, is far removed from social reality, as we shall find in the next chapters. The result of a fairly high "elasticity" of labor requirements combined with a low "elasticity" of the supply of labor is that districts are often found — even some with an extremely dense agricultural population — in which there is little or no surplus manpower ready to be "skimmed off" from agriculture when new demands for labor arise.

Therefore, we must conclude that the attempts in recent decades to devise a concept, underemployment, which would define a labor reserve in terms of a "static comparison," and so permit accurate measurement of the waste of labor in South Asian countries — a situation described in an earlier

---

[1] Appendix 6, Section 7.

[2] For a fuller discussion, see Chapter 10, Section 6; Chapter 22, *passim;* and Chapter 26, Sections 3 and 11 *et passim.*

[3] Chapter 10, Section 4, and Chapters 22 and 26, *passim.*

[4] This all means that the marginal productivity of labor cannot be assumed to be zero; see in Appendix 6, Section 7.

era as "overpopulation" — have been abortive. The concept is meaningless and the figures calculated have no significance. What we can attempt to study empirically is the readily available labor supply. Even though that labor supply cannot be precisely measured, the concept is at least consistent and clear. It refers to the way people would, or might, behave in a different situation and is not bound by *a priori* assumptions.

We know also that, from the point of view of the planner and the policy-maker, the labor reserve in South Asian countries — unlike that in Western economies — is very much bigger than this readily available labor supply. This is one of the most crucial facts of South Asian economic life. But this fact cannot be established, still less be given quantitative formulation, within the framework of the modern approach. It has to be studied realistically as a functional relationship, between policy measures and labor utilization, during a period of time and in a particular situation.

III

Outline of a More Realistic Approach

15 *Definitions*

We now turn to the task of constructing an alternative conceptual framework for the study of labor utilization — one we believe to be logically consistent and adequate for the study of actual conditions in South Asia.

This framework will first be stated in bare and skeletal form. The remaining chapters in this part of the book are intended to put flesh on the skeleton. Insofar as possible we shall fill it out with concrete data. But because of the paucity of data and the irrelevance of much of it we can often only highlight problems that urgently require further research. In large measure, the lack of relevant material results from the fact that most efforts to collect and analyze data on labor utilization have been guided by the logically invalid and unrealistic modern approach.

When the conceptual blinders of the modern approach are removed, the problem of labor utilization emerges as a highly intricate one — much more so than is implied in the simplifications of the modern approach. The framework presented below and utilized in the following chapters should be understood as tentative. But, for the time being, it has an important negative recommendation: it is not afflicted with the inhibiting assumptions of the modern approach but directs attention instead to the crucial issues obscured by that approach. As empirical research proceeds, it is to be expected that new, more realistic, and therefore more valid, generalizations will emerge, making it possible to frame theories to displace those contained in the modern approach. We can at least assert that future theoretical advances cannot build on the unrealistic foundations of the modern approach, but must break out in new directions.

Let us begin the formulation of our alternative approach by explaining what we mean by "potential labor force" or simply "labor force." In this study we shall use the term "labor force" to refer to the population of working age. The age limits for this group must be determined by an assumption. That assumption should, however, be realistic and consistent with the customs of the region; it should also take into account the way these customs might be changed according to value premises that should be made explicit.

Relatively speaking, the *size* of this labor force at a particular time — for instance, the beginning of a plan period — is among the magnitudes that can be fairly reliably approximated by thorough periodic censuses. Census compilations at present are not ideal for this purpose, as usually the age distribution in a census year is not accurately established, but is estimated within rather wide margins of error.[1]

With reservations concerning differential mortality rates in various age groups, estimates can also be made of the *increase* in the labor force during the period of the couple of decades falling within the perspective of planning. This increase will be composed of children now living and those who survive birth in the immediate future, minus persons who leave the labor force because of age or death. Natality does not enter crucially into the calculations but mortality does, and changes in mortality may be difficult to foresee.[2]

As stated at the beginning of this chapter, the level of development and its rate of change can be indicated by the average *productivity* of this potential labor force. The problem of planning is to devise politically feasible and practicable means to induce changes that raise average productivity as much and as fast as possible. Policy measures must be chosen and coordinated with this purpose in mind.[3]

Achievement of a productivity increase implies one or both of two broad types of changes:

(1) a higher total labor input;

(2) a higher productivity per unit of labor input.

The first of these variables, the total labor input, depends on:

(a) The *participation* rate, or that portion of the labor force normally performing some work, at least when the whole year is taken into account. The participation rate is lower than 1 everywhere in the world but, for various reasons, it is strikingly low in some South Asian countries.

[1] Chapter 27, Section 1 *et passim.*
[2] Chapter 28, Section 3.
[3] Appendix 2, Parts III and IV.

(b)   The *duration* of work by those who are participants (according to
      the above definition), in terms of months and weeks per year, days
      per week, and hours per day.

These distinctions permit us to determine the degree of *idleness* in the
following way. The total labor input achievable through complete participation of the population of working age at an assumed[1] standard of work
duration can be calculated. The degree of idleness can then be established
in two steps. First, the difference between the labor input obtained from
actual participation and duration and the labor input maximally achievable
under the assumed conditions can be established. Secondly, this magnitude
can be expressed as a proportion of maximum labor input assumed to be
achievable.

So far the reasoning is straight and simple, as we have treated the idleness of the labor force as a factual pattern of behavior, independent of assumptions about its causation or motivation. For many purposes it is appropriate that we stick to this behavioristic definition of idleness, though,
of course, in the analysis of idleness we must examine the factors responsible for it and distinguish among types of idleness.

In this examination we shall abandon the usual modern approach to non-
participation. Within its frame of reference, non-participation is related,
not to the labor force, defined as above, but only to that part of it which
can be characterized as *active*. As unemployment is assumed to be involuntary, there may indeed be a wide discrepancy between the potential
and the active labor force, with the difference accounted for by those who
are able but not willing to participate in work.

This distinction is bound to be utterly unclear in South Asia. Both in its
definition of the active labor force and of unemployment, the modern approach relies on the prevalence of a rational psychology and on the existence of a fluid labor market. As already pointed out, these presuppositions
are broadly realistic in the institutional and attitudinal setting of Western
countries, but are much less so in South Asia.

When ill health or climatic conditions make work impossible for sustained periods or make it so disagreeable that people are deterred from
working, idleness might in some sense be described as "involuntary." But
this characterization is valid only if and when it can be assumed that the
persons affected would otherwise be working or seeking opportunities for
work. In actuality, abstention from work is not dictated exclusively by
these objective facts but also by institutions, customs, and attitudes. When
people can be observed to prefer leisure, it might be held that their abstention from work is "voluntary" and that they should therefore be excluded
from the "active" labor force and from calculations of the "unemployed" —
to use the terminology of the modern approach.

[1] Here again an explicit value premise becomes necessary.

We must again insist, however, that the volitional approach to these matters in South Asia is unhelpful. People may not seek work because they believe none to be available; this in turn is a function of the lack of an effective market and of limited horizons imposed by life in stagnating and
largely isolated societies. Moreover, social and religious institutions and attitudes have a forceful effect in making some people indisposed to work at
all. Others are prepared to work, but only under certain conditions — for
example, if they can be self-employed or can participate in a family enterprise, but not as wage laborers. Even those of working age who are prepared to work for an employer may be available only locally or only in the
service of a particular kind of employer, or only for certain types of tasks.
Thus their mobility may be restricted both spatially and functionally.

The essential point is that the scope of rational planning cannot be restricted to those who respond to an opportunity to work, assuming for the
moment that this magnitude could be defined and ascertained, but must
also be directed toward raising levels of living, health, and stamina and,
in particular, toward changing institutions and attitudes and increasing
mobility in such fashion that more people will be prepared to become participants. Policy must, in other words, aim also at increasing the size of the
part of the labor force that participates in work.

This dynamic view thus makes still less feasible a clear-cut definition of
the active part of the potential labor force. When in the later discussion we
occasionally refer to the *active labor force*, we do so only in a very vague
sense, though it can always be understood as excluding the disabled and
persons who abstain from work because of institutional and attitudinal
constraints that the policy-makers do not at present seek to change.

The reasons why members of the labor force fail to participate in work,
and why the duration of work is often short, need to be intensively studied.
Fresh studies, however, should not prejudice the issue by loading the
definitions. The rationalistic concepts of "voluntariness" and "involuntariness," in any case, fail to provide a fruitful and realistic basis for study
in South Asia.

The second of the major variables — average output per unit of labor input — depends upon a number of factors.
(a)   One is directly related to the human factor of production, namely,
      labor efficiency, i.e., labor intensity and skill. Labor efficiency rep-
      resents a qualitative dimension of labor input and we shall define
      it as the worker's productivity, when all the conditions under (b)
      through (e) below are given.[1] Labor efficiency thus defined de-
      pends, in the first instance, on the worker's physical and mental

---

[1] Unlike labor input, labor efficiency cannot be measured directly when these conditions are changing. This circumstance may help to explain why labor efficiency has
been so neglected in the analysis of labor problems.

stamina — more generally, his health — which in turn is determined by available health facilities and, in addition, by nutritional and other levels of living; on his education and training for work at prevailing levels of technology; and on his attitudes toward life and work, as determined by climate, levels of living, customs, and institutions.

But the level of productivity is also influenced by a set of conditions that are not simply to be understood as qualities of workers. These are:

(b) *occupational distribution* of the labor force;

(c) *natural resources;*

(d) capital disposal, i.e., the volume of *capital resources* and *their allocation;* and

(e) *technology.*

Underutilization of the labor force is the non-achievement of those values of the three components of labor utilization which can reasonably be assumed to be brought about by feasible policy measures during a planning period. This comparison can also be stated in terms of output per member of the labor force, but only when conditions (b) through (e) are considered as given. It is closely related to the criterion we have chosen as an indicator of the level of underdevelopment and the rate of development.[1]

The level of actual labor utilization can thus be expressed as the product of the following three ratios, assuming occupational distribution, natural resources, capital disposal, and technology as given:

(1) participation $\left(\dfrac{\text{working members}}{\text{labor force}} \right)$

(2) duration $\left(\dfrac{\text{man-hours}}{\text{working members}} \right)$

(3) labor efficiency $\left(\dfrac{\text{output}}{\text{man-hours}} \right)$

Broadly speaking, the modern approach has been preoccupied with the first of these ratios, and then in only a partial and unrealistically biased way, whereas all three are essential to an understanding of labor utilization in South Asia.[2]

[1] See the introductory paragraphs in this part and Appendix 2, Section 7.

[2] Occasionally a reservation is made that an analysis in terms of idleness because of unemployment and underemployment does not exhaust the problem. A study of unemployment presented by the Indian Planning Commission thus starts out by noting the importance of "qualitative improvement leading to better work performance," and refers to "the existing pattern of intensity of work, attitudes or willingness for more work, the predominance of the household pattern of production [that] . . . introduces a peculiar difficulty in assessing the appropriate extent of the malady." (India, Government of, Planning Commission, *Outlook on Employment,* New Delhi, 1959, p. 1.) The source goes on, however, to present, and comment on, data on employment, unemployment, and underemployment.

16   Interrelationships

It is not sufficient to recognize the importance of the two additional variables in the analysis of labor utilization problems in South Asia and to purge unrealistic and *a priori* assumptions. That the three components of labor utilization are connected must also be appreciated. Duration of work and labor efficiency are, first, closely bound up with each other. This is true even from the standpoint of definition. When the unit in which labor input is reckoned — a day or an hour — contains periods of idleness shorter than that unit, labor efficiency covers not only skill and intensity of work during actual working time, but also varying elements of idleness. This idleness escapes statistical detection because it occurs in periods shorter than the unit of measurement.

Even apart from this, labor efficiency is, of course, causally associated with both participation and duration and is regularly lower when there is also much idleness and, more generally, when labor is abundant. Other factors may also affect the values of more than one variable. For example, climate — insofar as it is a deterrent to work — may reduce both the duration of work and its intensity. The same is true of low physical and mental stamina caused by bad health, which in turn results from low nutritional and other levels of living. Health deficiencies may prevent participation in work or cause workers to shorten their hours; poor health will usually also diminish labor efficiency during the time of actual work.

Similar multiple effects may arise from all those attitudes which may be called minimum-subsistence-mindedness and which in theoretical discussions have been represented by the backward-sloping supply curve. Institutional arrangements, such as the prevalence of tiny plots in agriculture, may mean that a high degree of efficiency should not be expected during the few hours and days of actual work performance.

However, "overstaffing" in employment is caused, among other things, by the cheapness of labor; the labor input in terms of participation may seem to be high quantitatively, but labor efficiency and, usually, work duration quite low. Improvements in labor efficiency may lead, at least in the short run, to increased idleness on the part of some or all workers. Large increases in participation could mean that duration and/or efficiency would be reduced, again particularly in the short run. All these factors and their interrelations can be changed; indeed, it is the purpose of planning to accomplish the desired changes in a coordinated way.

Even the variables affecting average productivity that are not directly related to the human factors — occupational distribution of the labor force, natural resources, capital disposal, and technology — can and must be altered. Natural resources, for example, may be fixed in quantity, but they need to be explored and the possibilities for their economic exploitation subjected to closer study.

These factors are also interdependent. A more productive occupational distribution of the labor force — brought, say, through industrialization — requires changes in the utilization of natural resources, capital investments in plants, machinery, power, and transportation, and the application of superior techniques. To be more advantageously utilized, natural resources must not only be explored but also supplemented by investment of capital and the application of new and more productive techniques. In most (though not all) cases, more productive techniques will raise demand for capital investments. Higher savings to pay for more investments will, to an extent, depend upon improvements in productivity that raise incomes. This result, in turn, is a function of changes in the factors mentioned above that could stimulate increases in labor input and improvement in labor efficiency.

The interrelationship between labor participation, work duration, and labor efficiency has been noted above. There is also a wider interrelationship. Labor efficiency does not depend simply upon stamina, training, institutions, and attitudes, but also upon the distribution of the labor force, the availability of capital equipment and natural resources, the levels of technology, and standards of managerial practice — factors themselves closely linked. Thus in many fields of work, not least in agriculture, the tools and the techniques employed govern a particular work process so narrowly that there is little scope for variation in labor efficiency.

The Indian peasant driving to market in his bullock cart at an average speed of three kilometers an hour is just as efficient — or inefficient — as his capital equipment and the technology embodied in it allow him to be. Similarly, changes in the occupational distribution of the labor force that favor more productive lines ordinarily require that other conditions be altered if labor efficiency is to rise. When, as often happens, a particular machine has to be run at a slower pace and/or requires more workers in the South Asian countries than in more advanced ones, this situation must be traced back to the fundamental determinants of labor efficiency: health and stamina, education and training, institutions and attitudes toward work.

Again, a higher input of labor arising from extension of the duration of work depends largely — though not exclusively — upon a changed occupational distribution and upon more effective use of natural resources, capital investments, and improved techniques. But it is also dependent upon changes in attitudes, as indeed are the changes required to advance labor productivity. This can be accomplished directly — by education, propaganda, and compulsion — and indirectly by changing the institutions under which the workers live. Further, attitudes and institutions are themselves likely to undergo some change under the influence of other changes, though with a lag that is sometimes considerable.

This reminder of the general interdependence in the social system, which is more fully described in Appendix 2, is inserted here for a purpose. The modern approach to underutilization of labor in terms of "unemployment" and "underemployment," because of its use of unrealistic assumptions, has suffered from a tendency to neglect this interdependence or to narrow unduly the relationships taken up for economic analysis.

To the policy problems raised by the waste of labor in the South Asian countries, which reveals itself in the very low average productivity of the labor force, we shall return in Chapters 24, 25, and 26. In the next two chapters we shall first try to use the available statistics and other empirical information to throw light on the underutilization of labor in South Asia and its causal and factual basis. We shall begin with traditional agriculture and then turn to other areas, particularly urban industries. Separate attention will also be given to persons with at least enough formal education to qualify them for clerical work, and to women in the labor force. Thereafter we shall examine the problems involved in attempting to raise the utilization of labor through industrialization and through agricultural advance.

In the remainder of this book, we shall avoid further use of the terminology of the modern approach, apart from those few cases in which labor market conditions in South Asia bear some resemblance to those typical in Western countries. As we shall find, the applicability of the conventional concepts of unemployment and underemployment is restricted mainly to the small "modern" segment of urban industries and to the position in the labor market of persons with some formal education. Even in these cases, the modern approach cannot be adopted without qualification. We shall, therefore, develop the argument of the following chapters around the concept of labor utilization discussed above.

17 The Inappropriateness of Western Conceptual Categories for the Compilation of Statistical Data

Let us now consider how the modern approach has distorted collection of the data that are essential to an understanding of the realities of labor utilization in South Asia.

Most of the official statistical inquiries dealing with the labor force have posed the wrong questions. This is the basic — though not the only — weakness in data collection to which we wish to draw attention. On labor force matters, the main statistical effort in these countries has been devoted to the compilation of data on "unemployment" and its appendage "underemployment." In view of the prominence of this topic in the modern approach, such a focus of effort is hardly surprising. Unemployment is one of the most relevant variables in contemporary Western analysis, and those who are immersed in the modern approach are naturally led to attempt measurements of its magnitude in the South Asian countries.

For the reasons spelled out in this chapter, this approach fails to come to grips with the essential realities. On the contrary, it tends to obscure them. Conditions in South Asia are so different from those in the Western countries where the modern approach originated that it is unreasonable to expect the same questions to be relevant in both contexts. By and large, preoccupation with the unemployment component of labor utilization has been legitimate in the West because the other two important components — duration of work and labor efficiency — have been institutionally standardized and regulated at high values. The same conclusion cannot be sustained with respect to South Asian economies.

The basic criticism, therefore, is that when the collection of empirical data is guided by the modern concept of unemployment, the questions raised are unreal, and consequently irrelevant. They do not illuminate the essential realities of the economies in question, which is, after all, the purpose of empirical inquiries. Instead, they have the unintended effect of camouflaging underutilization of labor. Underutilization is the important fact of economic life in the region; it deserves to be brought to the center of the stage and subjected to detailed analysis.

Despite this weakness in the orientation of statistical effort in South Asia, it still might be thought that in one respect the energies spent on unemployment measurement have not been altogether wasted. The existence of unemployment clearly affects the value of one of the three components of labor utilization, the participation ratio. Even so, the analysis of participation ratios cannot usefully be approached in the same manner in both types of environment.

In the modern West, a volitional approach to the concept of employment and unemployment is legitimate because high participation ratios are the socially expected norm. It is thus reasonable to assume that those who are able to work but are not employed are involuntarily idle. In South Asia, as we have argued above, the conventional distinction between "voluntary" and "involuntary" idleness is of little explanatory value.

But it must also be recognized that another factor in South Asia destroys comparability between worklessness there and open unemployment in the West. Throughout the region, there is no dole and no unemployment compensation to sustain those who are without gainful pursuits. Persons lacking a current source of income are obliged to find something to do (even at a very low level of earnings) if they cannot fall back on their reserves, throw themselves on the mercy of private charities, borrow for consumption purposes, or rely on friends or relatives for support. With some important exceptions, which we shall consider elsewhere, the mass of the population must find some means of eking out an existence, however unproductive their efforts may be from the society's point of view.

Nor is this "buried" unemployment identical to the "disguised unemployment" that has emerged as a by-product of the downswing in the business cycle in Western countries. "Disguised unemployment" in the latter sense refers primarily to the ineffective utilization of skills when members of the work force take up casual pursuits as a last resort. It cannot be assumed that those engaged in casual pursuits of low productivity in South Asia have been displaced from more productive jobs or possess, in fact, the skills that would raise their productivity if the demand for labor increased.

The foregoing considerations lead us to ask what the voluminous data collected on unemployment in the region can really mean. As we have indicated, they tell us virtually nothing about two fundamental magnitudes: the duration of work and labor efficiency. Moreover, they fail to convey a realistic approximation of aggregate participation ratios. Not only do studies guided by the modern approach fail to focus on the relevant questions, that is, those which would illuminate the important realities, but they fail to yield results to which a clear and precise meaning can be assigned.

Some of the sources of ambiguity can be understood more fully if we consider for a moment how the basic data on unemployment are compiled. In Western countries, estimates of the volume of unemployment are generally prepared from two primary sources of information — unemployment compensation rolls and sample surveys of the population of working age. In a Western context, these techniques yield reasonably valid measures of unemployment, though, of course, identical definitions are not used in all countries. Similar procedures are far from being even approximately reliable when transferred to South Asia.

Numerous obvious difficulties confront the preparation of any estimates of aggregate unemployment in the South Asian countries from registration with the labor exchanges. In the first place, the geographical coverage of these exchanges is limited. In the main, labor exchanges (offering enrollment on the "live registers") are established only in the larger urban centers. In some countries, new exchanges have been opened over the years; expansion in the services offered means that conclusions cannot be drawn from these studies about trends in unemployment over time. But even if the number of exchanges were stabilized, serious difficulties would remain in interpreting the significance of these registrations.

The absence of any unemployment compensation schemes removes much of the incentive to register. Many who might be regarded as "unemployed" in Western countries may be ignorant of the opportunity to register or skeptical of the value of registration.[1] Moreover, an unknown number of those who do register may hold jobs, but be seeking better ones.[2]

[1] Sample surveys in India have attempted to ascertain the number of unemployed who failed to register. Results for September 1953 indicated that nearly three-quarters of those without work in the urban areas did not register. The major reason was reported as "ignorance." See India, Government of, *National Sample Survey No. 16*, Report on Employment and Unemployment (Ninth Round), Calcutta, 1959, p. 44.

[2] In India, where the coverage of the employment exchange has been expanding, there has been at least one careful attempt to establish whether or not the increase in registrations reflects an actual rise in unemployment. The increase in gross registration

On the whole, the labor exchange returns are thus very unreliable indicators of the volume of unemployment in the urban centers, to say nothing of the economy as a whole.[1] In addition, the segment of the working-age population that makes use of these facilities is highly untypical, as registrations tend to be biased in the direction of those who have some education. The unemployment problems of this group, as we shall see later,[2] are very special ones.

The sample survey technique for measuring unemployment also faces formidable difficulties, though of a different kind. Quite apart from the technical problems of design of samples — problems that, in some degree, confront sampling procedures wherever they are used — a number of more basic sources of error are inherent in the use of this technique in South Asia. Any body of information collected through interviews or questionnaires — whether on a sampling basis or comprehensively, as is the case with the periodic censuses — will be useful and reliable only if two basic conditions are satisfied. First, the questions posed must be sharply defined in a way that eliminates both confusion on the part of the respondent and ambiguous classification and interpretation of the results. Secondly, it must be possible to check the reliability of answers in order to minimize error

---

figures was discounted by subtracting the registrants on newly opened exchanges, and by deducting the number of employed persons registering on the exchanges. In addition, an allowance was made for an increase in the proportion of the unemployed who actually registered because of the growing popularity of the service and the expansion in opportunities to take advantage of it. The latter estimate was, of course, subject to a margin of error of undetermined magnitude. While far from perfect, this approach is considerably superior to one which relies on the crude registration data. See India, Government of, Directorate General of Resettlement and Employment, Ministry of Labour and Employment, and Labour and Employment Division, Planning Commission (a Joint Study by), *Outlook on Employment, and Related Papers,* New Delhi, March, 1959, Appendix, pp. 17–19.

[1] The Second Pakistan Plan commented as follows on the labor exchange system: "The existing employment exchange system, a legacy from the past, has been built mainly along western lines suitable for countries at a relatively advanced stage of industrialization. In Pakistan the routine registration of large numbers of unskilled job seekers for whom few jobs can be found has been a largely futile task. The solicitation of vacancy notices from employers in occupations in which persons with skill and training are scarce or totally lacking, has likewise been a discouraging duty which has brought little co-operation from employers." (Pakistan, *Second Five Year Plan* (1960–1965), p. 373.)

To this should be added the I.B.R.D.'s strictures on labor exchanges as sources of employment data in Ceylon: "Official employment exchanges have only about 70,000 registered as unemployed; informed opinion places the real total at around 200,000. . . . Of the 70,000 registered, investigators of the I.L.O. estimate that 25% are really employed, and that 85% (including those employed) are simply using the registry as a means of seeking better jobs." (International Bank for Reconstruction and Development, *The Economic Development of Ceylon,* Johns Hopkins Press, Baltimore, 1953, p. 251.)

[2] Chapter 23, Section 6.

and bias in responses. Most of the sampling exercises conducted in the region satisfy neither of these conditions.[1]

If one considers for a moment the nature of the economic environment in South Asian countries, it is not difficult to understand why inquiries based on a Western-inspired set of concepts fail to produce worthwhile statistical data on the realities of labor utilization there. The problem of identifying the active labor force is a case in point. In South Asia, much of the population of working age maintains a connection with family enterprises and is largely detached from an organized wage labor market. Within this framework of organization, household members may make an important, though not a continuous, contribution to the output of the family unit. These circumstances further strip the Western concept of the active labor force — which is based on a volitional approach to work participation — of much of its meaning. Persons connected with such enterprises, though their labor contribution may be intermittent, are, not unnaturally, puzzled when asked such questions as: "Are you seeking employment?" or "Do you regard yourself as fully employed?" Within their range of vision no alternative to their present situation is likely to be comprehensible.

Some of the persons connected with the formulation of these surveys have in fact recognized the inapplicability of this type of questioning, though they have not always drawn the appropriate conclusions when devising subsequent inquiries. For example, the Census Commissioners in Pakistan have noted:

Only 131,484 agricultural and other workers in the whole of Pakistan reported themselves as having been unemployed during the whole month of January 1951. These figures are obviously too small and do not represent reality: to use them even as a standard of measurement will lead to quite wrong conclusions. . . . Many enumerators appear to have failed altogether to record the answer to the question of unemployment. Secondly, cultivators do not regard themselves as unemployed if their families own land and they are maintained by the general activities of the household. Among cultivators, therefore, only landless labourers are likely to regard themselves as unemployed. Thirdly, among non-agriculturalists there was evidence of considerable reluctance to admit unemployment and in the case of independent workers on own account, a category which represents a considerable proportion of skilled and unskilled labour, the whole conception of unemployment is indefinite. Moreover, persons seeking work in industry, business or services regard themselves, not as unemployed, but as still engaged in the general work of their family, particularly if their family owns or rents land. Lastly, the Census questions on unemployment were rather complicated and were probably properly handled only by the more intelligent and better trained enumerators.[2]

[1] For a fuller discussion of these problems, see Appendix 16.

[2] Pakistan, Government of, *Census of Pakistan, 1951*, Vol. I, Karachi, 1956, p. 114. The problems are too fundamental for us to share the Commissioner's view that "Now

Similar problems were found in connection with one of the rounds of the National Sample Surveys in India in which it was observed that "Many people living in villages would not regard themselves as unemployed so long as they were able to remain living on the earnings of other members of the family or taking part, even to a nominal extent, in the activities of the household, on the land, or in a family business."[1]

It might be thought that, outside the enterprises organized on a family basis, the conceptual problems involved in defining the labor force and, in turn, employment and unemployment would be less serious. In fact, however, the modern approach has only limited relevance to a substantial part of the wage labor force. In many countries of the region, but most especially in India and Pakistan, work performed outside the family enterprise cannot always be regarded as "voluntary" in the Western sense of the term. Many employees are "attached" to a particular employer, because of failure to repay debts or for other reasons. This form of bondage denies them freedom to move, or to select their own work engagements; and the work they do perform may be largely involuntary in character.

In a subtler sense, a high proportion of the minority ethnic groups manning the large plantations in Ceylon work under conditions only arbitrarily distinguishable as either voluntary or involuntary employment. "Volitional," in any meaningful sense, implies a freedom to choose. For many in the plantation labor force, freedom of choice is largely foreclosed. Their mobility may be restricted by long-term contractual commitments or, more importantly, by the strange — and perhaps even hostile — world in which they would find themselves outside the confines of the plantations. Effectively, they may have no option but to continue in the employ of the plantations.

These forms of immobility involve some type of restraint on the workers' maneuverability. But the relevance of Western approaches can be questioned in the absence of such obstacles as well. Ignorance may also be — and indeed is — a formidable bar to mobility in the labor force and to decisions to seek work. Even when knowledge is more complete, market conditions may discourage serious attempts to obtain work. As the Chief of the Indian Statistical Institute has observed, "Persons who are idle, especially in rural areas, [might] not be seeking work because they know that no work would be available."[2]

This view reinforces one aspect of our challenge to the relevance of Western modes of analysis. But the actual situation may often be more accurately characterized as one in which idle workers fail to seek jobs, not

that the difficulties in the conception of unemployment have been located, it should be possible to design a clear definition for use in the next Census." (*Ibid.*)

[1] India, *National Sample Survey No. 16*, p. 20.

[2] P. C. Mahalanobis, in *National Sample Survey No. 16*, p. iv.

because they know that none are available, but because they do not know of any that are available. Two issues — reasonably complete knowledge and labor force mobility — are inextricably interlocked in the conventional Western mold of thought with its volitional approach to unemployment. The absence of one of these foundation stones is sufficient to destroy the applicability of the Western approach. In South Asia, both foundation stones are often missing.

Along with these conceptual problems, another set of hazards confronts collectors of data on employment and unemployment in South Asian countries. These difficulties arise, in the main, from features of the social structure that tend to produce biases of types not readily eliminated from the results. In the preceding discussion, we have largely been concerned with confusions traceable to the posing of irrelevant questions, or questions that cannot be understood by those who are interrogated. We now turn attention to the separate, but related, matter of answers that convey inaccurate information, even though the questions themselves were understood. This problem is by no means unique to South Asia. Wherever interview surveys are conducted, some bias in responses is likely. But in South Asian conditions, not only is the bias likely to be greater, it is also less subject to control through cross-checks against other types of information.

The force of this point can be better appreciated if we consider briefly several sources of distortion in the available labor force statistics. Shy, illiterate villagers are apt to be highly suspicious of outside interrogators, particularly when they are connected with governments — and, hence, remotely with interference. This in itself is likely to preclude complete candor. But in some cases there are special reasons for refusal to divulge certain types of information. Religious influences — in Moslem Pakistan, for example — are likely to produce a substantial under-reporting of work participation by women. The weakening of purdah among the lower classes, especially in the Punjab, is often accompanied by a sense of religious guilt that leads to concealment of female work from interviewers.[1]

Distortions of a different type may often lead to over-reporting of the work participation of certain groups. One conspicuous example is the treatment of landowners in the Indian statistics. In general, even absentee landlords manage to find their way into the "cultivating classes" in the official classifications. The work participation of landowners tends to be systematically overstated, in part because, in order to protect themselves against the implementation of land reforms, they have a stake in creating the impression that they are active participants in farming operations.[2] That this leads

---

[1] John J. Honigman, "Women in West Pakistan," in Stanley Maron (ed.), *Pakistan: Society and Culture*, Human Relations Area Files, New Haven, 1957, p. 150.

[2] It is worth noting that the legal interpretation of "cultivator" has been widely stretched in India. The Report of U. P. Zamindari Abolition Commission noted, for ex-

to some distortion in the statistical reporting on employment patterns is suggested by the findings of the National Sample Surveys, one of which reported that approximately 20 percent of those gainfully employed in India's urban areas in 1955 were "engaged in agriculture."[1]

Such difficulties far from exhaust the potential sources of error. Much information pertinent to the measurement of unemployment or underemployment entails such questions as: "Have you been seeking work for more than a month?" or "How many days were you at work during the past year?"[2] In a Western context, these questions would appear to be straightforward. But among people who are unaccustomed to keeping written records, or, in many cases, are unable to read, write, or count, such questions cannot be expected to elicit accurate information. Often the questions posed would tax the powers of memory of persons with much higher education.

18   The Quality of Statistics on Labor Utilization

As was noted above, the official data-gathering on problems of the active labor force in South Asia has been preoccupied with the topics of unemployment and underemployment. Not only have these efforts been misconceived, but they have failed to produce results that can be judged as satisfactory by any standard. These shortcomings impose severe handicaps on the empirical analysis that we shall attempt in the following chapters of the factors influencing the values of the various components of labor utilization. The allocation of scarce statistical resources to the compilation of materials on irrelevant matters has meant that the body of useful information is slender.

---

ample, that it was not necessary to perform manual labor in order to qualify as a cultivator, nor was it necessary for the landowner to perform the functions of a supervisor himself or to live near his land.

As Daniel Thorner has noted: "What this formulation provides is a mode of considering the non-cultivating owner as contributing to production and accordingly entitled to a share of it even when, in practice, he leaves to others the functions of planning, of direction, of conducting, and of physically carrying out the entire round of agricultural operations." (Daniel Thorner, *The Agrarian Prospect in India*, University Press, Delhi, 1956, p. 21.) The problem is further discussed in Chapter 22, Section 6, and Chapter 26, Part III.

[1] India, *National Sample Survey No. 16*, p. 75.

An earlier survey, which excluded towns under 50,000 as well as the four largest cities, found that more than 11 percent of those gainfully occupied in this selection of urban areas were in agriculture, animal husbandry, forestry, fishing, and hunting. See India, Government of, Ministry of Finance, *National Sample Survey No. 8, Report on Preliminary Survey of Urban Unemployment, September, 1953*, Calcutta, 1956, p. 29.

[2] Some of the inquiries addressed to establishing the "days" worked during a preceding period of time have been unsatisfactory for other reasons as well; the Indian Agricultural Labour Enquiries are cases in point. See Appendix 16.

In practice, therefore, we shall be obliged to advance propositions as tentative conclusions without much support by the statistical documentation we should ideally possess. In many cases, for the lack of any alternative, we shall draw upon studies of the types we have criticized in the preceding section. When doing so, we shall proceed cautiously, fully aware of the inadequacies of the materials in question. For despite the confusions in concept and execution, a number of these studies, when examined critically and in detail, throw important light on relevant issues even though the studies themselves were not sharply focussed on them.

But again we shall be obliged to remind the reader — at times with a repetition that may seem excessive — of the gaps in the available store of useful information. *If we can succeed in defining the relevant issues with precision and in stating clearly what we do not know, a worthwhile purpose will have been served.* In this manner, research into the urgent problems of labor utilization may be stimulated and advanced.

We do believe that substantial progress can be made by behavioral techniques, and even by utilizing the method of questioning people, if the questions asked are adjusted to their actual life, are stretched over a short period, and are amenable to cross-checking. Even from a car or a bicycle one can observe, on one's daily rounds in a number of places, when people go to work, and how many are doing what in the fields.

Despite the perplexities confronting empirical measurement of the important variables involved in the utilization of labor, this approach is a clear and marked advance over the conceptual system underlying the great mass of official statistics. It does not attempt to superimpose Western categories of labor force analysis upon an environment for which they are totally unsuited. Instead, it attempts to look at the fundamental factors that condition participation in work and the duration and efficiency of the work performed. At base, *the labor utilization approach requires behavioral studies founded on observations of the raw realities.* Such studies are all too few in number, yet this line of investigation is far more promising and fruitful than one calling for interviewees to answer questions shaped by Westernized preconceptions.

In the ensuing discussion, we shall thus draw on such behavioral studies as exist, supplementing them with relevant portions of the official statistics. We shall devote considerable attention to the economic implications of the institutional pattern. This institutional emphasis will throw into bold relief the contrasts between the economic environment of South Asia and that now typical in the West. The limitations of "modern" theory will stand out clearly.

See the complete work for Chapters 22-23.

A CRITICAL APPRAISAL OF

THE CONCEPT AND THEORY OF

UNDEREMPLOYMENT

The concept and theory of underemployment will receive intensive analysis here, in terms of an immanent criticism, for two reasons. First, because of the importance of this concept and this theory in economic thinking, the whole approach should be annihilated if it is misdirected. Secondly, the concept and theory of underemployment are representative of a whole complex of concepts and theories in the modern approach to the problems of underdevelopment, development, and planning for development.

1 *The Concept Implies a Theory*

The term "underemployment" and its many synonyms — "hidden," "concealed," "invisible," "disguised," "potential," and "latent" unemployment — are used with considerable variation of meaning by different writers. Basically, however, these terms all represent an attempt to state the fact that the labor force actually engaged in a certain type of economic activity is idle during a part of the day, week, month, and year, or, if working, is unproductive. To that extent, the time spent by the workers is useless and dispensable. From this it is inferred that a proportionally decreased labor force in a particular line of production would be able to produce as much as the actual labor force does, if the remaining force worked full time. This inference establishes the theory that is implied in the concept of underemployment.

This waste of labor is "hidden" in the sense that the superfluous part of the labor force does not appear in the wage labor market as workers seeking, but not finding, employment. The theory of underemployment mainly concerns only that portion of the labor force that is "self-employed," usually within a family enterprise.[1] Like most writers who have dealt with the problem of underemploy-

[1] To the "self-employed" in agriculture should be added those farm laborers who are permanently employed, sometimes called "attached workers." "It may be argued that a permanent farm servant, being a wage-earner, cannot be said to be underemployed. But

ment, we shall in the following discussion be referring particularly to the labor force in the huge economic sector of small-scale, traditional farming. What we have to say, however, is equally valid for self-employed workers engaged in petty trading and other non-agricultural, individual, or family pursuits.[1]

There are serious difficulties in applying the Western concept of unemployment even to wage labor in South Asia.[2] For the "self-employed" the concept is,

---

there is an overwhelming evidence on overstaffing in all lines in the under-developed areas." (S. S. Gill, "Unemployment and Underemployment of Permanent Farm Workers," *Artha Vijñāna*, Vol. 2, No. 4, December, 1960, p. 249.) "Here the employer has to employ a man even though half-a-man-worth work is all that he can give him." (N. V. Sovani, "Underemployment Micro and Macro and Development Planning," *The Indian Economic Journal*, Vol. II, April, 1955, p. 303; cited in *ibid.*, p. 249, n.3.)

When, occasionally, the term "underemployment" is used also for employed wage labor, the waste of labor implied is assumed to be caused by low wages combined with "non-economic" motives on the part of the employers. Cf. Gustav Ranis and John C. H. Fei, "A Theory of Economic Development," *The American Economic Review*, Vol. LI, No. 4, September, 1961, pp. 536 ff. Following W. Arthur Lewis' rightly famous article, "Economic Development with Unlimited Supplies of Labour," *The Manchester School of Economics and Social Studies*, XXII, No. 2, May, 1954, Ranis and Fei explain in the article just cited (p. 536): "The persistence of this wage level is sustained by institutional or nonmarket forces since under competitive assumptions the real wage would fall to zero, at equality with . . . [marginal physical productivity]. We shall call this the institutional wage."

[1] The following quotation from W. Arthur Lewis (*The Theory of Economic Growth*, George Allen and Unwin, Ltd., London, 1955, p. 326) gives a representative formulation of the total situation in a typical underdeveloped country, as seen by those writers who have elaborated the concept and theory of underemployment; it also notes the connection of this concept and theory with the earlier speculation in terms of overpopulation (see Chapter 21, Section 5; Chapter 28, Section 6; and Appendix 7, Section 1):

"This extreme state of overpopulation is, alas, not unknown. It can usually be recognized from the excessive numbers attached to certain sectors of the economy, especially domestic service, petty trade, casual employments and agriculture. Domestic service swells because such economies adjust themselves to the need for each person to provide as much employment as he can; social prestige requires each person to have servants if he can, and the wealthier members of the community have to fill up their households with hordes of retainers who are little more than a drag on the purse. An extreme example of this is the island of Barbados, where sixteen percent of the population is recorded by the census as engaged in domestic service. Petty trading shows similar extension; market places are crowded with stalls, in which each seller makes only a very few sales — selling and passing the time away in gossip being almost indistinguishable. Then there are the hordes of porters, jobbing gardeners, and others who get such casual employment as they can, averaging perhaps a day a week or less. In agriculture the phenomenon shows itself in the smallness of the farms; the plot cultivated by the average family is so small that it cannot fully occupy all the time of members of the family. Whether the excess of population shows itself mainly in agriculture, or mainly in domestic service, trading and casual jobs, depends on whether agriculture is operated with wage labour or by peasants. If it is operated with wage labour (e.g. Barbados) it will not employ more people than are needed for cultivation, and the surplus must then find a living outside agriculture. But if it is operated by peasants, the surplus lives on the family farms, and there may be very little surplus in other occupations. The normal tendency in over-populated countries is for the great landowners to let their lands to peasants for rent, rather than to hire agricultural labourers. They get more this way, since the wage they would have to pay to labourers is more than is left to the peasants when rents have been extracted from them."

[2] Chapter 21, especially Section 11.

of course, still less adequate. This being so, the concept of underemployment was evolved in an attempt to give quantitative expression to the idleness or unproductivity of "self-employed" workers. To the extent that they are idle or unproductive, those workers appear to constitute a "surplus" or "excess" labor force. In planning, underemployment is thus an adjunct concept to unemployment in the wage labor market. Together, the unemployed and the underemployed are said to make up a "labor reserve," available as a resource for planning.[1] As Rosenstein-Rodan, an outstanding contributor to the development of the theory of underemployment, has observed: "Since the 1940's, it [this theory] has been made one of the cornerstones of the theory of development of underdeveloped countries."[2]

2 A Precarious Analogy

The concept and theory of underemployment are a recent development — steered in the particular direction we have called the modern approach[3] — of the old speculation in terms of overpopulation. The concept stems more directly from the Western concept of "disguised unemployment" as introduced by Joan Robinson in the unemployment discussion during the Great Depression.[4] She used this to denote the condition of those workers who were pushed down into less productive and remunerative occupations as self-employed in order to have something to live on, or something more to live on than the dole, personal savings, and family support. "It is natural," she said, "to describe the adoption of inferior occupations by dismissed workers as *disguised* unemployment."[5]

As used in the Western milieu, however, this concept carries the assumption that such unemployment is a rather exceptional occurrence, relatively small in scope, and, more particularly, of a temporary nature. The "disguised unemployed" in the Western setting really belong to another, more regular and better paid, occupation where they will reappear either as employed or as overtly unemployed workers, as soon as the labor market again gives them a chance to seek jobs there. Such a change of market conditions is normal and to be expected.[6] Except for product demand, which is temporarily deficient, all requisites for their employment in their regular occupation are present or will emerge when that demand has risen: on the one hand, enterprise, capital equipment, and other necessities for production; on the other, skills and aptitudes, preparedness to step back, and so on. All that is needed, therefore, to eliminate disguised unemployment, as well as ordinary unemployment, is an increase in the level of total effec-

---

[1] Chapter 21, Section 12.

[2] P. N. Rosenstein-Rodan, "Disguised Unemployment and Underemployment in Agriculture," *Monthly Bulletin of Agricultural Economics and Statistics*, Food and Agriculture Organization, Rome, Vol. VI, Nos. 7/8, July/August, 1957, p. 1.

[3] Chapter 21, Section 2 *et passim*.

[4] Joan Robinson, "Disguised Unemployment," *Economic Journal*, XLVI, No. 182, June, 1936, pp. 225 ff.

[5] *Ibid.*, p. 226. Miss Robinson cites some examples: "He takes up some occupation — planting potatoes if he can get an allotment, selling match-boxes in the Strand, hanging round railway stations to carry bags to hotels." (*Ibid.*, pp. 229–230.)

[6] "If a revival of investment were to occur, dismissed workers would be called back from the hedgerows and the street-curbs into their normal occupations." (*Ibid.*, p. 227.)

tive demand for labor, which in turn is a function of aggregate demand for (capital and consumption) goods and services.

But when the concept of underemployment — or its various synonyms, among them particularly "disguised unemployment" — is applied to the South Asian problem of labor utilization, it refers to something entirely different: the vast and long-term underutilization of human resources in which more laborers are tied up permanently and structurally in various lines of production than are necessary for the output of the product. Those workers "belong" where they are, not in a more remunerative occupation. They never had another type of job from which they were dismissed and to which they are expected to move back. Their vision of life cannot contain the idea of "return" to an occupation conceived by them as their regular and proper one. There is no potential employment for them once an increase in aggregate demand for goods and services becomes an effective demand for labor. The South Asian economies are typically "low-elasticity economies," and an increased aggregate demand does not translate itself readily into an all-round increase in production and demand for labor. Nor do the underemployed themselves have the skills, aptitudes, and preparedness to move. Behind these fundamental differences lies the whole complex of less favorable conditions — in levels and modes of production and of living and in attitudes and institutions — that constitute underdevelopment.[1]

3   *The Definition of "Underemployment"*

In tracking down a definition of underemployment we can start out from the definition of disguised unemployment given by the experts who wrote the classic U. N. report, *Measures for the Economic Development of Under-Developed Countries.*[2] After stressing that "rapid economic development is also the fundamental remedy for disguised unemployment" and that "the significance of the term 'disguised' is that it is applied only to persons who are not normally engaged in wage employment" but are self-employed, the authors state: "The disguised unemployed are those persons who work on their own account and who are so numerous, relatively to the resources with which they work, that if a number of them were withdrawn for work in other sectors of the economy, the total output of the sector from which they were withdrawn would not be diminished even though no significant reorganization occurred in this sector, and no significant substitution of capital."[3] A similar line is taken in a number of writings on the

---

[1] Appendix 2, Section 5.

[2] United Nations, Department of Economic Affairs, *Measures for the Economic Development of Under-Developed Countries* (Report by a Group of Experts appointed by the Secretary-General of the United Nations), New York, May, 1951.

[3] *Ibid.*, p. 7. The experts continue: "The term is not applied to wage labour; presumably employers will not employ a labourer for wages unless his labour increases the total product." (The implication is that marginal productivity is higher than zero; it would, however, need to equal, or be higher than, the wage; see Section 6 below.) "The use of the word 'unemployment' in this connexion is, therefore, somewhat misleading, since it is more often confined to wage-labourers whose status is recorded in unemployment statistics. We prefer to use, hereafter, the less precise but more familiar term 'underemployment,' which is used in our terms of reference." The definition is repeated later in the report (p. 41): "In many under-developed areas, the population on the land is so great that large numbers could be withdrawn from agriculture without any fall in agricultural output and with very little change of capital techniques."

Appraisal of Concept and Theory of Underemployment   2045

topic,[1] and is implied in practically all the literature on underdeveloped countries, including earlier contributions by the present writer. As already mentioned, the concept and theory of underemployment are an extension of the ideas of "overpopulation" and "population optimum"; indeed, they are meant to give a clearer and a measurable expression of these ideas.[2]

One point often left unclarified in the definitions is whether the waste of labor is thought to consist in idleness on the part of the workers or in their working without producing anything, or both.[3] Sometimes the assumption is apparently

[1] "If we take the size of the labour force as given, underemployment may be described as a situation in which the withdrawal of a certain quantity of the factor labour to other uses, will not appreciably diminish the total output of the sector from which it is withdrawn." (Alfredo de Navarrete, Jr., and Ifigenia M. de Navarrete, "Underemployment in Underdeveloped Economies," *International Economic Papers*, No. 3, London, 1953, p. 235.)

"These countries suffer from large-scale disguised unemployment in the sense that, even with unchanged techniques of agriculture, a large part of the population engaged in agriculture could be removed without reducing agricultural output. That is the definition of the concept of disguised unemployment as applied to the situation with which we are concerned. The same farm output could be got with a smaller labour force." (Ragnar Nurkse, *Problems of Capital Formation in Underdeveloped Countries*, Basil Blackwell, Oxford, 1953, p. 32.)

"Disguised unemployment may be defined as the part of the labour force which can be released from certain sectors of an economy *without changing the capital-intensity* and institutional framework, but by shifting some labourers to other productive work so that the remaining labourers may find full-time work (at least during that part of the year when season allows them to work), and further by improving the organization of work and division of labour, and also by introducing simple labour saving devices requiring little or no net addition to capital outlay." (Moti Lal Gupta, *Problems of Unemployment in India*, Nederlandsche Economische Hoogeschool te Rotterdam, 1955, p. 9.)

"By structural under-employment we mean that the total agricultural production will not fall even if a particular number of agricultural workers are taken away from it and given employment elsewhere in the economy." (P. K. Mukherjee, *Economic Surveys in Under-Developed Countries, A Study in Methodology*, Asia Publishing House, Bombay, 1959, p. 89.)

Rosenstein-Rodan, speaking about "the basic concept, which has a clear and unequivocal meaning," defines it as "that amount of population in agriculture which can be removed from it *without any change in the method of cultivation*, without leading to any reduction in output." (Rosenstein-Rodan, "Disguised Unemployment and Underemployment in Agriculture," p. 1.)

[2] Occasionally, the older terms are used as synonyms. For example: "Agricultural overpopulation means a situation in which there is, in a given region, a larger working population in agriculture than is necessary for the production of actual agricultural output by the prevailing methods. This means that a part of the labor may be withdrawn from agriculture, and this reorganization will not necessarily involve any change in the size and content of agricultural output. This definition implies the idea of a certain optimum of agricultural population at given conditions of place, time and agricultural technique." (Stanislas Swianiewicz, "The Problem of Agricultural Overpopulation," *Ekonomi dan Keuangan Indonesia* (*Economics and Finance in Indonesia*), Djakarta, No. 7, July, 1958, pp. 330–331.)

For a criticism of the theory of population optimum, see Gunnar Myrdal, *The Political Element in the Development of Economic Theory*, Routledge and Kegan Paul, London, 1953, pp. 33–39, and *idem, Population: A Problem for Democracy*, Harvard University Press, Cambridge, Mass., 1940, pp. 130 ff., esp. pp. 139 ff. See also Appendix 7.

[3] Rosenstein-Rodan is clear; he assumes idleness, and so do most of those who, like him, have actually "measured" underemployment.

that underemployment is a mixture of both, though in unspecified proportions. As underemployment commonly is assumed to imply a zero marginal productivity of labor, the alternative to idleness on the part of workers would in any case be unproductive work. The relation between underemployment and productivity of labor will be discussed in Section 6.

This whole trend of thinking in terms of underemployment observes the usual taboo in the modern approach to the problem of labor supply and labor input that takes into account only the quantitative dimension of labor.[1] Labor efficiency, that is, labor intensity and skill at the present level of technology and capital intensity, is entirely outside the scope of study. Labor efficiency is implicitly taken as given and constant, unchanged and unchangeable.

Again in conformity with the modern approach, it is also implied that underemployment, like unemployment, is entirely "involuntary," in the sense that the underemployed workers would want to work full time and productively, had they but the opportunity to do so.[2] This in turn implies the standardization of working conditions and rational attitudes toward life and work that in modern Western countries have become a social fact. The very special sense in which "involuntariness" has to be understood will be discussed in Sections 4, 6, and 8.

This line of definition, exemplified above from the literature, seeks to establish the meaning of underemployment in the "static" sense: the number of workers is the only variable, and everything else is assumed to be constant. But comparison could, of course, be made with a situation in which, by applying certain policy measures, a country expects to change some of these "givens."[3] The usual explanation of why the "static" approach has been adhered to — when such an approach is not simply taken for granted — namely, that it is the only one that is clear-cut and definite,[4] cannot be accepted.[5]

---

[1] Chapter 21, Sections 1, 10, *et passim.*

[2] Chapter 21, Sections 1, 10, *et passim.* Rosenstein-Rodan, with his usual clarity, makes this an explicit assumption: "It is assumed that those who are in surplus are involuntarily unemployed." ("Disguised Unemployment and Underemployment in Agriculture," p. 3.) It is always implied, however, by other writers as well.

[3] In defining underemployment it would be possible, of course, to assume instead increased capital intensity in terms of farm implements, working capital of various types and permanent investments, improved techniques, and a changed institutional structure, particularly in regard to the size of farm holdings. In Chapter 21, Section 13, we give examples of such a dynamic concept of underemployment. Many of the estimates made on more impressionistic lines also assume such changes. (See Section 4 below and Chapter 21, Section 13.) The extreme is represented by the unworldly statements sometimes made about the decrease in the labor force engaged in agriculture to some fraction of its present size that would be possible in a South Asian country, if agricultural production could be carried on in the same manner as in the United States or Western Europe.

[4] Rosenstein-Rodan, who defines the purpose of this attempt as "one of clarifying the definition and describing the method by which surplus population in agriculture can be measured or estimated" (p. 1), states that the static concept is the basic concept, which has a clear and unequivocal meaning. The dynamic concepts, which he points to, "are full of pitfalls and are made less exact and certain in their meaning and results." ("Disguised Unemployment and Underemployment in Agriculture," p. 2.)

[5] "Under very precise assumptions and in specific circumstances, a clear meaning can be given to the dynamic concept." (*Ibid.*, p. 2.) See below in Section 9.

A more plausible explanation of why most writers, without any theoretical misgivings, have taken the "static" approach is the force of theoretical conservatism, which is so strong because economic theory has never freed itself from the metaphysical legacy of natural law and utilitarian philosophy and hedonistic psychology. In line with the traditions of economic theory, this approach makes possible a definition of underemployment that is not dependent upon a policy premise, and thus appears to be purely "objective" and related only to the facts. It is supposed to give a definition of a "reserve" of unutilized labor that is available; the size of this reserve is assumed to be independent of the application of policy measures for its utilization. In Sections 8 and 9 we shall examine critically the logic of the "static" character of the concept and theory of underemployment. For the moment we shall not question it.

4 Measuring Underemployment

The definition of underemployment tries to delimit a magnitude that in principle — that is, insofar as relevant data are obtainable — can be measured. The important point is that this definition is normative; it assumes a standard of what full-time work should be in terms of hours per day, days per week, and weeks per year. Moreover, the abstraction from the qualitative dimension of labor input further implies that actual labor efficiency can be taken for granted and assumed not to be changed. Underemployment is the difference between this standard and the actual work performance — plus unproductive work performed, if this element of underemployment is taken into consideration.

The assumption of a standard introduces an outsider's point of view into the world of facts. There are different ways of introducing this norm. The most direct is to state the assumption in terms of a difference between the laborers available and those "required" to do the work.[1] Or the "surplus labor" may be calculated as the difference between the labor forces on farms of differing productivity, owing to more or less full labor utilization, with the more intensively cultivated farms (e.g., those with double-cropping) taken as the norm. Sometimes the standard is derived from the productivity of labor on farms having the highest output per laborer, and the labor requirement is translated to the less productive farms, which then have a labor surplus. Often, especially in general discussion, the methods of measuring underemployment have not been in the foreground, but only the idea that the same output could be produced by fewer workers even without any changes in capital input, technology, and institutional structure. The norm of "full-time" work and the assumption that anything short of it is involuntary are, however, basic to the concept of underemployment.[2]

5 The Causes of Underemployment

Once underemployment is assumed to be "involuntary," it becomes necessary to explain why workers, in spite of supposedly rational attitudes, waste their time

[1] *Ibid.* This is not a simple matter, as differences have to be considered in regard to ownership relations, types of agriculture, seasons, climate generally, and health, age structure, sex, etc., of the members of the labor force. See *ibid.*, pp. 2–5.

[2] Some illustrations of the attempts to measure underemployment are given in Chapter 21, Section 14.

in idleness or unproductive work. In line with classical theory, the explanation is regularly stated in terms of insufficiency of complementary resources and a low level of the arts, with stress usually on the first factor. The U. N. experts quoted above and other authors as well write this explanation into the definition itself. In regard to the first factor, the U. N. experts further explain:

Under-employment is due to a deficiency of the resources which are necessary to employ productively the available supply of labour. It is usually associated with family employment where, in agriculture or industry, the unit of production and of the supply of labour is the family; it exists because the resources of the family are too small to keep all working members of the family fully employed throughout the year and because there exist no opportunities for directing a part of the supply away into other occupations at appropriate times.[1]

As the opportunities for employment outside agriculture presumably depend on resources available there, lack of resources in the national economy as a whole simultaneously decreases the work opportunities in agriculture and the demand for labor outside agriculture, in both ways contributing to underemployment in agriculture.[2] Similar relationships naturally exist in regard to the level of the arts. Particularly as resources are generally translated into capital, the theory of underemployment is thus fit into the usual economic development models where an increase in output is made a function of capital input with reservation for the support rendered by progress in the arts.

There are two snags in this general line of explanation. First of all, it may be that — as the U. N. experts assume — lack of complementary resources (and presumably also primitive techniques) decreases the productivity of a greater labor input in agriculture, or even the possibility of an additional labor input; but the effect of raising levels of capital intensity and technology may be to release labor at an optimal level of production. This is in fact usually assumed to be the case, particularly when the changes in methods of production in agriculture take the form of greater mechanization.[3] But the theory of underemployment is stated in static terms of unchanged levels of capital equipment and technology. The point has importance only when it is used in a consideration of policy, which for realism must be in dynamic terms.[4]

---

[1] U. N., *Measures for the Economic Development of Under-Developed Countries*, p. 8. Cf. India, Government of, Planning Commission, *The First Five Year Plan — A Draft Outline*, New Delhi, 1951, p. 19: "Corresponding to idle labour, there are no adequate supplies of other cooperating factors of production, such as land and capital equipment."

[2] Occasionally the stress is put only on the latter causal relation: "The primary cause of underemployment in the non-industrial sector is the lack of demand for labour emanating from the industrial sector owing to the absence of complementary factors to enable industrial expansion." (N. Islam, "External Economies and the Doctrine of Balanced Growth," *Indian Economic Journal*, July, 1957, p. 51.)

[3] This view is criticized in Chapter 26, Sections 3 and 11. A rise in mechanization of a type that is at all practicable may on the whole present an opportunity for bigger productive labor input in agriculture, in which case there would be no difficulty on this point.

[4] Nurkse gives a specific reason why he believes that the static assumptions make sense, at least in the first approach to the problem: "Changes in technical methods are excluded from the definition of disguised unemployment. Improvements in methods are extremely important. Experts seem to be agreed, however, that it is rather hopeless to

The second difficulty is that, if only for logical reasons, some change in the way factors of production are combined must be assumed.[1] The general line is — explicitly or, more often, implicitly — to make a distinction between, on the one hand, technological advance and capital investment — which are understood to go together — and, on the other hand, the organization of production and work. The former category of changes are excluded by definition, while certain changes of the latter type must be obtained, though without major changes in the institutional framework.[2]

All writers who have gone deeper into the theory of underemployment have, of course, given consideration to the fact that some and in most cases a consid-

---

try to introduce better farming methods unless the excess population is drained off first. There is little chance of any substantial advance in agricultural technique until some of the factors of production now engaged in that activity have been removed. This may sound paradoxical, but there is some basis for this view." (Nurkse, *Problems of Capital Formation in Underdeveloped Countries*, p. 34.)

[1] This has been seen by Rosenstein-Rodan: "If one adheres rigidly to the assumption of *ceteris paribus*, under which nothing whatever can be changed in the method of cultivation, even a mere one-month peak load of work can substantially lower the amount of disguised unemployment. It is, however, convenient and also reasonable to deviate slightly from this assumption of no change, provided that the extent and the nature of the minimum change deemed compatible with static assumptions is described in detail. This is the same method as that which is applied in the theory of supply, where a minimum amount of imperfect competition is always assumed." ("Disguised Unemployment and Underemployment in Agriculture," p. 4.) With this motivation, Rosenstein-Rodan allows in his Italian inquiry that workers working for less than 51 days are assumed to be "removable," which, in turn, naturally assumes some change of organization; in his study the change consists in the employment of additional labor from the outside labor market.

[2] Nurkse says: "We exclude technological advance, more equipment, mechanization, better seeds, improvements in drainage, irrigation, and other such conditions. We exclude these things here only in order to isolate the possibilities that stem from the presence of large-scale disguised unemployment. There is, of course, no question of excluding them from any development programme in practice.

"One thing, however, one need not and probably cannot exclude and that is better organization. If the surplus labour is withdrawn from the land the remaining people will not go on working in quite the same way. We may have to allow for changes in the manner and organization of work, including possibly a consolidation of scattered strips and plots of land." (Nurkse, *Problems of Capital Formation in Underdeveloped Countries*, p. 33.)

Everett E. Hagen follows the same line: "By a strict definition, the term underemployment refers (in agriculture) to a condition in which, if some workers were removed from agriculture, the same total output could be produced by the remaining workers without any change in methods. I think it probable that this situation, strictly defined in this way, is fairly rare. Methods are in effect that make some use of all available labor. But if we modify the definition to what might be termed a practical one, namely that if some agricultural workers were withdrawn, the same total output could be produced by the remaining workers after a relatively simple adaptation of methods, then I think there can be little question that there is a large amount of agricultural underemployment in China, Japan, India, Ceylon, Malaya, Indonesia, Egypt, countries of southern and eastern Europe and a number of other countries." (Everett E. Hagen, "Economics and Economic Development," in *Economics and the Policy Maker, Brookings Lectures, 1958–1959*, The Brookings Institution, Washington, D.C., 1959, pp. 193–194.)

Also V. V. Bhatt, in "Underemployment in Underdeveloped Economies: Theoretical Considerations," *Indian Economic Journal*, July, 1957, p. 44: "*With appropriate re-*

erable part of underemployment is seasonal and is caused by the cyclical changes during a year in the need for labor input. Rosenstein-Rodan observes in addition that when the units of production are small, it becomes important that part of the underemployment is "fractional," and defines fractional unemployment as "labour hours not used throughout the whole year which do not add up to an entire labour unit."[1] In both cases there is true underemployment, though the utilization of the underemployed is limited spatially since alternative work opportunities must be near the farms where the underemployed now live and work part of the time.[2]

The modern theory of underemployment is, as we noted, an outgrowth of the old speculations about overpopulation. So far as the historical explanation of underemployment and the future prospects are concerned, most authors refer to the population increase, though this factor does not technically enter into the theory, which is static and by definition refers to a point of time. The assumption that, when there is underemployment, marginal net productivity of labor is zero (see Section 6) implies, however, that an increase in the labor force, following a population increase, will not raise output but only increase underemployment.

6 The Implications in Regard to Marginal Productivity

Almost all writers assert, usually in direct connection with the definition of underemployment, that the marginal productivity of labor is zero. This is apparently thought to be self-evident, and is therefore never argued.[3] Some writers

---

organization, the output of agriculture will not be significantly affected and in some cases may even increase by removing a certain quantity of labour from it." Italics added.

See also Gupta's definition of underemployment, quoted above in a footnote to Section 2, which spells out the assumption of such changes: "by introducing simple labour saving devices requiring little or no net addition to capital outlay." (Gupta, *Problems of Unemployment in India*, p. 9.)

[1] Rosenstein-Rodan, "Disguised Unemployment and Underemployment in Agriculture," p. 4. In Rosenstein-Rodan's calculation for Southern Italy about one half of total underemployment was considered "non-removable" on account of its seasonal or fractional character.

[2] "Even where disguised unemployment is mainly a seasonal matter, the question of making productive use of it still arises and still has important implications in regard to capital formation." (Nurkse, *Problems of Capital Formation in Underdeveloped Countries*, pp. 35–36.)

"Persons in fractional disguised unemployment cannot be moved out of agriculture, though they could be provided with more part-time work in handicrafts, community development, etc." (Rosenstein-Rodan, "Disguised Unemployment and Underemployment in Agriculture," p. 4.)

[3] "The marginal productivity of labor, *in other words*, is zero." (*Ibid.*, p. 1. Italics added.)

"This is as much as to say that the marginal productivity of these units of the factor labour in their original employment is zero, or very close to zero." (de Navarrete and de Navarrete, "Underemployment in Underdeveloped Economies," p. 235.) It is not explained why marginal productivity is not unreservedly zero, if that is implied.

Nurkse is occasionally a little more careful, and thus unclear: "And in this broad dynamic sense the marginal productivity of labour can perhaps be said to be negative." (Nurkse, *Problems of Capital Formation in Underdeveloped Countries*, p. 34.) On the

take the more extreme position that the marginal productivity of labor might be negative. This is supposed to imply that — under the ordinary assumptions of static capital, technology, and institutional framework — output would increase if the underemployed were removed[1] and in fact would increase even without removal if their labor input were decreased. Others suggest that the marginal productivity of labor may be positive but is very low.[2] It is somewhat disturbing to have a corollary to the definition that, though self-evident and therefore never argued, nevertheless turns out to hover uncertainly between "very low" and "negative."

The central position in the theory of underemployment of the thesis that marginal productivity is zero — or very low or negative — is indicated by the fact that those few writers who lately have been critical of the theory have directed their attack to this thesis, while apparently accepting its logical relation to the concept of underemployment.[3] By demonstrating that marginal productivity is

---

preceding page he says, however, in referring to an "overpopulated" country where the labor force on the land could be dispensed with without making any difference to the volume of output: "In technical terms, the marginal productivity of labour, over a wide range, is zero."

[1] "As the normal agricultural output can be obtained with a smaller labour force than is actually employed, the marginal productivity of the latent surplus of labour is zero, most probably, even negative. This implies that by removing some workers, agricultural output can actually be increased." (Gupta, *Problems of Unemployment in India*, p. 24.)

"When a country is over-populated, on this definition, [so as to cause disguised unemployment in agriculture] the marginal productivity of labour in agriculture is zero. It may even be negative. The Law of Diminishing Returns asserts that it is possible to have too many people on too little land, and this is not an uncommon phenomenon." (William Arthur Lewis, *Aspects of Industrialisation*, National Bank of Egypt, Fiftieth Anniversary Commemoration Lectures, Cairo, 1953, p. 8.)

Nurkse makes the point, however: "Some observers suggest that it [the marginal productivity of labor] may even be negative, which would imply that, by removing some people, farm output could actually be increased. The reason for this might be that under existing conditions people actually get into each other's way, so that if some go away those who remain are able to work more effectively. But this seems to me a doubtful and, in any case, unnecessary assumption, and I am not going to use it." (Nurkse, *Problems of Capital Formation in Underdeveloped Countries*, p. 33.)

[2] Occasionally, as a carry-over from the Malthusian and classical theory of population and wages, marginal productivity is related to the subsistence level. Thus we find: ". . . even at the existing level of technique there is redundant agricultural labour in the sense that the marginal product of labour is less than the minimum subsistence requirements of the workers. Since farming in most of these countries is largely on a family basis, the redundance of agricultural labour finds expression not so much in the existence of mass unemployment as in the phenomenon of chronic underemployment affecting the whole population." (United Nations, ECAFE, *Economic Survey of Asia and the Far East 1950*, New York, 1951, p. 66.) Presumably the meaning is that people in family enterprises are rewarded according to average product, which, of course, should be higher than marginal product, which then could fall under the minimum subsistence level. The lack of logical clarity in this reasoning is obvious.

[3] "The term 'disguised unemployment' is commonly used to designate a situation in which the removal from a working combination of factors of some units of labor, nothing else of consequence or worth mentioning being changed, will leave the aggregate product of the working combination undiminished, and may even increase it. To say that there is 'disguised unemployment' is therefore equivalent to saying that in that working combination the marginal productivity is zero or almost zero and may even be

not, or cannot be, zero, they believe that they have disposed of the concept of underemployment.

The astonishing thing is that in the large literature on underemployment, and also in the more recent controversy just referred to, little attempt has been made to clarify what is meant by marginal productivity, and why zero marginal productivity — or something close to it — is a condition for underemployment. Most writers seem to have in mind a situation where, under otherwise unchanged conditions, an addition to the labor force would result in a corresponding increase in idleness,[1] and consequently in a sharing of the work load with no addition to the actual labor input and no addition to output. In the reverse direction, the labor force could be decreased without lowering output, until all idleness would have been eliminated. This could, perhaps, be described as a *zero marginal productivity of an addition to the labor force*. But, first, it is not clear why this situation is described with reference to a margin, as it would obtain not only at the actual margin but far back on the scale of the number of workers available — to a point where the workers were so few that there would no longer be any idleness.

Secondly, productivity must logically be related, not to the number of workers, but to their labor input. Aggregate labor input, however, is by assumption held constant — as a corollary to the assumption of constant output under unchanged capital input, production techniques, and institutional conditions. Under this assumption the workers' *average productivity* is naturally a function — and a very simple one — of the size of the labor force. But what sense does it make to state that their *marginal productivity* is zero, when this only expresses the assumption that an increase in the labor force does not imply an increase in the labor input?

The concept of marginal productivity of labor must of course logically refer to the labor input, which in the ordinary way must be reckoned, not by the size of the labor force, whether it is working or not, but by the hours, days, and weeks of actual work. If that is clear, it cannot be taken for granted that underemployment in terms of actual idleness on the part of the labor force implies a zero marginal productivity of labor. On the contrary, there could of course be, and normally should be, underemployment at a marginal productivity of labor higher than zero, according to the definition given — and provided that this definition and the theory implied were logically consistent and realistic in other respects. How

---

a negative quantity." (Jacob Viner, "Some Reflections on the Concept of 'Disguised Unemployment,'" *Indian Journal of Economics*, July, 1957, p. 17.)

"A large literature has appeared in recent years based on the belief that countries, however poor the collection of resources at their disposal, can do wonders by recombining the resources already at hand. The mainspring of this view has been the notion that in agriculture one finds many workers whose marginal productivity is not only far below that in other sectors but that it is zero, and, of course, the agricultural sector bulks large in nearly all poor countries." (Theodore W. Schultz, "The Role of Government in Promoting Economic Growth," in Leonard D. White (ed.), *The State of the Social Sciences*, University of Chicago Press, 1956, p. 375.)

[1] "In agriculture the phenomenon shows itself in the smallness of the farms; the plot cultivated by the average family is so small that it cannot fully occupy all the time of members of the family." (Lewis, *The Theory of Economic Growth*, p. 326.)

high would depend on the level of marginal productivity at which the workers would not find it worthwhile to put in an extra unit of labor.

The whole discussion of marginal productivity in connection with the willingness of workers to exert themselves in South Asian agriculture is airy and unrealistic. This is so because of the assumption of rational attitudes, most flagrantly expressed in the assumption that underemployment is "involuntary." If in our immanent criticism we accept this common assumption, it is certainly not correct to assume that underemployment implies zero marginal productivity of labor. Why should workers continue to work though they are not producing anything? More particularly, why don't they stop working at a level above zero marginal productivity? Is it assumed that work does not represent any disutility? If so, why don't they go further, so that there is no idleness at all?

As was mentioned in Section 3, one sometimes finds allusions to another conception of underemployment — namely, as unproductive labor.[1] Again, the question must be raised: how can the writers who use the modern approach and who assume that underemployment is involuntary in a very specific and rational sense also assume that workers behave as if work performance had no element of "disutility"? Moreover, how can a situation in which workers are working unproductively be characterized as one of zero marginal productivity when this situation is meant to apply far inside the margin? It should be added that this construction does not make more sense in the mixed case, where underemployment is supposed to consist of both idleness and useless work.

[1] "This [disguised underemployment] includes the category of persons whose employment for a particular period is not really necessary . . . The farmer with a small piece of land is found to spend almost as much time on his land as a farmer with a larger piece of land because for lack of other employment opportunities he feels like doing some work during the day on his farm. . . . All this work is not necessary, all the same it does occupy a great deal of a person's time. In any enquiry such persons will never call themselves unemployed." (M. A. Telang, "Technique of Measuring Rural Unemployment," *Indian Journal of Agricultural Economics*, Vol. IX, No. 1, March, 1954, p. 150.)
Rosenstein-Rodan makes it clear that this is not his conception, but that underemployment for him has its reality in actual idleness. For most writers it is less easy to lay bare their understanding of the situation. The clear-cut formulation of the second conception is given by some of the critics of the underemployment theory, as when Viner points out that "The 'unemployment' in the term 'disguised unemployment' may be only metaphorical, since there may be hard work even at the margin, where 'unemployed' must mean 'unproductively employed.'" (Viner, "Some Reflections on the Concept of 'Disguised Unemployment,'" p. 17.) Cf. p. 21: "But for Lewis, the 'disguised unemployed' of agriculture may be working as hard as anyone else, and may in fact need more calories for farm-work than they would need for factory-work. They are 'idle' in the sense only that their work is unproductive."
The middle position — where there is a mixture of idleness and low productivity — is characterized by another critic of the underemployment theory. According to Schultz: "The idea that disguised unemployment is characteristic of poor countries is very widely held. It has become one of those self-evident propositions. Presumably anyone who has ever been about in poor countries is prepared to testify from his observations that it is true. Many people, so the proposition runs, are really working only part-time, doing little productive work, some work only seasonally, and others while they are employed most of the year are not kept busy, or, if they are, they are busy doing very little that contributes to production." (Theodore W. Schultz, *The Economic Test in Latin America*, New York State School of Industrial and Labor Relations, Bulletin 35, Cornell University, Ithaca, New York, 1956, pp. 13, 14.)

The conclusions we reach are the following. The proposition that underemployment as defined implies zero marginal productivity of labor makes no sense. It does not stand even when the assumption of rationality, on which it is based, is granted. Why then is this assertion so common? And why are there no attempts to clarify its meaning and to produce evidence that it is, or can be, a valid generalization? The only explanation is that this is theorizing within the blinkers of an ideology — in this case what we have called the modern approach, borrowed from the West and corresponding to Western conditions, and then "adapted" to serve the analysis of underdeveloped countries.

7   The Actual Level of Marginal Productivity in Underdeveloped Countries

In these circumstances, it is natural that the critics of the underemployment theory select for criticism the assertion about marginal productivity being zero. When they succeed in throwing doubt on the assumption of zero marginal productivity of labor they have not, however, disposed of the underemployment theory. For, as we have shown, there could be, and according to the rationalistic assumptions should be, underemployment at a higher than zero marginal productivity of labor.

So long as the idea of zero or near-zero marginal productivity of labor is widespread, both within and outside the formal theory of underemployment, the following observations are pertinent. Viner makes the point that zero marginal productivity would assume fixed technical coefficients "in a valid economic sense" and fixed crop patterns or uniform, fixed technical coefficients for all products. On logical grounds he denies that this is easily conceivable, and, on common-sense grounds, that it is likely ever to be the case in any country or any occupation.[1] He also points out that where the family labor supply is not adequate, or is unable to work, labor is employed for wages, and that this is not compatible with a zero marginal productivity of labor.[2]

[1] "As far as agriculture is concerned, I find it impossible to conceive of a farm of any kind on which, other factors of production being held constant in quantity, and even in form as well, it would not be possible, by known methods, to obtain some addition to the crop by using additional labor in more careful selection and planting of the seed, more intensive weeding, cultivation, thinning, and mulching, more painstaking harvesting, gleaning and cleaning of the crop. Even supposing that there were such a farm on which every product had technically and economically fixed ingredients, labor would still have positive marginal productivity unless there were not only fixed technical coefficients of production for all the economically relevant potential products of the farm, but the proportions between the technical coefficients were uniform for all of these products. For if these proportions are different as between different products, then it will always be possible by appropriate change in the product-mix, in the direction of more production of those products whose labor technical coefficients are relatively high, to absorb productively any increment of labor." (Viner, "Some Reflections on the Concept of 'Disguised Unemployment,' " p. 18.)

[2] "Unless one assumes non-economic motivation on the part of employers, there is difficulty in conceiving why they should hire at any wage-rate additional units of labor beyond the point at which they know the labor will add less in value to the product than the wage-cost, to say nothing of the case where the labor will add nothing to and may even subtract from the product." (*Ibid.*, p. 18.) Viner's assumption of rational economic motivation is justified in this particular argument, as the reasoning he is criticizing is carried out in terms of such motivation.

These criticisms[1] seem to be incontrovertible, so far as they go. In regard to the first argument, concerning technical coefficients and crop pattern, it must again be recalled that the whole discussion of underemployment is a continuation of the older discussion of overpopulation caused by population growth. What actually happened during this development toward an ever higher man/land ratio illustrates in fact how very wide the possibilities are of varying the labor intensity of cultivation — and thus the total labor input per unit of land — even within a given cropping pattern and without appreciable change in techniques. One consequence of population growth has very generally been a movement to more intensive utilization of the land resources. The same possibilities are demonstrated by the huge differences in the labor intensity in agricultural production in the South Asian region.[2] The marginal productivity is higher than zero.

Naturally both aggregate and marginal productivity are low in poor countries, and particularly in traditional self-sufficiency farming. As Viner puts it, "there is little or nothing in all the phenomena designated as 'disguised unemployment,' as 'hidden employment,' or as 'underemployment' which in so far as they constitute genuine social problems would not be adequately taken into account by competent, informed, and comprehensive analysis of the phenomenon of low productivity of *employed* labor, its causes, its true extent and its possible remedies."[3]

8   A "Static" Theory about the Results of a Big Change

The concept and theory of underemployment are developed in static terms[4] by assuming unchanged conditions of capital input, techniques, and institutional

---

[1] Schultz's criticism is less closely argued. He merely asserts that "The marginal productivity of labor in agriculture in poor countries is very low because of the poor collection of resources, but it is not zero. Moreover, in such a country it is very low for labor generally." (Schultz, in White, *The State of the Social Sciences,* p. 375.) He adds, without developing or proving the point: "And in situations, and there are many, where for many years, often for decades, agriculture has approximated a kind of stationary state, one is likely to find the average and the marginal values of labor more nearly the same than would be the case in a rapidly developing economy like that of the United States." (*Ibid.,* pp. 375, 376.) "I know of no evidence for any poor country anywhere that would even suggest that a transfer of some small fraction, say 5 percent, of the existing labor force out of agriculture, with other things equal, could be made without reducing its production." (*Ibid.,* p. 375.) "A poor country which has been virtually stationary for a long period is not likely to reveal any appreciable malallocation of factors, say, as between agriculture and the rest of the economy or within agriculture, whereas a country undergoing rapid economic growth, more likely than not, will have in it areas that have been bypassed and others that have become depressed as a consequence of its economic development." (*Ibid.,* p. 376.)

[2] Chapter 21, Section 14; Chapter 26, Section 3.

[3] Viner, "Some Reflections on the Concept of 'Disguised Unemployment,' " p. 23.

[4] As A. K. Dasgupta has pointed out, the concept is reminiscent of Marx's theory of primary accumulation. But Marx, of course, did not think in static but in dynamic terms. "Although the number of the tillers of the soil was decreased, the land produced as much fruit as before. . . . When, therefore, part of the rural population was set free from the land, the means of subsistence with which they had been nourished as land-workers were likewise set free. Such means of subsistence were transformed into the material elements of variable capital." (Karl Marx, *Capital,* Everyman's Library, p. 826, quoted by A. K. Dasgupta, "Tendencies in Economic Theory," *The Indian Economic Journal,* January, 1961, p. 204.)

framework. The assumption of minor changes in the organization of work,[1] necessary to carry out the analysis, does not by itself seriously infringe upon its
static character. It is carried out, however, by a comparison between two situations, both fulfilling the foregoing assumption of unchanged conditions but separated by a very big change — the decrease in the labor force. Underemployment is measured by the relative size of that part of the labor force that can be
"withdrawn," "released," or "removed" without causing a decrease in production. This change is thought of in purely abstract terms.[2] It is also timeless, as no
assumptions are made in regard to a period of time during which the change
should take place. One may then ask, however, what sense there can be, in pure
logic, in a "static" theory about the results of a very big change.

The change, of revolutionary proportions, is ordinarily assumed to affect from
20 to 50 percent of the labor force. Should this happen, it could not be abstract
any longer but must mean the shifting of a great many people. It can only take
place over a certain period of time, shorter or longer, and the length of time allowed for the change cannot be without influence on everything, including output. It is not legitimate, logically, to assume that conditions that *must* change in
the process will remain unchanged.

The change does not happen by itself; it must be thought of as the effect of
government policy. Can the government ever be assumed to undertake such a
policy while observing the *status quo* in regard to capital input, techniques, and
institutional framework? Indeed, what meaning can be given to a theory that
assumes this? The fact that traditional economic theory, as it is often expounded,
comprises many other concepts and theorems of the same doubtful character of
"comparative statics" cannot be invoked to support this particular one. They
may all be meaningless.

Let us assume, however, for the sake of the argument, that this static approach
with an implied, abstract and timeless, immense change, restricted to the "removal" of workers, can be given a meaning. The next question is: how can it be
assumed, as it is assumed, that the reduced labor force will exert itself and so
keep production at the level it was before the removal of the underemployed?
Only so could production remain unchanged under the assumed static conditions of capital input, techniques, and institutional framework. This in turn assumes that the remaining workers would suddenly begin to increase their labor
input exactly so much that there would cease to be any idleness. That they act

[1] See above in Section 5.

[2] "A number of people are working on farms or small peasant plots, contributing
virtually nothing to output, but subsisting on a share of their family's real income.
There is no possibility of personal identification here, as there is in open industrial unemployment. In industrial countries unemployment is a glaring waste of resources, visible to all, and has perhaps for this reason attracted more attention. In an overpopulated
peasant economy, *we cannot point to any person* and say he is unemployed in disguise.
The people may all be occupied, and no one may consider himself idle." (Nurkse, *Problems of Capital Formation in Underdeveloped Countries,* p. 33. Italics added.)

". . . the definition of chronic underemployment in macro terms considers not individual workers but abstract labour units and the extent of underemployment indicated
by it is that of so many man-hours." (Sovani, "Underemployment Micro and Macro
and Development Planning," p. 304.) Sovani, who is skeptical about the concept, notes
that "such a conversion seems to present no difficulty to many." (*Ibid.,* p. 308.)

in this way is apparently the more specific meaning of the assumption that underemployment is "involuntary." As we pointed out in Section 4, the concept of full employment, and consequently of idleness, in this analysis is injected as an outside norm, as is revealed whenever an attempt is made to actually measure underemployment.

Is this assumption about the "involuntariness" of idleness – defined in this very specific way – realistic? Can it be realistic in any society? To the extent that idleness is diminished, the workers remaining in agriculture would enjoy higher real incomes after the removal of a part of the labor force. In the extreme case assumed by this theory, the rise in incomes would be very substantial, amounting to 50 percent if, for instance, underemployment is supposed to be a third of the labor force. Would this rise in incomes have no effect on the remaining workers' ability and willingness to work?

In regard to their ability to work, it must be expected that in poor countries, where nutrition and other levels of living are sub-optimal for productivity, the change would raise the quality of labor when work is performed, and thus increase the productivity of the labor unit. But the whole approach to the employment problem typified by the concept and theory of underemployment is characterized by a neglect of labor efficiency.[1] If this causal relation between levels of income and labor efficiency were taken into account, and if, as the theory assumes, the remaining workers began to work full time, the total produce would increase, in contradiction to one of the assumptions. If, instead, unchanged production were assumed, a net of idleness would be left, corresponding to the rise in labor efficiency. From the point of view of the theory of underemployment, this would, in fact, mean the possibility of a still higher "removal" than corresponds to the actual idleness. Underemployment would have been underestimated. The theory is open, because its two assumptions – (1) liquidation of idleness, supposed to be "involuntary," and (2) unchanged production – are incompatible.[2]

In regard to willingness to work, any survival-mindedness on the part of the workers – of which there is much in the South Asian region – would clearly motivate them against full-time work if they could get the same income by clinging to their customary work habits. Aggregate production would then fall, though not of course production per head. If in addition there were decreasing returns, the remaining workers would be in a position to preserve their customary income levels while working even less than before part of the labor force was removed. From the point of view of the underemployment theory, this would imply that after the removal of a part of the labor force corresponding to the actual idleness, there would continue to be underemployment – perhaps a relatively large underemployment. This is an extreme case. But, more generally, it is an entirely unrealistic conception of conditions of and attitudes toward life and work in South Asia to take it for granted that removal of part of the labor force, corre-

[1] See above in Section 3.

[2] Leibenstein has touched on this problem, though only from the point of view of why wages can be positive when marginal productivity is zero. See Harvey Leibenstein, *Economic Backwardness and Economic Growth*, John Wiley & Sons, New York, 1957, pp. 58 ff. *et passim.*

sponding to the amount of actual idleness — measured by an arbitrary norm representing an outsider's view — would motivate the remaining workers to work full time in order to keep aggregate production unchanged, and also that income levels have no effect upon labor efficiency.

The upshot of all this is that the static concept and theory of underemployment are useless constructs. In spite of the thousands of pages devoted to their exposition by so many distinguished writers, and the calculations and estimates of actual underemployment carried out with sometimes considerable precision, this concept and this theory suffer from lack of clarity on crucial points. When the points are clarified, as we have tried to do in this immanent criticism, the concept and the theory are no longer tenable.

When underemployment is measured, the only accomplishment is to have ascertained the amount of actual idleness. In order to do this, a norm has to be introduced, defining full employment. This norm represents the outsider's view of how much people ought to work, not the view of the people concerned. In spite of the arbitrariness of this norm applied in the measurement of idleness, the exercise, by itself, is clearly of considerable interest. But the further manipulations that assume static conditions of capital input, techniques, and institutional framework; the attainment of full employment when a part of the labor force, corresponding to the amount of idleness ascertained, is removed; and unchanged production — all in terms of a static comparison implying that the vast change of removal is instantaneous and will not disturb any of the above assumptions — do not introduce any new elements of knowledge but rather a number of abstract notions that, when spelled out, are shown to be totally inapplicable to reality and therefore invalid.

These manipulations, which are preliminary to the definition of underemployment as that part of the labor force that under these assumptions can be removed and that, together with open unemployment, represents the labor reserve, constitute the theory of underemployment. The real function of that theory is to make it possible *to define underemployment with an implied policy relevance but without resort to a policy premise*, and at the same time to give credence to the preconceived, but seldom explicitly stated, ideas — which represent the modern approach (the ideological background of which we treat in Chapter 21, Part I) — that all idleness is "involuntary" in a specific and extreme sense and that labor can be dealt with in purely quantitative terms, disregarding the qualitative dimension.

As the failure to state value premises and the particular preconceptions discussed here are widely prevalent in other contexts as well, we have been prompted to use the case of underemployment illustratively.

9   An Escapist Approach

Much more intensive empirical research into the actual utilization of the labor force and the conditions of work in the South Asian countries is needed to supplement and validate our present knowledge. Meanwhile, on the theoretical level we can at least clarify what we are actually talking about, and raise meaningful questions in an attempt to render the empirical research more adequate and pertinent.

There is, and can be, no labor reserve *in abstracto*, independent of the time allowed, the foreseen changes, and particularly governmental policies.[1] To begin with, a change in labor input must be thought of in dynamic terms and must be related to a definite period of time. Labor input by the self-employed and the supply and demand of wage labor have a qualitative aspect — labor efficiency — that must be considered in the dynamic process. The utilization of the labor force in the period under consideration will depend on changes that are interdependent in their causation, some of which involve changes in workers' attitudes toward life and work. Among the strategic changes, from a planning perspective, are governmental policies operating by means of education and compulsion, subsidies, taxation, investments, and land reform. Output will, of course, not be unchanged, and the changed output belongs among the changes in the social system whose effect will have to be taken into account. Looked at *ex ante,* an increased labor utilization expected to be reached within a period of time by the application of governmental policies adapted to the specific — and changing — circumstances in a particular country may be regarded as a "labor reserve" or as "underemployment" to be cured. But these terms are by their present use so loaded with false association that we had better think in terms of utilization of the labor force — though, of course, the actual and expected partial idleness of workers is an important factor among many others.

The main point is that statements about the possibility of a better utilization of the labor force are senseless if made without a policy assumption — or, to be charitable, a policy assumption must have been made but not spelled out. When, for instance, Schultz asserts that he knows "of no evidence for any poor country anywhere that would even suggest that a transfer of some small fraction, say, 5 percent, of the existing labor force out of agriculture, with other things equal, could be made without reducing its production," he may be right in a sense. But he must then have either assumed such a short-term perspective that policies of the above-mentioned nature have little chance of changing conditions very much, or assumed that, even in the longer view, policies will not be of much importance because (1) the government follows a *laissez-faire* line in regard to economic development in general, (2) its development policies, for whatever reasons, are not specifically directed toward increasing and improving labor utilization, (3) the social setting — including workers' attitudes — is such that it will prevent governmental policies from having much effect on average labor input and labor efficiency, or (4) a specific combination of these three assumptions having that effect. Such policy assumptions are perfectly feasible and may be realistic in many underdeveloped countries; but they need to be spelled out, made specific, and their realism in the particular case needs to be established.

The opposite, and more common, view that the utilization of the labor force

---

[1] ". . . any estimate of the removable surplus is really inherent in the assumptions one makes regarding the existing situation and the change in it. A removable population surplus is not something which absolutely and independently exists but is what we create even theoretically by assuming certain specified changes. Any estimates of it in any particular context are all equally valid under their own assumptions." (N. V. Sovani, "Underemployment, Movable Surplus and the Saving Fund," *Artha Vijñāna,* Vol. 1, No. 1, March, 1959, p. 25.) Cf. Chapter 21, Section 12.

can be substantially increased, and thus that "underemployment" is very large, assumes instead a vigorous development policy that, by overcoming vested interests, administrative bottlenecks, adverse ingrained institutions and attitudes, and other factors of social inertia, would be directed toward accomplishing the better utilization of the labor force, and also assumes sufficient time for the policy to take effect. Such assumptions, of course, can be made. But again, they need to be stated as a basis for the calculations. As these assumptions are anything but simple and self-evident, they need to be spelled out in specific terms. And to render the calculations at all realistic, it must also be established that the policy assumptions are reasonable in the particular country under discussion.

What is most important is that by logical necessity the concept of "underemployment" is dependent upon assumptions about policy. As a rule neither party in the controversy referred to above has spelled out its assumptions in this regard. The concept is left floating and the arguments do not meet. It is quite possible that both parties may be "right": that in the short run, and also in the long run in the absence of a vigorous development policy directed toward "creating employment," stimulating labor input and supply, and raising labor efficiency, there might not be much of a "labor surplus" in the sense of an available supply of labor seeking opportunities for work and not finding an outlet; while at the same time, a big potential "labor reserve" actually exists and could be put to work and to more efficient work, if appropriate policy measures were taken and could be made effective (Chapter 21, Section 12).

That a definite meaning cannot be given to the concept of "underemployment" or "labor reserve" except in terms of policy holds true as a general proposition. In the concrete case of a particular country, the analysis must then be directed to ascertaining *the functional and operational relationships between policies and the more or less full and intensive use of the existing and foreseeable labor force*. A study of this functional relationship is, indeed, a crucially important analytical task in planning for development.

In regard to the valuations as to whether, to what extent, and by what means a specific policy line should be followed so as to reach a fuller and more intensive use of the labor force, there are, as a matter of fact, widely differing views in all the underdeveloped countries — as also among observers from Western countries. Whether and to what extent the development efforts should be concentrated on increasing the opportunities for work, now and in the more distant future, and on increasing labor input and supply and raising labor efficiency is not self-evident. To focus or intensify policy efforts in the direction of raising labor input and labor efficiency — that is, the productivity of the labor force — is to face a clash of interests on many issues. Institutions and attitudes would have to be changed through educational campaigns and/or compulsion. Vested interests in the *status quo*, firmly rooted in the existing power relations in the state and in the local communities, would have to be overcome. The entire complex of problems of land reform and tenancy reform is involved, as are the level and distribution of taxation.

In every underdeveloped country, the very diverse and conflicting political valuations in all these matters are merely concealed by the glib assertions that there is a large volume of "underemployment" and that it is of paramount interest to utilize that "labor reserve." To escape facing political issues by "objectifying" concepts and theories is an old tradition of economics and the social sciences generally. But it should be clear that the study of the functional relationship between policies and the utilization of the labor force, which is their task, cannot be assisted by the use of a concept of "underemployment" in general, allowed to be "objectively" established in relation merely to the facts, and perhaps even measured, in advance of any consideration of policy.

10 The Practicality of the Approach

One last remark should be added. The entire approach in terms of the "removal" of a labor surplus in agriculture assumes that the supposedly superfluous workers have somewhere to go. This is consonant with the common, glib preconception that industrialization, by also giving employment to labor moving out of agriculture, is the main solution to the development problem in underdeveloped countries, even in the fairly short run. In Chapter 24 (Sections 5 and 6) we show, however, that in South Asia industrialization, even if it were to proceed more rapidly, would not imply much more demand for labor for decades ahead. Moreover, in Chapter 27 and Section 3 of Chapter 28 we demonstrate that the labor force will increase very rapidly till the end of the century, independently of what happens in the field of birth control. Since in South Asia industrialization does not provide much of an outlet under any conceivable circumstances, this increase in the labor force will have to find its place mainly in agriculture. The whole idea of a "removal" is unrealistic (Chapter 26, Section 1).

The main practical problem facing the planners and the governments — which they can approach in different ways, depending on their value premises and their assessment of the facts and future prospects — is how to use more effectively the labor force that is now in agriculture and that is bound to increase at a foreseeable, very rapid rate for decades ahead. Policies aimed at increasing average labor input and improving the efficiency of that rapidly growing agricultural labor force must be formulated and implemented to raise the total output and also, as far as possible, output in relation to that (increased) labor input; all the conditions held constant in the theory of underemployment must be changed. We discuss this problem as an aspect of agricultural policy in Chapter 26; in this discussion we have, of course, no use for the concept and theory of underemployment.

Chapter 24

THE INDUSTRIALIZATION ISSUE

In the two preceding chapters, we concentrated on the crucial fact about underdevelopment in South Asia — the underutilization of labor — and found that all three components of labor utilization have low values. We attempted also to reveal the mechanism of social and economic forces that have created and perpetuated conditions inhibiting development.

Our inquiry led us to conclude that the problem of labor underutilization cannot realistically be approached in terms of "employment" and "unemployment" because these concepts presuppose institutional and attitudinal conditions that do not exist among the bulk of the South Asian labor force. More specifically, the modern approach neglects two important elements of this problem — the duration and the efficiency of work — and gives only inadequate attention to the third — participation in work. "Underemployment," a concept supposedly better adapted to South Asia, is equally unsatisfactory. When scrutinized, the theory implied in the concept of underemployment turns out to be both unrealistic and logically untenable.[1] With this inadequate treatment of labor utilization, the modern approach also becomes unrealistic in that it tends to interpret development as too simply a function of capital scarcity plus a low level of

[1] These theoretical arguments and their ideological roots are discussed in Chapter 21, Parts I and II; on the concept and theory of underemployment, see Sections 12–14 of that chapter and Appendix 6.

technology,[1] thereby neglecting the South Asian institutional and attitudinal setting. It is true that heavier inputs of capital and better techniques — changes themselves interrelated — are often necessary to raise labor utilization and, in particular, labor efficiency. But in the absence of simultaneous changes in institutions and attitudes, the effects on labor utilization and productivity throughout the economy may still be less consequential. Those changes do not occur automatically in response to increased capital and improved technology.

Against the background of the diagnosis of the central problem of underdevelopment presented earlier, we shall consider in this and the next two chapters the policy issues facing those who frame and implement plans for economic development. Throughout this discussion we shall be concerned with assessing the possible impact of alternative policies on the three components of labor utilization. Our approach to economic policy will thus be focussed on the extent to which various policy plans are likely to be successful in overcoming the vicious circle of low labor utilization that has perpetuated poverty in the region.

1 The Broad Appeal of Industrialization as an Imperative of Economic Policy

It is reasonable that a discussion of economic development policies in South Asia should begin with the ideology of industrialization. A clamor for industrialization is notable in all countries of the region. When the intellectually elite say their countries are underdeveloped, they mean, in the first instance, that they have too little industry.[2] Thus spokesmen for the South Asian countries frequently use the terms "pre-industrial" or "under-industrialized" as synonyms for "poor" or "underdeveloped."

The enthusiasm of the elite for industrialization is a manifestation of their general acceptance of the goal of modernization and the complex of ideas associated with it. In this view, the growth of modern industry will provide employment for an underutilized labor force now bottled up in agriculture and the loosely organized sectors of non-agricultural pursuits. Industrialization is held to be crucial to development strategy also because it will radiate stimuli throughout the economy and lift it out of stagnation. Directly and indirectly, modern industry is expected to raise the productivity of the labor force and increase national output and income; rising incomes are then expected to swell the volume of savings and thus finance further investments in industry. In this vision, industrial

---

[1] Chapter 21, Section 11 *et passim.*

[2] For instance, India's Second Five Year Plan stated bluntly that "rapid industrialization and the diversification of the economy" is "the core of development." (India, Government of, Planning Commission, *Second Five Year Plan*, New Delhi, 1956, p. 25.)

expansion, once started, touches off a progressive spiral. In currently popular jargon, it leads the economy from the "take-off" to "self-sustaining growth."

As Western economic history is commonly interpreted both by Westerners and by South Asia's intellectual leaders, the present high level of productivity and income in advanced countries — and the other concomitants of economic well-being — are the result of changes set in motion by the industrial revolution. Historically in Western countries, agriculture's claim on manpower has diminished; at first the decline was relative but it very soon became absolute. Progress toward rationality, equality of opportunity, democracy, and national consolidation has proceeded *pari passu* with industrialization and the higher levels of productivity and income made possible by it, or coming in the wake of it. More recently, an Asian country, Japan, has followed a similar course with striking success.

A further important influence on the ideology of industrialization in South Asia has been the recent rapid development of industry through government planning in the Soviet Union. In Communist ideology, industrialization embraces a theory and a program calling, in particular, for a fairly comprehensive industrial structure based on heavy industry. This pattern is now often accepted as a natural one for any large underdeveloped country to imitate. It has especially influenced the thinking of those many South Asian intellectual leaders who were at one time Communists or socialists with Communist leanings, among them Jawaharlal Nehru. Most of these leaders have had little respect for Communism as a political theory and, in the later years particularly, have rejected Communism's political methods. Nevertheless, they continue to hold Communist thought on the economic issues of industrialization in high regard. Almost all nontraditionalist intellectuals in the region have been decisively influenced by the Communist doctrine of planned and directed industrialization as a technique for engendering development. To them all, Soviet successes in planning convey lessons they would like to apply when charting their own course of development.

The appeal of industrialization to South Asia's leadership is powerfully buttressed by the desire to reverse the colonial economic pattern. Such economic development as occurred during the colonial period was restricted almost entirely to primary production for export and to the emergence of a few consumption goods industries producing mostly for the home market. This pattern is now commonly held to be the result of blind market forces operating in the absence of national planning, except insofar as it was shaped by colonial policies — policies that tended to hamper the growth of manufacturing and of heavy industry in particular.[1] Traditional

[1] Chapter 10, Sections 7–9.

laissez-faire policies worked in the interest of the metropolitan powers by assigning colonies a role as suppliers of raw materials and purchasers of finished goods. The result was an enclave economy that left the larger part of the population untouched by industrial impulses. This image of colonial economic history dominates the thinking of the intellectual elite who now subscribe to the industrialization ideology.

This argument is, in fact, the essence of the Communist doctrine of colonial exploitation. And, by implication, it contains the further view that colonies, once independent, can become genuinely free only through planned industrialization. In the absence of economic advance of this type, post-colonial economies are regarded as doomed to subservience to industrialized countries and to continued stagnation and poverty. This interpretation of history contains enough apparent realism to win wide acceptance among South Asian intellectual leaders far outside the Communist fold, just as in much the same form it is now widely accepted by Western economists. Communists are more clear and direct about it, and, with some justification,[1] they can point to Communist thinkers as originators of this argument. These facts undoubtedly add momentum to the spread of Communist ideas generally in South Asia. In the present context much of the importance of Communist ideology lies in its emphasis on a particular type of industrial development, namely, heavy industry, the priority of which is alleged to be almost self-evident.[2] But, more generally, the Communist view is also influential in breeding suspicion of Western governments and their attitude toward the order of priority of industrialization in planning. As an American economist has observed: "It has been said that the myth of the American development ideology is the community development program, while the Soviet myth is the steel mill. There is little doubt which myth is more highly esteemed in most of the underdeveloped world."[3] Consciousness of this suspicion has led most Western economists to adopt a more optimistic view than the facts would seem to warrant of the feasibility of, and the potential benefits from, industrialization in the region. That they are aided therein by an uncritical application of Western concepts and theoretical models has been stressed in various contexts in this book.

The ideology of industrialization in South Asia has, however, been further reinforced and solidified by two trends in the course of recent history. In the first place, deteriorating world market conditions for most of the region's traditional primary exports[4] have tended to intensify a feeling that

[1] Other theorists also contributed, the most conspicuous being the British Socialist, John A. Hobson, whose study of imperialism anticipated Lenin's writings.

[2] Section 3.

[3] Edward S. Mason, *Economic Planning in Underdeveloped Areas: Government and Business,* Fordham University Press, New York, 1958, p. 48.

[4] Chapter 13, Sections 5 and 13.

the international division of labor inherited from colonial times is increasingly prejudicial to aspirations for rapid economic development. Further concentration on production of staple primary commodities for export is thought to be futile. Even in countries like Malaya and Ceylon, where prospects for augmenting foreign exchange earnings through expanded output of traditional export products are better than average, this policy is regarded as insufficient in itself to spark development. Secondly, the case for industrialization draws fresh strength from a gradually mounting awareness of the implications of accelerated population growth. The need for new employment opportunities, which industrialization is assumed to provide, is, of course, strongest in those countries where the man/land ratio is highest — India, Pakistan, Indonesia (more specifically Java), and Ceylon.

Even before the acceleration of population growth registered by recent censuses, the discussion of "underemployment" — which is a continuation of the older discussion of "overpopulation" — focussed on the idea that huge labor surpluses, especially in agriculture, could be shifted into other sectors to increase labor utilization and aggregate output.[1] A major push toward industrial expansion is thus regarded as the main alternative to underemployment in agriculture. For example, a United Nations report states that "The reason for emphasizing industrialization is that industrial development would absorb rural under-employed persons into those fields of production where higher productivity is possible without reducing total agricultural output."[2] The plans of South Asian countries are equally expressive of this theme. Thus we find in India's Second Plan: "Development involves a transfer of part of the working force from agriculture to secondary and tertiary activities."[3] The Indian plan goes on to say:

The objective of policy from the long-term point of view should clearly be to keep to the minimum further increases in the working force in agriculture. . . . In fact, after a period, there should be a fall even in absolute numbers on the land. Similarly, there is little scope for increasing the working force in traditional small-scale industries, which are already burdened with excessive numbers; the problem here is to prevent too rapid technological unemployment and to maintain and raise incomes through improvements in equipment, techniques and organisation. The bulk of the new employment opportunities have, therefore, to be found in mining and in modern industry, large-scale as well as small-scale, in construction and in tertiary occupations. With the best effort that can be made, *some* increases in the working force in agriculture may be unavoidable for *some* years to come.[4]

---

[1] Chapter 21, Sections 12–14, and Appendix 6.

[2] United Nations, ECAFE, *Economic Bulletin for Asia and the Far East*, Vol. XII, No. 3, December, 1961, p. 11.

[3] India, *Second Five Year Plan*, p. 12.

[4] *Ibid.*, p. 14. Italics added. In this context, "traditional small-scale industries" means cottage industries.

Ceylon's Ten Year Plan makes the same case for industrialization:

The need for industrialisation stems from two basic conditions of the economy of Ceylon. The first is that the current rate of population growth and with it, of the work force, is very high by world standards. The rate of growth of the latter is indeed expected to become even higher after 1963. The second is that opportunities for absorbing this population growth within the traditional central industries of Ceylon — peasant agriculture and plantation crops — are strictly limited even when extensive irrigation works and land settlement are taken into account. This in turn means that expansion in the service industries, both public and private, based on these traditional activities is also limited.[1]

These views are becoming axiomatic in the region. The first statement below is that of a Pakistan economist and the second is that of an Indian economist, but the sentiments expressed are broadly representative:

. . . ours is the task of transferring the unemployed agriculturists to other sectors of the economy. In such circumstances, industrialization becomes an imperative need for the development of this economy. There is a potential source of economic surplus in the form of idle manpower which can be tapped only by industrialization.[2]

The existence of a large surplus labour force in agriculture is the main reason for industrialisation in India. . . . reasonable productive employment cannot be provided for additions to the labour force without a rapid expansion of industry.[3]

The logic of this position tends to seem self-evident also to Western economists, one of whom writes: "The improvement in the economic position of subsistence farmers who make up two-thirds or more of the people in many underdeveloped countries is dependent upon industrialization."[4] Although in recent years pending food crises have stirred an increasing number of economists in the West and in the region to give top priority to policy measures aimed at increasing agricultural yields, the pressure on food supply has not changed their conviction that a radical improvement in the utilization of labor in agriculture can come about only through industrialization. This seems to them all the more evident as, according to the theory of underemployment, there is "abundant" labor in agriculture with zero marginal productivity.[5] And industrializa-

---

[1] Ceylon, Government of, National Planning Council, *The Ten Year Plan*, Colombo, 1959, p. 345.

[2] Khurshed Husain, "Problem of Unemployment in Pakistan Economy," *Enterprise*, November 14, 1959.

[3] V. K. Ramaswami, "The Promotion of Industrial Development," in *Industrialisation in Developing Countries*, Ronald Robinson, ed., Cambridge University Overseas Studies Committee, Cambridge, 1965 p. 122.

[4] Bert F. Hoselitz, "The City, The Factory, and Economic Growth," *American Economic Review*, Vol. XLV, No. 2, May, 1955, p. 166.

[5] Chapter 3, Section 14; Appendix 6, Section 6.

tion will raise productivity in agriculture both by increasing the demand for agricultural produce and by furnishing the tools and equipment needed to improve agricultural techniques with decreasing labor demand.

While strong and pervasive in its appeal in South Asian countries, industrialization as an imperative of economic policy has not been unchallenged. Instead it competes with a traditionalist ideology. Identified as it is with modernization, industrialization is primarily associated with the establishment of large-scale enterprises, equipped with power and machines and using modern technology. The rival ideology does not demand an industrial revolution; rather it seeks to preserve and strengthen forms of traditional economic organization. Both, however, protest against the results of colonial economic experience. Those who support the industrialization ideology complain principally that modern industrial growth was hampered by the colonial powers' policies — or lack of policies. Subscribers to the traditionalist ideology, on the other hand, are obsessed with the deterioration of the ancient crafts caused, in their view, by imports of manufactured goods, and partly also, at a later stage, by the local production of machine-made products.

The traditionalist ideology has taken different forms and commands varying degrees of support in the several countries of the region. Ironically, the industrialization ideology has firmer roots and has received more sophisticated intellectual formulation in India than elsewhere in South Asia at the same time that the traditionalist ideology has been most forcefully expressed there. As we shall see, actual policies toward industrial growth have often been compromises between these competing ideologies.[1]

2 The General Productivity Argument

Part of the support for rapid industrialization is based on a conclusion that is obvious: in the larger and most populous parts of the region, substantial improvements in average levels of living by the end of this century — when the labor force will probably be more than twice its present size[2] — are out of the question unless considerably larger numbers of workers are engaged in productive activities outside agriculture. Advances in agriculture — within the limits set by technical knowledge now available and foreseeable and by the prospects for its practical application — will not in themselves be sufficient to ensure higher levels of living for such rapidly increasing populations or even to prevent a lowering of present levels.[3]

This conclusion applies most particularly to India and Pakistan and

[1] Chapter 25.
[2] Chapter 27, Section 15.
[3] Chapter 26; Chapter 28, Sections 3 and 4.

to Java, where more than two-thirds of Indonesia's people live.[1] In Ceylon it is almost impossible to augment substantially the area used for growing plantation crops, but yields per acre can be increased. And, as in India and Pakistan, the output of food crops can be raised through more intensive cultivation and, to a lesser extent, through the expensive alternative of bringing more land under cultivation. Even so, this increment is small in relation to the anticipated growth in the labor force.[2]

Burma and Thailand, with plenty of land, need have less fear about their ability to maintain, or even raise, levels of income per head, provided that effective policies are adopted for expansion of the cultivated area. Malaya is in a still more favorable position. Not only does it have more land available; its primary exports may not face such a bleak future as do the traditional primary exports of most other South Asian countries. But while traditional levels of income per head can easily be maintained and even raised for some time, in the longer run significant improvement in average income for the rapidly increasing population will require substantial industrial expansion.

This simple conclusion in itself provides *a rational basis for the strivings of these countries to industrialize as rapidly as possible.* And although we shall be concerned with the conditions limiting an industrialization drive, with the restricted possibilities it offers for raising labor utilization in the near future, and with the very compelling need for development efforts in many other directions, this discussion should not be construed to mean that South Asian countries should forego industrial expansion. Analysis of the hazards and limitations points rather to the importance and urgency of overcoming the obstacles to successful industrialization.

Underlying the general argument for industrial expansion presented above is the assumption that transferring members of the rapidly growing labor force from agriculture to modern industry will increase the general level of productivity. This assumption is related to a tenet of classical theory: that agriculture is subject to diminishing returns whereas increasing returns prevail in industry. In the static form in which it has often

---

[1] The force of this statement with respect to Java would be weakened if migration to the sparsely populated outer islands could be stepped up heavily. Experience to date, however, provides little basis for confidence that rapid outward migration will occur. See Chapter 26, Section 6, and Appendix 11.

[2] After taking account of all foreseeable prospects for absorbing labor productively in more intensive agricultural operations, the drafters of Ceylon's plan concluded that "The total of direct employment opportunities in the long-term amounts to 1,197,000 persons. This compares with a projected rate of increase in the workforce of 1,219,000 persons over the next 10 years alone." (Ceylon, *The Ten Year Plan*, p. 24.)

In India, the drafters of the First Five Year Plan asserted that "Improvement in agriculture cannot proceed beyond a point unless the surplus working force on the land is progressively diverted to industries and services." (India, *The First Five Year Plan*, New Delhi, 1953, p. 420.)

been presented, the assumption has serious limitations. As a dynamic generalization about long-term prospects under conditions such as those in South Asia, however, it contains an important element of truth.

The first part of this doctrine — that diminishing returns are the rule in agriculture — has been modified in the West during the past century and a half. Investment and new techniques, in combination with measures to alter institutions and attitudes, improved the utilization of the rural labor force so that agricultural employment declined not only in relative terms but also absolutely. In South Asia the present extreme underutilization of the labor force and the prospective rapid growth in its size will make a satisfactory utilization of labor in agriculture increasingly difficult to achieve if agriculture retains the major part of the natural increase in the rural population. In industry larger and more rapid advances in productivity are possible, partly because it is easier to circumvent attitudinal and institutional obstructions to effective utilization of labor. Moreover, in industry there is no limiting factor analogous to the availability of land in agriculture to impede the realization of increasing returns.[1]

The argument outlined does not require that productivity be higher in industry than in agriculture at the present time. Rather it rests on an inference about differentials that might be expected to arise over time as the labor force expands. It is usually assumed, probably correctly, that a substantial inter-sectoral differential in productivity already exists. Nevertheless, statistical calculations purporting to measure its magnitude are not very illuminating. In crude fashion, we have examined elsewhere the gap in average productivity that appears to exist between agricultural and non-agricultural pursuits in South Asia,[2] and stressed the weakness of the statistics on which the comparison is based.

For present purposes, a more relevant basis of comparison would be the value of product per worker in modern manufacturing industry and traditional agriculture. Such a comparison cannot readily be drawn from available materials. Even if accurate data could be assembled, their meaning would be far from clear. Several factors tend to exaggerate the probable productivity advantage of modern forms of manufacturing. In the first place, the much higher capital intensity of large-scale industry means that the higher average output per worker in that sector cannot be attributed solely to a fuller and more efficient utilization of labor. Furthermore, the product per agricultural worker may be underestimated, even in the most careful analyses. Not only does an unknown volume of output directly consumed within agriculture probably escape enumeration, but, more important, the output of agriculture and the output of industry are priced under different sets of rules. Agricultural products are regularly priced

---

[1] We shall reserve for Section 8 consideration of the argument that dynamic external economies also favor industrialization.

[2] See Chapter 11, Sections 3 and 4.

no higher than world market levels – and in some cases and periods, mostly in India, Pakistan, and Burma, below them – while the prices of manufactured products are usually well above those prevailing in international markets.[1]

Manufactured products for the home market are generally heavily protected by tariffs and import restrictions that tend to inflate their prices.[2] As we have shown in earlier contexts,[3] there are reasons why protection in South Asia tends to be exceedingly high. Import restrictions are designed primarily to close the exchange gap; the fact that they protect production for the home market is in a sense incidental. Thus the profits to which they give rise are "unplanned" and generally "too high" from a planning point of view. The governments have, on the whole, been unwilling or unable to expropriate by internal excise duties or other devices the profits over and above those needed to make production for the home market a profitable venture. Instead they have relied largely on direct controls in order to prevent protected industries from expanding too much. But edicts barring expansion do not eliminate featherbedding in those enterprises that have become established. Generally speaking, the result is high prices and high costs in the home market, which in turn are deterrents to the growth of export industries and a reason for subsidizing such industries. This sketch best describes the situation in India and Pakistan, where for a long time the authorities have prevented practically all imports except essential consumer goods and development goods. But with the advent of a generally unfavorable export situation

[1] This does not hold true in the case of manufactured goods produced for export and sold without benefit of subsidy. In any event, export activity by the modern component of South Asia's manufacturing sector is negligible outside the textile industry in India and Pakistan and threatens to remain so; see Chapter 13, Sections 3, 14, and 17.

[2] Ceylon's Ten Year Plan presents the case for protection: "Despite the desirability of import substitution it is hardly likely that Ceylon, lacking as it does so many of the overheads of a developed industrial economy, could find more than a very limited range of items whose local production would be cheaper than imports. A programme of development confined to only these items cannot be particularly large. If Ceylon is to pursue industrialisation on a substantial scale there would appear to be no alternative but to initiate a serious and effective policy of protection. Such a policy would have to go beyond that envisaged in the familiar 'infant industry' argument. Protection in Ceylon may be needed for a longer period than is required for only the initial commencement of particular ventures. It may in fact need to be sustained over the whole period during which an effective 'infra structure' for an industrial economy is built up. In the field of industry, in contrast to agriculture, favourable comparative costs are more the result of such a structure than of advantages in geographical position. They are based in effect on a well developed network of technology and skills, of power supplies and transport systems, of efficient business and commercial practices and a host of other factors. Until these have evolved, efficiency and hence costs in industrial production would tend to fall behind that of advanced countries. Unless, therefore, local industries have the shelter of a protective policy industrialization may not make an effective beginning." (Ceylon, *The Ten Year Plan*, p. 34.)

[3] Chapter 13, Section 17; Chapter 19, Section 7 *et passim;* and Appendix 8, Part I.

the trend is toward a spread and intensification of import restrictions in the region. Particularly if the industrialization drive is stepped up, all of the South Asian countries will soon be in the position of having to extend "unplanned" and excessive protection to their home industries, with similar effects on the industrial price and cost structure.

Although statistics that might throw a clear light on the cost-price structure of enterprises supported in this manner have not been produced, there is no doubt that many such enterprises run at high costs and charge prices incapable of standing the test of international competition. Static comparisons based on what appears at the moment to be a substantial differential in productivity between modern manufacturing and agriculture can therefore easily be misleading. The fact that wages are found to be considerably higher in industry does not prove that labor productivity is higher there; it may only signify that labor is sharing in the benefits of protection.

Despite these cautions in regard to statistical computations, there can be little doubt that labor utilization and labor productivity reach higher levels in modern manufacturing industry than elsewhere in the South Asian economies. Probably a basic explanation of this disparity is to be found, on the one hand, in the extremely low levels in other sectors and, on the other hand, in the institutional organization of modern manufacturing industry and its accompanying controls over labor performance.[1] The crucial test, however, as we pointed out above, is not the present situation but the situation that can be expected several decades hence when the modern industrial sector has grown substantially.

3   *The Direction of Industrial Growth*

Before exploring the effects of industrialization on labor utilization in greater detail, we must examine two aspects of industrial expansion: the choice of products to be produced by modern industry and the techniques and technology to be used. This section will be devoted to the first of these problems.

In the first instance, the choice of the product mix in the modern manufacturing sector is powerfully influenced by the international trading position of South Asian countries, which we analyzed in Chapter 13. Without repeating that analysis, a few conclusions pertinent to the present problem should be recalled. One is that it is vitally important for these countries to expand their export trade. The growth of exports has been sluggish since the First World War.[2] The main reasons for this are to be found on

---

[1] As noted elsewhere (see Chapter 23, Section 3 and Part II), labor efficiency in South Asia's large-scale manufacturing sector seldom reaches levels comparable to those found in Western countries using the same capital equipment and techniques.

[2] Chapter 13, Section 5.

the demand side and include: low income elasticity in importing countries, the substitution of synthetic products for the raw materials historically supplied from this region, technical innovations permitting users to economize in their use of those raw materials, and tariffs and import restrictions on South Asia's limited range of offerings in secondary product lines. On the supply side, population growth has increased domestic claims on exportable supplies or the factors used in their production. Except possibly for rubber and tin, Malaya's major exports, the prospects as far as traditional exports are concerned are dim.[1] As import needs have generally been rising — because of the population increase and the endeavors to promote development — most South Asian countries have experienced a widening foreign trade gap. This has been partly filled by foreign gifts and loans, but has increasingly necessitated stringent import controls, as mentioned above.

In this situation the promotion of exports other than the traditional ones would seem to be imperative. Such a program would have to be directed mainly toward the creation of opportunities to export manufactured products. As we pointed out in Chapter 13 (Section 14), it would encounter formidable difficulties, most of them deriving from the fact that the South Asian countries are underdeveloped and have not as yet made any great strides toward a higher level of economic activity. Nevertheless, the effort to gain a place in the world market with manufactured goods cannot be given up. Particularly as the region's debt charges are rising rapidly,[2] no increase in net foreign capital inflow that can reasonably be expected will be sufficient to ensure a balance of foreign exchange that will allow for essential imports. Naturally, this conclusion is reinforced by the fact that the need for imported goods is rising while prospects for traditional exports are discouraging.

As there are great obstacles to the successful penetration of the world trading network in manufactured goods, South Asian countries have concentrated their efforts on import substitution rather than on export promotion. Import substitution frees planners from major worries about organizing markets for industrial output at home. While there may be troublesome bottlenecks on the supply side, there are no serious problems on the demand side. A market already exists;[3] it does not have to be created

---

[1] Chapter 13, Section 13; cf. Section 15.

[2] Chapter 13, Section 16.

[3] This point has been explicitly stated, for example, in the draft of Ceylon's development plan: "The availability of a pre-existing market for industrial products (and of labour) affords a point of commencement in planning for industrial development. In 1957 industrial products of an approximate total value of Rs. 1,543 million were used in Ceylon for purposes of consumption or investment. Local production, however, accounted for only Rs. 380 million or 15 percent of this amount. The remaining 85 percent amounting to Rs. 1,163 million in value was supplied through imports from abroad. To put this in another way, though the productivity basis for the initial establishment of a market for manufactures has already been established through the development of

from scratch, though it may require reshaping. This task of reshaping is likely to be a fairly straightforward one in the case of reasonably standardized types of producer goods, especially in the larger countries. In the case of consumption goods, it may be more difficult if consumers have developed a preference for imported items.[1] There are, however, more serious limitations to the possibility of import substitution in South Asia. In their gestation phases, modern manufacturing industries increase a country's need for foreign exchange. Machinery must be imported for new industrial plants and for extensions of the power and transport network. Even after indispensable facilities have been constructed, machinery installed, and manufacturing operations begun, the drain on foreign exchange is likely to continue. In many cases, both raw materials and spare parts must be imported. Import substitution may ease the foreign exchange position in the long run, but in the short run it usually aggravates it.

There are other drawbacks as well. The fact that import substitution is not so much a policy choice as an adjustment to import restrictions that are designed primarily to combat a strained foreign exchange situation implies, as we have already hinted, that incentives for enterprise are created in the "wrong" fields and in the "wrong" proportions — wrong from the planning viewpoint.[2] Efforts to correct the situation by means of direct controls have a deleterious effect on efficiency and honesty in administration and business, as we demonstrated in Chapters 19 and 20. And the high cost, price, and profit levels created by import controls negate the efforts to stimulate entrepreneurs to enter the competitive export market.

In the circumstances of all the South Asian countries, there are other serious restraints on the prospects for successfully launching a large variety of modern industries. By Western standards all of these countries are economically small. Even when a domestic market already exists or can be created by import restrictions, it may not be large enough to justify the construction of many types of plants. A coordinated regional approach to industrial specialization with an international division of labor would simplify some of these problems. But the prospects for such arrangements in South Asia are slim. Indeed, the trend since independence has consistently been in the direction of autarky. Virtually all planning has

---

plantations and other sectors of the economy, this market has hitherto been satisfied largely through imports. A process of import substitution could therefore afford a basis for industrial development through the production locally of manufactured goods that were hitherto imported." (Ceylon, *The Ten Year Plan*, pp. 29–30.)

[1] The importance of consumer preferences is occasionally recognized. For example, Ceylon's Plan cites the conclusion of a government report on the problems of strengthening and renovating local cottage industries to the effect that "the preference of people generally for a foreign article" is a serious obstacle to development of manufacturing on the island. (*Ibid.*, p. 394.)

[2] Chapter 13, Section 17, and Appendix 8, Section 3.

been done on narrow national lines, with individual countries protecting their own industrialization programs. The barriers erected have made it difficult for potential exporters to find markets in neighboring countries.[1]

Limitations of size affect various countries in the region quite differently. India, though still economically minute by modern Western standards,[2] has a larger amount of aggregate purchasing power within its political boundaries than any other South Asian country. In addition, it is much more favorably endowed with the natural resources required by modern industry;[3] in particular, the local availability of coal and iron ore provides a base on which heavy industry can be built. By contrast, a country like Ceylon must concentrate largely on consumer goods industries for which there is relatively large local demand.

In India the existence of coal and iron deposits and the fact that even the import of development goods may have to be restricted are pragmatic reasons for assigning major emphasis to heavy industry in the planning of industrial production and, of course, are recognized as such. Nevertheless, the concentration on heavy industry can only be fully understood against the background of ideological inspiration. In part, the prevailing ideology has been influenced by Communist theory and practice, as adapted to India's colonial heritage. Thus the case for the priority of "basic industry" is often stated in terms of developing a "self-reliant economy." Reduced to its essentials, the argument in this guise holds that independence can only be consolidated when most of the capital goods required in domestic investment programs are produced at home. Otherwise, the fate of domestic investment plans may tend to slip beyond the control of the planners and be tied instead to an export surplus or an inflow of foreign capital, both highly uncertain quantities.[4] This amounts to saying that national sovereignty demands concentration on heavy industry — like the earlier policy choice of the Soviet government.

But it also argued in India that capital goods industries are "basic" because they come earlier in the production process. Thus Nehru maintained:

Unless we start from the base, we cannot build the third or fourth storey. We can advance in minor sectors of the economy, but if we do not build the basic structure, it will not make any difference to the hundreds of millions of our people.

---

[1] Chapter 13, Sections 6 and 15.

[2] In this context economic size is measured in terms of monetized incomes and demand.

[3] Chapter 11, Section 7.

[4] This point of view has been forcefully expressed by K. S. Gill, Assistant Chief, Perspective Planning Division of the Indian Planning Commission, in "Priority Development of Basic Industry," *A.I.C.C. Economic Review*, New Delhi, August 22, 1960, pp. 51–52.

The strategy governing planning in India is to industrialise, and that means the basic industries being given the first place.[1]

The plans often refer to heavy industries in this manner. The Chief of the Indian Statistical Institute has stated the case as follows:

In a big country it is possible and desirable to push back the manufacturing process to the utmost limit in order to expand continually its capacity to make investments increasingly out of its own domestic resources.

We may consider the case of India as an example. In India it would be economical to establish a heavy machine building industry which would manufacture heavy machines and equipment required for the installation of factories for the production of steel, fertilizers, aluminium, etc., or for the production of heavy electrical equipment like big generators, transformers, switchgear, etc. It would be also economical gradually to establish large-scale industries for the manufacture of synthetic raw materials of many kinds (including the production of petrol from coal in case an adequate supply of oil is not discovered). Once such basic industries are established it would be possible to expand the production of electricity, coal, steel, aluminium, fertilizers, mining and transport equipment, etc.; and then, with the help of such heavy machinery, producer goods, and energy, to manufacture machinery for the increasing production of consumer goods.[2]

This view has been elaborated in various formal models, the intellectual ancestry of which can be traced to the model produced by the Soviet economist, Feldman, in 1928. The case worked out at that time for the priority of heavy industry has influenced the strategy of planning in India and provided a general guide for contemporary "Marxist" economists on the problems of planning in underdeveloped economies.[3]

---

[1] Prime Minister Jawaharlal Nehru, "Strategy of the Third Plan," in India, Government of, Ministry of Information and Broadcasting, *Problems in the Third Plan — A Critical Miscellany*, Delhi, 1961, p. 35. Cf. Tarlok Singh, "Jawaharlal Nehru and the Five Year Plans," *Yojana*, June 7, 1964, pp. 5 ff. Singh points out that this thought has guided plan-making ever since the preparation of the Second Five Year Plan.

[2] P. C. Mahalanobis, "Industrialization of Underdeveloped Countries — A Means to Peace," *Bulletin of the Atomic Scientists*, Vol. XV, No. 1, January, 1959, p. 15.

[3] The following observations of a prominent Polish economist are pertinent:

"The first sub-problem is the most important one. It is concerned with choosing such types of investment as will most rapidly increase the productive power of the economy. This implies a concentration of investment in fields which increase the capacity of further production: that means building up the industries which produce means of production. It is only through development of the industries which produce means of production that the production capacity of the economy can be raised.

"This can be done, however, either directly or indirectly. It is done directly through investing in the construction of, say, power plants, steel plants, machine industries, raw material production and so on. It is done indirectly through foreign trade: instead of investing directly in the production say, of certain machines, it may be possible to get these machines from abroad by investing in the production of such commodities which can be sold abroad in order to import the machines required. Thus the productive power of the economy can be increased either directly through investing in the production of means of production, or indirectly through developing export industries which make it possible to import in the future the needed means of production. Which

Some of the ramifications of this doctrine can be observed in a 1958 presentation by Professor Mahalanobis. His words merit quotation at some length:

... in order to feed the fresh additions to the population at the rate of 5 million persons per year, it would be necessary to provide an additional quantity of 700,000 tons of foodgrains *every year* which would require Rs. 450 crore of foreign exchange over a period of five years. The cost can be reduced to Rs. 135 crore of foreign exchange in a 5-year period, if an additional quantity of 350,000 tons of ammonium sulphate is ordered from abroad *every year*, at least two years in advance of the crop season. The cost can be further reduced to Rs. 125 crore (out of which the foreign exchange component would be Rs. 50 crore) over a five-year period, if a new fertilizer factory of 350,000 ton capacity is started *every year;* this would call for decision 4 or 5 years ahead of the crop season concerned. The apportioned cost of a heavy machine building factory which would manufacture machinery in India to instal *every year* a new fertilizer factory of 350,000 ton capacity would be, however, so small as Rs. 12 or 15 crore with a foreign exchange component of perhaps Rs. 8 or 10 crore. Such a decision would have to be made only once but eight or ten years in advance of the season in which the fertilizer would be used. . . . Similar considerations hold good in other crucial sectors. An investment of Rs. 150 crore, including Rs. 80 crore of imported machinery, would be required to instal a million-ton steel plant with a product value of Rs. 40 or 45 crore. A heavy machine building factory with an investment of Rs. 80 crore, with foreign imports worth about Rs. 50 crore, would produce *every year* machinery worth roughly Rs. 80 crore or the equivalent of imported machinery needed to set up a million-ton steel plant. Once such a heavy machinery factory gets into production, it would be possible to start a new million-ton steel plant *every year* out of our own resources.[1]

This statement of the case for the development of a capital goods industry — or the "basic" industries in this terminology — has had a considerable influence on the strategy of planning in India. When examined more closely, however, the supporting arguments can be shown to be fallacious. Essentially, they depend on two propositions: (1) that development costs can be reduced, foreign exchange conserved, and, in consequence, the "savings" potential of the home economy increased through promotion of capital goods industries; and (2) that urgent requirements for a heavier volume of home-produced foodstuffs can be satisfactorily met by augmenting the capacity for fertilizer production and the manufacture of its re-

---

of these two methods is used depends on all kinds of circumstances, of existing facilities for developing either directly the output of means of production, or for producing commodities for export. However, if investment in exportable commodities is undertaken then obviously it must be associated with importation in exchange for these exports of machinery, steel, and other means of production to increase the country's productive power." (Oskar Lange, *Economic Development, Planning and International Cooperation,* Central Bank of Egypt, Cairo, 1961, pp. 11–12.)

[1] P. C. Mahalanobis, "Science and National Planning," *Sankhyā, The Indian Journal of Statistics,* Vol. 20, Parts 1 & 2, September, 1958, p. 85. Italics added.

quired inputs. This assumes that the provision of fertilizers is sufficient to raise food output. We shall defer consideration of the last very questionable assumption[1] and consider only the internal logic of this case for the promotion of heavy industry, assuming the relationship posited between the availability of fertilizers and food production.

The most important of the several flaws in this argument is the failure to take adequate account of the demands that must be fulfilled *simultaneously* if a link is to be established between the investment goods industries and the production of food. Professor Mahalanobis argues that the productive pattern can be steadily pushed toward a heavier proportionate emphasis on capital goods through the progressive displacement of imports and the build-up of home capacity. In fact, however, a link between steel plants and foodstuffs can only be established when all the intermediate steps are taken simultaneously. Without stating it, he assumes that food, fertilizers, and, behind them, plants, machines, and steel are produced *at the same time*, which implies a very substantial increase in the volume of investment.

Obviously, all of these intermediate links cannot be created overnight. As Mahalanobis recognizes, planning targets must be set well in advance, particularly for the most capital-intensive projects. Even though all the planned additions to industrial capacity are unlikely to reach the production stage simultaneously, the mere attempt to build up the whole range will create concurrent and competing claims on foreign exchange and disposable capital resources. Nor is it demonstrated that aggregate output will be maximized through this set of investment priorities as opposed to alternative ones. These points seem to have been neglected in his analysis.[2] The examples of the annual cost and foreign exchange reductions expected from pushing back the productive chain presuppose that such "savings" can be calculated simply by comparing the foreign exchange requirements of imported and home-produced goods when each item in the chain is examined independently. This method leads to a serious underestimation of total investment costs and of claims on foreign exchange in any one year. If, for example, it is decided to create the capacity required to

[1] See Chapter 26, Section 10.

[2] M. Mukherjee in his "Scientific Approach in Planning" (*Essays on Econometrics and Planning*, Pergamon Press Ltd., Oxford, 1965) recapitulates Mahalanobis' thoughts and is guilty of the same curious oversight as to the extra savings and foreign exchange required; he sees the problem only as one of foresight and planning. He writes (p. 168): "To sum up, [the] earlier a decision is taken, it is possible to choose a variant which is more economical to the country in the long run, both from saving of foreign exchange and also for other reasons. Of course, choice of each variant is associated with a particular complex of associated tasks not all of which are easy. But supposing decisions are taken and the tasks are squarely faced and fulfilled reasonably well, then it is always better to take decisions as early as possible and in general, choose a variant in which the basic capital goods are produced in the country. In fact, this is a quintessence of the philosophy of planning, and is probably profoundly true, provided there is planning in a real sense. . . . Some risks are involved in taking early decisions; but such risks should be calculated ones."

supply a fertilizer factory with machines eight or ten years hence, the costs of this decision would begin to make themselves felt immediately. Meanwhile, the growing population would still have to be fed, while the ability of the economy to buy imported foodstuffs during the gestation period would be diminished by the claims of nascent investment goods industries on foreign exchange.

Bewildering, also, is the manner in which "savings" are implicitly treated. The suggestion is that anticipated economies in foreign exchange expenditure can be regarded as "savings." As we have indicated, estimates of the savings (in this sense) that can be realized in any particular year are exaggerated. But the inference that development of heavy industry will raise the savings potential of the economy is misleading for yet another reason. Even if foreign exchange could be conserved, it would not necessarily follow that savings — in the sense of income that is not consumed — would rise for the economy as a whole.

Nevertheless, there is a sense in which investment goods provided out of capacity installed at home can be said to raise the savings of a South Asian economy, though this point is not treated explicitly in the argument criticized above. An allocation of industrial activity favoring capital goods (rather than consumer goods) at least produces a volume of output that the economy cannot consume. The physical composition of output itself imposes a form of forced saving by preventing increases in output from being directed in their entirety to current consumption. There can be no doubt that in India the production of more consumption goods would tend to increase consumption. This, then, is another reason for initiating heavy industry in addition to the availability of raw materials and the fact that investment goods production is one of the important avenues still remaining for import substitution, although it is not one that Indian advocates of a high priority for the capital goods sector have had in mind.[1] It is valid with the important reservation that in a very poor coun-

---

[1] Others, though, have made this point, among them M. H. Dobb: "If the more quick yielding forms of investment are chosen, then of course the consumable income of the near future will tend to be larger to the extent that new clothing factories, etc., come into operation and begin to pour their products into the shops. On the other hand, the rate of future development will be restricted by the limited capacity of the industries producing machines and equipment; so that expansion in, say, the second quinquennium and the third quinquennium cannot be so great (leaving aside the question of imports from abroad) as it could be if priority had been given in the first place to expanding the capacity of the industries which produce capital goods. By contrast, if the constructional programme is initially geared so as to give priority to the latter . . . then the flow of consumer-goods in the first few years will grow more slowly (and will be smaller than under the alternative scheme). But future developments in, say, the second quinquennium and after can be much more rapid." (M. H. Dobb, *Some Aspects of Economic Development*, p. 51, as quoted in A. H. Hanson, *Public Enterprise and Economic Development*, Routledge & Kegan Paul, London, 1959, p. 103.)

try consumption, and particularly certain types of consumption, is productive;[1] this is regularly forgotten by Western as well as South Asian
economists.

Unfortunately, much of the discussion of these important questions regarding the direction of industrial growth is clouded by an indiscriminate
use of the word "basic." This term is never clearly defined, though its emotional overtones are often exploited. Capital goods production is not inherently more basic to the economy than any other line of productive activity. In Ceylon, for example, as strong a case could be made for the view
that tea is "basic" for it provides resources the economy can use to obtain
the goods it chooses.[2] The view that heavy industry is basic may indeed be
characterized as an inverted form of physiocracy, the eighteenth-century
doctrine that agriculture is the basic economic activity.

The emphasis on heavy industry in the Indian development plans may
be rational nevertheless, for the reasons given,[3] even if the main supporting arguments are weak.[4] Also, in spite of its poverty, India has an internal market large enough to make possible the exploitation of the
economies of scale normally associated with heavy industry. The other
South Asian countries would, in varying degrees, gain less from heavy
industry; and they lack the raw material resources of India. Many of
them also still import numerous consumer goods and can benefit from
import substitution, while India has developed beyond this stage. Nevertheless, in all these countries the trend of opinion is strongly in favor of
venturing into heavy industry.[5]

[1] Appendix 2, Section 21.

[2] Oskar Lange, in the passage quoted on p. 1163, footnote 3, makes allowance for
this by stating that the development goods can be acquired "indirectly" by exports paying for imports. (Lange, *Economic Development, Planning and International Cooperation*, pp. 11–12.)

[3] To those reasons should be added the fact that foreign finance may be more readily available for large-scale enterprises of the heavy-industry type; cf. United Nations, ECAFE, *Economic Survey of Asia and the Far East 1965*, Bangkok, 1966, p.
25. India was able to get foreign loans for the construction of new steel mills; she
might have been less successful in raising money had the purpose been a build-up
of small-scale industries in the consumer goods sector.

[4] Chapter 17, Section 6 *et passim.*

[5] "The traditional capitalist pattern of development, building up consumer goods industries first, then gradually following with the capital goods to support them, did not
appeal to the Asian appetite for rapid economic growth. They believed, in other words,
that modern technology made it possible to skip some of the stages of industrialization
historically experienced in the West. Burma, Ceylon, Indochina, Indonesia, Pakistan,
and the Philippines were all considering specific projects for developing an iron and
steel industry." (David Wightman, *Toward Economic Cooperation in Asia*, published
for the Carnegie Endowment for International Peace, New Haven and London, Yale
University Press, 1963, p. 112.)

4   The Choice of Technologies and Techniques

An essential element of the industrialization ideology is the hope and expectation that newly launched industrial establishments will bring with them the powerful modern techniques used in advanced countries. Modern industry, using power and machines, is, of course, much more capital-intensive than are traditional methods of production that do not utilize power and machines. Indeed, this is one of the crucial facts about modern technology. Heavy industry requires especially large and expensive installations. But whatever the type of output chosen, modern industrialization will raise the average level of capital intensity for the economy as a whole. This will occur not simply because of the investment poured into individual plants but also because of heavy supplementary outlays on power and transport facilities, which are inherently capital-intensive.

When introduced in countries with very low levels of labor utilization, industrialization creates a dichotomy between technologies used in various parts of the economy, and produces an intricate set of theoretical and practical problems. A large and growing divergence between the "factor-mix" of new industries (and the modernized older ones) and that of customary activities is to be expected. This has been the starting point for a considerable controversy and a voluminous literature on the "optimal" combination of productive factors in underdeveloped countries. This discussion has been largely confined to factor combinations in industries — particularly the new or rationalized ones — and in construction work on plants, dams, ports, and roads.[1] As for traditional pursuits, that is, agriculture, crafts, and trade, it has commonly been assumed that *more* capital should be employed in order to improve techniques and raise productivity. In such fields as transportation, capital requirements are usually taken as given; discussion of factor combinations in the transport sector is thus focussed on reducing the number of workers by eliminating inefficient practices. In this section we shall follow the main line of recent discussion by considering only the question of the technology to be applied in the newly created or freshly rationalized modern types of large-scale industrial establishments.

On this point there are two prominent schools of thought, with many variations. One starts from the fact that labor is abundant — if it can be organized for higher levels of participation, duration, and efficiency — while capital is scarce. From this factor endowment it is inferred that, in augmenting modern industrial capacity, labor-intensive technologies that make little claim on scarce capital resources should be chosen. This

[1] One of the exceptions is the discussion of the choice of technologies and techniques for commodities currently produced by traditional methods of manufacturing. We shall postpone discussion of this problem until Chapter 25. The basic question is less which technology to apply than which sectors to promote.

approach has drawn its inspiration from neo-classical competitive equilibrium theory. The other school of thought assigns more importance to several dynamic considerations. It argues that capital-intensive methods may be preferable, despite the relative abundance of labor and scarcity of capital, because they produce a distribution of incomes favorable to profits and, in turn, to capital accumulation. As inadequacies in the supply of capital are considered to be a basic inhibition to economic growth, the inference is drawn that the rate of growth over the long run is advanced through the use of capital-intensive technologies and techniques in new industries.[1] Underlying this controversy are a number of assumptions we shall not elaborate here. But apart from the questionable relevance of these assumptions, the fundamental weakness of these approaches is their failure to come to grips with the practical issues.

One essential fact must be kept in the foreground of the discussion: part of the attractiveness of industrialization stems from its promise to bring modern techniques to a backward economy and to embody them in power and machines, particularly in heavy industry but also in industries producing consumption goods. These techniques are closely, though not rigidly, linked with the type of technology used. For the most part, machinery used in South Asia must be imported from the advanced countries. India, of course, is attempting to reach a position in which it can supply part of its own capital goods requirements, but the designs adopted are usually copies of those developed in advanced countries. Once the direction of industrialization has been chosen, there is little latitude in the choice of techniques. As the Indian Planning Commission has observed:

In many cases the choice appears to be obvious, dictated purely by technological facts of production. There is no choice, for instance, in the case of heavy industries, where no one would suggest that considerations of size and technology should be set aside to emphasize employment. Again, the need for the setting up of such industries cannot be questioned in view of their place in the larger interests of developing the employment potential of the economy in the long run.[2]

Within limits not easily definable, however, more scope remains for varying the proportions in which capital and labor are combined than is alleged in the foregoing observations. Indeed, much of the current discussion fails to consider how technologies are used. It is usual in this region for machines identical with those of advanced countries to be run at a slower pace and/or with more workers tending them. This is partly the result of the relative cheapness of labor, partly a consequence of the in-

---

[1] The influence of this line of thought is detectable in the observation of India's Second Plan that "the use of labour-intensive methods often implies that a smaller proportion of the incomes generated is available for saving and reinvestment. Steps must be taken to ensure that this does not happen on any significant scale." (India, *Second Five Year Plan*, p. 26.)

[2] *Ibid.*, p. 113.

experience of the South Asian labor force with industrial disciplines, and partly a reflection on the quality of management. In these circumstances, it is conceivable that the training of workers and managers could produce a rise in the capital/labor ratio even without a change in technology — that is to say, without a change in the technical processes and capital equipment used.

Potentially, however, substantial variation in factor proportions might be accomplished if different technologies, better suited to the factor endowments of the region, were devised.[1] This would call for a much higher degree of technological creativity than these countries have yet demonstrated. There are, of course, a few exceptions. But in the immediate future, countries launching an industrialization drive are mainly faced with the choice of using technologies worked out in the highly industrialized countries and adapted to their economic environment or rejecting modern machines altogether.

This is not to say that it is necessary to import or imitate only the latest and most up-to-date Western models. Considerable possibilities, which to date have hardly been touched, exist for developing a trade in second-hand machinery from advanced countries. Although there has been some discussion of such trade in Western circles, the South Asian countries have been less than enthusiastic about this prospect — partly because procedures for valuing used equipment have not been perfected, partly because of uncertainties about the continued availability of spare parts, and partly because the suggestion that they should accept "second-best" goods offends their sensibilities.

Even when factor proportions in the basic processes of production are rather rigidly determined by existing technologies, many types of operations in modern industrial firms still permit wide flexibility. This is especially true of such operations as the handling, packaging, and shipment of raw materials and finished products. In South Asia these tasks can easily be, and for the most part are, performed by labor-intensive methods, even when the direct processes of production are themselves capital-intensive.

But rigidities elsewhere in the economic system also affect choices of factor combinations — rigidities more complex than arguments about the technological constraints on the choice of productive combinations usually suggest. In particular, there is typically a deficiency of skills in these countries. Not only are persons with high technical qualifications few relative to demand, but complex administrative and managerial skills are also in short supply. It can thus be plausibly argued that husbanding these scarce resources and concentrating them in large and capital-intensive undertakings where their talents are likely to be most effectively used is a rational approach to policy.

[1] Chapter 14, Section 6.

The non-homogeneity of the labor force required in modern industrial processes tends, unfortunately, to be overlooked in highly simplified abstract discussions that regard units of capital and labor as readily substitutable for one another. In many cases, concentration of skills in capital-intensive undertakings also means that the bulk of the labor force can remain almost totally unskilled and can be assigned to routine and repetitive tasks. When this aspect of the factor combination problem is taken into account, technologies of high capital intensity may be better suited to the availability of productive factors than would otherwise be apparent. In this fashion, economies in the use of skills — a resource even scarcer than physical capital in the region — can be achieved. At the same time, of course, it is highly desirable that supplies of top skills be rapidly increased through training and that social restraints on their effective use be overcome.

The consequences of concentrating skills in large-scale capital-intensive enterprises are not, however, uniformly favorable. This course may serve to speed up the growth of industrial output. But it calls for minimal disturbance of the established institutional framework and minimal diffusion of skills throughout the labor force. In effect, it implies a perpetuation of a modernized enclave economy familiar from colonial economic experience. In some quarters, this effect of capital-intensive operations is viewed as a positive recommendation for their adoption. It is much simpler and less trying to bypass the social and institutional inhibitions and obstacles that have traditionally suppressed high levels of economic performance than it is to meet them head on.[1] The use of modern technologies that minimize the impact of industrial expansion on the economy as a whole, whatever their merits in other respects, evades direct confrontation with the social and institutional obstacles that have long inhibited economic performance and perpetuated low levels of labor utilization. More-

[1] This point has been recognized by Edward S. Mason:

"It is a truism that, in all countries, machines are easier to manage than men. This fact exercises its influence on planning in India and Pakistan in many ways, some inevitable and some probably representing the course of least resistance. It is easier, given the requisite skills, to secure a given output by administering a capital-intensive process than a labor-intensive process. Moreover, with an engineering orientation in management, it is probably more fun. A private entrepreneurial regard for costs tends to hold these preferences in check, but there is little check on the preferences of public management. A good deal of evidence supports the view that both in Pakistan and India public management shows little concern for the economies of labor-using techniques or for saving foreign exchange by the substitution, where possible, of local materials and labor.

"These administrative considerations probably also strengthen somewhat the already strong ideological predilections for growth through large-scale industrialization. The administrative burden per unit of development expenditure appears to be much less in the building of large dams and the erection of steel mills than in schemes for increasing agricultural output in land already in use. Also, it appears to be easier to recruit administrative talent for the former than for the latter undertakings. Yet the agricultural situation in India is close to desperate, and in Pakistan it is indeed desperate." (Mason, *Economic Planning in Underdeveloped Areas*, p. 73.)

over, at least in some quarters, capital-intensive techniques that minimize labor requirements may be viewed as advantageous on the ground that they enable employers to avoid labor troubles in the future.

Another and more purely economic factor also favors the introduction of capital-intensive technologies in modern industry. This is the failure of prevailing price ratios to reflect the relative scarcity and abundance of factors of production. For state enterprises and for many private ones with access to various public credit and development agencies, interest rates are held artificially low.[1] At the same time, industrial jobs generally yield earnings higher than workers could obtain elsewhere with the same skills and effort. These factors, in turn, tend to reinforce entrepreneurial preferences for factor combinations favoring capital.[2]

When all this has been said, it is still important to emphasize that the question of factor proportions, related as it has been in the recent discussion to the modern industrial sector, has little aggregative significance. Even if highly labor-intensive techniques were adopted in South Asia's modern industrial sector, there would be little change in the proportion of the total labor force it absorbed.[3]

We shall return shortly to a consideration of a number of other forces influencing the technologies, techniques, and productive combinations actually chosen in the industrial segment of South Asian economies. In particular, we shall consider in some detail the significance of the powerful political and social pressures in various South Asian countries in support of small enterprises as vehicles for producing manufactured goods.[4] At this point, however, it will be worthwhile to interrupt this discussion in order to examine the impact of an expanded modernized industrial sector on the volume of work opportunities in the economy.

5 *"Direct" Effects on Labor Demand and "Backwash"*
Effects on Existing Industry

Expansion of the modern industrial sector, of course, has consequences for participation ratios extending well beyond its immediate and direct impact on job opportunities in the industrial sector proper. In this section, however, we shall restrict discussion to the direct effects on the demand for labor within the manufacturing sector, both modern and traditional.

Analysis of the effects of industrialization on labor utilization is usually

---

[1] Appendix 8, Part II.

[2] This situation provides the point of departure for proposals to make "shadow" or "accounting" prices the basis for decisions regarding factor combinations. We discuss the limitations of this approach in Appendix 5.

[3] Section 6.

[4] Chapter 25.

approached in terms of the amount of "employment" industrial growth "creates." Within the modern part of the industrial sector, the term "employment" — and its antonym "unemployment" — may seem not altogether inappropriate, as conditions there bear some resemblance to those familiar in the West.[1] As we have pointed out, this is not so for manufacturing activity as a whole, since the bulk of it is not large scale and modernized. Moreover, when the indirect effects on other economic sectors are considered, even greater care must be taken to examine all three components of labor utilization.

With these reservations we shall examine in a preliminary way the "employment-creating" effects of industrialization. As we indicated in Section 1, these effects are regularly presented as a reason for the industrialization drive, and one that is particularly important because of the rapid increase in the labor force. In the literature on the development of South Asia and of underdeveloped countries in general it is usually taken for granted that industrialization has a substantial impact on employment, even in the short run.[2] In Chapter 21 (Section 1) it was pointed out that the "creation of employment" is a major preoccupation of planners in all countries of the region. It was also noted, however, that the objectives established in this area have been very modest — surprisingly so in view of the priority given to "full" and "fuller" employment in the general goals of planning — and that achievements have usually fallen far short of targets.

The unorthodox view to be expounded in the rest of this chapter is, instead, that *in South Asia the employment effects of industrialization cannot be expected to be very large for several decades ahead,* that is, until the region is much more industrialized. For a considerable time the net employment effects may even be negative. This dimension of the problem, as well as the wider consequences for labor utilization outside the modern sector, is overlooked in the vision that sees industrialization as the remedy for "unemployment" and "underemployment."

Generally speaking, the impact of industrialization on the growth of the direct demand for labor in manufacturing is a function not only of the

[1] This judgment is subject to the qualifications noted elsewhere, especially in Chapter 21, Section 11, and Chapter 23, Section 3 and Part II.

[2] "Industry also provides the openings which may draw away increasing proportions of rural workers, thus enabling those who remain behind to raise their levels of productivity and enjoy larger real incomes." (Tarlok Singh, "Agriculture and Industry in National Development," *A.I.C.C. Economic Review,* February 15, 1960, p. 31.) Similar statements are ubiquitous in the literature on economic development, whether by Western writers or writers from underdeveloped countries — or, of course, Communist countries. The belief that employment is to be had outside agriculture and the other traditional occupations is naturally basic to the concept and theory of "underemployment," as is the assumption that underemployed workers can be "removed"; see Chapter 21, Sections 12–14, and Appendix 6. Cf. Section 1 above.

speed of industrialization but also of the position in the economy already achieved by modernized industry. This proposition holds even when the backwash effects of industrialization on traditional manufacturing are disregarded. Even a very rapid rate of industrial growth will not for a considerable time generate sufficient demand for labor to increase substantially the percentage working in the industrial sector. The labor force is growing too rapidly.

The relationships involved may be seen most clearly if we consider a hypothetical example. Let us assume that one percent of the labor force is employed in *modern* industry at the beginning of a planning period and that *no traditional* manufacturing exists. (This proportion engaged in modern industry is slightly lower than that in India and Pakistan but substantially higher than that in other countries of the region.) Let us also assume that the population of working age is simultaneously increasing at 2 percent per year. (This rate of growth has been exceeded in India and Pakistan and is much below the rate in Ceylon and the Southeast Asian countries.) In these circumstances, a 10 percent annual expansion of employment in modern industry — which *per se* is a very considerable increase not reached in any South Asian country — would mean that direct employment in that sector would absorb only 5 percent of the increment in the labor force. In other words, 95 percent of the entrants to the labor force would be obliged to find a livelihood in some form of economic activity outside it. Given these assumptions, the task of absorbing in modern industry the full natural increase in the population of working age would, in the first year, impose the unreasonable requirement of tripling the number employed in industry in a single year. The proportionate rate of increase required would, of course, decline over time, but for a lengthy period this decline would be very slow.

In this hypothetical example, we have ignored the likely backwash effects on existing manufacturing industry. Apart from its effects on traditional manufacturing, the extension of modern industrial enterprise can be expected to entail some rationalization of established industry in the modern or quasi-modern sector. Rationalization normally implies that less labor is used to produce a given quantity of output. Even if output is increased, labor requirements will not grow proportionately, and in some cases may actually diminish. Just to maintain the prevailing level of demand for labor may require a rapid rate of industrial expansion in terms of investment and output when rationalization of older manufacturing plants within the modern sector occurs simultaneously with industrial expansion. More serious backwash effects are implied in industrialization when existing manufacturing enterprises are pushed out of business and not simply obliged to rationalize their processes. This displacement effect will be emphasized when modern technologies favoring units of large scale are introduced in order to take advantage of technical economies.

In the realistic case (as opposed to the one we have thus far assumed), backwash effects are also likely to be felt by the traditional manufacturing sector when new enterprises, using up-to-date techniques and equipped with power and power-driven machines, turn out goods competing with goods produced by traditional methods in small-scale enterprises and crafts. Through planning, traditional manufacturing can be shielded from much of this backwash.[1] Nevertheless, there is a real risk that the slight increase in demand for labor from new modern enterprises will be more than offset by reductions in labor demand in traditional manufacturing.

This is, of course, an old story and one often identified with colonial exploitation. In earlier periods, the competitive challenge to indigenous enterprises occurred in two rounds. In the first, competition came from imports of machine-made manufactures produced in metropolitan countries. In this round, the expansionary effects on labor demand were confined to the exporting countries; the colonies felt only the backwash. Later, traditional modes of manufacturing were further threatened by some locally based industrial establishments. At this stage the colony itself reaped at least some partially compensating advantages.

Backwash effects of the type described do not, of course, occur when newly formed manufacturing units either produce import substitutes or direct their output to export markets. As a practical matter, however, export promotion by South Asian countries — except as it involves primary commodities supplied primarily by plantations and mines — encounters serious difficulties.[2] Import substitution, by contrast, is open to new manufacturing industry without risk of internal backwash effects, a fact that adds to its appeal.

If, on the other hand, new or enlarged industrial enterprises are brought into direct competition with the remnants of the traditional crafts or with producers in other non-modernized units, the over-all effects of industrialization on labor demand may for a long time be negative. More opportunities for economic forms of participation may be lost in crafts and non-modernized industry than can be created by newly initiated or rationalized industrial enterprises.[3]

---

[1] Chapter 25, Section 3.

[2] Section 3 and Chapter 13, Section 14.

[3] An example of this process can be found in the experience of the Soviet Central Asian Republics of Uzbekistan, Kirgizia, Tadzhikistan, and Turkmenia where extremely rapid expansion in modern industry has occurred in the past few decades. The gross value of industrial output (excluding handicrafts) is believed to have risen by more than twelve times between 1926 and 1940, by nearly twice between 1940 and 1950, and by about two-thirds between 1950 and 1955. At the beginning of this period, factory-type industrial employment was extremely limited, though certain types of handicrafts were well developed. Despite the speed of growth in the modern industrial sector, the proportion of the population engaged in manufacturing (including both modern industry and handicraft production) was believed to be lower in 1955 than in 1897. Only in recent years — when a high level of industrial development had already been

The effects of these forces during the colonial phase of South Asian economic history cannot be adequately illustrated by statistics. That backwash effects, of both types mentioned above, did occur is clear beyond question. The importance of those effects is indicated by the concern South Asian governments now express about the possible repetition of similar displacements in the future. Rationalization of modern or quasi-modern, large-scale manufacturing units already in existence has seldom been greeted with enthusiasm, and in most countries special efforts have been made to protect and revivify traditional crafts.[1] Part of the desire to protect the traditional crafts springs from fear lest existing rural-urban disparities be magnified. Further deterioration in the crafts located in rural districts will depress incomes and levels of living, perpetuate poor educational and health conditions, and generally dim the prospects for rural progress.

The problem of backwash effects on labor demand raises several other important issues. As already mentioned, it provides a strong supplementary argument for restricting both new industry and the modernization of existing enterprises to sectors that produce export goods or import substitutes. Heavy industry is a particularly safe bet, as these countries begin their independent existence with no modern capital goods industry worthy of the name. But even a country like India, which for compelling reasons has stressed heavy industry, cannot possibly channel all its modernization efforts into export-oriented or import-substituting manufacturing.

In this situation, planners and governments face a serious dilemma. Their long-term goal is to use industrial expansion as a device for modernizing the entire economy. But their short-term interest in preventing serious deterioration in traditional manufacturing, and particularly in crafts, conflicts with this long-range objective. India has attempted to resolve this dilemma not only by concentrating as much new investment as possible in import-substituting large-scale industry but also by imposing restrictions on rationalization in certain lines of large-scale manufacturing that compete with traditional handicraft production.[2]

Measures of the latter type are particularly welcomed by workers, and concern for their interests has led the government to seek "rationalization without tears" — that is, without depriving anyone of a job, though the size of the work force may shrink when vacancies created by normal attri-

---

achieved — has the industrial sector been able to absorb a significant share of the natural increase in the rural population of working age. See United Nations, Economic Commission for Europe, "Regional Economic Policy in the Soviet Union: The Case of Central Asia," *Economic Bulletin for Europe*, Vol. 9, No. 3, Geneva, November, 1957, pp. 49–75.

[1] For more on these points, see below, Section 10 and Chapter 25.

[2] For a fuller discussion of these policies in India, see Chapter 25, Sections 3–4.

tion are not filled.[1] New enterprises are not subject to such restraints. Beginning fresh, they have no commitments to a labor force. And their awareness of the government's interest in protecting employment and of the risk of friction with workers should they later attempt to reduce the work force gives entrepreneurs an added inducement to adopt capital-intensive, labor-saving techniques from the start. This creates a tremendous gap between techniques used in new and in old establishments. The gap is widened when, at the same time, investment in older establishments is suppressed by governmental policy.

6 Statistical Estimates of the Employment-Creating Effects of Industrialization

The general points stressed above — that the *direct* employment effects of modern industrialization are small in the early stages, while the *backwash* effects may be considerable, unless industrialization is restricted to production of exports or import substitutes — have not been overlooked in the detailed planning in South Asia, though curiously enough the insight implied has not had much effect on the general pronouncements that hail industrialization as the means by which the underemployed in agriculture and elsewhere can be absorbed.

Very little explicit attention is given to the backwash effects. Instead, employment projections in the plans focus mainly on the gross additional demand for labor that new industries are expected to generate. This emphasis can be partially defended when, as in India, the government takes deliberate steps to block the backwash, both by selecting lines of output for expansion that do not conflict seriously with established production and by promoting specific protective measures. Even so, the possibility that some backwash will occur should be recognized. Moreover, the enlargement in employment opportunities expected to result from expansion in the modern industrial sector should not be confused with the net change in work opportunities in manufacturing throughout the economy as a whole. As we shall note when examining the specific statistical estimates presented in the plans, this distinction is regularly neglected.

For purposes of a clear analysis of the employment effects of industrialization, calculations presented in the various plans have another important weakness. In several cases, the form of presentation makes it impossible to

[1] In general, the Indian government has discouraged rationalization in existing large-scale industry, whether through the introduction of higher technologies or through increasing work norms on machines presently in use, unless industrialists have been prepared to absorb workers threatened with displacement in other operations or unless agreement can be reached between management and labor interests. In this connection, see Charles A. Myers, "Labour Problems of Rationalisation: The Experience of India," *International Labour Review*, Vol. LXXII, No. 5, May, 1956.

draw a line of demarcation between the primary or direct effects of industrial expansion and its secondary or spread effects.[1] Admittedly, distinctions of this sort are difficult, even in advanced economies, and projections of future demand for labor are always hazardous. In South Asia, the difficulties are compounded by the fact that the planners are obliged to base their estimates on totally inadequate statistics. For these reasons, calculations of the employment effects of industrialization are necessarily highly conjectural. The estimates produced are nevertheless worth reviewing, as they serve to illustrate that the impact on labor demand of expansion in the modern industrial sector, even on the most optimistically unrealistic assumptions, cannot be expected to make more than an extremely modest contribution to improvement in the demand for labor.

The limited scope for direct expansion in employment opportunities in the early phases of industrialization is indicated in estimates prepared for the Indian plans. In the First Plan period, modern industrial establishments were believed to be capable of generating only about 400,000 new jobs.[2] This figure was based on crude information about anticipated labor requirements collected from employers' organizations that was supplemented where necessary by projections built on the assumption that "additional production will lead to proportionate rise in employment."[3] The estimate can thus be understood as an attempt to establish merely the gross gain in job opportunities in the modern industrial sector when possible effects of rationalization within this sector and backwash effects outside it are ignored. The total rise in job opportunities necessary to absorb the natural increment in the labor force plus the uncalculated backlog of unemployment was not estimated in the first Indian plan. Even with the implicit, unrealistic assumptions mentioned and in the absence of detailed aggregative target, it is clear that the expected rise in labor demand generated directly within modern manufacturing industry could not absorb more than an insignificant fraction of the increment in the population of working age during the plan period.

The second Indian plan was more specific in its presentation of estimates. Industry — apart from small-scale and cottage industries — and mining combined were expected to contribute 750,000 new jobs in the period 1956–61.[4] The method of estimation, though different, was again necessarily crude. The basic estimates of gains in employment were derived from the assigned output targets as adjusted to allow for a 20 percent improvement in average productivity assumed for the plan period.[5] Even

[1] Sections 7–9.

[2] India, *The First Five Year Plan*, pp. 653–654.

[3] *Ibid.*, p. 653.

[4] India, *Second Five Year Plan*, p. 115.

[5] *Ibid.*, p. 117.

so, modern industry and mining combined were expected to assimilate only 7.5 percent of the natural increment in the labor force anticipated during the five-year period. In fact, the estimate of expansion in the labor force — placed at about 10 million in the Second Plan[1] — turned out to be much too low.[2] Cottage and small-scale industries were expected to provide jobs for an additional 450,000 persons, apart from an anticipated increase in work duration for some already occupied in this sector.[3] Backwash effects were thus excluded though some allowance for rationalization within the modern industrial sector could be interpreted as included in the planners' assumption about improvement in average productivity.

In the third Indian plan the increment in jobs expected from modern manufacturing and mining was the same as the figure projected in the Second Plan — 750,000. But a goal of expanding total employment by 14 million brought the relative share of industry and mining down to 5.3 percent of the over-all aim.[4] Within this composite segment of the economy, mining was expected to contribute one-third (250,000) of the increase in jobs and large and medium-scale manufacturing industries the remainder of only 500,000.[5] The technique of estimating employment gains in manufacturing had again been modified. In this round of planning, calculations of capital requirements per worker in key segments of manufacturing served as a basis for deriving estimates. These calculations, though admittedly crude, were then set against investment targets in particular industries and an estimate of changes in labor requirements was thus reached. The possible sources of error in this procedure are serious.[6] Not only are the data on capital requirements per worker subject to a wide margin of error; estimates of investment in particular industries are likely to be inaccurate.

This is not to suggest that projections of employment growth over a five-year period are simple to prepare or that there is any ideal technique for making them. The point is rather that, as shown by any of the three techniques used in the Indian plans, the modern manufacturing sector could not be expected to make more than a very slight contribution toward absorbing the expansion of population in the working age groups.

[1] *Ibid.*, p. 75.

[2] Chapter 27, Section 2.

[3] India, *Second Five Year Plan*, pp. 115–117.

[4] India, Government of, Planning Commission, *Third Five Year Plan, A Draft Outline*, New Delhi, June, 1960, p. 753. As before, the planners seriously underestimated the growth in the labor force.

[5] *Ibid.*, p. 757.

[6] In the words of the planners: "It should, however, be stated that the data on which the calculations given above are based, are on the whole very meagre. The conclusions which are drawn are, therefore, intended only to suggest broad dimensions. Indeed, precision in this field can only come from prolonged study." (*Ibid.*, p. 757.)

It would be useful to compare the targets for employment creation set out in the Indian plans with the changes in industrial employment that actually occurred. Unfortunately, the statistical evidence bearing on this important matter is cloudy. The Indian planners, in their periodic reviews of the degree of plan fulfillment, have reported only changes in employment for the economy as a whole and have not subdivided the aggregate by sectors; the estimates of aggregate changes are, moreover, crude and very unreliable, as we shall point out in Section 7.

It might be expected that some light would be thrown on this question by the surveys conducted by the statistical organs of the Indian government. The findings of various studies, however, are far from unambiguous, as will be readily apparent from a brief comparison of the results of a series of National Sample Surveys on manufacturing industries. These studies, which have been conducted on a continuing basis, have attempted to use uniform methods throughout. They have followed the definition of manufacturing enterprises adopted in the Factories Act of 1948: establishments employing 20 or more workers without the aid of mechanical power and 10 or more with power. This definition is not restricted solely to modern industry; it embraces some traditional manufacturing where some, though not all, of the backwash effects are felt. On the other hand, manufacturing units under the jurisdiction of the Ministries of Railways and Defence have been excluded.

The calculations of the volume of employment offered within this range of manufacturing enterprises do not inspire confidence. The survey covering 1951 indicated that total employment in the class of manufacturing defined above was roughly 3,068,000.[1] The 1953 study reported a lower volume of employment — 2,982,000 employees — with the bulk of the reduction occurring in establishments using power.[2] In 1954, data "for the factories where employment figures were available" indicated that the number of workers in manufacturing enterprises was 2,785,603.[3] This finding, however, referred only to workers; employees in supervisory and managerial jobs were thus excluded, as were persons who were at work but not employed for wages. In the survey of the preceding year workers in the manufacturing labor force were shown as numbering 2,611,000.[4] Unfortunately, the 1954 study failed to report the aggregate volume of manufacturing employment. This omission destroys comparability with the 1956

[1] India, Government of, *National Sample Survey No. 15, Report on Sample Survey of Manufacturing Industries, 1951,* Calcutta, 1958, p. 17.

[2] India, Government of, Indian Statistical Institute, *National Sample Survey No. 26, Report on Sample Survey of Manufacturing Industries, 1953* (Draft), Calcutta, 1957, p. 28.

[3] India, Government of, The Cabinet Secretariat, *National Sample Survey No. 28, Report on Sample Survey of Manufacturing Industries, 1954* (I), Calcutta, 1960, p. 5.

[4] India, *National Sample Survey No. 26,* p. 28.

study, which did not distinguish between workers and employees other than workers but simply reported total employment. Its estimate of total employment in manufacturing came to 3,145,000.[1]

These calculations, spanning the period of India's First Plan, hardly provide a basis for a confident conclusion that employment in manufacturing expanded or that it even held its own. Despite their weaknesses, these data certainly lend no support to the view that any substantial growth in modern industrial employment was achieved during the period in question.[2]

Other South Asian countries have followed various practices in their assessments of the employment-creating potential of industrial expansion. The calculations of all those that have published detailed sectoral estimates have much in common. In Pakistan, the First Plan estimated that the labor force "was likely to grow by about 2 million persons during the Plan period" (1955–60).[3] Large-scale industrial establishments, defined as those employing 20 or more workers and using power, were expected to provide some 200,000 new jobs by 1959–60. This rate of expansion would represent an increase of nearly 50 percent in industrial employment. But even such an impressive expansion in the industrial sector would absorb only 10 percent of the projected increase in the labor force, and this target was far from being fulfilled. Whereas the First Plan estimated the labor force in large-scale establishments at nearly 400,000 in 1954–55,[4] the Second Plan came to the conclusion that large and medium-scale industries had reached a figure for average daily employment of only 440,000 in 1959–60.[5] It is notable that the estimate of employment gains from the modern industrial sector in the Second Plan was only 180,000[6] — an even more modest figure than was set out in the First Plan. In both cases, backwash effects were apparently assumed to be nonexistent, as it was antici-

[1] India, Government of, Planning Commission, *Occupational Pattern in Manufacturing Industries, India, 1956*, Calcutta, 1959, p. 42.

[2] In another context, the views of the Indian Statistical Institute, the body that conducts the National Sample Surveys, on changes in employment in factories employing 50 or more workers with power and 100 or more without power, have been presented as follows:

"It may be noted that employment provided by those industries [i.e. as defined above] did not vary widely between 1951 and 1954, the rationalisation of certain industries having offset the additional employment provided by newly started industries." (India, Government of, Indian Statistical Institute, *National Sample Survey No. 21, Report on Small Scale Manufacturing Establishments* (Draft), Ninth Round, May–November, 1955, Calcutta, 1957, p. 13.)

[3] Pakistan, Government of, National Planning Board, *First Five Year Plan, 1955–60*, Karachi, 1958, p. 145. In fact, this projection turned out to be a gross underestimate.

[4] *Ibid.*, p. 594.

[5] Pakistan, Government of, Planning Commission, *The Second Five Year Plan (1960–65)*, Karachi, June, 1960, p. 260.

[6] *Ibid.*, p. 260.

pated that the numbers employed in traditional lines of manufacturing would grow.

Ceylon's plan, which is more oriented to manpower problems than the other plans, has never become operational. It was projected over the ten-year period to 1968, during which time it was estimated a substantial absolute growth in the industrial work force could be achieved. Employment in all industries — including cottage and small enterprises and thus backwash effects — was expected to rise from 291,000 in 1957 to 528,000 in 1968, an increase of more than 81 percent.[1] But, in the words of the plan, "the major portion of the increase in employment in this field will be due to the expansion of small-scale and cottage industries. The contribution to employment from the more capital intensive large and medium scale industries is naturally small."[2] The planners do not, however, present detailed estimates of the employment gains expected from these two components of the manufacturing sector.

In its Second Plan, covering the years 1961 to 1965, Malaya assigned a high priority to industrial growth, as the other governments of the region have done. The plan asserted that "for the future, the importance of manufacturing to the Federation's long-run development and economic diversification can hardly be over-emphasized."[3] But there were few illusions about the extent to which the expansion of the modern manufacturing sector would directly create new jobs. This is apparent from the manner in which the planners discussed the experience during the First Plan. They noted that employment in all types of manufacturing had risen by only about 12,000 between 1955 and 1960. Although the number of factory jobs had increased by a larger figure, about half of this gain was offset by losses in handicraft enterprises.[4] The probable backwash effects were not examined with equal clarity in preparing projections for manufacturing employment in the Second Plan. Within the modern industrial sector it was anticipated that the average level of capital intensity would be raised. This conclusion emerged from the planners' "reasonable expectations" concerning changes in the volume of industrial output and employment in the ensuing five years. While the output of the modern industrial sector was expected to increase by 50 to 75 percent, "the rise in industrial employment would be proportionately less with the trend toward more capital-intensive kinds of production."[5] Even if further backwash effects on traditional manufacturing were assumed to be nonexistent, the increase in demand for labor arising directly from modern manufac-

[1] Ceylon, *The Ten Year Plan*, p. 89.

[2] *Ibid.*, p. 90.

[3] Malaya, Government of the Federation of, *Second Five Year Plan, 1961–65*, Kuala Lumpur, 1961, p. 59.

[4] *Ibid.*, p. 4.

[5] *Ibid.*, p. 20.

turing would provide for less than 10 percent of the natural increment in the labor force.[1]

In Burma, the modest employment-expanding effects of industrialization were also understood. Burma's four-year development plan contained the following observation:

Even after all the industrial projects included in the Four Year Plan are completed and in operation, they will employ only a small fraction of the manpower in Burma and will yield only a small part of the national product. It is estimated that the industrial plants listed above will employ about 18,000 men to operate them, or less than 1 percent of the employable population of urban Burma.[2]

The foregoing examples of the planners' calculations of the employment potential of modern manufacturing are sufficient to illustrate the general point. However inaccurate these estimates may be in detail, they consistently support the conclusion that, in the absence of spread effects, industrialization can produce only a very small immediate expansion in demand for labor. This situation, of course, is an inescapable consequence of the low base from which modern industrial expansion begins and the backwash effects that are certain to occur unless the output of modern industry is directed exclusively to newly created markets, either in foreign countries or in home territory. When a start must be made from such modest beginnings, as it must in all South Asian countries, even a big push toward industrial expansion cannot for decades ahead be expected to provide employment opportunities directly for more than a very small fraction of the labor force, and even that gain may be partly, wholly, or more than wholly offset by backwash effects. This point needs to be emphasized in order to dispel the quite unrealistic expectation still widely entertained that a rapid transformation of the occupational structure will come about once an industrialization program is launched.

As we indicated in Section 4, the scope for utilizing substantially more labor-intensive technologies in the manufacturing sector is not wide, unless the goal of industrializing along modern lines is compromised. Nevertheless, it may well be asked whether the application of technologies substantially more labor-intensive than those actually employed (or than those assumed in the planners' projections) would have made a big difference in the employment impact of industrial expansion. A detailed study of Indian industry sheds some interesting light on this question. Capital/labor coefficients were calculated for five of India's largely modernized industries: cement, paper, iron and steel, sugar, and the Bombay and Ahmedabad cotton textile firms. One of the conclusions reached was:

[1] *Ibid.*, pp. 16, 20.

[2] Burma, Government of, Ministry of National Planning, *Resources for the Four Year Plan*, Rangoon, 1957, P.H. 2.

Even doubling the labour per unit of investment, as compared with the coefficients computed . . . would only increase the labour force in the five industries studied by about 100,000 more workers than projected in the Second Plan, assuming the same investment plans; the effect upon *all* organized manufacturing industry would increase employment in all factory manufacturing industries by less than one million workers in the Second Plan period (in contrast to a projected expansion in the labour force by ten million workers). Investment in this sector has today probably one of the lowest direct employment-expansion effects, compared with an equal investment within other sectors of the economy.[1]

Therefore, the adoption, even on a major — and totally impracticable — scale, of technologies and techniques favoring heavier employment of labor would not have made a substantial change in the direct impact of industrial expansion on participation ratios. This is so because modern industry forms — and will form for a long time to come — a very small part of the total economy in India and a still smaller one in the other countries of the region. This situation, it may be added, further reduces the practical significance of the widely discussed problem of factor-mix considered in Section 4.

7 The "Spread" Effects: A General Characterization of a Vision

Obviously, an industrialization program has indirect effects on the entire economy and on the demand for labor extending far beyond the industrial sector proper. We must attempt to analyze these further implications of the South Asian industrialization plans and the high hopes attached to them. We have already touched on one of the indirect effects of industrialization — the negative one of backwash on job opportunities in traditional enterprises. This backwash goes beyond job opportunities, spreading to wider social reaches; levels of living tend to be depressed, particularly in rural areas, and inequalities in incomes to be aggravated. Even governments that have attempted to dam up the backwash from modern industrialization have seldom adequately appreciated this dimension of the problem.

But if planners in South Asia have tended to underestimate the likelihood and the impact of backwash effect, they have also tended to exaggerate the force of expansionary stimuli radiating from industrial starts. This has given rise to excessive optimism and has distracted attention from the rigidities and inhibitions likely to swamp potential spread effects. This bias is not very difficult to understand. Western theories, as adopted in South Asia, have encouraged unrealistic expectations about the indirect

[1] George Rosen, *Industrial Change in India*, Free Press, Glencoe, Illinois, 1958, pp. 182–183.

effects of industrial starts. In the countries of the region, however, the climate for diffusion of expansionary impulses from industrialization is far less favorable than it is, or has been, in the West. In the present discussion of the wider ramifications of industrial starts in South Asia, we shall restrict our attention to the nature and strength of potential spread effects.

As noted in Section 1, the general discussion of development problems in South Asian countries holds industrialization to be the remedy for underdevelopment and for the vast underutilization of labor that, from the point of view of the human factor of production, is the essence of underdevelopment. Our analysis started out from the proposition that no substantial development in South Asia — especially in India, Pakistan, and other countries with a high man/land ratio — is possible *over the long run* unless these countries can employ a much larger part of their labor force in modern industry or other productive non-agricultural occupations. This is not to suggest that such a change in the economic structure can be easily accomplished, or even that it is feasible with measures now deemed practicable in the region. Behind the widespread optimistic view that such a change is possible without great delay and that, *even in the shorter run,* the launching of an industrial build-up will radiate powerful expansionary stimuli raising labor utilization and productivity, lies a vision of dynamic impulses penetrating all parts of the economic system. These impulses, in turn, are expected to give momentum to a cumulative process of expansion and to spur development all around.[1]

Industrial growth is thus seen not only as important in itself but as the vital catalyst for a larger economic transformation. Very little analysis, even on the abstract and theoretical level, has been devoted to clarifying the mechanism through which the momentum expected from industrial starts is transmitted. Often, however, general reference is made to the effects industrial growth has on demand. These effects are viewed in the macro-economic setting of Keynesian or post-Keynesian theory, but this conceptual apparatus is not very helpful. In the more sophisticated reasoning about development prospects in these countries, it is now generally recognized that theirs are typically low-elasticity economies. Increased demand does not lead to increases in supply after only a brief time lag. Rather, potential multiplier effects are often killed at the start of the process.[2] Sometimes emphasis is placed instead on the creation of external economies in the widest meaning of the term, including such institutional and attitudinal changes as the development of markets, the rationalization of attitudes, the spread of skills and the spirit of enterprise, and in-

---

[1] This vision is occasionally stated explicitly in the plans. For example: "Once industrial growth commences, it contributes towards its own expansion and also assists further improvements in agricultural productivity." (Ceylon, *The Ten Year Plan,* p. 29.)

[2] Appendix 2, Section 23 *et passim.*

creased mobility. But on the whole the mechanism through which the initiation of an industrialization program will produce these desirable consequences is left foggy and unexplained.

This crude vision is often implicitly dependent on a loose analogy with the earlier experience of Western economies. There the industrial revolution began with a number of small and, occasionally, some large industries. The success of these bred conditions that made further new starts possible and they, in turn, spurred still others. The cumulative development touched all aspects of economic and social life. In analogy with this experience, it is thought that similar results can be achieved in South Asia if only an expanding industrial sector can be created. New demands will then be stimulated, and costs will at the same time be reduced. The volume of profits will increase, generating savings that can be plowed back into productive investments to sustain and strengthen the economy's dynamic momentum. It is now generally realized that in South Asia this process is unlikely to start spontaneously. The inference is therefore drawn that industrialization will have to be planned. Although the initiating force may be different from the one that took hold in the West, it is nevertheless assumed that industrial expansion, once begun, will engender a similar — and virtually automatic — mechanism of growth.

On closer inspection, this image of Western economic history appears over-simplified and idealized. In retrospect, it is easy to overlook the risks and uncertainties that attended success. In the early stages of Western industrial expansion there were in fact many inhibitions and obstacles to the diffusion of growth impulses. But even so, conditions prevailing in the West a century or a century and a half ago were more favorable to strong and effective spread effects than are the conditions prevailing in South Asia today.

In the following sections, we shall consider the several ways in which the introduction of modern industrial enterprises could radiate impulses for cumulative expansion throughout the economic system, and we shall also examine the obstructions to the diffusion of such stimuli.

8   *The Spread Effects via Changes in Demand and Supply*

One type of impulse may, for lack of a better term, be labelled "logistical." This refers to requirements imposed directly on the economic system by the newly initiated modern industrial establishments and the opportunities opened up.

On the demand side it can be expected that two types of spread effects will — to some degree — make themselves felt as a consequence of industrialization. New plants must be constructed; machinery and other equipment must be acquired; raw materials must be obtained. Usually extensions in the infrastructure of power, transport, and communications facilities are also necessary. Acquisition of the entire range of inputs essential to the successful functioning of new industries will obviously increase the demands on the economy. To the extent that these inputs can be provided from domestic resources, other sectors of the economy will feel an impetus to expand output and employment. Not all of the logistical requirements can be supplied at home, naturally; some must be obtained abroad. Nevertheless, types of stimuli formerly absent will be felt by the domestic economy.

At the same time, the process of industrialization will create added potential for expansion in other sectors of the economy by virtue of the incomes it generates. Expenditures on industrial starts inevitably swell the local money stream, even when there is some leakage abroad. Local money incomes will be further augmented when new plants reach the production stage and make payments to workers engaged in current operations and to suppliers of raw materials and other essential inputs obtainable at home. A considerable proportion of this increase in money incomes is likely to accrue to wage earners whose expenditures are mainly for consumption goods. Unless restrictions on imports can be effectively imposed, part of this increase in consumption demand will at first probably be met by imports. If imports are curbed, heavier demands will be imposed on local producers of consumption goods.

There is nothing mystical about this transmission of spread effects through demand. In schematic form, it is the familiar multiplier process. Reduced to its essentials, it is a cumulative process of expansion triggered by domestic investment. Incomes thus generated increase consumption demand while at the same time requirements for raw materials and other essential inputs are increased. In Western countries, it has become usual to expect all sectors of the economy to be touched by this process, either directly or indirectly. Established manufacturing enterprises, whether they produce consumption goods or investment goods, receive fresh inducements to expand output, either by using existing capacity more fully or by extending their productive facilities. Agricultural producers find new requirements placed on them, both as suppliers of foodstuffs and of raw materials. Increased activity will also be stimulated in the tertiary sector as the process of expansion places additional tasks on the transport and distribution system. To meet these new demands, further increases in investment may be necessary. The process of economic uplift, once initiated, thus tends to be self-perpetuating. If sustained industrial expansion is planned for — or indeed merely expected with some confidence — additional investment may be induced. On the supply side, industrialization is conventionally regarded as having substantial spread effects through the reduction in the cost structure that occurs as industrial growth gains momentum. It is usually expected that the costs facing industrial entrepreneurs will decline over time as the infrastructure for manufacturing is extended and its operation is improved, and as new skills and discipline are diffused throughout the labor force.

This image of the spread effects expected from industrial expansion is a familiar one. But it is important to stress that it is an interpretation of the economic process worked out and adapted to conditions in Western countries. So far as the countries of South Asia are concerned, it refers to the potential secondary changes that industrial investment may generate and induce under certain hypothetical conditions, rather than to those that can actually be achieved. Even in Western countries, multiplier-accelerator types of conceptual schemes are normally hedged with qualifications about time lags, fractions, and leakages, all of which dampen the effectiveness and immediacy of spread.

The general structure of South Asian economies suggests that the inhibitions and obstacles to the effective spread of growth-inducing impulses through increased demand are much more formidable there than in the West. This is clearly apparent, in the first place, from a consideration of the relative importance of import leakages in the two environments. Both now and for a considerable time to come, South Asian countries will be obliged to obtain abroad a large proportion of their requirements for modern industrial equipment and spare parts. Apart from India no country in the region has even the rudiments of a machine tool industry capable of serving a growing local market for capital goods. The same generalization applies to semi-manufactured goods and, to some extent, to raw materials. Even when raw materials to support an industrial build-up can be supplied locally, the potential for spread may be dissipated by the diversion of materials from export to domestic markets. Genuine spread effects occur only when new demands are met by net increases in home production.

But the broader social situation in South Asia is an even more basic obstacle to spread because of demand changes. Even if the economic stimuli resulting from industrial starts could be retained within the domestic economy — which, realistically, is not completely and sometimes not even largely possible — the spread effects would still be likely to be weak. This situation is a by-product of the low level of development in the region and the fact that "elasticity of supply" is, as a result, "low." Stimuli for expansion are soon checked by bottlenecks that reduce the potential spread effects at an early stage. The more important of the barriers to effective and sustained spread can be easily catalogued: deficiencies in the supply of technical and administrative personnel, inadequacies in the supply and mobility of skilled labor, bottlenecks in the availability of raw materials and semi-manufactured goods, and deficiencies in the transport and power systems. Through intelligent planning, these problems can eventually be solved. Certainly the existence of a robust demand encourages efforts to overcome deficiencies. Meanwhile, however, the initial propulsive force toward expansion may be spent.

In addition to the factors listed above, several other features of the system reduce the spread potential of South Asian economies. In these countries, it cannot be automatically assumed — as it can be with reasonable assurance in Western countries — that economic stimuli for expansion will be accompanied by favorable behavioral responses. Societies that have for long accommodated themselves to stagnation cannot be expected to re-adapt dramatically to unfamiliar opportunities. This is notably so in agriculture where much of the initial domestic impact of industrialization should be felt. A sizeable share of the newly created wage income is likely to be spent for foodstuffs. For reasons hinted at in Chapter 22 and spelled out in Chapter 26, increased demands and higher prices for foodstuffs are not very conducive to an expanded volume of marketable produce. But even in the more highly organized modern industrial sector of the economy, where market sensitivity is most acute, the response mechanism may be inhibited by an institutional structure that has failed to encourage dynamic entrepreneurial zeal. Furthermore, entrepreneurs spirited enough to want to expand are often unable to do so because of difficulty in acquiring needed supplies. This is the fundamental reason why the Keynesian model does not apply to these economies.[1] Although they have a huge supply of underutilized labor, their essential economic properties are, in a special sense, analogous to those of full employment economies in the West. In both cases, the economic system as a whole has no slack from which increases in output can quickly be made available to match increments in demand. In order to minimize a possible source of confusion between two situations that, though vastly different in other respects, possess this element of similarity, it may be preferable to describe the South Asian economies as "quasi-full employment" economies.[2] Unlike the full employment situation in Western countries, the "quasi-full employment" situation in South Asian economies and the limitations on rapid economic expansion it implies cannot be usefully depicted in aggregative terms. The bottlenecks are all specific, while there is "oversupply" or "underutilization" in other respects; the situation cannot be represented realistically in a simple equation or index. Specific policies of intervention must be applied to each bottleneck in order to create additional supplies. The simple expedient of increasing aggregate demand is ineffective.[3]

One of the important attributes of underdeveloped economies — and one of the explanations for their state of underdevelopment — is the fail-

[1] Appendix 2, Section 23.

[2] For a discussion of this concept in a different context, see William J. Barber, *The Economy of British Central Africa*, Oxford University Press, London, 1961.

[3] Appendix 2, Section 23.

ure of supply to adjust to demand through the "normal" functioning of a market system. This weakness has been recognized by the proponents of "balanced growth" as an approach to planning.[1] The need for specific policies to foster spread effects from increases in demand applies in all segments of the economy. Nor are the issues involved in specificity limited to the problems involved in creating a needed supply. Specificity often leads to quite different difficulties when new enterprises are started. Nascent manufacturing enterprises face the risk of early death for lack of a sufficient market. Supply does not create its own demand, either in an aggregative sense or in the sense of assuring individual producers of market outlets for their products just as demand creates its supply. This important truth has also been emphasized in the recent literature on "balanced growth."[2] When newly initiated lines of manufacturing fill a market space formerly occupied by imported commodities and are given protection when doing so, this problem need not be serious. Nevertheless, a warning should be added that home-produced goods are not always perfect substitutes for imported goods.

The foregoing observations deserve restatement because economists are all too frequently disposed to over-simplify matters by thinking in terms of relationships between aggregate supply and aggregate demand. This thinking is reflected in the way officials have responded to the situation confronting them in the first stages of industrial expansion. For reasons already indicated, the ubiquity of bottlenecks gives rise to inflationary price increases, particularly for foodstuffs and for other staple consumption goods, soon after the first injections of additional incomes. When this has occurred, South Asian governments — and particularly the Indian government — have used direct and indirect controls to block the initiation of some enterprises, and thus checked forms of secondary expansion that might otherwise have taken place. This amounts to an unintentional killing off of spread effects. Underlying these measures of restraint is the concept of a "ceiling" — the height of which is rather rigidly determined — that limits the volume of aggregate demand the economy is thought capable of tolerating.[3]

One form in which limitations on spread are observable is in underutilization of industrial capacity. Precise judgments about its magnitude are difficult if not impossible to make. Measurements of "excess capacity" are far from unambiguous, even in the most advanced economies. Businessmen often plan deliberately to carry a certain amount of idle machinery as a strategic reserve, to be drawn into use in the event of mechanical break-

---

[1] Appendix 2, Section 24.

[2] Indeed, even the most extreme advocates of Say's law have never maintained that supply created its own demand in individual markets.

[3] In Appendix 2, Section 23, we discuss the limitations of this approach.

downs or temporary increases in the demand for their product. Moreover, ambiguities arise from the absence of homogeneity in interpretations of normal capacity in various sectors of the economy.[1] Nevertheless, in parts of the modern industrial sector idle capacity far exceeds anything that could be considered normal, and this fact has given rise to concern.[2]

No simple explanation of this phenomenon is possible. In most cases, underutilization of capacity is the result of specific bottlenecks. In some instances, crucial inputs have been cut off by shortages of foreign exchange. In others, strains on the transport system or on port facilities have held production below its potential.[3] At times, shortages of skilled personnel and occasionally industrial disputes have led to inadequate utilization. In addition, the troubles that accompany the launching of any large enterprise have meant that new additions to plant and equipment have not been fully

---

[1] In India, for example, the calculation of "normal shift" scheduling used by the Central Statistical Office in 1959 assumed three shifts and a 300-day year in 5 industries; continuous operation throughout the year in 4 industries; two shifts and a 300-day year in 3 industries; and one shift and a 300-day year in all others. See Jagdish Bhagwati, *Notes on Excess Capacity in the Indian Economy*, Planning Unit, Indian Statistical Institute, New Delhi, 25 November, 1959, roneod, p. 8.

The economies to be realized by shift work are occasionally noted: ". . . even if there is no increase in capital equipment labour by simply working longer or harder might produce a bigger output. This need not mean a longer working day. Aggregate man-hours may be increased by adopting multiple shifts. In an economy which is capital-short and labour-abundant, this should be particularly important, since it will not only increase aggregate output (plant depreciation would not rise proportionately) but also expand employment. Even if all costs rose proportionately, there would be a net gain to the economy in the form of greater output per unit of time." (Ceylon, *The Ten Year Plan*, p. 161.)

[2] See, for example, the memorandum prepared by India, Government of, Central Statistical Organisation of the Planning Commission, *Utilisation of Installed Capacity in Selected Industries of India, 1957–1961*, New Delhi, July, 1962, roneod. This study indicated that a high proportion of Indian industries operated with "substantial unutilised capacity" (defined as a rate of utilization below 65 percent) during the period in question. Satisfactory interpretation of this finding is hampered, however, by the statistical and conceptual ambiguities noted above.

"Over-investment in industry or neglect of agricultural development has actually caused such strain (especially through the shortage of foreign exchange), that in several countries of the region the existence of a sizeable idle capacity has become rather serious. In the Philippines, it is estimated that the average level of operation of existing industrial plants is only about 50 percent of rated capacity. It was estimated in the current plan that raising the operating capacity from 52 percent in 1957 to 70 percent in 1960/61 would raise foreign exchange requirements for imports of raw materials from 55 to 73 percent of merchandise imports in the corresponding years. Again, in Pakistan, at the end of the fourth year of the first Five-Year Plan period, the rate of capacity utilization for some consumer goods industries, engineering and electric industries, making up about 25 percent of the value added in large-scale industries, was on the average 50 percent. Idle industrial capacity in India . . . also appears to be substantial." (United Nations, ECAFE, *Economic Bulletin for Asia and the Far East*, Vol. XII, No. 3, December, 1961, p. 12.)

[3] The high degree of underutilization reported in West Pakistan's synthetic fertilizer factories, for example, was alleged to be the result of congestion in the East Pakistan port of Chittagong, which had impeded the distribution of the finished product.

used in the initial stages of operation. Deficiencies in effective demand
have been held partially responsible for unutilized capacity in several important industries.[1]

Complications of this sort underscore the basic point stressed earlier,
that the low elasticity characteristics of these economies threaten to stifle
the potential spread effects of industrialization at an early stage. Effective
planning can reduce many of these impediments. But planning of a purely
aggregative type cannot be expected to accomplish the desired results.
Policy intervention must be directed to specific bottlenecks in individual
sectors of the economy.[2]

In view of these difficulties, it is not surprising that most South Asian
governments have been reluctant to forecast the secondary impact industrial starts will have on demand for labor. Some projections have been
published, though they are of necessity largely conjectural. The conceptual
problems involved in such estimates are formidable. *Ex ante* assessments
of the strength of potential spread effects are speculative; *ex post* it is
impossible to isolate the changes in the demand for labor induced by
industrial starts from those resulting from other policy measures and non-
planned changes.

These perplexities can be observed in the calculations prepared by several governments on the expected changes in the demand for labor in
building and construction, a sector highly sensitive to the first phases of
logistical spread from industrial starts. The second Indian plan, for example, estimated that construction would provide work for roughly 21 percent
of the anticipated natural increment in the labor force during the planning
period.[3] Only about one-fifth of the growth in demand for labor in these
trades was related to industrial building, even when the industrial sector
was construed broadly.[4] The bulk of the demand for construction workers
was expected to arise from fulfillment of other plan objectives, particularly
in the development of social overheads. In the third Indian plan, construction was estimated to contribute only about 16 percent of the new jobs
foreseen during the planning period.[5]

In the abortive Ceylon plan, construction was thought to be capable of

[1] This factor was said to explain the disappointing performance of several sectors in
the course of the first Indian plan: "In one group of industries, shortfalls in production
were on account of lack of adequate domestic demand. These include some of the
light engineering industries such as diesel engines and pumps, radios, batteries, electric
lamps and hurricane lanterns. In some industries, production remained below target
levels on account of reduced export demand (jute manufactures) or low demand for
indigenous industries which cater for exports (plywood for tea chests)." (India, *Second
Five Year Plan*, p. 390.)

[2] Appendix 2, Section 22.

[3] India, *Second Five Year Plan*, p. 115.

[4] The planners' calculations on demand for labor in construction show industries and
minerals (including cottage and small-scale industries) as one category. (*Ibid.*)

[5] India, *Third Five Year Plan, A Draft Outline*, p. 159.

absorbing about 16 percent of the expected expansion in the population of working age during the course of the ten-year planning period.[1] The planners did not report how much of this added employment would be attributable to industrial starts rather than to the general demands placed on this sector by other parts of the development program and by the population increase. Nor was a classification along these lines attempted by planners in Malaya. The second Malayan plan, however, expected construction to expand its work force more rapidly than any other sector of the economy and to provide nearly 18 percent of the projected increment in jobs during the years 1961–65.[2]

Calculation of the possible spread effects of industrialization on the demand for labor in other sectors of the economy is even more hazardous. In the service trades, where a high degree of underutilization of labor is chronic, the problems are especially intricate. Such secondary effects on the demand for labor as may occur could be met by extending the work period of those already engaged and improving their efficiency; they would not necessitate any increase in the number of workers employed. If the number of workers in the service trades increases, this is more likely to be the result of pressures from underemployed persons, particularly migrants from the rural areas, than of impulses stemming from industrialization.

This point appears to have been slighted in the preparations of projections presented in India's Second and Third Plans. These documents divided the expected growth in employment opportunities into two categories: expansion resulting directly from the implementation of plan objectives and expansion from other sources (labelled "others including trade and commerce"). In the Second Plan, growth in employment in the latter category was expected to amount to 52 percent of that achieved in the former, while in the Third Plan the figure was raised to 56 percent.[3] This procedure was based on the assumption that the occupational pattern shown in the 1951 census would be perpetuated. Specifically, it was assumed that the ratio of employment in non-governmental services to other forms of employment outside agriculture would remain approximately constant.[4] These calculations are dubious, not only because of imperfections in statistical coverage in the base period but, more important, because of the implicit premise that employment ratios in the various sec-

[1] Ceylon, *The Ten Year Plan*, p. 90.

[2] Malaya, *Second Five Year Plan*, pp. 20–22.

[3] India, *Second Five Year Plan*, p. 115; and India, *Third Five Year Plan, A Draft Outline*, p. 159.

[4] The rationale offered for this procedure deserves to be cited in detail. The second Indian plan explained it as follows:

"Employment estimates for 'others including trade, commerce and other services' is much less firm. This has been based on the occupational pattern revealed in the 1951 census. The group 'others' comprises commerce, transport (other than railways), stor-

tors would be basically stable. Increases in investment and in output will indeed place new burdens on the economy's transport and distribution networks. But it cannot be presupposed that employment in these lines will have to expand just because demand is growing. The distributive trades particularly have long been a sponge for underutilized labor in all the South Asian countries, and they could easily increase their output by working their existing labor force longer and harder.

Even so, the planners' assumption of roughly constant proportions in occupational distribution may not prove to have been entirely inaccurate. In the absence of major reforms that succeed in raising the utilization of the rapidly growing labor force in agriculture, the migration from rural districts to cities continues, with a substantial proportion of the new arrivals in urban areas drifting into the distributive trades and other services where conditions of relatively free entry prevail. Even if this should occur, it would not justify the planners' approach to measuring the indirect effects of industrial expansion on employment opportunities. As we emphasized at some length in Chapter 21, a basic weakness of such aggregative calculations is their failure to distinguish carefully between changes in the number of work participants and changes in the utilization of labor.[1]

---

age, warehousing and miscellaneous services not elsewhere specified and general labourers. According to the 1951 Census, these groups provide employment for 12,876 millions of the working force. The total of these groups when compared to persons occupied in activities except cultivation consisting of primary occupations, mining and quarrying, industry, railway transport, construction and utilities, health, education, public administration and communications, which account for 22,447 millions, gives a ratio of 0.52. It is assumed that the same ratio would prevail in 1961. The omission of purely agricultural occupations in working out the employment ratio is justified on the assumption that in the Second Five Year Plan it is intended that additional employment should be largely in the non-agricultural sector. With the increase in production in the agricultural sector, persons already in the category 'others including trade and commerce' will find fuller employment by handling greater volume of work from their existing clients. The ratio 0.52 is likely to be considered as conservative." (India, *Second Five Year Plan*, pp. 117–118.)

The third Indian plan introduced the usual *caveats*, but produced an even higher estimate of secondary employment effects. It noted that much of the secondary impact would be felt by the self-employed and stated that "self-employment accounts for the occupation of a major portion of the working force. Considerable uncertainty would, therefore, attach to such estimates because in the self-employed sector the distribution of additional work as between those who are at present engaged in it and consider themselves to be under-employed and others who seek new entry is difficult to make with our present knowledge of the mechanism of employment generation in these fields. However, from such studies as have been undertaken, it appears that at present additional employment of this type might be of the order of 56 percent of the increase in employment. . . . This estimate is based on the analysis of the 1951 Census data. When the result of the latest census becomes available, it will be possible to arrive at a closer approximation of such employment effects." (India, *Third Five Year Plan, A Draft Outline*, p. 758.)

[1] Malaya's Second Plan (for 1961–65) observed in this connection: "The value of commercial and personal services can be expected to rise at least in correspondence

The major flaw in all these calculations is, as we have shown in Chapter 23 (Section 14),[1] the implicit assumption that the influx of population to the urban areas is a response to an increased demand for labor, which, in turn, is assumed to emanate from industrialization. These assumptions are not valid. The urban labor force is swelling and many of its members are finding "employment" in occupations characterized by a low level of labor utilization and productivity, but this has other explanations; it would probably happen without any industrialization at all. In any case, the "impact" of industrialization is minor. Or, to put it in another way, it would be possible to sustain a degree of industrialization greater than any now occurring in South Asia simply by using the present urban labor force more efficiently; no new workers from rural areas would be needed. Urbanization in all probability will continue, but this urbanization will not be to any large extent the result of industrialization.

In view of the calculations quoted and the general assumption that the increased demands for consumption goods and services generated by industrialization will create new employment, it is somewhat surprising that the planners intend that new consumer demand be supplied out of existing capacity. India's decision to concentrate new industrial starts on heavy industry and simultaneously to encourage an expansion in the output of cottage enterprises and crafts was based in part on the assumption that this would be done.[2]

There has been some increase in the output of hand-made goods, but this increase probably owes more to direct policy intervention than to spontaneous adaptations by traditional producers to any industrialization spurts.[3] More important, the rise in the flow of money incomes may be

---

with the general growth of the economy. On the other hand, employment in these service activities may rise more slowly in view of existing underemployment in many kinds of commercial and personal service." (Malaya, *Second Five Year Plan*, p. 21.)

[1] See also Chapter 10, Section 11, and Chapter 11, Section 4.

[2] See Chapter 25, Sections 3 and 5.

India's First Plan, for example, asserted that "an increase in the supply of consumer goods has, under present conditions, to come mainly from fuller utilisation of existing capacity." (India, *First Five Year Plan*, p. 427.)

The Second Plan was more explicit in expressing the hope that cottage and small-scale enterprises would fill part of the expected gap in the demand for manufactured consumer goods. Thus, for example: "Investment in basic industries creates demands for consumer goods, but it does not enlarge the supply of consumer goods in the short run; nor does it directly absorb any large quantities of labour. A balanced pattern of industrialisation, therefore, requires a well-organized effort to utilise labour for increasing the supplies of much needed consumer goods in a manner which economises the use of capital." (India, *Second Five Year Plan*, p. 25.)

And again: "If cottage and small industries have not fared well so far, one reason is the stagnancy of the economy and the consequent lack of demand. The increase in investment activity which development planning involves will increase existing demands and create new ones." (*Ibid.*, p. 32.)

[3] See Chapter 25, Section 7.

expected to increase demand for marketable foodstuffs. The intricacies of the agricultural situation are such, however, that there is little basis for the view that demand stimuli will suffice to call forth larger production and heavier deliveries of foodstuffs.[1]

9 Spread Effects and "External Economies" in a Wider Sense

The external economies expected from industrialization are often visualized only in the narrow sense touched upon in the preceding section — they are identified with the reductions in the cost structure that occur because of fuller utilization of facilities with heavy overheads and improvements in the efficiency and training of the labor force. There is also a wider sense in which consideration of external economies is relevant. The ideas involved in this broader concept are often stated quite unsystematically. Despite their great vagueness, they are an important element in the vision of industrialization as a source of expansionary momentum for the economic system. Industrialization is expected to instill a new spirit of rationalism, enterprise, discipline, punctuality, mobility, and efficiency. People will be stirred to become mechanically minded and master unfamiliar skills, not merely within new industrial enterprises but elsewhere in the economy as well. More competitive and more perfect markets will be called forth and superior commercial and financial institutions developed. All in all, the organization of work and people's attitudes toward it will be altered in ways that raise the efficiency of work performance throughout the economy. Bottlenecks will be more easily eliminated and the potential for diffusion of spread effects of the logistic type will be extended. All these happy results are expected to follow as a direct consequence of industrial expansion. Similar qualitative changes in the outlook, attitudes, and skills of the population are not regarded as obtainable from other forms of economic expansion, say from the development of agriculture along capitalist lines.

Whether external economies such as these can be quickly and effectively realized in South Asia is uncertain, however. In the first place, the prevailing institutional structure and the popular attitudes associated with it, which we analyzed in the two preceding chapters, inhibit changes conducive to substantial effects of this type. *The extent to which spread effects along these lines can be transmitted is, in fact, a function of the cultural, social, and economic levels already attained.* Poor countries with a long history of economic stagnation and fairly static social conditions thus face formidable obstacles when they attempt to achieve a

---

[1] Chapter 26, Section 4 *et passim.*

higher level of development. Potential spread effects of all types are easily smothered.

This lesson has been forcefully demonstrated in the limited experience of South Asian countries with rationalized and highly organized modern industries. The small islands within which Western forms of economic organization have been imitated have not made much lasting impression on the sea of tradition surrounding them.[1] In colonial times, plantations, mines, and the limited number of power-using manufacturing enterprises were not notable for their transmission of stimuli for adaptation to other segments of the economy. They remained enclaves surrounded by stagnation.[2] Often much of the labor force engaged in the modern sector was segregated and isolated, either physically or culturally, from persons living nearby. *There is an obvious danger that industrial starts now planned will perpetuate this colonial pattern.* "The effects of large investments in industry, both at existing centres and at new centres, have been largely limited to these centres. So far 'the spread effects' of these investments have been comparatively small," complains Tarlok Singh,[3] who has been the coordinating force in the Indian Planning Commission since its inception. Every open-eyed visitor to South Asia must notice that primitive modes of living and traditional patterns of work prevail within a few miles of cities where there are modern industrial establishments, as well as in the huge slums in those cities themselves.[4]

Nor indeed have modern industries always succeeded in producing permanent changes in attitudes toward work or in the standards of skills of laborers they have directly engaged. Typically, little provision has been made for training, and the bulk of the labor force has remained with few skills. Moreover, among those who have returned to their native villages after a period in wage employment, the effects of contact with more intri-

[1] The following account has been offered of a district in India that has enjoyed a substantial development of heavy industry: "No industrial 'ladder' seems to have been developed over the last few decades which could bring step by step the steel, fertilizers and pesticides produced in the area to the small farmer even 20 miles away in such forms and for such uses as could induce and enable him to modernize his farming techniques. The industrial development is, as it were, an island — nowhere integrated as part of area development with the agricultural sector. The experience of Chota Nagpur would seem to indicate that there is no automatic relationship between heavy industry and modernization of agriculture at least until certain complementary developments have taken place." (S. R. Sen, "The Strategy for Agricultural Development," Presidential Address to All India Agricultural Economic Conference, New Delhi, 1959, p. 9.)

[2] Chapter 10, Section 8.

[3] Tarlok Singh, *Economic Growth and Disparities in Levels of Development*, Brij Narain Memorial Lectures, February 7–8, 1964, roneod, p. 6.

[4] Indeed, there are reasons to believe that small-scale industry, if it were modernized, might give rise to more spread effects of this type; see Chapter 5, Section 8.

cately organized forms of economic activity and more regular work discipline have been short-lived.

It might be argued that the record of modern industry in instilling a better attitude toward work performance can and will be substantially improved upon as the alien orientation of these enterprises diminishes. To some extent this may be so. In recent years, the upper limit on posts to which local peoples might aspire has been raised. The proportion of Europeans in higher positions has been reduced and — particularly in Burma and Indonesia, and, to a lesser extent, the other Southeast Asian countries and Ceylon — the dominance of Asian aliens in skilled and semi-skilled positions in the modern sector has diminished. Greater opportunities to acquire skills have thus been opened to members of the indigenous population. But it would be naive to expect these changes to affect the masses. The fact that industrialization will for decades ahead have very weak direct employment-creating effects but will have backwash effects with negative consequences for incomes and income distribution and levels of living in traditional industry gives particular force to this conclusion.

In attempts to evaluate the pace and extent of this type of spread effect in South Asia, comparisons with Western experience in the early stage of industrialization are not very relevant. With the partial exception of England, all of the now highly developed Western countries possessed the great asset of nearly universal literacy before their industrialization drives were launched. In some cases, this level of educational attainment had been reached decades or even generations earlier. The significance of this inheritance for the adaptability of an industrial labor force and for its assimilation of training and discipline was profound. South Asian countries lack this advantage, though some are better off in this respect than others.[1] In addition, the social structure was far less rigidly stratified in the preindustrial West than it is in contemporary South Asia and in India particularly; the environment was thus more propitious for the generation and absorption of spread effects.[2]

In the Soviet Union, mass education had hardly begun when the major push toward industrialization was undertaken. Indeed, tzarist Russia was in some respects almost as backward as the South Asian countries. However, the social revolution and the totalitarian regime created by it set about to change popular attitudes and institutions by force. Particularly intensive energies were directed into improvements in education and health. Ironically, the Soviet practice did not conform to Marx's theory; the government did not rely on changes in the "modes of production" to alter institutions and attitudes, but intervened directly to reshape them.[3]

---

[1] Chapter 32, Section 3; Chapter 33, Sections 2, 3, and 7.

[2] There are other differences in initial conditions as well; see Chapter 14.

[3] See Appendix 2, Sections 19–20.

These considerations point once again to the conclusion that the conditions for effective spread effects from industrial starts are far from ideal in South Asia and in fact less satisfactory than they were in the West at the time of its industrial emergence. When thought through, the industrialization ideology fails to lend convincing support to the belief that institutional and attitudinal changes of types healthy for economic advancement will be produced *because of* industrialization. The appropriate inference is rather that specific policies in all fields — even far outside the industrial sector proper — must be pursued if spread effects are to be both forceful and sustained. This point is often stressed by D. R. Gadgil, who sees it in an even broader perspective than that of the industrialization issue:

In highly developed and integrated economies it can be taken for granted that forces of development generated in one place will soon have a decisive impact on other areas and activities. This is especially evident in the rural sectors even of some advanced industrial countries. The experience of the last decade in India has shown that there is very little of automatic transmission or spill-over of effects of development started in particular locations and activities.[1]

10 *Industrialization and the Components of Labor Utilization*

The analysis we have provided of the effects of industrialization on labor utilization has been directed to the broad effects of industrial growth on demand for labor and thus on participation ratios particularly. This is the component of labor utilization to which planners, following modern Western patterns of thought, have given their attention including that of a statistical nature. The estimates produced by the planners, as we have noted,[2] are crude, and the procedures used in reaching them are subject to considerable conceptual criticism. Nevertheless, an important conclusion about the employment-creating potential of industrial expansion can be sustained by the statistical calculations of governments — namely, that industrial expansion, when beginning from a low base, cannot directly have more than a peripheral uplifting effect on participation ratios during a very considerable early period.

Nor would this conclusion, which we reached on grounds of general reasoning, require serious qualification if production methods in the modern industrial sector were much more labor-intensive than those chosen to date. Labor-intensive methods, within the limits of feasibility set by presently available technologies for the production of modern lines of industrial output, could not aspire to raise demand for labor in the modern in-

---

[1] D. R. Gadgil, "Approach to Indian Planning," *The Economic Weekly*, Special Number, July, 1961, p. 1129.

[2] Section 6.

dustrial sector enough to absorb more than a minor fraction of the natural increment in the population of working age.

Calculations of the impact of industrial expansion on participation ratios should not, of course, be restricted to the volume of jobs created in new industrial enterprises but should embrace the indirect effects of this expansion as well. It will be recalled from the earlier discussion that the secondary impact of modern industrial starts on demand for labor cannot be unambiguously identified in official estimates. These secondary effects work in two directions: on the one hand, the backwash on traditional forms of manufacturing, and also on rationalized newer ones, is likely to mean reduction in participation ratios; on the other, spread effects may tend to raise participation ratios. We have set out our reasons for believing that, in general, spread effects are likely to be considerably weaker than they are often alleged to be.[1] Some diffusion effects tending to raise participation ratios will still occur in activities directly supporting industrial expansion — for example, in construction of new plants and in extension of the infrastructure of power and transport facilities — especially when they are deliberately planned with this end in view.

The changes in occupational distribution registered in the new censuses generally confirm our conclusions.[2] Tarlok Singh has summarized the findings with regard to the Indian labor force during the fifties, a time when planning was better organized in India than in any other country of the region, and was increasingly directed toward industrialization:

According to the final population totals for the 1961 Census, during the decade 1951–61, as against an increase of 34 percent in the total number of workers and of 35 percent among non-agricultural workers, the addition in agriculture was of the order of 33 percent. In terms of absolute figures, this has meant an increase in the number of agricultural workers from about 98 million to about 131 million, the proportion of agricultural workers to the total working force remaining at about 70 percent.[3]

The changes actually recorded thus stand in glaring contradiction to the goals expressed.[4]

Analysis of the possible impact of industrialization on labor utilization should not, however, be confined to consideration of participation ratios. Generally speaking, South Asian planners, like practically all Western and Communist economists, have not given sufficient attention to the

[1] Sections 8 and 9.

[2] The weaknesses of these statistics were commented on in Chapter 11, Sections 3 and 4.

[3] Tarlok Singh, *Indian Journal of Agricultural Economics*, Vol. XVIII, No. 1, Bombay, January–March, 1963, p. 12. "The proportion of population dependent on agriculture . . . has declined marginally only or remained much the same in most of the developing countries." (U. N., *Economic Survey of Asia and the Far East 1965*, p. 49.)

[4] Section 1.

relationship between industrialization and the duration and intensity of work, though some mention is made of the possibility that stimuli radiating from industrial starts will induce the indigenous sector of the economy, both in agriculture and in traditional manufacturing, to take up part of the slack. Such spread effects have not occurred to any appreciable extent. Within the modern sector itself, on the other hand, industrial expansion may have favorable effects on the duration and intensity of work for quite different reasons. At least the modern industrial sector can apply some forms of institutional discipline, largely lacking elsewhere, over punctuality and periods of work attendance. Small, informally run enterprises relying heavily on family labor have a built-in bias against the exercise of strict work discipline. Even when working hours are long, the intensity of work is low. These points are substantiated in Chapter 23 (Sections 3 and 9). On balance, it would be reasonable to expect some net gains in standardization of the duration and intensity of work to follow an enlargement of work opportunities in the formally structured segment of manufacturing industry. But even within the modern manufacturing sector, it would be a mistake to expect standards of duration and intensity generally to match those typical in the West. Besides, even rapid industrialization will create only a relatively small number of work opportunities.

Deeply ingrained rituals leave their stamp on work arrangements even when these are organized on modern lines. For instance, the many traditional holidays will continue to be honored and the daily work schedule may be interrupted in deference to religious observances. As the majority of factories cannot be air conditioned, climatic disadvantages will cause frequent interruptions in work and a lower intensity of work.[1] Inferior nutritional, housing, and health standards will have the same effect. It is therefore only realistic to expect that in general the intensity of work performance will fall short of the standards achieved in the West with identical or similar facilities. Nevertheless, by comparison with conditions in less modernized forms of manufacturing in South Asia, modern industrial establishments — by virtue of the pace of work dictated by mechanized processes — do standardize and raise the intensity of the labor input. But the improvement in work intensity may not extend to all factory workers; it may be confined to that part of the industrial labor force that works directly with machines. This point is worth restating, as prevailing low wage levels and the social prestige attached to the maintenance of large staffs encourage a substantial amount of padding even in the industrial enterprises in the organized sector.

Thus far, we have considered the problem of the duration and intensity of work primarily from an institutional and organizational point of view. Broader economic forces — from which the more traditional employments

[1] Appendix 10, Section 3.

are largely immune — influence these variables in modern types of manufacturing. While most industrial work, apart from the processing of agricultural products, is not subject to seasonal variations, it is more sensitive to fluctuations in market conditions. In this respect, manufacturing employments are more vulnerable than most other types of work in South Asia. These fluctuations can produce some open unemployment of a Western type, thus shortening the work year, even though its full force will be blunted by the pressure on discharged workers to seek an alternative livelihood. But the impact of declining demand may also be felt in the form of shortened working time for those who retain industrial jobs. Similarly, when demand is buoyant, the duration of work in the organized manufacturing sector of the economy may be extended by overtime work. It is not our purpose to attempt to forecast the occurrence or the magnitude of these cyclical changes. For present purposes, we wish merely to observe that the creation and extension of large-scale industrial undertakings introduces another dimension into the discussion of the duration of work — a dimension familiar from Western economic experience but largely absent from the traditional South Asian pattern.[1]

11   Conclusions

We are now in a position to discuss the broad conclusions arising from this discussion of industrialization in South Asia. These conclusions stretch beyond the industrial sector proper and concern the economy as a whole — indeed, the entire program of modernization.

Beginning with the ideology that views industrialization as the cure for the underutilization of labor in South Asia, we first reached the conclusion that all these countries — and particularly those with a high man/land ratio, which are also the largest and most populous — urgently need to build up manufacturing industry as fast as they can. Given the rapid and accelerating increase in the labor force in these countries, there is no prospect that incomes and levels of living can be substantially improved, or even that deterioration in standards thus far achieved can be prevented in the longer run, unless a much larger proportion of the labor force can be effectively utilized outside agriculture and especially in modern industry.

But because of the low level of industrialization from which these countries begin and the rapid population increase, modern industry, even if it grows at an extremely rapid rate, cannot absorb more than a small

---

[1] This conclusion must of course be qualified in the case of the plantation form of "industrialization." Most of these large estates suffered severe buffeting during the depression of the 1930's. Their response to this reduction in demand, however, sometimes took the form of dismissal of employees rather than shortening of the working day. See Chapter 23, Section 5.

fraction of the natural increment in the labor force for decades ahead. In the initial stages of industrialization, it may even be difficult to keep the absolute size of the labor force engaged in all types of manufacturing from falling. Only at a much later stage can modern industry begin to increase its claim on the labor force. This situation arises both because the direct expansionary impact of modern industrial growth on employment is likely to be slight in the early phases and because the risk of backwash on traditional manufacturing is substantial.

This does not mean that the South Asian countries should give up their industrialization drive. On the contrary, the fact that industrialization will have an important employment-creating effect only gradually, when it has reached a much higher level, means that these countries should industrialize as soon and as fast as they can. However, it also means that they should complement the industrialization drive with vigorous policy measures aimed at raising labor utilization and productivity in the other sectors including agriculture, which is the largest and most important of all. Otherwise there is a genuine danger that industrialization drives in South Asia will leave by far the larger part of the economy in stagnation. This would amount to a continuation of the economic pattern established in colonial times.

As we have seen, little confidence can be placed in the efficacy of favorable spread effects emanating from industrial starts. The diffusionary force of logistic spread effects is weak, but at least equally important is the high resistance of the indigenous economy to change. Generally speaking, the extent to which stimuli for change and improvement can be assimilated is a function of levels of mass education and the ability to change attitudes and the institutions in which they are rooted. South Asian countries now run the risk of creating petty islands of highly organized Western-type industries that will remain surrounded by a sea of stagnation. If this fate is to be averted, industrialization must be so directed, and so complemented by policies in other fields, as to permit simultaneous development outside the sphere of modern large-scale industry.

With respect to the direction of industrial starts, we have concluded that it is a rational course to develop an industrial sector that either produces for export or manufactures import substitutes. In general, however, the obstacles to export promotion in manufactures are so great that import substitution usually offers a more promising prospect. It follows that — particularly in the poorer and larger countries — domestic producers must turn increasingly to the production of capital goods. Malaya, Thailand, the Philippines, and Ceylon — countries in which import controls have been less rigid, though they have been tightened in Ceylon — still import consumer goods that might be manufactured locally. But as planning for development proceeds and the population increases, it is likely that even these better situated countries will be obliged to restrict the import of less essential consumer goods and at a later stage turn increasingly to the production of capital goods when they become the only imports of consequence. Focussing the industrialization drive upon exports and import substitution is, of course, rational for other reasons as well — particularly because it minimizes the backwash effects of modern industrial growth on established traditional industries.

But clearly, industrialization in this form is not enough to accomplish a significant change in the economic structure of these countries and to give real momentum to development. Indeed, if not accompanied by direct interventionist policies toward other sectors of the economy, it would merely bolster the enclave pattern of colonial economic experience. By itself, industrialization can do little to raise labor utilization in the more tradition-bound sectors of the economy, especially in rural areas. These problems must be attacked in their own right by specific policies designed to promote reform.[1] Success with these reforms requires, in turn, a major push in the direction of health and educational improvement.[2] Such measures are necessary not only to compensate the rest of the economy for the absence of sizeable automatic spread effects from industrial starts but also to support the industrialization drive itself. In particular, the modern industrial sector cannot thrive unless increasing quantities of consumption goods — particularly foodstuffs — can be produced and made available for sale.

The magnitude and pervasiveness of these problems naturally raises questions of priorities. Too often the selection of priorities is discussed solely in terms of the competition of different sectors of the economy for the same resources. As we have argued at some length in other contexts, this way of viewing the problem — which is linked to the tendency of the modern approach to regard such aggregates as savings and investment as significant and unambiguously quantifiable — is misleading. The influence of this reasoning is reflected in the plans when investments in industrial plants and in overhead capital for industry and expenditures for agriculture, education, health, and community development are added together and juxtaposed as "investments" or "development expenditures" against available financial resources.[3] The picture that emerges is a false one. For instance, it conveys an erroneous impression that internal savings and funds supplied from abroad are substitutable for one another. This is far from being the case. Reductions in consumption at home, for example, cannot create foreign exchange — particularly in countries like India and Pakistan, where few consumption goods are imported, other than those essential to survival.

[1] Chapters 25 and 26.
[2] Chapters 30–33.
[3] Appendix 4.

The modern approach also lends itself to another misconception, namely, an implicit view that the specific subjects requiring attention if development is to be fostered compete for the same resources. Many policy measures — especially those pertaining to rural areas — require firm direction and the implementation of institutional reforms and enthusiastic efforts in health and education, but need only limited amounts of funds and these can often be mobilized within the rural areas themselves without imposing any burden on the modern industrial sector. When the significance of these factors is appreciated, it becomes clear that considerable unexploited scope remains for pushing industrial drives — and the policy measures outside the industrial field necessary to support them effectively — without jeopardizing development in other sectors of the economy. In short, one of the most serious shortcomings of policy in the countries in which comprehensive planning has been undertaken is the failure to plan more ambitiously and on a larger scale, and to supplement the industrialization drive with equally determined efforts in other fields. Undoubtedly, the industrialization drive, which meets very little resistance from vested interests, has often served as an excuse for not pushing harder for reforms in other fields. What these countries need is a program that will induce changes simultaneously in a great number of the conditions that hold down their growth; fundamentally, the task of the planners is to coordinate all of these changes in such a way as to spur development. It is easy to lose sight of this when goals and targets are assigned "priorities."[1]

[1] Appendix 2, Section 19.

See the complete work for Chapters 25-27.

Chapter 28

POPULATION POLICY

From our discussion in the preceding chapter it is clear that the rate of population growth in the South Asian countries is now largely independent of their rate of economic development. It could affect the speed and extent of decline in mortality rates, since it determines the level of living and may influence the amount of public expenditure devoted to improving health conditions. But fertility, if left to spontaneous forces, will remain at traditionally high levels, or may even increase slightly, whether or not there is economic development. As there is no prospect of significant migration out of South Asia or between the countries, their populations will tend to grow at an accelerating pace. The reverse line of causation — *from* population growth *to* economic development — is strong, however. Generally speaking, the rapid and accelerating population increase in South Asia is retarding economic advance and holds the threat of economic stagnation if not deterioration — sooner or later, depending on the conditions in each country. As emigration is not a feasible policy, and as no government can but choose to decrease mortality (Section 9), the practical problem facing the governments in South Asia is whether they should attempt to induce a fall in the fertility rate that will not come spontaneously.

In the first part of this chapter we shall lay the basis for the discussion of such a population policy by examining the economic effects of different rates of fertility. Part II will then trace the ideological background of such a policy. In Part III the rationale of population policy in the South Asian countries and in economically advanced countries today will be compared. Inhibitions and obstacles standing in the way of a policy of the

kind the South Asian countries must choose will be the subject of the
fourth and last part of the chapter.

I

Economic Consequences of Population Trends

1 *Two Types of Effects*

Basic to our analysis of the economic consequences of population trends
is the fact, demonstrated by Coale and Hoover, that a decline in fertility
rates would have no substantial influence on the size of the labor force in
underdeveloped countries, for as long as twenty or even thirty years. For
fifteen years ahead this is self-evident; but even for some fifteen years beyond that, Coale and Hoover's calculations indicate the effect to be gradual and slow.[1] Thus the impact of a decline in fertility on the number of
producers is delayed for almost a generation. Its impact on the number of
consumers, however, is immediate: the relative number *outside* the labor
force begins to fall as soon as the fertility rate declines.

An analysis of the influence of population trends on economic development must therefore distinguish between two types of effects, one arising
from *changes in the size of the labor force* and the other from *changes in
the age distribution.* The two sets of effects will be discussed separately
in the next two sections. Since, however, the economy responds to changes
in both the size of the dependent population and the size of the labor
force, we must combine the two types of comparison, and this we shall do
in Section 4. We shall first limit our perspective to a period of twenty or
thirty years; some observations on the course of population and economic
development in the longer run will be made in Section 4. Our analysis will
concentrate on fertility because, by contrast, a further decline in mortality rates in South Asia — even one somewhat more concentrated on the

---

[1] Ansley J. Coale and Edgar M. Hoover, *Population Growth and Economic Development in Low-Income Countries,* Princeton University Press, Princeton, 1958. Coale
and Hoover estimated in this study (p. 232) that a decline of 50 percent in fertility in
India between 1956 and 1986 would reduce the number in the 15–64 age group at the
end of the period by only about 8 percent below what it would be under conditions of
constant fertility throughout the thirty years.

Age limits for the labor force cannot be rigidly demarcated. The custom of defining the range as 15 to 60 or 65 years is not altogether realistic. In the Western countries more and more young people attend school beyond 15 years of age, thus remaining outside the labor force, and many people over 60 or 65 are productively employed.
In South Asia as well the limits are, for different reasons, far from clear-cut. As we
have observed elsewhere (Appendix 16 and Chapters 22 and 23), many of the very
young and very old work, particularly in agriculture, at least during certain periods of
the year, while many in the normal working ages are idle or work very little.

early years of life — would have only insignificant and temporary effects on the age structure of the population.[1]

Economic development will, of course, be influenced by many factors other than the population trends. The South Asian countries will continue, with varying effort and success, to strive for development. There will be more or less radical changes in their social and political organization. Entrepreneurial and other initiatives will be taken, inventions and discoveries made, and existing knowledge and techniques put to greater use, for the better utilization of each nation's resources. Many factors outside the countries themselves will also help to determine the economic space within which their populations will grow, most notably the future markets for their export products, the terms of trade, and the amounts of grants and credits that will be made available to them. A precise relationship of population trends to a future reality in all these and other respects cannot be established; assumptions would have to be made about conditions in the future that simply cannot be known. Our analysis therefore cannot yield a forecast of alternative economic development patterns under different assumptions in regard to future fertility rates; it will have to be limited to the kinds of economic repercussions that can be expected to follow from broad changes in population size and age composition.

This first part of the chapter can be brief. The facts of life in the South Asian countries that determine the effects of a growing labor force on their economies have been dealt with in Part Five of the book and need not be summarized; those that determine the effects of a decreased dependency burden are more speculative in the absence of intensive empirical studies. Conclusions from such non-specific premises can only be very general and uncertain unless they are to represent what we have referred to as illusory precision. In Appendix 7 a criticism is made of some other approaches to the problem of the economic effects of population trends.

2   *Change in the Age Structure*

As a result of the very high fertility rates experienced in the relevant past period, the age distribution of the populations of the South Asian countries is skewed in the direction of a high dependency burden.[2] The proportion of children in these populations is large. Reduction of fertility rates would have the direct effect of decreasing the dependency burden. There would immediately be fewer children to support, and if the lower fertility were maintained, this decrease in the dependency burden would continue until the children began to reach working age. The decrease in

---

[1] Chapter 27, Section 5.
[2] Chapter 27, Section 4.

the proportion of children would be progressive if the decline in fertility rates were gradually intensified. A couple of decades hence, when the depleted age cohorts entered the reproductive period, there would also be a decline in the relative number of people in the reproductive ages. Still further ahead, if fertility should be stabilized, at a lower level than now, the age distribution would tend to become "normal"; it would not return to the present high dependency ratio.

With a lower dependency burden, income per head, however we calculate it, would rise. If all of the rise in average income were devoted to increased consumption, if the average child and adult maintained the same relative shares of consumption, and if public expenditure for consumption purposes were kept at a constant figure, there would be a general rise in levels of living corresponding to the increase in income per head. Everyone would eat better and be better housed; all would have a larger share in the educational and health facilities and other benefits provided for in the public budget.[1]

The static assumptions made above are, of course, not realistic because of the cumulative effects of circular causation. Thus a secondary effect of the higher consumption levels would be to raise productivity by increasing both labor input and labor efficiency.[2] This effect would be most pronounced in the poorest countries, where particularly low levels of nutrition, health, and education depress the duration and efficiency of work, and participation in work, even more than elsewhere. Moreover, at progressively higher levels of income per head, more could be saved or devoted to direct investment, and the government could squeeze out more in "forced savings" through taxation or other means. Both forms of saving would, after some delay, tend to increase income per head still further, with cumulative effects similar to those of the initial rise in income per head due to lower fertility. With lower fertility rates, costs and interruptions of work incidental to births would also decrease. We have, in addition, to reckon with other, more subtle effects of rising levels of living. The great poverty in India and Pakistan and in large sections of the pop-

---

[1] As children require food, clothing, and services but are assumed not to produce anything, every prevented birth would imply a yearly "saving" of expenditure, until the new generation entered the labor force. Taking into account that children consume less than adults in rough proportion to their age group, and discounting future "saved" consumption by a rate of interest of 10 percent, Stephen Enke calculates the value of "saved" consumption per birth for twenty years ahead in India at 537.6 rupees ($113) and for fifteen years at 442.3 rupees ($93). ("The Gains to India from Population Control: Some Money Measure and Incentive Schemes," *Review of Economics and Statistics*, Vol. XLII, No. 2, May, 1960, p. 117; cf. "The Economic Aspects of Slowing Population Growth," *The Economic Journal*, Vol. LXXVI, No. 301, March, 1966, pp. 44 ff.) In those South Asian countries with higher average incomes and levels of living the figures would be correspondingly higher. Enke's figures are minimum figures since his calculation does not allow for the cumulative effects of circular causation, discussed below.

[2] Labor input, labor efficiency, and labor productivity are defined in Chapter 21, Section 15.

ulation in the other South Asian countries must account, at least in part, for the apathy of the masses and their unresponsiveness to efforts to change attitudes and institutions, spread modern technology, improve hygiene, and so on.

Also, relatively more of total national income could then be devoted to raising the living levels of children, with especially beneficial effects on productivity in the long run. Thus public expenditures for educational and training facilities could be increased. Larger efforts could also be devoted to improving health facilities. Better health standards for adults as well as children would result, and still further improvements of labor input and efficiency would be possible. Finally, we must note that nearly all these direct and indirect effects of a decline in fertility would facilitate the productive integration of the expanding labor force into the economy.

We have so far disregarded the effects that a decline in fertility rates would have on mortality rates. Lower fertility rates could be expected to speed up the decline in the mortality rate for several reasons: fewer maternal and infant deaths, higher levels of living, and, with progressively higher income levels, a broadened financial base for public health work. Declining mortality rates, in turn, tend to raise economic levels because of the decrease in illness associated therewith. And not to be entirely overlooked are the economic inconveniences and the costs following upon every death, among them funeral costs — which, as in all poor countries, are inordinately high in South Asia.

It seems apparent, then, that *the effects of a decline in fertility would be favorable in both economic and more broadly human terms and that these effects are very considerable and cumulative, gaining momentum over the years.* They would also be *independent of the man/land ratio:* the same causal mechanism must operate in sparsely as in densely populated countries.

3 Increase in the Labor Force

In all South Asian countries the labor force is now increasing much more rapidly than it ever did previously in these countries, and two or three times as fast as it did in Western Europe before the effects of birth control made their influence felt; and the increase will accelerate. Coale and Hoover's estimates for India, published in 1958, indicated an increase in the labor force over three decades, beginning in 1956, of 87 percent.[1] This projection was based on the highest fertility rate Coale and Hoover used, but today it is a conservative projection since mortality has declined faster than they assumed while fertility has not fallen. For Pakistan they projected an increase of the same order. For Burma and Indonesia the projected increase

[1] Coale and Hoover, *Population Growth and Economic Development in Low-Income Countries*, p. 232.

was even greater. In the other Southeast Asian countries and Ceylon the growth in the labor force by 1986 would be still higher.

When we inquire into the significance of these projections for the economies of the South Asian countries, one brute fact already alluded to must be remembered: whether our vantage point is 1956 or 1966, most of those who will be of working age fifteen or twenty years hence are already born. For a generation ahead, indeed, the size of the labor force will not be very greatly changed by any reduction in fertility rates that might occur. The labor force in the South Asian countries is certain to increase rapidly during the next few decades because of the high birth rates in the recent past, and its increase will be magnified by the continuing decline in mortality. It is possible, therefore, to isolate the problem of the growth in the labor force from the question of a possible decrease in fertility.

In Appendix 7 (Section 2), we find that the economic effects of this tremendous rise in the labor force cannot be satisfactorily analyzed either by the static law of diminishing returns or by any other simple measure, such as the additional capital investment needed, given a fixed capital/output ratio, to keep aggregate income unchanged. Rather, the economic effects of the increase in the labor force must be studied in the light of levels of living, attitudes, institutions, and the entire complex of conditions in the several countries. An approach to such a study was attempted in Part Five; the following observations merely recall some of the especially pertinent conclusions.

Typically in South Asia today, the labor force is greatly underutilized. Efforts to raise labor input and efficiency, and thereby the productivity of the labor force, meet with extreme difficulties, political, institutional, and attitudinal. A rapid increase in the labor force must aggravate these difficulties of planning for development, particularly as, by itself, this increase tends to make the social and economic structure more inegalitarian and rigid. Given the heavy concentration of labor in agriculture, industrialization seems the evident solution. And it is undoubtedly true that *in the long run,* particularly in the more densely populated countries, the absorption of a much larger part of the labor force into modern manufacturing industry offers the only hope for a substantial rise in labor utilization and in economic levels. But the potential increase in the number of workers engaged in industry is a function not only of the rate of industrial growth but also of the present state of industrialization. In addition, industrialization normally has backwash effects on employment opportunities in existing enterprises that sometimes offset, or more than offset, the increase in demand for labor. Therefore, *in the short run* — which is to say the next few decades — it is not realistic to expect industrialization to offer employment to any significant proportion of the natural increase in the labor force, even if industrialization efforts were to be sharply stepped up. The spread effects of industrial development are also generally weak in South Asia, precisely because of the initial state of underdevelopment. A movement of labor from rural districts into urban services and trades cannot be a substitute for its absorption into industry; like agriculture, they are already plagued by underutilization of labor and low productivity.

Consequently, for the next few decades — the time perspective in this analysis — a major premise of planning in all the South Asian countries must be that agriculture will have to absorb by far the larger part of the expected rapid increase in the labor force. There can be no question, within that period, of an actual decrease in the size of the agricultural labor force, or even of its stabilization at a higher level. *The aim of agricultural planning must be to raise labor utilization, and to do so while the labor force is increasing rapidly.*

Were it true, as is commonly asserted, that the marginal productivity of labor in traditional agriculture is zero, or near zero or even negative, the task would be virtually impossible to accomplish. Fortunately it is not true: yields are generally very low and differ widely within and among countries. There are considerable opportunities for increasing agricultural output through a larger labor input and greater efficiency of work, even with present techniques; moreover, higher capital intensity and improved techniques need not replace labor, but have rather the opposite effect of calling for a larger and more efficient labor input. The main obstacle to such a development is, as already suggested, the institutional conditions, particularly in regard to land tenure, fortified by the attitudinal and political conditions; we have already pointed out that the growth of the labor force by itself tends to worsen the institutional conditions for reforms.

The opportunities to succeed in agricultural planning aimed at augmenting labor utilization and productivity while the labor force is rapidly expanding should be greater in the countries where much new land can be brought under cultivation, as in Laos, Cambodia, Burma, Thailand, and the outer islands of Indonesia, than where the land reserves are smaller, as in India and Pakistan.[1] The cultivation of new land requires,

---

[1] The reasons for believing this are threefold. First, there is in the former countries a considerable amount of land available for cultivation at presumably little, if any, decline in average output from agricultural labor, even without any change in capital intensity and techniques. Secondly, in these sparsely populated lands, a larger labor force means a better utilization of basic investments, especially of transport facilities. Thirdly, an increase in the labor force concomitant with placing more land under cultivation should often imply extra savings-*cum*-investment in land improvement and house construction. There is often also a fourth reason: with a less cramped land situation, the rural institutional structure is usually less inegalitarian and less rigid; concerning the general relationship between poverty and social inequality, see Chapter 33, Section 11, in particular p. 1806, footnote 1.

As noted earlier, birth control will have the same effect of raising incomes, levels of living, and productivity in sparsely as in more densely populated countries. The often expressed view that countries like Laos and Cambodia are "underpopulated," in the sense that a higher fertility would be advantageous, must assume that, say a generation hence, with higher fertility productivity of labor would not only have been maintained but raised so much that it would more than compensate for the rise in productivity which would result from a lower fertility. Knowing what we know about these countries, this does not seem probable.

however, clearing and settlement and often large public investments in irrigation or drainage and in organized migration.

It must be made clear that any intensification in the utilization of labor in agriculture, keeping pace with the increase of the labor force, can offer, in the best case, no more than a respite. Eventually a situation must be reached where more labor cannot be absorbed by agriculture or can be absorbed only at very low productivity rewards. If industrialization has not by then reached the level where it can more massively give work to a growing part of the increase in the labor force, this implies greater misery for the masses in agriculture and stagnation or even retardation of economic development generally — if it is not counteracted in time by the favorable effects along the first line of causation following a decrease in fertility. That dismal situation is nearer in countries like India and Pakistan where there is less possibility of increasing the area of cultivation, and even in Indonesia and Ceylon where this requires large-scale effective administrative exertions and substantial public investments. When this situation ripens depends also on the relative effectiveness and success of planning and government policies in general, on the aid and trade policies of the rich countries, and all other conditioning factors in the outside world — including the presence or absence of military conflicts or dangers of conflict and the consequent increase or decrease in military expenditures — and, indeed, on everything else that happens of importance for the economies of these countries, as, for instance, the outcome of the monsoons. As these other conditions not only differ among the countries, but vary in time in each country, it is not likely that a turn toward stagnation and retardation will be apparent as a sudden and clear-cut occurrence, which can be identified with a specific point of time. Only in retrospect will it be possible even to specify a period during which — with some intermittent ups and downs — economic development efforts became frustrated. It is, indeed, not excluded that future economic historians looking back on what is now happening in countries like India, Pakistan, and Indonesia will identify these recent years, or some years not far in the future, as that period — if fertility does not decrease substantially at an early date.

Many factors will be seen to have contributed to that course of events, including not only population policies and their effectiveness, but all other policies pursued or not pursued in these countries and in other countries interested in their fate. Nevertheless, one important factor will be the adverse condition of a very rapidly increasing labor force that is difficult to utilize. In any case, it is entirely unrealistic to assume that a growth in the labor force, corresponding to present and prospective rates of births and deaths, can be absorbed indefinitely in any South Asian country without causing calamity.

4 Combining the Two Types of Effects

We must now combine the conclusions we have reached in the two last sections. In Section 2 we found that a decline in fertility would raise average incomes and levels of living; it would also help in many ways to raise labor utilization and productivity. It would thus help to counteract — and in some countries perhaps more than counteract — the adverse effects on labor utilization and productivity, and thereby on income, exerted by the growth in the labor force due to high fertility in earlier years and declining mortality rates as discussed in Section 3. We know that the favorable effects of a lower fertility rate along the first-mentioned line of causation are very substantial and cumulative. They would mount for at least fifteen years if the lower rate were kept low; if birth control were gradually intensified, the gains would become progressively bigger and continue longer. In Appendix 7 (Section 3) we explain why we have not attempted to construct a theoretical model to account for the net effects on the economy accruing from the two sources: the decline in the dependency burden and growth in the labor force.

In the longer time perspective, a decline in fertility would be even more advantageous. This is true, first of all, because some of its effects are cumulative: circular causation does not occur instantaneously; it takes time to gather momentum. Secondly, as the smaller cohorts of children reached working age, a brake would begin to be put on the growth in the labor force. Thirdly, growth in the size of the procreative age group would also begin to be slowed down — and more rapidly, since a woman's childbearing period is over earlier than the normal working life — with the result that fewer children would be born even at a given age-specific fertility rate.

Population policy by its very nature needs to be viewed in the very long time perspective, and the need is the greater in South Asia because of the youthfulness of the population.[1] As some 40 percent of the population in South Asia is below 15 years of age, contrasted with 20–25 percent in Western countries, and as the age distribution even in the procreative age group is correspondingly skewed, the braking distance is extremely long before population growth and, especially, labor force growth can be significantly slowed down. Even if for one or another of the South Asian countries the prospective growth in the labor force would not seem likely to cause great difficulties for some period ahead, this could not be an argument for postponing efforts to reduce the birth rate. And it must not be forgotten that a period of mass education will be needed before a policy of spreading birth control can have significant effects on fertility rates.

The danger is that the long "running-in" period of any policy to induce

[1] Chapter 27, Section 13.

a decline in fertility will be underestimated. If a major and successful effort in population policy, corresponding to Coale and Hoover's most optimistic assumption in regard to fertility, were begun in India in fifteen years, reckoned from 1956, as opposed to five, there would be a difference of about 7 percent in the size of the total population after thirty years.[1] This difference may appear trivial, particularly as the labor force thirty years hence would be almost the same in both cases. But the population increase thereafter would be significantly slowed down ten years earlier; and what is certainly not trivial is the considerable savings on the maintenance burden in the average family that would immediately follow a decline in fertility and the cumulative effects of this change that would follow. The sooner fertility is reduced, the sooner will the cumulative effects of the decrease in the dependency burden be felt. Moreover, each postponement of effective birth control measures increases the potential growth rates in later years because, as the larger cohorts of children grow up, it allows the continued rapid increase in the procreative age group — which is, after all, the basic determinant of the future size of population. The longer time perspective — far on the other side of any perspective planning actually attempted in any South Asian country — is the only realistic one.

Although our treatment of the problem has been in general terms, and although we have consistently avoided making it more specific than our knowledge of the facts and the relationships between the facts permits, we believe we can conclude that *a consideration of the economic effects of population trends should give the governments of the South Asian countries strong reasons for instituting as soon and as vigorously as possible policy measures to get birth control practiced among the masses of the people.*

A NOTE ON INADEQUATE

APPROACHES TO THE ECONOMIC

EFFECTS OF POPULATION CHANGES

To clear the deck for the analysis in Chapter 28 (Part I) of the economic effects of population growth in South Asia, this brief note will seek to demonstrate the limitations of some theoretical approaches to this problem that are met frequently in both popular and scientific discussions.

1 Population Optimum and Similar Concepts

One such approach makes use of the concept of *population optimum*. Although this concept is heard of less often than it used to be, it still underlies much of the discussion of population problems. The postulation of an optimum size of population for a particular country represents an attempt to define "objectively" an ideal. In modern times the basis of this definition has been the maximization of income or output per head.[1]

[1] To cite but two examples: "The concept, 'optimum population,' is employed to signify that under given conditions in a country there is a population size that is preferable to any other larger or smaller size. What this size is depends upon the conditions that supposedly are given and upon what it is that a population wants. For purposes of the present discussion it will be supposed that what a population seeks to maximize is per capita income over the relatively long run, or the present value of future per capita income, or some other such indicator of economic 'welfare.'" (Joseph J. Spengler, "The Economics of Population Growth," in *The Population Crisis and the Use of World Resources*, Stuart Mudd, ed., W. Junk Publishers, The Hague, 1964, p. 87.) ". . . there will be at least one point in which productivity is a maximum. This point of density is called the optimum density or optimum population point." (Jan Tinbergen, *International Economic Integration*, Elsevier, Amsterdam, 1954, p. 37.)

The normative arbitrariness of this supposedly "objective" definition of population optimum is illustrated by the fact that in earlier days an alternative was occasionally put forward. Henry Sidgwick, for instance, postulated maximum total against maximum average satisfaction; see Gunnar Myrdal, *The Political Element in the Development of Economic Theory*, Routledge & Kegan Paul Ltd., London, 1953, pp. 38ff., especially p. 38, f.n. 6. Also, J. E. Meade, in Chapter VI of his *Trade and Welfare* (Oxford University Press, London, 1955), proposes, against current fashion, the maximization of

The idea of an optimum population not only objectifies implicit valuations, as does all welfare theory, but also illustrates the illegitimate *ceteris paribus* assumption which leads to logical contradictions. It implies a comparison between the present size of a population and its optimum size, in terms of maximum income (or output) per head. In this comparison all conditions relevant to income and output, other than population size, are assumed to remain unchanged, including the amount and kind of capital equipment, the state of the arts (technical knowledge) and all production functions, and the amount and terms of foreign trade. In addition to these conditions, conventionally held constant in short-term, static economic analysis,[1] all attitudes and institutions affecting productivity must also be assumed to remain constant.

The change-over from the present size of a population to its optimal size cannot occur instantaneously. It must involve changes in one or several of the determinants of population change: natality, mortality, migration. Changes in these occur gradually and are interrelated through their combined effects on age distribution. Different combinations of constancy and changeability in natality, mortality, and migration and different rates of change in these determinants will result in differences in the time period required to achieve a change in population size. During the transition period the age distribution and the other conditions mentioned in the previous paragraph relevant to output and income are bound to change. The assumption of constancy is both unrealistic (for autonomous changes and changes induced by future policies) and logically invalid (for changes resulting from the population changes themselves).

---

total welfare as the ultimate criterion of the optimum population (p. 83). (Like most modern welfare theorists, Meade ignores the old discussions, in which the utilitarian theory was worked out with greater conviction and in clearer terms; a closer reading of the exchanges between Sidgwick and Edgeworth and some of J. S. Mill's writings would have given his abstract normative reasoning greater depth and a wider historical perspective.) Recently P. T. Bauer has also shown leanings toward the alternative norm, though without expressing his thoughts very clearly; see P. T. Bauer, *Some Economic Aspects and Problems of Under-Developed Countries*, Forum of Free Enterprise, Bombay, 1959, p. 15, and P. T. Bauer and B. S. Yamey, *The Economics of Under-Developed Countries*, University Press, Cambridge, 1957, pp. 63, 152 *et passim*.

Concerning the doctrinal origin of the concept of "population optimum" in classical economic theory and its relation to the philosophies of natural right and utilitarianism, and for a general criticism of the concept, see the writer's *The Political Element in the Development of Economic Theory*, pp. 38ff. *et passim;* and *Population, A Problem for Democracy*, Harvard University Press, Cambridge, Mass., 1940, pp. 131ff., especially pp. 139ff.

[1] A host of specific assumptions, rarely spelled out, are necessary if the analysis is to have precise meaning. Since income (output) per head can be defined unambiguously only in a one-commodity world, the index number problem arises, and with it the question of how the heterogeneous collection of products is to be weighted. There are also the questions of how income is and "should be" distributed, of the direction of demand, the homogeneity and quality of the labor force, and so on. If inequalities of income distribution are substantial and if some factors of production are specific, it is impossible, over a wide range of outputs, to state without ambiguity what constitutes an increase in output per head. These implicit assumptions, like those mentioned in the text, acquire importance because the comparison is of the relatively long-run variety (see the first footnote).

Here is a particularly striking instance of the inadmissibility of the *ceteris paribus* assumption. Since changes in population size cannot be instantaneous, we must specify what population determinants are to be changed and at what speed. The choice between the different possibilities involves valuations. During the period of transition, "other things" cannot be assumed to stay constant and the process by which and the time in which the optimum size is reached are themselves bound to affect the conditions that would have to be assumed constant in order to make sense of the "optimum."[1]

Apparently in order to avoid the logical difficulties — felt but never properly spelled out — of the static *ceteris paribus* assumption, resort is sometimes had to the idea of *optimum population growth*. But this does not solve the problem. It implies, of course, the concept of a population optimum at a particular point of time. If in the initial situation the actual size of the population is other than optimum, one would perhaps be tempted to conclude that optimum population growth would be the rate that would most speedily change the actual population to an optimum. But that problem cannot be discussed without considering the factors discussed above in connection with the concept of optimum population size. It might seem, then, that the way to salvage the concept of optimum population growth would be to assume that the initial population size corresponds to the optimum size. Its optimum growth would then, however, be determined by all the other social and economic conditions as they change autonomously and through population growth. In other words, the optimum remains indeterminate until changes in other conditions and inter-relationships are made explicit. Moreover, to assume that the population initially is of the optimum size and thereafter moves along an optimum curve is to beg the question; all the difficulties mentioned in the foregoing paragraphs arise again.

We should not be surprised that in spite of the ubiquity of these concepts, it has never been possible to apply them effectively in analyzing a real situation or a process. A critical analysis would have exposed the futility of such an attempt. Indeed, the very idea that the population problem in the extremely poor countries in South Asia can be analyzed with practical benefit in terms of optimum population size or optimum population growth is fanciful and attests the sterility of social and economic speculation that has no contact with reality. The approach is as absurd as would be a discussion of the housing problem in South Asia in terms of "optimum housing accommodation." The practical problem for population policy, as for other issues, is how to achieve an *improvement*, not an *optimum*.[2] The valuations involved should be stated and the desired situation should be compared with a specified situation, either present or potential, with full account taken of the consequences of the process of transition — normally through a reduction in fertility rates — to the improved situation.

The concepts of *overpopulation* and *underpopulation*, when related to a concept of population optimum, are indeterminate for the reasons given. But we

---

[1] In this book we have repeatedly found it necessary to discard concepts and theories that use static comparisons. The grounds for their rejection have always been logical inconsistency and inadequacy to reality. See, in particular, Appendix 6, Section 8.

[2] Appendix 2, Sections 7 and 13.

have also found "overpopulation" used as a synonym for "underemployment,"[1] a concept we have discarded as logically invalid and not adequate to reality in South Asia.[2] It is not easy to give a clear meaning to the concept of overpopulation even if it is freed from associations with concepts of population optimum or underemployment. When related to the practical problem of a population policy based on an analysis of the facts and postulated value premises, "overpopulation" simply means that a reduction in fertility rates is desirable, because it would improve development prospects. As we show in Chapter 28 (Part I), all South Asian countries are in this sense "overpopulated" in various degrees — as are, indeed, most poor countries. It is difficult to see the scientific purpose of the term, given this very wide, even if clear, meaning. It is, in any case, the *degree* of "overpopulation" that is of interest. In practice, when the term is not related to the logically faulty and unrealistic concepts of population optimum or underemployment, it is used to indicate in a broad and general way that a population is very much "too large" to allow "decent" levels of living and "reasonable" prospects for development. We have no use for the term or for the related term "population pressure."

All these concepts and theories, stated in terms of "population," are also misleading because they abstract from changes in age distribution, which inevitably accompany a primary change in fertility rates (and most non-imaginary cases of migration). One service of the study of population growth by Coale and Hoover[3] is that it stresses this point and illustrates it by realistic projections. Too often, birth control in South Asia is advocated only because of the difficulties foreseen in *creating employment* for the growing population, without recognizing that for a long time to come the rate of increase in the labor force will be determined by births that occurred in an earlier period. Those who do recognize this fact sometimes draw the opposite conclusion that the spread of birth control is *not an urgent concern* because a lower birth rate cannot give much economic relief in the next few decades. This reasoning, of course, puts things upside down. By reducing the dependency burden, a reduction in the birth rate will immediately begin to improve levels of income and living. In many direct and indirect ways it will also make it easier to accelerate development policies by improving labor utilization and productivity. A lower current birth rate will, in addition, have important effects in the next generation, both on the reproduction potential and on the rate of increase in the labor force.[4]

2   *The Simple Model*

Most of the approaches to the problems of population growth — whether they are embellished by the concepts exemplified above or not — have usually this in common: the economic effects of a population increase are considered in terms

---

[1] Appendix 6, Sections 1, 3, esp. pp. 2042 (note 1), 2045; Chapter 21, Section 14.

This is an aberration of the classical doctrine that assumed full employment in the long run when there would be equilibrium between supply and demand. See Chapter 21, p. 974, footnote 1.

[2] Chapter 21, Sections 12–14; Appendix 6.

[3] Ansley J. Coale and Edgar M. Hoover, *Population Growth and Economic Development in Low-Income Countries,* Princeton University Press, Princeton, 1958.

[4] Chapter 28, Section 4.

of the man/land ratio and the static law of diminishing returns. They recognize the possibility that the "population pressure" could be reduced by a movement of labor from agriculture to industry, where increasing returns are assumed to prevail, and by investments and technical improvements in agriculture. The principal innovation in the modern approach has been to reduce to one — capital — the scarce factors cooperating with labor and to assume a definite relationship between capital input and total product, both considered in aggregate terms. An increase in the labor force raises the demand for a certain amount of capital investment — often called, after Sauvy,[1] the purely "demographic investment" — simply in order to keep total product per head unchanged. This model is now reproduced in almost every scientific[2] or popular discussion of economic development in underdeveloped countries; as we shall point out in the next section, it is implied in the more complicated model that takes age distribution into account as well. With some variation in the numerical values chosen, it is expressed in this standard form:

> If population increases by 2 percent annually and if the marginal capital/output ratio is 3 to 1, 6 percent of the national income must be saved and invested per year in order to maintain the present level of income per head. If it is desired to increase income per head by 2 percent a year, another 6 percent of the national income must be saved and invested.

A more careful formulation would assume, among other things, a constant ratio of labor force to population. This would imply an unchanged age distribution and therefore a constant birth rate over a long period and an equal incidence of the decline in the mortality rate in all age groups, if there is such a decline.

Let us, for the sake of the argument, make the assumption of a constant ratio of labor force to population and concentrate on the economic effects of an increase in the labor force. The model shows that the increase in the labor force has an adverse effect on average income, because, in order to provide the labor force with capital at unchanged levels of average productivity, a certain amount of net savings is used that would otherwise be available to invest for development. Assuming, further, *ceteris paribus*, constant return, and a given capital/output ratio, the model provides a very simple measure of this adverse economic effect of an increase in the labor force: the extra capital required merely to keep average income at the initial level.

This kind of analysis, in terms of capital investment and output, is typical of the modern approach to the economic problems of the South Asian countries. In our opinion it is too mechanistic and schematic. It gives the appearance of knowledge where none exists, and an illusory precision to this pretended knowledge. By overemphasizing investment — usually physical investment — it tends to direct research along lines that are largely unrealistic for South Asia. Because this modern approach represents a major bias in planning and policy we have criticized it in several contexts in this book.[3] A few of these criticisms are worth

[1] Alfred Sauvy, *Théorie générale de la population*, Vol. I. *Économie et Population*, Presses Universitaires de France, Paris, 1952, pp. 288–290.

[2] For an example see Jan Tinbergen, *The Design of Development*, Johns Hopkins Press, Baltimore, 1958, p. 14.

[3] See in particular Appendix 2, Sections 19–21, and Appendix 3.

noting here because they are of special importance for the study of population growth.

As we show in Part Five of the book, the present situation in the South Asian region is one of severe underutilization of the labor force, though not to the same degree in every country. Economic development must be thought of primarily as the achievement of greater labor input and labor efficiency (for agriculture, see particularly Chapter 26, Section 1). Economic development means, in the first place, that more people will work, that they will work longer and more efficiently, and that they will cooperate in order to create institutions that make this possible and rewarding. Changes in these respects will increase the productivity of the labor force. The availability of more capital can, of course, also increase labor productivity; if wisely invested according to a plan designed for that purpose, it may even facilitate and hasten fuller and more intensive labor utilization. The same effect can also be expected from many specific policies: for instance, policies directed at effective land and tenancy reforms; at rising levels of nutrition, health, and education; providing a larger and better trained cadre of managerial and supervisory personnel at all levels of responsibility; improving efficiency and honesty in public office; and, generally, promoting a consolidated nation ruled by an informed and determined government.

These policies cannot meaningfully be expressed in terms of capital invested. Neither can a realistic analysis proceed from the assumption that the conditions these policies seek to change are constant. The assumption of *ceteris paribus* would, indeed, be logically impossible, since some of these conditions will be altered by the increase in the labor force – the primary change whose economic effects on income per head the model is intended to measure. Besides, except for capital inflow from abroad, the actual limits of savings and investment are set by the same factors that limit the scope and effectiveness of the policies mentioned for increasing labor input and efficiency – levels of living, attitudes, and institutions, precisely the things from which the modern approach, as exemplified by the model quoted above, abstracts. Also, the economic effects of investment, as of any other policy, cannot be analyzed in isolation; they depend on the combination of policies applied. Finally, the age distribution cannot be disregarded when, as ordinarily, the model is used to motivate a policy of spreading birth control.

We cannot regard the modern theoretical approach as an advance.

3   The More Inclusive Model[1]

Increased attention has recently been paid to the economic effects of the change in age distribution resulting from reduced fertility rates, and in consequence more complicated models have been constructed.[2] Because the demographic determi-

---

[1] George Peterson kindly made suggestions for clarifying and strengthening the argument of this section and helped draft certain parts of it.

[2] Coale and Hoover have presented such models (*Population Growth and Economic Development in Low-Income Countries*, pp. 259ff.), and so have others, particularly among the French demographers (see, for instance, George Balandier, ed., *Le Tiers Monde*, Institut National d'Etudes Demographiques, Cahiers No. 27, Paris, 1956). See

nants — births, deaths, and migration — and the resulting population size, population growth, and age distribution lend themselves to the construction of models with determinate and predictable relationships, it has been tempting to graft onto this demographic mechanism those economic relationships that are thought to be determined by the demographic changes, particularly by the changes in age structure and their effect on the labor force and the dependency rate. By tracing the effects not only of the change in size of the labor force, which for a generation is almost a datum, but also of the changing dependency rates on consumption, saving, and investment and on the allocation of investment, it is hoped to show how income per head changes over time, largely as a result of different assumptions about fertility rates and the consequent modification of the age distribution. The behavior of mortality rates, although determined in part by the age structure, has a much less important effect on it than do changes in fertility rates (Chapter 27, Section 5). International migration can be disregarded as insignificant for the South Asian countries (Chapter 28, Section 14).

In projecting the effects of reduced fertility on Indian economic growth in the period 1956–86, Coale and Hoover assume (1) that the rate of growth of output is determined largely by public development outlays and private investment; (2) that the amount of funds available for these expenditures depends both on national income and on income per head; (3) that these expenditures fall into two categories — "direct growth" investment and public "welfare" outlays — the former contributing more to output than the latter (the direct growth investment contributes directly to output whereas the public welfare outlays do so by enhancing the incentives and energy of the labor force); (4) that welfare outlays can be subdivided into those providing facilities for the existing population and those adding to facilities because of population growth, and that these two categories make different contributions to output; (5) that only welfare outlays that assist the existing labor force increase present output, while there is a lag of fifteen years before those assisting the rest of the population affect output.

Coale and Hoover justify the assumption that the rate of growth of output depends largely on (1) public developmental outlays and public and private productive investment that affect output directly and (2) the indirect effects of welfare outlays on the incentives and energy of the present and future labor force on the grounds that these two types of determinants are the ones most clearly affected when alternative assumptions are made about rates of population growth; other determinants, such as government policies, technical assistance, and administration, are considered to be relatively unaffected. Coale and Hoover are aware that to ignore the effects of consumption levels on the vigor, efficiency, and adaptability of the labor force is a serious omission, but plead ignorance in defense. They stress that they are not making forecasts, but projections intended only to show the effects of different assumptions about fertility. Their projections contain substantial refinements of the simpler model, criticized in the previous section. Like savings in the simpler model, investment and public

---

also "Growth Models for Illustrating the Effects of Alternative Employment and Investment Policies," United Nations, ECAFE, *Economic Bulletin for Asia and the Far East*, Vol. IX, No. 1, New York, 1958.

developmental outlays, including governmental welfare expenditures, determine the growth of national income according to an "incremental developmental outlay/output" ratio — a sophistication of the more familiar incremental capital/output ratio. This coefficient is first assumed to rise from 3:1 in 1956 at the rate of 2 percent per annum. Finally, Coale and Hoover vary the parameters in several ways, changing the coefficient of investment and developmental outlays to incremental consumer income, changing the weights of the growth contribution made by welfare outlays, and changing the assumptions about the rise of the developmental outlay/output ratio. Although these changes yield widely varying *incomes* in 1986, the percentage *difference in income* associated with reduced fertility is said to be persistent and stable. In 1986 this differential ranges only from 38 to 48 percent.[1]

The main feature of Coale and Hoover's model is its quantitative illustration that a decrease in fertility accelerates the rise in total national income and, even more, in income per head, because (1) a larger proportion of income is available for growth expenditure and (2) a smaller proportion of this larger ratio goes into low-yielding and late-yielding welfare expenditure on extra population. Coale and Hoover are careful to point out that "This array of results should suffice to show the inapplicability of any of these projections as a forecast of likely economic growth, since we have no real basis for defending any one of the seven combinations of underlying assumptions as the best." They claim, however, that "The main body of the table . . . does give a positively significant result. It shows that through this whole gamut of projections, despite the wide variation in rates of progress that they imply, the *differential associated with reduced fertility* is remarkably persistent and stable."[2] In view of their modest claims and pioneering effort, it seems churlish to find fault with this conclusion. But despite their disclaimers, they create a false air of precision and a false confidence in their model. A critical examination is therefore justified. For the sake of argument, we shall assume that several aggregative concepts, and in particular, income, savings, and development outlay, can be given a clear meaning.[3]

First, Coale and Hoover are fully aware of leaving out of consideration a number of important variables, simply because they are difficult or impossible to quantify. Since the largest variation is associated with the distribution of imputed growth effects among different types of outlays, it is plausible to assume that the growth effects of policies and of changes in other conditions left out of consideration would make a substantial difference. We shall return to this point at the end of this section.

Secondly, the apparent stability of the income differential associated with reduced fertility is largely spurious. It is the result of their altering the parameters, which they list one at a time rather than in groups or all together. Thus if one inserts simultaneously all the values that lower the differential, or, *a*

[1] Coale and Hoover, *Population Growth and Economic Development in Low-Income Countries*, p. 281.

[2] *Ibid.*

[3] See Chapter 11, Section 1; Chapter 12, Section 2; and see Appendix 4, Section 3 *et passim*.

fortiori, all values that raise it, the differential is greatly increased. Coale and Hoover themselves say that there is "no real basis" for preferring one of the listed values of their parameters to any other. It follows that there is no real basis for choosing any single combination of parameters over any other single combination. Assume that the ratio Y_L/Y_H, where L indicates low and H high fertility, is a function of three parameters A, B, and C and that for each parameter there are three possible values, denoted by subscripts 1, 2, and 3. Assume that when the other two parameters are held constant, the ratio Y_L/Y_H is greatest when the variable parameter is evaluated at 1, second greatest at 2, and least at 3. What Coale and Hoover show is that if we start with a function of the form

$$Y_L/Y_H = f(A_2, B_2, C_2)$$

and substitute new values for the parameters A, B, C, *one at a time,* the ratio does not change much. That is, $f(A_2, B_2, C_2)$ is approximately equal to $f(A_1, B_2, C_2)$, which again is approximately equal to $f(A_2, B_1, C_2)$, and so on. But they have *not* shown that $f(A_1, B_1, C_1)$ is approximately equal to $f(A_3, B_3, C_3)$. It is obvious that this difference is much greater than the differences obtained by changing the parameters one at a time. Coale and Hoover give the impression that their variation of parameters is representative of all possible variations, for they speak of not computing ratios for all 27 possible combinations because this would take too much time and space. But the 7 computations they present cluster around the minimum variations. The apparent stability of the income differential when the parameters are varied is therefore due to a highly selective procedure.

Thirdly, the variations in their assumptions are arbitrarily confined to a narrow area. It can easily be shown that widely varying income differentials will result if quite plausible assumptions are made about, say, different capital/output ratios for the low-fertility than for the high-fertility projection, or about the savings function, or the welfare effects. A higher fertility rate necessitates a larger diversion of funds into welfare expenditure. Not only does this reduce the funds available for direct growth expenditure, but it may also raise the capital/output ratio for the direct growth investment that does take place. The use of identical capital/output ratios for the alternative projections is therefore not the only plausible procedure. For a number of reasons, spelled out elsewhere,[1] the amount of investment will influence the size of the capital/output ratio. If we now compare the two projections that use the same capital/output ratios with those assuming different ratios, the differential Y_L/Y_H is seen to be quite different for the two cases. The developmental outlay/output ratio may differ even more. It thus appears that a slight variation in the assumptions is sufficient to cast doubt on Coale and Hoover's principal conclusion. Their argument is that economists do not know precisely the functional relationships between outlays and income, but that whichever of several assumptions about these is made, the percentage by which low-fertility income exceeds high-fertility income is roughly the same. But if we consider the possibility that different capital/output ratios and developmental outlay/output ratios for the

---

[1] Appendix 3, Sections 13, 17 (iii), 18, and 22.

members of each pair of projections are as plausible as are the same capital/ output ratios, the conclusion no longer holds. We arrive at considerable differences in the differential.

Since even when based on the authors' own highly restricted views of the determinants of growth, the stability of the differential for low- and high-fertility projections is largely spurious, it follows that if we include the possibility of institutional and attitudinal changes and of different policies, there is little reason to assume stability of the differential. We have seen in our discussion of the importance of coordinating policies,[1] especially investment projects, that development contributions depend on a set of complementary and supplementary measures. The evidence from the Coale and Hoover projections, which impute different growth effects to different outlay distributions, supports the view that the range of the differential would be widened if other determinants of growth were considered.

Fourthly, insofar as there is a constant differential when the purely economic parameters are varied, it should be noted that labor force size does not respond to these variations, since all those persons are already alive who will enter the labor force in fifteen years or who will bear children in the next fifteen years; that is, the potential increment to the labor force over the next thirty years has an upper limit. The scope for economic changes over three decades is therefore strictly circumscribed, despite wide variations in the economic parameters. Changes in the age structure of the population due to variations in fertility rates are slow compared with the quasi-constancy of the size of the labor force, which dominates Coale and Hoover's thirty-year model. Even over a period longer than thirty years, the effects of the different fertility rates dominate over the effects of varying the purely economic parameters. For although it is true that after thirty years the increase in the labor force will add substantially to total production, this will not be sufficient to compensate for the depressing legacy of the high fertility. This depressing influence is due to three factors. (1) Output per worker will be lower than would be the case in the low-fertility projection, where, instead of duplicating facilities, each worker would be equipped with more capital. (2) The greater burden of dependency reduces the resources available for raising productivity per worker. (3) The lower level of income reached after thirty years will reduce the saving and investment ratio below what it would be on the low-fertility assumption. For all three reasons the gap in output per worker and income per consumer between the two projections will continue to widen, even if economic parameters were varied within a wide range.

Fifthly, the striking thing about Coale and Hoover's calculations, even under their arbitrary assumptions that minimize the range of the differential, is not the stability of the differential but its change from stability over the first ten years to increasing variation in the two succeeding decades. The relative superiority of total income under the low-fertility assumption over that under the high-fertility assumption is the same for projections 4 and 5 at the end of the first decade; at the end of the second decade, projection 4 exceeds projection 5 by 3 percent; and at the end of the third decade, by 10 percent. This suggests, as

[1] Appendix 2, Section 19; Appendix 3, Section 4 and Part II.

one would expect, that changes in economic parameters, while slow in affecting the differential associated with reduced fertility, work with accelerating speed at later stages.

We turn now from the alleged stability of the income differential associated with reduced fertility to the basic formula by which the size of growth funds is determined, which is open to certain objections. The formula is fundamental because government outlays plus private investment are assumed in the model to be the necessary and sufficient generators of growth. The formula is

$$F = C \left[\frac{F_o}{C_o} + a \left(\frac{Y}{C} - \frac{Y_o}{C_o} \right) \right] = aY - \left(\frac{aY_o - F_o}{C_o} \right) C$$

where F is public outlays plus private investment, a is the incremental propensity to save for the economy, Y is national income, C the number of consumers, and the subscript o denotes the base year. The authors assume that a is 30 per cent. The $\frac{aY_o - F_o}{C_o}$ term is estimated to be 49.27 for 1956. The formula for the funds available for government outlay plus private investment then becomes

$$F = .3Y - 49.27 C$$

The figure for India's incremental propensity to save has subsequently been shown to be too high. But the real question is not what figure to put into the formula, but whether in a country like India savings can reasonably be made a function exclusively of total income levels and of income per head. There are three main savings sectors in the Indian economy: government, individuals and small businesses, and corporations. Coale and Hoover exclude non-monetized savings and investment — a serious omission in the Indian setting. The personal sector accounts for somewhat less than three-sevenths of the total monetized savings, government for most of the rest, and corporations for a small but growing share. For each of these sectors the Coale and Hoover assumption that savings become an increasing proportion of rising income per head is open to grave doubts.

The assumption of a growing savings ratio for individuals is retained without any attempt to render it plausible, and despite evidence of a tendency to constancy of this ratio in other countries. Coale and Hoover reject this evidence on the ground that their projections are concerned not so much with change over time as with the income differential at any one time, according to different population assumptions. But their assumptions imply at least a doubling, and in some cases a tripling, of the average propensity to save between 1956 and 1986. If, instead, we were to assume a constant average propensity to save, total savings by individuals and small businesses would be the same for any given total income, irrespective of population size and income per head. Such an assumption would greatly reduce the superiority of the low-fertility projection over the high-fertility one.

The assumption that government savings increase as income per head increases is also questionable. The size of government savings, primarily through taxes but also through the surpluses of public enterprises, depends on many factors other than income per head. As the Indian Taxation Enquiry Commission and the Second and Third Five Year Plans have made clear, India's prevailing tax structure does not guarantee that tax receipts will increase even in proportion to the rise in income per head in the next thirty years. Progressive income tax rates play a much less important role than they do in Western countries and are not effectively enforced. The future proportion of national income saved by the Indian government depends much more on the kind of tax laws, the quality of the tax administration, and the political acceptability of the laws than on income per head.

Similarly, the amount of savings originating in the corporation sector depends largely on the opportunities for profitable investment, which in turn depend on a large number of forces besides growth of income per head. If, in view of these criticisms, a recalculation is made, for instance, on the assumption of a constant ratio of savings to income, it reduces the differential in total income between the low- and high-fertility assumption by some two-thirds.

Nothing of what has been said must be understood to suggest that savings and investment cannot or should not constitute an increasing proportion of rising income per head. Of course they can and they should. But it is important to remember that this does not happen automatically. In a model that abstracts from government policy and other "non-economic" determinants of growth, it would be more plausible to make savings depend on total income than on both total income and income per head. Again, it may be that rapidly growing income per head contributes to the breakdown of traditional attitudes, to a change in the pattern of demand, and to changes in the attitudes of active and potential businessmen toward innovation. Moreover, it is easier for governments to raise tax rates if incomes per head are rising. But none of this is consistent with assuming that these other conditions will remain constant while the average savings propensity will rise. Nor can one assume, as Coale and Hoover do, that all "non-economic" factors, such as government policy, will automatically adjust to rising income per head, or that government policies to raise the savings level cannot, or should not, precede such growth in income per head. Savings in general and taxes in particular are functions of public policy and of many interrelated conditions and cannot be relied on to rise without changes in these. The abstraction from government policies and institutional changes cannot yield the required rise in the savings ratio.

We have concentrated on the assumptions regarding the savings ratio. Similar considerations apply to the proportion of funds devoted to welfare expenditures. Policies in this field, especially those relating to the capital-intensive sectors of housing and construction and the dispersal or concentration of towns and industries, can have widely varying effects on economic growth. These variations influence the capital/output ratio of the welfare expenditures and, therefore, for given welfare requirements, the proportion of funds that can be allocated to direct growth investment. Once again a choice between different types of policies opens up a substantially wider range in the income differential for different assumptions.

To conclude, it is, of course, a considerable advance to use different incremental capital/output ratios for different types of investment and different types of developmental expenditure, including expenditure that improves the quality of the labor force, and to vary these ratios over time. Nevertheless, the arbitrary selection of parameters yielding the minimum range in the differential, the setting of the analysis in the frame of the relationship between capital input and product output — with its inherent bias toward overemphasis on investment and toward abstraction from other conditions, and thus toward isolation from all other policies and the consequent ignoring of the importance of how policies are combined — and the abstraction from effects of different levels of consumption on labor input and labor efficiency create the illusion that the demographic model so amplified can yield more inferences about the economy than its limitations permit. And even so we have not spelled out our objections to the main aggregative concepts used.

In our analysis of the economic consequences of population trends in Part I of Chapter 28, we began by experimenting with the construction of numerical models of the type criticized here. When finally we gave up the attempt and found ourselves restricted to much more general conclusions,[1] this was due not only to the lack of empirical data but also to the logical imperfections described briefly in this appendix.

Indeed, the point of our criticism of both the simple model and the more inclusive one is not the lack or inadequacy of empirical data for the estimation of the parameters intended to trace the economic effects of population movements. Were this the only deficiency, either model could still serve as a "theory" in our sense: a logically coordinated system of questions to be answered by further research. Such systems have their use in the organization and direction of research. The criticism is rather that these models are not appropriate systems of questions and so are not adequate to the South Asian reality. Their conclusions do not add to our knowledge since they are contained in the questionable simplifications of their premises.

We would not exclude the possibility of constructing models more adequate for this purpose. But such models would have to contain many more parameters and account for many more interrelationships. They would have to be very much more complex in order to be logically consistent and adequate to reality. With the present dearth of empirical data, indulging in this type of preparatory macroanalysis does not seem to be a rewarding endeavor.

[1] See, in particular, Chapter 28, Section 2.

Chapter 29

"INVESTMENT IN MAN"

---

1 Conceptual Clarifications

Both health and education can be conceived of in either static or dynamic terms — in other words, as a stock or as a flow. Where necessary, we shall use the word "conditions" to indicate that our interest is in things as they are. References to an "improvement" or a "deterioration" in health or education mean, of course, that we are thinking in terms of change.

In the preamble of the Constitution of the World Health Organization, health is defined as "a state of complete physical, mental, and social well-being and not merely an absence of disease or infirmity." Such a state cannot be regarded as a practical goal, for even in the richest country there is no limit to the proportion of national resources that could be devoted to keeping people alive, and many persons, the elderly in particular, could not be endowed with perfect health no matter how much was spent for this purpose. As the world's most advanced countries have failed to establish anything even approaching an ideal condition of health, a notion that the countries of South Asia could accomplish this feat would be totally unrealistic. Therefore, we shall focus our attention on the relative "level" of health.

Health shares with the concepts of quantitative demography the property of relating to biological facts,[1] which are of the same nature in South Asia as anywhere else. Thus in treating this subject we do not have to be concerned about logical difficulties of the type that arise when South

[1] Chapter 27, Section 1.

Asian conditions are analyzed in terms of Western economic concepts like income, saving, investment, and employment. Nevertheless, we do have to contend with the fact that health is a complex and many-faceted thing. Even if perfect health could be defined in a precise way — and this is by no means as simple as defining a total absence of health, or death — it would still be necessary to characterize the conditions in between. These intermediate conditions have no common denominator that would enable us to generalize about them. Instead, we are forced to consider the incidence of different health deficiencies, their consequences for life and work, their duration, and their prognosis. In comparison, the quantitative properties of a population — its size, its sex and age structure, and the changes in these due to births and deaths — can be summed up in simple and unequivocal figures.

Added to the logical difficulty in the way of any aggregation that would make it possible to ascertain the level of health in a nation is the fact, which we shall stress in Chapter 30, that information about health conditions is deficient and often totally lacking. Even when there are estimates of the prevalence of specific diseases with known symptoms, only the crudest guesses can be made about the prevalence of so-called incipient diseases and general psychic or physical weaknesses due to malnutrition and the diffusion among the population of pathogenic agencies. In South Asia these hard-to-diagnose health deficiencies may be more important for national development than the more obvious ones. The quantity of the various types of medical facilities available — medical personnel, hospitals, clinics, medicines, and so on — bears no definite relation to health conditions or their improvement, and this is even more true of expenditures allotted to health work. As recent experience shows, some illnesses, such as malaria, can be conquered at a small cost in terms of health facilities or financial expenditure, while others require a much greater effort. Life expectancy tables, death rates in specific age groups, and statistics on causes of death do not shed much light on morbidity (Chapter 30, Section 1), and even less on the general level of health.

It is equally if not more difficult to define a relative level of education. Education takes many forms, and again there is no common denominator. One may attempt to determine the percentage of literates in the South Asian countries. Similarly, one may seek to ascertain how many children in a certain age group attend schools of various types, how regularly they attend, for what period of time and with what results in terms of grades and examinations passed. Literacy and other skills may be imparted by means other than formal schooling. Important educational efforts, such as agricultural extension work and attempts to disseminate technical information to workers in industry, may be undertaken even though all or most of the people taught are illiterate and remain so. In all forms of education, improving attitudes is at least as important as imparting skills. These observations are only meant to illustrate the diversity of factors that an analysis of education must take into account. There is a great dearth of factual information in regard to all aspects of education in South Asia — even such simple items as literacy and school attendance are largely unknown — but even if data were available they would not afford a basis for calculating a level of education or a change in such a level.

Any attempt to measure educational levels in terms of the financial resources devoted to education — or the facilities provided, such as the teachers employed — is bound to fail for a number of reasons. To measure the "output," the "inputs" of resources would have to be more specifically defined. But even if a certain "education-mix" were assumed, the output of education — both in the imparting of abilities and the improvement of attitudes — would bear no definite relation to the inputs of resources. As we shall discover in Chapters 32 and 33, there is great wastage in all forms of education in South Asia; much of it is plain miseducation — given modernization and development as the goals, the wrong types of abilities and the wrong attitudes are imparted or preserved. This implies that improvement of education requires a better use of resources, not simply an increase in the volume of resources used for that purpose.

Moreover, neither health nor education can be dealt with in insolation. To begin with, conditions of health and education are closely interdependent. On the one hand, a child's ability to take full advantage of the schooling provided him depends on his health, and an adult's ability to use the knowledge and skills he has acquired depends on his mental and physical fitness. On the other hand, the extent to which health conditions can be improved depends on people's knowledge of and attitude toward hygiene. Standards of both health and education depend, in turn, on the whole societal milieu, especially the prevailing attitudes and institutions. Reforms in the fields of health and education are of necessity social — or even communal and familial — reforms. For technical reasons, they are usually wasteful unless undertaken on a large scale and integrated into a planned development. In this connection it should be noted that attitudes, in particular, can be improved through legislative and administrative measures that make certain behavior patterns subject to rewards or penalties. The effectiveness of such policies can be increased by directing educational efforts toward the same goal. Thus a propaganda campaign, directed toward a specific purpose — for instance, the spread of birth control — may be launched. If the purpose is achieved, this is, of course, an educational improvement, even though brought about by means not usually thought of as educational efforts.

Any attempt to analyze the impact of health or education measures without taking other policy measures into consideration involves the logical fallacy of illegitimate isolation.[1] Any attempt to abstract from

[1] Appendix 3, Section 2; cf. Section 6.

prevalent attitudes and institutions, and from all the items in the level of living other than health and educational facilities themselves, entails another logical fallacy, that of adapted *ceteris paribus* or automatic *mutatis mutandis*.[1] Any attempt to find a common denominator for conditions of health or education and their improvement, in terms of resources devoted to these purposes, implies a third logical fallacy, that of misplaced aggregation.[2] These fallacies cannot be removed by any amount of mathematical manipulation. The concepts "levels" and "rates of change in levels" of health and education give a semblance of precision that is entirely unwarranted, and models and theories that do not take account of this fact are based on faulty reasoning.

Since health and education are such unruly subjects, our treatment of them will encompass a very wide variety of phenomena and stress interrelationships in the entire social system, including the legacy from the past. It will not yield a clear-cut summary statement about the relative levels of health and education in the South Asian countries and rates of change in those levels. Moreover, because of the lack of reliable statistics, even on specific elements in the situation, our analysis will have to be based largely on estimates, the opinions of experts with first-hand experience, and our own impressions and conjectures.

2 *The Value Premises*

As in the rest of this study, our value premises are the modernization ideals as epitomized in the desirability of development.[3] Not only have these ideals informed our conclusions as to the nature and practicality of needed reforms; they have also determined the viewpoint from which we have observed and analyzed existing conditions and trends. There are, however, some complications in the use of these value premises in regard to health and education that justify a few remarks.

Every individual regards health as an important element of his well-being and the well-being of those close to him; the health facilities made available to him are an item in his level of living. Indeed, the enjoyment of health has come to take a place among the "human rights" — a position in accord with the modernization ideal of equality.[4] Thus the preamble of the Constitution of the World Health Organization states that "the enjoyment of the highest attainable standard of health is one of the fundamental rights of every human being without distinction of race, religion, political belief, economic or social condition." Doing everything possible

[1] Appendix 3, Section 2; cf. Section 3.
[2] Appendix 13, Section 2; cf. Section 5.
[3] Chapter 2, in particular Section 4.
[4] Chapter 2, Section 4; Chapter 16, Part I, particularly Sections 1 and 2.

to improve health conditions in all strata of the population stands, therefore, as a moral imperative, and is increasingly perceived as such in South Asia and throughout the world (Chapter 28, Section 9).

Besides having an independent value, health advances have an instrumental value in the development process in that they affect other social and economic conditions.[1] At first glance, this influence would appear to be wholly favorable, since the input and efficiency of labor, and, consequently, the volume of output, depend in part on the state of a nation's health. However, improved health conditions are likely to be accompanied by a decline in mortality rates and even some rise in fertility rates, and hence by a population increase with detrimental effects on development.[2] A conflict thus exists, but the improvement of health conditions is, as we noted, a moral imperative. In the preceding chapter (Section 9) we observed that anxiety about the economic effects of a high and rising rate of population increase in South Asia cannot be used as an argument against policies directed toward improving health conditions and preventing premature deaths.[3]

Education also has an independent value. Certainly an individual benefits from the development of his faculties, and anything that enlarges his opportunities to participate in the life and culture of his nation and the world enriches him personally. While the instrumental value of education attaches to its results — knowledge, skills, and changed attitudes — the educational process itself may have an independent value. On a more practical plane, education is important to individuals because it gives them a chance to increase their incomes and raise their levels of living. Like health facilities, educational facilities are an item in the level of living. Like the enjoyment of health, access to education — interpreted to mean access to elementary education and equal opportunities to climb the educational ladder — has gradually acquired recognition as a "human right." Article 26 of the Universal Declaration of Human Rights is very explicit on this score:

Everyone has the right to education. Education shall be free, at least in the elementary and fundamental stages. Elementary education shall be compulsory. Technical and professional education shall be made generally available and higher education shall be equally accessible to all on the basis of merit.

UNESCO's Constitution binds it to attempt to raise the level of education and strive to achieve "the ideal of equality of educational opportunity without regard to race, sex or any distinctions, economic or social."

[1] The other side of this circular causation (Appendix 2, Part II) is that health itself is affected by socio-economic factors, notably income, levels of living, and, in particular, nutrition.

[2] Chapter 27, Sections 6, 11, *et passim;* Chapter 28, Part I.

[3] We also noted that moral urgency becomes a relative matter when public funds are claimed for competing policy purposes.

In the nature of the case, educational improvements should lead to an improvement in social and economic conditions. For education implies the imparting of knowledge and skills that make possible increases in output. Education also implies — or rather it should imply — the inculcation of rational attitudes toward life and work that raise labor utilization and productivity directly, or contribute to this end by facilitating institutional reforms. But education in South Asia does not always have these beneficial results. This is not because of any untoward effect on population; if education makes people more eager and able to avoid ill health and premature death, it should also make them more receptive to propaganda for birth control. Rather, it is because education is sometimes valued by students (and their families) for reasons that are inimical, or not very conducive, to development. For instance, there is throughout the region a dislike for manual work, and this affects the way people approach education and the use they make of it. The notion that education is valuable because it affords an avenue of escape from manual work cannot be regarded as legitimate from a development point of view. This implies that we give preponderant weight to the instrumental value of education. However, as we assume development to be highly beneficial to all, or in any case to the great majority, the individual's own best interests would be served by such a policy. If, as a result of educational efforts, attitudes can be changed so that individuals come to identify their own ambitions with the nation's striving for development, the conflict of valuations will have been resolved and the independent value of education would justify extending efforts in this field somewhat further than development interests alone would indicate.[1]

---

[1] In the literature it is generally assumed that attitudes are, in fact, already rationalized, so that the instrumental value of education and, more particularly, its ability to raise the rate of economic growth represent a minimum value to which the independent value can be added. A representative statement, chosen at random, reads as follows:

"I do not intend to suggest that the amount spent on general education and public health should be determined solely by reference to a comparison of costs and returns in the form of additional [national] income. Certainly there are other and more fundamental reasons for providing these services. Noneconomic considerations may justify carrying expenditures on education and health beyond the point at which the return [to the national economy], narrowly construed, equals that from other outlays. Surely there is not a good case for stopping short of that point." (Richard B. Goode, "Adding to the Stock of Physical and Human Capital," *American Economic Review: Papers and Proceedings*, Vol. XLIX, No. 2, May, 1959, p. 154.)

This quotation also illustrates the logical errors discussed in the preceding section. First, various educational and health efforts, however directed, are measured in terms of financial cost and then added together (misplaced aggregation); secondly, no consideration is given to the influence of the attitudinal and institutional milieu on the return anticipated from these efforts (adapted *ceteris paribus* or automatic *mutatis mutandis*); thirdly, the instrumental value of improved education and health is assessed without taking into account other measures in effect at the same time (illegitimate isolation).

3   Rising Interest in Improving Health and Education: Obstacles and Inhibitions

In recent times a number of developments have conspired to stimulate interest in health and education in South Asia. The South Asian states formulated their planning goals in terms of the ideals of the modern Western welfare states,[1] and in so doing were impressed by the importance these states attach to health and educational improvements. The Communist countries have placed even greater emphasis on improving conditions of education and health for the masses of people, so ideological influences from this source have only strengthened the esteem in which these objectives are held. The planning ideology itself[2] has to some degree directed attention to the instrumental value of advances in these fields.

The formation in 1948 of the World Health Organization and the activities of that organization, which have been directed very largely toward ameliorating conditions in the underdeveloped countries, have strengthened the zeal for an improved level of health in South Asia. Of particular importance in this connection has been the availability since the Second World War of cheap but effective means of fighting many of the area's most disastrous diseases. The work of UNESCO has been important in the field of education. If this organization has occasionally exerted a less positive influence than the World Health Organization,[3] it must be remembered that the task of raising educational standards is more complex and difficult and that UNESCO has had nothing to offer comparable to the new wonder drugs.

These influences have had their impact on the educated and articulate strata in the South Asian countries — except insofar as their thinking has been distorted by conventional economic theory (see below). But the broad masses of people in these countries have been touched only slightly as yet by the heightened interest in improving health conditions. An indication of this is the fact that the authorities encounter difficulties when they attempt to induce people to behave more rationally in regard to sanitation and hygiene. The masses are perhaps more interested in better schooling, even though they often resist the changes in attitudes that are intended to be among its effects. Governments have shown an increased readiness to take action in both fields, but on a limited scale. Except for a few measures, like anti-malaria campaigns, which have been, predictably, inexpensive but highly productive of results, health policies have not been given a high priority. Measures to raise educational standards have been more promi-

[1] Chapter 16, Sections 1 and 2.
[2] Chapter 15, Section 1.
[3] See, for instance, Chapter 32, Section 4.

nent in the plans. That they have not had a greater effect on development is due partly to the explosive rise in the school-age population and partly, as we shall find, to faults and weaknesses in the direction of the educational effort.

The relatively low priority given to genuine and radical reforms in the fields of health and education is traceable to the prevailing philosophy of development, which stresses the over-riding importance of physical investment. As we have noted throughout this study, the economic literature and the plans have been dominated by theories based on an uncritical application of Western concepts and analytical models to the South Asian situation. Models centered on the concept of a capital/output ratio have dictated the direction of economic planning in underdeveloped countries.[1] One implication of this "modern approach" is the assumption that "non-economic" factors — not only institutions and attitudes but also levels of living, including health and educational facilities — can be disregarded. The primary and often exclusive importance given to investment in physical capital for economic development requires this assumption.

4   *The Recent Economic Theory of "Investment in Man"*

The capital/output approach was in line with neo-classical economic theory, where an "unchanged state of the arts" in a very inclusive sense was often assumed. In the post-war years this approach gained in popularity among economists because of several studies that purported to show a close relationship between capital formation and economic growth in the United States and certain highly developed West European countries. In fact, the capital/output ratio came to be regarded as akin to the constants that have made it possible to advance knowledge of the physical universe by purely abstract mathematical reasoning.[2] In very recent years, however, more intensive studies of economic growth in the same advanced countries revealed that only a part of it could be explained by the amount of investment in physical capital (and the increase in the labor force).[3] While estimates of the unexplained residual vary within a wide range, they generally support the view that it is considerably bigger than that part of economic growth which is explained by capital investment.

This important negative finding demolished the foundations of the planning model cast in terms of physical investment alone, and threw the door wide open to speculation about other operative factors in develop-

---

[1] Appendix 2, Sections 20–21; Appendix 3, particularly Sections 2 and 10; Prologue, Sections 5 and 6.

[2] Appendix 3, particularly Sections 2 and 8.

[3] For this and the next sections see Appendix 3, Section 7.

ment. A wide variety of factors presented themselves: education, health, research, technology, organization, management, government, administration, and so on. Significantly, economists were not prepared to abandon the capital/output model; instead, they widened the concept of capital investment to include, besides physical investment, "investment in man," sometimes labelled "investment in human capability" or "investment in human resources."[1] To accomplish this, it was necessary to reduce the wide variety of specific factors exemplified above to one or a few categories for which definite amounts of expenditure could be calculated. From the beginning, interest has focussed on education, though health has occasionally shared the spotlight; the more elaborate models all reduce investment in man to the one factor, education. Improvements in the other factors must then be thought of as effects of education — part of its "return." Another consequence of treating education as investment — and the same would hold true of health or any other factor if it was similarly treated — is that it must then be described in the separate and aggregate form of financial expenditure.

Once economists identified the residual factor in economic growth with investment in man and the latter with education, this approach derived support from various research undertakings that were themselves inspired by it. A positive correlation was found to exist between the level of development and literacy or some other easily available measure of educational "level" in different countries and during different periods. Although it was, of course, recognized that statistical correlation does not establish what is cause and what is effect, these calculations served to confirm in a general and vague way the theory that education is a form of investment and a vital one.

Events themselves gave support to the view that education is an important developmental factor, lending further spurious support to the new theory. When W. Leontief found that, as far as international trade was concerned, the United States specialized in selling labor-intensive rather than capital-intensive products, this invited the explanation that the United States had a greater comparative advantage in the skills possessed by its labor force (including organizational abilities, assumed to be imparted by education) than in its abundance of capital. The Marshall Plan

[1] "Without waiting for the completion of the lengthy investigations that will be required to bring information on human capital to parity with that now available on physical capital, economists and policy-makers can perhaps begin to try to introduce human capital more systematically into their growth models and development plans. These efforts may lead to a reconciliation of the usefulness of analytical devices such as capital-output ratios which take into account only physical capital and saving rates which equate savings with investment in physical capital in the monetized sector of the economy." (Goode, "Adding to the Stock of Physical and Human Capital," *American Economic Review: Papers and Proceedings,* p. 155.)

in Western Europe turned out to be a greater and more rapid success than most economists had foreseen, while economic aid to underdeveloped countries generally proved to be less effective than had been expected. It seemed reasonable to suppose that the accumulated "educational capital" of the West European countries was a factor in this result. Another influence was the delayed realization[1] that the Soviet Union had made strenuous efforts to increase educational facilities on all levels, and the inference that her rapid emergence from a state of relative underdevelopment was partly attributable to these efforts.

Not only the initial finding of a "residual" in development, impossible to explain by physical investment, but also all of the various calculations inspired by and vaguely supporting the theory that education can be treated as investment in the conventional capital/output model of development were based on statistics relating to some of the highly advanced Western countries: no underdeveloped country compiles statistical series of the kind needed for such studies. Nevertheless, economists have not hesitated to apply this theory to the underdeveloped countries. Some economists point to the fact that since the underdeveloped countries must use modern techniques as worked out in the advanced countries, if they are to progress, investment in education is even more important to them than it was to the Western countries when they were in the early stages of development.[2] Except for such general considerations, there has been little interest in determining the effect of education under the very different conditions that prevail in the underdeveloped countries. The new theory has simply been applied by analogy.

As far as underdeveloped countries are concerned, the newest approach — as we shall call it in order to distinguish it from the "modern approach" in the post-war period that has treated development as a function of physical capital investment — has thus remained merely a new approach and has hardly been used in any real research. The situation is somewhat paradoxical. While most of the planning in South Asia and the other underdeveloped regions, and most of the economic literature on development, continues to be based on the notion that physical investment is the engine

---

[1] Appendix 2, Section 20.

[2] Chapter 14, Section 6.

"The issue to ponder here lies in the fact that poor countries now entering upon industrialization are not employing the simple, primitive machinery and equipment of that period, and they are not adopting techniques of production of a century or two ago. Nor could they do so even if they wished to, because such equipment and techniques have become collectors' items for our museums." (Theodore W. Schultz, "Investment in Human Capital in Poor Countries," *Foreign Trade and Human Capital*, Paul D. Zook, ed., Southern Methodist University Press, Dallas, 1962, p. 4.)

of development,[1] there are today an increasing number of economists who denounce that view and who regard development, particularly in underdeveloped countries, as primarily an educational process.[2] The members of this newest school of thought are aware of the fact that they are thereby repudiating the dominant trend of economic thinking about development in underdeveloped countries as it evolved since the end of the Second World War; before that time there had been little interest in the development issue, particularly in regard to underdeveloped countries.[3] Of fresh research, guided by the newest theory and going deeply into their educational problems, very little has been seen.

The vision is there, however. To quote one exegesis of the newest school:

Much of the past discussion of economic growth — in developed as well as in underdeveloped countries — appears to be as obsolete as the abandoned and useless furniture in the attic of an old family homestead. . . . Clearly . . . a new concept of "capital" — and a new *political* economy — is in the process of formulation since the old concepts, which were limited to tangible property, are now manifestly inadequate. The main shift in the present development is characterized by the tendency to think of the cause of economic growth as the *capacity* to create wealth rather than the creation of wealth itself. The direction of the change in thought is suggested by the question: Can we formulate a theory of human capital which accounts for economic growth in terms of changes in the quality of human beings?[4]

The same spokesman contrasts this view to the still dominant one:

. . . orthodox economic and fiscal opinion continues to ignore the drift of current development and the significance to public policy of the new insight which is emerging. We continue to build models of economic growth on strictly materialist assumptions which overlook the role of capital investment in human beings in our own experience. . . . We disregard the role of the development of

[1] This is regularly noted by members of the newest school of economists. "In spite of the importance attached to investment in man by a number of economists and their efforts to bring it within the realm of economic theory, most economic-development planners usually give only peripheral consideration to the analysis of human resources. . . . When . . . confronted with problems of development which lie beyond the scope of his familiar analytical framework, the economic-development planner quite naturally brushes them aside with an expressed recognition of their probable importance and a vague hope that somehow or other they will solve themselves in the course of economic growth." (Frederick Harbison and Charles A. Myers, *Education, Manpower, and Economic Growth,* McGraw-Hill, New York, 1964, p. 11.)

[2] "Countries are underdeveloped because most of their people are underdeveloped, having had no opportunity of expanding their potential capital in the service of society." (Adam Curle, "Some Aspects of Educational Planning in Underdeveloped Areas," *Harvard Educational Review,* Vol. 32, No. 3, Summer, 1962, p. 300.)

[3] Prologue, Section 2.

[4] Harry P. Gideonse, "Economic Growth and Educational Development," *College and University,* Summer, 1963, pp. 424, 425–426.

human skills and trained imagination in our own achievements . . . by presenting a picture of exclusive preoccupation with physical and material achievement.[1]

Against the background of the common approach to development problems in the post-war period the idea that education can be treated as investment in the conventional model takes on the character of a discovery.[2] The newest school can, however, point out that the orthodoxy
they fight against was not always the ruling one. Alfred Marshall regarded
education as a "national investment" — although, unlike members of the
newest school, he used the word "investment" only in a figurative sense as
he repudiated calculations of returns — and he was only following in the
tradition established by many of the classical economists, among them
John Stuart Mill, Malthus, and Adam Smith. The basic practical and
political valuation inherent in this view is illustrated by the following
quotation from Theodore W. Schultz:

When poor countries . . . enter upon the process of developing a modern agriculture and industry, with some notable exceptions they invest too little in human capital relative to what they invest in nonhuman capital; skills and knowledge useful in their economic endeavor are neglected as they concentrate on
new plants and equipment. Thus, an imbalance arises and as a consequence they
fail, often by a wide margin, to attain their optimum rate of economic growth.[3]

Leaving aside for the moment the question whether it is possible and
correct to treat education in financial terms as simply an investment (Section 5), educationists in South Asia and elsewhere certainly agree with
the newest school of economists that education is important for development. And they formed this opinion long before a group of economists in
very recent years hit on the idea, though they have never been able to effectively challenge the modern materialist orthodoxy.[4] It is a remarkable
fact, testifying to the damaging compartmentalization of the social sciences and, in particular, the insularity of traditional economics, that economists after the Second World War could build up a theory of development based solely on physical investment — a theory so incapable of
explaining the process of economic growth that a group of them later

[1] *Ibid.*, pp. 428–429.

[2] "There is an 'egg of Columbus' quality to the challenge of received ways of thinking which is involved." (*Ibid.*, p. 421.)

Godfrey Hodgson, in a report from Washington dated February 29, 1964 in the
Observer (March 1, 1964), writes: "The idea that education, at every level, is the key
to the abolition of poverty, is described . . . as 'so revolutionary that if social scientists
had more self-confidence [sic!] they would call it a discovery.'"

[3] Schultz, "Investment in Human Capital in Poor Countries," in *Foreign Trade and
Human Capital*, pp. 14–15.

[4] Prologue, Section 8.

"discovered" investment in man — while all the time they were apparently unaware of the thinking and writings of students and practitioners who specialized in this field (and also of the theorizing by earlier members of their own profession). As one commentator has observed, "the economists have not properly taken account of a long history of pedagogical research and practice."[1]

This history is long indeed. When the Scandinavian countries began to legislate universal and compulsory elementary education in the beginning of the nineteenth century, this great reform movement was spurred by the argument that education was a prerequisite for improving agriculture, promoting industrialization, and for a general speed-up of what we now call "development." Another motivating factor was the belief that only a broadening of the educational base could make popular participation in government more effective. Somewhat later, similar reasoning led several states of the United States to include in their constitutions the right of all children to free elementary education. The French were inclined to trace their defeat in the war of 1870–71 to the superiority of German training programs, especially in the vocational and technical fields, and this belief helped to bring about a reform of the French educational system. Closer to South Asia, Japan has long acted on the belief that educational improvement would help it to emulate the industrial progress of the West.[2] In fact, with the major exception of the post-war economic theorizing and planning for development in underdeveloped countries, nowhere in the world in modern history has there been any discussion of economic development that did not give educational improvement a predominant role. Indeed, for well over a century education for development has been a central theme of pedagogical literature. Economic historians have regularly paid a great deal of attention to education and educational reform when seeking to explain why the rate of economic development has varied in different epochs and in different countries. As one writer observes: "It might seem somewhat surprising that such a common-sense hypothesis [that education can raise productivity of workers] should not have been accepted by economists until quite recently."[3] But none in this tradition has tried to put educational reform into the conceptual strait jacket of a quantity of financial investment, accounted for in a capital/output ratio. This is the only innovation in the newest economic approach.

[1] R. Diez-Hochleitner, "Educational Planning," *Economic and Social Aspects of Educational Planning*, UNESCO, Paris, 1964, p. 85.

[2] It is rather odd that until recently Japan's educational development effort has attracted little attention in South Asia, though there has been a great deal of interest in that country's methods of rice planting.

[3] M. Debeauvais, "The Concept of Human Capital," in Economics of Education, Part One, *International Social Science Journal*, Vol. XIV, No. II, 1962, p. 661.

5 *Critical Comments on the Newest Western Approach*

The present writer, who for more fundamental reasons has felt it necessary to apply an out-and-out institutional approach to the development problems in the nderdeveloped countries of South Asia, can only welcome the newest school's repudiation of the orthodoxy of the modern and still prevalent theory, which awards to physical investment the role of engendering development. Nevertheless, he has reservations concerning this school. In his opinion its members do not go far enough, either in their criticisms or in their innovations.

Economists of the newest school restrict themselves to widening the concept of investment in the capital/output model, so as to include investment in man, usually simplified to mean only education. But, as we point out in Appendix 3 (Section 7), the model itself is based on a number of unwarranted assumptions. In this instance it requires the assumption that education is a homogeneous magnitude, measurable in terms of financial expenditures.[1] The model also implies that prevailing attitudes and institutions, items in the levels of living other than educational facilities, are of no consequence for the problem,[2] and that the effect of all other policy measures applied at the same time can be completely disregarded.[3] As these assumptions are logically inconsistent and inadequate to reality, use of the capital/output model can only block the way to realistic and relevant research.

In the present context this criticism will be spelled out solely in regard to the invalid and unrealistic assumption made about institutions — specifically, those in agriculture. Our study of this sector (in Chapters 22 and 26) clearly indicates that the low productivity of labor and land is related to the social structure and the attitudes supported by that structure, the widespread existence of absentee land ownership and tenancy being of particular importance. Because of these institutions the peasants have little possibility or incentive to avail themselves of new techniques or otherwise try to increase their output. If productivity in agriculture is to increase, there must be institutional reform. Unless land reform of one type or another is introduced, improved farming methods have little chance of being

---

[1] This is an example of misplaced aggregation; see Section 1. Among other things, this approach implies that the eminently practical problems of the "education-mix" and wastage and miseducation can be ignored.

[2] The assumption must be that these factors are either fixed but of no consequence (adapted *ceteris paribus*) or easily adaptable to changed circumstances (automatic *mutatis mutandis*); see Section 1.

[3] Illegitimate isolation; see Section 1.

applied.[1] More precisely, the productivity-raising effects of education, and even people's interest in acquiring education, will depend on the extent to which institutional reforms take place. Such reforms can come about only through legislative and administrative means, and they require many additional policy measures to make them effective.

The tendency to exclude this institutional policy factor when planning is done in terms of even an extended capital/output model is plainly evident in the writings of members of the newest school. Thus James G. Maddox defines his "prescription for increasing agricultural productivity" as "the mixture of education, research, fertilizer, insecticides, high yielding seeds, and a few tractors."[2] Lee R. Martin explains that "the full productive potential of a country is a joint function of its natural resources (defined by worldwide technology, not technology in local use), the number of workers, and the most advanced state of the production arts."[3] Theodore W. Schultz has recently published a book, *Transforming Traditional Agriculture*,[4] which, while interesting, entirely bypasses the problems of the institutional setting and the need for institutional reform.[5]

Much more generally, the treatment of education in terms of investment implies a bypassing of the inequality issue. In Chapter 33 — especially Section 11 — we demonstrate how decisively social and economic inequality determines the effects of attempts to improve education, and also how educational advance often serves to stratify inequality. This newest theory of investment in man is, consequently, heavily biased, and in a way that conflicts with our value premises.

[1] See particularly Chapter 26, Part II.

The reference is to land reform in the broadest sense. In the case of India we reached the conclusion that perhaps some form of capitalist system — supplemented so far as possible by welfare policies in the interest of the now landless — might be the most practical institutional setting for a more progressive agriculture; see Chapter 26, Section 25. More generally, the assertion that the institutional framework is not conducive to agricultural progress does not imply that every attempt at land reform is meritorious.

[2] "Allocating Public Expenditures for Education in Underdeveloped Countries," in *Foreign Trade and Human Capital*, p. 24.

[3] "Productivity and Social Costs of Human Capital in Underdeveloped Countries," in *Foreign Trade and Human Capital*, p. 34.

[4] Yale University Press, New Haven, 1964.

[5] Schultz touches on the problem in relation to absentee ownership, which he regards as "in general inefficient." However, he sets down the "hypothesis," supported by data for the United States, that "under competitive conditions, as farmers adopt and learn how to use modern agricultural factors an increasingly larger part of all farming is taken over by owner-operators." He continues: "This means, to state it another way: where there is competition, that part of farming under absentee arrangements decreases relatively because of inherent inefficiencies." (Theodore W. Schultz, "Farm Size, Control, and Incentives," in *Transforming Traditional Agriculture*, pp. 118–119.) However, absentee ownership is only one of many institutional arrangements that are inimical to agricultural progress; in the larger part of South Asia there is nothing like effective competition; more particularly, generalizations based on United States experience can have little bearing on events in South Asia.

The critique in the last three paragraphs is not, of course, meant to deprecate efforts in the educational field, or, for that matter, to deny the importance of physical investment. The point is that an analysis which does not fully take into account the institutional framework within which the economic variables operate, and which aggregates disparate activities, while isolating them from other, complementary activities, is bound to be not only superficial but misleading. In the Prologue and in various other contexts we have pointed out that abstraction from the institutional frame-work — and from the attitudes that are molded in that framework and, in turn, support it — is opportunistic both in South Asia and in the West;[1] it is a biased approach. In a brilliant paper, Thomas Balogh suggests that calculations made about the profitability of education are "not merely fallacious in a technical economic sense but . . . immoral politically"; what he says about a particular species of model can be generalized to the whole genus of development models we are now discussing.

I admit the attractiveness of this mathematical approach. Land reform, the crea-tion of agricultural extention services and of an adequate agricultural credit system, the reorganisation of the civil service, the establishment of state indus-trial corporations — all these are complex matters. They involve a change of attitudes, a reform of institutions. They hurt vested interests. They cause polit-ical difficulties. How much simpler to lift out of a residual, representing com-plex conditions of progress, a particular factor — in this case 'the vast heavy investment which all countries undertake at all times in the development of their human resources' — and assign to it a definite causal force, having obtained the residual after accounting for the equally complex influence on economic progress of the growth of 'land, labour and capital' in a most cavalier and ille-gitimate way.[2]

6   Added Difficulties When Health Is Included in the Model

The tendency has been to restrict the category investment in man to financial expenditures on education. The question must at last be raised: why have economists focussed their attention on education and almost entirely ignored the other dimension of population quality, health?

The answer cannot be the difficulty of defining health or health objec-tives, as it is at least equally difficult to define educational levels.[3] Meas-

[1] Prologue, Section 6; Appendix 2, Section 14; Chapter 21, Sections 7 and 9 *et passim*.

[2] Thomas Balogh, "Education and Economic Growth. Comments on Professor Tin-bergen's Planning 'Model,'" *Kyklos*, Vol. XVII, 1964, Fasc. 2, pp. 261ff.; cf. the same author's "The Economics of Educational Planning: Sense and Nonsense," *Comparative Education*, Vol. 1, No. 1, October, 1964, pp. 5ff.

[3] Occasionally, though, a differential is said to exist. "Units of quality change through human capital formation by health programs cannot be defined as tidily as units of education embodied in the labor force. There is no quality unit comparable to that of

uring efforts put forth and their effectiveness in financial terms is no more feasible in the case of education than in the case of health. Factual information is about equally lacking in both instances. In any event, neither definitional difficulties nor a lack of empirical data have ever deterred economists, and least of all the model-builders among them, from tackling problems and presenting solutions that pretend knowledge. The fact that improved health is regularly accompanied by demographic changes (a fall in the death rate and perhaps a rise in the fertility rate) which exert a downward pressure on income per head and living levels, does not justify leaving the health factor out of development theories, especially since allowance could be made for these secondary changes by slightly complicating the models.

Some clue may be found in the fact that the concept of investment in man had its origin largely in the analysis of the recent growth history of certain highly developed countries. It can be assumed that health conditions in these countries have been so relatively favorable in recent decades that an improvement in health facilities — with the application at any point of time of the then known medical techniques — has not at the margin made any very great contribution to the utilization and productivity of the labor force. However, the same is true of education, particularly elementary schooling. Further speculation along these lines would seem profitless. There can be no warrant for leaving health out of the development picture. Ill health is a very serious deterrent to a rise in labor input and efficiency in the underdeveloped countries in South Asia.

But if we do add investment in health to investment in education and define human resources in terms of the two dimensions of population quality — as occasional references invite — we must include all costs involved in improving conditions of health, not just expenditures on health facilities. In all South Asian countries and particularly in the biggest and poorest of them, India and Pakistan, a major cause of ill health — specifically, of incipient disease, apathy, and bodily and mental weakness — is serious undernutrition and malnutrition among the masses of the people.[1] The majority of South Asians spend much more than half their income on food, and still they are undernourished. Nor do they have access to the clothing, housing, and sanitary facilities they need to keep them reasonably fit. On the margin, then, increases in the consumption of essentials, food especially, or the expenditures that make such increases possible, are bound to be productive of better health, which is not the case in the highly de-

---

the number of years of schooling, devised by Schultz as a measure of educational stock in the labor force." (Selma J. Mushkin, "Health as an Investment," *Journal of Political Economy*, Vol. LXX, No. 5, Supplement: October, 1962, Part 2, p. 133, citing T. W. Schultz, "Education and Economic Growth," in *Social Forces Influencing American Education*, N. B. Henry, ed., Chicago, 1961.)

[1] Chapter 12, Section 4; Chapter 30, Section 11.

veloped countries.[1] The implication is that the new term "investment in man" should include not only the consumption of educational and health facilities, but *practically all essential consumption,* if the underlying reasoning is to be logically consistent. The *productivity effect on the margin of the various items of consumption differs, however* — some consumption is relatively unproductive, and some has a negative value for health. The *real planning problem* is how to squeeze and twist consumption in such a way as to speed up development.[2] This problem would not be clarified to any degree by the statement that much of the consumption in these poor countries constitutes investment in man. What the planners need to know is the effect on productivity of increases in the consumption of various items, and here the model offers no guidance at all.

7   Concluding Remarks

To sum up, the most recent opposition of some economists to the modern approach is certainly wholesome, insofar as it challenges the exclusive role given in the post-war period to physical investment in the models that still form the basis for planning in South Asian countries. The general policy judgment of the rebel school — though it is usually not indicated, or is indicated only by a few illustrations of what educators have been hammering at for many decades — that greater efforts to improve education, if wisely planned and directed, can be more conducive to development than some physical investment, is probably correct, though it does not follow as a conclusion from use of the conventional model with only a broadened definition of capital investment. The same probably holds true of greater efforts to improve health, though these efforts would have to have as a major objective the increasing of essential consumption and, in particular, food intake. Again, this would not follow from the use of a capital/output model, even if the model took health measures into account. The investment approach entirely ignores the fact that institutional and attitudinal reforms, which depend on political decisions rather than budgetary considerations, are needed to make investments in education "pay off," and the broader consideration that the success of educational programs depends on the policies pursued in all other fields as well as the direction of the educational programs themselves. It is possible that some members of the school of economists whose views have been discussed in the preceding two sections would agree generally with our evaluation. But *if the concept "investment in man" is revised to take account of these criticisms, it becomes virtually empty of theoretical content; it becomes*

---

[1] Appendix 2, Section 21.

[2] Chapter 2, Section 4; Appendix 2, Section 21; Appendix 8, Section 8.

merely a vague propaganda term for a more rational and circumspect development planning that takes into account not only physical investment but all other induced changes. That concept does not by itself contain even the beginning of a valid theory, and should not invite the type of abstract and carelessly constructed models referred to above and in Section 7 of Appendix 3.

To avoid any misunderstanding it should again be stressed that we are not averse to the use of models.[1] Still less are we opposed to efforts to make quantitative judgments. We are not in sympathy with the view that some factors are "qualitative"; in principle, social scientists must strive constantly to translate all of their knowledge into measurable quantities. However, *both models and quantitative pronouncements must be logically consistent and thoroughly grounded in facts.* We need much more specific and precise information about actual health and educational conditions in South Asia and their relationship to a vast number of other socio-economic conditions. In particular, we need research to shed light on the effect of various programs on physiological and mental vigor, skills, knowledge and attitudes, labor input and efficiency. We need to know more about how different development efforts affect one another and how they are affected by institutional settings. When more data become available there will be plenty of room for models that are clear, specific, logically consistent, and adequate to reality.

The judgment that the South Asian countries would be well advised to devote more resources to improving health and education is probably correct as far as it goes, but it is vague and it does not clarify the really important issues, namely: where should health and educational programs be directed, how far should they be pushed, what means should they employ, and what other policy measures are needed? The criticism of the modern, conventional approach to planning, which relates development to physical investment alone, is valid — but for reasons more fundamental than those advanced by the newest school of economists. These two assertions are not in the slightest degree strengthened or rendered more precise by a general "theory" of investment in man as the engine of economic growth. The quantitative inferences frequently arrived at by the use of the new, extended models are as fictitious as, for instance, the calculations of the percentage of the labor force that is "underemployed";[2] by presenting an elegant appearance of knowledge, where none exists, they make it easy to avoid the laborious task of studying reality in all its complexity. The abstract criticism in this chapter is intended to help clear the deck of useless theories, based on preconceptions, that obstruct and misdirect scientific advance.

[1] Prologue, Section 8; Appendix 2, Section 14; Appendix 3, Section 8 *et passim.* For the following see also Thomas Balogh's two papers, cited in Section 5.

[2] Appendix 6; Chapter 21, Sections 12–14.

See the complete work for Chapters 30-33.

APPENDIX TO THE VINTAGE EDITION

Contents of Volume I

PART THREE: ECONOMIC REALITIES

Contents of Volume II

Contents of Volume III

APPENDICES

VINTAGE POLITICAL SCIENCE
AND SOCIAL CRITICISM